Introduction to International Disaster Management

Introduction to International Disaster Management

Second Edition

Damon P. Coppola

ELSEVIER

AMSTERDAM • BOSTON • HEIDELBERG • LONDON
NEW YORK • OXFORD • PARIS • SAN DIEGO
SAN FRANCISCO • SINGAPORE • SYDNEY • TOKYO
Butterworth-Heinemann is an imprint of Elsevier

Acquiring Editor: Pam Chester
Development Editor: Greg Chalson
Project Manager: Paul Gottehrer
Designer: Kristen Davis

Butterworth-Heinemann is an imprint of Elsevier
30 Corporate Drive, Suite 400, Burlington, MA 01803, USA

Library of Congress Cataloging-in-Publication Data
Coppola, Damon P.
  Introduction to international disaster management / Damon Coppola.
     p. cm.
  Includes index.
  ISBN 978-0-12-382174-4
1. Disaster relief—International cooperation. 2. Emergency management—International cooperation. 3. Hazard mitigation. I. Title.
  HV553.C693 2011
  363.34'526—dc22

                                                                    2010047428

British Library Cataloguing-in-Publication Data
A catalogue record for this book is available from the British Library.

Printed in China
11 12 13 14 15   10 9 8 7 6 5 4 3 2 1

For information on all BH publications visit our website at www.elsevierdirect.com/security

Dedication

This text is dedicated to my brother, Dr. Christopher Paul Coppola, who risked life, limb, and livelihood to treat children caught in the midst of war. His work reminds us to pay attention to the plight of individuals, no matter how great the disaster.

Contents

Foreword

Damon Coppola's book is a major contribution to understanding the universal principles of emergency management. Had it been available in 1978, it would have helped me become a better emergency manager. I joined the Office of U.S. Foreign Disaster Assistance (OFDA) in 1978 after serving three years in Viet Nam and a year in Ghana with the development program of the Agency for International Development. My qualifications were that I had common sense and street smarts because I survived Viet Nam, had traveled the world, and worked in Africa. If I applied for the same disaster job today with those qualifications, I would be rejected, fortunately.

Today's emergency managers have a wealth of information available to them and can benefit from the many academic courses offered to build a solid foundation of expertise in disaster preparedness and response. This know-how aids them in their profession and strengthens their decision-making capability. Damon has compiled an impressive collection of facts, statistics, and checklists that can help a motivated person become a skilled emergency management technician. Chapter 11, Special Considerations, is an insightful look at future challenges and possible solutions. His lessons, combined with field experience and good mentoring, can transform a technician into a competent professional. Insights gained through experience and difficult decision making are how one becomes a leader in the struggle against disasters.

Patterns emerge as I look back on 46 years of international experience, including 28 years and 375 disasters. Leadership and politics play an inordinate role in disaster planning and response internationally as well as in the United States. The recent failures following Hurricane Katrina were predictable, not only because of the known vulnerability of the Gulf Coast, but also because of ineffective leadership. The appointment of political supporters with no emergency management experience and weak interpersonal skills was a formula for failure. Unfortunately, it is always the disaster victims who pay the price of inept leadership and flawed decision making.

OFDA and the Federal Emergency Management Agency (FEMA) have been rivals for years, with the smaller OFDA wary of the larger FEMA. However, it was OFDA's smallness, its clear mandate, a short chain of command, and almost unlimited resources that enabled it to become so successful and well known in the 1980s and early 1990s.

OFDA's other critical ingredient for success was leadership. Outstanding leaders willing to take risks to assist disaster victims worldwide were appointed. OFDA's directors—Julia Taft, Julius Becton, and Andrew Natsios—were experienced managers and self-confident individuals who hired strong, experienced, and creative international disaster leaders and then took their advice. Fred Cuny battled the bureaucracy as much as he fought disaster threats. Paul Bell developed a cadre of Latin American emergency managers whose influence has transcended him. Bob Gersony, the remaining OFDA genius, plumbed the depths of many complex international situations to bring clear action recommendations to OFDA directors.

All disasters are local, but also political. Internationally, political influences take different forms than the political aspects in domestic disasters. OFDA prided itself on being "nonpolitical" and responding to all victims' needs. One example, the rapid and generous U.S. government's response to the El Asnam earthquake in Algeria (1980), has been cited by some as the reason that the Government of Algeria offered to negotiate the return of the U.S. hostages held by Iran. The only exception to nonpolitical assistance that I experienced was the failure of the U.S. government to respond to a major hurricane in Sandanista-ruled Nicaragua (1992). Despite severe damage to the eastern coast of Nicaragua, populated primarily by Misquito Indians friendly to the United States, the Reagan administration refused to allow the U.S. Embassy to declare a disaster. A declaration would have enabled OFDA to provide immediate assistance to needy hurricane victims.

As Damon documents, international disaster programs have had a significant influence on U.S. emergency management. The most well known is the U.S. Urban Search and Rescue Program (USAR Task Forces from Fairfax County, Virginia, and Metro Dade County, Miami, Florida), which was developed by OFDA. FEMA developed and expanded the teams into more than 25 USAR Task Forces that respond to disasters in the United States.

The probability forecasting system used by the National Hurricane Center originated with a U.S. Navy system supported by OFDA to alert and warn vulnerable populations through American embassies around the world. The Bangladesh early warning system, funded by OFDA and enhanced by others, continues to save thousands of lives.

The management of spontaneous donations (Chapter 6) is a continuing problem after U.S. and international disasters. Recognized by OFDA and FEMA in the 1980s, nongovernmental organizations (NGOs) and the U.S. government designed activities to educate potential donors and provided guidance to disaster-stricken country embassies. Today, the Center for International Disaster Information (CIDI) and InterAction work with FEMA, NVOAD members, and the Business Civic Leadership Center (U.S. Chamber of Commerce) to educate donors and foster cooperation to better manage offers of goods, services, and spontaneous volunteers.

Despite the similarities between the U.S. and international disaster needs and principles, there is limited cooperation between U.S. emergency managers working on domestic activities and U.S. emergency managers working on international programs. Although international coordination and the role of the United Nations described in Chapter 10 has improved cooperation, significant gaps remain between domestic and international emergency management programs in many donor countries. Damon's excellent use of universally recognized approaches may successfully forge more cooperation as both adherents recognize that they are using similar templates.

James Lee Witt, FEMA's famous and successful director, provided valuable guidance for emergency managers worldwide:

> ... we need to take a common-sense, practical approach to reducing the risks we face and protecting our citizens and our communities.
>
> We need to identify our risks, educate and communicate to our people about those risks, prepare as best we can for the risks, and then, together, form partnerships to take action to reduce those risks. This approach applies whether we are dealing with a flood, a tornado, a hazardous materials spill, a wildfire, a potential suicide bomb explosion, or a pandemic flu outbreak.

Good luck to the next generation. You will need to learn the basics and be willing to withstand the constraints of a bureaucracy. Perhaps you will be as lucky as I have been and work for outstanding leaders and with courageous colleagues. You will need all this book can provide and lots of personal courage.

Thanks, Damon, for a good start.

Ollie Davidson
Private-Public Partnerships for Disaster
Loss Reduction

Acknowledgments

The author would like to express profound gratitude to George Haddow and Jane Bullock for continuing to freely share their invaluable expertise and experience—much of which is captured in the pages of this text—and for their friendship and constant support. Special thanks also go to Ollie Davidson, Jack Harrald, Greg Shaw, J. René van Dorp, Joseph Barbera, Ryan Miller, Erin Ngo, and Robert McCreight. Their research, practice, publications, and experience, which have unquestionably made the world safer from the consequences of disasters, served as both a resource and an inspiration in the writing of this text.

I would also like to thank Pam Chester, Greg Chalson, Paul Gottehrer, and Kelly Harris at Elsevier for the tremendous assistance they provided in the development of this book. For their contributions to the content of this text, I would like to thank Ann Patton, David Alexander, Rae Zimmerman, Vicki Bier, George and Sharon Ketchum, Wayne Blanchard, Barbara Johnson, Gunnery Sergeant Shannon Arledge (USMC), Greg Guibert, Claire Reiss, Gilbert Burnham, Gaye Cameron, Niels Holm-Nielsen, Juan Edwardo Donoso, Meredith Golden, Amy Sebring, Avagene Moore, Sanjaya Bhatia, Irmak Renda-Tanali, Sarp Yeletaysi, Louise Comfort, Stephen Carter, David Gilmore, Alan Kirschenbaum, Jack Suwanlert, Cate Moore, Chris Schraders, Caroline McMullan, John Borton, Darcy Whiteside, Jessica Hill, Georg Pflug, Ralph L. Keeney, Clark Chapman, Anatoly Klypin, and W. Kip Viscusi.

And finally, I would like to extend a very special thank you to my wife, Mary Gardner Coppola, who dedicated countless hours to providing invaluable editorial and material assistance that made this book possible.

Introduction

The basis for the writing of this book is the juncture of two separate trends: (1) All countries face increased risk from a full range of known and previously unknown hazards and (2) disaster consequences are having greater adverse effects on populations and environments. To the degree that they are able, governments pass legislation and take action to prepare for and mitigate the effects of these natural, technological, and intentional hazards. Despite even the best efforts, however, the fury of nature or the folly of man regularly results in disastrous events that overwhelm not only local response capacities but also the response capacities of entire nations or even entire regions. When this happens, the full range of players from the international community is called on to intervene, requiring international disaster management.

The international response to disasters is convoluted, at times chaotic, and always complex. Every country has its own hazard profile, vulnerability fluctuation, and evolution or demise of emergency management systems, as well as unique cultural, economic, and political characteristics. Each of these qualities influences the country's interaction with international disaster management agencies and organizations.

Disaster management as a practice and as a profession is rapidly expanding and improving. Such change is necessarily driven by the modern needs of governments and nongovernmental organizations involved in one or more of the four phases of emergency management—mitigation, preparedness, response, and recovery.

This book was written to serve as a guide and a reference for students, practitioners, and anyone interested in disaster management and its application to the international community.

Chapter 1 provides a general background on the impact and management of disasters worldwide. Included in this discussion is a brief history of emergency management. Several of the issues unique to international disaster management are touched upon, while in-depth coverage is included in later chapters. Finally, several key terms are defined and discussed.

Chapter 2 addresses hazards. The various natural, technological, and intentional hazards are defined, and disaster-specific information is provided. Where applicable, the threat ranges of hazards are illustrated with charts, maps, and figures.

Chapter 3 examines the existence and assessment of vulnerability and risk. The disparity in these values between countries in relation to their variable levels of wealth is addressed in detail, as is risk perception, an important and influential component of vulnerability and risk.

Chapter 4 covers the mitigation of hazard risk. Mitigation is explained and then followed by definitions and examples of forms of structural and nonstructural mitigation. Insurance, as a mitigation option, is addressed. Finally, various obstacles to effective mitigation are identified and explained.

Chapter 5 addresses disaster preparedness. A general overview of preparedness is followed by several practical topics, including communications, social marketing, training, animals in disasters, public warning, and preparedness obstacles.

Chapter 6 examines the very complex response to international disasters. Following an overview of response, topics addressed include recognition of disasters, disaster assessments, the various components of disaster response (including search and rescue; the provision of food, water, and medical supplies; shelter, sanitation; social services; security; evacuation and relocation; medical treatment; and fatality management), and coordination, among many others.

Chapter 7 covers the recovery period following the disaster response. Components of disaster recovery addressed include the opportunity factor, sustainability, reconstruction of infrastructure, debris removal, rebuilding homes and lives, economic recovery, debt relief, and other related issues.

Chapters 8 through 10 discuss the various players involved in the management of international disasters. These include governmental disaster management agencies (Chapter 8), nongovernmental organizations (Chapter 9), and the various multilateral organizations and international financial institutions (Chapter 10).

In conclusion, Chapter 11 discusses several special topics that must be considered in the management of international disasters. These include coordination, minimum standards, sovereignty, capacity building, equality in distribution of relief, terrorism, emerging epidemics, funding, and the future of international disaster management.

1

The Management of Disasters

Introduction

Disasters have adversely affected humans since the dawn of our existence. In response, individuals and societies alike have made many attempts to decrease their exposure to the consequences of these disasters, developing measures to address initial impact, as well as post-disaster response and recovery needs. Regardless of the approach adopted, all of these efforts have the same goal: disaster management.

The motivating concepts that guide disaster management—the reduction of harm to life, property, and the environment—are largely the same throughout the world. However, the capacity to carry out this mission is by no means uniform. Whether due to political, cultural, economic, or other reasons, the unfortunate reality is that some countries and some regions are more capable than others at addressing the problem. But no nation, regardless of its wealth or influence, is advanced enough to be fully immune from disasters' negative effects. Furthermore, the emergence of a global economy makes it more and more difficult to contain the consequences of any disaster within one country's borders.

This chapter examines basic concepts of disaster management and expands upon those concepts to specifically address the management of international disasters. A brief history of disaster management is provided for context. To illustrate the disparity in the effects of disasters around the world, an examination of the global impact of disasters will follow. Finally, several relevant terms used throughout this text will be defined.

Disasters Throughout History

Disasters are not merely ornamental or interesting events that adorn our collective historical record—these disruptions have served to guide and shape it. Entire civilizations have been decimated in an instant. Time and time again, epidemics and pandemics have resulted in sizable reductions of the world's population, as much as 50% across Europe during the fourteenth century bubonic plague (Black Plague) pandemic. Theorists have even ventured to suggest that many of history's great civilizations, including the Mayans, the Norse, the Minoans, and the Old Egyptian Empire, were ultimately brought to their knees not by their enemies but by the effects of floods, famines, earthquakes, tsunamis, El Niño events, and other widespread disasters (Fagan, 1999). A worldwide drought in the eighth and ninth centuries, caused by shifts in the yearly monsoons and resulting in mass crop failure and subsequent starvation, is now believed to have been behind the fall of both the Mayan empire in Mexico and the Tang dynasty in China (Sheridan, 2007). From a modern perspective, each of the catastrophic events that has occurred as of late, including the December 26, 2004, earthquake and tsunami (over 230,000 killed), the 2005 Kashmir earthquake (80,000 killed), the 2008 Sichuan earthquake in China (68,000 killed), and the 2010 Haiti earthquake (perhaps as many as 200,000 killed), might seem anomalous, but these disastrous events are not close to record-breaking, or even unique, in the greater historical context (see Table 1–1).

The History of Disaster Management

Ancient History

Hazards, and the disasters that often result, have not always existed. To qualify as a hazard, an action, event, or object must maintain a positive likelihood of affecting man or possibly have a consequence that may adversely affect man's existence. Until humans existed on the planet, neither the likelihood nor the consequence factors of hazards were calculable; thus their presence is negated.

With the appearance of man, however, followed the incidence of hazards and disasters. Archeological discovery has shown that our prehistoric ancestors faced many of the same risks that exist today: starvation, inhospitable elements, dangerous wildlife, violence at the hands of other humans, disease, accidental injuries, and more. These early inhabitants did not, however, sit idly by and become easy victims. Evidence indicates that they took measures to reduce, or *mitigate,* their risks. The mere fact that they chose to inhabit caves is testament to this theory.

Various applications of disaster management appear throughout the historical record. The story of Noah's ark from the Old Testament, for example, is a lesson in the importance of warning, preparedness, and mitigation. In this tale, believed to be based at least partly upon actual events, Noah is warned of an approaching flood. He and his family prepare for the impending disaster by constructing a floating ark. The protagonist in this story even attempts to mitigate the impact on the planet's biodiversity by collecting two of each species and placing them within the safety of the ark. These individuals are rewarded for their actions by surviving the disastrous flood. Those who did not perform similar actions, the story tells us, perished.

Evidence of risk management practices can be found as early as 3200 BC. In what is now modern-day Iraq lived a social group known as the Asipu. When community members faced a difficult

Table 1–1   Selected Notable Disasters Throughout History

Disaster	Year	Number Killed
Mediterranean earthquake (Egypt and Syria)	1201	1,100,000
Shaanzi earthquake (China)	1556	830,000
Calcutta typhoon (India)	1737	300,000
Caribbean hurricane (Martinique, St. Eustatius, Barbados)	1780	22,000
Tamboro volcano (Indonesia)	1815	80,000
Influenza epidemic (world)	1917	20,000,000
Yangtze River flood (China)	1931	3,000,000
Famine (Russia)	1932	5,000,000
Bangladesh cyclone (Bangladesh)	1970	300,000
Tangshan earthquake (China)	1976	655,000

Source: St. Louis University, 1997; NBC News, 2004.

decision, especially one involving risk or danger, they could appeal to the Asipu for advice. The Asipu, using a process similar to modern-day hazards risk management, would first analyze the problem at hand, propose several alternatives, and finally give possible outcomes for each alternative (Covello & Mumpower, 1985). Today, this methodology is referred to as *decision analysis,* and it is key to any comprehensive risk management endeavor.

Early history is also marked by incidents of organized emergency response. For example, when in AD 79 the volcano Vesuvius began erupting, two towns in its shadow—Herculaneum and Pompeii—faced an impending catastrophe. Although Herculaneum, which was at the foot of the volcano and therefore directly in the path of its lava flow, was buried almost immediately, the majority of Pompeii's population survived. This was because the citizens of Pompeii had several hours before the volcano covered their city in ash, and evidence suggests that the city's leaders organized a mass evacuation. The few who refused to leave suffered the ultimate consequence, and today lie as stone impressions in an Italian museum.

Modern Roots

All-hazards disaster and emergency management, wherein a comprehensive approach is applied to address most or all of a community's hazard risks, are relatively new. However, many of the concepts that guide today's practice can be traced to the achievements of past civilizations. While the management of disasters during the past few thousand years was limited to single acts or programs addressing individual hazards, many of these accomplishments were quite organized, comprehensive, and surprisingly effective at reducing both human suffering and damage to the built environment. See the following examples.

Floods have always confounded human settlements. However, archeologists have found evidence in several distinct and unrelated locations that early civilizations made attempts to formally address the flood hazard. One of the most celebrated of these attempts occurred in Egypt during the reign of Amenemhet III (1817–1722 BC). Amenemhet III created what has been described as history's first substantial river control project. Using a system of over 200 "water wheels," some of which remain to this day, the pharaoh effectively diverted the annual floodwaters of the Nile River into Lake Moeris. In doing so, the Egyptians were able to reclaim over 153,000 acres of fertile land that otherwise would have been useless (Quarantelli, 1995; Egyptian State Information Service, n.d.).

The roots of the modern fire department trace back 2000 years to when the city of Rome was nearly destroyed by fire. Before this event, slaves had been tasked with fighting fires and their poor training, lack of equipment, and understandable lack of motivation made them highly ineffective. Following the great fire, Emperor Augustus established a formal, citywide firefighting unit from within the Roman army called the Corps of Vigiles. As a result, the firefighting profession became highly respected and, likewise, highly effective, and was emulated throughout the vast Roman Empire for 500 years. The structure of this organization was quite similar to many fire departments today with members fulfilling job-specific roles (see Exhibit 1–1). With the fall of Rome, however, came the disappearance of the Corps of Vigiles, and organized firefighting did not appear anywhere in the world for another 1,000 years.

The Incas, who lived throughout the Andes mountains in South America during the thirteenth to fifteenth centuries, practiced a form of urban planning that focused on their need to defend themselves from enemy attack. Many of the Incan cities were located at the peaks of rugged, although easily defensible, mountains. The prime example of their architectural achievement is the fortress of Machu

---

EXHIBIT 1–1: JOB TITLES WITHIN THE ROMAN CORPS OF VIGILES

Aquarius: A firefighter whose main tasks included supplying water to the *siphos* (pumps) and organizing bucket brigades.

Siphonarius: A firefighter responsible for the supervision and operation of the water pumps.

Uncinarius: An operator of a firefighting hook, which was designed to remove the flammable roofs of houses or buildings.

Source: Gloucestershire Fire and Rescue Service, n.d. *A Roman Fire Service.* Gloucestershire City Council.

Picchu. However, in locating their cities upon mountaintops and other similar areas, the Incas merely replaced one man-made hazard with a whole range of environmental hazards. To facilitate life on this extreme terrain, the Incas developed an innovative form of land terracing that not only conserved water in their unpredictable climate but also protected their crops—and thus their existence—from the landslides that occurred during periods of heavy precipitation.

As later eras are examined, still more examples of methods created to address specific hazards and their consequences emerge. One of the greatest and most effective forms of disaster mitigation in history is the collective effort of the British and Indian governments, which sought to reduce Indians' annual suffering and starvation that occurred as result of regular drought patterns. These famines became so devastating during the late nineteenth century that up to a million people were dying of starvation each year. Government officials commissioned a study and found that sufficient food existed throughout the country to feed the nation's entire population at all times, but that the problem lay in insufficient distribution capacity to address location-specific needs. To correct these shortfalls, planning committees were formed to develop various preventive measures, including a rapid expansion of the extensive railway system that crisscrosses the country (to quickly transport food), the adoption of a method by which indicators of emerging needs were identified and logged in a central repository, and greater monitoring of public health. So effective at controlling famine were these measures that many remain in force today. India's acclaimed railroad, which connects almost every one of that nation's settlements, is a legacy of these efforts (IRFCA, n.d.).

Civil Defense: The Birth of Modern Emergency Management

There is no global formula for how the countries of the world developed their disaster management capacities. However, there is one particular period in recent history that witnessed the greatest overall move toward a centralized safeguarding of citizens—the Civil Defense era (Figure 1–1).

Modern disaster management, in terms of the emergence of global standards and organized efforts to address preparedness, mitigation, and response activities for a wide range of disasters, did not begin to emerge until the mid-twentieth century. In most countries, this change materialized as a response to specific disaster events. At the same time, it was further galvanized by a shift in social philosophy, in which the government played an increasing role in preventing and responding to disasters. The legal foundation that allowed for such a shift was the result of advances in warfare technology.

In response to the threat posed by air raids and the ever-present and dreadful prospect of a nuclear attack, many industrialized nations' governments began to form elaborate systems of civil

FIGURE 1–1 Civil defense era poster, Pennsylvania, United States. (From Library of Congress, 2000)

defense. These systems included detection systems, early warning alarms, hardened shelters, search and rescue teams, and local and regional coordinators. Most nations' legislatures also established legal frameworks to guide both the creation and maintenance of these systems through the passage of laws, the creation of national-level civil defense organizations, and the allocation of funding and personnel.

Despite these impressive efforts, surprisingly few civil defense units evolved over time into more comprehensive disaster or emergency management organizations (Quarantelli, 1995). But the legal framework developed to support them remained in place and formed the basis for modern disaster and emergency management as we know it today. For example:

- Great Britain's disaster management agency traces its roots to the Civil Defense Act of 1948.
- Canada's Office of Critical Infrastructure Preparedness and Emergency Preparedness (OCIPEP) grew out of the Canadian Civil Defense Organization created in 1948.
- The United States Federal Emergency Management Agency (FEMA) grew out of the Federal Civil Defense Act of 1950.
- France's civil protection is a product of that nation's 1950 Ordinance and the 1965 Decree Relating to Civil Defense.
- Algeria Civil Protection grew out of the 1964 Decree on the Administrative Organization of Civil Defense.

While emergency management structures vary from country to country, having formed largely independent and irrespective of each other, patterns do exist. Many countries developed their disaster management capabilities out of necessity and their government's subsequent acceptance of the need to formalize both the authority and budget for an agency to address that risk. Other countries formed their disaster management structures not for civil defense, but after being spurred into action by popular criticism for poor management of a natural disaster (e.g., Peru in 1970, Nicaragua in 1972, and Guatemala in 1976 following destructive earthquakes in each country).

And still others, regardless of their disaster history, have no real emergency management structure to speak of.

The International Decade for Natural Disaster Reduction

On December 11, 1987, the United Nations General Assembly declared the 1990s as the "International Decade for Natural Disaster Reduction" (IDNDR). This action was taken to promote internationally coordinated efforts to reduce material losses and social and economic disruption caused by natural disasters, especially in developing countries. The stated mission of the IDNDR was to improve each United Nations (UN) member country's capacity to prevent or diminish adverse effects from natural disasters and to establish guidelines for applying existing science and technology to reduce the impact of natural disasters.

On December 22, 1989, through UN Resolution 44/236, the General Assembly set forth the goals they wished to achieve during the IDNDR. In addition to establishing a special UN office in Geneva to coordinate the activities of the IDNDR, the resolution called upon the various UN agencies to:

1. Improve each country's capacity to mitigate the effects of natural disasters expeditiously and effectively, paying special attention to assisting developing countries in the assessment of disaster damage potential and in the establishment of early warning systems and disaster-resistant structures when and where needed.
2. Devise appropriate guidelines and strategies for applying existing scientific and technical knowledge, taking into account the cultural and economic diversity among nations.
3. Foster scientific and engineering endeavors aimed at closing critical gaps in knowledge in order to reduce loss of life and property.
4. Disseminate existing and new technical information related to measures for the assessment, prediction, and mitigation of natural disasters.
5. Develop measures for the assessment, prediction, prevention, and mitigation of natural disasters through programs of technical assistance and technology transfer, demonstration projects, and education and training, tailored to specific disasters and locations, and to evaluate the effectiveness of those programs (United Nations, 1989).

It was expected that all participating governments would, at the national level:

1. Formulate national disaster-mitigation programs, as well as economic, land use, and insurance policies for disaster prevention, and particularly in developing countries, integrate them fully into their national development programs.
2. Participate during the IDNDR in concerted international action for the reduction of natural disasters and, as appropriate, establish national committees in cooperation with the relevant

scientific and technological communities and other concerned sectors with a view to attaining the objective and goals of the decade.

3. Encourage their local administrations to take appropriate steps to mobilize the necessary support from the public and private sectors and to contribute to achieving the purposes of the decade.

4. Keep the Secretary-General informed of their countries' plans and of assistance that could be provided so that the UN could become an international center for the exchange of information and the coordination of international efforts concerning activities in support of the objective and goals of the decade, thus enabling each state to benefit from other countries' experience.

5. Take measures, as appropriate, to increase public awareness of damage risk probabilities and the significance of preparedness, prevention, relief, and short-term recovery activities with respect to natural disasters and to enhance community preparedness through education, training, and other means, taking into account the specific role of the news media.

6. Pay due attention to the impact of natural disasters on healthcare, particularly to activities to mitigate the vulnerability of hospitals and healthcare centers, as well as the impact on food storage facilities, human shelter, and other social and economic infrastructure.

7. Improve the early international availability of appropriate emergency supplies through the storage or earmarking of such supplies in disaster-prone areas (United Nations, 1989).

The Yokohama Strategy—Global Recognition of the Need for Disaster Management

In May 1994, UN member states met at the World Conference on Natural Disaster Reduction in Yokohama, Japan, to assess the progress attained by the IDNDR. At this meeting, they developed the Yokohama Strategy and Plan of Action for a Safer World. Through this document, the UN affirmed the following:

1. Impact of natural disasters in terms of human and economic losses has risen in recent years, and society in general has become more vulnerable to natural disasters. Those usually most affected by natural and other disasters are the poor and socially disadvantaged groups in developing countries as they are least equipped to cope with them.

2. Disaster prevention, mitigation, preparedness, and relief are four elements that contribute to and gain from the implementation of sustainable development policies. These elements, along with environmental protection and sustainable development, are closely interrelated. Therefore, nations should incorporate them in their development plans and ensure efficient follow-up measures at the community, national, subregional, and international levels.

3. Disaster prevention, mitigation, and preparedness are better than disaster response in achieving (disaster reduction) goals. Disaster response alone is not sufficient, as it yields only temporary results at a very high cost. We have followed this limited approach for too long. This has been further demonstrated by the recent focus on response to complex emergencies, which, although compelling, should not divert from pursuing a comprehensive approach. Prevention contributes to lasting improvement in safety and is essential to integrated disaster management.

4. The world is increasingly interdependent. All countries shall act in a new spirit of partnership to build a safer world based on common interests and shared responsibility to save human lives, since natural disasters do not respect borders. Regional and international cooperation will

significantly enhance our ability to achieve real progress in mitigating disasters through the transfer of technology and the sharing of information and joint disaster prevention and mitigation activities. Bilateral and multilateral assistance and financial resources should be mobilized to support these efforts.

5. Information, knowledge, and some of the technology necessary to reduce the effects of natural disasters can be available in many cases at low cost and should be applied. Appropriate technology and data, with the corresponding training, should be made available to all freely and in a timely manner, particularly to developing countries.

6. Community involvement and their active participation should be encouraged to gain greater insight into the individual and collective perception of development and risk, and to have a clear understanding of the cultural and organizational characteristics of each society as well as of its behavior and interactions with the physical and natural environment. This knowledge is of the utmost importance to determine those things that favor and hinder prevention and mitigation or encourage or limit the preservation of the environment from the development of future generations, and to find effective and efficient means to reduce the impact of disasters.

7. The adopted Yokohama Strategy and related Plan of Action for the rest of the decade and beyond:

    A. Will note that each country has the sovereign responsibility to protect its citizens from natural disasters.

    B. Will give priority attention to the developing countries, particularly the least developed, land-locked countries and the small island developing states.

    C. Will develop and strengthen national capacities and capabilities and, where appropriate, national legislation for natural and other disaster prevention, mitigation, and preparedness, including the mobilization of nongovernmental organizations and participation of local communities.

    D. Will promote and strengthen subregional, regional, and international cooperation in activities to prevent, reduce, and mitigate natural and other disasters, with particular emphasis on

    - Human and institutional capacity-building and strengthening

    - Technology sharing—the collection, the dissemination, and the utilization of information

    - Mobilization of resources

    E. The international community and the UN system in particular must provide adequate support to (natural disaster reduction).

    F. The Yokohama Conference is at a crossroad in human progress. In one direction lie the meager results of an extraordinary opportunity given to the UN and its member states. In the other direction, the UN and the world community can change the course of events by reducing the suffering from natural disasters. Action is urgently needed.

    G. Nations should view the Yokohama Strategy for a Safer World as a call to action, individually and in concert with other nations, to implement policies and goals reaffirmed in Yokohama, and to use the International Decade for Natural Disaster Reduction as a catalyst for change (ISDR, 1994).

The participating member states accepted the following principles to be applied to disaster management within their own countries. The tenth, and final, principle formalized the requirement that each nation's government accept responsibility for protecting its people from the consequences of disasters:

1. Risk assessment is a required step for the adoption of adequate and successful disaster reduction policies and measures.
2. Disaster prevention and preparedness are of primary importance in reducing the need for disaster relief.
3. Disaster prevention and preparedness should be considered integral aspects of development policy and planning at national, regional, bilateral, multilateral, and international levels.
4. Development and strengthening of capacities to prevent, reduce, and mitigate disasters are a top priority to be addressed during the 1990s to provide a strong basis for follow-up activities after that period.
5. Early warnings of impending disasters and their effective dissemination using telecommunications, including broadcast services, are key factors to successful disaster prevention and preparedness.
6. Preventive measures are most effective when they involve participation at all levels from the local community through the national government to the regional and international levels.
7. Vulnerability can be reduced by the application of proper design and patterns of development focused on target groups by appropriate education and training of the whole community.
8. The international community accepts the need to share the necessary technology to prevent, reduce, and mitigate disasters; this should be made freely available and in a timely manner as an integral part of technical cooperation.
9. Environmental protection as a component of sustainable development consistent with poverty alleviation is imperative in the prevention and mitigation of natural disasters.
10. Each country bears the primary responsibility for protecting its people, infrastructure, and other national assets from the impact of natural disasters. The international community should demonstrate strong political determination required to mobilize adequate and make efficient use of existing resources—including financial, scientific, and technological means, in the field of natural disaster reduction—bearing in mind the needs of the developing countries, particularly those least developed (ISDR, 1994).

Modern Disaster Management—A Four-phase Approach

Comprehensive disaster management is based upon four distinct components: mitigation, preparedness, response, and recovery. Although a range of terminology is often used in describing them, effective disaster management utilizes each component in the following manner:

1. *Mitigation.* Involves reducing or eliminating the likelihood or the consequences of a hazard, or both. Mitigation seeks to "treat" the hazard such that it impacts society to a lesser degree. See Chapter 4 for more information.
2. *Preparedness.* Involves equipping people who may be impacted by a disaster or who may be able to help those impacted with the tools to increase their chance of survival and to minimize their financial and other losses. See Chapter 5 for more information.
3. *Response.* Involves taking action to reduce or eliminate the impact of disasters that have occurred or are currently occurring, in order to prevent further suffering, financial loss, or a

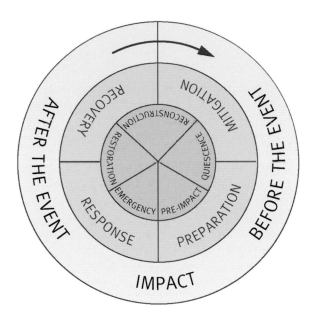

FIGURE 1-2 The disaster management cycle. (From Alexander, 2002)

combination of both. Relief, a term commonly used in international disaster management, is one component of response. See Chapter 6 for more information.

4. *Recovery.* Involves returning victims' lives back to a normal state following the impact of disaster consequences. The recovery phase generally begins after the immediate response has ended, and can persist for months or years thereafter. See Chapter 7 for more information.

Various diagrams illustrate the cyclical nature by which these and other related factors are performed over time, although disagreement exists concerning how such a "disaster management cycle" is visualized. These diagrams, such as the one in Figure 1-2, are generalizations, and it must always be understood that many exceptions can be identified in each. In practice, all of these factors are inter-mixed and are performed to some degree before, during, and after disasters. Disasters tend to exist in a continuum, with the recovery from one often leading straight into another. And while response is often pictured as beginning immediately after disaster impact, it is not uncommon for the actual response to begin well before the disaster actually happens.

What Is International Disaster Management?

Two separate but interrelated concepts are represented by the term "international disaster management":

1. The study of the diverse emergency and disaster management systems and structures that exist throughout the world.
2. The study of disaster management in scenarios where the capacity of a single nation's response mechanisms is overwhelmed.

Every country, every government, and every society is unique regarding:

- Its vulnerabilities and the root causes of such.
- The perception of risk and the methods used to identify and analyze it.
- The institutions, systems, and structures created to manage risk.
- The statutory authorities that guide the management of risk and the management of events that do actually occur.
- The mechanisms developed to respond to disaster events and the response capacity of those mechanisms.

Several times each year, the response requirements of disaster events exceed the disaster management abilities of a single nation or several nations. In these instances, the governments of the affected countries call upon the resources of the international response community. This cooperative international response is, by definition, international disaster management.

Over time and through iteration, a recognized and systemic process for responding to international disasters has begun to emerge. Standards for response have been developed by multiple sources, and a recognized group of typical participants has been identified (see Exhibit 1–2). Through practice and study, formulaic, methodical processes for assessing both the affected nations' damage and their various response needs have been identified, tried, and improved upon. What was only 20 years ago a chaotic, *ad hoc* reaction to international disasters has grown with astounding speed into a highly effective machine.

It is important to add that disasters do not become international just because they have overwhelmed a country's capacity to respond. There must be a commitment on the participants' part to recognize the need for international involvement and to accept the appeal made by the host nation's government. The sad truth is that, in practice, not all disasters elicit the same level of international interest and response, whether because of donor fatigue (see Chapter 11), media interest, diverted priorities, or other events that may dilute public interest. The Mozambique floods of 2000 are but one example of a situation in which the international community has been accused of sitting idly by as hundreds of people died (see Exhibit 1–3).

EXHIBIT 1–2: INTERNATIONAL DISASTER MANAGEMENT PARTICIPANTS

- Victims
- Local first responders
- The governments of the affected countries
- Governments of other countries
- International organizations
- International financial institutions
- Regional organizations and associations
- Nonprofit organizations
- Private organizations—business and industry
- Local and regional donors

EXHIBIT 1–3: 2000 MOZAMBIQUE FLOODS TIMELINE

February 9	Heavy rain begins falling across most of southern Africa, with Mozambique hit the hardest. The capital, Maputo, is submerged. Throughout the country, hundreds of thousands of families are left homeless and stranded. Damage to crops and infrastructure is severe.
February 11	At least 70 people have died due to the flooding. The UN reports that 150,000 people are in immediate danger due to starvation and disease. Dysentery outbreaks are reported outside the capital.
February 22	Tropical cyclone Eline makes a direct hit on the country, worsening the condition in many areas already submerged by the floods. The South African Air Force begins making airlifts to over 23,000 desperate victims.
February 24	The UN makes an appeal for $13 million in immediate relief and $65 million for recovery assistance. The appeal goes unanswered. Rainfall draining from other parts of southern Africa begins to flow into Mozambique, worsening already poor conditions.
February 27	More rainfall causes flash floods throughout the country, destroying much of the remaining farmland.
March 2	Floodwaters have risen by up to 26 feet (8 m) in many parts of the country. International aid workers report that 100,000 people are in need of immediate evacuation, and over 7000 are trapped in trees and need to be rescued (many have been trapped in the trees for several days without food or clean water). Finally, more than 3 weeks after the crisis began, international disaster management agencies begin to send responders and relief assistance.

Source: BBC News, 2000.

Response and recovery alone, however, are not effective means of managing disasters if they are performed in the absence of a comprehensive regimen of preparedness and mitigation activities (see Table 1–2). An important focal shift among the world's international disaster management organizations, agencies, and interest groups from disaster response to disaster prevention is evidence of widespread recognition and acceptance of this. Although many national governments, especially in the developing world, have yet to make a dedicated effort toward initiating or improving their pre-disaster management activities, many international development and disaster management agencies are working to address this issue. The UN, whose members consist of almost every country in the world, has made a sustained effort to lead its member nations in addressing their shortfalls: first by dedicating the 1990s to the IDNDR (producing the Yokohama Strategy and the Plan of Action for a Safer World), and then by following up with the International Strategy for Disaster Reduction (ISDR) to ensure that forward momentum is maintained.

Today, the United Nations International Strategy for Disaster Reduction (UNISDR) guides the efforts of the international community's overall disaster management mission. Specifically, the UNISDR seeks to build "disaster resilient communities by promoting increased awareness of the

Table 1–2   Response and Recovery-based Management versus Prevention and Risk Reduction-based Management

Response and Recovery-based Efforts	Prevention and Risk Reduction-based Efforts
Primary focus on disaster events	Focus on vulnerability and risk issues
Single, event-based scenarios	Dynamic, multiple risk issues and development scenarios
Basic responsibility to respond to an event	Fundamental need to assess, monitor, and update exposure to changing conditions
Often fixed, location-specific conditions	Extended, changing, shared or regional, local variations
Responsibility in single authority or agency	Involves multiple authorities, interests, actors
Command and control, directed operations	Situation-specific functions, free and open association and participation
Established hierarchical relationships	Shifting, fluid, and tangential relationships
Often focused on hardware and equipment	Dependent on related practices, abilities, and knowledge base
Dependent on specialized expertise	Focused on aligning specialized expertise with public views and priorities
Urgent, immediate, and short time frames in outlook, planning, attention, and returns	Moderate and long time frames in outlook, planning, values, and returns
Rapidly changing, dynamic information usage, which is often conflicting or sensitive in nature	Accumulated, historical, layered, updated, or comparative use of information
Primary, authorized, or singular information sources, need for definitive facts	Open or public information, multiple, diverse, or changing sources, differing perspectives and points of view
In–out or vertical flows of information	Dispersed, lateral flows of information
Relates to matters of public security, safety	Matters of public interest, investment, and safety

Source: Adapted from Jeggle (2001).

importance of disaster reduction as an integral component of sustainable development, with the goal of reducing human, social, economic, and environmental losses due to natural hazards and related technological and environmental disasters" (UNISDR, n.d.).

In January 2005, in Hyogo, Japan, the UN held the World Conference on Disaster Reduction. More than 4000 participants attended, including representatives from 168 governments, 78 UN specialized agencies and observer organizations, 161 nongovernmental organizations, and 562 journalists from 154 media outlets. The public forum attracted more than 40,000 visitors. The outcome of the conference was a 24-page "framework for action," adopted by all member countries, that outlined members' resolve to pursue "the substantial reduction of disaster losses, in lives and in the social, economic and environmental assets of communities and countries by 2015."

The framework outlined three strategic goals to achieve this:

- The more effective integration of disaster risk considerations into sustainable development policies, planning, and programming at all levels, with a special emphasis on disaster prevention, mitigation, preparedness, and vulnerability reduction.
- The development and strengthening of institutions, mechanisms, and capacities at all levels, particularly at the community level, that can systematically contribute to building resilience to hazards.

- The systematic incorporation of risk reduction approaches into design and implementation of emergency preparedness, response, and recovery programs in the reconstruction of affected communities (ISDR2, 2005).

The framework also outlined general considerations and key activities in the following five areas, identified as priorities for 2005–2015:

- Ensuring that disaster risk reduction is a national and local priority with a strong institutional basis for implementation.
- Identifying, assessing, and monitoring disaster risks and enhancing early warning.
- Using knowledge, innovation, and education to build a culture of safety and resilience at all levels.
- Reducing underlying risk factors.
- Strengthening disaster preparedness for effective response at all levels (ISDR2, 2005).

With the adoption of this framework, which coincided with some of the most devastating hazards and disasters in recent memory, international disaster management has climbed to the forefront of the international policy agenda. UNISDR, through the Global Platform for Disaster Risk Reduction, has only increased the international activity to address the growing hazard risk (see Exhibit 1–4). For years, the nations of the world have watched as country after country, both rich and poor, have suffered the consequences of terrible disasters. However, it has not been until recently that world leaders have begun to fully grasp that many of these consequences could have been reduced through better mitigation and preparedness efforts and more effective response capabilities. As a result, the field of international disaster management is now in a position to influence these leaders in a way previously not possible.

Disasters, Poverty, and Development

Research and practice support the theory that there exists a strong correlation between disasters and poverty. It is well documented that those developing countries repeatedly subject to disasters experience stagnant or even negative rates of development over time (see Figure 1–3). Hurricane Mitch, which destroyed as much as 70% of the infrastructure in Honduras and Nicaragua (UNISDR, 2004), is a prime example, having been blamed with reversing the rates of development in these and other Central American countries by at least a decade (and as much as 20 and 30 years in some areas; Oxfam, 1998). The same effect also has been witnessed in many of the areas affected by the 2004 tsunami and earthquake events in Southeast Asia and the 2010 earthquake in Haiti (see Exhibit 1–5). For countries with developing economies, the financial setbacks these events inflict can be ruinous, in contrast to their industrialized counterparts where a robust economy absorbs such impacts. In 2001, for example, earthquakes occurred both in El Salvador and in the United States (Seattle), each causing approximately $2 billion in damages. While this amount had little or no noticeable impact on the U.S. economy, the financial consequences in El Salvador amounted to 15% of that country's GDP (UNDP, 2004b).

The aftermath of a disaster exacerbates the debilitating causes of poverty in developing countries. Each disaster is unique in its consequences, so there is no single formula that can be used to characterize precisely how these problems will play out. The following list, however, provides a

---

EXHIBIT 1–4: GLOBAL PLATFORM FOR DISASTER RISK REDUCTION

The Global Platform for Disaster Risk Reduction (GP) was established by mandate of the UN General Assembly. The GP is an international meeting that occurs every 2 years and is attended by the international disaster risk reduction community, which includes governments, international organizations (including the UN and other regional organizations and institutions), NGOs, scientific/academic institutions, and the private sector. By mandate, the GP:

- Assesses progress made in the implementation of the Hyogo Framework for Action
- Enhances awareness of disaster risk reduction
- Enables the sharing of experiences and lessons from good practice
- Identifies remaining gaps and recommends targeted action to accelerate national and local implementation.

The first and second sessions of the GP, which occurred in 2007 and 2009, respectively, were attended by more than 152 governments and 137 organizations. These sessions helped to build momentum for national commitments to perform disaster risk reduction, culminating with the May 2011 GP meeting in Geneva, Switzerland. The benchmarks set out in the first two meetings focused on five main areas, including to

1. Harmonize disaster risk reduction and climate change adaptation in the broader context of poverty reduction and sustainable development
2. Reduce community and local-level risk through partnerships that better recognize the mutual dependence of governments and nongovernmental organizations (NGOs), and to promote the role of women as drivers of action (with special consideration to youth and children's roles)
3. Move toward full implementation of the Hyogo Framework for Action through several action targets (e.g., assessments of and mitigation for educational and health facilities)
4. Increase the disaster risk reduction component of national budgets and international development funding (including humanitarian relief and recovery expenditures), and to improve measurements of the effectiveness of investment in risk reduction
5. Continue the efforts of the ISDR in supporting governments and NGOs in their disaster risk reduction efforts.

Source: Prevention Web (2010).

---

general overview of the many ways in which disasters harm poor countries beyond the initial death, injury, and destruction:

- National and international development efforts are stunted, erased, or even reversed.
- Sizable portions of GDP often must be diverted from development projects, social programs, or debt repayment to manage the disaster consequences and begin recovery efforts (see Figure 1–4).
- Vital infrastructure is damaged or destroyed—including roads, bridges, airports, sea ports, communications systems, power generation and distribution facilities, and water and sewage plants—requiring years to rebuild.

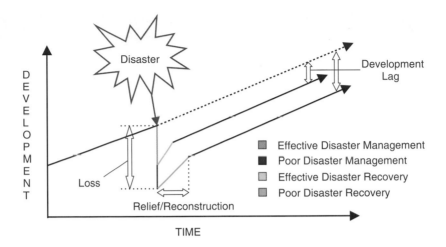

FIGURE 1–3 Impact of disasters on development. (Adapted from ADRC, 2005)

EXHIBIT 1–5: TSUNAMI SETS BACK DEVELOPMENT 20 YEARS IN MALDIVES

Within minutes of the December 2004 tsunami in the Indian Ocean, much of the economic and social progress in the Maldives was washed away.

According to government officials, the tsunami caused a 20-year setback in the development of this small country, an island nation off the coast of India, which only 6 days before the disaster had been removed from the UN's list of least-developed countries. In particular, the tsunami and its resulting floodwaters dealt a serious blow to the tourism sector, the country's main source of income. Nearly one-fourth of the 87 resorts in the Maldives were severely damaged and declared unable to operate. Tourism directly accounts for one-third of the country's economy, with the resorts alone providing between 25,000 and 30,000 jobs. When tourism-related tax and customs revenues are included, tourism contributes up to 70% of the economy, with the sector expanding each year. These earnings had helped to improve living standards in the Maldives, including increased school enrollment, lower unemployment, and more students seeking higher education abroad.

The Maldivians hope to get their fair share of the international aid pledged to help tsunami-affected countries. But most of all they hope to see tourists returning, as this is key to getting their country's socioeconomic development back on track. Schools, health clinics, jetties, power stations, and telephone lines were all badly damaged due to the tsunami, and repairing them will put a strain on the state budget for years to come.

Source: UNDP (2005).

- Schools are damaged or destroyed, leaving students without an adequate source of education for months or even years.
- Hospitals and clinics are damaged or destroyed, resulting in an increase in vulnerability to disease of the affected population.
- Formal and informal businesses are destroyed, resulting in surges in unemployment and decreased economic stability and strength.

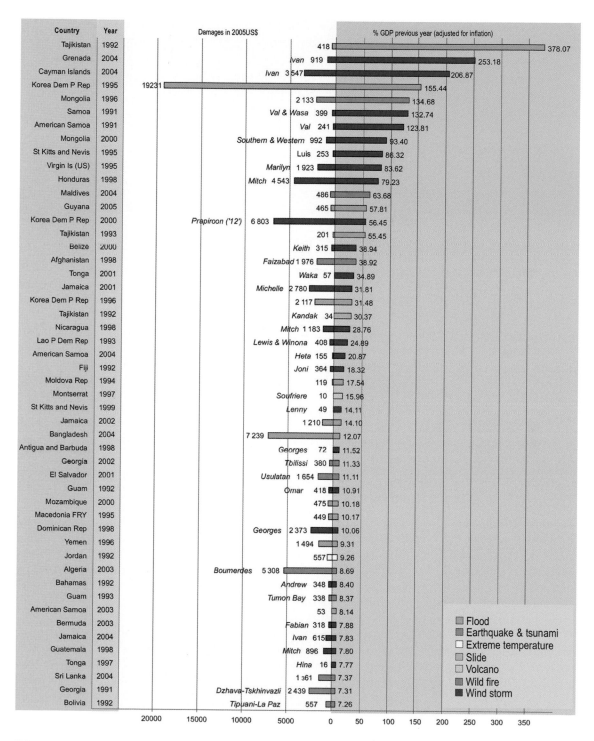

FIGURE 1–4 Selected natural disasters: total damage and share of the GDP: 1991–2005. (From EM-DAT: The OFDA/CRED International Disaster Database; www.em-dat.net) Université Catholique de Louvain, Brussels, Belgium.

- Reconstruction efforts result in shortages of materials and labor, which in turn drive up construction costs, inflate salaries, and draw workers away from other sectors where they are needed.
- Residents are forced or impelled to leave the affected zone, often never to return, extracting institutional knowledge, cultural and social identity, and economic viability from areas that cannot afford to spare such resources.
- Desperation and poverty lead to a rapid upsurge in crime and insecurity.
- A general feeling of hopelessness afflicts the affected population, leading to increased rates of depression and a lack of motivation to regain independence from outside assistance.

Disaster Trends

Increased accuracy in the reporting of disaster statistics has helped to provide both greater visualization and confirmation of something many scientists and disaster managers have been warning of for decades; the nature of disasters is rapidly changing. These changes are generally regarded as a result of human actions and development patterns. What is troubling is that these trends indicate that more disasters are occurring each year, with greater intensity, and that a great many more people are affected by either indirectly or directly. And while these disasters are becoming less deadly worldwide, they are causing a much greater financial impact on both affected and unaffected nations. Finally, and what may be the most disturbing of these trends, is that the poor countries of the world and their citizens are assuming a much greater proportion of the impacts of disasters. In sum, recent trends indicate that

1. The number of people affected by disasters is rising.
2. Overall, disasters are becoming less deadly.
3. Overall, disasters are becoming more costly.
4. Poor countries are disproportionately affected by disaster consequences.
5. The number of disasters is increasing each year.

Trend 1: The Overall Number of People Affected by Disasters Is Rising

Human settlement has always been directed by the needs of individuals and societies, such as the need for food, water, defense, and access to commerce. Almost without exception, increased natural hazard risk has been assumed in favor of these needs, often as result of a confidence that hazard risk can be accepted as "part of life" or can be effectively managed. Evidence of such behavior is apparent in almost any example of previous human settlement: communities along rivers build levees; those located along the sea coasts construct sea walls and jetties; farmers place their houses and sow their crops upon the fertile slopes of active volcanoes.

However, as the population and size of these settlements grow, the assumed risk becomes more and more concentrated. The overall rates by which people have relocated from rural areas into cities (urbanization) have continued to increase over time. Rising populations in almost all countries of the world amplify the urbanization effect. In 1950, less than 30% of the world's 2.5 billion people lived in an urban setting. By 1998, the number of people on earth had grown to 5.7 billion and 45% of them lived in cities. UN estimates state that by 2025 there will be 8.3 billion people on earth, and over 60% of them will live in cities (Britton, 1998).

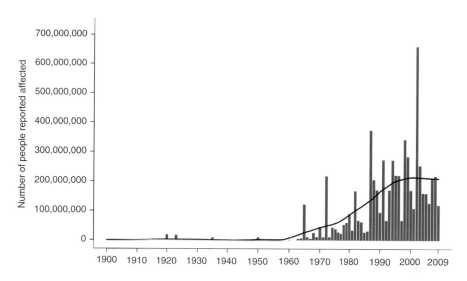

FIGURE 1–5 Total number of people affected. World: 1900–2009. (From EM-DAT: The OFDA/CRED International Disaster Database; www.em-dat.net) Université Catholique de Louvain, Brussels, Belgium.

When humans settle in high-risk urban areas, the hazard risks they face as individuals increase. As of the year 2000, it was estimated that at least 75% of the world's population lived in areas at risk from a major disaster (UNDP, 2004b). And because these high-risk areas periodically experience major disasters, it logically follows that the number of people who are annually affected by disasters (defined as having their home, crops, animals, livelihoods, or health impacted) is equally high (UNISDR, 2004).

Figure 1–5 displays the observed total number of people annually affected by disasters during the twentieth and early twenty-first centuries. Note that, beginning in 1954, there is a significant rise in the number of people affected. It was during this decade that the mass transition toward urbanization began in the industrialized nations, a trend that repeated soon after in most other nations of the world.

Trend 2: Overall, Disasters Are Becoming Less Deadly

The seismic, meteorological, hydrological, and other forces that result in natural hazards are natural processes that occur irrespective of the actions or existence of humans. Water has overflowed the banks of rivers since before man lived beside them. Archeologists and geologists have unearthed evidence that earthquake events occurred during every era of the planet's history. Volcanic activity has been given as much credit for its role in generating life on earth as it has for destroying it. Natural disasters, it has therefore been suggested, are merely the result of humans placing themselves directly into the path of these normal events (see Figure 1–6). United States Geological Survey (USGS) scientists Susan Hough and Lucile Jones aptly captured this line of thought when they wrote that "earthquakes don't kill people, buildings do" (Hough & Jones, 2002).

Humans are adaptable and quickly adjust to the pressures exerted upon them by nature. People have modified their behavior and their surroundings to accommodate their surrounding climate and topography, often proving successful at counteracting the negative consequences of common daily hazards such as rain or extreme temperatures. For less common events, such as earthquakes and

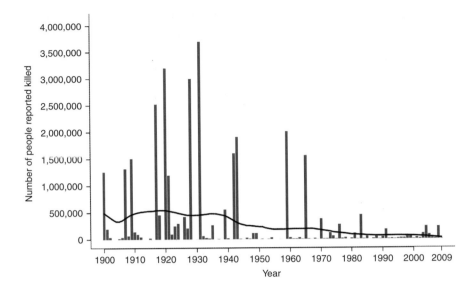

FIGURE 1–6 Total number of deaths reported in the world: 1900–2009. (From EM-DAT: The OFDA/CRED International Disaster Database; www.em-dat.net) Université Catholique de Louvain, Brussels, Belgium.

hurricanes, humans have had lower levels of success. Fortunately, modern science has helped to change this fact significantly, at least in those countries in which the technology and technical expertise is within reach. Table 1–3 illustrates the success achieved by the United States in adjusting to hurricane risk during the course of the twentieth century, where death rates fell steadily until the end of the century as explained by several driving forces (including better preparedness, storm tracking, public education, response, etc.). What is most interesting about this trend is that as we move into the second decade of the twenty-first century, there is an obvious trend reversal with the number of U.S. hurricane fatalities reaching levels that exceed the aggregate of the preceding 60 years. While there are varied theories to explain such a change, what draws the most support is the belief that this is an unintended consequence of a post-9/11 shift in U.S. emergency management policy that boosted terrorism prevention at the cost of natural hazard mitigation and preparedness. Such a consequence only reinforces the theory that global disaster fatality reduction is the result of our risk reduction efforts.

Table 1–3 Deaths Attributed to Hurricanes in the United States, 1900–2010

Period	Number Killed
1900–1919	10,000 (approximate; exact 1900 Galveston death toll is unknown)
1920–1939	3751
1940–1959	1119
1960–1979	453
1980–1999	82
2000–2010	2100

Source: Thoreau Institute, 2005; FEMA, 1997 (along with other multiple dates).

Globalization and increased international cooperation have helped the world community to more effectively address risk reduction and limit the human impacts of disasters. Although the number of disasters has more than tripled since the 1970s, the number of people worldwide who have perished has fallen by 50% (UNISDR, 2004). Greater recognition of the importance of emergency management and sustainable development is turning the tide on disasters. The efforts of the United Nations, the many nongovernmental agencies involved in development and disaster preparedness and response, and the efforts of individual governments have shown that humans can effectively influence their vulnerability.

There are several explanations for the falling fatality rates of disasters. These include:

1. More organized and comprehensive preparedness campaigns are helping individuals and communities to decrease their vulnerability and to react more appropriately in the face of disaster.
2. Early warning systems are giving potential victims more time to leave the dangerous situations associated with impending disasters.
3. Special disaster-specific protection structures, such as tornado safe rooms, are mitigating the impact that disasters have on human life.
4. Building code creation and enforcement are helping to increase the resilience of the various structures and systems upon which humans depend.
5. Secondary, post-disaster consequences, such as famine and disease, are more effectively managed by modern public-health response mechanisms.
6. Proper zoning procedures and enforcement are helping to prevent people from moving into the path of disasters and helping to remove those who are already there.
7. Sustainable development processes are helping to reduce population movement into areas of highest risk.

Trend 3: Overall, Disasters Are Becoming More Costly

The cost of disasters worldwide is increasing at an alarming rate. Twenty-five years ago, the economic damage from any given disaster rarely topped the billion-dollar mark, even after accounting for inflation. Now, several disasters top this mark each year (see Figure 1–7). By the year 2000, the cost of disasters worldwide had topped $60 billion per year, as measured by the international reinsurance firm Munich Re.

There are many reasons disasters are getting more expensive, including many of the previous explanations: there are more people in the world, there are more disasters, people are more concentrated together, and so forth. The fact remains that people continue to move toward urban centers, to build expensive structures and infrastructure in the path of hazards, and try to overcome the risk of disaster by building structures designed to resist damage. Take hurricanes in the United States, for example. Their basic power and natural characteristics have not changed significantly over time. However, human settlements in high-risk coastal areas have increased. The result of this human behavior is the rising costs of hurricane damage during the past 20 years (Riebeek, 2005).

There are several explanations for the rising financial cost of disasters, which include:

1. Increasing urbanization in high-risk zones is occurring throughout the world, concentrating wealth, physical structures, and infrastructure together in high-risk zones.

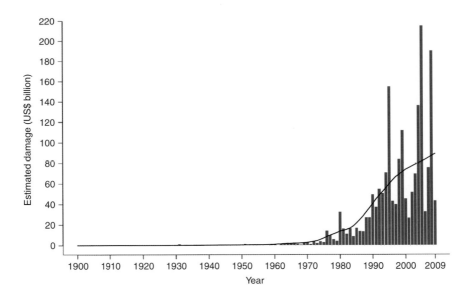

FIGURE 1–7 Total amount of reported damages (billion USD at 2009 prices) in the world: 1900–2009. (From EM-DAT: The OFDA/CRED International Disaster Database; www.em-dat.net) Université Catholique de Louvain, Brussels, Belgium.

2. Economies are much more dependent upon technologies that tend to fail in times of disaster; one example is the 2003 northeastern U.S./Canadian electrical blackout, which resulted in as much as $6 billion in damages.
3. Areas not directly affected are experiencing secondary economic consequences of disaster, as with many world economies following the September 11, 2001, terrorist attacks in the United States.
4. A greater number of less deadly but financially destructive disasters are occurring throughout the world as a result of climate change or other factors.
5. Increasing population; the U.S. Census Bureau estimates that the world's population grew from 3.8 to 6.8 billion between 1950 and 2010.

Trend 4: Poor Countries Are Disproportionately Affected by Disaster Consequences

Disasters of all kinds literally strike every nation of the world; they do not differentiate between rich and poor countries. However, developing countries suffer the greatest impact and also most often experience subsequent internal civil conflict that leads to complex humanitarian emergencies (CHEs; see section Definitions). Between 1980 and 2000, 53% of the deaths attributable to disasters occurred in countries with low human development ratings, although these countries accounted for only 11% of the world's "at-risk" population (UNDP, 2004b; see Figure 1–8). In fact, on average, 65% of disaster-related injuries and deaths are sustained in countries with per-capita income levels that are below $760 per year (UNEP, 2001; see Figure 1–9).

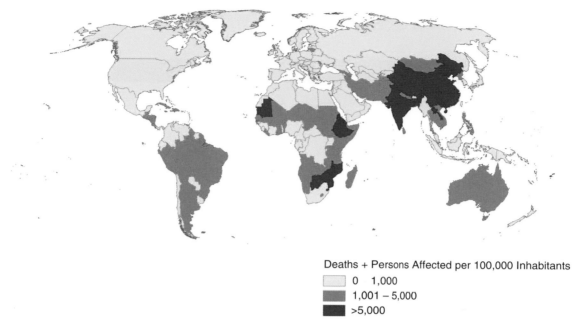

Deaths + Persons Affected per 100,000 Inhabitants

☐ 0   1,000
▨ 1,001 – 5,000
■ >5,000

FIGURE 1–8 Total number of deaths and of people affected by natural disasters by 100,000 inhabitants: 1974–2003. (From EM-DAT: The OFDA/CRED International Disaster Database; www.em-dat.net) Université Catholique de Louvain, Brussels, Belgium.

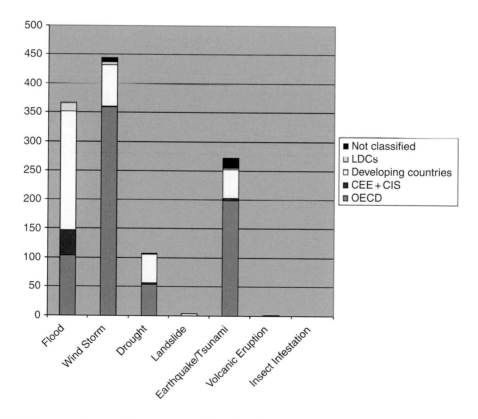

FIGURE 1–9 Total amount of economic damages reported in major world aggregates 1991–2005 (billion USD, 2006). (Adapted from EM-DAT: The OFDA/CRED International Disaster Database; www.em-dat.net) Université Catholique de Louvain, Brussels, Belgium.

OECD member countries: Australia, Austria, Belgium, Canada, Czech Republic, Denmark, Finland, France, Germany, Greece, Hungary, Iceland, Ireland, Italy, Japan, Luxembourg, Mexico, Netherlands, New Zealand, Norway, Poland, Portugal, Slovakia, South Korea, Spain, Sweden, Switzerland, Turkey, United Kingdom, United States

Central and Eastern Europe (CEE) and Commonwealth of Independent States (CIS) countries: Albania, Armenia, Azerbaijan, Belarus, Bosnia and Herzegovina, Bulgaria, Croatia, Czech Republic, Estonia, Georgia, Hungary, Kazakhstan, Kyrgyzstan, Latvia, Lithuania, Macedonia, Moldova, Poland, Romania, Russian Federation, Serbia and Montenegro, Slovakia, Slovenia, Tajikistan, Turkmenistan, Ukraine, Uzbekistan

Developing countries: Algeria, Antigua and Barbuda, Argentina, Bahamas, Bahrain, Barbados, Belize, Bolivia, Botswana, Brazil, Brunei, Cameroon, Chile, China, Colombia, Congo, Costa Rica, Côte d'Ivoire, Cuba, Cyprus, Dominica, Dominican Republic, Ecuador, Egypt, El Salvador, Fiji, Gabon, Ghana, Grenada, Guatemala, Guyana, Honduras, Hong Kong, China, India, Indonesia, Iran, Iraq, Jamaica, Jordan, Kenya, Kuwait, Lebanon, Libya, Malaysia, Marshall Islands, Mauritius, Mexico, Micronesia, Mongolia, Morocco, Namibia, Nauru, Nicaragua, Nigeria, North Korea, Oman, Pakistan, Palau, Palestinian Territories, Panama, Papua New Guinea, Paraguay, Peru, Philippines, Qatar, Saint Kitts and Nevis, Saint Lucia, St. Vincent and the Grenadines, Saudi Arabia, Seychelles, Singapore, South Africa, South Korea, Sri Lanka, Suriname, Swaziland, Syria, Thailand, Timor-Leste, Tonga, Trinidad and Tobago, Tunisia, Turkey, United Arab Emirates, Uruguay, Venezuela, Vietnam, Zimbabwe

Least-developed countries: Afghanistan, Angola, Bangladesh, Benin, Bhutan, Burkina Faso, Burundi, Cambodia, Cape Verde, Central African Republic, Chad, Comoros, Dem. Rep. of the Congo, Djibouti, Equatorial Guinea, Eritrea, Ethiopia, Gambia, Guinea, Guinea-Bissau, Haiti, Kiribati, Laos, Lesotho, Liberia, Madagascar, Malawi, Maldives, Mali, Mauritania, Mozambique, Myanmar, Nepal, Niger, Rwanda, Samoa (Western), São Tomé and Principe, Senegal, Sierra Leone, Solomon Islands, Somalia, Sudan, Tanzania, Togo, Tuvalu, Uganda, Vanuatu, Yemen, Zambia

Source: UNDP, 2004a.

Based on these facts, inferences can be drawn about a nation's disaster risk by considering its development status. Public health expert Eric Noji (1997) identified four primary reasons why the poor in general are often most at risk:

1. They are least able to afford housing that can withstand seismic activity.
2. They often live along coasts where hurricanes, storm surges, or earthquake-generated tsunamis strike or live in floodplains subject to inundation.
3. They are forced by economic circumstances to live in substandard housing built on unstable slopes that are susceptible to landslides or are built next to hazardous industrial sites.
4. They are not educated as to the appropriate life-saving behaviors or actions that they can take when a disaster occurs.

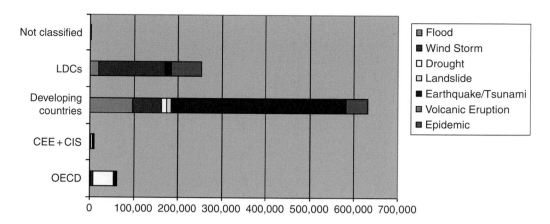

FIGURE 1–10 Number of people killed by disasters by income class: 1991–2005. (Note that *drought* includes extreme temperature hazards.) (From EM-DAT: The OFDA/CRED International Disaster Database; www.em-dat.net) Université Catholique de Louvain, Brussels, Belgium.

There are also many secondary reasons that contribute. For instance, injuries sustained in disasters, and the disease that often follows, are much more likely to lead to death in poor countries, where acute care may be substandard or nonexistent and the control of disease outbreaks more difficult. The poor are also likely to suffer greater disaster consequences as the result of minimal or nonexistent enforcement of safety standards, building codes, and zoning regulations (see Figure 1–10). The full range of explanations is both extensive and diverse.

Although the importance of disaster preparedness and mitigation is widely recognized by almost all of the world's countries, and although these principles are widely applied on a growing basis by international development agencies, it still comes as no surprise that countries ranking lower on development indices place disaster management very low in budgetary priority. These nations' resources tend to be focused on social interests such as education and infrastructure or on their military, instead of on projects that serve a preparatory or mitigation need, such as retrofitting structures with hazard-resistant construction. Because all disasters, even those that tend to repeat, are chance events and thus not guaranteed to happen, disaster management programs in poor countries tend to be viewed as a luxury or even superfluous. Compounding this situation, poverty and uncontrolled urbanization force large populations to concentrate in perilous, high-risk areas that have little or no defense against disasters. Thus, the difference in the effect of a disaster's impact in a rich versus poor country is remarkable. Table 1–4 illustrates these differences.

Trend 5: The Number of Disasters Is Increasing Each Year

All statistics on the annual number of disasters appear to indicate that, over time, the number of significant interactions between man and nature resulting in significant loss of life or property is increasing (see Figure 1–11). Furthermore, all evidence suggests that, despite a recent drop in the number of annual events, this trend will only continue over time without significant changes in settlement and development patterns.

There are two primary explanations for the increasing number of annual disasters. The first, a subject of much debate, is that climate change (both natural and human-influenced) and environmental

Table 1–4 Differences in Disaster Impact Between Rich and Poor Countries

Rich Countries	Poor Countries
Tend to suffer higher economic losses, but have mechanisms in place to absorb these costs	Have less at risk in terms of financial value, but maintain little or no buffer to absorb even low financial impacts Economic reverberations can be significant, and social development ultimately suffers
Employ mechanisms that reduce loss of life, such as early warning systems, enforced building codes, and zoning	Lack the resources necessary to take advantage of advanced technologies, and have little ability to enforce building codes and zoning even if these mechanisms do exist
Have immediate emergency and medical care that increase survivability and contain the spread of disease	Sustain massive primary and secondary casualties
Transfer much of personal, private, and public risk to insurance and reinsurance providers	Generally do not participate in insurance mechanisms. Divert funds from development programs to emergency relief and recovery

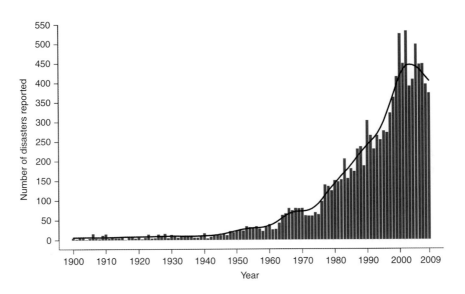

FIGURE 1–11 Total number of natural disasters reported in the world: 1900–2009. (From EM-DAT: The OFDA/CRED International Disaster Database; www.em-dat.net) Université Catholique de Louvain, Brussels, Belgium.

degradation are together resulting in a greater overall number of hazard events. Disaster managers have noticed a strong correlation between the loss of natural buffer zones (dunes, mangroves, wetlands), the destabilization of slopes, and unnatural increases and decreases in average global temperatures, among other related factors, with the changing dynamics of several major natural hazards. A few examples of hazards that can be heavily influenced by these human actions include landslides, floods, mudslides, extreme heat, and drought. The British NGO Oxfam released a report in 2008 that showed the number of disasters has increased fourfold in just two decades. Oxfam's research found that natural disaster events increased from 120 per year in the early 1980s to about 500 per year in 2008. What is particularly interesting about these findings is that while the number of geologic hazards (e.g., earthquakes, volcanoes) has remained relatively constant, the number of weather-related events (e.g., cyclonic storms, floods) has risen significantly (Gutierrez, 2008).

The second explanation pertains to patterns of increased human settlement in more vulnerable areas. As humans congregate in more urbanized centers, their collective vulnerability to disasters of all origins increases as a result. And when the hazard's risks are realized, its consequences have a much greater potential to result in a disaster than they otherwise would. In other words, incidents that may have been managed locally, with few deaths and only minor damages, will exhibit increasingly greater likelihoods of becoming devastating events with higher population density of the affected areas.

Considerable research has focused upon the phenomenon of marginalization of the urban poor. During mass migrations from rural regions into the cities, the poor are often faced with a shortage of available space within which to live, and are therefore forced to settle in very dangerous hazard zones such as unstable hillsides or floodplains. These groups, often living in disorganized informal settlements, effectively increase the chance that a disaster will result from any number of hazards that threaten the city. Chapter 3 will cover this topic of vulnerability in more depth.

Technological disasters, like their natural counterparts, are also increasing in number each year. In fact, this purely man-made form of disaster is growing at a rate much greater than natural disasters. Figure 1–12 shows that, from 1900 to 2005, the average number of reported technological disasters occurring worldwide grew and skyrocketed from under 50 per year in 1980 to almost 350 per year in 2000. This is a more than sevenfold increase in just 20 years. This graph also displays a recent drop in annual technological disaster events beginning in 2006. It is too early to tell if this is an actual trend reversal or whether the longer term rise in technological events will continue.

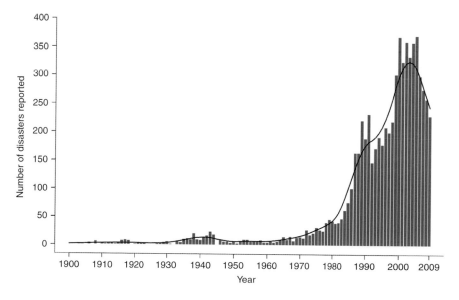

FIGURE 1–12 Total number of technological disasters reported in the world: 1900–2009. (From EM-DAT: The OFDA/CRED International Disaster Database; www.em-dat.net) Université Catholique de Louvain, Brussels, Belgium.

Definitions

Following is a list of defined terms that will be used throughout the text.

Hazard

There is dispute about the origin of the word *hazard*, but it likely came from either the French *hasard*, a game of dice predating craps, or the Arabic *al-zahr*, which means "the die." Clearly, the term is rooted in the concept of chance. In the modern sense of the word, hazards are events or physical conditions that have the *potential* to cause fatalities, injuries, property damage, infrastructure damage, agricultural loss, damage to the environment, interruption of business, or other types of harms or losses (FEMA, 1997). What determines whether a hazard becomes a disaster are risk and vulnerability.

Our lives are full of hazards, which exist in many forms, defined (in this case) according to their source. Chapter 2 will address the following three hazard types:

- Natural hazards
- Technological hazards
- Intentional hazards

The focus in Chapter 2 will be those hazards that have the potential to cause an international disaster. Cigarette smoke, for instance, is a hazard to public health, but would be unlikely to precipitate an event requiring the international disaster management community. A dam failure, however, very well could.

Risk

Just as all life is full of hazard, all life is full of risk. However, the concept of risk can have varying meanings depending on the context. Just as it is used differently by insurance specialists versus stockbrokers or physicians, disaster managers employ their own deviation on *risk*. It is not uncommon, for example, for the term to be used in a positive manner to denote "venture" or "opportunity" (Jardine & Hrudey, 1997, p. 490). Such variance in use may come from the word's multiple origins. The Arabic *risq* means "anything that has been given to you [by God] and from which you draw profit" (Kedar, 1970), possibly explaining why some may use the term in relation to fortune or opportunity. However, the Latin *risicum*, which describes a specific scenario faced by sailors attempting to circumvent the danger posed by a barrier reef, seems a more appropriate derivation for use in relation to disaster management, where the term's connotation is always negative.

Unfortunately, even among risk managers, there is no single accepted definition for the term. One of the simplest and most common definitions of risk preferred by many disaster managers, which will be used throughout this text, is one that displayed through the equation stating that risk is the likelihood of an event occurring multiplied by the consequence of that event, were it to occur: RISK = LIKELIHOOD × CONSEQUENCE (Ansell & Wharton, 1992).

Likelihood is expressed either as a probability (e.g., 0.15; 50%) or as a frequency (e.g., 1 in 1,000,000; 5 times per year), whichever is appropriate for the analysis considered. Consequences are a measure of the effect of the hazard on people or property. Expanding upon this definition, it can be said that by reducing either the likelihood of a hazard or the potential consequences that might result, risk is effectively reduced. Likewise, any action that increases the likelihood or consequences of a hazard increases risk.

Vulnerability

There is a reason that two identical events will present as a minor issue in one country and a disaster in another. This reason comes to mind when, in assessing damages from a hurricane, one comes across a house completely destroyed right next to an unscathed structure. We must also consider why two earthquakes, of almost equal magnitude and intensity, could cause less than 100 deaths in Los Angeles but over 20,000 in Gujarat, India. The answer to all of these issues is vulnerability.

Derived from the Latin term *vulnerabilis,* which means "to wound," vulnerability is a measure of the propensity of an object, area, individual, group, community, country, or other entity to incur the consequences of a hazard. This measurement results from a combination of physical, social, economic, and environmental factors or processes. Vulnerability can be decreased through actions that lower the propensity to incur harm, or it can be increased through actions that increase that propensity. For instance, retrofitting a building to withstand the shaking effects of an earthquake will lower that building's vulnerability to the hazard, lowering risk (*resilience,* the opposite of vulnerability, is a measure of propensity to avoid loss). Populations have vulnerabilities as well, which are raised or lowered according to their practices, beliefs, and economic status. Chapter 3 will expand upon this concept.

Disaster

The term *disaster* is derived from the Latin roots *dis-* and *astro,* meaning "away from the stars" or, in other words, an event to be blamed on an unfortunate astrological configuration. Disasters occur when a hazard risk is realized. There is a caveat to this definition, however: To be considered disastrous, the realized hazard must overwhelm the response capability of a community. An international disaster, as defined by the UN, is "a serious disruption of the functioning of society, causing widespread human, material, or environmental losses which exceed the ability of the affected society to cope using only its own resources" (UN, 1992).

There is an important distinction between an event and a disaster. Not all adverse events are disasters, only those that overwhelm response capacity. For instance, a simple house fire requires response by a jurisdictional fire department. There is surely property loss, and likely the possibility of injury or loss of life. However, as fires are routine occurrences that are easily managed, they normally are not considered disasters. In the great Chicago fire of 1871, however, more than 2000 acres of urban land were destroyed over the course of 3 days. Overall, the destruction included 28 miles of roads, 120 miles of sidewalk, 2000 lampposts, and 18,000 buildings, all totaling over $200 million in property damage (one-third of the value of all property in the city at the time; Wikipedia, 2005). Between two and three hundred people died. While both events are fires, only the Chicago fire can be called a disaster.

Disasters also grow in intensity as they overwhelm progressively larger response units. A local disaster is not a national disaster, for instance, if a state or provincial response entity can manage the consequences. If not, only then does the disaster become national, requiring the intervention of the national government. In situations in which a national government or several national governments are unable to manage the consequences of an adverse event, the event becomes an international disaster, requiring intervention by a range of international response and relief agencies.

Disasters are measured in terms of the lives lost, injuries sustained, property damaged or lost, and environmental degradation. These consequences are manifested through both direct and indirect means, and can be tangible or intangible. Understanding each of these measures is of great importance in assessing vulnerability, as will be shown in Chapter 3.

Disasters may be sudden onset or "creeping." Sudden-onset disasters often happen with little or no warning, and most of their damaging effects are sustained within hours or days. Examples include earthquakes, tsunamis, volcanoes, landslides, tornadoes, and floods. Creeping disasters occur when the ability of response agencies to support people's needs degrades over weeks or months, and they can persist for months or years once discovered. Examples are drought, famine, soil salination, the AIDS epidemic, and erosion.

Safe

While the term *safe* may seem so obvious as not to require clarification, its context in regard to disaster management is not evident without a solid understanding of risk. Most people assume that referring to something as "safe" implies that all risk has been eliminated. However, because such an absolute level of safety is virtually unattainable in the real world, disaster managers and societies must establish thresholds of risk that define a frequency of occurrence below which those societies need not worry about the hazard. A realistic definition is provided by Derby and Keeney, who contend that a risk becomes "safe," or "acceptable," if it is "associated with the best of the available alternatives, not with the best of the alternatives which we would *hope* to have available" (emphasis added; Derby & Keeney, 1981).

All aspects of life involve a certain degree of risk. However, as a global society, we are constantly assessing and reassessing what risk levels are acceptable for each and every hazard, considering that which science, technology, and law can offer to treat those risks. For many hazards, especially the natural, technological, and intentional examples provided in Chapter 2, this is true—as evidenced by the vast disparity between the number of people per population unit affected in the rich and poor countries of the world.

Compound (Combination) Disaster

Disasters are not always limited to a single hazard. Sometimes two or more completely independent disasters occur at the same time; for instance, an earthquake strike during a flood. It is more common that one disaster triggers a *secondary hazard*. Some secondary hazards only occur as result of a primary hazard, such as a tsunami (from earthquakes, volcanoes, or landslides), while others can occur either because of or independent of other disasters (such as landslides, which can be triggered by heavy rains, earthquakes, volcanoes, or other reasons, or occur purely on their own). Compound disasters, which can occur either sequentially or simultaneously with one or more disasters, have a tendency to exacerbate consequences and increase victims' issues (such as stress and isolation). They can make search and rescue and other response and recovery tasks more difficult, and, most important, can significantly increase the risk of harm to victims and responders alike.

Humanitarian Crisis

A humanitarian crisis is a special situation that results from a combination of the realized consequences of a hazard and the severely diminished coping mechanisms of an affected population. In these situations, the health and life of a very large number of people are threatened. Characteristics of humanitarian crises generally include mass incidence of

- Starvation/malnutrition
- Disease
- Insecurity
- Lack of shelter (exposure)
- A steadily growing number of victims

Humanitarian crises tend to only worsen without outside intervention.

Complex Humanitarian Emergency

There is a special type of humanitarian emergency that has response needs extending well beyond the normal scope of disaster management activities. These CHEs are the result of a combination of factors directly related to war and insecurity. The Inter-Agency Standing Committee (IASC) describes CHEs as a

> *humanitarian crisis in a country or region where there is a total or considerable breakdown of authority resulting from the internal and/or external conflict and which requires an international response that goes beyond the mandate or capacity of any single agency. (IASC, 1994)*

Andrew Natsios, director of the U.S. Agency for International Development (USAID), identifies five characteristics most commonly seen in CHEs in varying degrees of intensity. They are:

1. Civil conflict, rooted in traditional, ethnic, tribal, and religious animosities (usually accompanied by widespread atrocities).
2. Deteriorated authority of the national government such that public services disappear and political control dissolves.
3. Mass movements of population to escape conflict or search for food.
4. Massive dislocation of the economic system, resulting in hyperinflation and the devaluation of the currency, major declines in gross national product, skyrocketing unemployment, and market collapse.
5. A general decline in food security, often leading to severe malnutrition and occasional widespread starvation (Natsios, 1997).

CHEs, which will be described in further detail in Chapter 2, often result in the creation of both refugees and internally displaced persons (IDPs), who bring to the table entirely new response requirements.

Refugee versus Internally Displaced Person

In many situations related to war or internal strife, people are forced to flee their homes to escape anticipated or realized violence, often leaving behind all of their possessions. These groups are referred to as *forced migrants*. Where these migrants end up gives them further categorization, which significantly affects how international organizations are able to assist them.

If forced migrants are able to leave their country to seek asylum abroad, they become *refugees* (see Exhibit 1–6). When this happens, the host country generally provides them, as a group, with basic life needs. More important, international response agencies are granted access to them and are able to offer them food, shelter, and medical assistance. Refugees are also defended by a set of universally accepted laws that offer them a considerable degree of protection. Eventually, following the end of whatever conflict forced them from their homes, they are given assistance in returning to their former lives as best as possible. The United Nations High Commissioner for Refugees (UNHCR) estimates that there are more than 10 million refugees throughout the world today.

When forced migrants are unable or unwilling to cross the borders of their country, they become IDPs. There are many reasons why IDPs do not leave their country, including war in neighboring countries, little ability to travel long distances, and impassable border regions. IDPs have very little physical protection, and often face severe shortages of food, water, and other basic life necessities. They are afforded little protection under international law, and widely recognized agreements (like the Geneva Convention) are often difficult to apply. Mere recognition of IDP crises can be difficult and, once identified, access by international response and relief agencies can be both cumbersome and dangerous. The domestic government, which may view the uprooted people as "enemies of the state," retains ultimate control over their fate. UNHCR estimates that there are currently over 25 million internally displaced people in at least 50 countries throughout the world (Moore & Shellman, 2002; UNHCR, 2004).

Conclusion

International disaster management is a complex discipline. Like disaster management on the national level, it involves actions that seek to mitigate the effects of hazards, ensure that populations are prepared for disasters should they occur, facilitate the response to disasters that do occur, and help

---

EXHIBIT 1–6: CONVENTION RELATING TO THE STATUS OF REFUGEES: JULY 28, 1951

A *refugee* is someone who:

> Owing to well-founded fear of being persecuted for reasons of race, religion, nationality, membership of a particular social group or political opinion, is outside the country of his nationality and is unable, or owing to such fear, is unwilling to avail himself of the protection of that country; or who, not having a nationality and being outside the country of his former habitual residence as a result of such events, is unable or, owing to such fear, is unwilling to return to it.

Source: UNHCR, 1951.

nations and people recover in the months and years following disaster events. The remaining chapters of this text will explain what these actions are, how they are performed, and what organizations and individuals perform them.

References

Alexander, D. (2002). *Principles of emergency planning and management*. New York: Oxford University Press.

Ansell, J., & Wharton, F. (1992). *Risk: Analysis, assessment, and management*. Chichester, UK: John Wiley and Sons.

Asian Disaster Reduction Center (ADRC). (2005). *Total disaster risk management: Good practices*. http://web.adrc.or.jp/publications/TDRM2005/TDRM_Good_Practices/Index.html.

BBC News. (2000). Mozambique: How the disaster unfolded. *Africa: World. February 24*. http://news.bbc.co.uk/1/hi/world/africa/655227.stm.

Britton, N. R. (1998). *Managing community risks*. Wellington, New Zealand: New Zealand Ministry of Civil Defense.

Covello, V. T., & Mumpower, J. (1985). Risk analysis and risk management: An historical perspective. *Risk Analysis, 5*(2), 103–118.

Derby, S. L., & Keeney, R. L. (1981). Risk analysis: Understanding how safe is safe enough? *Risk Analysis, 1*(3), 217–224.

Egyptian State Information Service (ESIS). n.d. *Pharaonic Egypt: 12th dynasty. Encyclopedia of the rulers of Egypt*. http://www.sis.gov.eg/rulers/html/en12p.htm.

Fagan, B. (1999). *Floods, famines, and empires*. New York: Basic Books.

Federal Emergency Management Agency (FEMA). (1997). *Multi hazard identification and assessment*. Washington, DC: FEMA.

Gloucestershire Fire and Rescue Services. n.d. *A roman fire service*. Gloucestershire City council. http://www.glosfire.gov.uk/sections/schools/schoolrcroman/html.

Gutierrez, D. (2008). Natural disasters up more than 400 percent in two decades. *Natural News* (June 5).

Hough, S., & Jones, L. (2002). United States Geological Survey, 2002. Earthquakes don't kill people, buildings do. *San Francisco Chronicle* (December 4).

Inter-Agency Standing Committee (IASC). (1994). 10th meeting. FAO Field Programme Circular. December.

International Strategy for Disaster Reduction (ISDR). (2005). Examples of countries which have a Disaster Risk Reduction Policy. ISDR Media Room. http://www.unisdr.org/eng/media-room/facts-sheets/fs-good-policies.htm.

International Strategy for Disaster Reduction (ISDR). (1994). In: *Yokohama strategy and plan of action for a safer world*. UN World Conference on Natural Disaster Reduction. May 23–27, Japan.

ISDR 2. (2005). *Hyogo framework for action 2005–2015*. World Conference on Disaster Reduction. January 18–22. Hyogo, Japan.

Jardine, C., & Hrudey, S. (1997). Mixed messages in risk communication. *Risk Analysis, 17*(4), 489–498.

Jeggle, T. (2001). The evolution of disaster reduction as an international strategy: Policy implications for the future. In U. Rosenthal, R. A. Boin, & L. K. Comfort (Eds.), *Managing crises: Threats, dilemmas, opportunities*. Springfield, IL: Charles C Thomas.

Kedar, B. Z. (1970). *Again: Arabic risq, medieval Latin risicum, studi medievali*. Spoleto: Centro Italiano Di Studi Sull Alto Medioevo.

Library of Congress (U.S.). (2000). *By the people, for the people: Posters from the WPA, 1936–1943*. http://memory.loc.gov/ammem/wpaposters/wpahome.html.

Moore, W. H., & Shellman, S. M. (2002). *Refugee or internally displaced person? To where should one flee?* Florida State University, November 22. www.google.com/url?sa=U&start=2&q=http://www.ccis-ucsd.org/PUBLICATIONS/wrkg65.pdf&e=9888.

Natsios, A. (1997). *U.S. foreign policy and the four horsemen of the apocalypse*. Westport, CT: Praeger Publishers.

NBC News. (2004). *Worst natural disasters in history*. December 28. www.nbc10.com/news/4030540/detail.html.

Noji, E. (1997). *The public health consequences of disasters*. New York: Oxford University Press.

Oxfam. (1998). *Central America after Hurricane Mitch: Will the donors deliver?* December 3. www.google.com/url?sa=U&start=2&q=http://www.oxfam.org.uk/what_we_do/issues/conflict_disasters/downloads/CENTRALA.rtf&e=9888.

Prevention Web. (2010). *Global platform 2011*. http://www.preventionweb.net/english/hyogo/GP/2011/?pid:47&pil:1.

Quarantelli, E. L. (1995). *Disaster planning, emergency management, and civil protection: The historical development and current characteristics of organized efforts to prevent and respond to disasters*. Newark, DE: University of Delaware Disaster Research Center.

Riebeek, H. (2005). *The rising cost of natural hazards*. NASA Earth Observatory. March 28. http://earthobservatory.nasa.gov/Study/Risingcost/.

Sheridan, M. (2007). Climate change killed off dynasties in China, Mexico. *The Australian*, 10. January 8.

Smith, K. (1992). *Environmental hazards: Assessing risk and reducing disaster*. New York: Routledge.

Thoreau Institute (TI). (2005). *Lack of automobility key to New Orleans tragedy*. September 4. www.ti.org/vaupdate55.html.

United Nations. (1989). *Resolution 44/236*. United Nations General Assembly. 85th Plenary Meeting. December 22.

United Nations, Department of Humanitarian Affairs. (1992). *Internationally agreed glossary of basic terms related to disaster management (DNA/93/36)*. Geneva: United Nations.

United Nations Development Programme (UNDP). (2004a). *Human development report 2004*. http://hdr.undp.org/reports/global/2004/.

United Nations Development Programme (UNDP). (2004b). *Reducing disaster risk: A challenge for development*. New York: Bureau for Crisis Prevention and Recovery.

United Nations Development Programme (UNDP). (2005). *Tsunami sets back development by 20 years in Maldives*. United Nations Press Release. January 19. www.undp.org/dpa/pressrelease/releases/2005/january/pr19ja n05.html.

United Nations Environmental Panel. (2001). *Climate change 2001: Impacts, adaptation and vulnerability. Intergovernmental panel on climate change*. Cambridge: Cambridge University Press.

United Nations High Commissioner for Refugees. (1951). *Convention relating to the status of refugees*. www.unhchr.ch/html/menu3/b/o_c_ref.htm. July 28.

United Nations High Commissioner for Refugees. (2004). *Internally displaced persons: Questions and answers.* www.unhcr .ch/cgi-bin/texis/vtx/basics/opendoc.pdf?tbl=BASICS&id=405ef8c64.

United Nations International Strategy for Disaster Reduction (UNISDR). (2004). *Living with risk: A global review of disaster reduction initiatives.* http://www.unisdr.org/eng/about_isdr/bd-lwr-2004-eng.htm.

United Nations International Strategy for Disaster Reduction (UNISDR). n.d. *Mission and objectives.* www.unisdr.org/eng/ about_isdr/isdr-mission-objectives-eng.htm.

Wikipedia. (2005). *The Great Chicago Fire.* http://en.wikipedia.org/wiki/Great_Chicago_Fire.

2

Hazards

Introduction

All facets of life include some form of risk, and the source of that risk is the wide range of hazards that we are just beginning to understand. As a global society, we must contend with an array of hazards that may seem limitless, but in actual practice are considerably limited owing to our genetics, spatial movements, habits, activities, geographic locations, and a measure of pure chance.

For nations, many of these factors of hazard origin also hold true. Physical location dictates exactly what portfolio of natural hazards a nation must face. Economic, industrial, and sociopolitical factors dictate hazards of technological and intentional origin. And with globalization, the speed and ease of international travel, and the emergence of global climate change patterns, it is apparent that every nation may be considered a neighbor of every other nation on the planet.

This chapter begins with a short description of the disaster management processes of hazard identification and hazard analysis (sometimes referred to as *hazard profiling*). This will be followed by a listing and description of many of the hazards that possess catastrophic potential—in other words, those hazards that are capable of causing a disaster. The analysis and management of risk arising from these hazards is the focus of Chapter 3.

Hazard Identification and Hazard Profiling

The first steps that must be taken in any effective disaster management effort are the identification and profiling of hazards. It is only logical that a disaster manager concerned with treating the risk of a community or a nation must first know what hazards exist and where they exist.

The actual number of possible hazards throughout the world is staggering, and the list is by no means limited to what is found in this or any other text. However, disaster managers must be able to identify those hazards that are most likely to occur and that are most devastating should they occur. Understandably, it is impossible to plan for or prevent every possible contingency, so most government and other organized emergency management entities will focus their efforts upon those hazards that would result in the greatest undesirable consequences.

Disaster managers must attempt to identify every scenario that could possibly occur within a given community or country as a result of its geologic, meteorological, hydrologic, biological, economic, technological, political, and social factors. This hazard assessment, as it is often called, must include not only the actual physical hazards that exist but also the expected secondary hazards, including social reactions and conditions.

To begin the processes of risk analysis and risk assessment, which is covered in Chapter 3, community leaders must identify all of the hazards that the community has experienced in the past and could possibly experience in the future. It is also important, at least in the initial stages of the process, to identify all other possible hazards, regardless of how small their likelihood of occurrence. As will be discussed in Chapter 3, many hazards are extremely unlikely to occur but, due to the nature of their consequences, their mitigation measures must be considered.

The goal of hazard identification is to establish an exhaustive list of hazards upon which further analysis can be performed. Again, it is not the concern of those identifying the hazards to consider what their likelihood or consequences may be. This is a process in which more is definitely better.

A hazard, as defined in Chapter 1, is a source of potential harm to a community, including its population, environment, private and public property, infrastructure, and businesses. For ease of description, hazards can be categorized into several subgroups: natural hazards, technological hazards, and intentional hazards. These categories are but one of many ways in which hazards can be subdivided. Other classification systems may involve more or fewer categories and may use different terminology. What is important, however, is that the categories chosen accommodate the full range of hazards so that no group is overlooked.

It is common for hazards from one of the chosen categories to cause a secondary hazard or disaster in that same category or one of the others. Hazard sequencing, described in the following sections, helps to determine these secondary, tertiary, or further disasters. Additionally, some hazards may be correctly placed in more than one category, which can lead to confusion. The division of hazards into these respective lists, however, helps to provide direction to governments or groups tasked with hazard identification, and adds logic to the thought process by which the hazards are identified.

For most countries, natural hazards are the primary concern of disaster managers. The kinds of natural hazards a country may face depend upon that country's climate, geography, geology, and land use practices. Natural hazards fall under the subcategories of tectonic (seismic) hazards, mass movement hazards, hydrologic hazards, meteorological hazards, and biological/health-related hazards.

Technological, or "man-made," hazards are an inevitable product of technological innovation. These hazards, which can occur after the failure of existing technology, tend to be much less understood than their natural counterparts and are increasing in number as the scope of and dependence on technology expands. The most common technological hazards arise from various components of transportation, infrastructure, industry, and buildings/structures.

Intentional hazards are the third category, and include those hazards that result from the conscious decision of man to act in an antisocial or anti-establishment manner. Like technological hazards, many of these hazards are new and emerging, such as modern biological, chemical, and radiological weapons. Others, such as war, have existed for almost as long as humans.

Hazard identification must be exhaustive to be effective. The product of this process, which is a detailed list of all past disasters and all possible future hazards within the country or community, will be the basis upon which effective disaster management policies and projects may be based. The breadth of knowledge and experience of the team assembled to complete such a process will ultimately be a determining factor guiding how complete and accurate the generated hazard list will be. Also, because of risk perception (explained in Chapter 3), which defines how different people perceive hazard *significance,* a wide range of viewpoints is highly beneficial.

When identifying hazards, it is important to remember that the process is used simply to identify all of the hazards that might affect the country. It is not concerned with the severity of their impact or the likelihood of occurrence. Ideally, all hazards with likelihood greater than zero would be identified and their associated risks reduced. However, determining which hazards are treated comes later, and only after hazards are compared (as will be explained in Chapter 3) can hazard priorities be ranked. Additionally, it is often difficult to understand whether even a seemingly insignificant hazard could trigger a much larger secondary hazard.

There are several methods by which hazard identification can be conducted. Ideally, a number of these will be used in conjunction. Some methods can be performed simultaneously, while others follow a logical step-by-step approach. Hazard identification is often used to initiate hazard profiling, which is a process of describing the hazard in its local context. This includes a general description of the hazard, its local historical background, local vulnerability, possible consequences, and estimated likelihood.

Checklists, which are comprehensive lists of hazards, consequences, or vulnerabilities, provide reference information to those performing risk analyses. It is often recommended that the use of checklists be limited until the process has reached an advanced stage. If they must be used to start the hazard identification process, their importance should be downplayed. The experience and knowledge of the assembled team and the discovery of historical records should be relied upon the most heavily, as these resources will reveal the most accurate depiction of the community's hazards (Reiss, 2001). Many studies relating to hazard identification (and other nonrelated tasks) have found that the existence of checklists can block the assessment team's creativity, may limit the ability to "see matters that have never been seen before," and can cause other errors in judgment. Therefore, checklists should be brought in at a later time to ensure that nothing has been left out of consideration or overlooked.

Hazard identification methods can be grouped into two categories: prescriptive and creative. Whichever method is chosen, it is important that a cost- and time-effective overall methodology is established that caters specifically to the needs and capabilities of the government agency or organization performing the hazard risk assessment. This methodology should incorporate several of the methods listed below, either in part or completely. Because this process could be performed indefinitely, the disaster management team must establish a goal that defines when the process has reached a satisfactory end point. These hazard identification methods include:

- *Brainstorming.* This creative process, in which disaster managers use their own knowledge and experience to develop a list of possible hazards, is one of the most effective methods of hazard identification. There are several ways in which the process can be conducted, including workshops, structured interviews, and questionnaires. Whatever methods are used, the quality of the end product will correlate directly with the background, diversity, and experience of the individuals involved in the exercise.

- *Research of the country's disaster and emergency history.* This information can be found by searching newspapers, town/city government records, the Internet, public libraries, local historical societies, and community elders. Presumably, incident reports on past events exist and will generate a list of known hazards. Many of these resources will provide dates, magnitudes, damages, and further evidence of past disasters in the community or state.

- *Reviews of existing plans.* Various types of plans exist within the government (local to national) that may contain information on hazards. National or local transportation, environmental, dam, or public works reports or plans are often useful. Others sources include local police, fire, or emergency management action plans; land use plans; capital improvement plans; building codes; land development regulations; and flood ordinances.

- *Investigation of similar hazard identification efforts in neighboring countries.* Many disasters will extend beyond country borders. Especially in the case of small countries or ones that share regional climatic, geologic, or hydrologic characteristics, the neighboring countries are likely to share many of the same hazard risks. Investigations of neighboring countries also may turn up natural or technological hazards not present in the original country but that could result in a regional disaster within the country of focus (as with the Chernobyl disaster, in which fallout was carried by wind and weather to many adjacent countries).

- *Use of maps.* Disaster managers can use maps to overlay known settlement, topographic, hydrologic, and other environmental and technological characteristics to determine whether interactions between these factors could result in unforeseen hazards.

- *Interviews.* Interviews with local citizens, risk managers, community leaders, academics, nonprofit relief agencies, international organizations, and other municipal and private sector staff (many of which are described in later chapters) that regularly perform disaster management tasks can provide a wealth of information. Floodplain managers; public works departments; and engineering, planning, zoning, and transportation departments commonly keep records on past and possible future hazards. Fire departments, police departments, and emergency management offices are bound to have a wealth of insight and information.

- *Site visits to public or private facilities.* Public or private facilities that serve as a known source of risk for the community are likely to provide information not only on the hazards they create but also about external factors identified by their own risk management departments as a source of risk for the facility.

Determining the secondary hazards that can arise from the hazards already identified is commonly done using simple brainstorming, or hazard sequencing. Hazard sequencing is most often performed using event trees or fault trees.

There are two primary methods of creating event trees. The first method, shown in Figure 2–1, begins by focusing on the effects of a single identified hazard and then focuses on the subsequent effects of those effects, and so on. The process is repeated until the disaster managers feel all possible secondary effects have been listed.

The second method is very similar to the first, except that it examines all of the events that may occur over the course of a hazard scenario. This scenario-based event tree begins with a timeline depicting the disaster scenario from start to finish, and then examines the various "initiating events" that may occur during the course of the disaster by tracing each event to its possible end state. Figure 2–2 depicts the analysis of one of many possible initiating events. (For more information on event trees, see Kaplan, 1997.)

Fault trees differ from event trees in that they focus on the end state, or consequence, and trace back to the possible initiating events (hazards) that could have triggered the consequence. The first of two methods, shown in Figure 2–3, begins by focusing on the possible causes of a single identified consequence and then focuses on the subsequent causes of those causes, and so on. The process is repeated until all possible causes of the consequence have been listed.

The second method, depicted in Figure 2–4, is similar, except that all of the causes, or initiating events, of a consequence are mapped according to a timeline-based scenario. This fault tree method begins by identifying the consequence, and then examining the scenario for any possible triggering events that could eventually lead to that end state.

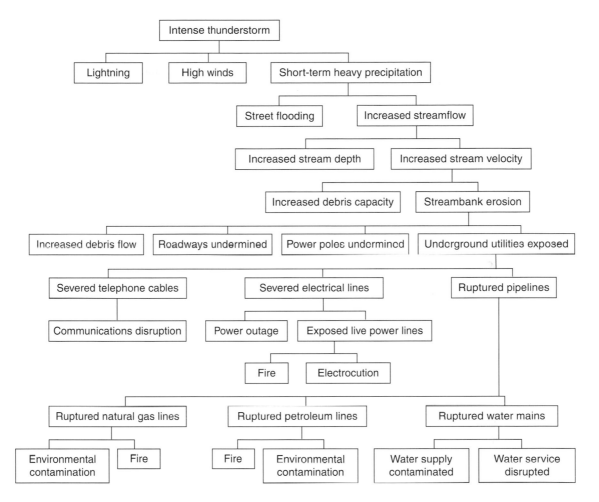

FIGURE 2–1 Event tree. (Adapted from NRC, 1991)

Hazard Analysis

Although the list of hazards generated through these processes will allow disaster managers to know what hazards threaten the community, it tells them little more. Once a hazard has been identified, it must be further described for later use in risk analysis. This descriptive process, called hazard analysis or hazard profiling, allows disaster managers to make more informed calculations of risk, upon which disaster management actions are ultimately taken.

To analyze a hazard, disaster managers must determine exactly how that hazard exists within the specific community or country. Each hazard will be different in this respect, due to climate, geography, settlement patterns, and regional and local political stability, among many other factors. Disaster managers commonly create what is called a risk statement, which serves to summarize all of the necessary information into a succinct report for each identified hazard. With these reports, disaster managers can more accurately address each hazard in the specific context of the community or country.

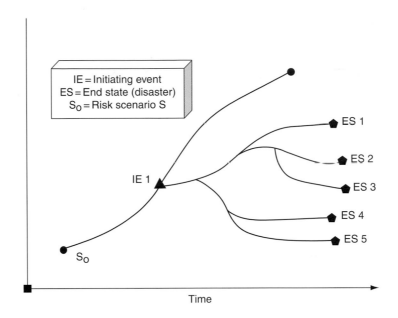

FIGURE 2–2 Event tree 2. (Adapted from Kaplan, 1997)

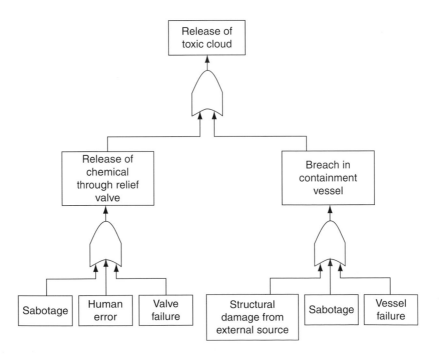

FIGURE 2–3 Fault tree. (Adapted from Slovic, Fischhoff, & Lichtenstein, 1979)

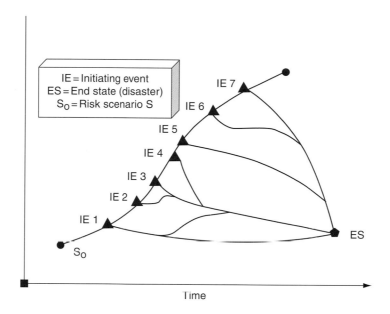

IE = Initiating event
ES = End state (disaster)
S_o = Risk scenario S

IE 7

IE 6

IE 5

IE 4

IE 3

IE 2

IE 1

S_o

ES

Time

FIGURE 2–4 Fault tree 2. (Adapted from Kaplan, 1997)

Risk statements, or hazard profiles, are described by Emergency Management Australia (EMA) as tools that "describe the possibility of a hazard (source of risk) affecting an element at risk" (EMA, 2000). In disaster management, a risk statement tells the disaster manager how each hazard impacts that community.

All hazards identified through hazard identification have unique characteristics that may not be fully understood by those who have identified them. Even people with extensive backgrounds in hazards may have little or no understanding of how those hazards affect a community or country. This knowledge requires information about a combination of general hazard information and descriptions, community and environmental factors, and vulnerability factors (described in Chapter 3).

There are several methods of generating risk statements and the main elements of this process are described in the following list. If done properly, the profiles that are generated outfit disaster managers with a powerful tool with which they can adequately assess the community's risk and determine mitigation and preparedness priorities. However, if done incorrectly, they can cause unnecessary confusion and be counterproductive to the disaster management process as a whole.

To begin profiling hazards, it is vital that a base map be obtained or created. A base map contains important geographical, political, population, and other information upon which hazard information may be overlaid. It is essentially a geographic representation of the community or country as a whole, sometimes called a community profile. Community profiles should include each of the following (adapted from FEMA, 1998):

- *Geography.* Includes topography, mountains, bodies of moving and standing water, canyons, coastal zones, tectonic faults, and other features.
- *Property.* Includes land use, construction type, essential facilities, and hazardous materials facilities, among others.

- *Infrastructure.* Includes roads, rail lines, airports, utilities, pipelines, bridges, communications, and mass transit systems, among others.
- *Demographics.* Includes population size, density, income levels, and special population designations (such as elderly, children, prisons), among others.
- *Response agencies.* Includes the locations, facilities, services, and assets of fire, police, emergency management, military, public health, and other response systems.

Each hazard that threatens a community affects it in a unique way. For instance, while heavy rain may be expected to uniformly affect a whole community, landslides and mudflows will only be a problem where there are steep, unstable slopes. The base map is the best way for disaster managers to analyze the spatial extent of hazards and thus plan for the possibility of interaction between hazards and people, structures, infrastructure, the environment, and so on.

To truly compare and analyze risks, it is important that risks are represented individually on a base map, as well as together on a single aggregate risk map. If a standardized map is used for all hazards profiled, disaster managers can maximize the possibility that all the mapped hazards account for timeliness and that there are no errors made due to scale of size, and they can simplify the task of comparing or combining two or more risk maps.

Once hazard maps are generated, disaster managers may move on to creating risk statements. Risk statements, like risk maps, are most effective if data are collected using a standardized format of information retrieval and reporting. A standardized display format ensures that detailed information is both easily readable and understandable to those involved in future steps of the disaster management process. The contents of the risk statements should include (but are not limited to, and not necessarily in the order presented):

1. *Name of the hazard.* Many hazards have different names, so it is important that a risk statement clearly identify exactly what type of hazard is being profiled. For instance, "storms" could be interpreted as windstorms, snowstorms, hurricanes, torrential rainfall, or other hazards. Providing a descriptive hazard identifier minimizes confusion.
2. *General description of the hazard.* The range of individuals involved in the exhaustive disaster management process probably will have many different levels of knowledge and understanding about the hazards to be analyzed. Additionally, many measurement and rating mechanisms for hazards have changed over time, and others may be extremely useful in determining the local context of a hazard.
3. *Frequency of occurrence of the hazard.* This includes:
   a. *Historical incidences of the hazard.* This could be displayed in a standardized format, either as a spreadsheet, chart, or list. If the hazard happens regularly, it may be indicated as such, with only major events listed. This is often true with floods and snowstorms.
   b. *Predicted frequency of the hazard.* Actual frequencies will be expanded upon in the risk analysis step detailed in Chapter 3.
   c. *Magnitude and potential intensity of the hazard.* Based upon the hazard maps, this measure may be a single figure or a range of possibilities. The magnitude and possible intensity will be important during risk analysis, as these figures help disaster managers to determine the possible consequences of each hazard and to determine what mitigation measures are appropriate.

d. *Location(s) of the hazard.* For most hazards, the basic hazard map will be both sufficient and highly informative during risk analysis. However, when there are individual areas or regions within the community or country that require special mention and, likewise, special consideration, this may be included as a separate comment or detail. This helps to ensure that those special areas are not overlooked in subsequent processes.

e. *Estimated spatial extent of impact of the hazard.* This information is also likely to be found on hazard maps. However, there may be special additional comments or facts for some hazards that need to be included separately from the visual representation provided by the map.

f. *Duration of hazard event, emergency, or disaster.* For hazards that have occurred frequently in the past, it will be possible to give an accurate estimation of the hazard's duration, based on previous response efforts. However, for disasters that rarely occur or have never occurred, such as a nuclear accident or a specific type of hazardous material spill, estimations are often provided based upon the hazard description, community vulnerability (see Chapter 3), emergency response capability (Chapter 6), and anticipated international response assistance. This figure will generally be a rough estimate, measured in days rather than hours or minutes, but will be very useful in subsequent steps that analyze possible consequences.

g. *Seasonal pattern or other time-based patterns of the hazard.* This is simply a description of the time of year that a hazard is most likely to appear, if such a pattern exists. Knowing seasonal patterns allows disaster managers to analyze interactions between hazards that could occur simultaneously.

h. *Speed of onset of the hazard event.* The speed of onset of a hazard can help planners in the mitigation phase determine what actions are possible, impossible, and vital given the amount of pre-disaster time they are likely to have. The public education and communications systems that are planned will be drastically different for each action. Warning systems and evacuation plans must reflect the availability or lack of time within which action can be taken. If responders can be readied before the disaster, the speed of response will be increased significantly. For these reasons and many more, knowing the speed of onset of a hazard is vital in planning.

i. *Availability of warnings for the hazard.* This information is indirectly related to the speed of onset of a hazard, but is also independent in some ways. Each hazard is distinct and has certain characteristics that either do or do not lend themselves to prediction. Some hazards that have a fast onset, such as a volcanic eruption, can be predicted with some degree of confidence (although not always), while some hazards with slower onset times, such as biological terrorism, cannot be predicted accurately. Yet other hazards provide no advance warning, such as a chemical accident. Even if advance knowledge of a disaster is possible, the capabilities of the local warning system further determine the possibility of adequately informing the public about an impending disaster. Local warning systems are more than the physical alarms, sirens, or announcements; they are also the public's ability to receive, understand, and act upon the warnings they receive. All factors must be considered when determining warning availability. The risk statement may include both the available technology that could provide warnings of the hazards and the local system's current status of warnings for each specific hazard.

Once the obtainable information in the preceding list has been collected, it should be presented in a standardized, easy-to-read display format.

The Hazards

Natural Hazards

It has been said before that no disaster is natural, because any disaster event by definition requires inter-action with either man, his built environment, or both. However, the many forces that elicit these disas-ters are in fact natural phenomena that occur regardless of the presence of man. It is possible, and is often the case, that human actions exacerbate the effect of these natural processes, such as increased flooding after the destruction of wetlands or landslides on slopes where anchor vegetation has been removed. The following section identifies the most common of these natural processes and briefly describes each.

Tectonic Hazards

Hazards that are associated with the movement of earth's plates are called tectonic hazards or seismic hazards. Plate tectonics is a study of the movement of these plates, and combines the theories of con-tinental drift and seafloor spreading. Research in this field has discovered that the lithosphere (the planet's outer shell) is broken up into a pattern of constantly moving oceanic and continental plates, each of which slides over the underlying asthenosphere. Where the plates interact along their margins, many important geological processes occur: mountain chains are formed and lifted, earthquakes begin, and volcanoes emerge.

We now know that there are seven major crustal plates, shown in Figure 2–5, which are subdi-vided into a number of smaller plates. They are about 80 km thick and are all in constant motion rel-ative to one another at rates varying from 10 to 130 mm per year. Their pattern is neither symmetrical nor simple. The specific type of interaction between plates, including collision, subduction (one plate sliding under another), or separation, determines the kind of tectonic hazard. These hazards occur most often at the boundaries of the great plates, where the interactions originate, but they are by no means limited to these convergent zones.

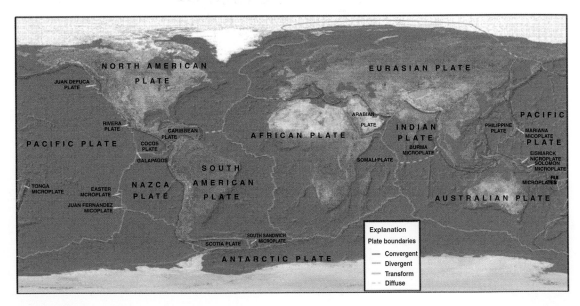

FIGURE 2–5 Plates of the earth. (From USGS, 2005a)

Earthquakes, which as their name suggests are sudden movements of earth, are caused by an abrupt release of strains that have accumulated over time along fault lines. The rigid, constantly moving plates often become stuck together at points along their boundaries, and are unable to release the energy that slowly accumulates. Eventually, this snag is released and the plates snap apart. The reverberation of energy through the plate from the point where the plates had become snagged is the earthquake (see Figure 2–6).

Seismic waves are generated by the jolting motion of the plates, and extend outward from the origination point, or epicenter, like ripples formed by a stone thrown into a pond. The speed of those waves depends upon the geologic makeup of the materials through which they are passing. For particularly large earthquakes, such as the event that caused the 2004 tsunami events in Asia, the entire world can vibrate for several seconds or minutes.

Fractures within the crust of the earth along which the plates have slipped with respect to each other are called faults, and are divided into three subgroups as determined by movement:

- *Normal faults* occur in response to pulling or tension; the overlying block moves down the dip of the fault plane.
- *Thrust (reverse) faults* occur in response to squeezing or compression; the overlying block moves up the dip of the fault plane.
- *Strike-slip (lateral) faults* occur in response to either type of stress; the blocks move horizontally past one another.

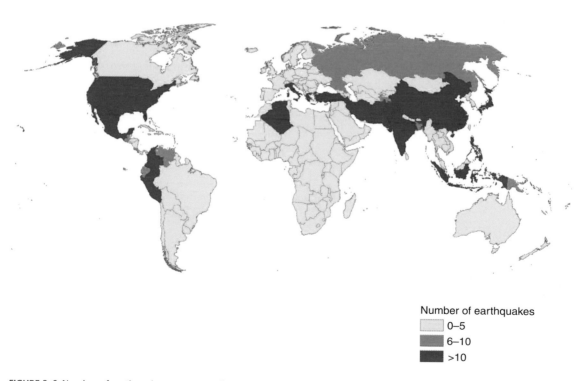

Number of earthquakes
- 0–5
- 6–10
- >10

FIGURE 2–6 Number of earthquakes per country from 1974 to 2003. (From the International Disaster Database, www.em-dat.net)

Most faulting along spreading zones is normal, along subduction zones is thrust, and along transform faults is strike-slip (in spreading zones, plates move away from each other; in subduction zones plates move toward each other, with one sliding beneath the other; transform faults occur when plates slide laterally against each other in opposite directions).

Earthquakes can occur at a range of depths. The focal depth is the distance below the earth's surface at which energy from the event was released, while the energy release point is called the focus of the earthquake (not to be confused with the epicenter). Finally, the earthquake's epicenter is the point on the earth's surface directly above the focus. Focal depths from 0 to 70 km (43.5 miles) are considered shallow, from 70 to 300 km (43.5 to 186 miles) are considered intermediate, and anything beyond 300 km is considered deep. The focal point may be as deep as 700 km (435 miles). The foci of most earthquakes are concentrated in the earth's crust and upper mantle (Shedlock & Pakiser, 1994).

Earthquakes have also been known to occur within plates, though less than 10% of all earthquakes occur away from plate boundaries. The powerful New Madrid earthquakes of 1811–1812 in the United States occurred within the North American plate. Although earthquakes can be generated by volcanic activity (see the following section) or by man-made explosions, the most destructive events are those resulting from plate slippage.

Earthquakes are generally measured according to their magnitude and intensity. The well-known Richter scale, named after its creator Charles Richter, is an open-ended logarithmic scale that measures the magnitude, or amount of energy released, by the earthquake as detected by a seismograph. Most events below 3 are imperceptible to humans, whereas those above 6 tend to cause damage. Very few earthquakes exceed 9 on the Richter scale. Table 2–1 illustrates the average number of quakes that occur per year within each point on the Richter scale.

The second scale used to measure earthquakes is the Modified Mercalli Intensity scale (MMI). This scale, which measures the effect of the earthquake on the earth's surface, is based upon observations rather than scientific measurements, and uses Roman numerals ranging from I to XII. The MMI is useful in determining how a single earthquake affects different geographical areas because, unlike the Richter scale where the event has a single magnitude, different intensities can be assigned to any variant of geographic determination. Also, because the scale does not depend upon instruments, it is possible to assign an MMI figure to past earthquakes based upon historical descriptions of the event. Exhibit 2–1 describes the observations associated with each level of intensity on the MMI scale.

Table 2–1   Annual Occurrence of Earthquakes

Descriptor	Magnitude	Average Annually
Great	8 and higher	1[a]
Major	7–7.9	17[b]
Strong	6–6.9	134[b]
Moderate	5–5.9	1,319[b]
Light	4–4.9	13,000 (estimated)
Minor	3–3.9	130,000 (estimated)
Very minor	2–2.9	1,300,000 (estimated)

[a]Based on observations since 1900.
[b]Based on observations since 1990.
Source: USGS, 2005a.

EXHIBIT 2-1: DESCRIPTION OF THE TWELVE LEVELS OF MODIFIED MERCALLI INTENSITY

I. Not felt except by a very few under especially favorable conditions.

II. Felt only by a few persons at rest, especially on upper floors of buildings.

III. Felt quite noticeably by persons indoors, especially on upper floors of buildings. Many people do not recognize it as an earthquake. Standing motor cars may rock slightly. Vibrations similar to the passing of a truck. Duration estimated.

IV. Felt indoors by many, outdoors by few during the day. At night, some awakened. Dishes, windows, doors disturbed; walls make cracking sound. Sensation like heavy truck striking building. Standing motor cars rocked noticeably.

V. Felt by nearly everyone; many awakened. Some dishes, windows broken. Unstable objects overturned. Pendulum clocks may stop.

VI. Felt by all, many frightened. Some heavy furniture moved; a few instances of fallen plaster. Damage slight.

VII. Damage negligible in buildings of good design and construction; slight to moderate in well-built ordinary structures; considerable damage in poorly built or badly designed structures; some chimneys broken.

VIII. Damage slight in specially designed structures; considerable damage in ordinary substantial buildings with partial collapse. Damage great in poorly built structures. Fall of chimneys, factory stacks, columns, monuments, and walls. Heavy furniture overturned.

IX. Damage considerable in specially designed structures; well-designed frame structures thrown out of plumb. Damage great in substantial buildings, with partial collapse. Buildings shifted off foundations.

X. Some well-built wooden structures destroyed; most masonry and frame structures destroyed with foundations. Rails bent.

XI. Few, if any (masonry) structures remain standing. Bridges destroyed. Rails bent greatly.

XII. Damage total. Lines of sight and level are distorted. Objects thrown into the air.

Source: USGS (2005b).

Soil liquefaction is a phenomenon that can occur within certain types of soil during an earthquake's shaking period. When loosely packed, waterlogged sediments are exposed to a certain degree of seismic strength (depending on the exact soil makeup), that land becomes jelly-like and loses its ability to support structures. Buildings can lean, topple, or collapse quite easily under these conditions.

Many secondary hazards and, likewise, disasters are known to occur in the aftermath of an earthquake. These include:

- *Landslides, rockslides (rockfalls), and avalanches.* The shaking can cause unstable slopes to give way, resulting in landslides that can be more devastating than the actual quake. The 2001 El Salvador earthquakes, in which the vast majority of the 1100 victims died from a series of resulting slides, is but one example. Rockslides and avalanches, both described later in this chapter, are common secondary hazards to earthquakes.

- *Tsunamis.* When the focus of an earthquake is along a fault under a large body of water and the movement causes a major deformation of the earth's surface, the water's resulting movement can result in a tsunami thousands of miles away. A single, high-magnitude (9.1) earthquake off the coast of Indonesia resulted in the widespread and devastating tsunami events that followed, affecting 15 countries throughout Asia and Africa. Tsunamis are described in greater detail later.

Beneath the earth's crust lie superheated gases and molten rock called magma. At certain points along the planet's crust, most notably in the seismically active zones along the plate boundaries, this magma can escape to the surface to become lava. These fissures, or "vents," are known as *volcanoes*. There are currently over 500 active volcanoes throughout the world (see Figure 2–7). There are three main categories, determined by their geologic environment:

- Subduction volcanoes occur when one plate dips beneath another. The plate can then melt into magma, creating a buildup of pressurized material that is thrust to the surface, often explosively. Subduction volcanoes tend to be the most disastrous, and often create the cone-shaped mountains characteristic of the world's most famous volcanoes. Mt. St. Helens in the Northwest United States is a subduction volcano.

- Rift volcanoes occur when two plates move away from each other, allowing magma to rise to the surface through the intervening space. These volcanoes tend to be associated with low

Number of volcanoes
- 0
- 1–2
- >2

FIGURE 2–7 Number of volcanoes per country from 1974 to 2003. (From the International Disaster Database, www.em-dat.net)

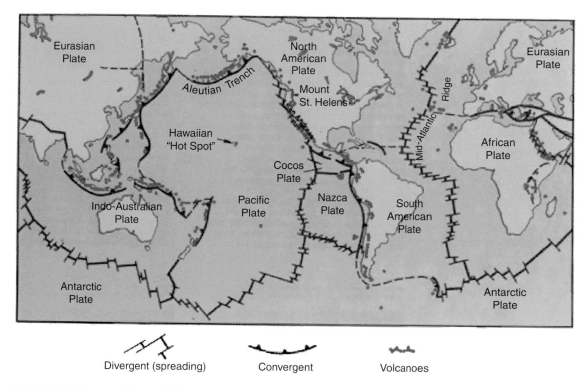

FIGURE 2–8 Volcanoes of the world. (From USGS, 1997)

magma pressure and therefore are not often explosive. Mt. Kilimanjaro in Africa is a rift
volcano.

- Hotspot volcanoes occur when there is a weak spot within the interior of a plate under which
  magma can push through to the surface. Many of the Pacific islands, including the Hawaiian
  island chain (see Figure 2–8), are hotspot volcanoes (Smith, 1992).

These three categories can be further subdivided according to their shape and composition:

- *Calderas.* When very large and explosive volcanic eruptions occur, ejecting tens to hundreds of
  cubic kilometers of magma onto the earth's surface, the ground below can subside or collapse
  into the emptied space. The resulting depression is called a caldera. These spaces can be more
  than 25 km in diameter and several kilometers deep.
- *Cinder/Scoria cones.* Cinder cones are simple volcanic structures formed by particles and
  congealed lava ejected from a single vent. As the gas-charged lava is blown violently into the
  air, it breaks into small fragments that solidify and fall as cinders around the vent, forming a
  circular or oval cone. Most cinder cones have a bowl-shaped crater at the summit and rarely rise
  more than 1000 feet above their surroundings.
- *Composite volcanoes and stratovolcanoes.* Many of the earth's great mountains are composite
  volcanoes, also called stratovolcanoes. These structures typically are very large, steep-sided,

symmetrical cones made from alternating layers of lava flows, volcanic ash, cinders, blocks (greater than 64 mm diameter rock fragments ejected from the volcano in a solid form), and bombs (volcanic material ejected in a liquid state that cools to a solid form before falling to the ground). Composite volcanoes can rise as much as 8,000 feet above their bases, and most have a crater at the summit that contains a central vent or a clustered group of vents. The essential feature of a composite volcano is a conduit system through which magma from a reservoir deep in the earth's crust rises to the surface, exiting through the volcano's central crater and/or side walls. The volcano is built up by the accumulation of material erupted through the conduit and increases in size as lava, cinders, ash, and so forth are added to its slopes.

- *Continental volcanoes.* These volcanoes are located in unstable, mountainous belts that have thick roots of granite or granite-like rock. Magma is generated near the base of the mountain root, and rises slowly or intermittently along fractures in the crust.

- *Island-arc volcanoes.* When one plate thrusts under another, usually below the ocean's surface, volcanic activity appears several hundred miles forward of the subduction zone in the shape of the leading edge of the underlying plate. A chain of islands is often thrust up in an arc shape from the ocean floor. Examples include the Aleutian Islands and Japan. Eruptions associated with these processes tend to be highly explosive.

- *Lava plateaus.* In some shield-volcano eruptions (see later in the list), basaltic lava pours out slowly from long fissures instead of central vents and floods the surrounding countryside, forming broad plateaus. Iceland is an example of this kind of volcano.

- *Lava domes.* These structures form when lava that is thrust from a vent is too sticky to flow very far and forms a steep mound.

- *Maars (tuff cones).* These structures are shallow, flat-floored craters that likely have formed above vents as a result of a violent expansion of magmatic gas or steam. Maars range from 200 to 6,500 feet across and from 30 to 650 feet deep, and most are filled with water, forming natural lakes.

- *Oceanic volcanoes.* These structures are aligned along the crest of a broad ridge that marks an active fracture system in the oceanic crust.

- *Shield volcanoes.* These structures are built almost entirely of highly fluid basaltic lava flows. Thousands of flows pour out in all directions over great distances from a central summit vent or a group of vents, building a broad, gently sloping cone with a profile much like that of a warrior's shield. The Hawaiian Islands are shield volcanoes.

- *Submarine volcanoes, ridges, and vents.* These undersea structures are common features on certain zones of the ocean floor along plate boundaries. Some are active and can be seen in shallow water because of steam and rock debris blasted high above the ocean surface. Many others lie at such great depths that the water's tremendous weight results in high, confining pressure and prevents the formation and explosive release of steam and gases.

- *Tuyas.* These volcanoes are formed under a glacier and are commonly found in Canada.

Each year, approximately 50 volcanoes erupt throughout the world, with fatalities occurring in about 1 of every 20 eruptions. Volcanoes cause injury, death, and destruction several ways. Eruptions can hurl hot rocks, ash, and other debris (airfall tephra) as far as 20 miles away. Airborne ash and noxious fumes can spread for hundreds of miles, contaminating water supplies, reducing visibility, instigating electrical storms, collapsing roofs, and causing health problems. Lava flows, which can be slow (aa lava) or fast moving (pahoehoe lava), burn everything they contact. Explosions of gas and lava have been known to flatten entire forests. Especially dangerous are pyroclastic flows (also called nuées ardentes), which are superheated (up to 1,000 °C), fast-moving clouds of gas, dust, glass, and other material that can travel many miles, incinerating everything in their way. Pyroclastic flows account for over 70% of the deaths that have occurred in modern (1900 or later) volcanic eruptions.

Many secondary hazards are associated with volcanoes, including:

- *Earthquakes.* The great changes that occur within the earth that are associated with the movement of lava often affect the pressure built up between surface plates, causing minor earthquakes to occur. The explosive nature of the volcano can also cause the plates to shake. Although these events are not often associated with widespread damage, they can cause structural damage to the volcano or surrounding land, leading to rockfalls, landslides, or other hazards.

- *Rockfalls and landslides.* As volcanoes erupt, they often shake and become unstable. Sections of the volcano may collapse inward or slough away completely. This results in the release of debris that becomes subject to the forces of gravity and moves in massive quantities, covering great distances.

- *Mudflows (lahars).* Volcanic eruptions are often accompanied by the generation of large volumes of water. This water can come from a range of sources, including snow pack that accumulated on the volcano during periods of inactivity, cloudbursts resulting from the eruption, or water stored in a crater lake. The water, which mixes with ash from the eruption and soil from the mountainside, turns to a thick mud and rushes quickly down the slopes of the volcano, burying whole towns and cities as it moves. Lahars are second only to pyroclastic flows in terms of their devastating potential (see Figure 2–9). Flash floods are also possible if the water generated does not mix with other materials before descending the slopes of the volcano.

- *Tsunamis.* When a volcanic eruption causes major changes to the ocean floor or along ocean shores, a tsunami may be generated. The famous 1883 eruption of Krakatoa resulted in a tsunami up to 135 feet in height when the volcanic structure collapsed into the ocean. Over 36,000 people living nearby were drowned (see the following discussion for more information).

FIGURE 2–9 Melting snow and ice from the 1982 eruption of Mount St. Helens triggered this lahar on the north flank of the volcano. (From Casadevall, 1982; USGS)

- *Poisonous gases.* Noxious gases, including carbon monoxide, hydrogen, and sulfur-related compounds, are often released in combination with a volcanic eruption, but they can also spontaneously release from a volcano that is not erupting. When these releases overcome a human or animal population, very few survive.

A *tsunami* (pronounced "soo-nah-mee") is a series of waves generated by an undersea disturbance such as an earthquake. The word is Japanese in origin, represented by two characters: "tsu" (harbor) and "nami" (wave). Tsunamis are often incorrectly referred to as tidal waves. In truth, tides result from the gravitational influences of the moon, sun, and planets, a phenomenon that has absolutely nothing to do with the generation of tsunamis (although the ultimate height of a tsunami striking a coastal area is determined by the tide level at the time of impact).

There are many events that result in the generation of a tsunami, but earthquakes are the most common. Other forces that generate the great waves include landslides, volcanic eruptions, explosions and, although extremely rare, the impact of extraterrestrial objects, such as meteorites.

Tsunamis are generated when a large area of water is displaced, either by a shift in the seafloor following an earthquake or by the introduction of mass from other events. Waves are formed as the displaced water mass attempts to regain its equilibrium. It is important to note that not all earthquakes generate tsunamis; to do so, earthquakes must occur underneath or near the ocean, be large in magnitude, and create vertical (up/down) movements in the seafloor. While all oceanic regions of the world can experience tsunamis, the countries lying in the Pacific Rim region face a much greater frequency of large, destructive tsunamis because of the presence of numerous large earthquakes in the seismically active "Ring of Fire" (see Figure 2–10).

The waves that are generated travel outward in all or in limited directions from the area of the disturbance, depending on the type of deformation. The time between wave crests can range from as little as 5 min to as much as 90 min, and the wave speed in the open ocean averages a staggering 450 miles per hour. Wave heights of more than 100 feet have been recorded. In the open ocean, tsunamis are virtually undetectable to most ships in their path. As the waves approach the shallow coastal waters, they appear normal but their speed decreases significantly. The compression of the wave resulting from the decrease in ocean depth causes the wave to grow higher and crash onto land—often resulting in great destruction, injuries, and death (NTHMP, 2003).

Strange phenomena that precede a tsunami, such as the ocean receding for hundreds of feet and exposing the ocean floor, have resulted in the death of those who ventured out to explore only to be drowned by the water's sudden return. Most deaths during a tsunami result from drowning. Other risks associated with the tsunami hazard include flooding, contamination of drinking water, destruction of crops, business interruption, loss of infrastructure (roads, electrical lines, etc.), and damaged gas lines. Locally generated tsunamis tend to be the most dangerous, because they can reach a nearby shore in less than 10 min. Even with the advent of tsunami warning systems, that is not enough time for local authorities to issue a warning.

The most destructive tsunamis are generated from large, shallow earthquakes with an epicenter or fault line near or on the ocean floor, which can tilt, offset, or displace large areas of the ocean floor from a few kilometers to as much as 1,000 km or more. Less frequently, tsunami waves can be generated by displacements of water from rockfalls, icefalls, volcanoes, or sudden submarine landslides or slumps (the instability and sudden failure of submarine slopes) sometimes triggered by the ground motions of a strong earthquake. The tallest tsunami wave ever observed was caused by a rockfall in Lituya Bay, Alaska, on July 9, 1958. Triggered by an earthquake, a rockfall of approximately

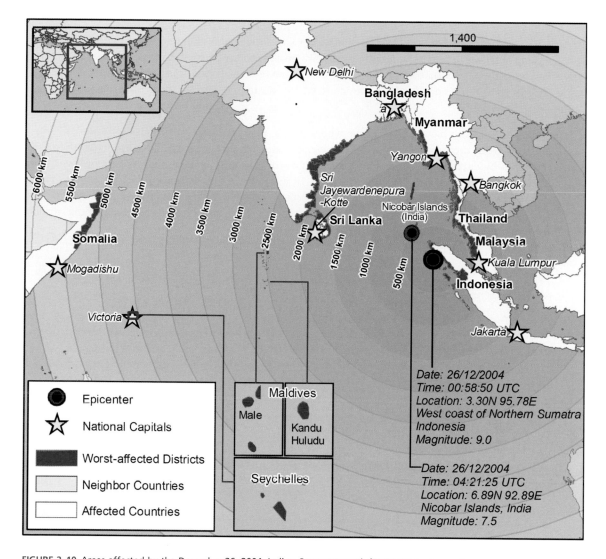

FIGURE 2–10 Areas affected by the December 26, 2004, Indian Ocean tsunami. (From www.usgs.gov)

40 million cubic meters at the head of the bay generated a wave that reached the incredible height of 1720 feet (520 m) on the opposite side of the inlet.

Mass-Movement Hazards

Mass-movement hazards include those events that are caused either by the rapid, gravity-induced downward movement of large quantities of materials (debris movements) or by the contraction (subsidence) or expansion of the Earth from nonseismic means.

Debris movements can be generated by a variety of mechanisms, including intense rainfall or snowfall, rapid snow melt, gradual erosion, a loss of anchoring vegetation, earthquakes, volcanoes, or human interaction. These hazards exist in almost every country of the world, and result in hundreds of deaths worldwide each year. There are three types of movements that can occur: falls that involve mostly vertical travel through the air; slides that involve tumbling of rock, soil, or other solid material down a slope; and flows that involve the downslope movement of fluid masses.

Debris movements are further characterized by the materials that form their mass. The most common include:

- *Landslides*. These hazards can occur whenever the physical mechanisms that prevent soil or bedrock from moving down a slope are weakened or disturbed. Landslides are most often triggered by earthquakes and other seismic hazards, but can be generated by loss of vegetation (especially after fires), human modification, or excessive water saturation of the ground. They can move at very high speeds, or they may occur slowly over days, weeks, or even longer. Landslides can travel great distances and result in very large runoff zones, where the bulk of their devastating effects tends to occur (see Figure 2–11).

- *Rockfalls*. These hazards involve the freefall, rolling, and tumbling of very loose material. They are usually the result of seismicity but can occur without external seismic pressures, especially on slopes exceeding 40°. Other common instigators of rockfalls are construction (most notably road construction through mountainous areas), ground freeze, and patterns of animal movement.

- *Debris flows*. These hazards, also referred to as mudflows or mudslides, are less common than landslides but often much more destructive. Debris flows are dependent upon the introduction of great amounts of water from prolonged rainfall, flash flooding, or very rapid snowmelt. The lubrication provided by the liquid content of the debris allows for much faster descent down the affected slope and, likewise, greater overall distances traveled from the source of the flow.

- *Avalanches*. Avalanches, or snowslides, are movements of debris composed of snow, ice, earth, rock, and any other material picked up as they progress down the affected slopes (see Figure 2–12). An avalanche occurs when the gravitational stress pulling downward on the snow exceeds the ability of the snow cover to resist it. Four factors are required for an avalanche to occur: (1) a steep slope, (2) snow cover, (3) a weak layer in the snow cover, and (4) a trigger. Common triggers are heavy

FIGURE 2–11 Fresh landslide scars in the Ecuadorian Andes.

FIGURE 2–12 "Battleship Avalanche," located in the San Ivan Mountains in Colorado. (From Colorado Avalanche Information Center, n.d.; photo courtesy of Tim Lane, February 28, 1987)

alternating periods of snowfall, rain, and melting, or an external increase in pressure (e.g., skiers, animals, or explosions). About 90% of all avalanches start on slopes of 30–45° (Colorado Avalanche Information Center, n.d.). Failures on slopes of less than 20° rarely occur; on slopes above 60°, the snow rarely accumulates to a critical mass. It is estimated that over 1 million avalanches occur each year worldwide. They typically follow the same paths year after year, leaving scarring along their course. Trained experts thus can easily identify, with a high degree of accuracy, areas that are prone to this hazard (see Figure 2–13). However, unusual weather conditions can produce new paths or cause avalanches to extend beyond their normal paths, and identifying these risk areas takes greater expertise and speculation (see Figure 2–14).

Flooding is a common secondary hazard associated with debris movements, especially when the runoff zone impedes the flow of a river or stream, forming a natural dam. Debris movements can also trigger a tsunami if its runoff zone terminates in a large body of water.

Land subsidence is a loss of surface elevation caused by the removal of subsurface support. Sinkholes are a form of subsidence. The affected area can range from a broad, regional lowering of the land surface to a pronounced, localized collapse (see Figure 2–15). A prevalence of sinkhole hazards in Guatemala was highlighted in 2010 when the second major event to occur in just 3 years swallowed a multistory building and created what appeared to be a bottomless hole (60 feet diameter and over 330 feet deep). The Guatemala sinkhole problem is caused by the interaction of human

FIGURE 2–13 Avalanche warning sign, Cotopaxi volcano, Ecuador.

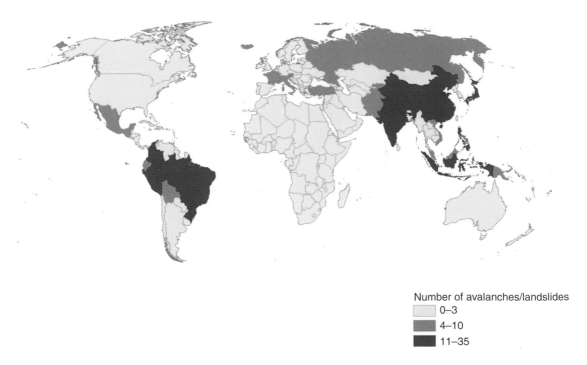

Number of avalanches/landslides
- 0–3
- 4–10
- 11–35

FIGURE 2–14 Number of disasters caused by debris movement per year throughout the world, 1974–2003. (From the International Disaster Database, www.em-dat.net)

FIGURE 2–15 A sinkhole almost 330 feet deep opened up in Guatemala City on May 31, 2010. (From Echavera, 2010)

development—such as leaking water and sewer pipes—and the pumice and limestone that lie below the city that is eroding from leakage points upward toward the surface, each hole growing in size as it progresses. Subsidence is almost exclusively (although not entirely) the result of human activities, including mining (predominantly coal mining), the removal of groundwater or petroleum reserves, and the drainage of organic soils. Other natural factors, such as the composition of the soil or underground aquifers, can contribute to this phenomenon.

Expansive soils are, as their name suggests, soils that tend to increase in volume when they are influenced by some external factor, especially water. The most common type of expansive soil is clay, which expands or contracts as water is added or removed. Adobe is the most significantly affected clay. Expansive soils that have high overlying weight, thus limiting upward expansion, tend to "ooze" in all horizontal directions, leaving a weakened area once the soil returns to its contracted state.

Subsidence and expansion, which (generally) occur gradually over extended periods of time, do not pose the same risk to life as sudden-onset types of events. Someone viewing an area affected by subsidence or expansion would probably not detect that anything had occurred. However, when structures are built upon land affected by subsidence or expansion, the damage inflicted tends to be severe. Wells, pipes, and other underground infrastructure, as well as overlying power lines, can be damaged or destroyed. These hazards can make geological survey records obsolete, because reference points can change significantly. Urban centers are most severely affected by these processes, as are transportation routes such as train tracks, roads, and bridges. Farmers also face considerable risk from subsidence, which can alter irrigation patterns and disrupt leveled fields. Any structure or infrastructure built upon land affected by subsidence or expansion faces grave risk (Gelt, 1992).

Hydrologic Hazards

Either excess or a severe lack of water causes hydrologic hazards. The major hydrologic hazards include flooding (and flash flooding), coastal erosion, soil erosion, salination, drought, and desertification.

Floods, which are by far the most common natural hazard, occur throughout the world. Annually, more people are killed by flooding than any other hazard, with an average of 20,000 deaths and 75 million people affected each year (see Figure 2–16). Floods can be either slow or fast rising, generally developing over days or weeks. Most often they are a secondary hazard resulting from other meteorological processes, such as prolonged rainfall, localized and intense thunderstorms, or onshore winds (see Figure 2–17). However, other generative processes, including landslides, logjams, avalanches, icepack, levee breakage, and dam failure can also generate rapid and widespread flooding. Flash floods, which occur with little or no warning, are the result of intense rainstorms within a brief period of time.

The five most commonly flooded geographic land types are:

- *River floodplains*. These include the low-lying, highly fertile areas that flank rivers and streams. They tend to be highly populated because of their ample irrigation and fertile soil. However, these regions are also the most likely to flood in any given year.

- *Basins and valleys affected by flash flooding*. In basins and valleys where runoff from intense rainstorms collects and concentrates, flash flooding is a significant risk. More lives are lost in

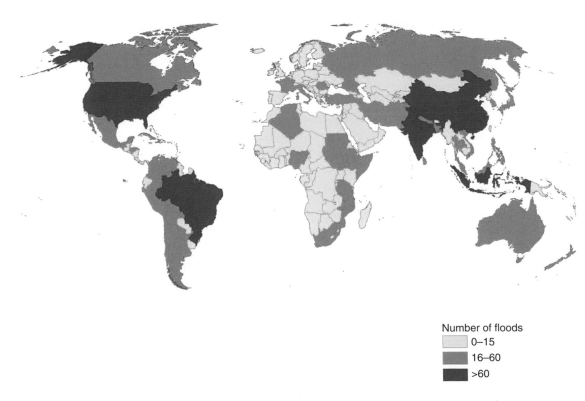

Number of floods
- 0–15
- 16–60
- >60

FIGURE 2–16 Flood events per year, 1974–2003. (From the International Disaster Database, www.em-dat.net)

FIGURE 2–17 Flooding in the town of Iba, Zambales, Philippines, due to multiple tropical storms and a break in the dike along the Bucao river. (From Trees for the Future, 2009)

this kind of flooding than any other because very little warning is possible, and evacuation can be difficult due to the surrounding terrain.

- *Land below water-retention structures (dams).* Dam failures, which can occur due to poor maintenance or as a secondary disaster from other natural or man-made processes, often cause flooding downstream from the dam as it releases a torrent of retained water. The United States has over 30,000 dams and most countries have as many or more, most of which are privately built and maintained.

- *Low-lying coastal and inland shorelines.* Coastal shorelines often flood as a result of a storm surge preceding hurricanes, cyclones, and other major windstorms. The storm-surge flooding can be more dangerous than the windstorm. Low-lying inland shores surrounding large lakes can be negatively affected when water levels rise significantly.

- *Alluvial fans.* This type of landscape, often the result of previous periods of hydrologic activity, can become very dangerous during flash floods when unpredictable water drainage patterns emerge. The Middle East is especially prone to this type of disaster (Smith, 1992).

Flash flooding is often the result of rapid, unplanned urbanization, which can greatly reduce the land's ability to absorb rainfall. The resulting runoff has nowhere to go and accumulates as quickly as the rain can fall. Drainage systems can be built to alleviate some of this problem, but very heavy rains will often exceed the capacity of even the best designed systems of the developed countries.

Deforestation is another causative factor of floods. Soil once anchored by vegetation quickly turns to runoff sediment, which is deposited into drainage systems such as rivers and streams, decreasing their holding capacity. As sediment builds up, successive floods occur more rapidly. The water-retention capacity of soil anchored by vegetation is greater than that of deforested land, leading to greater overall amounts of runoff that ultimately results from deforestation.

Secondary effects of flooding include coastal erosion and soil erosion. Erosion effects can increase the chance of future flooding, resulting in a vicious cycle of repeat flooding and further erosion.

A *drought* is a period of unusually dry weather that persists long enough to cause serious problems such as crop damage and water supply shortages. The severity of the drought depends upon its duration, the degree of moisture deficiency, and the size of the affected area. Drought is a hazard that requires many months to emerge and may persist for many months or years thereafter. This type of hazard is known as a "creeping" hazard. The causes, or triggers, of drought are not well understood, and are often part of constantly changing global climate patterns.

What defines a drought has not been established through any standardized measure. In general, any unusual shortage of useable water can be considered a drought, but whether the drought becomes a hazard is a factor of the affected region's coping mechanisms. A simple lack of rain does not necessarily constitute a drought, nor does the appearance of a rainstorm indicate the end of a drought. Additionally, what is considered to be an ample quantity of water resources in one geographic area may be considered drought in another area, where more water is required for individual, agricultural, and other needs. Therefore, drought is defined not by any global measure but by the capacity of the affected area to accommodate the changes brought about by the changes in available water (see Exhibit 2–2 for further discussion).

Droughts are categorized into four distinct groups:

- *Meteorological drought.* A measure of the difference between observed levels of precipitation and the normal range of values for precipitation in that same area.
- *Agricultural drought.* A situation in which the quantity of moisture present in the soil no longer meets the needs of a particular crop.
- *Hydrological drought.* When surface and subsurface water supplies fall well below normal levels.
- *Socioeconomic (famine) drought.* Refers to the situation that occurs when physical water shortages begin to affect people. This type of drought is caused more by socioeconomic factors (such as restrictive governments, poor farming practices, breakdown of infrastructure, or a failed economy) than by environmental factors, and as such can be the most devastating.

The lack of rainfall associated with drought can cause debilitating effects to both agricultural and urban centers. Crops quickly fail once irrigation systems run dry, and many industrial processes that depend upon water resources must cut back or stop production completely. Hydroelectric power is reduced significantly as river flow rates are reduced, and river-based commerce and transportation can come to a standstill as water levels drop. In poor countries, drought is often, but not always, associated with the emergence of famine (this is never the case in developed countries, where mechanisms to prevent famine are well established; see Figure 2–18). The Sahelian drought that began in 1968 was

EXHIBIT 2-2: THE PALMER DROUGHT INDEX

The Palmer Drought Index is a formula developed by Wayne Palmer in the 1960s to measure drought, using temperature and rainfall information to determine relative dryness. It has become the semi-official drought index.

The Palmer Index is more effective in determining long-term drought (months) than short-term forecasts (weeks). It uses 0 as normal. Drought is shown in terms of negative numbers; for example, –2 is moderate drought, –3 is severe drought, and –4 is extreme drought. The Palmer Index can also reflect excess rain using a corresponding level reflected by positive figures; 0 is normal, 2 is moderate rainfall, and so on.

Its advantage is that it is standardized to local climate, so it can be applied to any geographic location to demonstrate relative drought or rainfall conditions. Unfortunately, it is not very useful for short-term forecasts, nor is it particularly useful in calculating supplies of water reserved in snow or other similar reservoirs.

The Crop Moisture Index (CMI) is also a formula developed by Wayne Palmer. The CMI responds more rapidly than the Palmer Index and can change considerably from week to week, so it is more effective in calculating short-term abnormal dryness or wetness affecting agriculture. CMI is designed to indicate normal conditions at the beginning and end of the growing season; it uses the same levels as the Palmer Drought Index. It differs from the Palmer Index in that the CMI formula places less weight on the data from previous weeks and more weight on the most recent week.

Source: NOAA, n.d.(a).

---

responsible for the deaths of 100,000 to 250,000 people and 12 million cattle, the disruption of millions of lives, and the collapse of the agricultural bases of five countries.

Desertification is a creeping hazard that can be caused by natural processes, human or animal pressures, or as a secondary hazard associated with drought. The world's great deserts came into being long before man and have grown and shrunk according to natural long-term climatic changes affecting rainfall and groundwater patterns. However, since the appearance of man, desert growth has changed significantly, and has become a major concern for many of the world's governments and nongovernmental organizations focused upon environmental health and development (see Exhibit 2–3).

Poor land management is the primary cause of anthropomorphic desertification. Increased population and livestock pressure on marginal lands accelerate the process. In some affected areas, nomads trying to escape the desertified land for less arid regions exacerbate the problem by placing excessive pressures on land that cannot handle it (Watson, 1997). The process of desertification is not one that is easily predictable, nor can it be mapped along expected patterns or boundaries. Areas of desert land can grow and advance in erratic spurts and can occur great distances from natural, known deserts. Often, a geographic area suffering from desertification is widely recognized only after significant damage has occurred. It is still unknown if global-change patterns associated with desertification are permanent, nor are the processes required to stop or reverse desertification well understood.

Droughts are a cause of desertification, but not all droughts automatically result in the creation of desert conditions. In fact, well-managed lands can recover from drought with little effort when rains return. Continued land abuse during droughts, however, increases land degradation.

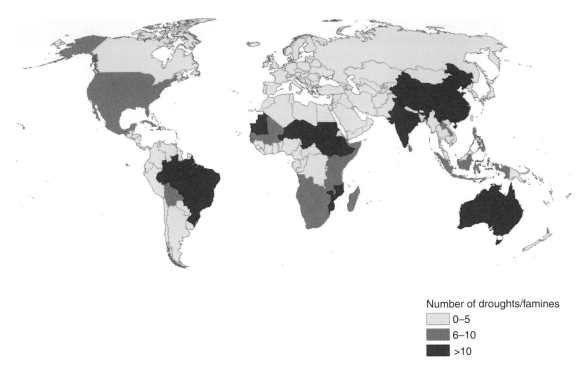

Number of droughts/famines
0–5
6–10
>10

FIGURE 2–18 Drought and famine events per year, 1974–2003. (From the International Disaster Database, www.em-dat.net)

Meteorological Hazards

Meteorological hazards are related to atmospheric weather patterns or conditions. These hazards are generally caused by factors related to precipitation; temperature; wind speed; humidity; or other more complex factors. As all of the world's people are subject to the erratic nature of weather, there exists no place on earth that is truly safe from the effects of at least one or more forms of meteorological hazards.

The greatest range of natural hazard types falls under this general category. The following section examines common meteorological hazards.

Tropical cyclones are spinning marine storms that significantly affect coastal zones, but they may also travel far inland under certain conditions. The primary characteristics of these events are their deadly combination of high winds, heavy rainfall, and coastal storm surges (see Figure 2–19).

Tropical cyclones with maximum sustained surface winds of less than 39 mph are called tropical depressions. Once attaining sustained winds of at least 39 mph they are typically called tropical storms and assigned a name (see Exhibit 2–4). If winds reach 74 mph, they are called:

- Hurricane in the North Atlantic Ocean, the Northeast Pacific Ocean east of the dateline, or the South Pacific Ocean east of 160E
- Typhoon in the Northwest Pacific Ocean west of the dateline
- Severe tropical cyclone in the Southwest Pacific Ocean west of 160E or the Southeast Indian Ocean east of 90E
- Severe cyclonic storm in the North Indian Ocean

EXHIBIT 2–3: UNITED NATIONS LAUNCHES INTERNATIONAL YEAR OF DESERTS AND DESERTIFICATION 2006 TO PROFILE DESERTIFICATION AS A MAJOR THREAT TO HUMANITY

In its resolution A/Res/58/211 of December 23, 2003, the United Nations General Assembly proclaimed 2006 as the International Year of Deserts and Desertification (IYDD) to raise public awareness of the issue and protect the biological diversity of deserts as well the traditional knowledge of those communities affected by desertification.

The main objective of the year is to profile desertification as a major threat to humanity, reinforced under the scenarios of climate change and loss of biological diversity. Dry lands constitute about 41% of the earth's surface and support more than 2 billion people. Between 10 and 20% of dry lands are degraded or unproductive. Land degradation affects one-third of the planet's land surface and threatens the health and livelihoods of more than 1 billion people in over one hundred countries.

Desertification is one of the world's most alarming processes of environmental degradation, and each year desertification and drought cause an estimated $42 billion in lost agricultural production. The risks of desertification are substantial and clear. It contributes to food insecurity, famine, and poverty, and can give rise to social, economic, and political tensions that can cause conflicts, further poverty, and land degradation. The great scope and urgency of this challenge led the United Nations General Assembly to proclaim 2006 to be the International Year of Deserts and Desertification.

The United Nations Convention to Combat Desertification (UNCCD) is the only internationally recognized, legally binding instrument that addresses the problem of land degradation in dry land rural areas. It enjoys a truly universal membership of 191 parties, and through the Global Environment Facility as its funding mechanism, it is able to channel much needed resources to projects aimed at combating the problem, particularly in Africa.

The IYDD provides a major opportunity both to strengthen the visibility and importance of the dry lands issue on the international environmental agenda and to highlight the truly global nature of the problem. All countries and civil society organizations have been encouraged to undertake special initiatives to mark the IYDD, and preparations are now well under way around the world.

The International Year of Deserts and Desertification is a strong reminder of the urgent need to address the far-reaching implications of this problem. The United Nations General Secretary recently summarized the goal of UNCCD in this way: "I look forward to working with Governments, civil society, the private sector, international organizations and others to focus attention on this crucial issue, and to make every day one on which we work to reverse the trend of desertification and set the world on a safer, more sustainable path of development."

Source: United Nations Convention to Combat Desertification (2005).

- Tropical cyclone in the Southwest Indian Ocean

Several environmental factors must exist for a tropical cyclone

- Warm ocean waters (at least 80 °F) extending at least 150 feet deep
- An atmosphere that cools quickly enough and is high enough to be potentially unstable to moist convection; the resulting thunderstorm activity allows the heat stored in the ocean waters to be transformed into a tropical cyclone

FIGURE 2–19 The devastation along the beach at Biloxi, Miss., September 15, 2005, following the storm surge of Hurricane Katrina. (From U.S. Air Force photo by Senior Master Sgt. David H. Lipp)

EXHIBIT 2–4: THE SAFFIR-SIMPSON HURRICANE SCALE

The Saffir-Simpson Hurricane Scale assigns ratings of 1–5 to cyclonic storms based upon a measurement of the storm's present intensity. The scale, which was designed for hurricanes but can be used for any cyclonic storm, is used to give an estimate of the potential property damage and flooding expected along affected coastal and inland regions. Wind speed is the determinant factor in the scale, as storm surge values are highly dependent on the slope of the continental shelf in the landfall region. Similar scales, based upon the Saffir-Simpson Hurricane Scale, have been developed specifically for the measurement of typhoons and cyclones.

- *Tropical storm.* Wind speed: 39–73 mph. Minor wind and water-related damage. A storm is given a name at this point.
- *Category 1.* Wind speed: 74–95 mph. No real damage to buildings. Damage to unanchored mobile homes. Some damage to poorly constructed signs. Some coastal flooding and minor pier damage.
- *Category 2.* Wind speed: 96–110 mph. Some damage to building roofs, doors, and windows. Considerable damage to mobile homes. Flooding damages piers, and small craft in unprotected moorings may break their moorings. Some trees blown down.
- *Category 3.* Wind speed: 111–130 mph. Some structural damage to small residences and utility buildings. Large trees blown down. Mobile homes and poorly built signs destroyed. Flooding near the coast destroys smaller structures; larger structures damaged by floating debris. Terrain may be flooded well inland.
- *Category 4.* Wind speed: 131–155 mph. More extensive curtain wall failures with some complete roof structure failure on small residences. Major erosion of beach areas. Terrain may be flooded well inland.
- *Category 5.* Wind speed: 156 mph and up. Complete roof failure on many residences and industrial buildings. Some complete building failures with small utility buildings blown over or away. Flooding causes major damage to lower floors of all structures near the shoreline. Massive evacuation of residential areas may be required.

Source: National Hurricane Center (2005).

- Relatively moist layers near the mid-troposphere (3 miles)
- A minimum distance of at least 300 miles from the equator (to allow for a minimum amount of Coriolis force, or the force caused by earth's rotation on its axis) to provide near-gradient wind balance
- A preexisting near-surface atmospheric disturbance; tropical cyclones require development of a weakly organized storm system with sizable spin and low level inflow
- Low vertical wind shear values (less than 23 mph) between the surface and the upper troposphere; vertical wind shear is the magnitude of wind change with height that can disrupt or destroy a cyclone (AOML, 2004)

Each year, approximately 80 tropical cyclones form throughout the world. Those that make landfall often have devastating consequences, leaving many people dead and injured and severely damaging all unprotected structures. They are the deadliest of all natural hazards. Due to these storms' dependence upon the oceans for energy, people who live far inland are generally not at risk from these hazards, nor are people in especially cold climates. It is estimated that 15 to 20% of the world's population is at risk from these hazards.

Monsoons are strong seasonal winds that exist throughout the world, and reverse in direction at predictable intervals each year. They are often associated with heavy rainfall when they cross over warm ocean waters before heading to cooler landmasses. As the wind blows over the warm water, the upward convection of air draws moisture from the ocean surface. When it passes over the cooler landmass, the moisture condenses and is deposited in heavy rainfalls that can last for weeks or months.

Monsoons are most marked and most intimately associated with the Indian subcontinent, which truly depends upon the annual cycle of winds for relief from the long, dry winter months. Without the monsoons, agriculture and many other basic life processes would be impossible. The monsoons in this region have two distinct seasons: a dry season that runs from September to March, blowing from the northeast, and a wet season that runs from June to September, blowing from the southwest. During the wet summer monsoon in India, the country receives 50–90% of its annual rainfall, depending upon location.

Disasters related to monsoons are associated with secondary effects from either monsoon failure or excessive monsoon rainfall. During years of monsoon failure, severe drought can ensue, leading to famine in the lesser developed countries. Crops struggle or fail and food shortages may follow without implementation of pre-established contingency plans. The economy tends to suffer as well during these years, as is true during all forms of drought. In years of excessive monsoon rainfall, severe flooding may result, leading to drowning, homelessness, and the destruction of infrastructure, property, and agriculture.

Tornadoes, or funnel clouds, are rapidly spinning columns of air (vortexes) extending downward from a cumulonimbus cloud (see Figure 2–20). To be classified as a tornado, the vortex must be in constant contact with the ground. Thousands of tornadoes are formed throughout the world each year but, thankfully, most do not touch ground and therefore remain harmless. The United States is the country most susceptible to these atmospheric hazards, with approximately 1,000 occurring each year. However, based upon landmass, other countries such as Italy experience proportionally more events (Smith, 1992).

Tornadoes form when warm, moist air meets cold, dry air, although the presence of these factors in no way guarantees that a tornado will form. The most destructive tornadoes form from supercells, which are rotating thunderstorms with a well-defined radar circulation called a mesocyclone. While the conditions necessary for their generation are well known and serve as indicators to when warnings should be issued, very little is known about how exactly tornadoes form. Tornadoes can be as short as seconds or persist for over an hour. The mean length of time is less than 10 min.

FIGURE 2–20 Undated photo of a tornado in the American Midwest. (Photo courtesy of the National Weather Service Historic Collection)

When a tornado occurs over a body of water, it is called a *waterspout*. These phenomena occur over seas, bays, and lakes worldwide. Although waterspouts are always tornadoes by definition, they are not officially counted in tornado records unless they contact land. They are smaller and weaker than most tornadoes but still can be quite dangerous—overturning small boats, damaging ships, and killing people.

Tornadoes differ between the Northern and Southern hemispheres in that they generally rotate in opposite directions—clockwise in the Southern Hemisphere and counterclockwise in the Northern (cyclonic). However, there are many known exceptions to this rule called "anticyclonic tornadoes." Tornadoes can also occur as a single funnel or as a series of many funnels.

Tornadoes average about 300 feet in diameter, and cause a path of destruction about that wide as they travel. Disasters resulting from tornadoes are caused by the damaging winds they generate. Most of the deaths associated with tornadoes are caused by secondary hazards, such as debris missiles and large hail. Tornado damage is rated according to the Fujita-Pearson Tornado Scale, or the F-Scale. This scale relates the degree of damage caused with the intensity of the wind and is assigned after the tornado is generated. Assignment of intensity is largely subjective and, therefore, arbitrary. However, the F-Scale is the most widely used and recognized rating system. It is shown in Table 2–2.

Straight-line winds are often confused with tornadoes because their damaging consequences appear the same to the untrained eye. Unlike the rotating vortex of a tornado, a straight-line wind is typically associated with a thunderstorm and moves in a linear fashion. Meteorologists often classify any thunderstorm-related winds as falling within this category. Straight-line winds are classified as "severe" if moving at or over 58 miles per hour. Experts can distinguish between a tornado and straight-line wind by the damages, given that debris associated with straight-line winds will lie in the same direction while tornado damage is much more scattered. Different categories of straight-line winds include (NOAA, 2010a):

- *Downdrafts*. Small-scale columns of air that rapidly sink toward the ground (a "downburst" is a result of a strong downdraft)
- *Downbursts*. Strong downdrafts with horizontal dimensions larger than 4 km (2.5 miles) resulting in an outward burst of damaging winds where it meets the ground (akin to how poured

Table 2–2   The Fujita-Pearson Tornado Scale

Scale	Wind Estimate (mph)	Typical Damage
F0	<73	**Light damage.** Some damage to chimneys; branches broken off trees; shallow-rooted trees pushed over; sign boards damaged.
F1	73–112	Moderate damage. Peels surface off roofs; mobile homes pushed off foundations or overturned; moving autos blown off roads.
F2	113–157	**Considerable damage.** Roofs torn off frame houses; mobile homes demolished; boxcars overturned; large trees snapped or uprooted; light-object missiles generated; cars lifted off ground.
F3	158–206	**Severe damage.** Roofs and some walls torn off well-constructed houses; trains overturned; most trees in forest uprooted; heavy cars lifted off the ground and thrown.
F4	207–260	**Devastating damage.** Well-constructed houses leveled; structures with weak foundations blown away some distance; cars thrown; large missiles generated.
F5	261–318	**Incredible damage.** Strong frame houses leveled off foundations and swept away; automobile-sized missiles fly through the air in excess of 100 meters; trees debarked; incredible phenomena will occur.

Source: Storm Prediction Center, n.d.

water reacts when making contact with the ground). Downburst damage can be as severe as that which results from a strong tornado.

- *Microbursts.* Small concentrated downbursts, generally less than 4 km across, lasting only 5 to 10 min, and with maximum wind speeds of 168 mph. Microbursts can be wet or dry, with wet microbursts accompanied by heavy surface precipitation and dry microbursts occurring with little or no precipitation reaching the ground.

- *Gust fronts.* The leading edge of rain-cooled air that meets the warm air of a thunderstorm. Gust fronts are characterized by a wind shift, temperature drop, and gusty winds out ahead of a thunderstorm.

- *Derechoes.* Widespread thunderstorm wind events caused when new thunderstorms form along the leading edge of the outer boundary of the storm-cooled air. These phenomena typically occur in the summer when thunderstorms form over the wide plains. Derechoes, which often produce severe rainfall, can produce strong winds that persist for a long time and cover a very large geographic area.

- *Bow echoes.* Radar echoes that are linear but bent outward in a bow shape. Damaging straight-line winds often occur near the "crest" or center of a bow echo, which can extend over 300 km in length, last for several hours, and produce extensive swaths of wind damage at the ground.

Ice storms are precipitation events involving freezing rain that accumulates on exposed surfaces to a thickness greater than one-quarter of an inch. These storms can extend for hundreds of square miles, and are highly destructive due to the damage caused by the weight of the accumulated ice.

Certain conditions must be present for freezing rain to occur. Two layers of cold air must be present, each less than or equal to 32°F, with a warm layer greater than 32°F in between. The position of the warm layer in this arrangement is important, because it determines whether precipitation will fall as freezing rain, sleet, or snow. Relative humidity must be near 100%, and upward-moving air is needed to keep the relative humidity at that level.

Precipitation that begins under these conditions is generated as snow, because the uppermost layer of air is usually cold enough to create flakes. As these snowflakes descend into the warm layer, they begin to melt, sometimes completely. These water drops continue to fall through the lowest cold layer, where they likely do not have sufficient time to refreeze before reaching the ground. They then fall on objects in the bottom-most layer of cold air, which has a surface temperature less than or equal to 32°F, and quickly freeze to form a coat of ice (see Figure 2–21).

The damage associated with ice storms results from the weight of the ice accumulation, which causes tree limbs to break, power lines to fall, and roofs to collapse. Icy roads lead to transportation accidents. Power outages can lead to exposure to extremely cold temperatures and can cause economic impacts due to business interruption and agricultural damage.

Severe winter storms (*snowstorms*) are extratropical, cold-weather cyclonic weather hazards associated with excessive precipitation of snow, sleet, and ice (see Figure 2–22). Many classifications of winter storms dictate that at least 4 inches of accumulation must occur within 12 hours, or 6 in. within 24 hours. These storms are dangerous because they can make travel very difficult or impossible, are accompanied by dangerously cold temperatures, and can cause many secondary hazards such as avalanches, snow drifts, and floods. The longer term effects of successive snow accumulation can be disastrous: snow melts and runs off once temperatures begin to rise, leading to mudslides and wide-spread flooding. *Blizzards* are a type of severe snowstorm accompanied by very low temperatures (below 20°F) and high winds (35 mph or greater).

Hailstorms are meteorological events characterized by the precipitation of balls or lumps of clear ice and compact snow. Cold ground temperatures are not necessary for hailstorms to occur, and these events commonly occur throughout the world, including in the tropics. The process by which hail-stones form and grow is not entirely understood, but it is believed that ice crystals form within a cloud and then are covered in layer upon layer of frozen water and suspended in strong updrafts until the holding capacity of the cloud is exceeded. Hailstones are generally spherical or irregularly spherical and generally vary in diameter from pellet size to half an inch. On rare occasions, giant hailstones have formed; some up to 5 in. in diameter.

The primary negative consequence of hail is damage and injury to crops. In Canada, although no human death has ever been attributed to hail, hailstones' damage to crops makes them one of that

FIGURE 2–21 Ice storm, Lexington, Kentucky, February 2003. (From Hornsby, 2003)

FIGURE 2–22 Cars buried after a blizzard in Washington, DC, 2003.

nation's most costly hazards. One event in 1991 in Calgary, Alberta, caused over $450 million in damages in a matter of minutes. Livestock also are at risk due to injuries and fatalities sustained during the storms. Humans usually escape death but can be injured by falling hail. Property (buildings and cars) often sustains severe damage, and roof collapses are common when the heavy hailstones accumulate quickly. Airplanes have also been damaged by hailstorms.

Frost is a hazard related to agriculture. Frost crystals form when water vapor freezes upon contact with a surface that is below the frost point. Frost is most common in low-lying valleys where heavier, cooler air collects, especially at night. It also can occur when the air temperature is higher than freezing, but just above the surface is below freezing because of this heavier cold air. Crops often can survive freezing temperatures in the absence of frost, as their cells remain in a liquid state as much as 10 °F (12 °C) below the freezing point of water. However, once frost forms on the plant, the cells begin to sustain damage and often die. Worldwide crop losses from frost have been estimated to be as high as $2.5 billion each year.

Frost is known to change the shape of topsoils, which can cause ground deformation and damage to overlying structures. Roads often deteriorate more quickly in areas where frost frequently forms. In Finland, Norway, and Sweden, where frost damage to roads is common, an annual average of $10 million in damages per country is normally sustained. Frost can also lead to rockfalls when boulders on high precipices are loosened by frost in the surrounding soil or in cracks on the stone.

Extreme cold temperatures, which may be fleeting or may persist for days or weeks, can have severe negative consequences. What constitutes extreme cold and its effects vary across geographic regions. For example, in regions relatively unaccustomed to winter weather, near-freezing temperatures are considered "extreme cold." Generally, a significant drop below the average low temperature for an area will cause adverse affects to unprepared people, animals, or property.

Extreme cold is a dangerous situation that can bring on health emergencies in susceptible people, such as those who are without shelter or stranded, or who live in a home that is poorly insulated or without heat. Wind chill, which is a measure of apparent temperature relative to actual temperature based upon observed wind speed, can exacerbate the effects of extreme cold (see Table 2–3). Hypothermia is a dangerous condition that is observed much more frequently during periods of extreme cold.

Table 2–3   Wind Chill Chart

		Temperature (°F)																	
	Calm	40	35	30	25	20	15	10	5	0	−5	−10	−15	−20	−25	−30	−35	−40	−45
Wind (mph)	5	36	31	25	19	13	7	1	−5	−11	−16	−22	−28	−34	−40	−46	−52	−57	−63
	10	34	27	21	15	9	3	−4	−10	−16	−22	−28	−35	−41	−47	−53	−59	−66	−72
	15	32	25	19	13	6	0	−7	−13	−19	−26	−32	−39	−45	−51	−58	−64	−71	−77
	20	30	24	17	11	4	−2	−9	−15	−22	−29	−35	−42	−48	−55	−61	−68	−74	−81
	25	29	23	16	9	3	−4	−11	−17	−24	−31	−37	−44	−51	−58	−64	−71	−78	−84
	30	28	22	15	8	1	−5	−12	−19	−26	−33	−39	−46	−53	−60	−67	−73	−80	−87
	35	28	21	14	7	0	−7	−14	−21	−27	−34	−41	−48	−55	−62	−69	−76	−82	−89
	40	27	20	13	6	−1	−8	−15	−22	−29	−36	−43	−50	−57	−64	−71	−78	−84	−91
	45	26	19	12	5	−2	−9	−16	−23	−30	−37	−44	−51	−58	−65	−72	−79	−86	−93
	50	26	19	12	4	−3	−10	−17	−24	−31	−38	−45	−52	−60	−67	−74	−81	−88	−95
	55	25	18	11	4	−3	−11	−18	−25	−32	−39	−46	−54	−61	−68	−75	−82	−89	−97
	60	25	17	10	3	−4	−11	−19	−26	−33	−40	−48	−55	−62	−69	−76	−84	−91	−98

Frostbite Times   □ 30 min   □ 10 min   □ 5 min

Wind chill (°F) = 35.74 + 0.6215T − 35.75($V^{0.16}$) + 0.4275T($V^{0.16}$), where T = air temperature (°F), V = wind speed (mph)

Effective 11/01/01

Source: NOAA (2010).

FIGURE 2–23 A 2007 ice jam on the Assiniboine River in Winnipeg, MB, Canada, caused localized flooding in the surrounding floodplain. (Photo courtesy of Daniel McKay, April 14, 2007)

Extreme cold can cause damage to structures from frozen pipes, including fuel lines, and may lead to bursting or breakage. Fires are common during periods of extreme cold because more people use fireplaces to heat their homes. This effect is increased when power outages accompany the extreme cold. Carbon monoxide poisoning is another related hazard of indoor wood-fired heat.

With extended periods of extreme cold, secondary environmental hazards can occur, such as ice jams on major rivers (see Figure 2–23). Flooding behind the jammed ice can be disastrous, especially in conjunction with the extremely cold temperatures that threaten anyone without shelter.

Extreme heat, like extreme cold, is a temperature-related hazard associated with a significant deviation above normal high temperatures for a given geographical area. Periods of extreme heat are often called "heat waves." Extreme heat most significantly affects humans, although stresses upon electrical infrastructure related to intense demand caused by widespread overuse of air conditioners often causes secondary, exacerbating disasters. Power outages leave people without any option for cooling down and health effects skyrocket.

Between 1979 and 2001 excessive heat exposure was attributed to almost 10,000 deaths in the United States. That accounts for more deaths than from hurricanes, lightning, tornadoes, floods, and earthquakes in the same period combined. Europe was affected by one of the worst heat waves in history in 2003, leading to a catastrophic public health disaster. In total, over 40,000 people died from related causes. Exhibit 2–5 describes the effects of the heat wave by country, including secondary hazards that appeared.

At greater risk are the elderly, children, and people with certain medical conditions, such as heart disease. However, even young and healthy individuals can succumb to heat if they participate in strenuous physical activities during hot weather. Some behaviors also put people at greater risk, such as drinking alcohol, taking part in strenuous outdoor activities in hot weather, and taking medications that impair the body's ability to regulate its temperature or inhibit perspiration.

Windstorms are periods of high wind not associated with convective events (severe local storms, hurricanes, and winter storms). They are considered severe if sustained winds of 40 mph or more persist for an hour or longer, or if sustained winds of 58 mph or more are sustained for any amount of

EXHIBIT 2–5: DESCRIPTION OF THE 2003 EUROPEAN HEAT WAVE BY COUNTRY

France
In France, 14,847 people, mostly elderly, perished from the heat. In France, where very hot summers are uncommon, most of the population was unprepared to protect themselves and avoid overheating and dehydration. Additionally, most homes (including retirement homes) are not equipped with air conditioning. Because extreme heat had not been previously identified as a hazard risk, no contingency plans existed for its management. Further compounding the issue was that the heat wave struck during the August vacation season, when many government employees and doctors were away.

Italy
In Italy, 20,000 people died when temperatures varied between 38 and 40 °C in most cities for weeks.

United Kingdom
In the United Kingdom, the highest temperature since records began in 1911 (38 °C/100.4 °F) was recorded at London's Heathrow airport on Sunday, August 10, 2003. This was surpassed later the same day at Gravesend, Kent, with a temperature of 38.1 °C (100.6 °F). By August 15, 907 people were estimated to have died because of the heat.

Portugal
There were extensive forest fires in Portugal related to the heat wave. Five percent of the countryside and 10% of the forests were destroyed, an estimated 4000 km². Eighteen people died in the fires.

Germany
In Germany, a record temperature of 40.4 °C was recorded at Roth, Bavaria. With only half the normal rainfall, rivers were at their lowest in over a century, and shipping could not navigate the Elbe or Danube Rivers.

Switzerland
Melting glaciers in the Alps caused avalanches and flash floods in Switzerland.

Total Dead
A total of 40,000 people died from the 2003 European heat wave.

Source: United Nations Environmental Programme (2003).

time. At higher elevations, these wind speed minimum limits are increased due to the lower air density, which results in less damage from equal wind forces. Categories of windstorms include:

- *Gradient high winds.* High winds that usually cover a large area, caused by large-scale pressure systems.
- *Mesoscale high winds.* High winds that tend to occur after organized convective systems have passed and are associated with barometric "wake depressions" or strong mesoscale high pressure.
- *Channeled high winds.* In mountainous areas or in cities with tall buildings, air can be channeled through constricted passages, producing high winds. Channeled high winds are local in nature but can be extremely strong.

- *Tropical-cyclone-associated high winds.* High winds can occur a few hundred miles from where a tropical cyclone has made landfall and are forecast independent of the tropical cyclone.
- *Chinook or foehn winds.* Warm, dry winds that occur on the lee side of high mountain ranges, developing with great strength in well-defined areas.

Windstorms cause damage primarily because of their powerful wind forces and secondarily from flying debris. Damage associated with windstorms includes impaired visibility, crop damage, damage to or destruction of buildings and vehicles, power outages and other infrastructure damage, and felled or broken trees. These storms often accompany major winter or early spring blizzards, can affect multiple jurisdictions, and may cover a range of hundreds of square miles. The storms can last anywhere from a few hours to three days with lulls in intensity during the night. They worsen during the late morning and become most intense during the late afternoon when atmospheric mixing is most pronounced (UCAR, 2005).

The Beaufort scale is the most common measurement of wind force. The original version of this scale, designed in the 1830s, was a sailing tool that did not include wind speed. However, these speeds were added later to make the tool more useful for meteorologists. Hurricanes are often listed as Beaufort numbers 12–16, with a Category 1 hurricane labeled a Beaufort 12. This scale is shown in Table 2–4.

Sandstorms (called *duststorms* in the United States) occur when very strong winds blow over loose soil or sand, picking up significant amounts of material in the process. In desert regions, sandstorms become a frequent occurrence at certain times of the year due to the intense heating of the air over the desert surface, which in turn causes instability in the lower atmosphere. This instability produces higher winds in the middle troposphere, which are drawn downward and produce much stronger winds at the surface.

Areas where the ground is extremely dry and has very little vegetation are most susceptible to sandstorms (see Figure 2–24). Once particles become airborne, they can reduce visibility to a few feet; cause respiratory problems; and have a damaging, abrasive effect on machinery and structures. Any sandstorm or duststorm that reduces visibility to less than a quarter of a mile tends to pose hazards for travelers, causes damage and injury, and affects commerce. Damage caused by these storms includes:

- Impaired visibility and breathing difficulties, especially for outdoor workers, people in recreational activities, and motorists
- Crop damage
- Destruction to buildings, vehicles, and trailers
- Power outages and other infrastructure damage
- Broken trees
- Scouring damage to buildings and automobiles
- Damage to electronics, computers, and communications equipment from accumulated dust

In 2008, research showed that duststorms also have the potential to pick up contaminants and industrial pollutants as well as harmful living organisms (such as fungi, bacteria, and viruses). The growing threat is considered significant enough that the World Meteorological Organization (WMO) has established a worldwide monitoring and notification system that is capable of warning geographic areas in the path of advancing storms (Struck, 2008).

Table 2–4 The Beaufort Wind Scale

Beaufort Number	Wind Speed (mph)	Description	Wave Height (m)	Sea Conditions	Land Conditions
0	0	Calm	0	Flat	Calm
1	1–3	Light air	0.1	Ripples without crests	Wind motion visible in smoke
2	4–7	Light breeze	0.2	Small wavelets	Wind felt on exposed skin; leaves rustle
3	8–12	Gentle breeze	0.6	Large wavelets	Leaves and smaller twigs in constant motion
4	13–18	Moderate breeze	1	Small waves	Dust and loose paper raised; small branches begin to move
5	19–24	Fresh breeze	2	Moderate (1.2 m) longer waves; some foam and spray	Smaller trees sway
6	25–31	Strong breeze	3	Large waves with foam crests and some spray	Large branches in motion; umbrella use becomes difficult
7	32–38	Near gale	4	Sea heaps up and foam begins to streak	Whole trees in motion; effort to walk against the wind
8	39–46	Gale	5.5	Moderately high waves with breaking crests forming spindrift; streaks of foam	Twigs broken from trees
9	47–54	Severe gale	7	High waves (2.75 m) with dense foam; wave crests start to roll over; considerable spray	Light structure damage
10	55–63	Storm	9	Very high waves; the sea surface is white and there is considerable tumbling; visibility is reduced	Trees uprooted; considerable structural damage
11	64–74	Violent storm	11.5	Exceptionally high waves	Widespread structural damage
12	75 or more	Hurricane	14+	Huge waves; air filled with foam and spray; sea completely white with driving spray; visibility very greatly reduced	Massive and widespread damage to structures

Source: NOAA, 2010.

Wildfire, which is a brush or wildland fire burning out of control over great geographic range, is often considered a meteorological event because it is so closely associated with the weather conditions necessary to sustain and spread it (called fire weather). Other factors also contribute to the generation and spread of wildfire, including hydrological conditions, topography, and vegetation (fuel). The following weather conditions promote ignition and rapid spread of fires:

FIGURE 2–24 Sandstorm approaching a U.S. military base in Iraq, 2005. (Photo courtesy of Gunnery Sergeant Shannon Arledge, USMC)

- Low humidity
- High winds (over 10–20 mph)
- Dry thunderstorm (i.e., lightning without rain)
- Unstable air

Other factors that impact the spread and severity of fires include:

- *Dry antecedent conditions.* Prolonged hot, dry conditions greatly increase fire danger. In drought conditions, forests can ignite from a weak source that normally would not be a threat.
- *Urban-wildland interface.* The spread and severity of residential areas into wildlands mean the human population faces a greater risk of forest fires.
- *Available fuel.* The spread of fire depends on the amount of burnable material. Trees that contain oily sap, such as eucalyptus, provide tremendous fuel when dry.
- *Hilly terrain.* Fire spreads much faster uphill than downhill and spreads faster uphill than across level terrain.

Wildfires can cause incredible environmental damage, both during the fire and after they have burned. They often burn any unprotected structure that lies in their path, and many deaths are attributed to people who become stranded within zones of major burning. They can also cause transportation problems when they occur along major road and railway routes. Smoke from wildfires tends to cause severe respiratory problems in susceptible individuals. Once the fires have passed or have been extinguished and a major loss of vegetation has occurred, secondary hazards can occur, including mudslides, landslides, river silting, and flooding.

Forecasters use the Haines Index, shown in Exhibit 2–6, to indicate the potential for large fire growth. The Haines Index is a stability index especially designed for fire weather use. It is determined by combining the stability and moisture content of the lower atmosphere into a single number that correlates with large fire growth. Dry air affects fire behavior by lowering fuel moisture, which results in more fuel available for fire, and by increasing the probability of spotting (new, isolated fires caused by

EXHIBIT 2–6: HAINES INDEX POTENTIAL FOR LARGE FIRE GROWTH

2 or 3—very low
4—low
5—moderate
6—high

Source: USDA (2006).

airborne sparks emitted by the primary fire or fires). Instability affects fire behavior by enhancing the vertical size of the smoke column, resulting in strong surface winds as air rushes into the fire to replace air evacuated by the smoke column. Because the index is derived from the combination of these two factors, which each has a minimum value of 1, the index has a minimum value of 2. When the index is 5 or 6, the probability of extreme fire behavior is moderate to high.

The United Nations Environmental Program monitors worldwide wildfires on their Global Wildfires monitoring site www.grid.unep.ch/activities/earlywarning/fires/index.php.

Thunderstorms are local storms accompanied by lightning and thunder; are produced by cumulonimbus clouds; and are usually accompanied by gusty winds, heavy rain, and occasionally hail. Three factors are required for a thunderstorm to develop. The first, which serves to fuel the storm, is moisture in the form of water vapor that must lie in the lowest atmospheric levels. Second, there must be a rapid cooling of air above these low, wet levels, decreasing in temperature with altitude, up to 2 to 3 miles. Finally, there must be a force strong enough to lift the low moist air to the higher, colder atmospheric layers—usually a cold front (the boundary between where the cold air from one thunderstorm meets the air outside the storm, called an outflow boundary). As the moist air rises, it begins to cool, and after some time, the water vapor begins to condense into liquid drops. This process causes warming of the cloud mass, which in turn generates rising currents of air that can extend up to 10 miles in altitude.

Thunderstorms are classified as nonsevere and severe. Nonsevere thunderstorms rarely last longer than 2 hours. A typical nonsevere thunderstorm life cycle consists of three stages:

1. _Cumulus stage._ Warm, moist air rises (updraft) and condenses into tiny water droplets that make up the visible cloud. Outside air is pulled into the cloud. Supercooled droplets of water are carried far above the freezing level.
2. _Mature stage._ The cloud grows above the freezing level; precipitation forms and becomes heavy enough to fall back to the earth. Friction caused by the falling precipitation generates downdrafts of cool air that reach the earth's surface. Very heavy rains are associated with this stage. The cloud extends upward to the tropopause, causing a characteristic flat (anvil) top to form. Strong periods of lightning are likely during this stage, which typically lasts from 10 to 20 min.
3. _Dissipation stage._ The downward motion of air overcomes the storm, depriving it of moist air. Precipitation begins to subside, and the cloud evaporates.

Thunderstorms become severe when their wind speeds exceed 58 miles per hour and hail forms in balls greater than three-quarters of an inch in diameter. Several different kinds of thunderstorms can form:

- *Single cell.* These are short-lived storms, lasting only 20–30 min from formation to dissipation covering only a limited area of generally a few square miles. These storms are relatively uncommon.

- *Multicell.* These are the most common type of thunderstorm, consisting of an organized cluster of two or more single cells. The storm cells fuel each other with the air that flows between them and cause new cells to form in succession on the flank or rear sides about every 5–15 min.

- *Supercell.* These storms, which are always severe due to observed wind speeds, are relatively uncommon. Supercells cause significant damage, last for a long time (generally, 1–6 hours), and travel great distances (200 miles or more; see Figure 2–25). These storms can cause hurricane-force winds, giant hail (2 in. in diameter or more), and significant tornado activity. A supercell produces updrafts of 56–112 mph that combine with sustained downdrafts to extend the storm's duration.

- *Squall lines.* These are lines or bands of active thunderstorms that can extend over 250–500 miles, can be 10–20 miles wide, and consist of many laterally aligned cells that do not interact or interfere with one another. The cells involved in the squall line may be a combination of types. These phenomena often form along cold fronts, but they also can form as far as 100 miles ahead of an advancing cold front in the warm sector of an extratropical storm. They often trail a large, flat cloud layer that brings significant rain after the storms pass (UCAR, n.d.).

Thunderstorms cause most of their damage through the rain and wind that they generate. Flash floods are common due to the rapid precipitation, which cannot be absorbed by the ground and quickly becomes runoff. Hail can cause damage to buildings and crops. Lighting can cause fatalities and generate fires. Less common but very damaging are tornadoes that can form as result of these storms.

Fog is essentially a cloud that forms at ground level. However, it is formed by very different processes from those that form clouds in the upper atmosphere. Like clouds, fog consists of airborne condensed water droplets, the result of moist air being cooled to the point at which it can no longer hold all of the water vapor it contains, known as the dewpoint. With fog, this cooling may happen

FIGURE 2–25 A supercell in Texas. (Photo courtesy of Jason Hunter, 2010)

for a variety of reasons, including the cooling and moistening of surface air by rain; infrared cooling of a cloudless, humid air at night (also called radiation fog); and the passage of a warm, moist air mass over a cold surface (usually snow or ice), which produces so-called advection fog. The various types of fog are listed in Table 2–5.

The primary danger associated with fog is reduced visibility. Major destructive and often fatal highway pileups are often blamed on thick, rapidly developing fog. Aviation accidents also are commonly blamed on this hazard. Constant fog near steep mountain slopes can either cause or be an indicator of high moisture content in the water, which leads to more rapid erosion and subsequent landslides, mudslides, and mountain road collapse.

El Niño and La Niña are related weather phenomena characterized by a disruption in the ocean-atmospheric system of the tropical Pacific (see Figure 2–26). Both of these events are associated with severe negative consequence around the world. The most significant consequence is increased rainfall across the southern parts of the United States and in the northwestern coast of South America (Chile,

Table 2–5   Types of Fog

Type of Fog	Factors	Description	Effects
Ground fog	• Clear nights • Stable air (winds less than 5 mph) • Small temperature-dewpoint spread	Heat radiates away from the ground, cooling the ground and surface air. When the air cools to its dewpoint, fog forms (usually a layer of less than 100–200 feet)	Common in many areas, ground fog burns off with the morning sun
Valley fog	• Cold surface air and weak winter sun • May follow a winter storm or prolonged nighttime cooling	Fog can build to a height of more than 1500 feet. Weak sun may evaporate lower levels of the fog but leave upper levels in place	Found in valleys during the winter, valley fog can last for days, until winds are strong enough to push out the cold air
Advection fog	• Horizontal wind • Warm, humid air • Winter temperatures	Wind pushes warm humid air over the cold ground or water, where it cools to the dewpoint and forms fog	Advection fog can cover wide areas of the central United States in winter. It may be thick enough to close airports
Upslope fog	• Winds blowing up hills or mountains • Humid air	As humid air pushes up hills and mountains, it cools to its dewpoint and forms fog, which drifts up the mountain	Upslope fog is common and widespread in most of the world's great mountain chains
Sea smoke, steam fog	• Body of water • Air much colder than water • Wind	As cold air blows over warmer water, water evaporates into the cold air, increasing the humidity to the dewpoint. Vapor condenses, forming a layer of fog 1–2 feet thick over the water	This type of fog forms most commonly over oceans, lakes, ponds, and streams on fall days
Precipitation fog	• Warmer air • Cool rain	Some rain evaporates, and the added vapor increases the air to its dewpoint. The vapor then condenses into fog	Precipitation fog forms on cool, rainy days

Source: UCAR (2005).

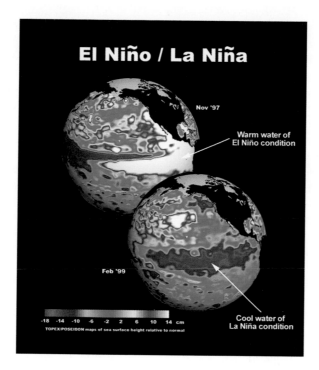

FIGURE 2–26 Image depicting sea surface heights relative to normal, for the 1997 El Niño and 1999 La Niña events. (From NASA, 1999)

Peru, and Ecuador). During years of El Niño, devastating drought and associated brush fires often occur in Australia. In normal, non-El Niño conditions, the trade winds blow toward the west across the tropical Pacific.

These winds literally "pile up" warm surface water in the west Pacific, so that the sea surface is about half a meter higher at Indonesia than at Ecuador. The sea surface temperature is about 46 °F (8 °C) higher in the west, with cool temperatures off South America, due to an upwelling of cold water from deeper levels. This cold water is nutrient-rich, supporting high levels of primary productivity, diverse marine ecosystems, and major fisheries. Rainfall is found in rising air over the warmest water, and the east Pacific is relatively dry.

During El Niño years, the trade winds relax in the central and western Pacific, leading to a depression of the thermocline (juncture of cold and warm water) in the eastern Pacific and an elevation of the thermocline in the west. Ocean water temperatures reach points well above normal in the eastern Pacific, and rainfall follows that warm water eastward, bringing the associated flooding to South America and drought in Indonesia and Australia. The eastward displacement of the atmospheric heat source overlying the warmest water results in large changes in the global atmospheric circulation, which in turn forces changes in weather in regions far removed from the tropical Pacific (see Exhibit 2–7).

La Niña is a phenomenon that is often described as being the opposite of El Niño. It is characterized *by cooler than normal sea surface temperatures* in the central and eastern tropical Pacific

EXHIBIT 2–7: WORLD METEOROLOGICAL ORGANIZATION REGION IV ADOPTS CONSENSUS EL NIÑO AND LA NIÑA INDEX AND DEFINITIONS

NOAA announced on April 28, 2005, that the 26 nations of the World Meteorological Organization's Regional Association IV had adopted a Consensus Index and Definitions of El Niño and La Niña conditions. By doing so, scientists and governments throughout the region are now better able to define potential impacts from these short-term climate shifts and prepare for remedial action.

The Consensus was agreed upon earlier that year by the NOAA National Weather Service, as the U.S. representative, and its meteorological service counterparts in Canada and Mexico. In adopting the North American Consensus, the Regional Association IV Member nations, located in North and Central America and the Caribbean, agreed that the index and definitions could be revised in the future based on further scientific research, and Member nations were urged to define local thresholds for impacts based on the index. The Consensus is now known as the WMO RA IV Consensus Index and Definitions of El Niño and La Niña. Worldwide consensus on this approach is being sought through the WMO.

By agreeing to the same operational definition for El Niño and La Niña events, members are better able to collaborate on understanding risks and mitigating impacts throughout the region. Scientists are now better able to focus on whether observations of the measurable changes in Pacific sea surface temperatures will lead to changes in the rain and temperature patterns around the world. The definitions focus more attention on these shifts and help governments in the region brace for periodic flooding or drought conditions.

As part of the agreement, the WMO Commission for Climatology established an expert team on El Niño and La Niña definitions. Led by NOAA, the expert team catalogs El Niño and La Niña definitions in operational use globally to further assist improving analysis of local and regional impacts. The index is defined as a three-month average of sea surface temperature departures from normal for a critical region of the equatorial Pacific (Nino 3.4 region; 120–170W, 5N–5S). This region of the tropical Pacific contains what scientists call the "equatorial cold tongue," a band of cool water that extends along the equator from the coast of South America to the central Pacific Ocean. Departures from average sea surface temperatures in this region are critically important in determining major shifts in the pattern of tropical rainfall, which influence the jet streams and patterns of temperature and precipitation around the world.

Operational definitions for El Niño and La Niña are:

- **El Niño:** A phenomenon in the equatorial Pacific Ocean characterized by a positive sea surface temperature departure from normal (for the 1971–2000 base period) in the Niño 3.4 region greater than or equal in magnitude to 0.5 °C, averaged over three consecutive months.
- **La Niña:** A phenomenon in the equatorial Pacific Ocean characterized by a negative sea surface temperature departure from normal (for the 1971–2000 base period) in the Niño 3.4 region greater than or equal in magnitude to 0.5 °C, averaged over three consecutive months.

Source: NOAA (2005).

Ocean and the impacts of the resulting global weather pattern. Like El Niño, La Niña recurs every few years and can persist for as long as 2 years.

Typically, a La Niña is preceded by a buildup of cooler than normal subsurface waters in the tropical Pacific. Eastward-moving atmospheric and oceanic waves help bring cold water to the surface through a complex series of events that are not well understood. Eventually, the easterly trade winds strengthen, cold upwelling off Peru and Ecuador intensifies, and sea-surface temperatures drop below normal. Like El Niño, La Niña tends to peak during the Northern Hemisphere winter.

La Niña years are marked by altered weather patterns in certain parts of the world. Abnormally high rainfall is observed in Southeast Asia, while dry to drought conditions occur in South America. Other impacts that have been observed during La Niña years include:

- Abnormally heavy monsoons on the Indian subcontinent.
- In the United States, colder and snowier winter in the northern states west of the Great Lakes, drier than normal winter in the Southeast, warmer and drier winter in the Southwest, and enhanced hurricane activity around the mid-Atlantic states.
- Torrential rains leading to floods in Southeast Asia.
- Wet weather in eastern Australia.
- Cool and wet winter in southeastern Africa.

Climate change is not a single hazard but an observed change in average global climatic conditions over time. Drastic climate changes have occurred throughout the earth's existence, but over very gradual periods of time. Recent scientific studies have indicated, however, that many of these gradual processes are speeding up significantly, and it is likely that human activities are to blame. As humans have adapted to a specific climate, it is only logical that any significant change in that climate system will cause primary and secondary effects that are very hazardous to human life and property.

While no conclusive correlations have been developed as of yet, it is certain that continued climate change will eventually increase the catastrophic potential of many meteorological hazards that exist today (and will likewise decrease the potential of others). Many interest groups feel that the observed increase in these hazards in recent history is actually a first indication of these increased effects, caused by global warming, air and water pollution, and other human-induced factors. These theories, which decades ago seemed far-fetched, are today attracting the attention of the world's nations, major multilateral groups, and private and nonprofit environmental groups.

Models for predicting climate change have been created, providing insight into what changes can be expected without intervention or behavioral change. Several trends have been recognized; for instance, increases in the amount of greenhouse gases released into the atmosphere will likely raise temperatures over most land surfaces with great regional variation. Increased drought and storm intensity is likely, including tropical cyclones with higher wind speeds, a wetter Asian monsoon, and, possibly, more intense mid-latitude storms.

Storm formation patterns could be altered by decreases in the temperature difference between the poles and the equator caused by global warming. The temperature difference would fuel mid-latitude storms, which would affect many of the world's highest density population centers. With warmer temperatures would come increased atmospheric water vapor and, thus, a hotter, more humid environment. These changes would be most pronounced at the poles. The result would be a lower number of storms generated overall, but those that form would be much more intense. They would also become more difficult to predict and track.

Other effects of climate change include much higher and lower average temperatures and longer periods of cold and heat waves. Environmental changes would occur, such as rising sea levels caused by melting of the world's snow and ice cover at the poles and in glaciers. Coastal flooding would be one of many negative results. Predictions by the Intergovernmental Panel on Climate Change have stated that global warming could cause sea levels to rise 0.11–0.77 m (0.36–2.5 feet) by 2100. In June and July of 2010, the governments of Thailand and Viet Nam, respectively, reported projections that both Bangkok and Ho Chi Minh City were facing the prospect of inundation caused by rapidly rising sea levels. In Bangkok, it is estimated that the city will be under water within a century due to a combination of up to 4 inches of land subsidence caused by aquifer drainage and a 3 to 4 cm annual rise in the Gulf of Thailand (Bernama, 2010; CNN, 2007a). In Viet Nam, it is feared that 61% of the city, representing land occupied by over 7 million people, will face constant risk of catastrophic flooding due to land falling below the level of the rising seas (*Viet Nam News*, 2010).

Biological/Health-Related Hazards

Biological hazards are the umbrella grouping for all hazards that cause or are related to disease in plants, animals, and humans. Daily life involves contact with many minor biological hazards, including bacteria, viruses, pollutants, chemicals, and toxins. Many of these do cause disease in individuals and are, worldwide, the single greatest cause of death. However, humans constantly seek ways of managing these hazards. Management mechanisms range from simple hand washing to highly complex vaccines and medical treatments. Unfortunately, on many occasions each year biological hazards become unmanageable and result in a disaster. This section describes the most common biological disasters faced today.

Human epidemics are illnesses caused by single pathogenic sources that affect a quantity of people rising at a rate faster than the disease is being controlled. Epidemics are not a factor of the total number of people with the disease; thus, for certain very rare diseases, a small number of people can constitute an epidemic (often called an *outbreak*). Epidemics are often defined by their geographical range, which can include a community, a country, or even the entire globe (called a *pandemic*). Pathogens can be present normally without causing an epidemic, but a change in certain conditions (such as climatic variance or mutations) may make their spread more effective and/or their treatment more difficult.

Epidemics can arise quickly or gradually, and can be halted quickly or persist for decades. The AIDS pandemic, for instance, which could be controllable (but not cured) with proper medication, public education, and policy, appears to have no end in sight. The SARS epidemic, however, which struck twice in two consecutive years, was quickly controlled through the action of a coordinated international public health effort. Fears about the possible spread of avian influenza (H5N1), should it mutate into a form transmissible between humans, generated estimates of possible deaths numbering in the hundreds of millions, although so far only dozens of people have died since it first emerged and the outbreak has largely passed. The most recent pandemic influenza threat, which is the H1N1 strain (also referred to as swine flu), was incredibly effective at passing through the human population but was ultimately less consequential than seasonal flu.

Controlling epidemics is difficult. It needs a complex set of requirements managed by public health and other government officials, nonprofit agencies, and private facilities such as hospitals and clinics. There are many components to this effort, including recognition of the epidemic (and the ability to test for the disease), the ability to locate victims and backtrack their actions, existing and available medical treatment options and facilities, mechanisms to control further spread of the disease (including quarantine if needed), public education, and short- and long-term disease prevention among those not afflicted (vaccination or other prophylaxis, if available). Self-reporting by those who are infected, which is not always conducted, makes controlling an epidemic much more effective.

Epidemics, statistically, have been the greatest killers of man. History is dotted with epidemic and pandemic events that have decimated populations (see Exhibit 2–8). Because the projected transmission and fatality rates are very difficult to establish with accuracy, public health organizations and agencies are typically overly careful in their warnings. In the initial weeks of the H5N1 outbreak, for example, the WHO declared the disease a worldwide pandemic. When the disease turned out to be less deadly than originally expected, the organization fell under intense scrutiny for being what many felt was alarmist (Jordans, 2010). However, the intense vaccination campaign that occurred following this declaration is likely what would be needed to drive the research, development, production, and administration of an effective vaccine should a more virulent strain arise. The event also pushed for greater pandemic preparedness planning on a global scale, which has driven a change in the way many businesses and governments operate.

Livestock, or *animal*, *epidemics*, including those in aquatic environments, refer to epidemics that affect the life of any animal other than humans (see Figure 2–27). Animal epidemics often strike

---

EXHIBIT 2–8: GREAT EPIDEMICS AND PANDEMICS

430 BC	An unknown pathogen that struck during four years of the Peloponnesian War killed one-quarter of the Athenian army, and a quarter of the surrounding population.
AD 165–180	Five million people were killed in Rome by either smallpox or measles in the Antonine Plague (also known as the Plague of Galen).
251–266	A second outbreak of the same or a similar disease that caused the Antonine Plague struck Rome again. Although total numbers of fatalities are not known, it is estimated that over 5,000 people per day were dying during the peak of the epidemic.
541–542	The Plague of Justinian, an early outbreak of bubonic plague, killed as many as 25 million people and reduced the population of the Mediterranean by a quarter.
1347–1350	The Black Plague, a pandemic of bubonic plague, affected many areas throughout the world, reducing the population of Europe by 20 million, or 33% (50% in some countries).
1629–1631	The Great Plague of Milan, an epidemic of bubonic plague, killed 280,000 people. The city of Milan lost about 45% of its population.
1918–1919	The Spanish Flu, a pandemic of influenza, killed an estimated 25–50 million people worldwide in a period of only 18 months, with a majority of deaths occurring during one 6-month period. 17 million people died in India alone.

Source: Wikipedia (2010).

FIGURE 2–27 Veterinarian Carole Bolin prepares to inject a cow with the new vaccine for bovine leptospirosis. (Photo courtesy of Keith Weller)

livestock on a large scale, with great economic consequences to affected regions and countries. Epidemics can cause a loss of confidence in food supplies from the afflicted areas, and even noncontaminated meat can be rendered valueless. A list of common diseases that affect animals throughout the world is provided in Exhibit 2–9.

In early 2008, research published in *Nature* magazine based on over six decades of infectious disease research showed that there are a number of hotspots throughout the world where new and

---

EXHIBIT 2–9: LIST OF WORLDWIDE ANIMAL DISEASES

African horse sickness: equine
African swine fever: porcine
Anaplasmosis: bovine
Anthrax: any species
Atrophic rhinitis: porcine
Avian infectious bronchitis: avian
Avian infectious laryngotracheitis: avian
Avian influenza: avian
Avian tuberculosis: avian
Babesiosis: bovine, porcine
Bluetongue: any species
Bovine spongiform encephalopathy: bovine
Brucellosis: any species
Caprine arthritis/encephalitis: caprine, ovine
Caseous lymphadenitis: caprine, ovine
Chlamydiosis: avian
Chronic wasting disease: cervids
Contagious agalactia of sheep and goats: caprine, ovine
Contagious bovine pleuropneumonia: any species

Contagious caprine pleuropneumonia: caprine, ovine
Contagious equine metritis: equine
Cysticercosis: bovine, porcine
Dermatophilosis: bovine
Dourine: equine
Duck virus enteritis: avian
Duck virus hepatitis: avian
Echinococcus/hydatidosis: any species
Enterovirus encephalomyelitis: porcine
Enzootic abortion of ewes: caprine, ovine
Enzootic bovine leukosis: bovine
Epizootic hematopoietic necrosis: aquaculture
Epizootic hemorrhagic disease: cervids
Epizootic lymphangitis: equine
Equine encephalomyelitis: avian, equine
Equine infectious anemia: equine
Equine influenza: equine
Equine piroplasmosis: equine
Equine rhinopneumonitis: equine
Equine viral arteritis: equine
Exotic myiasis: any species
Foot and mouth disease: any species
Fowl cholera: avian
Fowl pox: avian
Fowl typhoid: avian
Genital campylobacteriosis: bovine
Glanders: any species
Goat and sheep pox: caprine, ovine
Heartwater: any species
Hemorrhagic septicemia: bovine
Hog cholera: porcine
Horse mange: equine
Horse pox: equine
Infectious avian encephalomyelitis: avian
Infectious bovine rhinotracheitis/infectious pustular vulvovaginitis: bovine
Infectious bursal disease: avian
Infectious hematopoietic necrosis: aquaculture
Japanese encephalitis: equine
Leptospirosis: any species
Listeriosis: bovine, caprine, ovine
Lumpy skin disease: any species
Maedi-Visna/ovine progressive pneumonia: caprine, ovine
Malignant catarrhal fever: any species
Marek's disease: avian

(*Continued*)

EXHIBIT 2–9: LIST OF WORLDWIDE ANIMAL DISEASES (CONTINUED)

Mycoplasma gallisepticum: avian
Nairobi sheep disease: caprine, ovine
Newcastle disease: avian
Onchorhynchus masou virus disease: aquaculture
Ovine epididymitis: ovine
Ovine pulmonary adenomatosis: caprine, ovine
Paramyxovirus: avian
Paratuberculosis: any species
Peste des Petits Ruminants: any species
Porcine reproductive and respiratory syndrome: porcine
Pseudorabies: any species
Pullorum disease: avian
Q fever: caprine, ovine
Rabies: any species
Rift Valley fever: any species
Rinderpest: any species
Salmonella enteritidis enteritidis: avian
Salmonella typhimurium DT 104: bovine
Salmonellosis: caprine, ovine
Scabies: bovine, caprine, ovine
Scrapie: caprine, ovine
Screwworm: any species
Spring viremia of carp: aquaculture
Surra: equine
Swine vesicular disease: porcine
Theileriosis: bovine
Toxic substance contamination: any species
Transmissible gastroenteritis: porcine
Transmissible spongiform encephalopathy: any species
Trichinellosis: porcine
Trichomoniasis: bovine
Trypanosomiasis: bovine
Tuberculosis: any species
Venezuelan equine encephalomyelitis: equine
Vesicular exanthema: porcine
Vesicular stomatitis: any species
Viral hemorrhagic septicemia: aquaculture

Source: Michigan Department of Community Health (2005).

emerging infectious disease outbreaks are occurring at rising rates. While the majority of these hot-spots were located within the tropics and in developing countries, they extended as far north as Canada and Scandinavia and as far south as South Africa and Australia. What is surprising about these findings is that the majority of outbreaks are the result of pathogens crossing over from animal to human hosts (also known as zoonotic diseases; Kinver, 2008). More information on animal diseases can be found by accessing the British Agrifor Web site at http://agrifor.ac.uk/hb/06ce169e8d86491-b9454aa5769f41b64.html.

Plant and *agricultural epidemics* threaten to cause both economic and environmental damage. The great Irish potato famine of 1845 through 1850 (caused by *Phytophthora infestans* fungus), which resulted in the starvation of over 1 million people and the emigration of another 1.5 million, is possibly the most widely recognized example of a disaster caused by this very real hazard. Two million people died in South Asia as result of the Bengal rice epidemic in 1942. Much more recently, in 1970, the United States was affected by an epidemic that affected corn crops (corn leaf blight), although the result was more economic in nature ($1 billion in losses).

Plant and agricultural epidemics can be caused by a number of factors, many of which are not dependent upon an external biotic organism like pathogens, insects, or animals. Epidemics can be simply the result of a change in climate (including rainfall, temperature, sunlight, relative humidity, and wind). Exhibit 2–10 describes possible sources of plant and agricultural epidemics, and Exhibit 2–11 discusses a recurring agricultural epidemic and its impact.

There are five basic categories of plant diseases:

1. *New diseases.* Diseases introduced on a new host within the past 5 years in a new geographic area
2. *Emerging diseases.* Diseases whose incidence has increased within the past 10 to 15 years
3. *Reemerging diseases.* Diseases previously known in the area but that are gaining importance
4. *Threatening diseases.* Diseases not reported or with limited distribution in a new geographic area
5. *Chronic/spreading diseases.* Diseases whose presence has been known for a long period but that are still causing outbreaks

Plant and agricultural outbreaks can be spread by a number of means, including (but not limited to) the following:

- Vectors (insects, such as aphids, are common vectors)
- Propagation of diseased plants
- Planting of infected seeds
- Use of contaminated cattle manure
- Movement of crops in contaminated equipment
- Wind, including hurricanes and tornadoes
- Human transportation of infected plants and fruits (intentional and unintentional)

Controlling certain pathogens requires the complete destruction of a crop as well as crops in surrounding areas. Chemicals used to prevent or control plant and agricultural epidemics have been found on occasion to cause as much, if not more, environmental damage than the actual disease.

EXHIBIT 2–10: SOURCES OF PLANT AND AGRICULTURE EPIDEMICS

Nonparasitic
- High and low temperatures
- Oxygen deficiency
- Toxic gases: Air pollution
- Mineral deficiency and excess
- Drought
- Light (too much or too little)

Fungi

Bacteria
- Wilts
- Rots
- Blights
- Galls

Viruses
- Reduced growth
- Mosaics
- Ringspots

Algae

Other plants (toxicity and competition)

Protozoa

Insects

Snails

Rodents

Nematodes

Source: Chynoweth (2003).

Other Natural Hazards

In addition to these natural hazards, there are individual natural hazards that do not fit neatly into any single category. Although the list extends far beyond what is covered in this book, the following are examples of hazards that disaster managers must consider in light of their catastrophic potential.

Meteors and *meteorites* strike the earth many times each day, most often burning up in the atmosphere before they reach ground. However, on many occasions these extraterrestrial masses do make contact with the earth, but their decayed size results in minor or inconsequential impact. By 1990, there were still fewer than 5,000 known intact meteors found on the planet (SEDS, n.d.). Humans have been injured on a few occasions from meteorites, but the only known fatalities from space objects falling to earth are a horse in Ohio in 1860 and dog in Egypt in 1911. Property damage has also been negligible.

Large meteors, which could cause major disasters, including the extinction of all life on the planet, are what are referred to in risk management as a "very low probability, very high consequence" hazard. Although emergency managers could ignore them because the possibility of their striking is so

EXHIBIT 2–11: AFRICA FIGHTS LOCUST PLAGUES

Locust plagues may predate biblical times, but today scientists still struggle to fully understand and control the swarms that can bring famine to thousands. In Guinea-Bissau, West Africa, desert locusts (*Schistocerca gregaria*) currently threaten to decimate the cashew crop on which nearly two-thirds of the nation's farmers depend. The current outbreak comes on the heels of heavy locust damage in numerous West African countries this past summer and fall.

Food shortages loom in the hardest hit areas. In Mauritania, government officials estimate that one-third of the nation's 2.8 million inhabitants could go hungry next year. Others in the Sahel region, the semidesert southern fringe of the Sahara, will share the misery.

The recent plagues mark the worst locust upsurges in 15 years. "The last big infestation was between 1986–89," said Clive Elliott, a locust expert with the UN Food and Agriculture Organization (FAO) in Rome, Italy. "I've spoken to lots of people in the field this year who say that the size and density of the swarms they've seen [in western and northwestern Africa] is larger than in 1988."

If there is a pattern to the plagues, scientists have yet to find it. Twentieth-century plagues occurred in 1926–1934, 1940–1948, 1949–1963, 1967–1969, and 1986–1989. Plagues are spurred by recurrent rainfall during the insect's breeding season. "We've looked for regularities, but locust population dynamics are so driven by the weather we don't find [predictable cycles]," said University of Wyoming entomologist and locust expert Jeff Lockwood. "We can forecast locust [plagues] about as well as we can forecast the weather."

During massive plagues, desert locusts can appear over a land area of nearly 12 million square miles (30 million square kilometers) in some 60 nations—comprising over 20% of the earth's land surface. The insects inflict heavy crop damage that is devastating for subsistence farmers, many of whom must flee land that can no longer support their families. The FAO's Desert Locust Information Service reports that during the biggest plagues, the insects may endanger the livelihood of one in every ten people on earth.

Control Efforts

To control locust plagues, FAO coordinates international efforts and helps national authorities battle the ancient pests with modern technology that includes satellites, pesticides, and helicopters. "Part of our forecasting system is looking at satellite information on vegetation and identifying desert areas where locusts are likely to be found," Elliott said. "We provide information to countries, so that they can target their surveys to those areas. It doesn't always work, but it has proven useful."

Approximately 42,500 square miles (11 million hectares) of African land was sprayed last year with fixed-wing aircraft and helicopters. While the process may control locusts, it also introduces large amounts of environmentally harmful pesticides. It is a problem the FAO says it is attempting to address. "Most of the spraying has been done with conventional organophosphate pesticides," Elliott noted. "The FAO is trying to promote use of more environmentally friendly pesticides. But it's taking longer than we'd like to get it off of the ground."

One possible alternative control method uses a naturally occurring fungus, *Metarhizium anisopliae,* to create a bio-pesticide dubbed green muscle. The fungus is deadly to locusts and grasshoppers but has proven harmless to other insects, plants, and animals—including people.

(Continued)

EXHIBIT 2–11: AFRICA FIGHTS LOCUST PLAGUES (CONTINUED)

"Conveyor Belts"

Elliott reports that, while the desert locust plague situation remains serious, hopes are high that heavy control operations in fall 2004 have made an impact. "We don't know whether we could be into a plague by September of this year, or if by May the whole thing will have petered out," he said. While controlling locust plagues is the FAO's first priority, understanding the ecological role of the massive outbreaks is also important. Thus far, the latter goal has proven somewhat elusive. "We can think of locust swarms as giant conveyor belts of nutrients that move tons and tons of organic material from one place to another," Lockwood said. "Frankly, we have a poor understanding of how this fits into nutrient cycling in Africa."

Although not fully understood, the massive outbreaks are generally believed to have an important ecological role. "You could think of a locust outbreak as a sort of metabolic wildfire. We don't have the capability to do it, but ... the thought of totally eliminating locust outbreaks would give most ecologists a shiver up their spine," he said. "We just don't know enough about the possible effects."

Source: Handwerk (2005).

---

low, their consequences must be considered because they are so great (see Table 2–6). In the history of the earth, about 120 large craters have resulted from large meteors, including one whose diameter extends over 100 miles and is thought to be the cause of the extinction of the dinosaurs. Other large meteorites have exploded in the lower atmosphere before reaching ground, destroying everything below but causing no crater to form (including the 1908 Tunguska meteor, which flattened an entire forest over 30 miles across; see Figure 2–28).

Poisoning of large populations due to natural, nonpathogenic (e.g., *Escherichia coli* food poisoning) circumstances is rare, but it happens enough to merit mention as a potential catastrophic hazard. Disasters included in this category result from a poisonous material, such as a gas or a mineral, being introduced into the food supply, water, or the air. These hazards can strike in an instant or kill populations slowly over the course of years.

In 2000, the World Health Organization (WHO) released a press statement describing their urgent concern about the emergence of widespread contamination of wells in many countries throughout the world, including Argentina, Bangladesh, Chile, China, India, Mexico, Taiwan, Thailand, and the United States. The contamination was caused by naturally occurring arsenic in groundwater, and the people who were relying on this water were afflicted in high numbers with skin lesions, cancers, and other ailments. In Bangladesh alone, over 77 million (of the country's 125 million) people are at risk, and over 100,000 people have developed sicknesses so far. In India, the number of people sickened has exceeded 200,000. The WHO considers the events to be the worst mass poisoning in history (WHO, 2000).

Other means of natural poisoning include naturally occurring mercury from eating excessive amounts of certain fish, carbon monoxide poisoning from traditional indoor cooking practices, excess fluoride in groundwater, radon in groundwater, and sulfur clouds released from volcanic lakes.

Soil salination is a natural hazard caused by both natural and man-made processes. When soil salt content reaches certain levels above normal for a particular ecosystem or region, the soil's normal

Table 2–6   Possible Consequences from Impacts of Meteors of Various Sizes

Asteroid/ Comet Diameter	Energy, and Where Deposited	Likelihood of Occurrence during This Century	Potential Damage and Required Response
>0.3 m	2 tons TNT, upper atmosphere	1000 per year	Dazzling, memorable bolide or "fireball" seen; harmless
>1 m	100 tons TNT, upper atmosphere	40 per year	Bolide explosion approaching brilliance of the sun for a second or so; harmless, may yield meteorites
>3 m	2 kT, upper atmosphere	2 per year	Blinding explosion in sky; could be mistaken for atomic bomb
>10 m	100 kT, upper atmosphere	6 per century	Extraordinary explosion in sky; broken windows, but little damage on ground; no warning
>30 m	2 MT, explosion; stratosphere	40%	Devastating stratospheric shock wave may topple trees, weaken wooden houses, ignite fires within 10 km; deaths likely if in populated region (1908 Tunguska explosion was several times bigger); advance warning very unlikely, all-hazards advanced planning would apply
>100 m	80 MT, lower atmosphere or surface explosion affecting small region	1%	Low-altitude or ground burst larger than biggest ever thermonuclear weapon, regionally devastating, shallow crater—1 km across; after the fact national crisis management (advance warning unlikely)
>300 m	2000 MT, local crater, regional destruction	0.2%	Crater—5 km across and devastation of region the size of a small nation *or* unprecedented tsunami; advance warning or no notice equally likely; deflect, if possible; internationally coordinated disaster management required
>1 km	80,000 MT, major regional destruction; some global atmospheric effects	0.02%	Destruction of region or ocean rim; potential worldwide climate shock—approaches global civilization destruction level; consider mitigation measures (deflection or planning for unprecedented world catastrophe)
>3 km	1.5 million MT, global	<1 in 50,000	Worldwide, multiyear climate/ecological disaster; civilization destroyed (a new Dark Age), most people killed in aftermath; chances of having to deal with such a comet impact are extremely remote; mitigation extremely challenging
>10 km	100 million MT, global	<1 in a million	Mass extinction, potential eradication of human species; little can be done about this extraordinarily unlikely eventuality

Source: Morrison, Chapman, and Slovic (1994).

FIGURE 2–28 Forest destroyed by a meteor in Tunguska, Siberia, 1908. (Photo courtesy of Anatoly Klypin)

plant life can no longer survive and the ground becomes effectively "barren." Salination occurs because of three separate processes:

1. Naturally occurring salt within the composition of soil
2. Geographic conditions that promote the movement of salt in groundwater
3. Climatic and meteorological conditions that promote salt accumulation

These natural processes tend to occur slowly and surrounding ecosystems change in reaction as necessary (even if the change results in barren land, such as the natural salt flats found around the world). Human influence has sped up many of these processes, mostly through the use of irrigation, which tends to increase the rate by which water is filtered through the ground and water tables are replaced by an inflow of outside water. Other factors that affect groundwater levels, like the construction of dams, can have the same effect. The Aswan Dam, built in 1970 in Aswan, Egypt, allowed for increased irrigation below the dam, which, due to the high rates of evaporation in the Egyptian heat, has ultimately resulted in a dramatic increase in salt content in that soil.

Soil salination has several ultimate consequences. The most obvious is that arable land is eventually made infertile, leading to a decrease in a nation's ability to produce food. In countries like Egypt that have a shortage of arable land, salination can have a significant impact. Infrastructure is also affected. Salt naturally erodes many materials, including those used to fabricate roads, pipes, wires, and building materials. Additionally, groundwater can become saline if the soil salt content rises too high, making it unusable for humans and animals. Finally, if soil becomes barren because of salination, anchor vegetation will die and soil erosion will increase, resulting in a number of secondary hazards mentioned throughout this chapter.

Space weather refers to the conditions that exist outside of the earth's atmosphere that nonetheless have an influence on the planet's environmental and built environments. Space weather is caused by magnetism, radiation, plasma, and other matter. It impacts and even renders communication and navigation systems useless, or affects the in-flight machinery of airplanes and spacecraft. In 1989,

Canada experienced a widespread power failure when a March 9 solar flare resulted in a geomagnetic storm, which in turn influenced magnetic currents on the surface of the earth, and subsequently caused electrical transformers to fail a full 4 days later (Odenwald, 2005).

Animal attacks occur, from time to time, resulting in a major emergency or disaster. Large animals can cause significant damage to property and kill or injure many people. A weeklong rampage involving about 100 elephants in India in 2007 resulted in the destruction of dozens of homes, leading to more than 50 cases of homelessness. Elephants actually caused over 600 deaths in India in less than two decades (CNN, 2007b). In the United States, two stampeding horses injured 24 people during an Independence Day parade (Thomas, 2010).

Technological Hazards

The second major group of hazards explored in this chapter are technological hazards. These are the negative consequences of human innovation that result in the harm or destruction of life, property, or the environment. They range from chemical spills to power failures and from computer programming bugs to mass transportation accidents. By their very nature, they are generally new hazards in terms of the full spectrum of threats humans have faced, so relatively little is known about their consequences. They can be very difficult to predict, and a wide range of triggers tends to initiate them, including many natural disasters previously discussed. Depending on the circumstances, seemingly equal technological hazards can affect geographic areas from as small as a single city block to as large as an entire continent. As technology advances, the catalog of technological disasters only expands.

Technological hazards differ from natural hazards in that societies have chosen to assume technology's associated risks (known and unknown) in exchange for some realized benefit. Perhaps the best illustration of this cost/benefit gamble, as well as one of the single greatest technological hazards, is the automobile (NIH, 2004). On average, 1.2 million people worldwide die each year in traffic accidents, yet society has collectively decided to accept that risk for the benefit of rapid transit.

Since 1980, the number of reported technological disasters has skyrocketed, increasing at a rate that completely outpaces the increase of natural disasters. Furthermore, the number of people dying as a result of these technological disasters is also rising. Figures 2–29 and 2–30 illustrate these increases.

The following section explores many of the known technological hazards that often strike with catastrophic consequences and that most disaster managers are likely to face as technology progresses.

Transportation Hazards

Transportation hazards have become such a common part of global society that it seems only the truly tragic events merit international news coverage. Transportation is a technology on which the entire world now depends for travel, commerce, and industry. The vast system of land, sea, and air transportation involves complex and expensive infrastructure, humans or machines to conduct that infrastructure, and laws and policies by which the whole system is guided. A flaw or breakdown in any one of these components can and often does result in a major disaster involving loss of life, injuries, property and environmental damage, and economic consequences.

Transportation infrastructure disasters do not involve the vehicles but the systems upon which those vehicles depend. Vast engineering feats are often required to join the world's cities, to cross mountains and waterways, and to shorten the distances from point A to point B. As with all engineering projects, a certain risk is imposed by the very nature of the forces the projects must overcome,

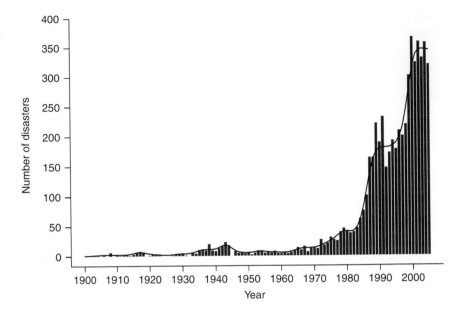

FIGURE 2–29 Total number of reported technological disasters, 1900–2005. (From the International Disaster Database, www.em-dat.net)

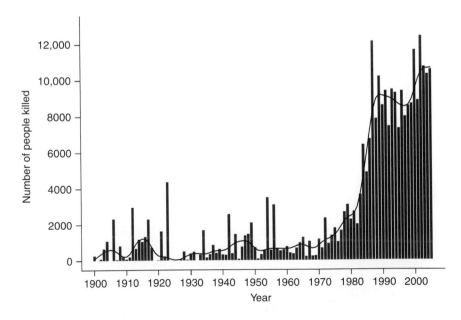

FIGURE 2–30 Total number of people killed in technological disasters, 1900–2005. (From the International Disaster Database, www.em-dat.net)

including gravity, tension, mass, resistance, and velocity. Bridges, tunnels, raised highways, mountain roads, overpasses, airport terminals, and other infrastructure components are all subject to the realization of that risk: failure.

A component of infrastructure can fail for many reasons. The most common causes are poor design, poor maintenance, or the introduction of unforeseen or unexpected outside forces (e.g., seismicity or hurricanes), which can cause the impacted structures to collapse or sustain significant damage, often harming or killing those inside or nearby. As the event usually renders these infrastructure components useless, transportation of all individuals and businesses dependent upon the overall system is instantly hindered or eliminated. It thus is not a surprise that transportation infrastructure disasters often result in economic collapse for towns and cities. The failure of even the simplest footbridges, tens of thousands of which have been constructed throughout the developing world, can have devastating effects by cutting off villagers from their fields or jobs. In many developing countries, where critical transportation routes must traverse very rugged, hazard-prone terrain, a significant amount of government money may be required to repair and maintain those routes. However, even in the industrialized countries, deterioration and age of infrastructure can lead to a buildup of components that together represent a monumental cost in terms of repair and update, and as such, accidents occur before allocations are made. In the United States alone, there are over 150,000 bridges considered either structurally deficient or functionally obsolete (CNN, 2010). The I-35 Mississippi Bridge collapse that occurred in Minnesota on August 1, 2007, resulted in the death of 13 people and the injury of 145 more. This is an example of the consequences of infrastructure aging and deterioration. This accident also had severe financial implications given that an average of 140,000 commuters and travelers used the bridge daily. Figure 2–31 illustrates the damages that resulted.

Airline accidents are relatively rare, but are often both spectacular and catastrophic due to the high number of people involved and the very low number of survivors. Air Safe, an airline safety advocacy Web site, examined 342 fatal accidents involving both jet and propeller-driven aircraft between 1978 and 1995. They found that mortality rates exceed 90% in 6 out of every 10 accidents (Air Safe, 2003). When airline accidents occur in cities, in addition to fatalities and injuries sustained by people on the ground, structure fires and collapses usually occur, requiring difficult response efforts. This

FIGURE 2–31 Collapse of the I-35 Mississippi Bridge in Minneapolis, Minnesota, August 4, 2007. (Photo courtesy of Kevin Rofidal, U.S. Coast Guard)

problem is especially troubling in cities undergoing massive growth, whose airports, constructed in once empty fields, are now completely surrounded by urban sprawl. Mariscal Sucre International Airport in Quito, Ecuador, where fatal crashes into residential areas have occurred, is such an example.

Rail accidents can occur for both passenger and freight trains with each posing unique problems for disaster managers. Accidents primarily occur because of contact between two trains, contact between a train and a foreign object (car, animal, debris), onboard fire, or faulty or misaligned tracks (due to external forces, human error, sabotage, or poor maintenance).

Rail accidents involving passenger trains are often mass casualty incidents (see Exhibit 2–12). Due to their sheer weight, it is difficult for trains to suddenly slow down, and accidents are often unavoidable. The increased production and implementation of high-speed train systems are increasing passenger risk. On April 25, 2005, a high-speed train in Japan derailed due to operator error, slamming into a building, killing 107 people and injuring over 450.

Trains are used extensively to transport cargo, much of which is classified as hazardous. Accidents involving train cars with flammable or poisonous gases or liquids have caused several major disasters and are a significant hazard for any urban area they pass. These accidents can involve explosions, fires, the release of deadly gases, and severe environmental degradation. Evacuations may be necessary to protect the surrounding population, and rescue efforts are difficult to impossible without proper equipment and training.

EXHIBIT 2–12: SELECT RAIL ACCIDENTS WITH OVER 100 FATALITIES, 1950–2010

- October 29, 2005: India (derailment caused by flood)—114 killed
- July 13, 2005: Pakistan (three trains collide)—over 100 killed
- April 25, 2005: Japan (high-speed train derails)—107 killed
- Dec. 26, 2004: Sri Lanka (train struck by tsunami)—about 2000 killed
- April 22, 2004: North Korea (two trains collide)—about 161 killed
- Feb. 18, 2004: Iran (HAZMAT train derails)—over 200 killed
- Feb. 20, 2002: Egypt (fire)—over 360 killed
- Aug. 2, 1999: India (two trains collide)—over 285 killed
- Aug. 20, 1995: India (two trains collide)—358 killed
- Sept. 22, 1994: Angola (mechanical failure causes derailment)—300 killed
- Jan. 4, 1990: Pakistan (two trains collide)—over 210 killed
- June 3, 1989: Soviet Union (fire)—575 killed
- June 8, 1991: Pakistan (two trains collide)—over 100 killed
- June 6, 1981: India (bridge collapse)—over 800 killed
- Oct. 6, 1972: Mexico (passenger train derails)—208 killed
- Feb. 1, 1970: Argentina (two trains collide)—236 killed
- Nov. 9, 1963: Japan (three trains collide)—161 killed
- May 3, 1962: Japan (three trains collide)—160 killed
- Sept. 29, 1957: Pakistan (two trains collide)—250 killed
- April 3, 1955: Mexico (train derails)—300 killed

Sources: The Associated Press (2005) and AllExperts (2010).

Maritime accidents, like rail accidents, may involve either passenger vessels or freight vessels, each posing a specific set of risk factors. The range of causes of maritime accidents includes weather-related accidents, mechanical failure, human error, overloading (passengers or freight), poor maintenance, fire, collision (other vessels, stationary objects, war, striking of floating or submerged objects or land), sabotage, and terrorism. Large passenger vessels that encounter serious trouble pose a significant challenge to disaster managers in that rescue requires numerous marine search-and-rescue resources deployed within a very short amount of time. Ships can sink quickly, and in cold waters survivors have only minutes before hypothermia proves fatal. Exhibit 2–13 lists selected maritime disasters with more than 500 fatalities over the past 150 years.

Roadway accidents are the most common type of transportation accident (see Figure 2–32). Although the number of injuries and deaths in individual events are normally much lower than for

---

EXHIBIT 2–13: SELECT MARITIME DISASTERS WITH MORE THAN 500 FATALITIES, 1865–2010

- 1865: *Sultana* (explosion)—1700 killed
- 1873: *Atlantic* (sank)—546 killed
- 1904: *General Slocum* (fire)—1,021 killed
- 1904: *SS Norge* (sank)—620 killed
- 1912: *Titanic* (sank)—1,503 killed
- 1914: *Empress of Ireland* (sank)—1,012 killed
- 1915: *Lusitania* (sank)—1,198 killed
- 1915: *Eastland* (sank)—845 killed
- 1940: *Lancastria* (sank)—up to 5,000 killed
- 1944: *Tango Maru* (sank)—about 3,000 killed
- 1944: *Ryusei Maru* (sank)—4,998 killed
- 1944: *Toyama Maru* (sank) – about 5,600 killed
- 1944: *Koshu Maru* (sank)—about 1,540 killed
- 1944: *Junyo Maru* (sank)—about 5,620 killed
- 1944: *Rigel* (bombed)—2,571 killed
- 1945: *Wilhelm Gustloff* (sank)—about 9,000–10,000 killed
- 1945: *Steuben* (sank)—about 4,000–4,500 killed
- 1945: *Goya* (sank)—over 7,000 killed
- 1945: *Cap Arcona* (sank)—about 8,000 killed
- 1945: *Thielbek* (sank)—2,750 killed
- 1955: *Novorossiysk* (sank)—608 killed
- 1987: *Doña Paz* (sank)—about 4,000 killed
- 1994: *M/S Estonia* (sank)—852 killed
- 2002: *Joola* (sank)—950 killed
- 2006: *Al Salaam Boccaccio 98* (sank)—846 killed
- 2006: *MV Senopati Nusantara* (sank)—over 500 killed

Source: Wikipedia (2010).

FIGURE 2–32 Bus involved in fatal accident, California, 2001. (Photo courtesy of NTSB, 2001)

other forms of accidents, the collective number is much greater: over 1.2 million deaths per year. Mass casualty accidents involving passenger transportation lines, such as intercity buses, are common, especially in developing countries where enforcement of safety standards is sparse, driver training and regulations lax, and rescue resources slim to nonexistent. Hazardous materials accidents involving tanker trucks or other forms of transportation are also common, and almost always pose a hazard risk to life, property, and the environment. Exhibit 2–14 lists several devastating roadway accidents that have occurred throughout the world.

EXHIBIT 2–14: SELECT ROADWAY ACCIDENTS EXCEEDING 75 KILLED, 1945–2010

- 1945: Thailand—Explosion of a dynamite truck; over 150 killed
- 1956: Colombia—7 ammunition trucks explode; over 1,200 killed
- 1965: Togo—Collision with 2 trucks; over 125 killed
- 1973: Egypt—Bus plunged into an irrigation canal; 127 killed
- 1978: Spain—Gasoline tanker exploded; over 120 killed
- 1982: Afghanistan—Gasoline tanker exploded in a tunnel; over 2000 killed
- 1992: Kenya—Bus crashed into a bridge; 106 killed
- 1995: South Korea—100 cars fell into a hole created by an explosion; 110 killed
- 2000: Nigeria—Gasoline tanker struck cars and exploded; over 150 killed
- 2003: South Africa—Bus drove into a reservoir; 80 killed
- 2004: Iran—Bus collided with a fuel tanker; 90 killed
- 2006: Benin—Overturned tanker exploded as people collect leaking gas; about 75 killed
- 2007: Nigeria—Fuel tanker truck exploded after catching on fire; 98 killed
- 2007: India—Bus crashed into a gorge; over 75 killed
- 2010: Congo—Fuel tanker overturned and exploded; 220 killed

Source: Wikipedia (2010).

Infrastructure Hazards

Infrastructure hazards are another type of technological hazard, and are primarily related to critical systems of utilities, services, and other assets (both state-run and private) that serve the public. The consequences of infrastructure hazards may include loss of vital services, injury, death, property damage, or a combination of these. As technological innovation, global communication, and global commerce increase, nations are becoming much more dependent upon their critical infrastructure. The primary types of infrastructure hazards are listed in the following sections.

Power failures can be caused by a breakdown in the power generation and/or distribution grid, or by an accident or preceding disaster that somehow damages the grid. Increased dependence upon electronic equipment for communications, management, commerce, and other vital systems has increased public and private entities' vulnerability to the consequences of this hazard. Extended power outages can quickly turn into public health emergencies when life safety systems begin to fail. Without power, citizens can find themselves unable to travel, purchase necessary supplies, heat or cool their homes, communicate, or work. Companies have discovered that power outages lasting as short as one hour can result in millions of dollars in losses and, if extended across a whole region's industry, can result in major economic damage. In 2003, a power outage struck 50 million people in Canada and the United States, resulting in over $6 billion in economic costs to those two countries and affecting businesses, water supplies, transportation systems, communications systems, food supplies, and much more. Figure 2–33 illustrates the geographic range affected by this single event. Experts predict that disasters like this will only increase in number and severity over time.

FIGURE 2–33 Geographic area affected by the 2003 blackout in Canada and the United States. (From the U.S. Government Accountability Office, 2003)

Telecommunications systems failures, which include telephone (land line and mobile), radio, satellite, and Internet, have economic and social impacts. Most businesses and governments depend upon reliable communications to function. When communications systems fail, citizens are unable to contact emergency resources and businesses are unable to sell their products or provide their services.

Computer network failures are becoming as costly as power and telecommunications failures. Most of the world's businesses and banks are wholly reliant upon the Internet, and public facilities and service providers (such as utilities, communications, public health facilities, traffic systems, and other government-related offices) are heading in that same direction. The interconnectedness of the global Internet has created the risk that a collapse of a portion of that network anywhere in the world could result in total collapse of the entire system. This risk is increasing in all countries of the world, rich and poor. Exhibit 2–15 describes the consequences of a 2005 Internet outage in Pakistan.

Critical water or sewer system failures can and do occur quite often, primarily as result of natural hazards. Humans depend upon a steady supply of useable water for basic survival, industry, and agriculture, and an interruption of as little as one day can result in a disaster. Many mechanisms can lead to failure of water resources, ultimately resulting in drinking water contamination, cessation of service, or environmental destruction. If reservoirs that populations depend on become

---

EXHIBIT 2–15: INTERNET LINK IN PAKISTAN RESTORED AFTER MORE THAN 11 DAYS' BREAKDOWN

ISLAMABAD: Pakistan's Internet users were back on line Friday after more than a week of disruptions caused by a faulty undersea communications cable that connects the country with the rest of the world, an official said. "The repair work has been completed and Internet supply has been restored," said Mashkoor Hussain, a senior official with Pakistan Telecommunications Co. Ltd. [PTCL], which operates the cable.

The cable stopped working on June 27, halting an estimated 10 million Internet connections. Days later, a fault in the cable in the Arabian Sea was located about 15 km (nine miles) southwest of Karachi, Pakistan's main seaport. Pakistan is normally connected to the Internet by a single undersea fiber link, called Southeast Asia, Middle East and Western Europe-3 (SEA-ME-WE-3). It was the second time in 3 months that Pakistan's Internet services came to a halt, with a similar cable glitch suspending service in April. PTCL officials have said a new cable would be laid by October this year to avoid similar Internet outages in the future.

Banks, brokerages, Internet service providers, and call centers were badly hit by the disruption. Telecom officials say they are now working on erecting a back-up link to avoid similar breakdowns in the future. The optic fiber cable is Pakistan's only telecommunications link with the outside world. Pakistan sought assistance from the 92-member consortium that operates the cable, since the country does not have the technology to deal with such problems on its own. But repairs were hampered by bad weather in the Arabian Sea delaying ships from reaching the problem area for several days.

While the immediate problem has been dealt with, Pakistan's budding IT industry is now pressing the government to give more thought to its communication infrastructure. The government is under fire from industry professionals on two counts:

- First, they are asking the government why a back-up system was not in place. So far, the 39,000 km cable—which links Pakistan to South East Asia, the Middle East and Western Europe—is the country's sole link to the outside world. At the time it was commissioned some four years ago, Pakistan rejected the proposal of linking up with India or Iran as a backup, citing security issues. Telecom officials at the time argued in favor of a satellite link as an alternative. After the breakdown the authorities acquired a back-up satellite system. But it turned out to be insufficient for the country's needs, providing only about half the bandwidth required.

- Second, IT professionals accuse the government of not taking Pakistan's growing commercial dependence on the Internet seriously. The Pakistan Call Centers Association says it may have lost deals amounting to $10 m with their counterparts in India because of the breakdown. There are no estimates of how much money the smaller businesses may have lost due to the disruption, the association says. But independent analysts say that the Pakistan economy's dependence on the Internet has not yet reached a point where such a disruption could lead to serious financial losses.

- Telecom officials say that the government has finally shed its security concerns and has agreed on a back-up cable link through India. The back-up is expected to be in place by October this year by the latest, they say. The submarine cable fault has been rectified and all communication services have been fully restored.

Pak Telecom Chief

Addressing a press conference here Friday, President/CEO of Pakistan Telecommunication Company Limited (PTCL) Junaid I. Khan said the organization is committed to support the telecom industry and did its best to meet the situation effectively. The PTCL president said the incident was the first during the last five years of operation of the cable in the leg of the 600 km SEA-ME-WE-3 Pakistan segment. Although such incidents occurred in the past in other sections of the SEA-ME-WE-3, the impact was not felt due to availability of diversity in related sections, he added.

Junaid said as regards the duration of the cable fault developed on June 27 at 20:56 hours, past history of the rectification period shows that incident localization period is the minimum amongst all occurred in the past and added in the best cases such faults are repaired in minimum 13 days and in the worst case it has taken 110 days in China. Answering a question, he said two special-built ships were involved for the localization and rectification of fault and added the major challenge faced by E-marine cable ships and their crew was weather, considering the monsoon in the region.

Alternate Connectivity

Replying to another question, he said PTCL has already invested Rs. 2.4 billion in arranging alternate connectivity through SEA-ME-WE-4 cable, which will be available by October or November this year. Additionally, terrestrial link with India by replacing the existing analogue system through optical fiber system is also under implementation, he said, and added discussions with Etisalat, UAE are also being held for up-gradation of the existing coaxial bilateral link to optical fiber system. He assured after the completion of these project, the problem like interruption of communication will not take place in future.

Source: Faisal (2005).

FIGURE 2–34 Fires rage in San Francisco after an earthquake severs several gas lines. (Photo courtesy of USGS, 1906)

contaminated and it is not quickly discovered, the contaminated water can quickly enter the public supply and cause a widespread public health disaster. Following heavy rains or flooding or during times of drought, water and sewer systems can become overloaded or damaged and fail altogether, adversely affecting both the served population and the surrounding environment.

Major gas distribution line (main) breaks are becoming more of a risk as intra- and intercity systems are established. These systems of pipes, which contain highly pressurized and flammable gas, are vulnerable to a range of natural and man-made influences that could ultimately result in their failure. Breach of a gas line can result in fire, environmental pollution (often requiring evacuation of the area), injury, and death. Special expertise is required to respond to a break in a gas distribution line, and significant populations can be affected. The 1906 earthquake that struck San Francisco is an example of the risk posed by gas lines. In this event, ruptured gas lines started fires that quickly spread throughout the city during a time when response resources were strained (see Figure 2–34). The resulting fires greatly contributed to 700 deaths—the greatest single death toll of all earthquakes to strike the United States. Sabotage or vandalism of oil and gas distribution occurs in very poor countries where groups or individuals attempt to steal flowing gas by intentionally breaching the pipes. One such event that occurred along the Abule Egba pipeline in Lagos, Nigeria, on December 26, 2006, resulted in the death of hundreds (though exact numbers are not known; BBC, 2006). This is but one of many similar events in Nigeria as shown in Exhibit 2–16.

Dam failure is a hazard that exists in almost every country of the world, posing serious danger to all people and property located downstream. Any structure constructed for the purpose of storing, withholding, or diverting water can be classified as a dam. They can be constructed using any number of materials, ranging from resilient concrete to soft earth. The number of dams that exist throughout the world is much greater than most people realize and recently stood at 845,000 (Jacquot, 2009). The vast majority of these are privately constructed, owned, and maintained. The United States alone has over 80,000 dams, with thousands classified as having the potential to cause loss of life and property in the event of failure. China has the greatest number of dams (22,000) classified as "large." Figure 2–35 and Exhibit 2–17 illustrate the global distribution of large dams.

EXHIBIT 2–16: SELECT NIGERIA PIPELINE DISASTERS

Date	Number Killed
May 2006	150
December 2004	20
September 2004	60
June 2003	105
July 2000	300
March 2000	50
October 199	1000

Source: BBC (2006).

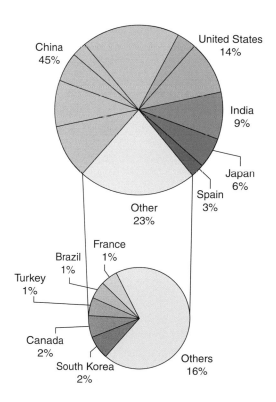

FIGURE 2–35 Share of world dams by country. (From World Commission on Dams, 2000)

EXHIBIT 2–17: NUMBER OF DAMS PER COUNTRY

Africa

South Africa	539
Zimbabwe	213
Algeria	107
Morocco	92
Tunisia	72
Nigeria	45
Côte d'Ivoire	22
Angola	15
D.R. Congo	14
Kenya	14
Namibia	13
Libya	12
Madagascar	10
Cameroon	9
Mauritius	9
Burkina Faso	8
Ethiopia	8
Mozambique	8
Lesotho	7
Egypt	6
Swaziland	6
Ghana	5
Sudan	4
Zambia	4
Botswana	3
Malawi	3
Benin	2
Congo	2
Guinea	2
Mali	2
Senegal	2
Seychelles	2
Sierra Leone	2
Tanzania	2
Togo	2
Gabon	1
Liberia	1
Uganda	1
Total	**1,269**

Western Europe

Spain	1,196
France	569
Italy	524
United Kingdom	517
Norway	335
Germany	311
Sweden	190
Switzerland	156
Austria	149
Portugal	103
Finland	55
Cyprus	52
Greece	46
Iceland	20
Ireland	16
Belgium	15
Denmark	10
Netherlands	10
Luxembourg	3
Total	**4,277**

South America

Brazil	594
Argentina	101
Chile	88
Venezuela	74
Colombia	49
Peru	43
Ecuador	11
Bolivia	6
Uruguay	6
Paraguay	4
Guyana	2
Suriname	1
Total	**979**

Eastern Europe

Albania	306
Romania	246
Bulgaria	180
Czech Rep.	118
Poland	69
Yugoslavia	69

(Continued)

EXHIBIT 2–17: NUMBER OF DAMS PER COUNTRY (CONTINUED)

Slovakia	50
Slovenia	30
Croatia	29
Bosnia Herzegovina	25
Ukraine	21
Lithuania	20
Macedonia	18
Hungary	15
Latvia	5
Moldova	2
Total	**1,203**
North and Central America	
United States	6,575
Canada	793
Mexico	537
Cuba	49
Dominican Republic	11
Costa Rica	9
Honduras	9
Panama	6
El Salvador	5
Guatemala	4
Nicaragua	4
Trinidad & Tobago	4
Jamaica	2
Antigua	1
Haiti	1
Total	**8,010**
Asia	
China	22,000
India	4,291
Japan	2,675
South Korea	765
Turkey	625
Thailand	204
Indonesia	96
Russia	91
Pakistan	71
North Korea	70
Iran	66
Malaysia	59

Taipei, China	51
Sri Lanka	46
Syria	41
Saudi Arabia	38
Azerbaijan	17
Armenia	16
Philippines	15
Georgia	14
Uzbekistan	14
Iraq	13
Kazakhstan	12
Kyrgyzstan	11
Tajikistan	7
Jordan	5
Lebanon	5
Myanmar	5
Nepal	3
Vietnam	3
Singapore	3
Afghanistan	2
Brunei	2
Cambodia	2
Bangladesh	1
Laos	1
Total	**31,340**
Australasia	
Australia	486
New Zealand	86
PNG	3
Fiji	2
Total	**577**

Source: World Commission on Dams (2000).

The most common cause of dam failure is flooding caused by excess amounts of precipitation, but other possible causes include:

- Prolonged periods of rainfall and flooding
- Inadequate spillway capacity, resulting in excess overtopping flows
- Internal erosion caused by embankment or foundation leaking or piping

- Improper maintenance, including failure to remove trees, repair internal seepage problems, replace lost material from the cross-section of the dam and abutments, or maintain gates, valves, and other operational components
- Improper design, including the use of improper construction materials and construction practices
- Negligent operation, including failure to remove or open gates or valves during high-flow periods
- Failure of upstream dams on the same waterway
- Landslides into reservoirs, which cause surges that result in overtopping
- High winds, which can cause significant wave action and result in substantial erosion
- Sabotage or terrorism
- Earthquakes, which typically cause longitudinal cracks in the tops of embankments that weaken entire structures

The worst disaster caused by dam failure occurred in China in 1975. During one chain-reaction event triggered by a typhoon, 62 interrelated dams failed, the largest of which was the Banquio Dam. These failures resulted in the immediate drowning of 26,000 people and another 100,000–150,000 deaths due to disease and exposure. Almost 6 million buildings were destroyed. Major dam disasters have also occurred in Italy (1961, 3,000 killed), the United States (1928, 400 killed; 1889, 2,200 killed), and England (1864, 270 killed). The total number of people killed by dams in the twentieth century, excluding China, is 13,500 (International Rivers Network, 1999).

Food shortage, defined as the situation that exists when available food supplies do not meet the energy and nutrient requirements of the affected population, can have disastrous consequences. When systems of food production, transportation, and reserve cannot accommodate the local population's needs, a *famine* becomes possible. Malnutrition, starvation, panic, and civil disobedience are often the consequences. Food shortages can be caused by food production crises, social, cultural, political, or economic factors, and environmental hazards. The World Food Programme calls famine the greatest threat to health worldwide, reporting that 797 million people, or 16% of the world's population, currently suffer from the effects of food shortages (WFP, 2005).

Famines are rarely caused by a single factor, but by rather a complex interaction of several ongoing and sudden onset issues (see Exhibit 2–18). The following list highlights four major food shortage factors:

1. *Food production crises.* Caused by changes in climate (temperature, humidity, and rainfall), soil content, biological competition, attack (insects, pathogens, rodents, competing plants), or poor farming practices.

EXHIBIT 2–18: EXAMPLES OF HISTORICAL FAMINES

- 1845–1849: Irish potato famine—potato disease and government policy; 1 million died
- 1847: Czech Republic—potato disease; 20,000 died
- 1932–1933: Ukraine—bad harvests and government policies; 3–6 million died
- 1943: Bengal—rice disease and government policies; 3 million died
- 1944: Dutch famine—extreme cold and war; 30,000 died
- 1945: Vietnam—war; as many as 2 million died
- 1984–1985: Ethiopia—drought and war; 1 million died
- 1988: Sudan—war and drought; 250,000 died
- 1998: Sudan—war; 100,000 died

2. *Social/cultural.* Caused by regional food production policy, crop choice (e.g., cotton vs. corn), labor cost and availability, and dietary preference.
3. *Political/economic.* Caused by a lack of incentive to farm, exporting too much of the crop, government-imposed price caps (which deter production), taxation and duty policies, availability of food aid, war, and genocide.
4. *Environmental.* Caused by drought, flood, storms, extreme temperatures, the El Niño phenomenon, and many more.

Conflict often results in food shortages. One warring faction controls food aid, and withholding such aid is used as a weapon. This occurred in Ethiopia in the 1980s and in Sudan in 1997. For this reason, famine is often a factor in complex humanitarian emergencies, described in greater detail in the section entitled "Intentional, Civil, and Political Hazards."

For additional information on food shortages currently affecting the various regions of the world, visit the World Food Programme Interactive Hunger Map at http://one.wfp.org/country_brief/hunger_map/map/hungermap_popup/map_popup.html. A map of malnutrition rates in 2009, developed by the World Food Programme, is provided in Figure 2–36.

Overburdened public health facilities can be either a cause or a consequence of disaster. Most public health facilities throughout the world are designed to accommodate noncrisis patient caseloads. However, following disasters or during epidemics, the physicians, support staff, facilities, and

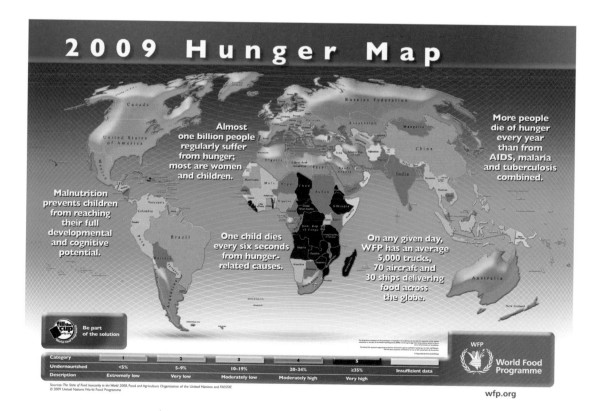

FIGURE 2–36 World Hunger Map 2009. (From World Food Programme, 2009)

inventories upon which these systems depend become quickly strained or overloaded, and a break-down in service may take place. The public health infrastructure can also break down due to labor issues (strikes), supply line breaks, loss of facilities, and increased demand without increased capacity as well as other reasons, the majority of which are related to poverty (see Exhibit 2–19).

Economic failure, which is caused by a collapse or serious downturn in the ability of a country, region, or community to sustain economic solvency, results in a wide spectrum of disastrous consequences that include but are not limited to

---

EXHIBIT 2–19: U.S. DEPARTMENT OF STATE ADVISORY ON THE RISK THAT HEALTH SERVICES COULD BE OVERWHELMED IN A PANDEMIC

Health care services likely will be overburdened if confronted by a pandemic. Hospitals and clinics could be overwhelmed by thousands of seriously ill patients, and health care workers might be in short supply because of their own illnesses. Communities and health care providers must plan in advance for maintaining a workable health care system during a crisis that could last several months. Planning should include the delivery of triage care, self-care, and telephone consultations.

Health Care Concerns

Health care planning for a potential pandemic should involve all levels of government, including specialists in policy development, legislative review and drafting, human and animal health, patient care, laboratory diagnosis and testing, disaster management, and communications. Health professionals must learn how to communicate risk effectively and be able to provide the facts to a frightened population. Experts at the World Health Organization (WHO) and in academia say that communities must prepare for

- Medical shortages of equipment and supplies such as ventilators, respirators, syringes, anti-bacterial soap, anti-virals, vaccines, clean water, and waste management
- Death management challenges: refrigerated trucks dedicated to transporting bodies and crematory and funeral service facilities that may be in short supply

Disruptions in routine health care services are likely, resulting in the need for alternative sites, such as gymnasiums, nursing homes, daycare facilities, and tents to provide health care. Plans should also address who could serve as alternates in medical positions.

According to WHO, community health care managers should make plans now to determine:

- Where patients will be treated
- What will be the admission criteria for existing and newly created health care facilities
- How specimens will be collected and transported to laboratories
- Who will get priority if there are limited quantities of protective masks and gloves
- How large a supply of chlorine for water purification is sufficient if shipments are delayed or suspended; many cities keep only enough chlorine on hand to last five days to seven days.

Source: U.S. Department of State (2006).

- Currency devaluation
- High unemployment
- Loss of basic government and private services
- Inflation
- Fuel shortages
- Civil unrest
- Hunger and famine
- Crime
- Political upheaval and instability
- Rising international debt
- Loss of foreign investment
- Deterioration of critical infrastructure

Industrial Hazards

Industrial hazards are the final area of technological hazards we will examine. Hazardous materials and conditions are a fact of life in the industrialized world. Our ability to extract, create, produce, and provide much of the goods and services we depend upon has introduced a whole new range of hazards that is expanding at an ever-increasing rate. This section details many of the hazards that exist as a result of industry and industrial processes.

Hazardous materials processing and storage accidents are common, affecting almost any private or public facility that works with these kinds of materials. Many of our industrial processes depend upon one or more hazardous materials (solids, liquids, or gases) that, when removed from their controlled setting, can cause injury and death to humans and animals and can devastate the environment. Although safety standards, procedures, and other measures are often in place, all of these are dependent upon a degree of enforcement and a level of environmental control. Therefore, any locality where fabrication, processing, storage, transport (including by pipeline), or disposal of hazardous materials occurs is at risk from these hazardous materials (HAZMAT) incidents (see Table 2–7).

The vast majority of hazardous materials events occur because of accidents during transportation on highways and railroads. The minority of events that do occur at industrial sites ("fixed sites") have a range of causes, including natural disasters, fire, human error, infrastructure deterioration or failure, accidents, sabotage, and terrorism. When the hazardous materials used are flammable or explosive, or when explosive conditions are created as result of certain storage, transportation, or processing methods, the risk of an *explosion* or *fire* exists. This risk extends to *military installations*, where it is very common for munitions and other hazardous or explosive materials to be stored. Nuclear storage, disposal, and electrical generation facilities, as well as many other industries and laboratories that use nuclear and radiological materials, pose a special industrial hazard. Accidents at these types of facilities can have catastrophic consequences that persist for decades or even longer.

In a free and open society, the presence of these hazards is often well mapped and well communicated to the at-risk public. However, there are many societies in which such openness does not exist. In these cases, people will often unknowingly place themselves at even greater risk by moving closer to the source of risk and doing nothing to protect themselves from a possible incident.

A notorious case of an industrial release accident without effective public disclosure took place in 1984 at Bhopal, India. After the release of methyl isocyanate from a Union Carbide plant, as many

Table 2–7   List of Select Industrial Accidents during the Past 30 Years

Year	Location	Industry	Description
1978	France	Oil tanker	Amoco Cadiz tanker ran aground off the coast of France, spilling 1.6 million barrels of crude oil
1979	Pakistan	Fireworks factory	32 people killed in a fire and resulting explosions
1979	Hungary	Chemical factory	Fire at the North Hungarian Chemical Works factory killed 13 workers
1979	United States	Nuclear	Three Mile Island nuclear power plant in Pennsylvania almost suffered a core meltdown. Over 140,000 people evacuated
1982	United States	Chemical waste	2242 residents of Times Beach, Missouri, were evacuated after dioxin found in soil
1984	Mexico City	Natural gas storage	Explosion at a liquefied natural gas storage plant within the city limits killed over 450 people
1984	Brazil	Pipeline	Oil pipeline near Cubatao exploded, killing 508
1984	India	Toxic chemicals	Explosion at Union Carbide pesticide plant in Bhopal released cloud of methyl isocyanate, killing at least 2000 and injuring hundreds of thousands
1985	United States	Fireworks factory	Fire at the Aerlex Corporation Fireworks plant in Oklahoma killed 21 workers
1986	Ukraine	Nuclear	Chernobyl nuclear power station in the Ukraine was struck by a chemical explosion at the station's fourth reactor and an uncontrolled graphite fire that led to the release of about 3.5% of the fuel stored in the reactor core. Official reports put the immediate death toll at 31, but it is widely believed that many more died in the first hours and weeks after the explosion. The Ukrainian government has estimated 7000–8000 deaths among clean-up workers alone
1988	North Sea	Oil platform	Platform explosion killed 168 people
1989	USSR	Gas pipeline	Pipeline explosion between Ula and Asha killed over 650 people
1989	United States	Oil tanker	Exxon Valdez spilled 11 million gallons of crude oil off the coast of Alaska
1991	Malaysia	Fireworks factory	21 killed in fires and explosions
1991	United States	Poultry plant	Fire at chicken processing plant in North Carolina killed 25 people
1993	Thailand	Toy factory	Fire killed 188 and injured over 400
1993	Hong Kong	Fireworks factory	27 workers killed in a factory fire
1998	Nigeria	Oil pipeline	Pipeline at Jesse Nigeria exploded, killing more than 500 people and severely burning hundreds more. Up to 2,000 people had been lining up with buckets and bottles to scoop up oil. The fire spread and engulfed the nearby villages of Moosqar and Oghara, killing farmers and villagers sleeping in their homes
1999	Mexico	Fireworks factory	Explosion in Celeya factory killed 56 people
2000	Holland	Fireworks factory	Explosion killed 22 and left thousands homeless
2001	France	Fertilizer factory	Explosion at Azote de France (AZF) agricultural chemicals factory near Toulouse killed 31 and injured at least 650
2004	Scotland	Plastic factory	ICL Plastic's Stockline Plastics plant in Glasgow exploded, killing 9 and injuring more than 40
2007	United States	Power plant	Testing at a yet-to-open combined oil and gas fired electric plant killed 5 and injured 27
2007	China	Steel plant	A ladle holding molten steel broke free, killing 32 and injuring 6
2010	United States	Oil well blowout	BP's Deepwater Horizon explodes while capping an undersea well, resulting in release of more than 400 million gallons of crude oil killing 11 and injuring 17

Source: Draffan, n.d.

as 4000 people in nearby communities died within days, and as many as half a million were injured. Twenty years later, much of the affected population still shows signs of illness caused by this accident. Prior to this catastrophic event, Union Carbide had taken out newspaper announcements warning people living near the plant of the risks of industrial release accidents. However, the company failed to reach their intended audience for various social and cultural reasons (see Chapter 5 for more information about risk communication).

Raw materials extraction accidents (including mining accidents), which are caused by fires, explosions, poisoning, flooding, and structural collapse, continue to be a hazard. Because of the underground, confined nature of many mines, associated accidents often result in mass casualty and require very difficult technical rescue. Collapse of overlying land can also occur, resulting in severe property damage. Raw material extraction accidents can also result in tremendous environmental damage, as occurred during the summer of 2010 when an explosion on a deepwater oil drilling rig leased by British Petroleum (BP) resulted in the release of as many as or even more than 400 million gallons of crude oil into international waterways (in addition to the death of 11 rig workers).

Mining kills more workers than any other industry, in both large and small accidents (Mining the Facts, 1998). More than 80% of the world's mine fatalities occur in China, where mining activity is extensive. In 2004 alone, more than 6,000 miners died in China (Davis & Speigel, 2005), although unofficial statistics have placed the annual average closer to 20,000 (BBC, 2004). Mining accidents often receive significant media coverage, and subsequent public attention, due to the extraordinary nature of the rescue efforts that must take place to spare the lives of any accident survivors. A mine accident that occurred at the Quecreek Mine in Pennsylvania on July 24, 2002, trapped nine miners behind 50 to 60 million gallons of water. Their rescue was accomplished by a highly complex recovery operation in which a relief tunnel was made by boring through 250 feet of rock, allowing all nine to escape alive only 4 days later (*The Daily American*, 2010, 9 for 9; a Site Dedicated to the Quecreek Mine Rescue, http://www.dailyamerican.com/quecreek/timeline/). As of the writing of this edition, one of the most spectacular mine rescues in history continues. Thirty-three miners remain trapped 2,200 feet below the surface in a collapsed mine in Chile. The ongoing rescue effort involves the drilling of a relief shaft wide enough to extract the miners—a task that will leave the men stranded for up to four months in a cramped space while receiving food, water, oxygen, electricity, and communications through multiple but tiny bore holes (Quilodran, Federico, 2010. Setback in Chile Mine Rescue, But No Delay Seen. Associated Press, http://www.msnbc.msn.com/id/39135920/ns/world_news-americas/).

This Web site, www.msha.gov/fatals/fab.htm, is maintained by the U.S. Department of Labor; it details individual mine accident fatalities in the United States.

Structural Fires and Failures

Structure fires and failures pose a significant risk that is universal among all countries of the world, rich or poor. The number of casualties from structure fires is greater than from many other hazards combined. This is mainly because almost everyone is dependent upon a built structure for their home, and probably for employment, education, government services, and commerce as well. Exposure to this risk, therefore, is extreme. This is an interesting risk, however, in that it is so common that most local agencies are prepared to manage fire or structural failure events, so the events rarely transform into disasters. When large structures burn or collapse, however, the chance of a disaster occurring is great, no matter what country is involved (see Exhibit 2–20).

EXHIBIT 2–20: HISTORICAL STRUCTURE FIRES WITH 50 OR MORE FATALITIES

1811—Richmond Theater fire kills 70, Virginia
1864—Church of La Compana fire kills about 2000, Santiago, Chile
1876—Brooklyn Theater fire kills 295, New York
1903—Iroquois Theater fire kills 602, Illinois
1908—Rhodes Opera House fire kills 170, Pennsylvania
1908—Lakeview Grammar School fire kills 175, Ohio
1919—Mayagucz Theater fire kills 150, Puerto Rico
1923—Cleveland School fire kills 77, South Carolina
1926—Movie theater fire kills 50, Drumcollogher, Ireland
1927—Laurier Palace movie theater fire kills 78, Quebec, Canada
1928—Teatro de Novedades theater fire kills 68, Madrid, Spain
1929—Cleveland Clinic fire kills 125, Ohio
1930—Ohio State Penitentiary fire kills 320, Ohio
1940—Rhythm Club fire kills 207, Mississippi
1942—Cocoanut Grove nightclub fire kills 492, Massachusetts
1944—Ringling Bros., Barnum & Bailey Circus tent fire kills 168, Connecticut
1946—Winecoff Hotel fire kills 119, Georgia
1946—LaSalle Hotel fire kills 61, Illinois
1946—Loebel's Restaurant fire kills 89, Berlin, Germany
1947—Select movie theater fire kills 88, Paris, France
1947—Joelma office fire kills 179, São Paulo, Brazil
1949—St. Anthony's Hospital fire kills 74, Illinois
1957—Katie Jane Nursing Home fire kills 72, Missouri
1958—Our Lady of the Angels school fire kills 95, Illinois
1960—Neuropsychiatric hospital fire kills 170, Guatemala City, Guatemala
1961—Gran Circus Americano fire kills 323, Niteroi, Brazil
1963—Golden Age nursing home fire kills 63, Ohio
1967—Innovation store fire kills 325, Brussels, Belgium
1970—Dance hall fire kills 145, Grenoble, France
1971—Taeyokale Hotel fire kills 163, Seoul, Korea
1971—Club Cinq Sept fire kills 143, St. Laurent du Pont, France
1973—Summerland Leisure Centre fire kills 50, Isle of Man, UK
1977—Beverly Hills Supper Club fire kills 165, Kentucky
1978—Cinema Rex theater fire kills 422, Abadan, Iran
1979—Hotel Coronade Aragon fire kills 74, Zaragoza, Spain
1980—MGM Grand Hotel fire kills 85, Nevada
1985—Soccer stadium fire kills 56, Bradford, UK
1986—Dupont Plaza Hotel fire kills 97, Puerto Rico
1990—Happy Land Social Club fire kills 87, New York
1993—Hasaka Prison fire kills 57, Damascus, Syria
2003—The Station nightclub fire kills 100, Rhode Island
2004—Prison fire kills 103, San Pedro Sula, Honduras
2004—Nightclub fire kills 188, Buenos Aires, Argentina

2005—Prison fire kills 133, Higuey, Dominican Republic
2006—Textile fire kills 65, Chittagong, Bangladesh
2007—Nursing home fire kills 63, Russia
2009—Santika nightclub fire kills 66, Bangkok, Thailand
2009—Daycare center fire kills 47, Hermosillo, Mexico
2009—Nightclub fire kills 125, Perm, Russia

Source: National Fire Protection Association, n.d.

Many natural and man-made factors influence the risk posed by this class of hazard, including design, geographic location, climate, seismicity, construction materials, maintenance, and safety standards employed. When buildings burn or collapse, they pose great risk not only to the inhabitants but also to the first responders.

One of the greatest structural failures due to nothing other than poor design was the collapse of the Sampoong Department Store in a South Korean mall in 1995. The ceiling on the five-year-old structure collapsed due to the weight of a rooftop water tank and poor quality concrete used in construction. The mall was packed with shoppers at the time and 500 were killed. Thousands sustained injuries, of which 900 were serious. Figure 2–37 shows the store following the disaster. Other notable structure fires and failures include:

- Hyatt Regency walkway collapse (July 17, 1981): Two thousand people were standing on a hotel atrium walkway in Missouri when the structure collapsed onto people below; 114 people were killed and over 200 were injured.
- Dubai Airport terminal collapse (September 27, 2004): Five were killed and 17 injured when part of the terminal under construction failed.
- Jerusalem wedding hall collapse (May 24, 2001): A four-story building collapsed while full of people attending a wedding party; 23 were killed and hundreds injured.

FIGURE 2–37 Sampoong Department Store, South Korea, June 29, 1995. (Photo courtesy of Institute of Historical Studies, 1995)

Intentional, Civil, and Political Hazards

Intentional, civil, and political hazards include those hazards that exist not due to an accident or an "act of God," but as a result of the conscious decision of man to act in an antisocial or anti-establishment manner. Assigning these hazards to this category does not imply that they are wrong or right, just that they are caused with intent. Like the technological hazards, many of these hazards are new and emerging, such as modern biological, chemical, and radiological weapons. Others, like war, have existed almost as long as humans.

Terrorism is the most salient hazard due to a remarkable upsurge in terrorist acts during the past decade (see Table 2–8). Terrorism is defined as "the unlawful use or threatened use of force or violence against people or property to coerce or intimidate governments or societies, often to achieve political, religious, or ideological objectives" (Globalsecurity.org, n.d.). It is important to note that terrorism does not have to involve an actual attack, as the mere threat of terrorism or a terrorism hoax can elicit many physiological and financial consequences of an actual event.

The Council on Foreign Relations has identified several different sources of terrorism, grouped into six major categories:

1. *Nationalist terrorism.* Groups seeking to separate from the government that they are targeting with terrorist acts in the hopes of forming an independent state of their own. The terrorist acts are performed to draw international attention and sympathy to their cause. Their acts seek a low level of violence in order to avoid appearing barbaric, but enough to garner media attention. Examples include the Irish Republican Army (IRA) and the Palestinian Liberation Organization (PLO).
2. *Religious terrorism.* Groups using terrorism as a means to carry out what they envision as a holy mission. This type of terrorism is especially dangerous because it is not constrained by national boundaries and often operates outside of normal civil systems. Examples include al Qaeda, Hamas, and Hezbollah.
3. *State-sponsored terrorism.* Groups, often working covertly, act as mercenaries. Their actions serve to inflict harm to enemy nations or to instigate conflict. Because of their government backing, these groups may be provided with steady and substantial funding. Examples of states that have been found to have sponsored terrorism include Iran, Libya, and Sudan.
4. *Left-wing terrorism.* Groups that seek to end capitalism in favor of communist/socialist regimes. These groups tend to avoid civilian casualties, favoring the destruction of capitalist symbols. Examples include the Red Brigade and the Japanese Red Army.

Table 2–8   Top 10 Countries Ranked by Terrorism Risk, 2010

Rank	Country
1	Iraq
2	Afghanistan
3	Pakistan
4	Somalia
5	Lebanon
6	India
7	Algeria
8	Colombia
9	Thailand
10	Philippines

Source: Maplecroft, 2010.

5. *Right-wing terrorism.* Groups that attempt to establish a fascist state by intimidating or removing liberal, democratic elements from government and society. They tend to have weak organizational structures and rarely garner support outside of their core group. They are most often racist. Examples include neo-Nazis, Skinheads, and the Aryan Nation.

6. *Anarchist terrorism.* Groups that attack any organized government structure, seeking a total destabilization of the global political framework. Though these groups have been only a minor threat since their decline in the early twentieth century, antiglobalization movements have brought about a resurgence in the anarchist movement (Council on Foreign Relations, 2004).

A seventh source, not included above, that is having an increased impact throughout the world is single-interest terrorism. These groups attempt to bring attention to a nonpolitical, nonreligious issue they believe needs to be addressed. Examples include environmental, animal rights, agrarian rights, and anti-abortion groups.

The means by which terrorists achieve their often disastrous ends are diverse. Although kidnappings, assassinations, shootings, robberies, and other tactics are regularly employed, the most feared incidents involve weapons of mass destruction (WMDs). WMDs are weapons designed specifically for causing mass casualty harm to humans as well as significant property damage.

WMDs can be subdivided into four principal categories: chemical, biological, radiological/nuclear, and explosive (CBRNE). While research is ongoing and new practices continue to be discovered, the worldwide emergency management community is largely unprepared and undertrained for dealing with WMDs. Knowledge of the properties and destructive qualities of the various chemical and biological threats is limited at best. The first-responder community, local emergency management organizations, and the general public remain almost completely uninformed about these hazards and have little or no experience in facing their consequences. The same is largely true with community and national leaders and the news media. The CBRNE weapons are described in the following sections.

Conventional explosives have existed for centuries, since explosive gunpowder invented by the Chinese for use in firecrackers was modified for use in weaponry. Both traditional and improvised explosive devices (IEDs) are the easiest weapons to obtain and use. Instructions for their assembly and use are widely available in print and on the Internet, as well as through the institutional knowledge of informal criminal networks. When skillfully used, they can inflict massive amounts of destruction to property and can cause significant injuries and fatalities to humans. Conventional explosives are most troubling when used as a WMD in light of their ability to effectively disperse chemical, biological, or radiological agents.

Conventional explosives and IEDs can be either explosive or incendiary. Explosives inflict damage or harm by the physical destruction caused by the expansion of gases resulting from the ignition of "high-" or "low-filler" explosive materials. The range of explosive devices includes simple pipe bombs, made from common plumbing materials; satchel charges, which are encased in an ordinary-looking bag such as a backpack and left behind for later detonation; letter or package bombs, delivered through the mail; and car bombs, which can be used to deliver a large amount of explosives. Incendiary devices, also referred to as firebombs, rely upon the ignition of fire to cause damage or harm. Examples include Molotov cocktails (gas-filled bottles capped with a burning rag) and napalm bombs.

Explosions and fires can be delivered as a missile or projectile device, such as a rocket, rocket-propelled grenade (RPG), mortar, or air-dropped bomb. Nontraditional explosive delivery methods are regularly discovered, and include the use of fuel-filled commercial airliners flown into buildings, as occurred on September 11, 2001. Because these weapons rely upon such low technology and are relatively easy to transport and deliver, they are the most commonly utilized terrorist devices. Although suicide bombings, in which the bomber manually delivers and detonates the device on or near his person, are becoming more common, most devices are detonated through the use of timed transmission, remote transmission (radio, cell phone), or other methods (light sensitivity, air pressure, movement, electrical impulse, etc.).

More than 70% of terrorist attacks involve the use of conventional explosives, but less than 5% of actual and attempted bombings are preceded by any kind of threat or warning. Conventional explosives can be difficult to detect because most easily attainable explosive materials are untraceable. Many commercial- and military-grade explosives are now required to contain a chemical signature that can be used to both trace their source should they be used for criminal means and make them detectable to trained dogs, but these account for only a fraction of the explosive materials available to terrorists. Because of the graphic nature of the carnage resulting from explosives and the widespread fear historically associated with their use, these weapons are very effective as a terror-spreading device (FEMA, 1999).

Like explosives, *chemical agents* have existed for centuries and have been used repeatedly throughout history. The most significant and first modern, organized use of chemical weapons was during World War I in Belgium. During an attack against Allied forces, German troops released 160 tons of chlorine gas into the air, killing over 10,000 soldiers and injuring another 15,000. In total, 113,000 tons of chemical weapons were used in World War I, killing over 90,000 and injuring 1.3 million.

Chemical weapons are created for the sole purpose of killing, injuring, or incapacitating people. They can enter the body through inhalation, ingestion, or through the skin or eyes. Many different kinds of chemicals have been developed as weapons; they fall under six general categories that are distinguished according their physiological effect.

1. Nerve agents (sarin, VX)
2. Blister agents (mustard gas, lewisite)
3. Blood agents (hydrogen cyanide)
4. Choking/pulmonary agents (phosgene)
5. Irritants (tear gas, capsicum [pepper] spray)
6. Incapacitating agents (BZ, Agent 15)

Terrorists can deliver chemical weapons via several mechanisms. Aerosol devices spread chemicals in liquid, solid (generally powdered), or gas form by causing tiny particulates to be suspended into the air. Explosives can be used to spread the chemicals through the air as well. Containers that hold chemicals, either for warfare or for everyday use (such as a truck or train tanker), can be breached, exposing the chemical to the air. Chemicals can be mixed with water or placed into food supplies. Some chemicals are easily absorbed through the skin and can be placed directly onto a victim to cause harm or death.

In general, chemical attacks are recognized immediately, although whether the attack is chemical or biological may be unclear until further testing. Chemical weapons can be persistent, remaining in the affected area long after the attack, or nonpersistent. Nonpersistent chemicals tend to evaporate quickly, are lighter than air, and lose their ability to harm or kill after about 10 or 15 minutes in open areas. In unventilated rooms, any chemical can linger for a considerable time.

The effect on victims is usually fast and severe. Identifying what chemical has been used presents special difficulties, and responding officials (police, fire, emergency medical services, hazardous materials teams) and hospital staff treating the injured are at risk from their effects. Without proper training and equipment, first-response officials can do little in the immediate aftermath of a chemical terrorist attack (FEMA, 1999).

A list of chemical agents compiled by the Centers for Disease Control (CDC) is presented in Exhibit 2–21.

EXHIBIT 2–21: CHEMICAL AGENTS CAPABLE OF TERRORIST USES

Abrin
Adamsite (DM)
Agent 15
Ammonia
Arsenic
Arsine (SA)
Benzene
Bromobenzylcyanide (CA)
BZ
Cannabinoids
Chlorine (CL)
Chloroacetophenone (CN)
Chlorobenzylidenemalononitrile (CS)
Chloropicrin (PS)
Cyanide
Cyanogen chloride (CK)
Cyclohexyl sarin (GF)
Dibenzoxazepine (CR)
Diphenylchloroarsine (DA)
Diphenylcyanoarsine (DC)
Diphosgene (DP)
Distilled mustard (HD)
Ethyldichloroarsine (ED)
Ethylene glycol
Fentanyls and other opioids
Hydrofluoric acid
Hydrogen chloride
Hydrogen cyanide (AC)
Lewisite (L, L-1, L-2, L-3)
LSD
Mercury
Methyldichloroarsine (MD)
Mustard gas (H) (sulfur mustard)
Mustard/lewisite (HL)
Mustard/T
Nitrogen mustard (HN-1, HN-2, HN-3)
Nitrogen oxide (NO)
Paraquat
Perflurorisobutylene (PHIB)
Phenodichloroarsine (PD)
Phenothiazines
Phosgene (CG)

(Continued)

EXHIBIT 2–21: CHEMICAL AGENTS CAPABLE OF TERRORIST USES (CONTINUED)

Phosgene oxime (CX)
Phosphine
Potassium cyanide (KCN)
Red phosphorous (RP)
Ricin
Sarin (GB)
Sesqui mustard
Sodium azide
Sodium cyanide (NaCN)
Soman (GD)
Stibine
Strychnine
Sulfur mustard (H) (mustard gas)
Sulfur trioxide-chlorosulfonic acid (FS)
Super warfarin
Tabun (GA)
Teflon and perflurorisobutylene (PHIB)
Thallium
Titanium tetrachloride (FM)
VX
White phosphorus
Zinc oxide (HC)

Source: Centers for Disease Control, www.bt.cdc.gov/agent/agentlistchem.asp.

Biological agents, or germ weapons, are live organisms, either bacteria, viruses, or toxins generated by living organisms. They are used to cause illness, injury, or death in humans, livestock, or plants. Awareness of the potential weapon use of bacteria, viruses, and toxins existed long before 2001, when anthrax was used in terrorist mail attacks in the United States. There is evidence of biological warfare as early as the fourteenth century, when the Mongols used plague-infected corpses to spread disease among their enemies. Because of advances in weapons technology that have allowed much more successful use of bioweapons over much wider geographic limits, biological weapons elicit great concern from counterterrorism officials and emergency planners alike.

Bioweapons can be dispersed either overtly or covertly. Their use can be extremely difficult to recognize because their negative consequences may take hours, days, or even weeks to emerge. This is especially true with bacteria and viruses; toxins generally elicit an immediate response. Recognition is made through a range of methods, including identification of a credible threat; the discovery of weapons materials (dispersion devices, raw biological material, or weapons laboratories); and correct diagnosis of affected humans, animals, or plants. Detection depends upon a collaborative public health monitoring system, trained and aware physicians, patients seeking medical care, and suitable equipment for confirming diagnoses. Bioweapons are unique in that detection is likely to be made not by a first responder but by members of the public health community.

Their devastating potential is confounded by the fact that people normally have no idea that they have been exposed. During the incubation period, when people do not exhibit symptoms but are contagious to others, the disease can spread. Incubation periods can be as short as several hours or as long as several weeks, allowing for wide geographic spreading due to the efficiency of modern travel. The spread of the SARS virus (which was not a bioterrorist attack) throughout all continents of the world is one example of an event when people did not realize they had been exposed to the virus and therefore unknowingly infected others.

Biological weapons are effective at disrupting economic and industrial components of society when they target animals or plants. Terrorists could potentially spread a biological agent over a large geographic area without being detected, causing significant destruction of crops. If the agent spread easily, as is often the case with natural diseases like Dutch elm disease, an entire industry could be devastated. Cattle diseases such as foot and mouth disease and mad cow disease, which occur naturally, could be used for sinister purposes without extensive planning, resources, or technical knowledge. In 1918, the German army spread anthrax and other diseases through exported livestock and animal feed. With globalization, such actions would require relatively little effort.

The primary defense against the use of biological weapons is recognition, which is achieved though proper training of first responders and public health officials. Early detection, before the disease or illness has spread to critical limits, is key to preventing a major public health emergency.

Biological agents are grouped into three categories: A, B, and C. Category A agents are those that have great potential for causing a public health catastrophe and are capable of being disseminated over a large geographic area. Examples of Category A agents are anthrax, smallpox, plague, botulism, tularemia, and viral hemorrhagic fevers. Category B agents are those that have low mortality rates but may be disseminated over a large geographic area with relative ease. Category B agents include salmonella, ricin, Q fever, typhus, and glanders. Category C agents are common pathogens that have the potential to be engineered for terrorism or weapon purposes. Examples of Category C agents are hantavirus and tuberculosis (Centers for Disease Control, 2010).

Some indicators of biological attack are

- Stated threat to release a biological agent
- Unusual occurrence of dead or dying animals
- Unusual casualties
  - Unusual illness for region/area
  - Definite pattern inconsistent with natural disease
- Unusual liquid, spray, vapor, or powder
  - Spraying, suspicious devices, packages, or letters (FEMA, 2002)

A list of biological agents compiled by the CDC is presented in Exhibit 2–22.

Nuclear and *radiological weapons* are those that involve the movement of energy through space and material. There are three primary mechanisms by which terrorists can use radiation to carry out an attack: detonation of a nuclear bomb, dispersal of radiological material, and attack on a facility housing nuclear material (power plant, research laboratory, storage site, etc.).

EXHIBIT 2–22: BIOLOGICAL AGENTS CAPABLE OF TERRORIST USES

Anthrax (*Bacillus anthracis*)
Botulism (*Clostridium botulinum* toxin)
Brucellosis (*Brucella* species)
Cholera (*Vibrio cholerae*)
E. coli O157:H7 (*Escherichia coli*)
Emerging infectious diseases such as Nipah virus and hantavirus
Epsilon toxin (*Clostridium perfringens*)
Glanders (*Burkholderia mallei*)
Melioidosis (*Burkholderia pseudomallei*)
Plague (*Yersinia pestis*)
Psittacosis (*Chlamydia psittaci*)
Q fever (*Coxiella burnetii*)
Ricin toxin from *Ricinus communis* (castor beans)
Salmonellosis (*Salmonella* species)
Smallpox (*Variola major*)
Staphylococcal enterotoxin B
Tularemia (*Francisella tularensis*)
Typhoid fever (*Salmonella typhi*)
Typhus fever (*Rickettsia prowazekii*)
Viral encephalitis (alphaviruses; e.g., Venezuelan equine encephalitis, eastern equine
    encephalitis, western equine encephalitis)
Viral hemorrhagic fevers (filoviruses; e.g., Ebola,
Marburg and arenaviruses (e.g., Lassa, Machupo)
Water safety threats (e.g., *Vibrio cholerae*, shigellosis (*Shigella*), *Cryptosporidium parvum*)

Source: Centers for Disease Control, www.bt.cdc.gov/agent/agentlist.asp

Nuclear weapons are the most devastating attack form. They are also the most difficult to develop or acquire, so they are considered the lowest threat in terms of terrorist potential. A nuclear weapon causes damage to property and harm to life through two separate processes. First, a blast is created by the bomb's detonation. An incredibly large amount of energy is released in the explosion, the result of an uncontrolled chain reaction of atomic splitting. The initial shock wave, which destroys all built structures within a range of up to several miles, is followed by a heat wave reaching tens of millions of degrees close to the point of detonation. High winds accompany the shock and heat waves. The second process by which nuclear weapons inflict damage is through harmful radiation. This radiation and radiological material is most dangerous close to the detonation area, where high concentrations can cause rapid death, but particles reaching high into the atmosphere can pose a threat several hundreds of miles away under the right meteorological conditions. Radiation can persist for years after the explosion occurs.

Radiological dispersion devices (RDDs) are simple explosive devices that spread harmful radioactive material upon detonation, without the involvement of a nuclear explosion. These devices are often called "dirty bombs." Some RDDs do not require explosives for dispersal. Although illnesses and fatalities are likely very close to the point of dispersal, these devices are more apt to be used to spread terror. As with many biological and chemical weapons, initially detecting that a radiological attack has occurred may be difficult. Special detection equipment and training in its use are prerequisites.

A third scenario involving nuclear/radiological material entails an attack on a nuclear facility. There are many facilities around the world where nuclear material is stored, including nuclear power plants, hazardous materials storage sites, medical facilities, military installations, and industrial facilities. An attack on any of these could release radiological material into the atmosphere, posing a threat to life and certainly causing fear among those who live nearby.

If a radiological or a nuclear attack were to occur, humans and animals would experience both internal and external consequences. External exposure results from any contact with radioactive material outside the body, while internal exposure requires ingestion, inhalation, or injection of radiological materials. Radiation sickness results from high doses of radiation and can result in death if the dosage is high enough. Other effects of radiation exposure can include redness or burning of the skin and eyes, nausea, damage to the body's immune system, and a higher lifetime risk of developing cancer (FEMA, 2002).

Terrorists can use *combined hazards* to achieve a synergistic effect. By using two or more methods, they can increase the efficacy of each agent in terms of its potential to destroy, harm, or kill, creating a more devastating total consequence than if each agent had been used individually. A dirty bomb, in which radiological material is added to a conventional explosive, is one example. The explosive causes physical damage from the expansion of gases, while the radiological material causes severe health effects. The combination causes both physical damage and harmful radiation, and it disperses the radiological material over a much larger area. Additionally, the debris from the conventional explosive becomes dangerous beyond the original explosion due to radiological contamination.

Explosives can be used to deliver chemical or biological weapons. This presents a dangerous scenario. Trauma resulting from the explosion will demand immediate attention from responders, who may enter a contaminated attack scene without first recognizing or taking the time to check if a biological or a chemical agent is present. Victims who are rushed to hospitals can cause secondary infections or injuries to emergency medical services and hospital staff. Additionally, contaminated debris can help to spread certain viruses that may not otherwise have entered the body as easily.

When multiple chemicals, biological agents, or a combination are used in an attack, the consequences can confound even those who are normally considered experts. The combination of symptoms resulting from multiple injuries or infections will make diagnosis extremely difficult, as these diagnoses often depend upon a defined set of effects. The multiple agents will cause physiological effects that do not fit any established human, animal, or plant models. The extra time required to identify the agents will undoubtedly cause an overall increase in the efficacy of the terrorist attack.

Terrorists have other options besides WMDs for which governments, businesses, and individuals must be prepared.

Cyberterrorism, which is described by the Federal Bureau of Investigation (FBI) as an "attack against information, computer systems, computer programs, and data which results in violence against non-combatant targets by sub-national groups or clandestine agents," can cause severe economic damage or result in a loss of critical services (about.com, 2006).

Narcoterrorism also deserves mention. Narcoterrorists are terrorist groups that fund their activities through the global drug trade (including cultivation, production, transport, distribution, and sales). The marriage between terrorist groups and the drug trade is a dangerous one, because each presents a special set of problems that are exacerbated when combined. They protect each other's interests, as their dependence is mutual. The most notorious narcotraffickers are the Revolutionary Armed Forces of Colombia (FARC), although many other terrorist groups participate in the practice to varying degrees (including the Shining Path, the Tamil Tigers, and the Taliban).

Civil unrest, including *protests*, *strikes*, and *rioting*, while daily and often non-newsworthy throughout the world, often leads to major property damage, economic damage, injuries, and death. Political and economic instability are very often either the cause or the consequence of this hazard, although apolitical and noneconomically motivated civil unrest does occur. Governments often take severe police or military measures to quell civil unrest and, in the process of doing so, can both sustain and inflict casualties. Crowds of demonstrators are as often to blame for instigating violence as they are victims of it, although it can be the actions of a select few seeking to incite a reaction that sets off a violent encounter. Exhibit 2–23 provides several examples during the past century of civil unrest that has turned deadly.

Stampedes, which are uncontrolled, often panicked movements of people, are unpredictable and deadly. They occur at sports venues, festivals, and other events where people congregate together within a facility that cannot accommodate a hurried exit or entrance or hurried movement within the structure or facility.

Most victims in stampedes die because of suffocation or crushing. The force of the crowd behind them places so much pressure upon their chest that breathing is impossible. The passing crowd often tramples those who fall. Exhibit 2–24 lists major stampedes (exceeding 100 fatalities) that occurred throughout the world during the past 110 years.

Crime, which affects hundreds of millions of people each year on a small, individual scale, results in disaster when criminals target or affect significant populations or property. Examples of criminal disasters are mass murders, arson, poisoning, illegal dumping, poaching, sabotage, and hostage taking. Many believe, for instance, that the Bhopal chemical disaster, described previously, was the result of one individual sabotaging the Union Carbide plant after having been transferred to a less

---

EXHIBIT 2–23: DEADLY INCIDENTS OF CIVIL UNREST

1907: German Southwest Africa (Namibia) massacres—40,000 killed

1919: U.S. race riots—an unknown number of people (in the hundreds) killed

1947: Taiwan 228 massacre—as many as 30,000 killed

1959: Tibetan uprising—approximately 87,000 killed

1964: Peruvian soccer game riots—300 killed

1965–1968: U.S. race riots—195 killed

1968: Mexico City, Mexico, Tlatelolco massacre—as many as 400 killed

1969: South Africa Sharpeville riot—69 killed

1972: Derry, Ireland "Bloody Sunday" events—13 killed

1980: Gwangju, South Korea protests—at least 207 killed

1985: Brussels, Belgium, soccer game riot—39 killed

1989: Tiananmen Square protests, China—approximately 1,000 killed, 7,000 injured

1989: Tbilisi, Georgia, protests—20 killed and 4,000 injured

1992: Los Angeles race riots—54 killed

2002: Gujarat, India, ethnic violence—over 1,000 killed

EXHIBIT 2–24: DEADLY STAMPEDES EXCEEDING 100 FATALITIES: 1900–2010

1943: London, England, a rush into a subway station to escape an air raid—173 killed
1956: Nilgata, Japan, New Year Procession—124 killed
1982: Moscow soccer game stampede—340 killed
1990: Mecca, Saudi Arabia, panic at the annual Hajj—1,426 killed
1994: Mecca, Saudi Arabia, panic at the annual Hajj—270 killed
1998: Mecca, Saudi Arabia, panic at the annual Hajj—119 killed
2001: Ghana soccer game stampede—120 killed
2004: Mecca, Saudi Arabia, Hajj stampede—244 killed
2005: Wai, India, religious procession stampede—265 killed
2005: Baghdad, Iraq, religious procession stampede—1,000 killed
2006: Mecca, Saudi Arabia, Hajj stampede—345 killed
2008: Himachal Pradesh, India, panic caused by rain shelter collapse—162 killed
2008: Jodhpur, India, religious procession stampede—147 killed

desirable job. Deranged individuals can massacre for irrational reasons, like the two students who terrorized a high school in Colorado in 1999, killing 12 classmates and teachers. In 1990, a man in New York City who was angry at his girlfriend set fire to a nightclub, killing 87 people. Exhibit 2–25 lists several disastrous criminal events. The crime associated with an escalation in drug gang activity in Mexico since Mexican President Calderon began a counternarcotic operation (2009) has led to destabilization of many areas of the country and thousands of deaths of civilians, police, and rival drug gang members. In total, it is estimated that more than 25,000 people were killed between December 2006 and July 2010 (Grillo, 2010).

War is perhaps the greatest of all man-made hazards, having resulted in hundreds of millions of deaths throughout history. As weapons technology has progressed, war's deadly consequences have increased, with the nuclear bomb retaining the distinction of being the deadliest weapon ever employed. War devastates populations, economies, and cultures, leaving a lasting mark on all parties involved for generations. The outcome of war is almost always significant in terms of deaths, injuries,

EXHIBIT 2–25: DISASTROUS CRIMINAL EVENTS

1966: Tasmania, Australia—Martin Bryant kills 35 people and injures 37
1987: Berkshire, UK—Michael Robert Ryan kills 17 people and injures 15
1996: Dunblane, Scotland—Thomas Hamilton kills 17 people
2001: Osaka, Japan—Mamoru Takuma kills 8 people and injures 18
2002: Thuringia, Germany—Robert Steinhauser kills 16 people
2004: Honduras—Criminal gang members massacre 28 people on a bus
2007: United States—Seung-Hui Cho kills 32 people and injures 25 in a shooting rampage
2009: Philippines—100 armed men kidnap and kill a political candidate and 56 supporters
2010: Jamaica—Resistance of extradition by drug lord Michael Christopher Coke leads to the death of 76 people, including police officers and civilians

damage and destruction of infrastructure, and homelessness, and often involves acts of genocide or other racial or ethnic violence. In almost all wars, the civilian population suffers the greatest consequences.

During and immediately following major conflicts, civilian populations in the war-affected countries are likely to be displaced from their homes and communities, and are subject to many of the threatening conditions associated with general humanitarian crises: shortages of adequate food, water, shelter, healthcare, and other basic services. However, they may also be threatened by violence or further conflict, qualifying their situation as something completely distinct from a regular humanitarian emergency. This special category of disaster that results from ongoing war or violence is the *complex emergency*, or as it is commonly known, the *complex humanitarian emergency* (CHE; see Chapter 1). The United Nations defines a complex emergency as follows:

> *A complex emergency is a humanitarian crisis in a country, region or society where there is a dramatic disruption in the political, economic and social situation, resulting from internal or external conflict or natural disaster, seriously disrupting the population's capacity to survive and the national authorities to respond, and which requires a consolidated multi-sectoral international response. (Wigdel, 2000)*

In the twentieth century alone, almost 170 million people died in the midst of CHEs (Stewart, 2000). These disasters are especially fatal due to intentional attempts to alienate or eliminate certain populations. They create large numbers of refugees and internally displaced persons (IDPs), as defined in Chapter 1, who are routinely grouped into camps for aid and/or protection. Under these conditions, their needs are absolute and their conditions generally abysmal.

Of all types of disaster responses, none is more difficult and involved than that directed at treating and ending a CHE. They truly require the full resources of the international response community. These efforts go above and beyond normal disaster responses due to the confounded variable of violence—a desperate lack of security due to the nature of the conflict that created the emergency in the first place. CHEs endanger not only the lives of the directly affected population but also those of the responders. Finally, a wide array of internal and external contextual influences push and pull in all directions, whatever response efforts are mounted, making stability and predictability an often unanswered wish (see Exhibit 2–26 for a list of common contextual influences). Although every CHE is distinct, there are many common characteristics including, but by no means limited to

- Substantial civilian casualties, displacement, and suffering
- The need for substantial international assistance to complement local efforts
- Involvement of a substantial number and type of relief organization
- Humanitarian assistance impeded, delayed, or prevented by politically or conflict-motivated constraints
- Significant security risks for relief workers in many areas
- The need for external political support and mediation to overcome obstacles to assistance, such as difficult access to those in need (McCreight, 2001)

There is much debate about what types of sociopolitical conditions lead to a CHE, and whether early warning indicators can be developed. It has been recognized, for example, that despite the

EXHIBIT 2–26: CONTEXTUAL INFLUENCES OF CHEs

- Host government/national leaders
- Host nation culture
- Roots of ethnic conflict
- Recent events
- Legal issues
- Desired end state
- Players-imperatives
- Media and public affairs
- Foreign interests
- Public health
- Donor states
- Military-civil cooperation
- NGOs
- Security
- Recovery
- UN mandate
- Stabilization
- Ethnic politics
- Multinational corporations
- Alliances
- The World Bank

Source: McCreight (2001).

presence of conflicts throughout the world, CHEs result only within the poorer countries. However, poverty alone by no means indicates a predisposition for CHE formation. A combination of factors is required, including several of the following:

- Income inequality
- Worsening poverty
- Military centrality (spending, power)
- A tradition of conflict
- Deteriorating political climate
- Passage of repressive legislation
- Hardening ideologies
- Scarcities of food, or unequal distribution
- Deteriorating public health conditions
- Flight of the educated class out of the country
- Increased internal military movements
- Massive movements of people

- Recurrent and devastating natural disasters
- Long-standing ethnic, religious, or cultural tensions (Auvinen & Nafziger, 1999; McCreight, 2001)

Complex humanitarian emergencies combine internal conflicts with large-scale displacements of people: mass famine and fragile or failing economic, political, and social institutions. Some CHEs are exacerbated by the conditions resulting after natural disasters or by inadequate or nonexistent transportation networks. Historically, an equal number of CHEs have developed very quickly as have developed over a more prolonged period, leaving any mechanism for prediction only moderately effective.

CHEs are becoming much more common and, likewise, more widespread in their global range. Before the end of the Cold War, only a handful of CHEs existed at any given time, but today these events are occurring in much greater numbers, in many different parts of the world. For example, between 1978 and 1985, there were an average of only five CHEs each year, but by 1985 that number had jumped to 20 (CIA, 1995), and has remained at that level ever since (see Figure 2–38).

Probably the most significant factor that must be considered by any agency responding to a CHE is security. This includes security of relief workers as much as security of the affected population. Peacekeeping missions are often required to ensure the safety of IDPs and marginalized members of the population. Without the security offered by the peacekeepers, it is impossible for relief agencies to do their jobs, as the warring factions targeting the affected population will likely see relief agencies as hindering their cause and target them as well. Other times, relief workers merely get caught in the crossfire of battle. Either way, the results are tragic and occasionally result in aid workers retreating from the crisis. Exhibit 2–27 provides a list of select events where aid workers have been killed or injured during the response to CHEs. Figure 2–39 shows the actual number of humanitarian aid workers killed from 1985 to 1998.

A database of aid worker fatalities is maintained by Patronus Analytical, with data reaching back to 1993. This site provides an updated listing of reported incidents, including accidents and violent encounters that have resulted in the death of one or more aid workers. This database can be accessed at http://www.patronusanalytical.com/aid%20worker%20fatalities/Fatal%20Incidents%20Aid%20Workers%20DB/Fatal%20Incidents%20data.html.

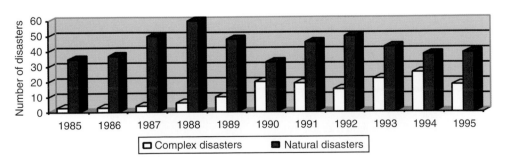

FIGURE 2–38 Number of natural and complex disasters worldwide, 1985–1995. (From Lynch, 1998)

EXHIBIT 2–27: SELECT FATAL INCIDENTS INVOLVING RELIEF WORKERS, 1991–2010

1991: Ethiopia—29 relief workers killed in separate incidents over 9 months

1993–1994: Somalia—125 U.S. and UN military personnel killed, 195 wounded

1998: Sudan—3 UN staff killed and 3 wounded in an attack on their vehicle

1999: Sudan—4 Red Cross workers kidnapped and executed

2000: Somalia—20 killed during an attack on a convoy of aid workers

2000: Iraq—2 Food and Agriculture Organization employees killed

2000: Afghanistan—7 UN mine clearance workers killed in an ambush

2000: Indonesia—3 aid workers killed

2001: Congo—6 Red Cross workers killed

2003: Iraq—24 UN employees killed in UN Headquarters bombing

2003: Iraq—12 Red Cross workers killed in a bombing

2004: Afghanistan—5 Doctors Without Borders workers killed

2005: Afghanistan—28 aid workers killed in 14 separate incidents

2006: Sri Lanka—17 Action Against Hunger workers executed

2007: Lebanon—2 Red Cross workers shot in a Palestinian refugee camp

2007: Algeria—17 UN staff killed in suicide bombings in Algiers

2008: West Bank/Gaza—2 UN staff killed in a shooting incident

2010: Afghanistan—10 aid workers with International Assistance Mission killed in an ambush in Afghanistan

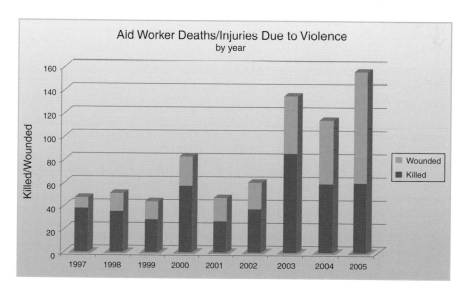

FIGURE 2–39 Number of humanitarian aid worker deaths and injuries due to violence, 1997–2005. (From Patronas International, 2006)

EXHIBIT 2–28: SELECTED CHEs AND ASSOCIATED MORTALITY FIGURES

Sudan (1983–present): over 2 million killed
Ethiopia (1984–1993): up to 2 million killed
Uganda (1987–present): 100,000 killed
Rwanda (1994–1997): up to 1 million killed
Cambodia (1975–1998): over 1 million killed
Somalia (1988–present): 500,000 killed
Colombia (late 1990s–present): 35,000 killed
Bosnia-Herzegovina (1992–1996): 200,000 killed
Congo (1998–2003): 3.8 million killed
Sierra Leone (2002): 20,000 killed

Civilians trying to flee war have much higher mortality and morbidity statistics. Refugees who are able to escape to neighboring countries (see Chapter 7) are usually placed into refugee camps in which conditions range from uncomfortable to squalid. While there, they are subject to outbreaks of communicable diseases, starvation, elevated stress, and violence. When the daily death rate reaches 1 per 10,000 people, refugee or IDP situations are classified as CHEs. This threshold is by no means absolute and thus, depending on the circumstances, a situation may be called a CHE much earlier.

A measure of mortality called the Crude Mortality Rate (CMR) measures the number of deaths per 10,000 people per day. This metric is used because it helps to standardize the effect of the emergency in terms of numbers dying per day over specific population blocks. This enables events of different sizes to be compared in terms of the effect sustained by the individual. (Absolute numbers are often irrelevant if the compared countries' populations greatly differ, such as 1,000 deaths in Jamaica vs. China.) Under normal circumstances, CMR rates in the developing world range from about 0.4 to 0.7 deaths per 10,000 people each day. During CHEs, these numbers can range from the baseline of 1 per day to 35 per day (as with Rwandan refugees in Zaire in 1994), and even higher. Mortality in CHEs is a factor of vulnerability to specific causes of death. In general, situations in which violence is the greatest cause of death show high mortality rates among grown men, while situations in which disease and famine are the greatest threat predominantly affect women, children, and the elderly (see Exhibit 2–28).

Under the provisions of the UN Charter, the United Nations is allowed to intervene in the event of a CHE. The role it takes on, as either a peacekeeper or a peace enforcer, depends upon the decisions of the UN Security Council and the rules outlined in its Charter. These security operations may be active or simply observatory. Exhibit 2–29 provides more insight into the difference between UN Chapter VI and VII Peace Operations.

Conclusion

There are many known hazards, whether natural, man-made, or intentional. It is likely that the list of man-made and intentional hazards will increase as technological discovery advances, although the range of natural hazards will probably remain static. Thankfully, most nations face only a select subset

EXHIBIT 2–29: UN CHAPTER VI AND CHAPTER VII PEACE OPERATIONS

The UN Charter allows for two different kinds of security activities during CHEs: peacekeeping and peace enforcement.

Peacekeeping, sometimes called "Chapter VI," allows for the introduction of forces, which are noncombatant in nature, on location to monitor peace agreements. It is intended to maintain an established pause in conflict to allow UN and other "peacemakers" the time they need to negotiate a permanent dispute settlement, or to assist in carrying out the terms of that negotiated settlement. There must be some degree of stability within the country or region in order for Chapter VI to be invoked. Chapter VI Peacekeeping is designed to support diplomatic endeavors to achieve or to maintain peace, and often involves the peacekeepers having to deal with and witness existing tension and violence without actually getting involved in any way as a participant. Peacekeeping forces require an invitation or, at the very least, full consent of all involved parties. Peacekeepers are required to remain impartial toward all of these parties. Chapter VI Peacekeeping forces may include unarmed observers, lightly armed units, police, and civilian technicians. Operations conducted by peacekeeping forces may include: observation, recording, supervision, monitoring, occupying a buffer or neutral zone, and reporting on the implementation of the truce and any violations thereof. Typical peacekeeping missions include:

- Observing and reporting any alleged violation of the peace agreement
- Handling alleged cease-fire violations and/or alleged border incidents
- Conducting regular liaison visits to units within their area of operation (AO)
- Continuously checking forces within their AO and reporting any changes
- Maintaining up-to-date information on the disposition of forces within their AO
- Periodically visiting forward positions; report on the disposition of forces
- Assisting civil authorities in supervision of elections, transfer of authority, partition of territory, and administration of civil functions

Force may only be used in self-defense. Peacekeepers are not permitted to prevent violations of a truce or cease-fire agreement by the active use of force, as their presence alone is intended to be sufficient to maintain the peace.

Peace Enforcement, on the other hand, or Chapter VII, allows for the use of "such action by air, sea, or land forces as may be necessary" to ensure compliance with UN resolutions and for the resumption of peace. Peace enforcement could include combat, armed intervention, or the physical threat of armed intervention. In contrast to peacekeeping, peace enforcement forces do not require consent of the parties to the conflict and they need not be neutral or impartial. Typical missions include:

- Protection of humanitarian assistance
- Restoration and maintenance of order and stability
- Enforcement of sanctions
- Guarantee or denial of movement
- Establishment and supervision of protected zones
- Forcible separation of belligerents

Source: U.S. Army, n.d.

of the exhaustive list provided in this chapter. Awareness of the hazards that affect a nation or region and full understanding of the causes and consequences of that hazard "profile" are the first steps in the disaster reduction process known as hazards risk management.

References

About.com. (2006). *Cyberterrorism*. Web site: terrorism.about.com/od/protectingtargets/a/cyberterror.htm.

Air Safe. (2003). *Top ten airline safety questions*. www.airsafe.com/ten_faq.htm.

AllExperts. (2010). *List of rail accidents*. www.associatepublisher.com/e/l/li/list_of_rail_accidents.htm.

Associated Press. (2005). *Some deadly train disasters since 1900*. (July 12). www.msnbc.msn.com/id/8557709/.

Atlantic Oceanographic and Meteorological Laboratory (AOML). (2004). *Hurricane frequently asked questions* (August 13). www.aoml.noaa.gov/hrd/tcfaq/tcfaqHED.html.

Auvinen, J., & Nafziger, E. W. (1999). The sources of humanitarian emergencies. *Journal of Conflict Resolution, 43*(3), 267–290.

BBC. (2004). *Life is cheap in China's mines*. (November 28). http://news.bbc.co.uk/1/hi/world/asia-pacific/4049253.stm.

BBC. (2006). *Lagos pipeline blast kills scores*. (December 26). http://news.bbc.co.uk/2/hi/africa/6209845.stm.

Beaufort Wind Scale. NOAA. Storm Prediction Center. NOAA. N.d. http://www.spc.noaa.gov/faq/tornado/beaufort.html.

Bernama. (2010). *Researchers warn Bangkok under threat to sink*.Bernama.com. July 23. http://www.bernama.com/bernama/v5/newsindex.php?id=515935.

Brun, S., et al. (1997). Coping with natural hazards in Canada. Environmental Adaptation Research Group and Institute for Environmental Studies, University of Toronto, June.

Centers for Disease Control (CDC). (2010). Bioterrorism Agents/Diseases. Emergency Preparedness and Response. CDC Website: http://www.bt.cdc.gov/agent/agentlist-category.asp.

Central Intelligence Agency (CIA). (1995). The CIA on global humanitarian emergencies. *Population and Development Review, 21*(4), 913–917.

Chapman, C. R. (2004). *The asteroid impact hazard and interdisciplinary issues*. Boulder, CO: Southwest Research Institute. www.boolder.swri.edu/clark/icsupb05.doc.

Chynoweth, D. P. (2003). *University Lecture Notes. Agricultural and Biological Engineering*. The University of Florida.

CNN. (2007a). *Rising seas, sinking land threaten Thai capital*. CNN Worldwide. October 22.

CNN. (2007b). *Elephant rampage frightens villagers in India*. CNN Asia. October 14.

CNN. (2010). *Family transformed three years after bridge disaster*. Building Up America. July 30. http://www.cnn.com/2010/LIVING/07/30/minneapolis.bridge.anniversary/index.html?hpt=C1.

Colorado Avalanche Information Center. n.d. *Avalanche facts*. http://geosurvey.state.co.us/avalanche/Default.aspx?tabid=56.

Council on Foreign Relations. (2004). *Types of terrorism*. http://cfrterrorism.org/terrorism/types.html.

Davis, S., & Spiegel, M. (2005). Take tough action to end china's mining tragedies. *Wall Street Journal* (February 18). http://hrw.org/english/docs/2005/02/23/china10203.htm.

Draffan, G. n.d. *Chronology of industrial disasters. Endgame Research Services.* www.endgame.org/industral-disasters.html.

Emergency Management Australia (EMA). (2000). *Emergency risk management: Applications guide.* Dickson: EMA.

Faisal, H. (2005). Internet link in Pakistan restored after over 11-days breakdown. *Pakistani Times,* (July 7). www.pakistantimes.net/2005/07/09/top3.htm.

Federal Emergency Management Agency (FEMA). (1998). *Introduction to mitigation independent study course.* Emmitsburg, MD: Emergency Management Institute.

Federal Emergency Management Agency (FEMA). (1999). *Emergency response to terrorism. Self-study course.* Emmitsburg, MD: National Fire Academy.

Federal Emergency Management Agency (FEMA). (2002). Managing the emergency consequences of terrorist incidents. In *Interim planning guide for state and local governments* July. Emmitsburg, MD: Emergency Management Institute.

Gelt, J. (1992). Land subsidence, earth's fissures change Arizona's landscape. *Arroyo, 6*(2). www.ag.arizona.edu/azwater/arroyo/062land.htm.

Global Security. n.d. *Glossary.* www.globalsecurity.org/military/library/policy/army/fm/100-20/10020gl.htm.

Grillo, I. (2010). *7 circles of Juarez.* Huffington Post. http://www.globalpost.com/dispatch/mexico/100702/ciudad-juarez-cartel-drug-war.

Handwerk, B. (2005). *Africa fights locust plagues* (January 7) www.ngnews.com/news/2005/01/0107_050107_tv_locust_plague.html.

International Rivers Network. (1999). *Dam index.* www.irn.org/pubs/damindex.html.

Jacquot, J. (2009). Dams, from Hoover to the Three Gorges to the crumbling ones. *Discover Magazine,* March. http://discovermagazine.com/2009/mar/08-dams-hoover-three-gorges-crumbling-ones.

Jordans, F. (2010). *Swine flu response: Alarmist or legit?* Associated Press. March 29.

Kaplan, S. (1997). The words of risk analysis. *Risk Analysis, 17*(4), 407–417.

Kinver, M. (2008). *Map pinpoints disease "hotspots."* BBC News. February 20.

Lynch, J. (1998). *Overview of humanitarian emergencies.* Military Medical Humanitarian Assistance Course, Uniformed Services University of the Health Sciences.

Maplecroft. (2010). *Iraq, India, and Colombia Top Maplecroft Terrorism List.* Maplecroft Press Release, February 16. http://www.maplecroft.com/about/news/terrorism_risk_index_feb_10.html.

McCreight, R. (2001). *Characteristics of complex emergencies.* Personal Vuegraphs, George Washington University.

Michigan Department of Community Health. (2005). *Reportable diseases in Michigan.* Bureau of Laboratories. Fact Sheet. January.

Mining the Facts. (1998). *New Internationalist,* March. www.newint.org/issue299/facts.html.

National Aeronautics and Space Administration (NASA). n.d. *El Nino – When the Pacific Ocean Speaks, Earth Listens.* Jet Propulsion Laboratory, California Institute of Technology. http://www.jpl.nasa.gov/earth/ocean_motion/el_nino_index.cfm.

National Tsunami Hazard Mitigation Program (NTHMP). (2003). *Frequently asked questions.* National Academy Press. www .pmel.noaa.gov/tsunami-hazard/tsunami_faqs.htm.

National Fire Protection Association (NFPA). n.d. *Important dates in fire history. NFPA Web site:* www.nfpa.org/itemdetail .asp?categoryid=954&itemid=23375&url=research%20&20reports/fire%20statistics/historical.

National Hurricane Center. (2005). *The Saffir-Simpson hurricane scale.* www.nhc.noaa.gov/aboutsshs.shtml.

National Institutes of Health (NIH). (2004). Vehicular manslaughter: The global epidemic of traffic deaths. *Environmental Health Perspectives, 112*(11). http://ehp.niehs.nih.gov/members/2004/112-11/spheres.html.

National Oceanographic and Atmospheric Administration (NOAA). (2010a). *Damaging wind basics.* National Severe Storms Laboratory. http://www.nssl.noaa.gov/primer/wind/wind_basics.html.

National Oceanographic and Atmospheric Administration (NOAA). (2010b). NWS Wind Chill Chart. Office of Climate, Water, and Weather Resources. http://www.nws.noaa.gov/os/windchill/index.shtml.

National Oceanographic and Atmospheric Administration (NOAA). (2005). *World Meteorological Organization Region IV Adopts Consensus El Niño and La Niña Index and Definitions.* NOAA Press Release, April 28. www.noaanews.gov/ stones2005/s2428.htm.

National Oceanographic and Atmospheric Administration (NOAA). n.d.(a). *The Palmer Drought Severity Index.* www.drought.noaa.gov/index.html.

National Research Council (NRC). (1991). *A safer future.* Washington, DC.

NOVA. (1997). *Avalanche!.* PBS. www.pbs.org/.../programs/2418_avalanche.html.

Odenwald, S. (2005). *Space weather: A conflagration of storms.* Solarstorms.org. http://www.solarstorms.org/SWChapter1 .html.

Patronus Analytical. n.d. Aid worker deaths due to violence. NGO Security. http://www.patronusanalytical.com/files/Air% 20Worker%20Deaths%20Due%20to%20Violence.php.

Perlin, D. (2002). *The complete idiot's guide to dangerous diseases and epidemics.* New York: Penguin Books.

Reiss, C. L. (2001). *Risk identification and analysis: A guide, Fairfax, Public Entity Risk Institute (PERI). Broadleaf Capital International. (1999). The Australian and New Zealand standard on risk management, AS/NZS 4360:1999.* Pymble, Australia: Broadleaf Capital International.

Slovic, P., Fischhoff, B., & Lichtenstein, S. (1979). Rating the risks. *Environment, 21,* 14–20, 36–39.

Smith, K. (1992). *Environmental hazards: Assessing risk and reducing disaster.* London: Routledge.

Stewart, F. (2000). The root causes of humanitarian emergencies. In W. E. Nafziger (Ed.), *War, hunger, and displacement (Vol. 1 Analysis).* Oxford, UK: Oxford University Press.

Storm Prediction Center. n.d. *The Fujita tornado scale.* www.ncdc.noaa.gov/oa/satellite/satellitesexe/educational/ fujita.html.

Struck, D. (2008). *Dust storms overseas carry contaminants to the U.S.* (p. A22). *The Washington Post,* February 6.

Students for the Exploration and Development of Space (SEDS). n.d. *Meteors, meteorites, and impacts.* http://seds.lpl.arizona.edu/nineplanets/nineplanets/meteorites.html.

Thomas, J. (2010). *Horse stampede injures 24 during Iowa parade.* Right Juris. http://news.google.com/news/search?aq=f&pz=1&cf=all&ned=us&hl=en&q=horse+parade+stampede+injures.

United Nations Convention to Combat Desertification. (2005). *United Nations launches International Year of Deserts and Desertification 2006 to profile desertification as a major threat to humanity.* UNCCD Press Release, December 23. www.unccd.int/publicinfo/pressrel/showpressrel.php?pr=press23_12_05.

United Nations Environmental Programme. (2003). *Impacts of summer 2003 heat wave in Europe. Environmental Alert Bulletin 2*. http://www.grid.unep.ch/product/publication/download/ew_heat_wave.en.pdf.

United States Department of Agriculture. (USDA). (2006). *Haines index.* USDA Forest Service. www.fs.fed.us.

University Corporation for Academic Research (UCAR). (2005). *Anticipating community weather and atmospheric risk.* National Center for Academic Research. www.meted.ucar.edu/hazwx/start.htm.

University Corporation for Atmospheric Research (UCAR). n.d. *Thunderstorm glossary. UCAR Web site:* www.ucar.edu/news/backgrounders/stormglossary.shtml.

U.S. Army. n.d. *Chapter 23: United Nations and Peace Operations.* www.jagcnet.army.mil/JAGCNETInternet/Homepages/AC/CLAMO-Public.nsf/0/1af4860452f962c085256a490049856f/%24FILE/Chapter%252023%2520-%2520UN%2520and%2520Peace%2520Operations.pdf&e=9888.

U.S. Department of State. (2006). *Health service could be overwhelmed in a pandemic, experts say.* March 10. http://usinfo.state.gov/gi/archive/2006/Mar/11-871715.html.

U.S. Geologic Survey. (1997). *Eruptions of Hawaiian volcanoes: Past, present and future.* http://pubs.usgs.gov/gip/Hawaii.

U.S. Geologic Survey. (2005a). *Earthquake facts and statistics.* http://neic.usgs.gov/neis/eqlists/eqstats.html.

U.S. Government Accountability Office. (2003). *Electricity restructuring: 2003* blackout identifies crisis and opportunity for the electricity sector. GAO-04-204. http://www.gao.gov/new.items/d04204.pdf.

Viet Nam News. (2010). *HCM City mulls climate change threat. Viet Nam News,* July 13. http://vietnamnews.vnagency.com.vn/Environment/201463/HCM-City-mulls-climate-change-threat-.html.

Watson, K. (1997). *Desertification.* http://pubs.usgs.gov/gip/deserts/desertification/.

Wigdel, J. (2000). A roadmap to collaborative relief and recovery. *Liaison, 1*(4), January.

Wikipedia. (2010). *List of Epidemics.* http://en.wikipedia.org/wiki/List_of_epidemics; and Perlin, D. (2002). *The Complete Idiot's Guide to Dangerous Diseases and Epidemics.* Penguin Books.

World Commission on Dams. (2000). *Dams and development: A new framework for decision-making.* www.dams.org/report/contents.htm.

World Health Organization (WHO). (2000). *Researchers warn of impending disaster from mass arsenic poisoning.* Press release, September 8. www.who.int/inf-pr-2000/en/pr2000-55.html.

3

Risk and Vulnerability

Introduction

Risk is an unavoidable part of life, affecting all people without exception, irrespective of geographic or socioeconomic limits. Each choice we make as individuals and as a society involves specific, often unknown, factors of risk, and full risk avoidance generally is impossible.

On the individual level, each person is primarily responsible for managing the risks he faces as he sees fit. For some risks, management may be obligatory, as with automobile speed limits and seatbelt usage. For other personal risks, such as those associated with many recreational sports, individuals are free to decide the degree to which they will reduce their risk exposure, such as wearing a ski helmet or other protective clothing. Similarly, the risk of disease affects humans as individuals, and as such is generally managed by individuals. By employing risk reduction techniques for each life hazard, individuals effectively reduce their vulnerability to those hazard risks.

As a society or a nation, citizens collectively face risks from a range of large-scale hazards. Although these hazards usually result in fewer total injuries and fatalities over the course of each year than individually faced hazards, they are considered much more significant because they have the potential to result in many deaths, injuries, or damages in a single event or series of events. In fact, some of these hazards are so great that, if they occurred, they would result in such devastation that the capacity of local response mechanisms would be overwhelmed. This, by definition, is a disaster. For these large-scale hazards, many of which were identified in Chapter 2, vulnerability is most effectively reduced by disaster management efforts collectively, as a society. For most of these hazards, it is the government's responsibility to manage, or at least guide the management of, hazard risk reduction measures. And when these hazards do result in disaster, it is likewise the responsibility of governments to respond to them and aid in the following recovery.

This text focuses on the management of international disasters, which are those events that overwhelm an individual nation or region's ability to respond, thereby requiring the assistance of the international body of response agencies. This chapter, therefore, focuses not upon individual, daily risks and vulnerabilities, but on the risks and vulnerabilities that apply to the large-scale hazards like those discussed in Chapter 2.

Two Components of Risk

Chapter 1 defined risk as the interaction of a hazard's consequences with its probability or likelihood. This is its definition in virtually all documents associated with risk management. Clearly defining the meaning of "risk" is important, because the term often carries markedly different meanings for different people (Jardine & Hrudey, 1997). One of the simplest and most common definitions of risk, preferred by many risk managers, is displayed by the equation stating that risk is the likelihood of an event occurring multiplied by the consequence of that event, were it to occur: RISK = LIKELIHOOD × CONSEQUENCE (Ansell & Wharton 1992).

Likelihood

"Likelihood" can be given as a probability or a frequency, whichever is appropriate for the analysis under consideration. Variants of this definition appear in virtually all risk management documents. "Frequency" refers to the number of times an event will occur within an established sample size over a specific period of time. Quite literally, *it tells how frequently* an event occurs. For instance, the frequency of auto accident deaths in the *United States* averages around 1 per 81 million miles driven (Dubner & Levitt, 2006).

In contrast to frequency, "probability" refers to single-event scenarios. Its value is expressed as a number between 0 and 1, with 0 signifying a zero chance of occurrence and 1 signifying certain occurrence. Using the auto accident example, in which the frequency of death is 1 per 81 million miles driven, we can say that the probability of a random person in the United States dying in a car accident equals 0.000001 if he was to drive 81 miles.

Disaster managers use this formula for risk to determine the likelihood and the consequences of each hazard according to a standardized method of measurement. The identified hazard risks thus can be compared to each other and ranked according to severity. (If risks were analyzed and described using different methods and/or terms of reference, it would be very difficult to accurately compare them later in the hazards risk management process.)

This ranking of risks, or "risk evaluation," allows disaster managers to determine which treatment (mitigation and preparedness) options are the most effective, most appropriate, and provide the most benefit per unit of cost. Not all risks are equally serious and risk analysis can provide a clearer idea of these levels of seriousness.

Without exception governments have a limited amount of funds available to manage the risks they face. While the treatment of one hazard may be less expensive or more easily implemented than the treatment of another, cost and ease alone may not be valid reasons to choose a treatment option. Hazards that have great consequences (in terms of lives lost or injured or property damaged or destroyed) and/or occur with great frequency pose the greatest overall threat. Considering the limited funds, disaster managers generally should recommend first treating those risks that pose the greatest threat. Fiscal realities often drive this analytic approach, resulting in situations in which certain hazards in the community's overall risk profile are mitigated, while others are not addressed at all.

The goal of risk analysis is to establish a standard and therefore comparable measurement of the likelihood and consequence of every identified hazard. The many ways by which likelihoods and consequences are determined are divided into two categories of analysis: quantitative and qualitative. Quantitative analysis uses mathematical and/or statistical data to derive numerical descriptions of risk. Qualitative analysis uses defined terms (words) to describe and categorize the likelihood and consequences of risk. Quantitative analysis gives a specific data point (e.g., dollars, probability, frequency, or number of injuries/fatalities), while qualitative analysis allows each qualifier to represent a range of possibilities. It is often cost and time prohibitive, and often not necessary, to find the exact quantitative measures for the likelihood and consequence factors of risk. Qualitative measures, however, are much easier to determine and require less time, money and, most important, expertise to conduct.

For this reason, it is often the preferred measure of choice. The following section provides a general explanation of how these two types of measurements apply to the likelihood and consequence components of risk.

Quantitative Representation of Likelihood

As previously stated, likelihood can be derived as either a frequency or a probability. A quantitative system of measurement exists for each. For frequency, this number indicates the number of times a hazard is expected to result in an actual event over a chosen time frame: 4 times per year, 1 time per decade, 10 times a month, and so on. Probability measures the same data, but the outcome is expressed as a measure between 0 and 1, or as a percentage between 0% and 100%, representing the chance of occurrence. For example, a 50-year flood has a 1/50 chance of occurring in any given year, or a probability of 2% or 0.02. An event that is expected to occur two times in the next 3 years has a 0.66 probability each year, or a 66% chance of occurrence.

Qualitative Representation of Likelihood

Likelihood can also be expressed using qualitative measurement, using words to describe the chance of occurrence. Each word or phrase has a designated range of possibilities attached to it. For instance, events could be described as follows:

- *Certain*: >99% chance of occurring in a given year (1 or more occurrences per year)
- *Likely*: 50–99% chance of occurring in a given year (1 occurrence every 1–2 years)
- *Possible*: 5–49% chance of occurring in a given year (1 occurrence every 2–20 years)
- *Unlikely*: 2–5% chance of occurring in a given year (1 occurrence every 20–50 years)
- *Rare*: 1–2% chance of occurring in a given year (1 occurrence every 50–100 years)
- *Extremely rare*: <1% chance of occurring in a given year (1 occurrence every 100 or more years)

Note that this is just one of a limitless range of qualitative terms and values that can be used to describe the likelihood component of risk. As long as all hazards are compared using the same range of qualitative values, the actual determination of likelihood ranges attached to each term does not necessarily matter (see Exhibit 3–1).

Consequence

The consequence component of risk describes the effects of the risk on humans, built structures, and the environment. There are generally three factors examined when determining the consequences of a disaster:

1. Deaths/fatalities (human)
2. Injuries (human)
3. Damages (cost, reported in currency, generally U.S. dollars for international comparison)

Although attempts have been made to convert all three factors into monetary amounts to derive a single number to quantify the consequences of a disaster, doing so can be controversial (How can one place a value on life?) and complex (Is a young life worth more than an old life? By how much?).

EXHIBIT 3–1: QUALITATIVE MEASUREMENTS: THE CONSIDERATION OF RISK PERCEPTION AND STANDARDIZATION

In brief, different people fear different hazards, for many different reasons. These differences in perception can be based upon experience with previous instances of disasters, specific characteristics of the hazard, or many other combinations of reasons. Even the word *risk* has different meanings to different people, ranging from "danger" to "adventure."

Members of assembled disaster management teams are likely to be from different parts of the country or the world, and all have different perceptions of risk (regardless of whether they are able to recognize these differences). Such differences can be subtle, but they make a major difference in the risk analysis process.

Quantitative methods of assessing risk use exact measurements and are therefore not very susceptible to the effects of risk perception. A 50% likelihood of occurrence is the same to everyone, regardless of their convictions. Unfortunately, there rarely exists sufficient information to make definitive calculations of a hazard's likelihood and consequence.

The exact numeric form of measurement achieved through quantitative measurements is incomparable. The value of qualitative assessments, however, lies in their ability to accommodate for an absence of exact figures and in their ease of use.

Unfortunately, risk perception causes different people to view the terms used in qualitative systems of measurement differently. For this reason, qualitative assessments of risk must be based upon quantitative ranges of possibilities or clear definitions. For example, imagine a qualitative system for measuring the consequences of earthquakes in a particular city, in terms of lives lost and people injured. Now imagine that the disaster management team's options are "None," "Minor," "Moderate," "Major," or "Catastrophic." One person on the team could consider 10 lives lost as minor. However, another team member considers the same number of fatalities as catastrophic. It depends on the perception of risk that each has developed over time.

This confusion is significantly alleviated when detailed definitions are used to determine the assignation of consequence measurements for each hazard. Imagine the same scenario, using the following qualitative system of measurement (adapted from EMA, 2000):

1. *None.* No injuries or fatalities
2. *Minor.* Small number of injuries but no fatalities; first aid treatment required
3. *Moderate.* Medical treatment needed but no fatalities; some hospitalization
4. *Major.* Extensive injuries; significant hospitalization; fatalities
5. *Catastrophic.* Large number of severe injuries; extended and large numbers requiring hospitalization; significant fatalities

This system of qualitative measurement, with defined terms, makes it more likely that people of different backgrounds or beliefs would choose the same characterization for the same magnitude of event. Were this system to include ranges of values, such as "1–20 fatalities" for "Major," and "over 20 fatalities" for "Catastrophic," the confusion could be alleviated even more.

Therefore, it is often most appropriate and convenient to maintain a distinction between these three factors.

Categories of consequence can be further divided, and often are to better understand the total sum of all disaster consequences. Two of the most common distinctions are direct and indirect losses, and tangible and intangible losses.

Direct losses, as described by Keith Smith in his book *Environmental Hazards,* are "those first order consequences which occur immediately after an event, such as the deaths and damage caused by the throwing down of buildings in an earthquake" (Smith, 1992). Examples of direct losses are:

- Fatalities
- Injuries (the prediction of injuries is often more valuable than the prediction of fatalities, because the injured will require a commitment of medical and other resources for treatment [UNDP, 1994])
- Cost of repair or replacement of damaged or destroyed public and private structures (buildings, schools, bridges, roads, etc.)
- Relocation costs/temporary housing
- Loss of business inventory/agriculture
- Loss of income/rental costs
- Community response costs
- Cleanup costs

Indirect losses (also as described by Smith, 1992) may emerge much later and may be much less easy to attribute directly to the event. Examples of indirect losses include:

- Loss of income
- Input/output losses of businesses
- Reductions in business/personal spending ("ripple effects")
- Loss of institutional knowledge
- Mental illness
- Bereavement

Tangible losses are those for which a dollar value can be assigned. Generally, only tangible losses are included in the estimation of future events and the reporting of past events. Examples of tangible losses include:

- Cost of building repair/replacement
- Response costs
- Loss of inventory
- Loss of income

Intangible losses are those that cannot be expressed in universally accepted financial terms. This is the primary reason that human fatalities and human injuries are assessed as a separate category from the cost measurement of consequence in disaster management. These losses are almost never included in damage assessments or predictions. Examples of intangible losses include:

- Cultural losses
- Stress
- Mental illness
- Sentimental value
- Environmental losses (aesthetic value)

Although it is extremely rare for benefits to be included in the assessment of past disasters or the prediction of future ones, it is undeniable that they can exist in the aftermath of disaster events. Like losses, gains can be categorized as direct or indirect, tangible or intangible. Examples of tangible, intangible, direct, and indirect gains include:

- Decreases in future hazard risk by preventing rebuilding in hazard-prone areas
- New technologies used in reconstruction that result in an increase in quality of services
- Removal of old/unused/hazardous buildings
- Jobs created in reconstruction
- Greater public recognition of hazard risk
- Local/state/federal funds for reconstruction or mitigation
- Environmental benefits (e.g., fertile soil from a volcano)

As with the likelihood component of risk, the consequences of risk can be described according to quantitative or qualitative reporting methods. Quantitative representations of consequence vary according to deaths/fatalities, injuries, and damages:

- *Deaths/fatalities.* The specific number of people who perished in a past event or who would be expected to perish in a future event; for example, *55 people killed.*
- *Injuries.* The specific number of people who were injured in a past event or who would be expected to become injured in a future event. Can be expressed just as injuries, or divided into mild and serious; for example, *530 people injured, 56 seriously.*
- *Damages.* The assessed monetary amount of actual damages incurred in a past event or the expected amount of damages expected to occur in a future event. Occasionally, this number includes insured losses as well; for example, *$2 billion in damages, $980 million in insured losses.*

Qualitative Representation of Consequence

As with the qualitative representation of likelihood, words or phrases can be used to describe the effects of a past disaster or the anticipated effects of a future one. These measurements can be assigned to deaths, injuries, or costs (the qualitative measurements of fatalities and injuries often are combined). The following list is one example of a qualitative measurement system for injuries and deaths:

- *Insignificant.* No injuries or fatalities
- *Minor.* Small number of injuries but no fatalities; first aid treatment required

- *Moderate.* Medical treatment needed but no fatalities; some hospitalization
- *Major.* Extensive injuries; significant hospitalization; fatalities
- *Catastrophic.* Large number of fatalities and severe injuries requiring hospitalization

Additional measures of consequence are possible, depending on the depth of analysis. These additional measures tend to require a great amount of resources, and are often not reported or cannot be derived from historical information. Examples include:

- *Emergency operations.* Can be measured as a ratio of responders to victims, examining the number of people who will be able to participate in disaster response (can include both official and unofficial responders) as a ratio of the number of people who will require assistance. This ratio will differ significantly depending on the hazard. For example, following a single tornado touchdown, there are usually many more responders than victims, but following a hurricane, there are almost always many more victims than responders. This measure could include the first responders from the community as well as the responders from the surrounding communities with which mutual aid agreements have been made. Emergency operations also can measure the mobilization costs and investment in preparedness capabilities. It can be difficult to measure the stress and overwork of the first responders and their inability to carry out regular operations (fire suppression, regular police work, regular medical work).

- *Social disruption* (people made homeless/displaced). This can be a difficult measure because, unlike injuries or fatalities, people do not always report their status to municipal authorities (injuries and deaths are reported by the hospitals), and baseline figures do not always exist. It is also difficult to measure how many of those who are injured or displaced have alternative options for shelter or care. Measuring damage to community morale, social contacts and cohesion, and psychological distress can be very difficult, if not impossible.

- *Disruption to economy.* This can be measured in terms of the number of working days lost or the volume of production lost. The value of lost production is relatively easy to measure, while the lost opportunities, lost competitiveness, and damage to reputation can be much more difficult.

- *Environmental impact.* This can be measured in terms of the clean-up costs and the costs to repair and rehabilitate damaged areas. It is harder to measure in terms of the loss of aesthetics and public enjoyment, the consequences of a poorer environment, newly introduced health risks, and the risk of future disasters.

It does not matter what system is used for qualitative analysis, but the same qualitative analysis system must be used for all hazards analyzed in order to compare risks. It may be necessary for disaster managers to create a qualitative system of measurement tailored to the country or community where they are working. Not all countries or communities are the same, and a small impact in one could be catastrophic to another, so the measurement system should accommodate these differences. For example, a town of 500 people would be severely affected by a disaster that caused 10 deaths, while a city of 5 million may experience that number of deaths just from car accidents in a given week.

Another benefit of creating an individualized system of qualitative analysis is the incorporation of the alternative measures of consequence (ratio of responders to victims, people made homeless/displaced).

Trends

Both the likelihood and the consequences of certain hazard risks can change considerably over time. Some hazards occur more or less frequently because of worldwide changes in climate patterns, while others change in frequency because of measures taken to prevent them or human movements into their path. These trends can be incremental or extreme and can occur suddenly or over centuries. Several short-term trends may even be part of a larger, long-term change.

Changes in Disaster Frequency

Changes in disaster frequency can be the result of both an increase in actual occurrences of a hazard and an increase in human activity where the hazard already exists. It is important to remember that a disaster is not the occurrence of a hazard, but the consequences of a hazard occurring. A tornado hitting an open field, for example, is not considered a disaster.

Changes in climate patterns, plate tectonics, or other natural systems can cause changes in the frequency of particular natural hazards, regardless of whether the causes of the changes are natural (El Niño) or man-made (global warming). Changes in frequency for technological or intentional hazards can be the result of many factors, such as increased or decreased regulation of industry and increases in international instability (terrorism).

Increases or decreases in human activity also can cause changes in disaster frequency. As populations move, they inevitably place themselves closer or farther from the range of effects from certain hazards. For instance, if a community begins to develop industrial facilities within a floodplain that was previously unoccupied, or in an upstream watershed where the resultant runoff increases flood hazards downstream, it increases its risk to property from flooding.

Changes in Disaster Consequences

Similar to changes in disaster likelihoods, changes in consequences can be the result of changes in the attributes of the actual hazard or changes in human activity that place people and structures at either more or less risk.

Changes in the attributes of the hazard can occur as part of short- or long-term cycles, permanent changes in the natural processes if the hazard is natural, or changes in the nature of the technologies or tactics in the case of technological and intentional hazards. The consequences of natural hazards change only rarely independent of human activities. One example is El Niño events, with intense flooding increasing in some regions of the world and drought affecting others, possibly for years. Technological and intentional hazards, however, change in terms of the severity of their consequences all the time. The high numbers of deaths and the structural damage associated with the bombings of the U.S. embassies in Kenya and Tanzania and the September 11 attacks on the World Trade Center and the Pentagon together display an increase in the consequences of terrorist attacks aimed at Americans. A mutation of a certain viral or bacterial organism, resulting in a more deadly pathogen, can cause a drastic increase in consequences, as occurred with HIV, the West Nile virus, mad cow disease, and SARS.

Changes in human activities are probably the most significant cause of increases in the consequences of disasters. These trends, unfortunately, are predominantly increasing. While the effects of disasters worldwide are great, their consequences are the most devastating in developing countries. Smith (1992) lists six reasons for these changes:

1. *Population growth.* As populations rise, the number of people at risk increases. Population growth can be regional or local, if caused by movements of populations. As urban populations grow, population density increases, exposing more people to hazards than would have been affected previously.
2. *Land pressure.* Many industrial practices cause ecological degradation, which in turn can lead to an increase in the severity of hazards. Filling in wetlands can cause more severe floods. Lack of available land can lead people to develop areas that are susceptible to, for example, landslides, avalanches, floods, and erosion, or that are closer to industrial facilities.
3. *Economic growth.* As more buildings, technology, infrastructure components, and other structures are built, a community's vulnerability to hazards increases. More developed communities with valuable real estate have much more economic risk than communities in which little development has taken place.
4. *Technological innovation.* Societies are becoming more dependent on technology. These systems, however, are susceptible to the effects of natural, technological, and intentional hazards. Technology ranges from communications (the Internet, cell phones, cable lines, satellites) to transportation (larger planes, faster trains, larger ships, roads with greater capacity, raised highways) to utilities (nuclear power plants, large hydroelectric dams) to any number of other facilities and systems (high-rise buildings, life support systems).
5. *Social expectations.* With increases in technology and the advancement of science, people's expectations for public services, including availability of water, easy long-distance transportation, constant electrical energy, and so forth, also increase. When these systems do not function, the economic and social impacts can be immense.
6. *Growing interdependence.* Individuals, communities, and nations are increasing their interdependence on each other. The SARS epidemic showed how a pathogen could quickly impact dozens of countries on opposite sides of the world through international travel. In the late 1990s, the collapse of many Asian economies sent ripple effects throughout all the world's economies. The September 11 terrorist attacks in the United States caused the global tourism market to slump.

Disaster managers must investigate the validity of the trends they identify. It is common for a trend to exist that is based on incomplete records. The technology used to detect many hazards has improved, allowing for detection where it formerly was much more difficult or impossible. Therefore, the lack of recorded instances of certain disasters could possibly be based on a lack of detection methods.

Computing Likelihood and Consequence Values

Because there is rarely sufficient information to determine the exact statistical likelihood of a disaster occurring or to determine the exact number of lives and property that would be lost should a disaster occur, using a combination of quantitative and qualitative measurements can be useful. By combining these two methods, the hazards risk management team can achieve a standardized measurement of risk that accommodates less precise measurements of both risk components (likelihood and consequence) in determining the comparative risk between hazards.

The process of determining the likelihood and consequence of each hazard begins with both quantitative and qualitative data and converts it all into a qualitative system of measurement that accommodates all possibilities that hazards present (from the rarest to the most common and from the least damaging to the most destructive).

Depth of Analysis

The depth of analysis undertaken by disaster managers depends on three factors: the amount of time and money available, the risk's seriousness, and the risk's complexity. According to the information they gather during the identification and characterization of the hazards, disaster managers must decide what level of effort and resources each individual hazard requires.

Each hazard analyzed can be considered according to the range of possible intensities it could exhibit. Depending on its characteristics, the hazard may be broken down according to intensity, with a separate analysis performed for each possible intensity. The likelihood and consequences for each category of intensity will be different, which in turn results in different treatment (mitigation) options (see Exhibit 3–2).

For instance, the general hazard of "earthquake" could be divided into events of magnitude 4, 5, 6, or 7, and so on. Generally, the lower the intensity of an event, the greater the likelihood of that event occurring, while its consequences tend to decrease. Several thousand earthquakes of very low intensity and magnitude occur daily with few or no consequences at all. However, the rarer large earthquakes must be treated differently because of their potential to inflict massive casualties and damages.

The degree of subdivision of hazards into specific intensities also depends upon the available time and resources. More divisions will give disaster managers a more comprehensive assessment, but a point will come when the added time and resources spent no longer provide enough added value.

In summary, effective qualitative risk analysis is performed using four steps:

1. Calculate the (quantitative) likelihood of each identified hazard (broken down by magnitude or intensity if appropriate).
2. Calculate the (quantitative) consequences that are expected to occur for each hazard (broken down by magnitude or intensity if appropriate), in terms of human impacts and economic/financial impacts.

EXHIBIT 3–2: f:N CURVES

f:N curves, which plot historical hazard intensities and likelihoods against the amount of damage inflicted, can provide an estimation of both the likelihood of events of specific magnitude and the consequences should those events occur. Examples of worldwide hazard f:N curves are shown in Figure 3–1.

Individual communities would plot f:N curves for their locality using local historical data. This graphical representation illustrates the justification for dividing hazards according to possible intensities.

3. Develop a locally tailored qualitative system for measuring the likelihood and consequence of each hazard identified as threatening the community.
4. Translate all quantitative data into qualitative measures for each hazard's likelihood and consequence.

Disaster managers begin their hazard analysis by calculating (to the best of their ability and resources) the quantitative likelihoods and consequences of each identified hazard risk. It does not matter whether the likelihood or the consequence is analyzed first, or if they are done concurrently, as neither depends upon the other for information. It is important, however, that the quantitative analyses are completed before the qualitative ones, as the qualitative rankings will be based upon the findings of the quantitative analyses.

The following section describes the methods by which the hazards risk management team can perform the quantitative analyses of hazard risks.

Quantitative Analysis of Disaster Likelihood

Quantitative analysis of the likelihood component of risk seeks to find the statistical probability of the occurrence of a hazard causing a disaster. These analyses tend to be based upon historical data gathered in the process of describing identified hazard risks (often called a risk statement). The disaster managers performing a quantitative analysis of disaster likelihood must first establish a standard numerical measurement by which the results of all analyzed hazards will be reported (see Figure 3–1).

One of the most common quantitative measures of likelihood, and the measure that will be used in this example, is the number of times a particular hazard causes a disaster per year. For example, "In country X, it is predicted that there will be three major snowstorms per year." (For major events that occur less frequently, like a major flood, this number may be less than 1. A 20-year flood has a 5% chance of occurring in any given year, or would be expected to occur 0.05 times per year.) The hazard can now be analyzed according to the chosen standard. If the hazard is one that has been divided into individual intensities and magnitudes, a separate figure will be required for each magnitude or intensity.

If records have been maintained for disasters that occur regularly, such as flash floods or snowstorms, it will be fairly easy to calculate the number of occurrences that would be expected to happen in a coming year or years. More often than not, however, sufficient information does not exist to accurately quantify the likelihood of a disaster's future occurrence to a high degree of confidence. This is especially true for hazards that occur infrequently and/or with no apparent pattern of behavior, such as earthquakes, terrorism, or nuclear accidents. This inability to achieve precision is a fundamental reason that qualitative measures are used in the final determination of a hazard's likelihood.

Rare and extremely rare hazards, such as terrorist attacks, nuclear accidents, or airplane crashes (outside of communities where airports exist) may have few if any data points to base an analysis upon. However, this does not mean that there is a 0% probability of the disaster occurring, even if there has been no previous occurrence. For these incidences, consulting with a subject matter expert (SME) is necessary to determine the likelihood of a disaster resulting from the hazard over the course of a given year and to gather any information on the existence of a rising or falling trend for that particular hazard. Organizations, professional associations, and other bodies, such as the United Nations (UN), national governments, and research facilities, maintain risk data on particular rare hazards. Modeling techniques also can be used to estimate the likelihood of infrequent events.

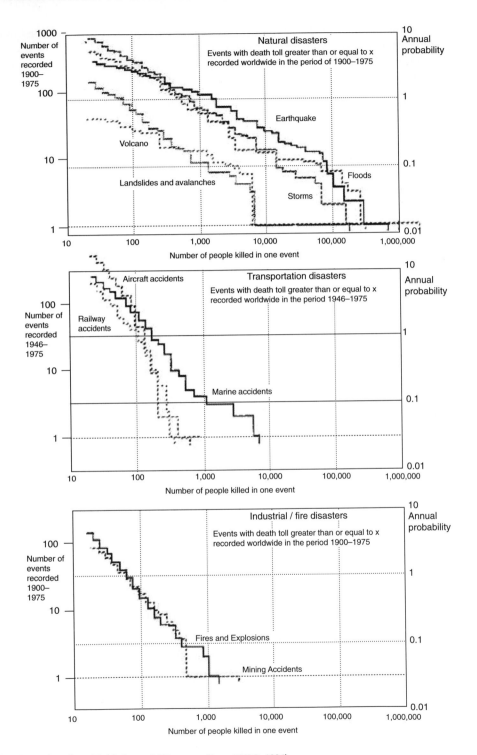

FIGURE 3–1 Examples of worldwide hazard f:N curves. (From UNDP, 1994)

The more often that a disaster occurs, the more data points those performing the quantitative likelihood assessment will have, and the more accurate the historical analysis will be (given that the collected data is accurate). However, more information must be examined than simply the number of events per year.

The concept of increasing and decreasing trends in hazard likelihoods and consequences was previously introduced. Both infrequently and frequently occurring disasters tend to exhibit either falling or rising trends over time, rather than having a steady rate of occurrence. These rising and falling trends must be accounted for if there is to be any accuracy attained in an analysis of likelihood.

For example, if a community has sustained approximately 35 wildfires per year for the past 40 years, it might easily be assumed that it is very likely there will be approximately 35 wildfires per year in the coming years. However, further inspection of historical records discovers that 40 years ago, there was one fire, and 39 years ago, there were three fires. The number of fires steadily increased until the historical record ended with 70 fires occurring in the past year. Over the 40-year period, the average number of wildfires is in fact 35 per year. However, the rate of wildfires has increased each year from 1 per year 40 years ago to 70 per year last year. Considering this trend, the expected number of wildfires next year cannot be expected to be 35, although the average per year is 35.

It must be assumed from these data that there is a rising trend in the occurrence of wildfires, and that there is likely to be 70 or more fires in the coming year. Why this rising trend is occurring and what can be done to counteract it will need to be examined in the process of determining vulnerability and generating mitigation and preparedness options.

Quantitative Analysis of Disaster Consequences

The quantitative analysis of disaster consequences seeks to determine the number of injuries, the number of deaths, the cost of direct damages to property and infrastructure, and the indirect costs associated with the disaster. (Depending on the scope of the analysis, other factors such as homelessness or displacement may be considered as well.) A standard form of measurement must be established for deaths, injuries, and damages. It is most useful if the measurement is per occurrence, as opposed to per year or other time frame.

It will be necessary to analyze the expected consequences of each magnitude or intensity of a hazard if it has been broken down into subcategories.

Historical Data

As with the likelihood component of risk, the calculation of hazard consequences should begin by examining the historical data on injuries, fatalities, and property/infrastructure damage and destruction that was gathered during the identification of hazards. However, as previously described, human behavior and/or changes in hazard characteristics often result in either increasing or decreasing trends in disaster consequences over time. Changes in settlement or new development, for example, can significantly increase community vulnerability for two different occurrences of a hazard.

Historical information does have its uses, however, especially with more common hazards for which data has been collected methodically and accurately for many years. Consequence data based upon historical information can act either as a benchmark to validate the findings of more in-depth analyses (described in the following section) or as the actual estimation of consequences, should disaster managers decide to perform a lower level of analysis.

In the section addressing vulnerability, we will explain the process of describing the community and the environment. In this process, information is gathered on the physical community, the built environment, and the social environment, as well as on the critical infrastructure and the interdependence of the community on surrounding and other external communities.

Using hazard maps created or obtained during the process of hazard identification, combined with the description of the community environment, disaster managers can develop numerical figures for the expected number of lives that will be lost, people who will be injured, and the dollar amount of the direct and indirect damages that may occur. (However, it is always important to keep in mind that even the most extensive analyses of consequences are imperfect, as they are heavily based upon assumptions and historical data that may or may not indicate future behavior of hazards.)

Consequence analyses must look not only at the location of structures in relation to the hazard but also at the vulnerability of each structure. For instance, imagine that a school is located in a floodplain. Disaster managers have obtained information indicating that the school has been raised to an elevation where it will only be affected by floods of magnitude greater than the 50-year (2% chance/year) flood. Using this information, disaster managers can deduce that such a structure will likely sustain no damage during the course of a 20-year (5% chance/year) flood event.

While disaster managers will likely not have the value of all structures within the community or be able to determine complete data pertaining to lost revenue and inventory, such data deficiencies probably will be consistent across all hazard consequence analyses and will probably not cause unreliable results; more data generally result in more accurate assessments. However, the amount of data that can be collected will always be a factor of available time and resources. Moreover, the process of translating the quantitative data resulting from these analyses into the qualitative determination of likelihood and consequence can be tailored to accommodate for almost any lack of accuracy.

Deaths/Fatalities and Injuries

Disaster managers can estimate the number of people who will be hurt or killed by using two methods: estimation based upon historical data and changes in population or modeling techniques.

To estimate the numbers of deaths and injuries using historical data, disaster managers must first assemble the data on historical incidences of disasters caused by the particular hazard. Then, using current data on the community, a conversion to current conditions can be made. For example, imagine that a Category IV hurricane struck a community in 1955, causing 4 deaths and 35 injuries. The population of the community at the time was approximately 10,000. Today, the population is estimated to be 15,000, increasing by a factor of 1.5. By multiplying the historical consequence data by this conversion factor, disaster managers could surmise that there would be approximately 6 deaths and 52 injuries if a Category IV hurricane struck today.

It must be kept in mind that these estimates do not account for mitigation measures taken or new development in the period between disasters. The more recently a comparable disaster has occurred, the more accurate the conversion will be. The use of modern modeling techniques, such as HAZUS-MH (Hazards United States Multi Hazard), a nationally standardized, GIS-based risk assessment, and loss estimation tool developed by the Federal Emergency Management Agency (FEMA), can increase the accuracy of injury and death estimations.

Modeling Techniques

Various computer-modeling techniques are available to assist disaster managers in estimating the injuries and deaths that would occur should a disaster strike. For instance, HAZUS-MH can be used to estimate the numbers of injuries and fatalities that would result from earthquakes of varying magnitudes, strong winds associated with cyclonic storms, and floods. There are many other models that give estimates for other hazards including tsunamis, storm surges, chemical releases, and explosions.

The data collected on base maps and the hazard-specific maps created during the hazard identification and description process also can be used to estimate the population affected by the hazard.

Regardless of the method used, a high degree of accuracy is very difficult to attain when estimating the numbers of injuries and deaths that would occur in future disasters. Many confounding variables affect human behavior and the ability to react to hazard events, including warning times and warning accuracies, the nature of the hazard, and the numbers, resources, and abilities of the emergency responders. These estimations should always be taken to be just that—estimations. The experience of the disaster management team and of other community experts such as first responders and the medical community can be just as valuable in making these estimates.

Abbreviated Damage Consequence Analysis

If disaster managers choose to perform a lower level of analysis on the consequences of the community's hazards, two pieces of information are needed. The first is the historical incidence of hazard damage for each disaster. The second piece of information is data on the population/structural changes in the community since the date of each historical disaster in order to compare to present-day data. Once that data are assembled, the team can calculate damages as they would be expected to affect the community as a comparison between the dates. For instance, imagine that a flood (of a specific magnitude) in 1955 caused $1 million in damages in a community. The community is found to have grown approximately 50% *in the floodplain* in the intervening years. Using this information, the hazards risk management team can estimate the consequences of a future event of similar magnitude to be approximately $1.5 million in 1955 dollars, or $11,884,047 in 2009 dollars. Currency inflation converters are widely available on the Internet: see www.westegg.com/inflation/.

If a certain hazard has not affected the community over a significantly extended period of time, or if it has never affected the community, the team may want either to use data from an example of the hazard affecting a community of comparable structure and size or to avoid performing a quantitative analysis for the rare hazard.

Full Damage Consequence Analysis

A full damage consequence analysis requires that disaster managers consider the current estimated cost of all physical assets within the country. These include:

- *Losses to structures.* Estimated as a percentage of the total replacement value. This figure is obtained by multiplying the replacement value of the structure by the expected percent damage to the structure.

- *Losses to contents.* Estimated as a percentage of the total replacement value. This figure is obtained by multiplying the replacement value of the contents by the expected percent damage.

- *Losses to structure use and function and cost of displacement.* The losses to structure use are a function of the number of days the structure is expected to be out of use multiplied by the average daily operating budget or sales (annual revenue or budget divided by 365 days). The cost of displacement is the product of the costs incurred as result of the business/service being displaced and the number of days that displacement is necessary. These calculations can apply to businesses, bridges, utilities, public services (libraries), and any other community asset.

To track calculated figures, a standardized worksheet is often created. One example of a standardized worksheet provided by FEMA is shown in Figure 3–2.

Each hazard will affect structures and their contents differently. Many organizations and institutions have made available tables to determine this information for specific hazards. To perform a full damage consequence analysis, disaster managers will need to have the following information (which is often gathered during the process of describing the community and environment and determining the vulnerability of the community):

- Replacement value of all community assets (homes, businesses, and infrastructure).
- Replacement value of inventory (business inventory, personal property in homes, contents of government offices and other buildings).
- Operating budgets/annual revenues of businesses and government assets.
- Costs of relocation of operations/services.

Once quantitative figures have been calculated for both the likelihood and consequence components of risk, the disaster managers can begin the process of determining the qualitative values assigned to the likelihood and consequence for each hazard (and hazard intensity or magnitude, if the hazard is subdivided into such). They should begin by selecting a system of qualitative measurement or by designing one that suits the needs of both the format of results in the quantitative analysis and the characteristics of the particular country or community.

A disaster, as defined in Chapter 1, is "a serious disruption of the functioning of society, causing widespread human, material, or environmental losses which exceed the ability of the affected society to cope using only its own resources" (UNDP, 1994). Therefore, a specific set of hazard consequences may constitute a disaster in one community but not in another. For instance, 10 injuries may exceed the capacity of the local clinic in a community of 500, but in a large city, 10 injuries could be easily managed.

Whether designing a new system of measurement or using an existing one, it is necessary for the disaster management team to be aware of the local capacity to know how many deaths and injuries and how much damage can be sustained before the local capacity is either stressed or exceeded. They will have the data collected in the hazard identification process and in the description of the community and the environment upon which to base their new or acquired system of measurement.

Creating two measures of consequence can be beneficial: one measuring the tangible physical/material losses associated with cost and another measuring the intangible losses of deaths/fatalities and injuries. Each qualitative term should have two measures associated with it, corresponding to deaths/injuries and costs. In many instances, the tangible and intangible rankings will not be the same. For instance, there may be no physical damages to structures in a chemical spill, but many people may be injured or die. Other events may cause no immediate deaths or injuries, but cause a great amount of physical loss, such as a large-scale power outage. In either case, the factor that achieves the qualitative

Date: _____   *How will these hazards affect you?*

Hazard _____

Structure Loss					Contents Loss				
Name/ Description of Structure	Structure Replacement Value ($)	x	Percent Damage (%)	=	Loss to Structure ($)	Replacement Value of Contents ($)	x	Percent Damage (%)	=	Loss to Contents ($)
		x		=			x		=	
		x		=			x		=	
		x		=			x		=	
		x		=			x		=	
		x		=			x		=	
		x		=			x		=	
		x		=			x		=	
		x		=			x		=	
Total Loss to Structure						**Total Loss to Contents**				

Structure Use and Function Loss									Structure Loss + Content Loss + Function Loss ($)
Name/ Description of Structure	Average Daily Operating Budget ($)	x	Functional Downtime (# of days)	+	Displacement Cost per Day ($)	x	Displacement Time ($)	=	Structure Use & Function Loss ($)	
		x		+		x		=		
		x		I		x		=		
		x		+		x		=		
		x		+		x		=		
		x		+		x		=		
		x		+		x		=		
		x		+		x		=		
		x		+		x		=		
Total Loss to Structure Use & Function										
										Total Loss for Hazard Event

FIGURE 3–2 FEMA standardized loss estimation worksheet. (From FEMA, 2001)

Table 3–1   An Example of a Qualitative Likelihood Measurement System

Descriptor	Description
Almost certain	Is expected to occur in most circumstances; and/or high level of recorded incidents and/or strong anecdotal evidence; and/or a strong likelihood the event will recur; and/or great opportunity, reason, or means to occur; may occur once every year or more
Likely	Will probably occur in most circumstances; and/or regular recorded incidents and strong anecdotal evidence; and/or considerable opportunity, reason, or means to occur; may occur once every 5 years
Possible	Might occur at some time; and/or few, infrequent, random recorded incidents or little anecdotal evidence; and/or very few incidents in associated or comparable organizations, facilities, or communities; and/or some opportunity, reason, or means to occur; may occur once every 20 years
Unlikely	Is not expected to occur; and/or no recorded incidents or anecdotal evidence; and/or no recent incidents in associated organizations, facilities, or communities; and/or little opportunity, reason, or means to occur; may occur once every 100 years
Rare	May occur only in exceptional circumstances; may occur once every 500 or more years

Source: EMA (2000).

measure of greater (higher) consequence is used to determine the consequence of the hazard. Tables 3–1 and 3–2 are examples of qualitative measures of likelihood and consequence.

Once a measurement system has been chosen, the disaster managers can assess each hazard according to its qualitative likelihood and consequences, using the quantitative data obtained in the previous steps of the hazard analysis process. These qualitative rankings are then recorded and assessed according to a risk assessment matrix (described next).

When assessing the qualitative ranking for a hazard consequence, two different types of consequences are usually examined: human impacts (injuries and deaths/fatalities) and material/physical losses. In determining the qualitative consequence ranking, the hazards risk management team will choose whichever ranking is greater. (Differences between the severity of human and material losses often exist. A poisonous gas leak is a good example of a hazard where few material or physical damages are likely, but many deaths and injuries could occur. In that case, the hazards risk management team would probably base their assessment on the human consequences of the hazard rather than the material/physical consequences.)

Risk Evaluation

Risk evaluation is conducted to determine the relative seriousness of hazard risks for the country or community being assessed by the disaster manager. Using the processes listed earlier and in Chapter 2 to identify hazards that threaten the community, characterize them, and determine their likelihoods and consequences, the disaster managers will have gathered the information necessary to carry out the risk evaluation.

By the time the risk evaluation process begins, each hazard will have been identified, described, mapped, and analyzed according to its likelihood of occurrence and its consequences should a disaster occur. All countries and communities undoubtedly face a range of natural, technological, and intentional hazards, each of which requires a different degree of mitigation and risk reduction.

Table 3–2   An Example of a Qualitative Consequence Measurement System

Descriptor	Human Life and Health	Property, Financial, Environmental
Insignificant	No injuries or fatalities	Inconsequential or no damage
	Small number or no people are displaced and only for a short duration	Little or no disruption to community
		No measurable impact on environment
	Little or no personal support required	Little or no financial loss
Minor	Small number of injuries but no fatalities; first aid treatment required some displacement of people (<24 hours)	Some damage
		Small impact on environment with no lasting effects
	Some personal support required	Some financial loses
	Some disruption (<24 hours)	
Moderate	Medical treatment required but no fatalities; some hospitalization	Localized damage that is rectified by routine arrangements; normal community functioning with some inconvenience
	Localized displacement of people who return within 24 hours	Some impact on environment with long-term effect
		Significant financial loss
Major	Fatalities	Significant damage that requires external resources; community only partially functioning; some services unavailable
	Extensive injuries, significant hospitalization	
	Large number displaced (>24 hours' duration)	
	External resources required for personal support	Some impact on environment with long-term effects
		Significant financial loss; some financial assistance required
Catastrophic	Significant fatalities	Extensive damage
	Large number of severe injuries	Extensive personal support
	Extended duration and large numbers requiring hospitalization	Community unable to function without significant support
	General and widespread displacement for extended duration	Significant impact on environment and/or permanent damage

Source: Cameron (2002).

Unfortunately, communities are rarely able to dedicate sufficient resources to mitigation to lower all of the community's risks to the lowest possible levels.

As will be shown in Chapters 4 and 5, there are hazards for which the technology exists for mitigation but are cost prohibitive. An example of a risk mitigation measure that is very expensive is the conversion (retrofit) at wastewater treatment plants to less dangerous chemicals, such as using liquid chlorine bleach or other disinfection technologies instead of the more volatile chlorine gas. Exhibit 3–3 illustrates the danger posed by chlorine gas, which is still widely used despite its known dangers.

Other risks may have many options available, each with an associated cost and benefit. Some have direct risk reductions with each incremental increase in cost. A classic example is the practice of increasing the number of firefighters or police officers in a community, which, until reaching a threshold, results in decreased fire hazard risk and decreased crime risk.

Fortunately, however, not all risks require immediate action, and some no action at all. These include those risks for which both the likelihood and the consequences of the risk are extremely low, such as a small meteor strike. While some risks can be reduced easily, others may require

---

EXHIBIT 3–3: DESCRIPTION OF THE DANGERS OF USING CHLORINE GAS TO PURIFY WATER

Chlorine is often used as a disinfectant in most of the world's water systems because of its cost-effectiveness. The chemical is usually stored in a pressurized, liquid state. When released, chlorine vaporizes into a highly toxic, invisible gas that concentrates at ground levels. Germany used chlorine gas during World War I for this reason, because it would settle into the trenches where British troops were hiding.

It has been estimated that anyone located within 2 or 3 miles from a ruptured 90-ton chlorine railcar would be killed if directly exposed to the ensuing cloud. Injuries, including fluid in the lungs and a permanently reduced breathing capacity, could result at distances as great as 10 miles.

Because of the increasing risk of terrorism and other criminal attacks on storage facilities, the [U.S.] Environmental Protection Agency has distributed guidelines that encourage U.S. chemical industry businesses to employ safer technologies. One such facility, the Washington, D.C.–based Blue Plains wastewater treatment plant, heeded this advice and fully converted from the use of chlorine-gas disinfectant to the safer liquid chlorine bleach. The plant's close proximity to the nation's capital placed it at high perceived risk of terrorist attack, but only as long as the highly volatile chlorine gas was stored on the site. In switching to liquid chlorine bleach, the threat has essentially been eliminated.

Many other drinking and wastewater treatment plants have also switched to safer technologies. In addition to liquid chlorine bleach, ultraviolet light and ozone may be used to purify the water.

Source: Davis (2002).

---

exorbitant cash resources, time, and a committed effort to achieve even slight reductions. These possibly limiting factors must also be considered by disaster managers.

In addition to actual reductions in risk related to the likelihood and consequences of a hazard, several risk factors must be considered that weigh heavily on the perceived "seriousness" of the risk and therefore affect mitigation priorities. For instance, a man-made risk is likely to be considered much less "acceptable" than one that is natural in origin. The degree to which these man-made risks are perceived to be unacceptable can be an important determining factor in assigning mitigation funding. Smith (1992) discusses voluntary and involuntary risks and states, "[T]here is a major difference between voluntary and involuntary risk perception with the public being willing to accept voluntary risks approximately 1000 times greater than involuntary risks."

Risk perception issues also weigh heavily upon such decisions. For instance, consider a rural community in which one person dies per year as result of cave-ins of abandoned mine shafts and approximately four people per year are drowned in a river that regularly experiences swift currents following storms. There is likely to be considerable public outcry over the yearly incidence of fatal accidents from the abandoned mines, while the river drowning is viewed as a controllable, easily reduced, voluntary, preventable, observable hazard whose effects are known to those exposed (risk perception concepts are described in greater detail later in the Section entitled "Vulnerability").

There are also risks that societies are able to eliminate altogether but choose not to because the benefits that result from such risks would also disappear (see Exhibit 3–4). This essentially implies

---

EXHIBIT 3–4: ACCEPTABILITY OF RISK

Almost everything that provides a benefit also creates some level of risk for either the benefactor(s) or others who do not necessarily enjoy those benefits. This risk ranges from barely measurable to severe. The side effects of certain prescription drugs, negative health effects from "fast food," or skin cancer from the sun are a few examples at the personal level. On a larger scale, more specifically related to disaster management, is the inundation danger associated with the construction of a power-generating dam. As a society, citizens have come to accept most of these risks without question, although many present much greater risks than some people are willing to accept.

For instance, tens of thousands of people are killed and over tens of millions suffer disabling injuries each year from falls while using stairs in their homes and elsewhere (Roderick, 1998). It is unlikely that stairways will be eliminated, despite the fact that they injure and kill many more people than hazards like saccharin, fluoroscopes (shoe-fitting X-ray machines), and extra-long tandem trailer trucks, for instance. Why are people willing to accept one risk and not another? The answer can be found in the perceived benefits of each risk. People perceive that the benefit of having multiple stories in a house or other building is worth the risk of injury or death from using stairways. Society does not perceive the risk of injury, illness, or death resulting from saccharin, fluoroscopes, or tandem trucks to be worth the benefits gained from each (low-calorie sweetener, an X-ray look at your foot inside a shoe, and the truck's greater carrying capacity), even though each of these three examples poses less of an absolute population risk than stairways.

---

that, when evaluating risks, disaster managers must also consider the negative consequences of mitigation or elimination. Eliminating certain beneficial risks results in adverse effects on the community or society. Examples of situations where the benefits are believed to outweigh the risks include the aesthetic value to homeowners and collected property taxes for the community from beachfront property construction; collected taxes and created jobs for a community that result from the existence of a factory that produces, stores on-site, or emits hazardous materials; and the reduced reliance on fossil fuels and cheaper power generation costs that exists as result of a nuclear power plant.

One of the primary goals of disaster managers is to formulate a prioritized list of hazard risks to be mitigated. This list should be based upon a combination of factors that includes the hazard's likelihood and consequences, the county's or community's priorities and criteria (regarding their views on the acceptability of different risks), the benefit-to-cost ratios of mitigating different risks, and the political and social ramifications of certain mitigation decisions.

Hazards were examined individually in each previous step of this process. During the risk evaluation step of the process, risks are compared to each other and questions of priority begin to be answered. Prioritization can take place by many methods, and while there is no single correct method, there are many that have been used with success in the past.

The following may be used to determine the prioritization of risk treatment:

1. Creating a risk matrix
2. Comparing hazard risks against levels of risk estimated during the analysis process with previously established risk evaluation criteria
3. Evaluating risks according to the SMAUG methodology (seriousness, manageability, acceptability, urgency, growth)

The final output of risk evaluation should be a prioritized list of risks, which will be used to decide treatment (mitigation) options.

Hazard analysis determines qualitative values describing the likelihood and consequence of each hazard. For those hazards known to exhibit a range of magnitudes or intensities, the likelihood and consequence values were determined for several magnitudes or intensities across the range of possibilities.

Assigning these qualitative values is the first step in a process that allows for a direct comparison of the risks faced by a community. Armed with both the likelihood and consequence values, disaster managers can now begin comparing and ranking the identified risks.

To compare hazards according to their likelihood and consequences, the team must select or create a risk matrix to suit the needs of the country or community. A risk matrix is a direct comparison of the two components of a hazard's risks. In other words, it plots the likelihood and consequence of hazards together in various combinations, with one risk component falling on the x axis and the other on the y axis.

While it does not matter which of these two risk components goes on which axis, the values used must exactly match the values used in the risk analysis qualitative assessments. Because the terminology must be consistent throughout the process of "calculating" risk from likelihood and consequence, much as if quantitative (numerical) values were being used. For instance, if the possible range of values for the likelihood of a risk included the values "Certain," "Likely," "Possible," "Unlikely," "Rare," and "Extremely Rare," then the risk matrix must include all of those values (on the appropriate axis) in logical consecutive order.

Plotting these values on the matrix results in individual boxes representing unique combinations of likelihood and consequence. The likelihood and consequence values upon which the individual boxes are based can be determined by tracing from that box back to the values indicated on each axis. The number of possible combinations will be the product of the number of likelihood values times the number of consequence values (i.e., if there are 5 values for likelihood and 6 for consequence, the matrix will have 30 possible combinations required to evaluate risk).

Disaster managers must decide whether to use a preexisting risk matrix or to make a custom risk matrix that suits their specific needs. If they choose to create their own systems of qualitative measurement in the risk analysis process, they must make their own risk matrix. However, even if they used an existing set of qualitative measurements in the risk analysis process, a risk matrix to evaluate each risk may not exist, in which case they would need to make one.

To create a risk matrix, disaster managers must first establish levels, or "classes," of risk representing increasing severity. The levels should range from those that are so low that mitigation is not necessarily needed to risks that are so high that efforts to mitigate them are of highest priority.

One example of such a system is described in the FEMA's "MultiHazard Identification and Risk Assessment" publication (1997). Their risk matrix values are:

1. *Class A*. High-risk condition with highest priority for mitigation and contingency planning (immediate action)
2. *Class B*. Moderate to high-risk condition with risk addressed by mitigation and contingency planning (prompt action)
3. *Class C*. Risk condition sufficiently high to give consideration for further mitigation and planning (planned action)
4. *Class D*. Low-risk condition with additional mitigation contingency planning (advisory in nature)

Emergency Management Australia (EMA, 2000) described risks according to the following breakdowns:

1. Extreme risk
2. High risk
3. Moderate risk
4. Low risk

Other systems include "Intolerable, Undesirable, Tolerable, Negligible," "Severe, High, Major, Significant, Moderate, Low," and "Trivial."

Once these values have been determined and defined as they apply to the disaster manager's priorities, they should be assigned to each combination of likelihood and consequence shown on the matrix. How they are assigned must be determined by personal judgment, expert knowledge, and previously established risk management criteria. An example of a risk matrix from FEMA is shown in Figure 3–3.

Class A. High-risk condition with highest priority for mitigation and contingency planning (immediate action)

Class B. Moderate to high-risk condition with risk addressed by mitigation and contingency planning (prompt action)

Class C. Risk condition sufficiently high to give consideration for further mitigation and planning (planned action)

Class D. Low-risk condition with additional mitigation contingency planning (advisory in nature)

Once the values have been assigned to each box on the matrix, each hazard can be evaluated accordingly and the derived values recorded. Because each "risk level" will likely be assigned to more than one matrix box, and because several risks could elicit the same combination of likelihood and risk, the hazards risk management team will not be creating an ordered list of risk priorities, but rather

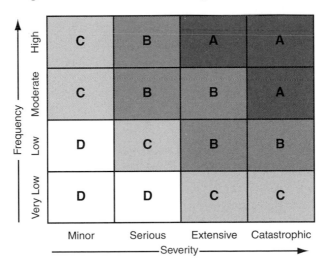

FIGURE 3–3 FEMA "MultiHazard Identification and Risk Assessment" risk matrix.

several categories of risk with several hazards falling within each category group. In other words, the disaster manager will have several "classes" of risks, each containing several risks for which no intra-class priorities have been determined. For instance, if a 50-year flood was determined to be a Class C risk, and an accident involving a truck carrying hazardous materials was determined to be a Class C risk, they would be considered equal risks according to the risk matrix. The results of the risk matrix allow disaster managers to further classify the hazards threatening their country or community but do not provide a definitive list of priorities for mitigation. Such a list requires further evaluation, as will be described.

It is helpful for disaster managers to begin recording the results of their evaluations on a concise form that allows fast and easy reference to risk evaluation output data so these data can be more easily compared in the prioritization step. Risk registers, as they are called, provide a useful tool, and should include the following information:

- Name of the risk (including specific magnitude and/or intensity if the risk has been broken down into these categories)
- Qualitative likelihood value
- Qualitative consequences value
- Level of risk as determined by evaluation on the risk matrix
- Priority rating
- Additional information, including any of the following:
  - Description of possible consequences
  - Adequacy of existing mitigation measures or controls
  - Known mitigation options and alternatives
  - Acceptability of risk

Because people have different risk perceptions, and because there may be more risks than there are resources to mitigate them, disaster managers must develop risk evaluation criteria before any risk identification or analysis takes place. Risk evaluation criteria help disaster managers and citizens make judgments about what they consider to be the most serious risks and set forth performance measures to judge progress in mitigating the community's risks.

In establishing these contextual criteria, disaster managers will also define the political, social, economic, legal, and physical environment within which all of the hazards can occur. Some of criteria include:

- Population issues
  - Death and injuries
  - Displacement
  - Loss of homes and property
  - Loss of jobs and income
  - Loss of sense of security
  - Loss of sense of community
- Business sector issues
  - Damage to facilities

- Loss of income
- Business disruption costs
- Insurance losses
- Loss of market share
- Loss of trained employees
- Bankruptcy
- Community issues
  - Damage or destruction of community infrastructure (i.e., roads, bridges, hospitals, jails, city halls, community service centers, etc.)
  - Loss of tax revenues
  - Disaster response and recovery costs
  - Reduced funding for other community priorities (i.e., education, social services, etc.)
  - Loss of population base
  - Increased community debt and borrowing
  - Economic repercussions
  - Environmental harm
  - Loss of culture/heritage

Disaster managers would also define their analysis as it relates to mitigating the country's or community's hazards. This could include several or all of the following:

- Legal requirements
- Cost and equity
- Risks that are clearly unacceptable
- Risks that should be kept as low as reasonably practicable

Additionally, risks that have been evaluated according to the risk matrix will need to be verified for accuracy. It is possible that a risk may have been placed in a category that defines it as either too great or not great enough—only further analysis can correct such errors.

The Purpose of Evaluating Risk

Gaye Cameron of the University of New South Wales (2002) wrote, "The purpose of evaluating risks is to determine that risk levels resulting from the risk analysis step [including the results of the risk matrix] reflect the relative seriousness of each risk." She mentions three tasks that are important to perform at this point in the hazards risk management process:

1. Identify which risks require referral to other agencies (i.e., is the risk one that is better mitigated by another local, regional, or national agency rather than one that needs to be considered for mitigation options by the disaster managers?).
2. Identify which risks require treatment by the disaster managers.
3. Further evaluate risks using judgment based upon available data and anecdotal evidence to determine the accuracy of the final risk value recorded.

A risk that might be better mitigated by another local, regional, or national agency is hazardous material exposure and other accidents that might occur at or from an extrajurisdictional utility (like a nuclear power plant) adjacent to a second country or community. Hazards created in one jurisdiction but whose consequences affect another have caused many cantankerous debates throughout history. These types of cross-jurisdictional problems are most severe on rivers and streams. Pollution content, increased flooding potential, and even decreased quantities of water can all occur in one jurisdiction but be caused by the actions of another. An illustrative example is changes in a river's hydrology brought about by the construction of man-made levees (water-retention walls built along the banks of rivers that allow for higher water levels before flooding occurs). Dams and levees are river structures that often cause these problems. They can cause flooding both upstream from rising water levels in reservoirs behind the dam and downstream from forced release or failure of the dam.

Cameron (2002) wrote that there are two overarching issues that need to be addressed in the risk evaluation process. First, risk levels must be confirmed. Through a process of stakeholder consultation, these levels are reviewed to ensure:

1. They reflect the relative seriousness of each risk.
2. The likelihood and consequence descriptions utilized for risk analysis are appropriate.
3. Local issues have been considered.

Cameron adds, "If, following stakeholder consultation, the risk level is considered inappropriate the risk should be subjected to further analysis using new information or data."

Second, risk acceptability must be addressed:

In almost all circumstances risk acceptability and treatment will be determined and/or carried out by the agency or agencies responsible for managing the treatment of risks. For those risks where no agency is responsible, the [disaster managers] will prepare treatment options for the management of the identified risks. (Cameron, 2002)

For each risk, the levels of risk acceptability (by both the public and the disaster managers) must be determined for the level of mitigation effort required to be determined. Risk acceptability will be discussed in greater detail in the Section entitled "Risk Perception."

Once the risk levels of each hazard have been compared to the previously established risk evaluation criteria, the risks must be prioritized, or ranked in the order that the disaster managers feel they should be addressed.

This prioritization can be accomplished in many ways, most of which rely upon the information gathered in the previous steps of the process and build upon the results of the risk matrix. Risk prioritization takes the evaluation of a country or community's hazards beyond merely comparing risks as factors of likelihood and consequence, and uses the expert judgment of the hazards risk management team to add experience, knowledge, and contextual influence to the final determination of mitigation priority.

In risk prioritization disaster managers must consider the degree of control over each risk and the cost, benefits, and opportunities presented by each risk, and decide which risks are unacceptable at any cost.

One such method for the evaluation of risk, the so-called SMAUG approach, designed by Benjamin Tregoe and Charles Kepner, has gained wide acceptance by emergency managers in Australia and New Zealand.

According to this methodology, disaster managers consider five individual factors in determining how a list of risks can be generated that reflects the established priorities of the community. This list includes (each factor is accompanied by the upper and lower extremes by which each risk could be evaluated):

1. **Seriousness**
   a. The risk will affect many people and/or will cost a lot of money (see Exhibit 3–5).
   b. The risk will affect few or no people or will cost little or nothing.
2. **Manageability**
   a. The risk could be affected by intervention.
   b. The risk cannot be affected by intervention.
3. **Acceptability**
   a. The risk is not acceptable in terms of political, social, or economic impact.
   b. The risk will have little political, social, or economic impact.
4. **Urgency**
   a. The risk urgently needs to be fixed.
   b. The risk could be fixed at a later time with little or no repercussions.
5. **Growth**
   a. The risk will increase quickly.
   b. The risk will remain static (Lunn, 2003).

Using the SMAUG criteria for evaluation, disaster managers can more precisely determine priorities for mitigating individual risks, beyond the characterizations that resulted from the risk matrix. After the risk matrix evaluation, risks were grouped into categories of seriousness. Now they can be assigned a numerical order defining specific priorities.

It is important to note that the list of priorities will likely change as the risk mitigation options are considered. Risk evaluation has given the hazards risk management team a better idea of those risks for which mitigation must be conducted at all costs, due to their absolute unacceptability. However, for risks with similar mitigation priority rankings, the factors of cost-effectiveness of mitigation, technological availability of mitigation options, and other risk treatment factors will require revisiting this priority list and re-ranking risks using additional information.

Risk Acceptability

In performing hazard risk assessments and analyses of risk, disaster managers must make decisions about what risks to treat, what risks to prevent at all costs, and what risks can be disregarded because of low consequence, low frequency, or both. These decisions are based upon the acceptability of risk.

Unfortunately, no disaster manager will ever have complete information about all risks faced by the country or community regarding the number of people and the area affected, the actual frequency of the hazard in the future, and the actual benefit to be attained through mitigation, among many other factors. If the disaster manager did have all of this information, determining risk acceptability and making mitigation decisions would be simple. However, in the absence of this perfect information, judgments must be made about the severity of risk for each hazard, and whether the community is willing to accept that risk in light of the known information.

EXHIBIT 3–5: CONSIDERING EXTREME EVENTS

Rae Zimmerman and Vicki Bier, in their Chapter "Risk Assessment of Extreme Events," shed some light on the extra considerations that must be made when prioritizing hazard lists that include extreme event hazards that are man-made and intentional, such as terrorism.

They write, "Predicting human behavior in emergency situations is already difficult. However, in attempting to estimate and manage the risks of intentional attacks, further difficulties become apparent. First, as pointed out by Woo (1992), some idea of event likelihood is needed for intelligent benefit-cost analysis. "However, estimating the likelihood and nature of intentional attacks is an area with which most risk assessors are not yet familiar, although there has been some related work on this problem in other fields. For example, Dickey (1980) interviewed bank robbers to understand the criteria that they used in choosing banks to rob; he found that they preferred banks located near major highways and banks with a single point in the lobby from which they could see all of the employees at once. Similarly, Crowe (2000) and de Becker (1997) report that criminals choose targets based not only on the attractiveness of the target but also on the likelihood that they would be discovered and apprehended. Interviews with incarcerated terrorists could presumably be used to explore the criteria they use in selecting targets, which could be factored into quantitative risk assessments."

"More significantly, protection against a knowledgeable and adaptable adversary is a fundamentally different challenge than protection against accidents or acts of nature. For example, earthquakes do not get stronger or smarter just because we defend our buildings against them. However, if adversaries know or can easily learn about their target's defensive measures, then they can actively choose to either bypass or circumvent those defenses. Progress in and increased reliance upon detection technologies has made this more important to take into account. For example, metal-screening devices prior to September 11th increased the security and safety of air travel. A network news report early in 2002 suggested that the box cutters used by the terrorists on September 11th to gain control of the hijacked airplanes fell just below the detection settings of such screening devices."

"As noted by Dresher (1961), optimal allocation of defensive resources requires that 'each of the defended targets yield the same payoff to the attacker.' Thus, even if some components can be shored up quite inexpensively, focusing protective investments there can lead to wasted resources if adversaries choose to attack targets that cannot be shored up cost-effectively. In other words, critical assets must be defended against all possible attacks, which is much more difficult than just shoring up a few 'weak links.' As a result, Ravid (2001) concludes that security improvements are generally more costly than safety improvements: '[I]nvestment in defensive measures, unlike investment in safety measures, saves a lower number of lives (or other sort of damages) than the apparent direct contribution to those measures.'"

Source: Zimmerman and Bier (2002).

Because disaster managers do not work in a vacuum, many factors—political, social, or economic—influence the collective determination of what risks are acceptable and what risks are not. The mechanisms by which they can begin to determine such categorization are explained next.

The disaster managers have thus far identified the risks affecting the country or community, analyzed them individually, and evaluated them collectively. They are now left with an ordered list of risks that they must consider for treatment. Ideally, they would treat all risks such that nobody would have to worry about them ever again, but that risk-free-world scenario is inconceivable despite modern technology and engineering. While most risks can be reduced by some amount, few can be completely eliminated, and rarely if ever do the funds exist to reduce all risks by an amount acceptable to everyone in the community. There will never be complete satisfaction with the ultimate decisions made by disaster managers, mostly because of differences in perception.

Two factors confounding the acceptability of risks are the benefits associated with certain risks, and the creation of new risks by eliminating existing ones. For instance, to completely eliminate the risk from nuclear power generation plants, they would need to be dismantled and taken out of service. The resulting shortage of power would require that fossil-fuel-burning plants increase their production, which in turn would create increased carbon-based pollution, which would likewise create increased health and environmental risks.

Alternatives

Derby and Keeney (1981), two risk management experts, wrote:

> *The key aspect of acceptable risk problems is that the solution is found by a decision among alternatives. The generic problem involves choosing the best combination of advantages and disadvantages from among several alternatives. The risk associated with the best alternative is safe enough.*

This is an important distinction—that risks deemed "acceptable" are not necessarily those with risk levels for which we are "happy." They continued:

> *We all would prefer less risk to more risk if all other consequences were held fixed. However, this is never the case. In a situation with no alternatives, then the level of safety associated with the only course of action is by definition acceptable, no matter how disagreeable the situation. Said another way, acceptable risk is the risk associated with the best of available alternatives, not with the best of the alternatives which we would hope to have available.*

There are several factors that together influence the determination of risk acceptability. They include personal, political/social, and economic reasons. Although the three are interrelated, different processes drive them. These processes are described next.

Personal

The personal factors that dictate whether a risk would be considered "acceptable" mirror the risk perception characteristics described in the following section. For example, a risk whose consequences are "dreaded," such as the radiation sickness that could result from a meltdown at a nuclear power plant, is likely to be found less acceptable to individual members of the public than the long-term effects of increased solar radiation (such as skin cancer), which may be caused by a decrease in the ozone layer from increased automobile emissions.

The United Nations Development Programme (UNDP) training program in Vulnerability and Risk Assessment (UNDP, 1994) described the differences in individual acceptance between risks that are voluntary and involuntary:

> Some risks are entered into voluntarily and a distinction is sometimes made between voluntary and involuntary risks. Many recreational activities and sports involve considerable levels of personal risk entered into voluntarily. Indeed the thrill of the risk is part of the enjoyment of the recreation. The benefits of the risk outweigh the costs and so the perception of the risk is reduced; i.e., the threat level that is deemed acceptable is much higher than a risk that is imposed from outside or involuntary.

Other factors that have been shown to affect public acceptance of risk include personal values, gender, ethnicity, education level, and the treatment of the risk by the media.

Political/Social

The political/social acceptability of risk is the product of either democratic processes or other collective mechanisms of determination. In other words, political and social influences are representations of many personal determinations of acceptability. While it is almost certain that not every individual citizen will be happy with the final decisions made concerning a risk's acceptability and treatment, the choice made will reflect the feelings of the majority if those choice are influenced by political and social acceptability.

Because of the differences in the makeup of different communities and populations, risk acceptance will not be universal. It is likely to change from place to place, from time to time, and from hazard to hazard (Alesch, 2001). Acceptability is likely to change even within individual communities over time as the makeup of that community changes. It is these differences that make public participation in the disaster management process important.

Economic

Because countries or communities can rarely support the level of funding required to mitigate all risks, the risk acceptability decision must be influenced by how much each mitigation alternative would cost and what other possible risk mitigation measures would be offset through funding of a specific mitigation effort.

In general, disaster managers will have to address the costs of reducing a risk in terms of the benefits (actual risk reduction) that would result. Some communities have chosen to simply live with a risk because the costs of mitigating its consequences are prohibitive, and eliminating the risk is unthinkable. For a simplified example, consider the use of the automobile, which highlights the cost-benefit scenario. At present, over a million road traffic fatalities occur throughout the world each year. This obviously presents a great risk. With increased cost, car manufacturers could easily make their cars much safer, and these fatality rates could be reduced significantly. However, such a cost would make automobiles too expensive for the average consumer. Thus, we accept the loss of over a million lives per year for the benefit of having affordable cars. Even if manufacturers spent the money to make cars completely "safe" for occupants, however, there would still be an inherent risk associated, as indicated by the great number of fatalities that are caused by pedestrians who are struck by cars (shown in Figure 3–4). The cost of totally eliminating this particular risk associated with automobiles is inconceivable.

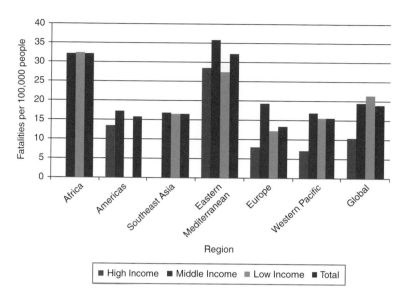

FIGURE 3–4 Worldwide road traffic fatalities. (From WHO, 2009)

W. Kip Viscusi, in the Chapter "Economic Foundations of the Current Regulatory Reform Efforts" (1996), described how the economics of an acceptability decision can be influenced by the political and social aspects of that decision. To illustrate his point, he produced a list of risk-reducing regulations that fail a cost–benefit "test" (cost is greater than the benefit), and a list of risk-reducing regulations that pass a cost–benefit test (benefit is greater than the cost). His results are shown in Tables 3–3 and 3–4.

"Injustices" are commonly seen in the disaster management decision-making process, especially concerning the treatment and acceptability of hazard risks (MPPP, 1999). Following are three criticisms of the processes by which risk acceptability is determined:

1. *Those with money and vested interests can influence the process of determining the acceptability of risk.* Because the process of determining risk acceptability (including mitigation spending and regulatory practices) is influenced by politics and may be shaped by political ideology, it is possible for corporate or interest groups to lobby and influence those decisions. This can be seen with hazards such as handguns and assault rifles, environmental degradation, soil and water pollution, or construction in hazardous areas. Increased citizen participation in the process can decrease this type of injustice. By increasing the decision-making power of the general public, a more democratic outcome is possible (although not guaranteed).

2. *Setting a dollar figure (in cost–benefit analyses) on a human life is unethical and unconscionable.* This is primarily a factor related to involuntary risks. To the individuals whose lives are being placed at risk, any dollar figure will seem low or inappropriate as a trade-off for the acceptance of the risk. Many people would (understandably) feel that their life is too great a price to pay for the existence of any involuntary risk. The cognitive processes that dictate these "price of a human life" determinations are often different for voluntary risks. As the automobile safety example illustrates, people are willing to accept a certain increase in risk to their own lives for the benefit of more affordable products. How much more affordable differs by person. But, as

Table 3–3   The Cost of Risk-reducing Regulations That Fail a Benefit-Cost Test per Life Saved

Regulation	Initial Annual Risk	Annual Lives Saved	Cost Per Life Saved (millions of $)
Grain dust	2.1 in 10,000	4	5.3
Radionuclides/uranium mines	1.4 in 10,000	1.1	6.9
Benzene	8.8 in 10,000	3.8	17.10
Arsenic/glass plant	8.0 in 10,000	0.110	19.20
Ethylene oxide	4.4 in 100,000	2.8	25.60
Arsenic/copper smelter	9.0 in 10,000	0.060	26.50
Uranium mill tailings (inactive)	4.3 in 10,000	2.1	27.60
Uranium mill tailings (active)	4.3 in 10,000	2.1	53.00
Asbestos	6.7 in 100,000	74.7	89.30
Asbestos	2.9 in 100,000	10	104.20
Arsenic/glass manufacturing	3.8 in 100,000	0.25	142.00
Benzene/storage	6.0 in 10,000,000	0.043	202.00
Radionuclides/DOE facilities	4.3 in 1,000,000	0.001	210.00
Radionuclides/elemental phosphorous	1.4 in 100,000	0.046	270.00
Benzene/ethylbenzenol styrene	2.0 in 1,000,000	0.006	483.00
Arsenic/low-arsenic copper	2.6 in 10,000	0.09	764.00
Benzene/maleic anhydride	1.1 in 1,000,000	0.029	820.00
Land disposal	2.3 in 100,000,000	2.52	3500.00
EDB	2.5 in 10,000	0.002	15,600.00
Formaldehyde	6.8 in 10,000,000	0.010	72,000.00

Viscusi (1996) assumed that $2.8 million per life saved was an acceptable cost. Any cost greater than $2.8 million per life fails the cost–benefit test.
Source: Viscusi (1996).

shown by relatively recent lawsuits against tobacco companies by smokers who became ill, people may be unwilling to accept some voluntary risks despite previous knowledge about those risks. Because of the controversial nature of placing a value on life, it is rare that a risk assessment study would actually quote a dollar figure for the amount of money that could be saved per human life loss accepted. Post-event studies have calculated the dollar figures spent per life during a crisis, but to speculate on how much a company or government is willing to spend to *save or risk a life* would be extremely unpalatable for most.

3. *Risk management is usually an undemocratic process, as those who may be harmed are not identified or asked if the danger is acceptable to them.* It is not difficult to recall a case in which a vulnerable or disadvantaged group of people was exposed to a risk whose benefits were enjoyed by others. Many toxic waste dumps are located in impoverished parts of towns, cities, and states, although the people in those communities had little say in deciding the location of such materials. Related to this injustice is the reality that the impoverished are usually less able to avoid such risks, as the property or jobs available to them are often associated with these very same risks. It is often the poor who must live in the highest risk areas of a floodplain, or under

Table 3–4   The Cost of Risk-reducing Regulations That Pass a Benefit–Cost Test per Life Saved

Regulation	Initial Annual Risk	Annual Lives Saved	Cost per Life Saved (millions of $)
Unvented space heaters	2.7 in 100,000	63	0.1
Oil and gas well service	1.1 in 1,000	50	0.1
Cabin fire protection	6.5 in 100,000,000	15	0.2
Passive restraints/belts	9.1 in 100,000	1850	0.3
Underground construction	1.6 in 1,000	8.1	0.3
Alcohol and drug control	1.8 in 1,000,000	4.2	0.2
Servicing wheel rims	1.4 in 100,000	2.3	0.2
Seat cushion flammability	1.6 in 10,000,000	37	0.6
Floor emergency lighting	2.2 in 100,000,000	5	0.7
Crane-suspended personnel platform	1.8 in 1,000	5	1.2
Concrete and masonry construction	1.4 in 100,000	6.5	1.4
Hazard communication	4 in 100,000	200	1.8
Benzene/fugitive emissions	2.1 in 100,000	0.310	2.8

Source: Viscusi (1996).

high-tension power lines, or along highways. These people bear a larger share of the population risk, while many others enjoy much lower risk levels from those particular hazards, even though they enjoy a disproportionate amount of the benefits. Thus, risk communication and public participation are important to counteract these injustices.

In determining the treatment of risks in a country or community, disaster managers must consider each hazard according to its current risk level and determine if the risk is too great to be left as is. If it is determined to be too great, they must analyze what can be done to reduce the risk, and then make another determination as to the acceptability of the new risk level.

Several methods for determining the acceptability of risks have been developed in the past, and are used to varying degrees (dependent upon the needs of those performing the risk evaluation). They include:

- *The "no go" alternative.* This alternative, which is not always available, is the complete elimination of the risk. Such action can be easier with technological hazards, especially those that are new. How easy depends on how dependent society has become on the technology in question. For example, when DDT was found to be bioaccumulating in birds and mammals and was feared to eventually lead to a "silent spring" (a silent spring, as described by Rachel Carson in her 1962 book of the same title, is what would result if DDT were used to the extent that all birds died as a result), the chemical was banned from use. There were alternatives to DDT, and while they may not have been as cost-efficient or -effective, they were not perceived as being as harmful. For some countries, the more expensive alternatives were acceptable, while in others DDT is still the preferred, cheap option.

     However, with hazards that have established a unique niche in society, such as the automobile, eliminating the risk is close to impossible. Eliminating risks is often only possible with the existence of viable alternatives. The possibility of eliminating the risk must always be considered in the assessment. (Because the option is to eliminate the *risk* and not the *hazard*, natural disasters can be considered for this option—if either the consequences or the frequency is lowered to zero, the risk becomes zero. However, this option is rarely possible given economic and technological constraints.) The emergence of hybrid cars that rely on a combination of gasoline and electric power is a sign of movement toward a viable alternative in terms of fossil-fuel dependence.

- *Accept the risk.* A second option is to simply accept the risk as it is—to do nothing. Certain risks may be so low that the money spent to reduce them would be better spent to treat a more severe hazard. In risk matrices, the risks that fall within the lowest category of both consequence and likelihood are generally the risks that are considered acceptable. After all other risks have been treated to the satisfaction of the hazards risk management team, the low risks can be revisited.

- *Establish a "de minimis risk" level.* De minimis risk dictates that a level of statistical risk for hazards exists, below which people need not concern themselves. This level is often set at either 1 in 100,000 or 1 in 1,000,000, and is set either for a 1-year period or for a lifetime (70 years). The term *de minimis* is a shortened version of the Latin phrase *de minimis non curat lex,* which means "the law does not care about very small matters." This concept is widely used throughout Europe to set guidelines for acceptable levels of risk exposure to the general population. An example of its use in the United States includes a regulation *de minimis* risk set by the Environmental Protection Agency (EPA) for human lifetime risk from pesticides of 1 in 1,000,000 over a 70-year lifetime (PMEP, 1997).

  De minimis does not seek to prohibit any risk above the levels set. The theory only states that, if a risk falls below that level, no resources need to be spent on its prevention. If a product poses less risk than the *de minimis* level, for example, then it should be authorized for production and/or distribution. However, if the risk associated with a product does not fall below the *de minimis* level, then risk managers need to assess if anything can be done to reduce its risk and if the costs outweigh the benefits, among many other issues.

  Proponents for *de minimis* feel that governments can avoid wasting their time trying to increase the safety of risks already satisfying *de minimis* requirements, thus freeing them up to spend their resources on other risks of greater concern. Opponents are concerned that some risks exist for which even a 1 in 1,000,000 risk would be too high (Mumpower, 1986). One of their contentions is that risks that affect huge populations would result in a high number of deaths even though the risk is so "low." The smallpox vaccine, for example, has a 1 in 1,000,000 risk of death. However, if the entire world population were to be vaccinated, approximately 6000 fatalities would occur. A third group feels that the *de minimis* strategy is effective only if there are two *de minimis* levels working in conjunction—one that measures absolute risk (e.g., 1 in 1,000,000), and another that sets the maximum number of allowable expected fatalities (e.g., X number of fatalities for country Y).

- *Establish a "de manifestis risk" level.* Related to *de minimis* risk is the concept of *de manifestis* risk, or "obnoxious risk." With *de manifestis* risk, there is a risk level above which mitigation is mandatory. In practice, this level is generally set at 1 in 10,000 per vulnerable individual. This practice is often cited regarding secondhand smoke exposure in the workplace (Ravid, 2001).

- *Perform cost–benefit analyses of risks.* Cost–benefit, or benefit-cost, analyses, are probably the most widely used and widely accepted method by which risks and alternatives are evaluated for acceptability. The Massachusetts Precautionary Principle Project (MPPP, 1999) wrote:

  [Cost–Benefit Analyses are] where the risks reduced by taking a protective action (like imposing a stricter regulation on emissions) are equated to benefits (such as a life saved or reduced health costs). The "benefit" is then compared to the estimated "costs" of implementing the protective action (cost to the industry to install better pollution controls). Often a determination is made as to how much "cost" it is worth to save that life, usually 2 million dollars.

  If the cost of controls greatly exceeds the cost of the life saved, regulatory actions may not be taken. Among other flaws, cost–benefit analysis fails to consider who reaps the benefits and who assumes the cost. It also perpetuates the myth that we must decide between economic growth and environmental protection. Cost–benefit analysis is also heavily biased toward costs of regulation today, discounting less quantifiable costs such as health damage and benefits of prevention. Cost–benefit analysis often overestimates the costs of regulation. It also tries to quantify the unquantifiable, or translate the noneconomic—pain and suffering, illness, and disease—into money. Many consider this unethical.

  Following the September 11 terrorist attacks, in which hijacked commercial airplanes were used as weapons, considerable effort went into (and continues to go into) securing airways around the world. As security measures increase, so does the cost of ensuring that security, and most of this cost is passed along to the consumer. Questions that require people to consider the financial cost of their own safety are often used to determine individual risk-seeking or risk-averse behavior.

  Related to cost–benefit decisions are cost-effectiveness decisions. In the case of cost-effectiveness decisions, the minimum "unit cost" to reduce maximum risk is favored in considering the alternatives for risk mitigation within and between risks.

- *Acceptable risk as the best choice among alternatives.* Derby and Keeney (1981) wrote that "The answer to 'How safe is safe enough?' depends upon [five steps]. ... Acceptable risk is determined by what alternatives are available, what objectives must be achieved, the possible consequences of the alternatives, and the values to be used." The five steps they are referring to are:

1. Define the alternatives.
2. Specify the objectives and measures of effectiveness to indicate the degree to which they are achieved.
3. Identify the possible consequences of each alternative.
4. Quantify the values for the various consequences.
5. Analyze the alternatives to select the best choice.

- Disaster managers will have already completed most of these steps by the time they are deciding which risks to treat. Derby and Keeney (1981) provided graphical illustrations of four factors that influence how risk alternatives are chosen and determined to be acceptable. These examples are shown in Figures 3–5 through 3–8.

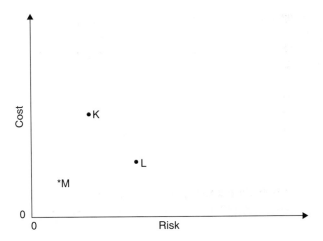

FIGURE 3–5 Risk acceptability Example A. (From Derby & Keeney, 1981)

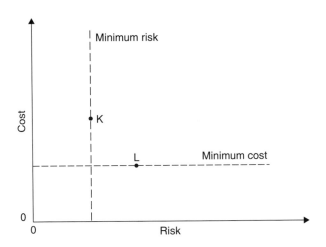

FIGURE 3–6 Risk acceptability Example B. (From Derby & Keeney, 1981)

In Example A, it is assumed that the benefits of all the alternatives are equal. The differences are only in their financial cost and the level of risk (with 0 being the optimal level for both cost and risk). If only alternatives K and L are available, then the choice is between high cost with low risk and low cost with high risk. The acceptable risk would be the level of risk associated with the particular alternative chosen, either K or L.

If another alternative, M, were introduced into the problem, then M with lower cost and lower risk would be preferred to either K or L. Consequently, acceptable risk is now the safety level of alternative M. This risk is different from the level associated with the other alternatives. Clearly, the appropriate level of risk depends on the alternatives available.

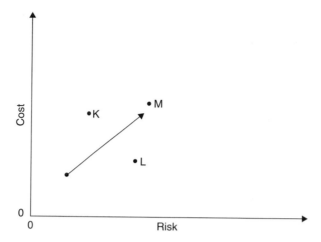

FIGURE 3–7 Risk acceptability Example C. (From Derby & Keeney, 1981)

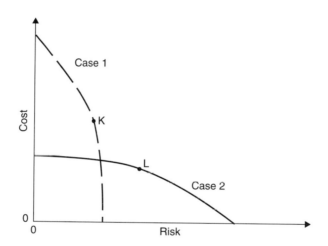

FIGURE 3–8 Risk acceptability Example D. (From Derby & Keeney, 1981)

Example B shows how acceptable risk changes with what objectives are achieved. In this example, only alternatives K and L are (known to be) available. If the sole objective is to minimize the risk, alternative K would be chosen. The acceptable risk would then be the risk level associated with K. However, if the sole objective is to minimize the cost, the alternative L would be chosen. Acceptable risk under this objective would be the risk level for L. Each objective leads to choosing different alternatives. In each case, the acceptable risk changes with the objective used to make the choice.

Example C shows how new information can change the determination of what is considered acceptable risk. In this example, we assume that alternative M determines the acceptable risk, as in Example A. However, additional information provided by experience, research, development, or analysis reveals that the initial assessment of alternative M must be revised. Instead of confirming that M has lower cost and lower risk than both alternatives K and L, the new information shows that M has both the high cost of K and the high risk of L. The acceptable risk is now determined by the choice between K and L.

Example D illustrates the effect of values and preferences on the choice between alternatives. In this example, different preferences for trading off increased cost for lower risk are represented by the two curves. In Case 1, the trade-off curve reflects the willingness to incur large costs to reduce risk by small amounts. Alternative K is the most attractive choice with this preference. In Case 2, the trade-off curve reflects less of a willingness to increase costs in exchange for specific reductions in risk. This preference selects alternative L as the best choice. Because acceptable risk is determined by the choice between the two alternatives, these different preferences change what is considered acceptable.

Vulnerability

The concept of vulnerability was first presented in Chapter 1 and defined as a measure of the propensity of an object, area, individual, group, community, country, or other entity to incur the consequences of a hazard. As this section illustrates, measurement of vulnerability results from a combination of physical, social, economic, and environmental factors or processes. These factors are the primary determinant features that dictate how the likelihood and/or consequences components of risk are increased or decreased.

It is important to first clarify the difference between the concepts of vulnerability and exposure, which are often confused. The two words are used interchangeably to describe how a country, region, or community is likely to experience a certain hazard. However, this is incorrect, as the discussion on vulnerability factors shows. The United Nation's risk reduction document *Living with Risk* embodies this concept, saying, "While most natural hazards may be inevitable, disasters are not" (ISDR, 2004).

While vulnerability defines the propensity to incur consequences, exposure merely suggests that the individual, structure, community, nation, or other subject will be *exposed* to the hazard. For instance, one might say, "The Spanish are vulnerable to drought," meaning that Spain regularly experiences the drought hazard. But this statement implies more than the speaker intended. The use of the word "vulnerable" implies that the population is likely to incur negative consequences as a result of factors that make it less likely to protect its citizens and built and natural environments from harm, not simply that drought happens there. The reality, as Figures 3–9 and 3–10 illustrate, is that while Spain is regularly exposed to drought, the nation is not vulnerable to its consequences.

Risk is composed of two components: likelihood and consequence. Exposure, or the measure of whether a person, building, population, or nation is likely to experience a hazard, looks only at likelihood. Vulnerability, however, is a factor of how small or great the consequences will be *should the hazard manifest*. Figures 3–9 and 3–10 illustrate that, although many different nations are exposed to drought, each experiences differing vulnerabilities. In light of this, it may be more accurate to say that the Spanish face a drought risk, because their exposure likelihood is greater than zero, and that because of measures the nation has taken to reduce drought consequences, it is no longer *vulnerable* to the hazard.

Vulnerability can be studied and measured. Likewise, it can be decreased through actions that lower the propensity to incur harm or increased through actions that increase that propensity—mitigation and preparedness. How these processes are conducted will be detailed below and in Chapters 4 and 7. As the definition in Chapter 1 states, two identical events may be presented as a minor issue in one country and a major disaster in another. Each country's vulnerabilities explain the difference. There are generally four different types of vulnerabilities: physical, social, economic, and environmental. Each is determined by a set profile of factors that are identifiable and measurable.

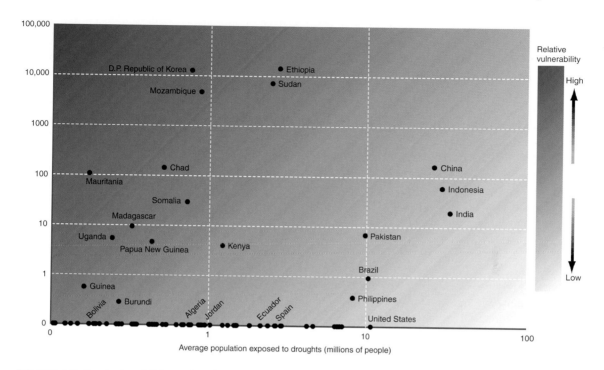

FIGURE 3–9 National vulnerabilities to drought risk as a factor of population exposure. (From the International Disaster Database, www.em-dat.net)

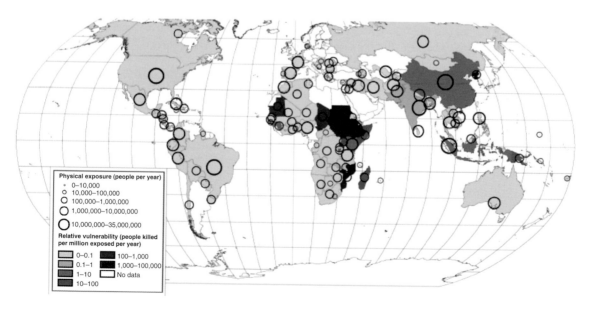

FIGURE 3–10 National vulnerabilities to drought risk as a factor of population exposure. (From the International Disaster Database, www.em-dat.net)

Physical vulnerability generally involves what in the built environment is physically at risk of being affected. The choices societies make about placing structures, transportation routes, and populations either in or out of harm's way effectively determine physical vulnerability. A majority of available mitigation measures are focused upon "hardening" these populations and structures to reduce their physical vulnerability to hazards. For instance, a building may be placed in a zone where a flood hazard is known, but raising the structure onto stilts reduces its physical vulnerability. People also are affected by physical vulnerability. As populations move into areas of high risk of disaster, their physical vulnerability increases.

Social vulnerability measures the individual, societal, political, and cultural factors that increase or decrease a population's propensity to incur harm or damage as a result of a specific hazard. Certain behaviors can contribute to or reduce that population's ability to protect itself from harm. Within populations may be groups, such as the elderly or the very young, who exhibit different vulnerability factors than the population as a whole.

Economic vulnerability refers to the financial means of individuals, towns, cities, communities, or whole countries to protect themselves from the effects of disasters. Within societies, there may be many economic delineations that further divide groups into economically vulnerable subgroups. As previously discussed, the poor are much more likely to suffer the consequences of disasters as they often do not have the financial means to avoid extreme hazards.

Environmental vulnerability refers to the health and welfare of the natural environment within the area of study that either contributes to or reduces the propensity of the affected population to incur the consequences of disasters. Poor environmental practices, such as deforestation, a lack of land-use planning, or management of hazardous materials, can turn what would have been minor events into major disasters.

Each of these vulnerability elements is interconnected. Economic vulnerability can lead to social vulnerability, which causes populations to build on dangerous land, causing environmental vulnerability and physical vulnerability. This is but one example, but it shows how each factor is equally important to consider when assessing the vulnerability of a country or community.

To better understand an area's vulnerability, disaster managers must attempt to develop a profile of the country's or community's physical, social, economic, and environmental profiles. These four factors will help them determine overall vulnerability, determining what consequences are likely to occur as result of each hazard and what mitigation and preparedness measures will be most effective at treating those hazard risks. Descriptions and samples of profile components are provided in the following section.

The Physical Profile

The physical profile of a country, which dictates its physical vulnerability, is generally considered to be a collective examination of three principal components: geography, infrastructure, and populations. The more known about each component, the better understood the physical vulnerability will be. Each component contributes to the hazards that are likely to occur and how those hazards' consequences will manifest themselves.

The geographic components of the physical profile include the natural makeup of the area of study. For instance, it is estimated that almost three billion people, or about half of the world's population, currently reside in what is classified as coastal territory. This includes all but two of the world's 15 largest cities (ISDR, 2004). The economic and industrial benefits provided by a seaside location prompted these populations to move into such zones, but by doing so, the residents increased their exposure to many different hazards, including severe windstorms, flooding, and tsunamis. As a result, they must now accommodate that exposure by taking risk-reduction measures, or else experience increased vulnerability to those hazards.

The following list provides several examples of what factors may be seen in a study of a country's geographic makeup:

- Land cover (vegetation)
- Soil type
- Topography
- Slope
- Aspect
- Water resources (lakes, rivers, streams, reservoirs, etc.)
- Wetlands and watersheds
- Faults
- Climate (wind, rainfall, temperature)

The infrastructure components of the physical profile primarily include the interaction between people and the land. This profile is diverse, and is often generalized for regions or segments (see Exhibit 3–6). Common components of the physical profile include those listed on pages 181 and 182.

EXHIBIT 3–6: SECTORING

Sectoring helps to further understand the ways in which a disaster would affect segments of a country or community. Not all areas of a community will be affected by an unforeseen event. Sectoring divides an area into manageable segments or portions based on local geography in relation to a specific hazard. It allows disaster managers to categorize parts of their study area in terms of response and impacts. It is used to identify local service areas in relationship to a hazard and physical features, and allows for the identification of especially vulnerable areas, evaluation of how an area could be or has been affected, and what can be done to respond to specific events.

Knowing the hazard and the potential of its impact in each sector allows for a more accurate identification of appropriate mitigation actions as well as warning and emergency response needs. Sectoring can also be used to organize and conduct emergency response needs within a sector or between adjacent sectors.

Sectors should be defined by easily identifiable boundaries that can be seen on the ground, such as bluffs, rivers, and major highways. These features often dictate who responds and how a response is managed. Things to think about in identifying sectors include:

- People
  - How many people in each sector
  - How many subdivisions in a sector
  - Where people work
  - Where people recreate

(Continued)

EXHIBIT 3–6: SECTORING (CONTINUED)

- - Where people live
  - Where people gather for civic events
  - Where the special needs populations are located
- Animals and livestock
  - Where animals are located
  - What types of animals are in a specific sector
- Housing and living quarters
  - How many housing units in the sector
  - What types of housing units are present
  - Whether all units are insured
- Critical facilities and response
  - Fire station locations
  - Ambulance locations
  - Hospital locations
  - Emergency first-response locations
  - Emergency coordination locations
  - What the responding zones are
- Special facilities and community resources
  - School locations
  - Nursing home locations
  - Health care service locations
  - Prison and jail locations
  - Important historical or cultural locations
- Infrastructure and lifelines
  - Utilities, including pipelines and power lines
  - Roads and bridges
  - Railroads and yards
  - Airports
  - Navigable waterways
  - Dikes, dams, and flood protection
- HAZMAT facilities/public health concerns
  - Leaking underground storage tank (LUST) sites
  - Municipal emergency services (MES) sites
  - Chemical storage sites
  - Hazardous materials locations
  - Funeral homes
  - Sites containing radioactive materials
- Commercial and industrial facilities
  - Commercial business areas defined
  - Industrial business areas defined
  - Agricultural business areas defined
  - Port facilities identified

- Land use
- Location and construction material of homes
- Location and construction material of businesses
- Zoning and building code delineations
- Critical infrastructure components
  - Hospitals and clinics
  - Schools
  - Senior citizen centers
  - Daycare/child care centers
  - Government and other public facilities
  - Prisons and jail facilities
  - Power generation facilities and transmission
  - Water purification facilities and pipes
  - Wastewater treatment and sewer lines
  - Gas lines
  - Oil and gas transport pipelines
  - Oil and gas storage facilities
- Transportation systems
  - Roads and highways
  - Railroads
  - Airports
  - Public transportation systems
- Waterways and port facilities
- Bridges
- Communication facilities
- Landfills
- Dikes and flood protection structures and facilities
- Nuclear power generation plants
- Dams
- Military installations
- Industrial sites that manufacture and/or store hazardous materials
- Emergency management systems
  - Ambulance services
  - Fire services
  - Law enforcement services
  - Emergency first response services

- Early warning systems
- Emergency operations centers
- Emergency equipment (fire trucks, ambulances, response vehicles, etc.)
- Hazardous materials (HAZMAT) equipment
- Weapons of mass destruction (WMD) detection teams
- Evacuation routes and shelters
- Historical and cultural buildings and areas

The population component of the physical profile looks at how people move throughout time. Disasters that occur at different times of the day often can have different consequences, and knowing where people are likely to be at certain times helps to determine vulnerability. At night, most people are likely to be in their homes, while during the weekday they will be at their jobs. For this reason, physical vulnerabilities vary throughout the day as population movements occur. Individual population factors may include:

- Population by jurisdiction (i.e., county, city)
- Population distribution within a county or city
- Population concentrations
- Animal populations
- Locations of major employers and financial centers
- Areas of high-density residential and commercial development
- Recreational areas and facilities

The Social Profile

The social makeup of a country plays a strong role in its vulnerability. Aspects of the social profile are diverse and comprise education, culture, government, social interaction, values, laws, beliefs, and other aspects of society. Within most countries, and even within individual communities, the vulnerability of different groups varies due to a range of sociocultural factors that help or prevent them from being able to protect themselves from disasters. The prevalence of epidemics, in particular, is heavily influenced by the social factors that vary from one country to another (see Figure 3–11).

Certain religious, cultural, or traditional practices and beliefs can help or hinder disaster management practices. Although it may not be evident to the people practicing such behavior, their practices may have been a product of adjustment to a hazard. In India, for instance, there is a group of people called the Banni who adapted to the use of a traditional style of single-story, round houses called *bhungas* after a particularly devastating earthquake in 1819. In 2001, when an earthquake struck in Gujarat, India, killing over 20,000 people (primarily as result of residential structure failure), not a single *bhunga* collapsed.

Disaster managers must be able to recognize when social interactions are either helping or hindering people in reducing their vulnerability to hazards, and must recognize what aspect of that social process is causing the alteration. People tend to be very attached to places and practices. An outsider recommending change without considering the original reasons for the social practices is unlikely to be taken seriously in that community. Additionally, changing certain social practices without regard for

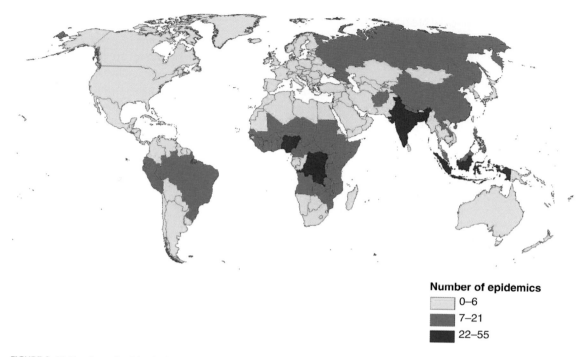

Number of epidemics

	0–6
	7–21
	22–55

FIGURE 3–11 Number of epidemics by country, 1974–2003. (From the International Disaster Database, www.em-dat.net)

their historical bases can actually increase vulnerability due to the common but unintended consequences resulting from a social reaction in response to the change.

Examples of factors that disaster managers must consider when scoping a social vulnerability include:

- Religion
- Age
- Gender
- Literacy
- Health
- Politics
- Security
- Human rights
- Government and governance (including social services)
- Social equality and equity
- Traditional values
- Customs
- Culture

The Environmental (Natural) Profile

The natural environment of a country or community plays a critical role in defining its hazard vulnerability (see Figure 3–12). It also helps to define what risk management practices and actions are possible and most effective. For instance, a mountainous country whose government does not or is not able to restrict clearcutting on unstable slopes is likely to have increased vulnerability to landslides, whereas a country that does not manage the filling in of wetlands may show an increase in flood propensity. Environments are also vulnerable to the consequences of hazards, and may increase the likelihood that a hazard event develops into a disaster.

The health and vitality of the natural environment of a country or community are critical when measuring its vulnerability to each specific hazard. A healthy and productive natural environment provides excellent protection from a variety of hazards, while a damaged and unhealthy natural environment can reduce protection from specific hazards and, in some cases, increase the hazard's potential impact. Healthy and productive wetlands provide invaluable flood protection by soaking up excess rainwater. Healthy forests are less vulnerable to catastrophic wildfires and reduce landslide dangers on slopes. Dunes on coastlines provide buffers from storm surges caused by hurricanes and severe storms. Figure 3–13, developed by the UN as part of the International Strategy for Disaster Reduction (ISDR), illustrates this process of risk augmentation through environmental degradation.

Understanding the direct link between a healthy and productive natural environment and a country's vulnerability to specific hazards is critical to developing an effective risk management strategy. Conducting an inventory of the features of the country's natural environment is an important step. Measuring the health of the country's natural environment is vital in understanding the role that the natural environment can play in protecting a community and reducing the impacts from hazard events (see Figure 3–14). Features of a community's natural environment include, but are not limited to,

- Health of waterways (rivers, streams, creeks, etc.)
- Status of wetlands
- Management of lakes
- Management of forests
- Health of coastal dunes
- Health of coral reefs

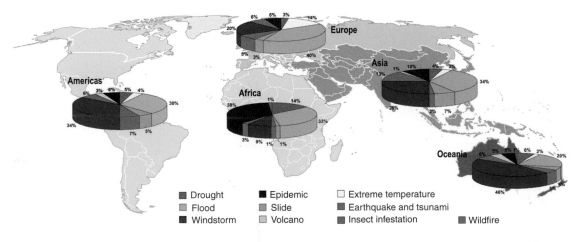

FIGURE 3–12 Regional differences in hazard portfolios (1991–2005). (From the International Disaster Database, www.em-dat.net)

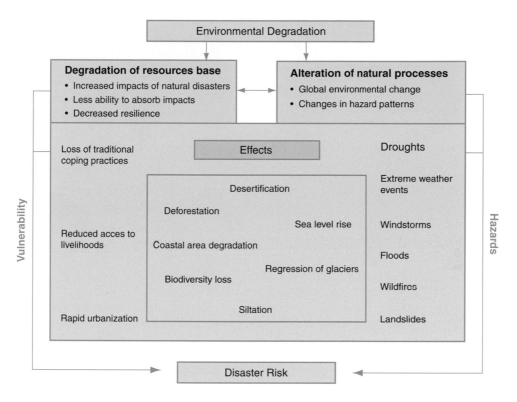

FIGURE 3–13 The link between environmental degradation, natural disasters, and vulnerability. (From ISDR, 2004)

Human practices that affect the environmental profile of a country (see Exhibit 3–7) include:

- Diking or damming of rivers and creeks
- Filling in wetlands for development
- Channeling of coastal areas such that marsh and wetlands areas are destroyed
- Clearcutting of forests
- Mismanagement of forests such that dead wood builds up (serving as fuel for a forest fire)
- Destruction of coastal dunes

Natural processes also affect the natural environment, such as:

- Rainfall averages
- Wind
- Snowfall and snowmelt averages
- Seasonal trends in severe storms and cyclonic storms
- Seasonal drought
- Lightning

Number of windstorms
- 0–10
- 11–30
- >30

FIGURE 3–14 Number of severe windstorm events by country, 1974–2003. (From the International Disaster Database, www.em-dat.net)

The Economic Profile

The financial status of a government and its populations deeply affects their ability to protect themselves from the consequences of disaster. Financial well-being, however, does not indicate that they *will* protect themselves; rather, it is just a measure of their ability to do so. Other factors may be learned from this economic profile. Trends and tendencies associated with wealth, or the lack thereof, can be deduced. For instance, the poor are often marginalized and forced to live on more dangerous land. Their housing is more likely to be constructed of materials that are unable to withstand environmental pressures. They are more likely to have zero tolerance to delays in basic necessities that often follow disasters.

Factors involved in the economic profile that affect vulnerability include:

- Gross domestic product
- Debt
- Access to credit
- Insurance coverage
- Sources of national income
- Funds reserved for disasters
- Social distribution of wealth
- Business continuity planning

EXHIBIT 3–7: ILLEGAL DESTRUCTION OF CORAL REEFS WORSENED IMPACT OF TSUNAMI

The illegal mining of corals off the southwest coast of Sri Lanka permitted far more onshore destruction from the December 26, 2004, tsunami than occurred in nearby areas whose coral reefs were intact. This is the principal finding of a team of researchers from the United States and Sri Lanka who studied the area earlier this year. Their report is published in the August 16 issue of *Eos,* the newspaper of the American Geophysical Union.

Some of the differences were startling. Lead author Harindra Fernando of Arizona State University reports that in the town of Peraliya, a 10-m (30 foot) wave swept 1.5 km (1 mile) inland, carrying a passenger train about 50 m (200 feet) off its tracks, with a death toll of 1700.

Yet, a mere 3 km (2 miles) south, in Hikkaduwa, the tsunami measured just 2–3 m (7–10 feet) in height, traveled only 50 m (200 feet) inland, and caused no deaths.

The researchers found this pattern of patchy inundation to be characteristic of the study area and was not related to such coastline features as headlands, bays, and river channels. Rather, the key factor was the presence or absence of coral and rock reefs offshore. At Hikkaduwa, the hotel strip is fronted by a rock reef and further protected by coral reefs that the local hoteliers protect and nurture, the researchers report. Relatively little damage and few deaths were recorded from there to Dodanduwa, around 6 km to the south.

From Hikkaduwa north to Akuralla, however, damage and loss of life were extensive. Local residents, interviewed by the authors, say that illegal mining had decimated coral reefs in that area, especially by use of explosives that result in harvests of both coral and fish.

Some eyewitnesses to the tsunami described a visible reduction in the height of the water wall and its deflection parallel with the shore as it approached the coral reef. The researchers concluded that waves blocked by the reef caused even more inundation and damage where they found low resistance gaps due to removal of coral by humans.

The scientists note that the brunt of the tsunami had hit Sri Lanka's eastern shore, but that the southwestern, or leeward, side had also been hit hard. Their analysis of the available data concluded that two or three waves hit the area within an hour, having been channeled and bent around the southern tip of the island, and that another wave struck around 2 hour later, having bounced back after hitting India or the Maldives. They say that existing computer models cannot adequately explain or predict the wave amplitudes in southwest Sri Lanka, likely due to small-scale ocean processes, including topographic variations due to coral removal, that are not yet well understood.

The authors noted that the low-lying Maldives islands directly in the path of the tsunami escaped destruction. They suggest that this may have been due to the presence of healthy coral reefs surrounding the islands. Apparently, in Sri Lanka, very little healthy coral was damaged by the tsunami.

Source: American Geophysical Union (2005).

It is recognized that poor countries experience more disasters than the wealthy ones. Figure 3–15 illustrates this. This is not surprising, however, when considering the definition of a disaster and the concept of vulnerability. An event only becomes a disaster when the local capacity to respond to the event is exceeded, requiring external assistance to manage the consequences. Because of their strong economic standing, wealthy nations are better able to develop the preparedness, mitigation, response, and recovery mechanisms before events occur, and thus are able to manage them effectively once they do happen. Identical events that occur in a high-income country and a low-income country may be recorded as a

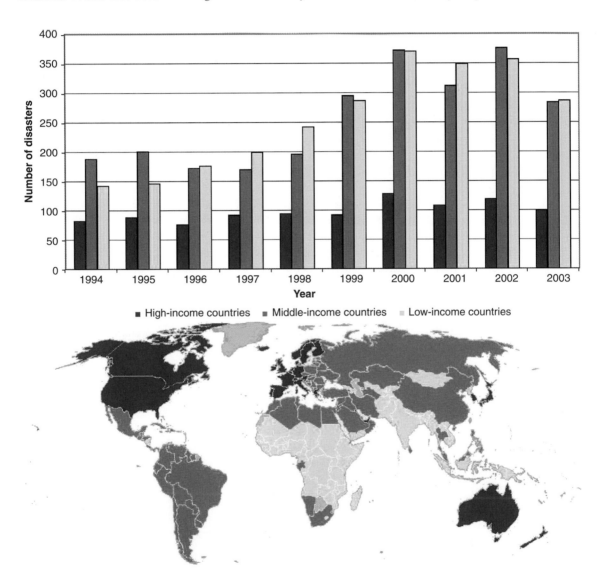

FIGURE 3–15 Total number of disasters by year, 1994–2003 (by income; reference map provided). (From the International Disaster Database, www.em-dat.net)

routine event in the high-income country while resulting in a full-scale disaster in the poor country. The income of these countries, therefore, results in their discrepancy in vulnerability.

Another income-related factor that determines how significantly an event affects a country is the gross domestic product (GDP), which is a measure of the value of all goods and services produced within a nation in a given year. When considered in the absence of a nation's GDP, the financial consequences of a disaster do not provide a great deal of information about how badly the country overall was affected. However, when presented as a percentage of GDP, this consequence figure gives much greater perspective on how deeply the nation's economy feels the impact. For example, a disaster that causes $2 billion in damages may represent upwards of 38% of total GDP for a country like Honduras, while it would be equal to less than one-tenth of a percent of Japan's GDP. Large-scale disasters that affect poor countries can literally wipe out their entire economy. Wealthy nations with strong economies can absorb the effects of disasters, and many even have reserve funds set aside for expected events. Poor countries, however, often must borrow significant amounts of funding while concurrently cutting vital social programs to pay for the relief and recovery from a major disaster. As a result, development continues to lag long after the disaster has struck, as debt payments draw heavily off of annual budgetary spending. Figures 3–16 and 3–17 illustrate how disaster events differently affect economies of different sizes.

Risk Factors That Influence Vulnerability

The United Nations Development Programme (UNDP, 2004), in their report *Reducing Disaster Risk: A Challenge for Development*, identifies two main factors that influence risk levels of nations and their populations: urbanization and rural livelihoods. Each factor contains associated processes that further influence a combination of the vulnerability factors previously discussed.

Urbanization

Populations are concentrating in urban centers throughout the world. The UN estimates that by 2007, more than half the world's population will live in cities. This trend toward the development of large "megacities" is evident upon examination of the world's great metropolises. Between 1950 and 1990, the average population of the largest 100 cities on the planet grew from 2.1 to 5.1 million. There are now six times as many cities with more than 1 million people in the developing world as there were in 1950, and 41 cities had populations that exceeded 5 million in 2000 (UNDP, 2004).

Urbanization, especially rapid urbanization, presents significant challenges for disaster managers and urban planners. In the most basic terms, the concentration of people concentrates risk. The absolute numbers of people who are exposed to individual hazards increases as those people settle in closer and closer proximity. As populations become denser, land pressures require the poor to settle in undesirable, often dangerous, parts of urban centers (e.g., unstable slopes, in floodplains, and on seismically unstable soil). Governments may not be aware for months or years that these groups are at such high risk without current census data and risk assessment.

In addition to concentrating populations, urbanization concentrates national wealth and resources into small, often vulnerable pockets. When disasters occur, the likelihood that a significant portion of the nation's infrastructure, industrial output, and governance will be affected greatly increases. Housing, distribution of food, transportation, communications, public health, and many other resources and services can be affected to a much greater degree as urbanization increases.

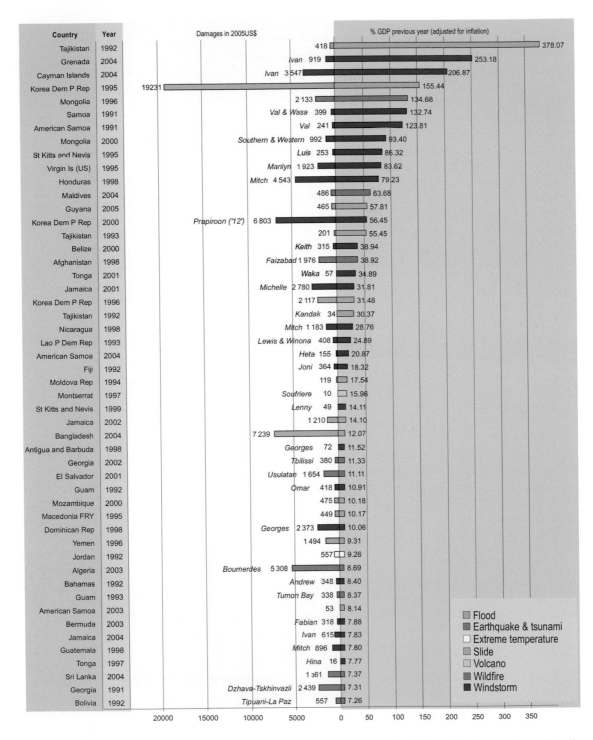

FIGURE 3–16 Disaster damages as a percent of GDP, 1991– 2005. (From the International Disaster Database, www.em-dat.net)

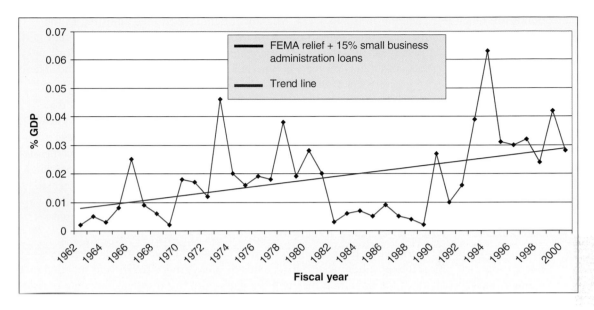

FIGURE 3–17 Disaster relief costs as a percentage of GDP in the United States. (From the Congressional Natural Hazards Caucus and Princeton University, 2001)

Governments' ability to ensure the safety of urban populations decreases significantly when surges in population occur in a haphazard, informal manner. It can be very difficult, if not impossible, for officials to prevent people emigrating from rural areas from building and operating in a way that increases their risk, most significantly in the short term. Disaster and emergency management services must grow with populations to ensure adequate protection. Even wealthy countries often have a lag in services as recognition and funding catch up, but in poor countries the situation can be much worse because political pressure and the competition of financial interests often rob disaster management programs of much needed funding.

The UNDP identified several characteristics of urbanization that contribute to risk and vulnerability, including:

- *Risk by origin.* Some cities are inherently risky because of their location. Mexico City, for example, is located very near active seismic faults and was built upon soft soil that amplifies seismic waves to dangerous levels in certain parts of the city. In this case, the vulnerability of the population is increasing through urbanization because the urban center itself is inherently risky.

- *Increasing physical exposure.* As mentioned earlier, when rapid urbanization occurs, marginalized groups are very often pushed to the more dangerous, riskier parts of the city, even to places where construction may previously have been prohibited. In this case, overall population exposure increases because people are moving into higher risk pockets that exist within the overall boundaries of the urban environment.

- *Social exclusion.* Rural areas often have community-based coping and support systems that allow for decreased overall vulnerability to the consequences of hazards. However, these bonds are much less common in urban areas. Migrants often have trouble adjusting to the new demands of city life, requiring them to disregard many of the protection measures they may have otherwise taken. Their social "safety nets" are reduced or eliminated when they move away from families and friends, and it may be years before they are able to fill the resulting void. These groups tend to face the greatest risk from disaster consequences.

- *Modification and generation of hazard patterns.* Rapid urbanization not only changes the character and size of a city but also affects its natural and built environments as well. Growing populations alter the way many services and resources, such as water, sewerage, garbage disposal, and hazardous materials generation, are managed. These increased pressures can easily create or modify existing hazards, or can result in completely new hazards. For instance, land pressure often results in the filling of wetlands to allow for new construction. The decreased hydrological holding capacity of the land may result in increased flooding where flooding was previously not a problem. This filled land may be less stable in the event of an earthquake because of the lack of bedrock below foundations.

- *Increasing physical vulnerability.* In addition to causing people to move into high-risk areas (increasing their physical exposure), urbanization tends to cause groups to live and function in a manner that increases the likelihood that they will become victim to a disaster. Moving into risky areas does not automatically imply that vulnerability has been increased. With the proper mitigation measures, the likelihood and consequence factors of risk can be reduced. However, because it is the poor who are most likely to move to these areas, expecting that the great (and expensive) measures required to compensate for the increased hazard risk in the area will be taken is unrealistic. As such, population vulnerability increases. It should be noted, however, that even in previously populated areas, increased density can result in conditions that increase vulnerability.

- *Urbanization of new regions.* It is not uncommon, in the modern age of transportation, commerce, and communications, for previously undeveloped areas to transform into large urban centers in a relatively short time. New markets, newly discovered resources, and increased population mobility can result in rapid settlement of people in an area at particular risk for one or more hazards about which few or no people are aware. The UN points out the disasters that resulted from earthquakes in Peru in 1990 and 1991, in Costa Rica in 1991, and in Colombia in 1992 were consequences of new region urbanization.

- *Access to loss mitigation mechanisms.* Rapid urbanization places increased pressure on the government to provide mitigation and other disaster reduction and response services. However, even if these services are increased or developed, there is always a lag in time between recognition of the increased vulnerability and the development of services to reduce that vulnerability. Apart from major disasters, marginalized groups, especially those in informal squatter communities, face the risk of devastating consequences from minor storms, fires, landslides, and other hazards that normally would cause little or no damage.

Rural Livelihoods

More than half the world's population and, according to the World Bank (2005), more than 70% of the impoverished live in rural areas. Like their urban counterparts, rural populations experience vulnerability from disasters because of a unique set of factors resulting directly from the classification of their living conditions as rural. The following lists several of these factors, as identified by the UNDP:

- *Rural poverty.* In the absence of large, organized government entities, rural communities may be left to fend for themselves for disaster mitigation and response resources. This is pronounced in the developing world. With little or no money to spend on prevention, the rural poor have few options to mitigate for disaster risk. When what little they are able to do ultimately fails as result of a disaster, the catastrophic loss of crops, equipment, livestock, housing, and possessions is devastating, and relief resources may be nonexistent. Although they may have developed long-established social systems to counteract the effects of disasters, those systems may fail for many reasons, including changes in the demographic makeup of the community, climate change, changes in markets, and environmental degradation.

- *Environmental degradation.* Many of the world's rural poor engage in environmentally destructive practices. Most often, these practices are directly related to agricultural or other income-generating practices. Deforestation, overgrazing of land, poor farming practices, and alteration of waterways can all lead to an increase in the likelihood or consequence factors of risk. In these cases, it is common for regular events, such as annual rains, to result in disasters that did not normally affect the region; for example, mudslides and flash floods.

- *Nondiversified economies.* Many rural areas rely on just a few sources or even one source of income. This increases the chance that a hazard will result in the destruction of much of the area's income-generation abilities. A plant epidemic is one example of a hazard that causes a disaster that would not have occurred with a more diversified range of resources. Shifts in global market prices can result in a drop in local income, increasing the vulnerability of the area's population. The worst-case scenario, which involves a drop in global prices in conjunction with a disaster, has happened on multiple occasions in the recent past.

- *Isolation and remoteness.* Rural populations that are far outside the reaches of national and regional government services often have little outside intervention to reduce their vulnerability from disasters. Poor transportation and communications infrastructure severely hinders pre- and post-disaster assistance. When disasters do occur, it can be days or weeks before news of it reaches the outside world and assistance is provided. War-torn areas are especially susceptible, as was evident after the 2004 tsunami events in Banda Aceh province in Indonesia.

Risk Perception

An important component of disaster management is the recognition that a hazard exists. However, recognizing the hazard is only the beginning, as one must also be able to judge the relative seriousness of that hazard in comparison to other hazards. The process of risk analysis helps disaster managers to do just that. For laypeople, however, and in the absence of such technical and involved analysis, the mechanisms by which they *perceive* the hazards that threaten them can be very different, and very complex.

The study of why people fear the things they do (and also why they do not fear other things) is called risk perception. Traditionally, people do not tend to fear the things that are statistically most likely to kill them, and an abundance of research has been dedicated specifically to finding out why. Understanding these trends in public risk perception can help disaster managers understand why people are disproportionately afraid of spectacular hazards they are statistically less vulnerable to than, for instance, automobile accidents, food poisoning, heart disease, or cancer.

In their Chapter "Rating the Risks," acclaimed risk perception experts Paul Slovic, Baruch Fischhoff, and Sarah Lichtenstein begin, "People respond to the hazards they perceive" (Slovic, Fischhoff, & Lichtenstein, 1979). This statement is important for two reasons. First, its opposite is true. People generally do not respond to the hazards that they do not perceive. Second, it has been found that these stated perceptions are based primarily upon inaccurate sources of information, such as mass media outlets, social networks, and other external sources, as opposed to personal experience and expert knowledge.

Slovic et al. (1979) identified four "Risk Perception Fallibility" conclusions to explain the ways in which people tend to inaccurately view the hazards in their world. These conclusions, which help to explain how populations decide which disasters to prepare for and why, are:

1. Cognitive limitations, coupled with the anxieties generated by facing life as a gamble, cause uncertainty to be denied, risks to be distorted, and statements of fact to be believed with unwarranted confidence. People tend to fear a specific risk less as they become better informed with more details of the risk. However, what a person can discover about a risk will almost never be complete, as the actual likelihood or consequence most risks pose cannot be quantified in a way that addresses the specific threat faced by individuals (even well-known risks such as cancer or heart disease; Ropeik, 2001).

   The more uncertainty a risk poses or, as Slovic et al. (1979) stated, "the more of a gamble something is," the more people will fear it. In the face of uncertainty, people will consciously or subconsciously make personal judgments based upon very imperfect information to establish some individual concept of the risk they face. Judgments based upon uncertainties and imperfect information often cause people to wrongly perceive their own risk in a way that overstates reality.

   In Mexico City, for instance, where a public insecurity crisis is a priority political topic and a constant subject in the press, but where no reliable crime statistics have been available for over 7 years, people have overestimated their personal risk from violent crime by up to 86%. According to a 2002 comprehensive countrywide poll measuring the incidence of crime, approximately 14 of every 100 citizens of Mexico City would fall victim to some form of crime in the 12 months following the survey (ICESI, 2002). However, when asked in a poll what they believed their chance was of falling victim to crime in that same time period, many people responded with an 80 to 100% chance.

2. Perceived risk is influenced (and sometimes biased) by the imaginability and memorability of the hazard. People, therefore, may not have valid perceptions about even familiar risks.

   People are more afraid of those things that they can imagine or remember. The likelihood of occurrence of these easily available risks, as they are called, tends to be overestimated. For instance, we rarely hear about a person dying from a "common" cause such as a heart attack, unless somebody close to us dies of that specific cause. However, the media will report heavily on a death that is the result of an "uncommon" cause, like the West Nile virus. The result tends to be that people underestimate common risks and overestimate rare risks.

   Social scientists Slovic, Fischhoff, and Lichtenstein performed a study to measure this phenomenon, and found that people greatly overestimated their risk from rare events such as botulism, tornadoes, pregnancy complications, and floods, while underestimating their risk from stroke, diabetes, cancer, and heart disease (Slovic et al., 1979). Generally, people tend to fear what they hear about repetitively or often. This phenomenon is referred to as the "availability heuristic," which states that people perceive an event to be likely or frequent if instances of the event are easy to imagine or recall. This perception bias can be correct when considering events that really are frequently observed, such as people who believe that automobile accidents are common because almost everyone they know has been involved in one. However, when a risk that is spectacular but not necessarily common receives constant media attention, people often wrongly assume that similar events are very likely to occur.

3. Disaster management experts' risk perceptions correspond closely to statistical frequencies of death. Laypeople's risk perceptions are based in part on frequencies of death with some striking discrepancies. It appears that the concept of risk for laypeople includes qualitative aspects such as dread and the likelihood of a mishap being fatal. Their risk perceptions are also affected by catastrophic potential.

It can be difficult for people to fully understand statistics they are given, and even more difficult to conceptualize how those statistics apply to them personally. Furthermore, statistics tend to do little to affect how people perceive the calculated risks. This is not to say that the average person lacks sufficient intelligence to process numbers; rather, the numbers are not the sole source of influence on public risk perception.

Extensive research has discovered that people rank their risks by using other, more heavily weighted *qualitative* factors, as well as the quantitative likelihood of a hazard resulting in personal consequence (Slovic et al., 1979). People are generally more concerned with the consequence component of risk than they are about the likelihood component (recall that Risk = Likelihood × Consequence).

It is important to examine the quality and usefulness of statistics provided to the public by the media regarding risks. Without complete information, media-provided statistics are meaningless and likely misleading. In the absence of complete information, people tend to over- rather than underestimate their vulnerability. Economists have classified this tendency to overestimate unknown or unclear risks as "risk-ambiguity aversion" (*The Economist*, 2002).

However, even if statistics provided by the media or other sources are straightforward, people have difficulty understanding how those numbers affect them as an individual, even if they are a risk "expert." Few people can conceptualize the difference between a "one-in-a-million" and a "one-in-one-hundred-thousand" chance of occurrence (Jardine & Hrudey, 1997).

People tend to need other clues to help them put these numbers into perspective. Many tend to view their chance of being affected by rare but spectacular hazards in a comparable fashion to how people believe that they can beat long odds to win a state lottery. James Walsh wrote in his book *True Odds:*

The odds are greater you'll be struck by lightning than win even the easiest lottery. They're better that you'll be dealt a royal flush on the opening hand of a poker game (1 in 649,739). They're better that you'll be killed by terrorists while traveling abroad (1 in 650,000). If you bought 100 tickets a week your entire adult life, from age 18 to 75, you'd have a 1 percent chance of winning a lottery. Lotteries really play on the inability of the general public to appreciate how small long odds are. (Walsh, 1996)

In Walsh's calculations, the odds of winning the lottery are 1 in $57 \times 52 \times 100 \times 100 = 29,640,000$.

It is the qualitative factors that people consider most heavily when weighing their personal risk. Slovic, Fischhoff, and Lichtenstein (1980) proposed that there are 17 risk characteristics that influence public risk perception. These characteristics fall under two subgroups (called "factors"): factors related to dread (Factor 1) and factors related to how much is known about the risk (Factor 2). A third factor, encompassing a single, eighteenth characteristic, which measures the number of people exposed to the hazard, will not be covered in this section.

Using these 17 characteristics, Slovic et al. (1980) examined public perceptions of 90 risks and plotted their findings on a two-dimensional graph depicting Factor 1 on the x axis and Factor 2 on the y axis. Characteristics of Factors 1 and 2 are described in the following lists:

Factor 1: Factors Related to Dread

- *Dreaded versus not dreaded.* People fear risks that cause painful, violent deaths more than risks that do not. David Ropeik, Director of Risk Communication at the Harvard Center for Risk Analysis, wrote, "What are you more afraid of: being eaten by a shark or dying of a heart attack in your sleep? Both leave you equally as dead, but one—being eaten alive—is a more dreadful way to go" (Ropeik, 2001). Of course, millions of people around the world die from heart attacks while sleeping every year, but fewer than 15 fall victim to sharks in the same time period (Wiggins, 2002).

- *Uncontrollable versus controllable.* People tend to be less fearful of risks that they feel they can control. For instance, most people feel safer as a driver in a car than as a passenger because they are controlling the movement of the vehicle, and they know their own skills in accident avoidance. When people lack control of a situation, a risk seems more pronounced. Examples of uncontrollable risks are airplane travel, street crime, pesticides in food, and terrorism.

- *Globally catastrophic versus not globally catastrophic.* Risks that have the potential to affect the entire world tend to be deemed greater than those that would only affect local or national populations. For instance, the effects of nuclear war, whose aftermath could include widespread nuclear fallout and long-term physiological effects beyond the borders of any one state, is far scarier than the effects a conventional war taking place in a country other than one's own.

- *Fatal consequences versus not fatal consequences.* A risk that results in death is more feared than other, nonlethal risks. For example, even though auto accidents are much more likely than airplane accidents, the chance of fatality is much greater for airplane accidents, and airplane accidents are thus more feared.

- *Not equitable versus equitable.* Risks that affect one group with a greater statistical likelihood and/or consequence than the general population tend to be considered greater than those that affect all people equally, especially to those within the groups more severely affected. This is especially true if the risk disproportionately affects children.

- *Catastrophic versus individual.* Risks that affect a great number of people in one location or at one time are more feared than those that affect individuals one at a time, over a wide location. Terrorism and earthquakes are examples of catastrophic hazards, while heart disease, auto accidents, and drowning are considered individual hazards.

- *High risk to future generations versus low risk to future generations.* A risk that extends across generations, especially one that will affect future generations, is considered scarier than ones that will be mitigated or prevented within our own lifetime. The most apparent example of this is nuclear radiation, which can remain dangerous for thousands of years. Because of this extended danger, there still are no agreements on where spent nuclear fuel will be stored in the United States after it is no longer useful for power generation.

- *Not easily reduced versus easily reduced.* People are more afraid of risks that cannot be easily mitigated. The effort required to reduce crime or drug use is much greater than the effort required to prevent drowning or bicycle injuries. Simply wearing a helmet on a bike, or a life preserver on a pleasure boat, greatly reduces the likelihood of injury or death. However, it takes months or years to combat a crime wave or drug problem plaguing a town or city.

- *Risk increasing versus risk decreasing.* A risk that appears to be growing in likelihood or consequence becomes more feared. However, if a risk appears to be more easily mitigated or is decreasing in likelihood or consequence, people begin to fear it less.

- *Involuntary versus voluntary.* Why are people more afraid of drunk drivers than of eating high-cholesterol food that will raise their risk of heart disease? How can some people smoke cigarettes, wholly unconcerned about their cancer risk, while those around them complain incessantly? The most obvious answer for both questions is that people are more concerned with risks that are involuntary than with those they bring upon themselves. Keith Smith, in *Environmental Hazards: Assessing Risk and Reducing Disaster,* discusses voluntary and involuntary risk and states, "there is a major difference between voluntary and involuntary risk perception with the public being willing to accept voluntary risks approximately *1,000 times greater than involuntary risks*" (emphasis added; Smith, 1992).

- *Affects me versus does not affect me.* Terrorism has been reported almost daily in the media for years, but until September 11, 2001, Americans who did not travel abroad did not worry about it. After that date, preventing terrorism became a national concern and a government priority. The *statistical* risk to the average person in the United States was raised only a minuscule amount, but the mere fact that people suddenly knew *for certain* that foreign terrorism could occur at home made them much more afraid.

- *Not preventable versus preventable.* A risk that cannot be mitigated or prepared for is more feared than one that can be. For instance, in the early 1980s HIV and AIDS were seen as always fatal, and were terribly feared. With modern medicine, people who are HIV positive can live for years without contracting AIDS. While the disease is still feared, it is not perceived to be as dangerous as it was 20 years ago.

Factor 2: Factors Related to How Much Is Known about the Risk

- *Not observable versus observable.* Risks that can be seen are less feared than those that cannot be seen or visualized. The dangers associated with radon or genetic manipulation are considered not observable, while secondhand smoke is observable.

- *Unknown to those exposed versus known to those exposed.* If people have no way of knowing whether they are exposed to a risk, they will fear that risk more. Food irradiation and biological terrorism are examples of risks where people may not be able to know if they have been exposed.

- *Effect delayed versus effect immediate.* Risks that cause immediate harm or damage tend to be less feared than those that cause negative effects at some future time following exposure. This is the primary reason people tend to fear the effects of biological terrorism more than conventional or even chemical warfare.

- *New risk versus old risk.* Risks we are facing for the first time are much scarier than risks that we have had plenty of time to become "accustomed" to. Few people fear cars for their accident risk or fear the risk posed by vaccines, as we have lived with these technologies for decades. When anthrax was mailed to news agencies and politicians in New York, Washington, DC, and Florida, people became extremely frightened when opening their mail, while today it is highly unlikely that anyone continues to wear a mask and rubber gloves while opening letters.

- *Risks unknown to science versus risks known to science.* When risks can be explained using scientific evidence, people fear them less because of increased understanding. Many diseases raise questions when they are first discovered, but once their methods of transmission, prevention, and cure are revealed, they become less of a concern.

4. *Disagreements about risk should not be expected to evaporate in the presence of "evidence."* Definitive evidence, particularly about rare hazards, is difficult to obtain. Weaker information is likely to be interpreted in a way that reinforces existing beliefs (Slovic et al., 1979).

Slovic et al. (1979) discovered that "people's beliefs change slowly and are extraordinarily persistent in the face of contrary evidence. New evidence appears reliable and informative if it is consistent with one's initial belief; contrary evidence is dismissed as unreliable, erroneous, or unrepresentative." They added, "Convincing people that the catastrophe they fear is extremely unlikely is difficult under the best conditions. Any mishap could be seen as proof of high risk, whereas demonstrating safety would require a massive amount of evidence," evidence that is sometimes impossible to obtain in an accurate or timely manner (Slovic et al., 1979).

This stubbornness is compounded by the fact that once people make their initial judgments, they believe with overwhelming confidence that they are correct. This phenomenon, called the "overconfidence heuristic," states that people often are unaware of how little they know about a risk, and of how much more information they need to make an informed decision. More often than not, people believe that they know much more about risks than they actually do.

Slovic and his colleagues (1979) conducted a study to determine whether people knew if homicides were more frequent than suicides. Of participants who answered incorrectly, 12.5% gave odds of 100:1 that their answer was correct, and 30% gave odds of 50:1 that their answer was correct. In fact, suicides happen much more frequently than homicides, with an incidence of 1.7 suicides per homicide (CDC, 2002).

The overconfidence heuristic has been linked to media coverage of other spectacular events, specifically regarding how people's rating of risks is dependent on the amount of media coverage a risk receives. For example, one study showed that a greater percentage of crimes covered by the media involve perpetrators and victims of different races than occurs in reality. In other words, a news story is more likely to describe a white victim of a black attacker than a black victim of a black attacker, even though the latter is more common. This inconsistency in coverage is seen as the main reason Caucasians overestimate their likelihood of being a victim of interracial crime by a factor of 3 (Twomey, 2001).

Paul Slovic wrote that "strong beliefs are hard to modify" and "naïve views are easily manipulated by presentation format" (Slovic, 1986). Often, only time will change people's opinions about the risks they personally face. One reason that people are more scared of a new risk than an old risk is that they have not been able to gather enough information to alter their initial fearful impression. After time has passed and they realize that their expectations for victimization have not been realized for themselves or anybody that they know, they can begin to question the validity of their views.

Elspeth Young of the Australian National University described social constructs of risk. These are human attributes that define how different people assess risk and determine personal vulnerability. They include:

1. *Socioeconomic characteristics (including age, gender, ethnicity, income, education, employment, and health).* "Older people and children may be much more vulnerable than active adults. Poorer people, with fewer capital resources, are likely to suffer far more from the effects of hazards such as flood invasion of their homes. Some specific ethnic groups may be much less able to take advantage of the assistance offered because of communication problems and cultural differences" (Young, 1998).
2. *People's knowledge of the environment and the hazards that the environment poses to them (traditional ecological knowledge).* "Traditional ecological knowledge may be effectively used to cope with a situation that outsiders perceive to be threatening, and generally provides much more detailed understanding of local environments. It can be valuable in predicting the threats posed by hazards (e.g., when significant floods are actually likely)" (Young, 1998).
3. *Their ignorance.* "For example, people who have newly moved into a vulnerable area often lack knowledge of the actual threats posed by hazards such as severe [wild]fires, and fail to take suggested precautions seriously" (Young, 1998).
4. *Their ability to cope with those hazards.* "[People are able to cope] through technology, financial attributes, education, political power, and having a voice. Knowledge, high levels of education, and high incomes generally give people more confidence in articulating their feelings and needs and hence they may be able to cope better with adversity" (Young, 1998).
5. *Their ability to access help from outside.* "Having confidence makes asking for assistance much easier" (Young, 1998).

The ways in which hazard risk is presented or reported greatly influence how people perceive the hazard. For instance, Slovic and Weber (2002) described several ways that a risk manager could describe the risk from a nearby factory to an exposed population. All of the measurements will describe the same risk factor, but each one is likely to produce a different number. The ways in which people perceive that number will be different as well. Such measurements include (Slovic & Weber, 2002):

1. Deaths per million people in the population
2. Deaths per million people within x miles of the source of exposure
3. Deaths per unit of concentration
4. Deaths per facility

5. Deaths per ton of air toxin released
6. Deaths per ton of air toxin absorbed by people
7. Deaths per ton of chemical produced
8. Deaths per million dollars of product produced
9. Loss of life expectancy associated with exposure to the hazard

Richard Wilson (1979) described ways in which risks can be compared by calculating risks that increase a person's chance of death by one in one million (0.000001). It must be noted that these risks are population risks as opposed to individual risks. These compared risks are provided as Exhibit 3–8.

Risk comparisons can also cause incorrect perception of risk if they are not presented in an appropriate manner. Kenneth Warner (1989) described how the media often use vivid comparisons to better explain risks to their audience. He gives the following three examples of comparisons provided by the media to describe the risks associated with cigarette smoking.

EXHIBIT 3–8: RISKS THAT INCREASE CHANCE OF DEATH BY 0.000001 (1 IN 1 MILLION), FOLLOWED BY THE CAUSE OF DEATH

- Smoking 1.4 cigarettes (cancer, heart disease)
- Drinking one-half liter of wine (cirrhosis of the liver)
- Spending 1 hour in a coal mine (black lung disease)
- Spending 3 hours in a coal mine (accident)
- Living 2 days in New York or Boston (air pollution)
- Traveling 6 min by canoe (accident)
- Traveling 10 miles by bicycle (accident)
- Traveling 300 miles by car (accident)
- Flying 1000 miles by jet (accident)
- Flying 6000 miles by jet (cancer caused by cosmic radiation)
- Living 2 months in Denver (cancer caused by cosmic radiation)
- Living 3 months in average brick or stone building (cancer caused by natural radioactivity)
- One chest X-ray taken in a good hospital (cancer caused by radiation)
- Living 2 months with a cigarette smoker (cancer, heart disease)
- Eating 40 tablespoons of peanut butter (liver cancer caused by aflatoxin B)
- Drinking Miami drinking water for 1 year (cancer caused by chloroform)
- Drinking 30 12 ounce cans of diet soda (cancer caused by saccharin)
- Living 5 years at the boundary of a typical nuclear power plant in the open (cancer caused by radiation)
- Living 20 years near a PVC plant (cancer caused by vinyl chloride)
- Living 150 years within 20 miles of a nuclear power plant (cancer caused by radiation)
- Eating 100 charcoal-broiled steaks (cancer from benzopyrene)

Source: Adapted from Wilson (1979).

1. "On average, cigarettes kill as many people as would die if three passenger-laden jumbo jets crashed every day, month after month, year after year."
2. "In one year, cigarettes kill more Americans than died in World War I, the Korean War, and the Vietnam War combined."
3. "The annual death toll associated with cigarette smoking is equal to that of a hydrogen bomb dropped in the heart of a city such as Miami, Kansas City, Cleveland, or wherever." (Warner, 1989)

Warner described how the conceptual differences between the slow death associated with smoking-induced cancer or emphysema and the immediate deaths associated with being shot in a war, incinerated in a hydrogen blast, or killed in a plane crash render such comparisons ineffective. These comparisons attempt to elicit the fear associated with the risk characteristics identified by Slovic et al. (1979). Studies have shown, however, that these types of comparisons lack the desired effect.

People's perceptions of risk can also be influenced by the emotions elicited by a particular report on a hazard. According to a report in the *Washington Post*, Jennifer Lerner of Carnegie Mellon University discovered that people who watched media reports framed in a way to cause fear, like one on bioterrorism, would likely overestimate their personal exposure to risk. However, people who watched reports that elicited anger, such as ones showing Palestinians and other people celebrating the 9/11 attacks, were likely to perceive their exposure to terrorism as relatively less than the fearful group's perception. Lerner attributed to the effects of these fear-inducing reports the fact that in surveys conducted after 9/11, Americans felt they faced a 20% chance of being a direct victim of future attacks, and felt that the "average American" faced a 48% chance of being a victim (Vedantam, 2003).

Lerner found that women tended to respond with more fear to terrorism risk-related articles, while men tended to respond more with anger. She contended, "the government and the media can unwittingly alter risk perception by making people either fearful or angry," and further stated, "[u]sed responsibly, that connection could also be used to better communicate the real degree of risk" (Lerner et al., 2003).

Risk Perception Is Necessary for Disaster Management and Communications

Most people do not rely on statistical likelihoods to determine what risks they fear but consider other qualitative aspects, which can be due to attributes of the hazard itself or each individual's personal experience and information exposure. The outcome of these risk perception effects is that there is no single, universal, agreed-upon ranking of hazard risks.

Disaster managers need to consider risk when performing their assessments, but also are influenced by the effects of risk perception, regardless of their knowledge or expertise in risk management. C. J. Pitzer wrote in the *Australian Journal of Emergency Management*:

> We make a fundamental mistake when we, as safety managers, deal with risk as a "fixed attribute," something physical that can be precisely measured and managed. The misconception of risk as a fixed attribute is ingrained into our industry and is a product of the so-called science of risk management. Risk management has created the illusion that risk can be quantified on the basis of probability, exposure to risk, and from the likely consequences of accidents occurring. Risk management science can even produce highly technical and mathematically advanced models of the probabilistic nature of a risk.

The problem with this is that risk is not a physical quantum. It is, instead, a social construction. Everyone has a unique set of assumptions and experiences that shape their interpretations of objects or events. People tend to ignore, "misperceive" or deny events that do not fit their worldview. People find what they expect to find. (Pitzer, 1999)

Elspeth Young (1998) wrote:

Risk should not be defined solely by pre-determined, supposedly objective criteria that enable its various levels to be gauged through quantification. It is also a social construct, interpreted differently by all of us. Some find certain events or situations unacceptably risky and will do their utmost to avoid being involved, while to others the same events may offer exhilaration and thrills that stimulate their whole purpose of living. There may even be others to whom the particular event is a non-issue, something to be totally ignored. These differences in perception and response, coupled with differences in people's socio-economic characteristics and circumstances, result in a wide range of vulnerability in any community. Social aspects of risk interpretation must be recognized if risk is to be effectively managed, and community participation in the practical management of the problem faced is a vital component of this approach.

When disaster managers perform the hazards risk management process, they take many steps during the process that require the use of both qualitative assessments and personal experience and opinions. Because of differences in risk perception, the hazards risk management process can be flawed if risk managers do not accommodate inconsistencies between their own and their constituents' perceptions and reality.

During hazard identification, a hazard first must be perceived as a risk before it is identified as one. Perception is not the same as awareness. An obvious example is a hazards risk management team that is *unaware* that chlorine is used to purify water in the community. Without this knowledge, they may not know that the hazardous chemical (capable of causing mass casualty disasters) is not only transported by truck through populated areas several times a year but also stored in a location where a leak or explosion could result in many fatalities. This is *not* an issue of risk perception. Now, imagine that the same team is aware of the above information but they have never heard of a disaster actually happening, or the one accident they have heard of did not result in any deaths, and they decide that the chlorine is something they do not need to worry about in their assessment. This is a result of the effects of risk perception (the availability and overconfidence heuristics, in this case).

Risk perception may have the opposite, compounding effect for disaster managers. For instance, it is possible that a risk that is essentially harmless or has extremely low likelihood or consequence is perceived to be much greater than reality by a manager or by the public. Such faulty perceptions on the part of the disaster management team could result in time or funding wasted in mitigation and preparation for a risk that may never happen at the expense of neglecting a more severe risk that threatens the population to a greater degree. However, if the disaster managers have an accurate impression of a risk and determine that it is low enough to not worry about, while the public perceives it to be significant, they run the risk of appearing negligent. Only effective public education and risk communication can counter the effects of public (mis)perception of risk.

Risk perception can also influence the way that the mitigation of a hazard is considered by decision makers or by constituents within a community. If a hazard is not perceived to be a significant risk by those who decide to fund mitigation projects, funding is unlikely to be provided without significant efforts to correct those perceptions. Likewise, if the public does not perceive a hazard to affect them personally, they are unlikely to take any personal measures to prepare or mitigate for that hazard. Once again, the presence of differing risk perceptions highlights the need for effective risk communication as a component of mitigation and preparedness.

Risk perception can lead to difficulties in making important decisions on the management of hazard risks. Slovic and Weber (2002) wrote:

Perceptions of risk play a prominent role in the decisions people make, in the sense that differences in risk perception lie at the heart of disagreements about the best course of action between technical experts and members of the general public, men vs. women, and people from different cultures. Both individual and group differences in preference for risky decision alternatives and situational differences in risk preference have been shown to be associated with differences in perceptions of the relative risk of choice options, rather than with differences in attitude towards perceived risk.

Managing risk perceptions is an important component of the hazards risk management process. With an understanding of the perceptions and misperceptions of risk made by their constituents, hazards risk managers can work to correct those misperceptions and address the public's fears and concerns. Failure to do so could easily lead to any of the mistakes discussed here.

Barry Glassner provided one example of the secondary effects of misperception of risk on a community. In the 1990s, the media widely reported on a "crime wave" against tourists in Florida that resulted in 10 murders. It was called a crime wave because the media labeled it as such.

Objectively speaking, 10 murders of 41 million visitors did not even constitute a ripple, much less a wave, especially considering that at least 97% of all victims of crime in Florida are Floridians. Although the Miami area had the highest crime rate in the nation during this period, it was not tourists who had most cause for worry. One study showed that British, German, and Canadian tourists who flock to Florida each year to avoid winter weather were more than 70 times more likely to be victimized at home (Glassner, 1999).

This widespread misperception of risk was not adequately managed and made many tourists think twice before traveling to Florida; the tourism industry suffered as a result.

It is important for risk managers to evaluate personal perceptions because they will undoubtedly influence the process of risk identification, subsequent analysis, and treatment. Because much of the risk identification and analysis processes are based upon qualitative information, great discrepancies can exist, even between experts.

Risk managers must be as certain as possible that their assumptions and perceptions concerning risk mirror reality as closely as possible. Risk managers who incorrectly overstate a hazard will devote a disproportionate and inappropriate amount of available resources and time to that hazard.

For hazards risk management to be effective, an overall philosophy of cost-effectiveness must be employed, and without accurate information and risk perceptions, such cost-effectiveness is unlikely.

Risk managers must not assume anything. They must utilize as many historical records and officially recognized hazard profiles as possible. Many public, private, and nonprofit agencies specialize in specific hazards and are likely to have the most accurate information concerning risk likelihood and consequence data.

The public is likely to overestimate some risks and underestimate others, depending upon the general risk perception characteristics listed above. If the public collectively overestimates the likelihood or consequence of a particular hazard, such as the presence of a nearby nuclear power plant, then they may demand from public officials a significant effort to decrease what they see as a great risk. While initiating an increased level of preparedness and mitigation may not be a particularly effective and efficient use of resources, simply ignoring the public's concerns can have significant political implications.

With an understanding of the public's perceptions, risk managers can initiate a program of risk communication and public education to increase understanding and steer public concern toward risks of greater consequence and likelihood, such as house fires or floods.

Conversely, disaster managers should be aware of a collective public risk perception that underestimates the incidence or consequences of a certain hazard, such as underground power lines. A significant number of people have been killed who made contact with underground power lines while performing construction or landscaping work. Public education campaigns have regularly stressed to citizens the significance of the hazard. Similar campaigns are employed for risks such as drug abuse, forest fires, smoking, poisons, and so on. These risks tend to be ones that kill many more people than all natural hazards combined, but are not considered appropriately "risky" by the public.

The Term Safe

Those involved in disaster management are often faced with defining what level of safety from hazard exposure is considered sufficient. There is not necessarily a correct answer to the question "How safe is safe enough?" (Derby & Keeney, 1981). Most people assume that referring to something as "safe" implies that all risk has been eliminated. However, because such an absolute level of safety is virtually unattainable in the real world, risk managers must establish thresholds of risk that define a frequency of occurrence below which society need not worry about the hazard. Derby and Keeney (1981) contended that a risk becomes "safe," or "acceptable," if it is "associated with the best of the available alternatives, not with the best of the alternatives which we would *hope* to have available" (emphasis added).

This definition can cause great disagreement between the public and disaster management officials. The public may expect a level of safety determined to be zero risk for some hazards, such as terrorism in the United States. Officials may need to continually recalibrate the public's perception of these hazards to let the public know that, while the risks are in fact still possible, they have been mitigated to the best of the country's or community's social, economic (available resources), and technological abilities. While the chances of a terrorist attack will always exist, governments strive to attain levels of security dictating that the risks are so low that people need not worry.

To determine what level of safety is most acceptable, Derby and Keeney (1981) contended that the best combination of advantages and disadvantages must be chosen from among several alternatives. For instance, although the risk of car accidents is one of the greatest we face on a daily basis, eliminating the risk by prohibiting the use of cars is impractical. However, we can make cars more resistant to impact, add seat belts and air bags, and enact laws and regulations that limit the ways in which cars are operated. The result is a level of safety upon which society agrees is acceptable in relation to the benefits (mobility) retained.

Paul Barnes of the Australia Department of Primary Industries explains the importance of establishing an agreement on what constitutes safety in the community. He writes:

Is our goal Community Safety or Safer Communities? As a societal outcome, Community Safety can be sought via efficient and effective regulation at an institutional level. Associated with this regulation must be similarly high standards of risk management applied at the community level. The establishment of safer communities, however, is a different matter. Before this can be sought as a goal, determinations must be made about what safety means to the communities themselves. To do this, institutional regulators must ensure that use of their expertise does not promote inflexibility in understanding the world-views of the public. (Barnes, 2002)

Conclusion

Risk and vulnerability reduction is paramount to reducing injuries, deaths, and damages associated with disasters. All nations may significantly reduce their risk and vulnerability, no matter their wealth or facilities. Yet for most nations, disaster management emphasis focuses only upon the post-disaster functions of response and recovery, rather than pre-disaster mitigation and preparedness. Fortunately, nations such as Australia, New Zealand, and the United States and international organizations such as the United Nations are working hard to reverse these reactive attitudes.

References

Alesch, D. (2001). *Acceptable risk: What is it and how do we measure it?* Presentation at the University of Colorado, 2001 Hazards Workshop, Boulder. June.

American Geophysical Union. (2005). *Illegal destruction of coral reefs worsened impact of tsunami.* Press Release, August 15.

Ansell, J., & Wharton, F. (1992). *Risk: Analysis, assessment, and management.* Chichester, UK: John Wiley & Sons.

Barnes, P. (2002). Approaches to community safety: Risk perception and social meaning. *Australian Journal of Emergency Management* (Autumn), 15–23.

Cameron, G. (2002). *Emergency risk management: What does it mean?* Presentation at ATEM-AAPPA 2002 Conference, Brisbane, Australia, September 29–October 2. www.aappa.com/infoservices/papers/2002_AAPPA_Brisbane/G_Cameron.pdf.

Centers for Disease Control (CDC). (2002). *Suicide in the United States.* www.cdc.gov/ncipc/factsheets/suifacts.htm.

Congressional Natural Hazards Caucus and Princeton University. (2001). *US vulnerability to natural hazards.* www.hazardscaucus.org/USHAZPOSTER.pdf.

Crowe, T. D. (2000). *Crime prevention through environmental design: Applications of architectural design and space management concepts.* Boston: Butterworth-Heinemann.

Davis, A. (2002). New alarm heats up debate on chemical risks. *Arizona Daily Star* (May 30). www.azstarnet.com/attack/indepth/wsj-chemicalrisks.html.

de Becker, G. (1997). *The gift of fear: Survival signals that protect us from violence.* Boston: Little, Brown and Co.

Derby, S. L., & Keeney, R. L. (1981). Risk analysis: Understanding 'how safe is safe enough?' *Risk Analysis, 1*(3), 217–224.

Dickey, T. S. (1980). *Bank robbery—Architectural implications from the criminal's point of view*. Unpublished Master's thesis, Georgia Institute of Technology College of Architecture.

Dresher, M. (1961). *Games of strategy: Theory and applications*. Englewood Cliffs, NJ: Prentice-Hall.

Dubner, S. J., & Levitt, S. D. (2006). How many lives did Dale Earnhardt save? *The New York Times* (February 19), http://www.nytimes.com/2006/02/19/magazine/19wwln_freak.html?pagewanted=print.

Economist, The. (2002). *The logic of irrational fear* (October 19), 29–30.

Emergency Management Australia (EMA). (2000). *Emergency risk management: Applications guide*. Dickson, Australia: Author.

Federal Emergency Management Agency (FEMA). (2001). *How-to guide #3*. www.Fema.gov/FIMA/planning_howta3.shtm.

Federal Emergency Management Agency (FEMA). (1997). *Multi-hazard: Identification and risk assessment*. Washington, DC: Author.

Glassner, B. (1999). *The culture of fear*. New York: Basic Books.

ICESI. (2002). *Primera Encuesta Nacional sobre Inseguridad Publica en las Entidades Federativas*. Mexico City: Instituto Ciudadano de Estudios Sobre la Inseguridad A.C.

International Strategy for Disaster Reduction (ISDR). (2004). *Living with risk*. Geneva: The United Nations Inter-Agency Secretariat.

Jardine, C. G., & Hrudey, S. E. (1997). Mixed messages in risk communication. *Risk Analysis, 17*, 489–498.

Lerner, J. S., Gonzales, R., Small, D., & Fischoff, B. (2003). Effects of fear and anger on perceived risks of terrorism. *American Psychological Association. Psychological Science, 14*(2).

Lunn, J. (2003). Community consultation: The foundation of effective risk management. *Journal of Emergency Management, 1*(1), 39–48.

Massachusetts Precautionary Principle Project (MPPP). (1999). *Risk assessment & risk management*. Boston: Massachusetts Precautionary Principle Partners.

Mumpower, J. (1986). An analysis of the *de minimis* strategy for risk management. *Risk Analysis, 6*, 437–445.

Pesticide Management Education Program (PMEP). (1997). *The Delaney Paradox and negligible risk 8/91*. http://pmep.cce.cornell.edu/issues/delaney-negrisk-891.html.

Pitzer, C. J. (1999). New thinking on disasters: The link between safety culture and risk-taking. *Australian Journal of Emergency Management* (Spring), 41–50.

Ravid, I. (2001). Theater ballistic missiles and asymmetric war. Unpublished manuscript.

Roderick, L. M. (1998). Slips, trips, and falls. *Safety and ergonomics manual*. www.trinity3.com/lmr/slipstripsfalls.htm.

Ropeik, D. (2001). *"Fear factors" in an age of terrorism* (October 15). www.msnbc.msn.com/id/3077306/.

Slovic, P. (1986). Informing and educating the public about risk. *Risk Analysis, 6*(4), 403–415.

Slovic, P., Fischhoff, B., & Lichtenstein, S. (1979). Rating the risks. *Environment, 21*, 14–20, 36–39.

Slovic, P., Fischhoff, B., & Lichtenstein, S. (1980). Facts and fears: Understanding perceived risk. In *Societal risk assessment: How safe is safe enough?* New York: Plenum.

Slovic, P., & Weber, E. (2002). *Perception of risk posed by extreme events.* Presented at Risk Management Strategies in an Uncertain World, Palisades, New York, April 12–13.

Smith, K. (1992). *Environmental hazards: Assessing and reducing disaster.* London: Routlege.

Twomey, J. (2001). Media fuels fear about youth crime. *Baltimore Sun* (May 13), 1C.

United Nations Development Programme (UNDP). (2004). *Reducing disaster risk: A challenge for development.* New York: Bureau for Crisis Prevention and Recovery.

United Nations Development Programme (UNDP). (1994). *Vulnerability and risk assessment.* www.proventionconsortium .org/files/undp/VulnerabilityAndRiskAssessmentGuide.pdf.

Vedantam, S. (2003). More afraid than we should be. *The Washington Post* (March 31), A6.

Viscusi, W. (1996). Economic foundations of the current regulatory reform efforts. *Journal of Economic Perspectives, 1*(3), 119–134.

Walsh, J. (1996). *True odds: How risk affects your everyday life.* Santa Monica, CA: Merritt Publishing.

Warner, K. E. (1989). The epidemiology of coffin nails. In *Health risks and the press: Coverage on media coverage of risk assessment and health.* Washington, DC: The Media Institute.

Wiggins, C. (2002). Warm waters attract people and sharks. *Standard (Baker County)* (March 27). www.bcstandard.com/ news/2002/0327/community/007.html.

Wilson, R. (1979). Analyzing the daily risks of life. *Technology Review, 81*(4), 41–46.

World Bank. (2005). *The World Bank and agriculture and rural development.* World Bank News and Broadcast. September.

World Health Organization (WHO). (2009). *Global status report on road safety: Time for action.* Geneva: World Health Organization. www.who.int/violence_injury_prevention/road_safety_status/2009.

Young, E. (1998). Dealing with hazards and disasters: Risk perception and community participation in management. *Australian Journal of Emergency Management,* (Winter), 14–16.

Zimmerman, R., & Bier, V. (2002). *Risk assessment of extreme events.* Columbia-Wharton/Penn Roundtable on Risk Management Strategies in an Uncertain World, April 12–13. www.ldeo.columbia.edu/CHRR/Roundtable/Zimmerman_WP.pdf.

4

Mitigation

Introduction

Mitigation, sometimes called prevention or risk reduction, is often considered the "cornerstone of disaster management" (FEMA, 2010). While the three other components of the disaster management cycle (preparedness, response, and recovery) are performed either in reaction to hazards or in anticipation of their consequences, mitigation measures seek to reduce the likelihood or consequences of hazard risk before a disaster ever occurs.

Mitigation is by no means a simple answer to the hazard problem, however. Because of the numerous difficulties associated with it, only in the last few decades, its full potential at controlling hazard risk has been recognized. Mitigation measures tend to be costly, disruptive, time-consuming, and in some cases socially unpalatable. They almost always carry their own inherent risk and do not always work as intended. Political will for mitigation is hard to come by in many situations, and the public's attention span tends to be too short to accommodate the significant life changes that may be necessary for mitigation to work. Furthermore, mitigation traditionally has been a luxury of rich nations, with many societies considering it to be something they cannot justify or afford in light of other, more immediate issues.

As the practice of mitigation grows throughout the world, in both wealthy and developing nations, it is emerging as a means of measurably reducing the incidence of many types of disasters. The International Decade for Natural Disaster Reduction and the subsequent International Strategy for Disaster Reduction have proclaimed its value. Following the 2004 tsunami events in Asia that resulted in the deaths of over 120,000 people, it was recognized that a simple, cost-effective early warning system like those currently in use in many nations around the globe could have prevented such a significant loss of life. Clearly, the solutions exist, but the problem lies in implementation.

This chapter provides an overview of mitigation and describes its various forms. Insurance as a mitigation option will be detailed. Finally, several of the many obstacles to mitigation will be presented.

What Is Mitigation?

Mitigation is defined as any sustained effort undertaken to reduce a hazard risk through the reduction of the likelihood and/or the consequence component of that hazard's risk. In other words, mitigation seeks either to make a hazard less likely to occur or to reduce the negative effects if it were to occur.

Each hazard is unique in its effect on humans and the natural and built environments. Likewise, each hazard has a unique set of mitigation options from which disaster managers may choose that have been developed or been conceived but remain to be developed. Each option carries an associated cost, a level of feasibility based upon several factors, and an expected success rate for actually reducing the risk as designed. What methods, if any, the disaster manager selects will be wholly dependent upon these and a range of other factors, including the amount of funds available, the anticipated social and physical consequences of such actions, and the receptiveness of the geographic environment into which the measure will be applied.

Once identified and analyzed, as explained in the preceding chapters, risks can be evaluated to determine methods to handle them. As part of this process, mitigation techniques are identified (or developed, if adequate mitigation does not exist for a specific risk) and considered according to their ability to reduce or eliminate hazard likelihood or consequence. While it is true that most risks can be reduced through proper mitigation, such efforts generally become increasingly expensive as the actual level of risk reduction increases. Therefore, depending on the nature of the risk, several different mitigation alternatives may need to be considered and applied to ensure a comprehensive examination of costs to benefits, as shown in the following sections.

Mitigation Goals

When considering the mitigation options suitable for treating a hazard risk, several general goals classify the outcome that disaster managers may seek: risk likelihood reduction, risk consequences reduction, risk avoidance, risk acceptance, and risk transfer, sharing, or spreading.

Risk Likelihood Reduction

It is possible to reduce the chance that many hazards will manifest themselves. For these hazards, risk is reduced through a reduction in likelihood. For some hazards, such as hurricanes, intervention obviously is not yet technically possible (despite many attempts to prove the contrary, including the proposal to detonate a nuclear device in a hurricane's eye). Other hazards, such as river flooding, have several mitigation options available to disaster managers, including dikes, levees, and buyouts (see the following sections), each with associated benefits and secondary risks.

Technological and intentional hazards tend to have a greater overall application of measures that seek to reduce hazard likelihood, simply because the very existence of these hazards is a direct result of human decision. For example, tandem trailers, developed for cargo transport, have been proven to be involved in more accidents than traditional single-trailer rigs. Restricting the use of these vehicles immediately reduces the risk likelihood. While we cannot feasibly "decide" not to have a natural hazard, we can do so with other hazard forms.

Mitigation measures that seek to reduce risk likelihood tend to be nonstructural in nature, but not without exception.

Risk Consequences Reduction

The second primary goal that disaster managers seek through mitigation is a reduction in the impact of a hazard to humans, structures, the environment, or any combination of these. Mitigation measures that address consequences assume that a hazard will occur with an associated intensity or magnitude, and they ensure that the protected structure, population, system, or other subject is able to withstand such an event without negative consequences. Again using the example of hurricane mitigation, we can see that there is a much greater chance of mitigation success with some hazards when disaster managers address those hazards' consequences. Mechanisms enabling structures to be raised above storm surge levels and strengthened against wind damage, storm shelters for affected populations, and regulations restricting actions and activities in high-risk areas all work to considerably reduce the consequences from hurricanes.

Most hazards have one or more options for disaster consequence reduction, which cannot always be said of likelihood reduction. For natural disasters, these measures tend to be structural and address the hardening of structures and systems and the protection of people. For technological hazards, consequence reduction revolves around the development of primary and redundant safety, containment, and cleanup systems. Consequence reduction for intentional hazards, especially terrorism, is still in the primary stages of development, although the increase in global attention to terrorism involving weapons of mass destruction (WMDs) has drastically quickened the pace of such research and development efforts.

Risk Avoidance

Some hazard risks are so great that even with a partial reduction in either their likelihood or consequence, the outcome is still unacceptable. For these risks, only total avoidance is considered, and so it is deemed necessary to take action to reduce either the likelihood or the consequence factor to absolute zero. One day, future discoveries may allow for manageability of these hazards such that they are tolerated, but current methods of mitigation are either nonexistent or prohibitively expensive.

Total risk avoidance for natural hazards usually means removing all people and structures out of the affected area. Such measures are understandably unrealistic for hazards that have a wide geographic range. Civilizations have tended to avoid such high-risk areas as is evident by the historical lack of development in harsh or dangerous climates such as the Antarctic continent. Risk avoidance may be possible for other hazards for which risk is not so all-encompassing and can be mapped within regions. For example, buyout programs seek to physically remove all structures within a floodplain and then restrict all future construction in that reclaimed area.

Risk avoidance is used most often in the treatment of technological disasters for which risk acceptability is subject to more critical consideration in society. For example, since the famed 1979 Three Mile Island nuclear reactor accident, not one new reactor has been approved for construction in the United States (an $8 billion loan guarantee approved in February 2010 by the U.S. government for two new reactors has not resulted in actual construction). In the case of natural disasters, implementing risk avoidance measures in areas that have already been settled can be very difficult due to sociocultural and legal matters. Avoidance mitigation often involves uprooting whole communities, at least a temporary reduction in services and quality of life, and the disruption of cultural and social frameworks. These measures are rarely conducted without resistance, ultimately requiring forced implementation by law enforcement or other government authority figures.

Risk Acceptance

For certain hazards, disaster managers, as well as societies and individuals, consider a certain risk to be acceptable "as is." It may be determined that any further reduction in risk is either too expensive or unnecessary. Several reasons might lead to this decision.

First, every community, country, or region has a whole range of hazards with which it must contend, and it assuredly has limited funding to treat that range of hazards. Certain risks, shown by their cost-benefit analyses, are better left untreated so that funding that would have been dedicated to that treatment may be applied to other hazards for which risk reduction will have greater value.

Second, some risk reduction measures will result in one or more undesirable consequences. These secondary consequences may simply be the reduction in an enjoyed benefit that existed because of the hazard, or undesirable consequences may be expected to arise as a direct result of the mitigation measure (in which case, the secondary consequences are considered more damaging or undesirable than the consequences of the hazard risk).

A third reason risk acceptance many be practiced relates to sociocultural patterns. Many cultures identify with a certain place or location, and would rather face a certain risk than leave for a "safer" option. Certain religious beliefs cause people to accept risks as the will of some higher power that is beyond their control, not as an avoidable option. These reasons pose especially difficult obstacles to disaster managers, as will be detailed in the section entitled "Obstacles to Mitigation."

Unlike risk avoidance, risk acceptance is rarely considered a luxury. Japan, for instance, spent more than $30 billion on mitigation-related projects in 2003 (UNISDR, 2005). In most cases, risk acceptance is entertained or applied not when risk reduction or avoidance measures are unavailable but when they are unaffordable. Understandably, risk acceptance, even if in a de facto manner, occurs most often in poor nations forced into such decisions by their lack of available funds.

Risk Transfer, Sharing, or Spreading

The final and most debated goal of mitigation is risk transfer, sharing, or spreading. The concept behind this goal is that the risk is not actually reduced, but its consequence or likelihood is diluted across a large group of people such that each suffers an average consequence (which may in fact be greater or less than what each would have suffered without participation in the measure).

The most common forms of risk transfer are insurance coverage and international reinsurance. Insurance reduces the financial consequence of a hazard risk by eliminating the monetary loss of property. Insurers charge a calculated premium, priced according to the hazard's expected frequency and consequence, which guarantees the repayment of losses in the event that the insured hazard occurs. The cost of the disaster is thereby shared by (or spread across) all customers through the payment of premiums. Victims and nonvictims alike pay the same premium (the consequence), with the common fund collected bearing the brunt of the disaster.

Risk sharing, spreading, and insurance schemes appeared as early as 1950 BC when shipping companies began practicing bottomry, the sharing of costs related to maritime risk among all vessels in a fleet (Covello & Mumpower, 1985). Insurance as a mitigation option is not without controversy, and is discussed in further detail in the section entitled "Risk Transfer, Sharing, and Spreading." Noninsurance forms of risk spreading do exist, including crop diversification and redundancy in lifeline systems. These will also be discussed.

More direct risk sharing and spreading measures are common in developing countries, where informal agreements exist within social groups to accommodate the particular needs of victims within those groups. One common practice is food sharing schemes, which ensure that all members of a community have enough to eat despite seasonal or unexpected shortages of their personal crops.

Types of Mitigation: Structural and Nonstructural

The mitigation measures employed to achieve the first two goals previously listed, a reduction in the likelihood or consequence of a hazard, are grouped into two primary categories: structural and nonstructural. Although these two terms are almost universally used to differentiate between the various options available to disaster managers, much disagreement exists concerning the actual delineation of what makes something structural or nonstructural.

For the purposes of this text, structural mitigation is defined as a risk reduction effort performed through the construction or altering of the physical environment through the application of engineered solutions. Nonstructural mitigation is defined as a measure that reduces risk through modification in human behavior or natural processes without requiring the use of engineered structures. It must be noted that, while there are several mitigation measures that will clearly fit into one category or the other regardless of the definition of the terms, there are also many that could go either way, and may appear as one form in this text and another form elsewhere. These two categories are described in detail in the following sections.

Structural Mitigation

Structural mitigation measures are those that involve or dictate the necessity for some form of construction, engineering, or other mechanical changes or improvements aimed at reducing hazard risk likelihood or consequence. They often are considered attempts at "man controlling nature" when applied to natural disasters. Structural measures are generally expensive and include a full range of regulation, compliance, enforcement, inspection, maintenance, and renewal issues.

Although each hazard has a unique set of structural mitigation measures that may be applied to its risk, these measures may be grouped across some general categories. Each category will be described with examples of how the mitigation type would be applied to one or more individual hazard types. The general structural mitigation groups to be described are

- Resistant construction
- Building codes and regulatory measures
- Relocation
- Structural modification
- Construction of community shelters
- Construction of barrier, deflection, or retention systems
- Detection systems
- Physical modification
- Treatment systems
- Redundancy in life safety infrastructure

Resistant Construction
Clearly, the best way to maximize the chance that a structure is able to resist the forces inflicted by various hazards is to ensure that it is designed in such a way *prior to construction* to do just that. Through awareness and education, individual, corporate, and government entities can be informed of the hazards that exist and the measures that can be taken to mitigate the risks of those hazards, allowing resistant construction to be considered. As a mitigation option, designing hazard resistance into the structure from the start is the most cost-effective option and the option most likely to succeed.

Whether or not builders choose to use hazard-resistant design depends upon whether they have access to the financial resources, the technical expertise necessary to correctly engineer the construction, and the material resources required for such measures.

FIGURE 4–1 House built on stilts above annual flood levels in Guayas Province, Ecuador.

Where cultures have adapted to living with a hazard, construction styles may incorporate hazard-resistant design. This is often seen in areas with annual flooding, where houses are built on stilts (see Figure 4–1). An example of a culturally adjusted hazard-resistant construction style is the houses built by the Banni in India (discussed in Chapter 3), which resist the shaking of earthquakes. Little funding and minimal added effort are required to design these mitigation measures into the construction from the start, but building a standard, nonresistant house and altering it at a later time is both cost- and ability-prohibitive.

Building Codes and Regulatory Measures

Hazard-resistant construction, as previously explained, is clearly an effective way to reduce vulnerability to select hazards. However, the builder of the house must apply these resistant construction measures for there to be an actual reduction in a population's overall vulnerability. One way that governments can ensure members of the population apply hazard-resistant construction is by creating building codes to guide construction and passing legislation that requires those codes to be followed.

Regulatory structures are one of the most widely adopted structural mitigation measures, used in almost every country of the world in some form. With sufficient knowledge about the hazards likely to affect a region or a country, engineers can develop building codes that guide builders to ensure that their designs are able to resist the forces of the relevant hazards. Although simple in theory, inherent problems with codes and regulations can drastically decrease their effectiveness.

Building codes ensure that structure designs include resistance to various forms of external pressure. Each hazard emits a unique set of external pressures on structures, including:

- Lateral and/or vertical shaking (earthquakes)
- Lateral and/or uplift load pressure (severe storms, cyclonic storms, tornadoes, windstorms)
- Extreme heat (structure fires, wildland fires, forest fires)
- Roof loading (hailstorms, snowstorms, ash falls)
- Hydrological pressure (floods, storm surge)

When properly applied, building codes offer a great deal of protection from a wide range of hazards. They are a primary reason for the drastic drop in the number of earthquake deaths in the developing world during the last century. They are so effective because they completely integrate protection measures into the structure from the design phase onward, rather than applying the measures after construction.

Unfortunately, these measures have several negative aspects that prevent them from being used more widely and more effectively. Most countries have building codes, but few use them to their fullest capacity. First, any increase in building resistance increases the subsequent cost of construction. Developers fight the creation of strict building codes because the need to use stronger and additional materials decreases the profit margins of their structures.

Second, for building codes to be successful there must be compliance. Compliance can only be ensured through enforcement, which creates a new budgetary expense for government officials. Even when enforcement is possible through building inspections, misconduct is always possible in the form of bribery, neglect, cronyism, and so forth. Inspectors may lack the proper training or expertise to adequately do their job, leaving them unable to correctly identify hazardous conditions or breaches in building codes.

Relocation

Occasionally, the most sensible way to protect a structure or a people from a hazard is to relocate it or them away from the hazard. Homes and other structures may be disassembled or transported intact.

Flooding is the most common reason that structures are relocated. Although destroying the original structure and rebuilding it elsewhere is often less expensive and technically more feasible, in certain circumstances such actions are either impossible or undesirable. For example, the structure in question may be a cultural heritage site that cannot be replaced. The Abu Simbel temple in Egypt, which would have been flooded after the damming of the Nile at Aswan, was moved 90 m from its original location to protect it.

In some instances where the hazard area is especially great, moving entire communities may be necessary. One such example is the town of Valdez, Alaska, which was relocated in 1967 after hazard assessments showed that the entire town was built upon unstable soil. Fifty-two of the original structures were moved to a new site 4 miles away, while the rest were destroyed and rebuilt in their new location.

Structural Modification

Scientific progress and ongoing research continually provide new information about hazards. This new information can reveal that structures in identified risk zones are not designed to resist the forces of a likely hazard. There are three treatment options for these structures. The first is to do nothing. Second, the structure may be demolished and rebuilt to accommodate the new hazard information. Third, often the most appropriate action, is to modify the structure such that it resists the anticipated external forces. This action is often referred to as retrofitting (see Figure 4–2).

How the retrofit affects the structure depends on the hazard risk that is being treated. Examples of hazards and their retrofits include:

- *Cyclonic storms.* Wind-resistant shingles; shutters; waterproofing (often called secondary water resistance; SWR); stronger frame connections and joints (including "roof straps," which help secure the roof to the main structure of the house); structural elevation; lateral support structures; stronger doorways (including garage doors)

FIGURE 4–2 Mexico City parking garage with external steel frame retrofit.

- *Earthquakes.* Sheer walls, removal of cripple walls, foundation anchor bolts, frame anchor connections, floor framing, chimney reinforcement, base isolation systems, external frames, removal of roof weight, soft-story reinforcement
- *Floods.* Structural elevation, first-floor conversion, "wet" and "dry" floodproofing, foundation flood vents
- *Wildfire.* Replacement of external materials, including decks, gutters, downspouts, paneling, doors, window frames, and roof shingles, with those that are fire-resistant
- *Hail.* Increase roof slope, strengthen roof materials, strengthen load-carrying capacity of flat or shallow-angle roofs
- *Tornadoes.* In addition to the modifications for cyclonic storms, construction of a "safe room" or basement shelter
- *Lightning.* Electrical grounding of the house with lightning rods or other devices
- *Extreme heat.* Air-conditioning systems
- *Terrorism.* Hardening of exterior walls, construction of blast walls, replacement of glass with shatter-resistant material, use of a filtered and restricted-access air system, restricted-access entryway

Construction of Community Shelters

The lives of community residents can be protected from a disaster's consequences through the construction of shelters designed to withstand a certain type or range of hazard consequences. Shelters are usually constructed when it is either unlikely or unrealistic for all or a majority of community members to be able to protect themselves from the hazard in their homes or elsewhere. Two systems must be in place for shelters to work. First, there must be an effective early warning system that would enable residents to have enough time to travel to the shelter before the hazard event. This immediately rules out several hazards for which warning is impossible or unlikely, such as earthquakes or landslides. Second, there must be a public education campaign that both raises awareness of the existence of the shelter and teaches residents how to recognize when to travel to the shelter.

During the Cold War, many countries built shelters or designated qualified buildings to protect citizens from the dangerous fallout effects of a nuclear attack. Shelters are much more likely to be utilized in poor communities throughout the world, where housing construction is especially deficient. For this reason, it is common for community development projects to design community buildings like schools that double as a shelter in the event of a disaster.

Construction of Barrier, Deflection, or Retention Systems

The forces that many hazards exert upon man and the built environment can be controlled through specifically engineered structures. These structures fall under three main categories: barriers, deflection systems, and retention systems.

Barriers are designed to stop a physical force dead in its tracks. Their job is to absorb the impact of whatever force is being exerted. They are, in other words, blocking devices. Barrier walls can be made of natural materials, such as trees, bushes, or even existing soil, or they can be constructed of foreign materials, such as stone, concrete, wood, or metal. Depending upon the hazard type, barriers may be built on just one side of a structure, or may completely surround it. Examples of barriers and the hazards they are designed to protect against include:

- Seawalls (cyclonic storm surges, tsunamis, high waves, rough seas, and coastal erosion) (see Figure 4–3)
- Floodwalls, dikes, berms (floods, flash floods)
- Natural or synthetic wind and particle movement barriers (strong seasonal winds, sand drift, dune movement, beach erosion, snow drift)
- Defensible spaces (wildfires, forest fires)
- Mass movement protection walls (landslides, mudslides, rockslides, avalanches)
- Security fences, checkpoints (terrorism, civil disturbances)
- HAZMAT linings (ground contamination)

Deflection systems are designed to divert the physical force of a hazard, allowing it to change course so that a structure situated in its original path escapes harm. Like barriers, deflection systems may be constructed from a full range of materials, both natural and manmade. Examples of deflection systems and the hazards they are designed to protect against include:

- Avalanche bridges (snow avalanches)
- Chutes (landslides, mudflows, lahars, rockslides)
- Lava flow channels (volcanic lava)
- Diversion trenches, channels, canals, and spillways (floods; see Figure 4–4)

FIGURE 4–3 Example of a seawall failure following Hurricane Jeanne in 2004, Melbourne Shores, Florida. (Photo courtesy of USGS, 2004)

FIGURE 4–4 Flood spillway in use on Hayes Lake, Roseau River, Minnesota. (Photo courtesy of U.S. NOAA, 2002)

Retention systems are designed to contain a hazard, preventing its destructive forces from ever being released. These structures generally seek to increase the threshold to which hazards are physically maintained. Examples include:

- Dams (drought, floods)
- Levees and flood walls (floods)
- Slit dams (sedimentation, floods)
- Landslide walls (masonry, concrete, rock cage, crib walls, bin walls, and buttress walls)
- Slope stabilization covers (concrete, netting, wire mesh, vegetation landslides, mudflows, rockfalls; see Figure 4–5)

Detection systems are designed to recognize a hazard that might not otherwise be perceptible to humans. They have applications for natural, technological, and intentional hazards. As more funding is dedicated to the research and development of detection systems, their ability to prevent disasters or warn of hazard consequences before disaster strikes increases. With natural disasters, detection systems are primarily used to save lives. With technological and intentional hazards, however, it may be possible to prevent an attack, explosion, fire, accident, or other damaging events. Examples of detection systems are

- Imaging satellites (wildfires, hurricanes, volcanoes, landslides, avalanches, floods, fire risk, terrorism, virtually all hazards; see Exhibit 4–1)

FIGURE 4–5 Slope covered with concrete and outfitted with drainage pipes to prevent landslides.

EXHIBIT 4–1: CHINA USES SATELLITES TO MONITOR NATURAL DISASTERS

Telecommunication and imagery satellites, launched for a number of reasons independent of disaster management, are being used to an increasing degree to provide advance and assessment information about hazards and disasters. Satellites are a constant source of accurate and up-to-date information about conditions on the ground in all countries of the world. When disasters happen, and access is limited, they may be the only means of understanding what damage has occurred and where.

The use of satellite imagery was used extensively in the aftermath of the September 11th terrorist attacks to estimate the amount of debris that required removal, and even as early as 1993 when imagery was used to accurately measure the extent of flooding around the Mississippi River in the U.S. Midwest. Satellites have been tracking storms for decades, providing days of advance warning for major cyclonic storms like Hurricane Katrina and Cyclone Nargis.

In the aftermath of disasters in the developing world, satellite imagery can be invaluable in assessing both damages and needs. After the Sichuan Earthquake in China in 2008, for instance, nearly 1300 satellite images were processed to monitor and evaluate damage, mitigate additional threats, and guide relief workers through affected areas. China had announced in January of 2008 that it would be developing the capacity to use satellites built to measure environmental resources to monitor natural disasters, and the decision helped considerably. Through imagery normally used for city planning, environmental protection, and land resource surveys, the Chinese government space agency was able to identify areas of greatest need, and even determine the number of structures and infrastructure components that had been damaged or destroyed.

Collaborations like the International Charter on Space and Major Disasters offer governments free satellite data, from cooperating space agencies, to help cope with ongoing disasters. But there are still costs for long-term monitoring and predicting risk. Sian Lewis, of SciDev.Net, wrote:

> Sometimes (but not always), the limited uptake comes from implementation barriers—countries may lack the institutional infrastructure or human expertise to quickly analyze and interpret satellite data, and disseminate it to emergency services. But arguably the most significant barrier in the world's poorest regions is a lack of political support. Very few politicians—particularly in Africa—have shown interest in remote sensing, or much understanding of how it can help manage natural disasters.

Sources: Lewis, 2009; China View, 2008.

- Chemical/biological/radiological/explosive detection systems (technological hazards, chemical leaks, pipeline failures, terrorism)
- Ground movement monitoring system (seismicity, volcanic activity, dam failure, expansive soils, land subsidence, rail infrastructure failure)
- Flood gauges (hydrologic hazards)
- Weather stations (severe weather, tornadoes)
- Undersea and buoy oceanic movement detection (tsunamis; see Figure 4–6 and Exhibit 4–2)
- Information systems (epidemics, WMD terrorism)

FIGURE 4–6 Tsunami buoy being deployed in the Pacific Ocean by the U.S. NOAA ship *Ronald H. Brown*. (Photo courtesy of NOAA)

Physical modification is the group of mitigation measures that alters the physical landscape in such a manner that hazard likelihood or consequence is reduced. This can be performed through simple landscaping measures or through the use of engineered devices. Ground modification examples include:

- Slope terracing—landslides, mudflows, erosion (see Figure 4–7)
- Slope drainage—landslides, mudflows, erosion
- Regrading of steep slopes—landslides, mudflows, rockfalls, erosion, avalanches
- Anchors and piling—landslides
- Removal and/or replacement of soils—expansive soils
- Wetland reclamation—flooding
- Dredging rivers and channelization—flooding
- Dredging reservoirs—drought
- Building culverts—flooding

EXHIBIT 4–2: THE AUSTRALIAN TSUNAMI ALERT SYSTEM (ATAS)

Australia faces extreme tsunami risk given that it is bounded on three sides by approximately 8000 km of seismically active plate boundaries that generate about one-third of all of the world's earthquakes. This zone is capable of delivering tsunamis to the Australian coast within 2 to 4 hours.

After the December 26, 2004, tsunami events, the Australian government wished to increase their ability to warn the Australian population if a tsunami were headed their way, in order to limit the loss of human life. The Australian Tsunami Alert System (ATAS) existed prior to this event, but had limited capabilities in tsunami monitoring and warning.

In 2005, the Australian government committed $68.9M over 4 years to establish an Australian tsunami warning system. This effort included:

- Establishment of the Joint Australian Tsunami Warning Centre (JATWC) with 24/7 monitoring and analysis capacity for Australia
- The upgrade and expansion of sea level and seismic monitoring networks around Australia and in the Indian and Southwest Pacific Oceans
- Implementation of national tsunami education and training programs
- Assistance to the Australian Intergovernmental Oceanographic Commission (IOC) in developing the existing Pacific Tsunami Warning & Mitigation System (PTWS) and establishing an Indian Ocean Tsunami Warning & Mitigation System (IOTWS)
- Technical assistance to help build the capacity of scientists, technicians, and emergency managers in Southwest Pacific and Indian Ocean countries

The system operates through the existence of an enhanced national network of seismic stations combined with data from international monitoring networks. Government officials are advised of the magnitude, location, and characteristics of seismic events that have the potential to generate a tsunami. Based on this information, the Australian government runs a tsunami model to generate an estimate of the tsunami size, arrival time, and potential impact locations. The existence of a tsunami is verified using information from an enhanced sea level monitoring network. Advice and warnings are then issued as needed on any possible tsunami threat to State and Territory emergency management services, media, and the public.

Source: Government of Australia, 2010.

Treatment systems seek to remove a hazard from a natural system that humans depend on. These systems may be designed for nonstop use or for use in certain circumstances where a hazard is known to be present. Examples include:

- Water treatment systems
- HEPA air filtration ventilation systems
- Airborne pathogen decontamination systems
- Hazardous materials (HAZMAT) decontamination systems

FIGURE 4–7 Slope terracing in Nepal. (Photo courtesy of Sharon Ketchum)

One last structural mitigation measure is *redundancy in life safety infrastructure.* As humans have evolved beyond subsistence living, they have become more dependent upon each other and on societal infrastructure. Today, private and government infrastructure may provide an individual with food, water, sewerage, electricity, communications, transportation, medical care, and more. With such great dependency on these systems, failure in any one could quickly lead to catastrophe. Examples of life safety systems into which redundancy may be built include:

- Electricity infrastructure
- Public health infrastructure
- Emergency management infrastructure
- Water storage, treatment, conveyance, and delivery systems
- Transportation infrastructure
- Irrigation systems
- Food delivery

Nonstructural Mitigation

Nonstructural mitigation, as defined previously, generally involves a reduction in the likelihood or consequence of risk through modifications in human behavior or natural processes, without requiring the use of engineered structures. Nonstructural mitigation techniques are often considered mechanisms where "man adapts to nature." They tend to be less costly and fairly easy for communities with few financial or technological resources to implement.

The following section describes several of the various categories into which nonstructural mitigation measures may be grouped, and provides several examples of each:

- Regulatory measures
- Community awareness and education programs

- Nonstructural physical modifications
- Environmental control
- Behavioral modification

Regulatory Measures

Regulatory measures limit hazard risk by legally dictating human actions. Regulations can be applied to several facets of societal and individual life, and are used when it is determined that such action is required for the common good of the society. Although the use of regulatory measures is pervasive, compliance is a widespread problem because the cost of enforcement can be prohibitive and inspectors may be untrained, ineffective, or susceptible to bribes.

Examples of regulatory mitigation measures include:

- *Land use management (zoning).* This is a legally imposed restriction on how land may be used. It may apply to specific geographic designations, such as coastal zone management, hillside or slope management, floodplain development restrictions, or microclimatic siting of structures (such as placing structures only on the leeward side of a hill).

- *Open space preservation (green spaces).* This practice attempts to limit the settlement or activities of people in areas that are known to be at high risk for one or more hazards.

- *Protective resource preservation.* In some situations, a tract of land is not at risk from a hazard, but a new hazard will be created by disturbing that land. Examples include protecting forests that serve to block wind and wetlands preservation.

- *Denial of services to high-risk areas.* When squatter and informal settlements form on high-risk land despite the existence of preventive regulatory measures, it is possible to discourage growth and reverse settlement trends by ensuring that services such as electricity, running water, and communications do not reach the unsafe settlement. This measure is only acceptable when performed in conjunction with a project that seeks to offer alternative, safe accommodations for the inhabitants (otherwise, a secondary humanitarian disaster may result).

- *Density control.* By regulating the number of people who may reside in an area of known or estimated risk, it is possible to limit vulnerability and control the amount of resources considered adequate for protection from and response to that known hazard. Many response mechanisms are overwhelmed because the number of casualties in an affected area is much higher than was anticipated.

- *Building use regulations.* To protect against certain hazards, it is possible to restrict the types of activities that may be performed in a building. These restrictions may apply to people, materials, or activities.

- *Mitigation easements.* Easements are agreements between private individuals or organizations and the government that dictate how a particular tract of land will be used. Mitigation easements are agreements to restrict the private use of land for the purposes of risk reduction.

- *HAZMAT manufacture, use, transport, and disposal.* Hazardous materials are a major threat to life and property in all countries. Most governments have developed safety standards and procedures to guide the way that these materials are manufactured and used by businesses and individuals, the mechanisms by which they are transported from place to place, and the methods and devices that contain them.

- *Safety standards and regulations.* Regulations that guide safe activities and practices are diverse and apply to more situations than could be described in this chapter. Safety regulations may apply to individuals (seatbelt laws), households (use of smoke detectors), communities, businesses, and governments. The establishment of building codes, as described in the section Structural Mitigation, is an example of a safety regulation.

- *Natural resource use regulations.* The use of common natural resources, such as aquifers, can be controlled for the purpose of minimizing hazard risk (in this case, drought).

- *Storm water management regulations.* Storm water runoff can be destructive to the areas where it originates (through erosion), and to the areas where it terminates (through silting), pollution, changes to stream flows, and other effects. Development, especially when large amounts of land are covered with impervious materials like concrete, can drastically increase the amount of runoff by decreasing the holding capacity of the land. Regulations on storm water management, imposed on private and public development projects, help to manage those negative effects, reducing both hazard risk and environmental vulnerability.

- *Environmental protection regulations.* Certain environmental features, such as rivers, streams, lakes, and wetlands, play an important part in reducing the vulnerability of a community or country. Preventing certain behaviors, such as dumping or polluting, helps to ensure that these resources continue to offer their risk-reduction benefits.

- *Public disclosure regulations.* Property owners may be required to disclose all known risks, such as flood or earthquake hazard risk, when selling their property. This ensures hazard awareness and increases the chance that purchasers will take appropriate action for those known risks when they begin construction or other activities on that land.

- *Mitigation requirements on loans.* Banks and other lending institutions have much at stake when they lend money to developers. Therefore, lenders can apply mitigation requirements or at the very least require that hazard assessments be conducted, and governments can require that such actions be taken by those lending institutions. Such policies limit the building of unsafe projects.

Community Awareness and Education Programs

The public is most able to protect itself from the effects of a hazard if it is first informed that the hazard exists, and then educated about what it can do to limit its risk.

Public education programs are considered both mitigation and preparedness measures. An informed public that applies appropriate measures to reduce their risk before a disaster occurs has performed mitigation. However, a public that has been trained in response activities has participated in a preparedness activity.

Often termed "risk communication," projects designed to educate the public may include one or more of the following:

- Awareness of the hazard risk
- Behavior modification
    - Predisaster risk reduction behavior
    - Predisaster preparedness behavior
    - Postdisaster response behavior
    - Postdisaster recovery behavior
- Warning

A more detailed description is provided in Chapter 5.

Warning systems inform the public that a hazard risk has reached a threshold requiring certain protective actions. Depending upon the hazard type and the warning system's technological capabilities, the amount of time citizens have to act varies. Some warning systems, especially those that apply to technological and intentional hazards, are not able to provide warning until the hazard has already begun to exhibit its damaging behavior (such as a leak at a chemical production facility, or an accident involving a hazardous materials tanker truck). The UN Platform for the Promotion of Early Warning (PPEW, n.d.) states that four separate factors are necessary for effective early warning:

1. Prior knowledge of the risks faced by communities
2. A technical monitoring and warning service for these risks
3. The dissemination of understandable warnings to those at risk
4. Knowledge by people of how to react and the capacity to do so

Warning systems, therefore, are dependent upon hazard identification and analysis, effective detection systems (as described in the section Structural Mitigation), dissemination of the message, and public education. A tsunami that occurred in American Samoa in 2009 illustrates the ineffectiveness of a system missing even just one of these components. The tsunami had been detected by the U.S. government and transmitted to the Governor of American Samoa, and that the people of American Samoa were trained in personal response to tsunamis, but the lack of an alert system prevented ample warning and many people who otherwise could have escaped were killed (American Samoa Government, 2009).

Early warning systems have been developed to varying capacities for the following hazards:

- Drought
- Tornadoes/windstorms
- Cyclonic storms
- Epidemics
- Landslides
- Earthquakes
- Chemical releases
- Volcanoes
- Floods
- Wildfires
- Air raids/attacks
- Terrorist threats
- Tsunamis
- Extreme winter weather

For an inventory of early warning systems, see http://database.unep.dkkv.org/.

Risk mapping involves presenting the likelihood and consequence components in the format of a physical map, with figures based upon a specific hazard or set of hazards. Risk maps are fundamental to disaster management, and are very effective as a mitigation tool. Using risk maps, governments and

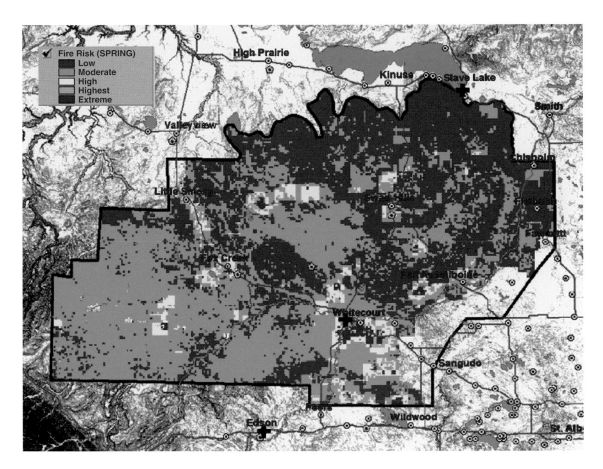

FIGURE 4–8 Map detailing the likelihood of fire determined by activities and presence of causative agents. (From Alberta Sustainable Resource Development)

other entities can most effectively dedicate resources to areas of greatest need, and plan in advance of incidents, so that adequate response resources are able to reach those highest risk areas without unforeseen problems. Risk maps are generally based upon the base maps discussed in Chapter 2, but include the added information acquired through the risk analysis and assessment described in Chapter 3 (see Figure 4–8).

Nonstructural Physical Modifications

Several different mitigation options, while not structural in nature, involve a physical modification to a structure or to property that results in reduced risk.

Examples include:

- *Securing of furniture, pictures, and appliances, and installing latches on cupboards.* In many earthquakes, the majority of injuries are caused by falling furniture and other unsecured belongings. Economic costs also can be reduced significantly through this very inexpensive, simple measure that generally requires little more than connecting items to walls through the use of a specially designed thin metal strap.

- *Removal or securing of projectiles.* During tornadoes, items commonly found outside the house, such as cooking grills, furniture, and stored wood, may become airborne projectiles that cause harm, fatalities, or further property damage.

Environmental Control

Structural mitigation involves engineered structures that control hazards. It is also possible to control or influence hazards through nonengineered structural means. These nonstructural mechanisms tend to be highly hazard specific, and include:

- Explosive detonation to relieve seismic pressure (earthquakes)
- Launched or placed explosives to release stored snow cover (avalanches)
- Cloud seeding (hail, hurricanes, drought, snow)
- Chemical surface treatment (ice and snowstorms)
- Controlled burns (wildfires)
- Bombing of volcano flows (volcanic eruption)
- Dune and beach restoration or preservation (storm surges, tsunamis, erosion)
- Forest and vegetation management (landslides, mudflows, flooding, erosion)
- Riverine and reservoir sediment and erosion control (flooding)
- Removal and replacement of soils (expansive soils)
- Hillside drainage (landslides, mudslides, erosion)
- Slope grading (landslides, mudslides, rockfalls, erosion)
- Disease vector eradication (epidemics; see Figure 4–9 and Exhibit 4–3)

Behavioral Modification

Through collective action, a community can alter the behavior of individuals; resulting in some common risk reduction benefit. Voluntary behavior modification measures are more difficult to implement than the regulatory measures previously listed, because they usually involve some form of sacrifice. However, through effective public education, behavioral modification is possible. Tax incentives, or subsidies, can help to increase the success of behavioral modification practices. Examples of mitigation measures that involve behavioral modification include:

- *Rationing.* Rationing is often performed prior to and during periods of drought. Because it can be very difficult for governments to limit vital services such as water to citizens, it is up to citizens to limit their individual usage. Electricity rationing is also performed during periods of extreme heat or cold to ensure that electrical climate control systems are able to perform as required.
- *Environmental conservation.* Many practices, in both urban and rural areas, are very destructive to the environment. Once the environmental feature—a body of water, a forest, or a hillside—is destroyed, secondary hazardous consequences may appear that could have been avoided. Through proper education and the offering of alternatives, destructive practices can be halted before too much damage is done. Examples of environmental conservation include

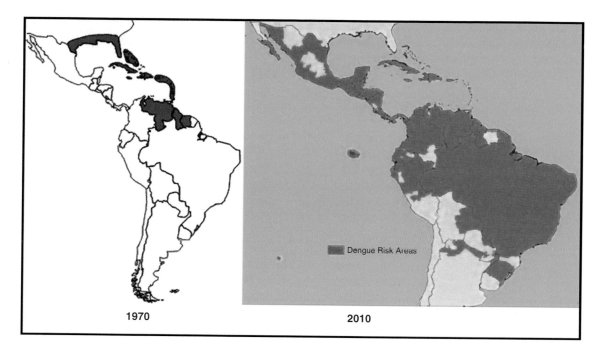

FIGURE 4-9 Incidence of dengue fever (in red) showing 1970 levels during a mosquito eradication campaign, and 2010 levels, decades after the eradication campaign was stopped. (From U.S. CDC, 2005) (For interpretation of the references to color in this figure legend, the reader is referred to the web version of this chapter.)

environmentally friendly farming practices, wood harvesting that does not cause deforestation, and protecting coral reefs from dynamite fishing and other fishing practices.

- *Tax incentives, subsidies, and other financial rewards for safe practices.* Individuals and businesses can be coaxed into safer practices that reduce overall risk through financial incentives. Examples of schemes that use financial incentives include lower insurance premiums, housing buyout programs to move out of high-risk areas, farm subsidies for allowing land to be used for flood control during emergencies, and environmentally friendly farming practices (no deforestation, responsible grazing practices, flexible farming and cropping).

- *Strengthening of social ties.* When a community strengthens its social ties, it is more likely to withstand a hazard's stresses. For many reasons, the largest of which is urbanization, these ties break and are not replaced. In Chicago in 1995, a heat wave caused the death of 739 people. It was later determined that weak social structures were primarily to blame for the deaths, which could have been prevented had friends, family, or neighbors checked on the victims.

Risk Transfer, Sharing, and Spreading

Risk transfer, sharing, and spreading are often considered mitigation measures, although they do absolutely nothing to reduce actual disaster consequences or reduce hazard likelihood. The concept behind these measures is that the financial disaster consequences that do occur are shared by a large group of

EXHIBIT 4–3: DENGUE FEVER ERADICATION—AN EXAMPLE OF FAILED MITIGATION

Dengue fever is caused by four closely related "flavoviruses": DEN-1, DEN-2, DEN-3, and DEN-4. When people are infected with one of these viruses, they gain lifetime immunity if they survive the illness. However, they will not have cross-protective immunity, and people living in dengue-endemic areas can actually have four dengue infections during their lifetime. Dengue fever occurs predominantly in the tropics, and is spread through a cycle of infection between humans and the *Aedes aegypti* mosquito.

Infection with dengue fever results in a full range of nonspecific viral symptoms spanning from mild to severe and fatal hemorrhagic disease. Important risk factors for the disease include the strain and serotype of the infecting virus, as well as the age, immune status, and genetic predisposition of the infected person.

The emergence of dengue fever has been most dramatic in Latin America. In an effort to eradicate yellow fever, which is also transmitted by the *Aedes aegypti* mosquito, the Pan American Health Organization (PAHO) organized a campaign that effectively eradicated the insect from most Central and South American countries during the 1950s and 1960s. As a result, epidemic dengue was also limited, occurring only sporadically in some Caribbean islands during this time. The eradication program was officially discontinued in the United States in 1970, and subsequently stopped elsewhere in the following years. As a result, the species began to re-infest countries from which it had been eradicated, and by 1997, the geographic distribution of *Aedis aegypti* was wider than its distribution before the eradication program (see Figure 4–9).

In 1970, only DEN-2 virus was present in the Americas. DEN-1 was introduced in 1977, resulting in 16 years of major epidemics throughout the region. DEN-4 was introduced in 1981 and caused similar epidemics. Also in 1981, a new strain of DEN-2 from Southeast Asia caused the first major dengue hemorrhagic fever (DHF) epidemic in the Americas. This strain has spread rapidly throughout the region and has caused outbreaks of DHF in Venezuela, Colombia, Brazil, French Guiana, Suriname, and Puerto Rico. By 1997, 18 countries in the region had reported confirmed DHF cases, and it is now endemic in many of these countries.

The DEN-3 virus reappeared in the Americas after an absence of 16 years, first detected in Nicaragua in 1994. Almost simultaneously, the strain was confirmed in Panama and, in early 1995, in Costa Rica. In Nicaragua, considerable numbers of DHF cases were associated with the epidemic. Gene testing from the DEN-3 strains isolated from Panama and Nicaragua showed that the new American DEN-3 strain likely came from Asia, since it is genetically distinct from the DEN-3 strain found previously in the Americas, but is identical to the DEN-3 virus serotype that caused major epidemics in Sri Lanka and India in the 1980s. As suggested by the finding of a new DEN-3 strain and the susceptibility of the population in the American tropics to it, DEN-3 spread rapidly throughout the region, causing major dengue epidemics in Central America in 1995.

As of 1997, dengue was the most important mosquito-borne viral disease affecting humans; its global distribution is comparable to that of malaria, and an estimated 2.5 billion people live in areas at risk for epidemic transmission. Each year, tens of millions of cases of dengue fever occur and, depending on the year, up to hundreds of thousands of cases of DHF. The case-fatality rate of DHF in most countries is about 5%, with most fatalities affecting children and young adults.

Source: CDC, 2005.

people, rather than the entire burden falling only on the affected individuals. The result is a calculated average consequence cost, such as an insurance premium.

Insurance, which is the most common mitigation measure in this category, is defined as: "A promise of compensation for specific potential future losses in exchange for a periodic payment" (InvestorWords.com, 2003). Insurance is a mechanism by which the financial well-being of an individual, company, or other entity is protected against an incidence of unexpected loss. Insurance can be mandatory (required by law) or optional.

Insurance operates through the use of premiums, or payments determined by the insurer. In exchange for premiums, the insurer agrees to pay the policyholder a sum of money (up to an established maximum amount) upon the occurrence of a specifically defined disastrous event. The majority of insurance policies include a deductible, which can be a fixed amount per loss (e.g., the first $1000 of a loss), a percentage of the loss (5% of the total loss), or a combination. The insurer pays the remaining amount, up to the limits established in the original contract. In general, the lower (smaller) the deductible associated with a policy, the higher the premiums. Common examples of insurance include automobile insurance, health insurance, disability insurance, life insurance, flood insurance, earthquake insurance, terrorism insurance, and business insurance.

Insurance allows losses to be shared across wide populations. To briefly summarize, insurance works as follows. For example, an auto insurer takes into account all of the policyholders it will be insuring. It then estimates the cost of compensating policyholders for all accidents expected to occur during the time period established in the premiums (usually 6 months to a year.) The company then divides that cost, adding its administrative costs, across all policyholders. The premiums can be further calculated using information that gives more specific definitions of risk to certain individuals. For example, if one policyholder has 10 moving violations (speeding tickets) in a period of 10 years and has been found at fault in 5 accidents during the same period, that policyholder is statistically a greater risk to the insurer than someone who has never had an accident or moving violation. It follows, then, that the first policyholder would be expected to pay a higher premium for equal coverage. Insurance companies make the majority of their profits through investing the premiums collected.

To cover losses in case the severity of accidents or disasters is greater than estimated when the policies were created, insurance companies rely on the services of reinsurance companies. Reinsurance companies insure insurance companies and tend to be internationally based to allow the risk to be spread across even greater geographical ranges.

Insurance industry researchers Howard Kunreuther and Paul Freemen investigated the insurability of risks, especially those associated with disastrous consequences. They found that two conditions must be satisfied for a risk to be insurable. First, the hazard in question must be identifiable and quantifiable. In other words, the likelihood and consequence factors must be well understood before an insurer can responsibly and accurately set insurance premiums such that they will be able to adequately compensate customers in the event of a disaster. Second, insurers must be able to set premiums for "each potential customer or class of customers" (Kunreuther & Freemen, 1997). Common hazards, such as house fires and storm damage, have a wealth of information available upon which insurers may calculate their premiums. For catastrophic but rare events, such as earthquakes, it can be difficult or impossible to estimate with any degree of precision how often events will occur and what damages would result (see Exhibit 4–4).

In the wealthier nations of the world, most property owners and renters have some form of insurance that protects the structure itself, the contents of the structure, or both (see Figure 4–10). However, for the reasons listed earlier, this coverage is often limited to common events, with specific

EXHIBIT 4–4: FINDINGS OF THE PROVENTION CONSORTIUM INTERNATIONAL CONFERENCE ON THE POTENTIAL OF INSURANCE FOR DISASTER RISK MANAGEMENT IN DEVELOPING COUNTRIES: CHALLENGES

Lack of information needed for underwriting. Many developing countries lack the data and information needed for sound underwriting and product development. The quality and availability of data may vary, such that in a capital city some information may be available, while in rural areas information may be held only locally and in forms that are not easily understood by noncommunity individuals. Insurance services require information about potential losses and client demand, including data on assets at risk and the vulnerability and hazard exposure of those assets.

Lack of local insurance expertise. In countries where insurance is not common, there is often a distinct lack of local expertise, ranging from actuarial science, underwriting, and risk assessment to claims management and client support.

Lack of awareness and understanding of insurance. It takes time to develop awareness among potential clients about the benefits and costs of insurance, whether the clients are national or local governments, community groups, or low-income individuals. Awareness is important not only for demand development and sales but also because the design of insurance products should be based on client needs. Potential clients need an awareness of basic insurance principles and how these tools could help them before they can articulate their needs and thus generate demand.

High opportunity cost of premiums for the poor. It is often asked if insurance is truly a viable option for the very poor, because premiums are not productive (unless a claim is made), and other needs may be more pressing. Paying premiums will generally not be a priority for a poor household if doing so would require foregoing essentials.

Lack of legal structure and financial services infrastructure. Many developing countries lack the regulatory framework that makes insurance provision possible. Some micro-insurance services are provided in semi-legal ways because the legal environment in host countries does not allow formal insurance. Community groups may be able to aggregate business and overcome moral hazard, adverse selection, and data needs, but formal insurance providers may not be legally allowed to offer services to these groups. Some developing countries' legal systems are developing toward market economy standards, but may not yet be mature enough to link with the international capital markets. Also, many developing countries lack the infrastructure to provide insurance services. Inadequate technological infrastructure such as communications may hinder insurance services and claims management.

Lack of a culture of risk reduction and mitigation. Insurance functions on the assumption that the underlying risk is reduced as much as possible, with insurance mitigating against the remaining unpreventable and unpredictable events ("residual risk"). Many developing countries lack a culture of predisaster risk reduction, or resources and incentives for action are often inadequate. Without a culture of risk reduction and insurance as forms of mitigation, establishing successful insurance will be challenging.

Partner differences in vocabulary, organizational operations, and timelines. Partners in different schemes that provide insurance services might include any mix of national and local governments, nongovernmental organizations (NGOs), civil society and the poor, commercial enterprises, and international organizations. Each potential partner may operate with different vocabularies, goals, and methods, and along different timelines. Different operational structures can also be a challenge: While national governments may need to run decisions through complex and time-consuming democratic decision-making processes, commercial entities need to make decisions based on profitability and other strategic concerns. There is the example of a partnership that fell apart when the involved national government could not provide insurance and reinsurance partners with necessary data by a certain deadline, even though products had been developed and the partnership was ready to move forward.

Need to define partner roles clearly. The word "partnership" among international organizations and national governments often signifies a broad willingness to engage in discussions, while in business the term often implies contractual obligations. Further to such basic differences of understanding and interpretation, there are examples of a national government establishing a pattern of "bailing out" disaster victims following earthquakes, thus creating a disincentive to purchase insurance from a scheme that the government supported as mandatory. International organizations have at times acted as reinsurers for client countries, which in many cases is inappropriate. Roles and agreements must be examined carefully and adjusted so that there is no confusion and detraction of the opportunities and responsibilities of each partner.

Lack of national stability and thus insurance industry confidence. Developing countries may lack the stability in government, regulatory framework, and economy that is required for the provision of sustainable insurance services. Constantly changing governments and regulatory frameworks make it difficult for the insurance industry to establish itself and develop a viable market. Unstable macroeconomies can affect the ability of potential clients to pay premiums over a long period of time. The insurance industry is aware of these risks and commensurately wary of doing business under such conditions.

Source: ProVention Consortium, 2004.

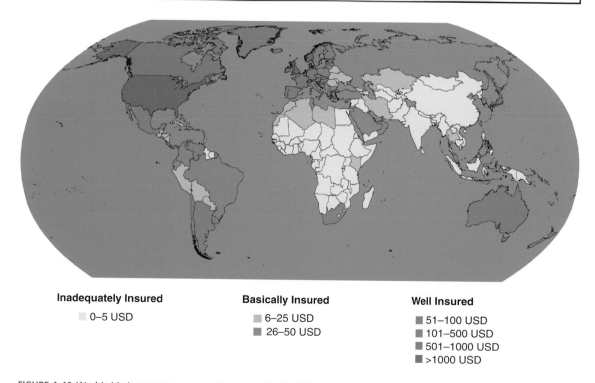

Inadequately Insured
  0–5 USD

Basically Insured
  6–25 USD
  26–50 USD

Well Insured
  51–100 USD
  101–500 USD
  501–1000 USD
  >1000 USD

FIGURE 4–10 Worldwide insurance coverage. (From Munich Re, 2004)

preclusions against more unlikely natural and technological disasters. These special disasters require the purchase of policies formulated to assume the specific risk for each causative hazard. In the poorer countries, insurance schemes are underutilized given the limitations on disposable income faced by most members of the population. The January 2010 earthquake in Haiti, for instance, is expected to amount to only $26 million in insurance payouts because there was so little private insurance that had been purchased by the impoverished Haitian population (News-Insurances.Com, 2010).

General homeowner and renter policies cover losses that commonly occur and are not catastrophic in nature, such as fires, wind damage, theft, and plumbing damage. Catastrophic hazards, like earthquakes, landslides, and floods, are often precluded because of the wide spatial damage they inflict. Hazard damages that affect a wide spatial territory present a special problem for insurance companies because of the mechanisms by which insurance functions. For example, in the event of a fire or theft in a single home, the cost of the damages or losses would be easily absorbed by the premiums of the unaffected policyholders. However, in the case of an earthquake, a large number of people will be affected, resulting in a sum total much greater than their collective premiums, such that the total funds collected from the premiums will be less than the capital required to pay for damages. The bankruptcy of insurance companies due to catastrophic losses has been prevalent throughout the history of the insurance industry.

Policies for specific catastrophic hazards can often be purchased separately from basic homeowners' or renters' insurance policies or as riders to them. However, these entail specific problems that deserve mention. In general, only those people who are likely to suffer the specific loss defined in the policy are likely to purchase that type of policy, creating the need for much higher premiums than if the specific hazard policy were spread across a more general population. This phenomenon, called "adverse selection," has made the business of hazard insurance undesirable to many insurance companies.

Several methods have been adopted to address the problems associated with adverse selection. Examples include:

- The inclusion of these disasters in basic/comprehensive homeowners and renters policies, regardless of exposure or vulnerability. This spreads out the risk across the entire population of policyholders in the country, regardless of differential risk between individuals. Additionally, controls are placed upon the minimum spatial zones within which each company can provide policies to ensure that the ratio of policies affected by a disaster to those unaffected are kept as low as possible.

- The introduction of government backing on insurance coverage of catastrophic events. In this scenario, the insurers are liable for paying for damages up to an established point, beyond which the government supplements the payments. Terrorism insurance, as discussed later in this section, is an example of government backing on insurance coverage of catastrophic events.

- Heavier reliance on international reinsurance companies. Buying reinsurance can spread the local risk to wider areas of coverage, reducing the chance that annual claims exceed collected premiums. Unfortunately, many companies are unable to purchase all the reinsurance they would like to have. Additionally, because many of these policies require the insurers to pay a percentage of total claims placed, the amount they ultimately pay in catastrophic disasters can be massive despite reinsurance coverage.

Several advantages gained through the use of insurance have been identified, including:

1. *Victims are guaranteed a secure and predictable amount of compensation for their losses.* With this coverage, they do not have to rely on disaster relief, and reliance on government assistance is reduced as well.
2. *Insurance allows for losses to be distributed in an equitable fashion, protecting many for only a fraction of the cost each would have incurred individually if exposed to hazards.* This can help the economy overall by reducing bankruptcies, reducing reliance on federal government assistance, and increasing the security of small businesses and individuals, often the most severely affected victims of disaster.
3. *Insurance can actually reduce hazard impact by encouraging policyholders to adopt certain required mitigation measures.* As policyholders reduce their vulnerability to risk, their premiums fall. The owners of automobiles that have airbags, antitheft devices, and passive restraint devices, for instance, will receive a discount on their premiums. Homeowners who develop outside of the floodplain or who install fire suppression systems will also receive these benefits. Additionally, this gives financial/economic disincentives for people or businesses to build in areas that are exposed to hazards.

Limitations on hazard insurance exist as well, and include the following issues:

1. *Insurance may be impossible to purchase in the highest risk areas* if the private insurance companies decide that their risk is too high. This is especially true for hazards like landslides that affect a very specific segment of the population.
2. *Participation in insurance plans is voluntary.* Although private insurance companies can earn a profit despite overall low participation, benefits in terms of mitigation value become limited by low participation. Furthermore, it is not uncommon for homeowners and renters to save money by purchasing policies that cover less than is needed for catastrophic losses, which increases their potential (although reduced) reliance on government relief.
3. *Participation in insurance has been known to encourage people to act more irresponsibly than they may act without such coverage.* For instance, if a person knows that his furniture is likely to be replaced if it is damaged in a flood, he is less likely to move that furniture out of harm's way (such as moving it to a second floor of his home) during the warning phase of the disaster. This phenomenon is termed "moral hazard." In the long run, this causes damage payouts to increase and, as a result, premiums to increase as well.
4. *Many insurance companies are pulling out of specific disaster insurance plans because the probability that they will not be able to cover catastrophic losses is too great.* Before 1988, there had never been a single disaster event for which the insurance industry as a whole needed to pay over $1 billion in claims. Since then, there have been over 20 events for which claims have exceeded that threshold (see Table 4–1). Hurricane Katrina has thus far required $45 billion in compensation, and estimates for insured losses in the September 11th terrorist attacks have been as high as $40 billion (International Insurance Society, 2003).
5. *Catastrophic losses that cover a wide but specific geographic space within a country may result in inequitable premium increases if coverage areas are too general.* For instance,

Table 4–1   The 10 Most Costly World Insurance Losses, 1970–2005

Rank	Date	Country	Event	Insured Loss in 2005 (USD millions)[a]
1	Aug. 29, 2005	United States	Hurricane Katrina	$45,000
2	Sept. 11, 2001	United States	9/11 attacks	$35,000
3	Aug. 23, 1992	United States, Bahamas	Hurricane Andrew	$22,300
4	Jan. 17, 1994	United States	Northridge earthquake	$18,500
5	Sept. 2, 2004	United States, Caribbean	Hurricane Ivan	$11,700
6	Oct. 15, 2005	United States, Mexico	Hurricane Wilma	$10,300
7	Aug. 11, 2004	United States, Caribbean	Hurricane Charley	$8,300
8	Sept. 27, 1991	Japan	Typhoon Mireille	$8,100
9	Jan. 25, 1990	Europe: France, UK, etc.	Winter storm Daria	$6,900
10	Dec. 25, 1999	Europe: France, Switzerland, etc.	Winter storm Lothar	$6,800

[a]Adjusted to 2005 dollars.
Source: Kunreuther & Erwann, 2007.

the Northridge, California earthquake cost insurers more than $12 billion in claims, but only $1 billion in premiums had been collected in the entire state of California. Therefore, the payment for this event and, likewise, the required increase in premiums were "subsidized" by other states that were not affected and were not at such high risk (Mileti, 1999).

Insurance has been denied status as a true mitigation measure by many experts because it is seen as redistributing losses rather than actually eliminating exposure to the hazard (which would effectively limit absolute losses). This is a widely debatable issue, which requires many assumptions. For instance, one must assume that an individual has the ability to move out of a risky situation or has other options that present less risk before stating that the mere presence of insurance encourages him to live in the riskier situation. One also must assume that we would be able to limit all losses, or that we could reach consensus as a society about which hazard risk should be considered insurable and at which level of risk insurance should be limited or prevented.

Throughout the world, more than $4.06 trillion was collected in the form of insurance premiums in 2009, representing an almost 13% increase over 2006 when this figure stood at $3.6 trillion, and indicative of the rising recognition of the importance of insurance coverage globally. The United States has the greatest amount of insurance coverage, with over $1.1 trillion in premiums collected, representing more than 28% of the entire world market. The United States is followed, in order, by Japan, the United Kingdom, France, Germany, Italy, China, the Netherlands, Canada, and South Korea (Insurance Information Institute, 2009). The International Insurance Institute maintains profiles on the insurance industry in most countries of the world, accessible at www.internationalin-surance.org/international/toc/.

The United States has a nationally managed insurance program designed to insure against the risk of flood hazards. Exhibit 4–5 describes this program in detail.

EXHIBIT 4–5: THE U.S. NATIONAL FLOOD INSURANCE PROGRAM—HISTORY OF THE PROGRAM

Up until 1968, federal actions related to flooding were primarily responses to significant events that resulted in using structural measures to control flooding. Major riverine flood disasters of the 1920s and 1930s led to considerable federal involvement in protecting life and property from flooding through the use of structural flood-control projects, such as dams and levees, with the passage of the Flood Control Act of 1936. Generally, the only available financial recourse to assist flood victims was in the form of disaster assistance. Despite the billions of dollars in federal investments in structural flood-control projects, the losses to life and property and the amount of assistance to disaster victims from floods continued to increase.

As early as the 1950s, when the feasibility of providing flood insurance was first proposed, it became clear that private insurance companies could not profitably provide such coverage at an affordable price, primarily because of the catastrophic nature of flooding and the inability to develop an actuarial rate structure that could adequately reflect the risk to which flood-prone properties are exposed. The U.S. Congress proposed an experimental program designed to demonstrate the feasibility of the private sector providing flood insurance by enacting the Federal Insurance Act of 1956, but this Act was never implemented.

In recognition of increasing flood losses and disaster relief costs, major steps were taken in the 1960s to redefine federal policy and approaches to flood control. In 1965, Congress passed the Southeast Hurricane Disaster Relief Act. The Act was as a result of the extensive damage caused by Hurricane Betsy in the Gulf states. The Act provided financial relief for the flooding victims and authorized a feasibility study of a national flood insurance program. The resulting report was entitled "Insurance and Other Programs for Financial Assistance to Flood Victims." Shortly thereafter, the Bureau of the Budget Task Force on Federal Flood Control in 1966 advocated a broader perspective on flood control within the context of floodplain development in House Document 465, "A Unified National Program for Managing Flood Losses." House Document 465 included five major goals:

1. Improve basic knowledge about flood hazards
2. Coordinate and plan new developments in the floodplain
3. Provide technical services
4. Move toward a practical national program of flood insurance
5. Adjust federal flood control policy to sound criteria and changing needs

The National Flood Insurance Act of 1968

Congressional Document 465 and the prior feasibility study provided the basis for the National Flood Insurance Act of 1968. The primary purposes of the 1968 Act creating the NFIP are to

1. Better indemnify individuals for flood losses through insurance
2. Reduce future flood damages through state and community floodplain management regulations
3. Reduce federal expenditures for disaster assistance and flood control

Section 1315 of the 1968 Act is a key provision that prohibits FEMA from providing flood insurance unless the community adopts and enforces floodplain management regulations that meet

(Continued)

EXHIBIT 4–5: THE U.S. NATIONAL FLOOD INSURANCE PROGRAM—HISTORY OF THE PROGRAM (CONTINUED)

or exceed the floodplain management criteria established in accordance with Section 1361(c) of the Act. These floodplain management criteria are contained in 44 Code of Federal Regulations (CFR) Part 60, Criteria for Land Management and Use. The emphasis of the NFIP floodplain management requirements is directed toward reducing threats to lives and the potential for damages to property in flood-prone areas. Over 19,700 communities presently participate in the NFIP. These include nearly all communities with significant flood hazards.

In addition to providing flood insurance and reducing flood damages through floodplain management regulations, the NFIP identifies and maps the nation's floodplains. Mapping flood hazards creates broad-based awareness of the flood hazards and provides the data needed for floodplain management programs and to actuarially rate new construction for flood insurance.

When the NFIP was created, the U.S. Congress recognized that insurance for "existing buildings" constructed before a community joined the program would be prohibitively expensive if the premiums were not subsidized by the federal government. Congress also recognized that individuals who did not have sufficient knowledge of the flood hazard to make informed decisions built most of these flood-prone buildings. Under the NFIP, "existing buildings" are generally referred to as Pre-FIRM (Flood Insurance Rate Map) buildings. These buildings were built before the flood risk was known and identified on the community's FIRM. Currently about 26% of the 4.3 million NFIP policies in force are Pre-FIRM subsidized, compared to 70% of the policies being subsidized in 1978.

In exchange for the availability of subsidized insurance for existing buildings, communities are required to protect new construction and substantially improve structures through adoption and enforcement of community floodplain management ordinances. The 1968 Act requires that full actuarial rates reflecting the complete flood risk be charged on all buildings constructed or substantially improved on or after the effective date of the initial FIRM for the community or after December 31, 1974, whichever is later. These buildings are generally referred to as "Post-FIRM" buildings.

Early in the program's history, the federal government found that providing subsidized flood insurance for existing buildings was not a sufficient incentive for communities to voluntarily join the NFIP or for individuals to purchase flood insurance. Tropical Storm Agnes in 1972, which caused extensive riverine flooding along the East Coast, proved that few property owners in identified floodplains were insured. This storm cost the nation more in disaster assistance than any previous disaster. For the nation as a whole, only a few thousand communities participated in the NFIP and only 95,000 policies were in force.

As a result, Congress passed the Flood Disaster Protection Act of 1973. The 1973 Act prohibits federal agencies from providing financial assistance for acquisition or construction of buildings and certain disaster assistance in the floodplains in any community that did not participate in the NFIP by July 1, 1975, or within 1 year of being identified as flood-prone.

Additionally, the 1973 Act required that federal agencies and federally insured or regulated lenders had to require flood insurance on all grants and loans for acquisition or construction of buildings in designated Special Flood Hazard Areas (SFHAs) in communities that participate in the NFIP. This requirement is referred to as the Mandatory Flood Insurance Purchase Requirement. The SFHA is that land within the floodplain of a community subject to a 1% or greater chance of flooding in any given year, commonly referred to as the 100-year flood.

The Mandatory Flood Insurance Purchase Requirement, in particular, resulted in a dramatic increase in the number of communities that joined the NFIP in subsequent years. In 1973, just over 2200 communities participated in the NFIP. Within 4 years, approximately 15,000 communities had joined the program. It also resulted in a dramatic increase in the number of flood insurance policies in force. In 1977, approximately 1.2 million flood insurance policies were in force, an increase of almost 900,000 over the number of policies in force in December of 1973.

The authors of the original study of the NFIP thought that the passage of time, natural forces, and more stringent floodplain management requirements and building codes would gradually eliminate the number of Pre-FIRM structures. Nevertheless, modern construction techniques have extended the useful life of these Pre-FIRM buildings beyond what was originally expected. However, their numbers overall continue to decrease. The decrease in the number of Pre-FIRM buildings has been attributed to a number of factors, such as severe floods in which buildings were destroyed or substantially damaged, redevelopment, natural attrition, and acquisition of flood-damaged structures, as well as flood control projects.

In 1994, Congress amended the 1968 Act and the 1973 Act with the National Flood Insurance Reform Act (NFIRA). The 1994 Act included measures, among others, to

- Increase compliance by mortgage lenders with the mandatory purchase requirement and improve coverage
- Increase the amount of flood insurance coverage that can be purchased
- Provide flood insurance coverage for the cost of complying with floodplain management regulations by individual property owners (Increased Cost of Compliance coverage)
- Establish a Flood Mitigation Assistance grant program to assist states and communities to develop mitigation plans and implement measures to reduce future flood damages to structures
- Codify the NFIP's Community Rating System
- Require FEMA to assess its flood hazard map inventory at least once every 5 years

Funding for the NFIP is through the National Flood Insurance Fund, which was established in the Treasury by the 1968 Act. Premiums collected are deposited into the fund, and losses and operating and administrative costs are paid out of the fund. In addition, the program has the authority to borrow up to $1.5 billion from the Treasury, which must be repaid along with interest. Until 1986, federal salaries and program expenses, as well as the costs associated with flood hazard mapping and floodplain management, were paid by an annual appropriation from Congress. From 1987 to 1990, Congress required the program to pay these expenses out of premium dollars. When expressed in current dollars, $485 million of policyholder premiums were transferred to pay salary and other expenses of the program. Beginning in 1991, a Federal policy fee of $25, which was increased to $30 in 1995, is applied to most policies to generate the funds for salaries, expenses, and mitigation costs.

The program currently has three basic components:

1. Identifying and mapping flood-prone communities
2. Enforcing the requirement that communities adopt and enforce floodplain management regulations
3. The provision of flood insurance

Source: FEMA and FIMA, 2002.

Risk-Sharing Pools

Claire Reiss of the Public Entity Risk Institute and author of *Risk Identification and Analysis: A Guide for Small Public Entities* describes an alternative for local governments and other small public entities that are considering purchasing insurance: risk-sharing pools. Reiss wrote:

> *A public entity that is considering purchasing traditional insurance may also consider public risk-sharing pools. These are associations of public entities with similar functions that have banded together to share risks by creating their own insurance vehicles. Pools sometimes structure themselves or their programs as group insurance purchase arrangements, through which individual members benefit from the group's collective purchasing power. Members pay premiums, which (1) fund the administrative costs of operating the pool, including claims management expenses and (2) pay members' covered losses.*
>
> *Pools can provide significant advantages to their members. For example, they offer insurance that is specific to public entities at premiums that are generally stable and affordable. Many pools also offer additional benefits and services at little or no extra charge, including advice on safety and risk management; seminars on loss control; updates on changes in the insurance industry; and property appraisal and inspection. Some pools offer members the opportunity to receive dividends for maintaining a good loss record.*
>
> *Some membership organizations for public entities sponsor pools or endorse insurance products that are then marketed to their members. However, sponsorship or endorsement by a membership organization does not guarantee that the insurance is broad enough to meet the needs of a given entity or that the insurance provider is financially stable. A public entity must apply the same due diligence to a consideration of these programs that it would apply to a comparison of available commercial insurance programs. (Reiss, 2001)*

Obstacles to Mitigation

Mitigation is not yet practiced to its fullest extent. The potential exists to reduce hazard risk throughout the world through the various mitigation measures discussed in the previous sections, but formidable obstacles stand in the way.

The first and primary obstacle is cost. Mitigation projects can be very expensive. Although governments may have the resources to carry out even very costly mitigation projects, they choose not to in favor of spending money on programs that are perceived to be more pressing. The reality is that governments maintain limited funds to support development, and many consider hazards to be chance events that might not occur. When drafting their budgets, they therefore tend to favor programs requiring regular funding, such as military, educational, economic, or infrastructure projects.

The second obstacle is low levels of political support or "buy-in." It is important for politicians to maintain their high public standing, so they tend to prefer projects that increase their stature over risky endeavors that may not offer a return in the short run. Mitigation, which is often conducted during periods where no imminent threat exists and which may require some level of sacrifice or hardship, may be hard to "sell" to the local politicians. Convincing the local decision-making authority of the need to undertake a mitigation measure is crucial to getting the project off the ground.

Sociocultural issues are a third potential obstacle. Mitigation measures almost always result in a change of some sort, whether to a place (location), a practice, or a physical structure. People and cultures may tie meaning to these factors and resist any project that involves an alteration they find undesirable. Disaster managers unaware of these sociocultural ties are likely to create mitigation measures that do not take these important issues into consideration, dooming their program to failure before it even begins.

Risk perception is the fourth major obstacle to mitigation. How people perceive a hazard that threatens them will play a large part in what they do to prevent it, and how much they are willing to sacrifice to avoid it. First, the hazard must be recognized. Second, the two risk components of consequence and likelihood must be accurately perceived. And third, there must be a belief that the hazard risk is reducible. Inaccuracies in any of these three areas can quickly derail a mitigation effort.

Assessing and Selecting Mitigation Options

Once a comprehensive hazards risk analysis and assessment have been completed, as described in Chapters 2 and 3, and risk mitigation options have been generated for each hazard on the prioritized list, disaster managers can begin assessing their options. Each hazard may have several risk mitigation options to choose from, each option resulting in different impacts upon society. Several factors must be considered when assessing each identified risk mitigation action, including:

- The expected impact that each risk mitigation option will have on reducing the identified hazard risks and vulnerabilities
- The probability that each action will be implemented
- Mechanisms for funding and leveraging of resources necessary to implement each option

Impact of Risk Mitigation Options on Community Risk Reduction

The most critical issue in assessing a risk mitigation option is determining its impact on reducing the identified risk or vulnerability in the community. Several factors must be considered when assessing the risk reduction to be accomplished through individual mitigation options or groups of mitigation options. These factors, each of which is analyzed according to the six categories of mitigation listed earlier, include:

- Reduced number of deaths and injuries
- Reduced property damage
- Reduced economic loss

Probability That Each Action Will Be Implemented

Determining the probability that an individual mitigation action or a group of mitigation actions will be implemented is critical in determining feasibility. Numerous factors impact the probability that an individual mitigation action or a group of mitigation actions will be implemented, including:

1. *Political support.* Without sufficient political support, it is difficult or impossible to implement mitigation actions. Strong political support, developed over the course of the planning process, increases the probability of implementation. Weak political support, as a result of limited or even no understanding of the risk management strategy, decreases the probability of implementation.
2. *Public support.* Support from the public is critical, especially when such support is needed to pass funding bills and regulatory restrictions to enable the implementation of particular

mitigation actions. Public support is most easily acquired through public participation throughout the entire disaster management process, including the implementation phase.

3. *Support from the business sector.* Business owners play a key role in their communities, and so their support for a community risk management strategy is critical for successful implementation. Businesses may have much to gain, but also have much to lose, from the consequences of a particular mitigation option. The business community generally plays a large role in any community in generating funding and public support for risk management actions and, likewise, is a good partner in mitigation.

4. *Support from nonprofit and interest groups.* A variety of groups are active in any community, including environmental groups, voluntary organizations, neighborhood and church organizations, and labor unions, to name a few. Their participation helps generate support among community members and their families. Conversely, their opposition can generate great resistance and even legal action that could delay or foreclose the implementation of mitigation actions.

5. *Cost.* The cost of a mitigation action can impact the probability of its implementation. The best way to mitigate cost issues is to educate political leaders, the public, the business sector, and nonprofit and community groups of the expected benefits of the action and the expected reduction in casualties and property losses when the next disaster strikes. If a mitigation option has been analyzed accurately and has been chosen because its benefits clearly outweigh its costs, then selling it to these stakeholders is possible. Changing risk perceptions to match reality is the primary obstacle.

6. *Long-term versus short-term benefits.* Political leaders and business executives are sensitive to the need to produce immediate results, either in their term of office or in the next business quarter. This may cause them to support short-term actions that will produce fast, identifiable results. The long-term, sustainable option is always the best, although convincing people may not be easy when cheaper, shorter term options exist.

The STAPLEE Method of Assessing Mitigation Options

There are many methods by which the hazards risk management team can assess the mitigation options that they have generated for each identified hazard risk. One method, or framework as it is often called, that has been developed by FEMA is the STAPLEE method.

STAPLEE guides the disaster managers in their assessment by utilizing a systematic approach for addressing options. The term "STAPLEE" is an acronym that stands for the following evaluation criteria:

- Social
- Technical
- Administrative
- Political
- Legal
- Economic
- Environmental

Each of these terms represents an opportunity or constraint to implementing a particular mitigation option. Because communities are generally very different in their overall makeup, a single mitigation option analyzed according to the STAPLEE criteria may produce very different outcomes in different places.

Each criterion considers a different aspect of the community and requires different methods of information collection and analysis. There is no definable or identifiable priority or weight assigned to any of these criteria—the order of the letters in the acronym was determined by the word they formed (which was meant to be easy to remember).

The criteria include (adapted from FEMA, 2005):

1. *Social.* A mitigation option will only be viable if it is socially accepted within the community where it is implemented. The public is instrumental in guiding decisions such as these through their support or lack thereof. Even with public support, a proposed mitigation option might not work, but without public support, the taken action will almost certainly fail

   Disaster managers must have a clear understanding of how the mitigation option will affect the population. They must investigate several questions that will guide their interpretation of this criterion, including:
   - Will the proposed action adversely affect any one segment of the population? Will it give some disproportionate benefit to only one segment?
   - Will the action disrupt established neighborhoods; break up legal, political, or electoral districts; or cause the relocation of lower income people?
   - Is the proposed action compatible with present and future community values?
   - Will the actions adversely affect cultural values or resources?

2. *Technical.* If the proposed action is investigated and found to not be technically feasible, it is probably not a good option. Additionally, it is important to investigate, when looking into the technical feasibility of each option, whether it will help to reduce losses in the long term and whether or not it has any secondary effects that could nullify its benefits. By addressing the following questions, the hazards risk management team can determine the suitability of their proposed actions based on the actual degree of help those actions will ultimately provide:
   - How effective is the action in avoiding or reducing future losses? It is important that the measures taken are able to achieve the anticipated results, not a fraction thereof.
   - Will it create more problems than it fixes?
   - Does it solve the problem or only a symptom?

3. *Administrative.* This measure investigates the community's capabilities for carrying out the projects that would be required to implement each of the mitigation options. Specifically, the disaster managers will look at each option's requirements in terms of:
   - Staffing
   - Funding
   - Maintenance

     The community may be able to implement some options on their own, using their own resources, whereas other options will require (often significant) outside assistance. The questions disaster managers must answer include:
   - Does the jurisdiction have the capability (staff, technical experts, and/or funding) to implement the action, and can it be readily obtained?

- Can the community provide the necessary maintenance work required to maintain the method of mitigation?
- Can the implementation project be accomplished in a timely manner, without excessive disruption to the community?

4. *Political.* Mitigation actions tend to be highly political. Like most other government actions, they tend to entail the spending of local funds and the use of local services, require permits and permissions, involve some alteration to the fabric of the community, may involve some use of public lands, and involve a certain amount of risk for the political leaders who authorize the actions. The political nature of each option will likewise be an influential decision-making factor when options are being chosen for implementation. Disaster managers will need to be aware of or will need to investigate how local, regional, and national political leaders feel about issues related to such agenda items as the environment, economic development, safety, and emergency management. Logically, actions that go against the current administration's political ideology in any of these areas are likely to receive less support than those that are in line with its beliefs. It is not uncommon for proposed mitigation actions to fail because they lack this much-needed political support.

Disaster managers can measure political support for their mitigation options by addressing the following questions:

- Is there political support to implement and maintain this action?
- Have political leaders participated in the planning process so far?
- Is there a local champion willing to help see the action to completion?
- Who are the stakeholders in this proposed action, and how do they feel about the changes that will occur as a result of the action?
- Is there enough public support, toward which political leaders are likely to lean, to ensure the success of the action?
- Have all of the stakeholders been offered an opportunity to participate in the planning process?
- How can the mitigation objectives be accomplished at the lowest "cost" to the public?

5. *Legal.* Many mitigation options will require actions to be taken that need legal authority to be lawfully conducted. Disaster managers must determine whether they will be able to establish the legal authority at the national, provincial, state, or local levels to implement the proposed mitigation actions. It even may be necessary to propose the passage of new laws or regulations to accommodate the needs of the mitigation measure if such legal authority is weak or does not exist. However, this legal authority is best established long before the mitigation action is taken because of the exhaustive process of making or changing laws.

Depending upon the country where the mitigation actions are being conducted, government entities at each structural level may operate under their own specific source of delegated authority. Local governments may operate under "enabling legislation" that gives them the power to engage in certain activities, or under informal governance systems based on tribal or other forms of law.

Disaster managers will need to identify the unit of government that will ultimately have the authority to grant or deny the permission to undertake the actions necessary to implement the mitigation action. They will be well served to understand the interrelationships between the various levels of government to better anticipate any political roadblocks or challenges that may arise. Much of this information can be obtained by asking:

- Does the government in question have the authority to grant permissions or permits for the work that is to be conducted?
- Is there a technical, scientific, or legal basis for the mitigation action (i.e., does the mitigation action "fit" the hazard setting)?
- Are the proper laws, ordinances, and resolutions in place to implement the action?
- Are there any potential legal consequences?
- Will there be any issues of liability for the actions or support of actions, or lack of action, by any of the mitigation stakeholders?
- Is the action likely to be challenged by stakeholders who may be negatively affected?

6. *Economic.* Like all community projects, mitigation options must prove to be cost-effective to the community before they are considered viable for implementation. The mitigation measures must also be affordable to those who will be funding the project. Mitigation projects often require maintenance long after the project is completed, at the expense of the community where it is implemented. For this reason, affordability means many things, including being fundable without restructuring local budgets, fundable but with some budget restructuring required, fundable but requiring a special tax to be imposed, fundable but requiring external loans, and so on.

Mitigation measures that are cost-free to the community or that can be financed within a current budget cycle are much more attractive to government officials who are making funding decisions than options that will require general obligation bonds or other forms of debt that will ultimately draw upon future community funds.

Those communities that have very little money to support mitigation actions (a common condition) are likely to be more willing to support a mitigation option if it can be funded, either in part or in whole, by some alternative (outside) source or sources. Disaster managers should ask the following questions when considering the economic aspects of mitigation options:

- Are there currently sources of funds that can be used to implement the action?
- What benefits will the action provide?
- Does the cost seem reasonable for the size of the problem and likely benefits?
- What financial burden will be placed on the tax base or local economy to implement or maintain this action?
- Will the result of the action negatively affect the economy in some secondary manner, such as reducing some form of income generation that was dependent upon the existence of the hazard?
- Does the action contribute to other community economic goals, such as capital improvements or economic development?

7. *Environmental.* Many mitigation measures affect the natural environment, either positively or negatively (and occasionally both positively and negatively to some degree). Disaster managers must consider these effects, as their actions could have long-term effects on the community and could negate any positive gains of the mitigation action.

Benefits to the environment often arise from the implementation of a mitigation measure, which must be considered in the choosing of options. Floodplain buyout programs, for instance, which include acquisition and relocation of structures out of identified floodplains, help to restore the natural function of the floodplain. Vegetation management, which is often performed to control the wildfire hazard risk to humans and property, also provides the same protection to the environment.

Questions that disaster managers should ask when considering the environmental factors associated with particular mitigation options include:

- How will this action affect the environment (including land, water, and air resources and endangered species)?
- Will this action comply with environmental laws and regulations?
- Is the action consistent with the community's environmental values and goals?

Emergency Response Capacity as a Risk Mitigation Measure

Development of a nation's emergency response capacity is often cited as one of the most important mitigation measures that can be taken. The ability of emergency and disaster response mechanisms to manage a disastrous event and prevent further injuries, fatalities, and destruction of property and the environment will play a large part in determining the vulnerability of that community or country.

To be truly effective, emergency capabilities must be tailored to the risks of the community. Even though they are primarily designed to handle the routine emergencies experienced by the community, the region, or the country, these resources can be developed to manage large-scale events as well. In general, emergency and disaster management systems will minimally include:

- Fire department resources
- Law enforcement resources
- Public health infrastructure (clinics, hospitals, ambulances, etc.)

Additional resources that help specialize emergency management and ensure that the community or country is prepared for major disasters include, but are not limited to,

- Search-and-rescue teams (wilderness and urban)
- Hazardous materials teams
- Special weapons and tactics teams
- Emergency management specialists or departments
- Disaster medical and mortuary teams
- Debris management teams
- Mass casualty management teams
- Infrastructure repair resources
- Communications coordinators
- Volunteer management teams

Developing an emergency management capacity also involves taking several important actions. These may involve:

- Creation of comprehensive emergency response plans for the range of known hazards that exist, detailing responsibilities, operational tasks, leadership roles, and administrative issues (such as what agency pays for what actions, and what reimbursement will occur)
- Establishment of statutory authority for response and recovery
- Creation of mutual aid agreements within countries (between communities) and around international regions to formalize assistance before disasters strike
- Development of a full training and exercise regimen

Preparedness and response actions and resources will be described in much greater detail in Chapters 5 and 6, while the components of an emergency response capacity will be described in Chapter 8.

Incorporating Mitigation into Development and Relief Projects

More and more each year, especially as a result of the United Nations' efforts during the International Decade for Natural Disaster Reduction and the International Strategy for Disaster Reduction, mitigation is recognized as an essential component of all pre- and post-disaster development projects. Development workers, be they national, international, or other, must be aware of the hazard risks that exist where they are developing and must incorporate those risks into their project designs.

Mitigation is costly, and for this reason its incorporation may be resisted. However, through education, regulation, and enforcement, it is easy to teach these officials that it may not be worth spending the money on the project in the first place if there is little chance the structure or system is unlikely to survive a disaster in the near or even distant future. This is especially true for projects that involve large amounts of national or foreign debt, because the debt will still exist even if the structure has been destroyed. Resilience is one of the fundamental bases of sustainable development.

The World Bank embraces this philosophy and has created the Disaster Risk Management Team to assess risks around the world and incorporate their findings into consideration for development projects. They are gradually gaining a greater awareness of site-specific risks that exist in many countries of the world, especially poor countries, where risk assessments were nonexistent, inaccurate, or severely out of date. With this tool in hand, they can more accurately assess large development projects, such as schools, hospitals, or other components of infrastructure, and determine if the project design accounts for the hazard risks with which the new structure will need to contend. It is in the best interest of both the lender and the borrower to take such actions, because both will ultimately suffer in the event of a disaster that results in loss of the structure or project.

Finally, mitigation must be incorporated into relief projects. It has often been said that disasters are opportunities in disguise. Despite the death, suffering, and destruction, the event allows for a fresh start, and with proper planning, the society that is rebuilt can be made resilient to the hazard that brought about its previous destruction (see Exhibit 4–6). There are conflicting goals in the aftermath of disasters—the goal to rebuild as quickly as possible, and the goal to rebuild as strongly as possible. It is vital that relief efforts fully assess the future risks of the region, based upon the new information gained in the aftermath of the disaster, and incorporate all of those findings into any relief and

EXHIBIT 4–6: INCORPORATING HAZARD-RESISTANT DESIGN IN RECOVERY

Recovery programs must ensure that all structures built are done so in a manner that accounts for known risk. Oftentimes, the anticipated hazard risk is re-evaluated in the aftermath of a disaster, and building (construction) codes are correspondingly made more stringent to address these changes. Building design is, after all, the cornerstone of the "Build Back Better" philosophy, and as such postdisaster recovery efforts demand ample study by qualified engineers. Efforts that neglect this step and rebuild to previous standards will do little to reduce future risk.

There are a number of challenges associated with achieving hazard-resistant design, including:

- As hazard resistance increases, construction cost often follows accordingly. In the case of housing, this may translate to a need for financial assistance by homeowners to support their risk-reduction efforts. Otherwise, these individuals may find it impossible to take such action despite their recognition of its value. With nonresidential projects, especially those utilizing contract work (such as large public works projects), modification of building codes and permitting procedures is effective in ensuring risk reduction.
- Hazard-resistant design demands construction-related technical expertise and training that exceeds what is normally held by local laborers—especially in the instance where owners are rebuilding or repairing their houses. It may be necessary to provide extensive training to ensure that laborers are capable of delivering final products that conform to the design specifications.
- Hazard-resistant construction can require materials that are either prohibitively expensive, not locally available, that change the appearance of the house so that it is no longer culturally acceptable, or any combination of these factors. Design needs to address these concerns if at all possible by relying on local products in every feasible instance. Plans drawn from foreign efforts may need to be adapted such that the appearance and/or functional preferences of the affected population are addressed by the new design.
- Hazard-resistant structures may be more difficult and/or more expensive to maintain in the long run. Owners may require training to prepare them for upkeep responsibilities and may need material or financial support in the future to address situations where repair can compromise the integrity of the structure.
- Structures built to more stringent standards can raise their value beyond the means of the victims who once lived in them, effectively pricing them out of the community. Resistant design must conform to the affordability of the housing it is replacing.

The following case, drawn from the housing recovery efforts that occurred after the earthquake in Yogyakarta and Central Java, Indonesia (2006), provides a good example of how risk reduction can be incorporated into a recovery program:

Many lives were lost in this earthquake because the prevailing housing design could not adequately resist the seismic forces sustained. The resulting loss of infrastructure occurred despite the introduction of earthquake-resistant building codes more than 30 years earlier. After the earthquake, the Indonesian government sought to address seismic risk by increasing the prevalence of hazard-resistant design in houses repaired or reconstructed in Yogyakarta. During reconstruction a government-sponsored training program called the Community Empowerment Program was initiated, focusing on raising awareness of earthquake-resistant building methods among construction workers. The program's goal was to increase the capacity of local laborers and contracted construction workers so that they were able to build back in a manner that addressed future seismic risk. This had the benefit of preparing individuals interested in rebuilding their own houses to do so in a resistant manner, even if they had no additional construction training or experience. The affected communities supported these training sessions and workshops, and as a result the pace of recovery increased and costs were minimized (mostly due to a reduction in contract labor requirements). The training further helped to ensure that houses built subsequent to the conclusion of recovery efforts would incorporate hazard-resilient design. To carry out this project, community members were organized into groups of 10 to 15 families, with each group selecting three members who would serve as leader, secretary, and treasurer. These individuals attended training sessions, and then transferred the knowledge they gained to the remainder of the group (allowing greater participation in a more limited number of training sessions). Together, the members of this group worked as a unit that constructed the houses of each of the 10 to 15 members.

Sources: Satyarno, 2009; OAS, 1991.

reconstruction project. For the structures that are left standing, this information may be used to retrofit, relocate, or perform other mitigation measures as listed earlier. Finally, the opportunity to fine-tune both public education efforts and response capabilities may be gained in this period as well.

Conclusion

Mitigation traditionally has been perceived as a luxury of the wealthy nations. Yet, through unilateral, multilateral, and nonprofit financial and technical assistance, many of the poorer nations of the world are beginning to not only recognize mitigation's benefits but to benefit from its practice as well.

References

American Samoa Government. (2009). *Governor Togiola said Homeland Security making positive progress in disaster education*. Press Release. http://americansamoa.gov/news/2009/gov-togiola-said-homeland-security-making-positive-progress-disaster-education.

Centers for Disease Control (CDC). (2005). *CDC dengue fever home page*. www.cdc.gov.

China View. (2008). *China to monitor global disasters through satellite*. January 25. http://www.china.org.cn/english/China/240681.htm.

Covello, V. T., & Mumpower, J. (1985). Risk analysis and risk management: An historical perspective. *Risk Analysis*, 5(2), 103–118.

Federal Emergency Management Agency. (2010). Federal Insurance and Mitigation Administration (FIMA). http://www.fema.gov/about/divisions/mitigation.shtm.

Federal Emergency Management Agency (FEMA). (2005). *How-to guide: Historic properties and cultural resources.* www.fema.gov/pdf/fima/386-6_phase_3.pdf.

Federal Emergency Management Agency (FEMA) and Federal Insurance and Mitigation Administration (FIMA). (2002). *National flood insurance program: Program description.* www.fema.gov/doc/library/nfipdescrip.doc.

Government of Australia. (2010). *Australian tsunami warning system.* Bureau of Meteorology. http://www.bom.gov.au/tsunami/about/atws.shtml.

Insurance Information Institute. (2009). *World insurance overview.* http://www2.iii.org/international/overview/.

International Insurance Society. (2003). *Overview of world insurance markets.* www.iisonline.org/London/PDFs/Ishihara.pdf.

InvestorWords.com. (2003). *Insurance.* www.investorwords.com/cgi-bin/getword.cgi?2510.

Kunreuther, H., & Erwann, O. (2007). Climate change, insurability of large-scale disasters and the emerging liability challenge, *NBER Working Papers* 12821, National Bureau of Economic Research, Inc.

Kunreuther, H., & Freeman, P. K. (1997). The insurability of risks. In V. Molak (Ed.), *Fundamentals of risk analysis and risk management.* Boca Raton, FL: CRC Press.

Lewis, S. (2009). *Spotlight on satellites for disaster management.* SciDev.Net. http://www.scidev.net/en/editorials/spotlight-on-satellites-for-disaster-management-1.html.

Mileti, D. S. (1999). *Disasters by design.* Washington, DC: Joseph Henry Press.

Munich Re. (2004). *Annual review: Natural catastrophes in 2003.* Munich. www.munichre.com/publications/302-03971_en.pdf?rdm=88865.

News-Insurances.com. (2010). *How much will Haiti earthquake cost to insurers?* January 14. http://www.news-insurances.com/how-much-haiti-earthquake-will-cost-to-insurers/016713331.

Organization of American States (OAS). (1991). *Primer on natural hazard management in integrated regional development planning.* www.oas.org/usde/publications/Unit/oea66e/begin.htm.

Platform for the Promotion of Early Warning. N.d. What is a Tsunami: In Brief. International Strategy for Disaster Reduction. http://www.unisdr.org/ppew/tsunami/what-is-tsunami/backinfor-brief.htm.

ProVention Consortium. (2004). *Solidarity and opportunity: The potential of insurance for disaster risk management in developing countries.* ProVention Consortium International Conference Report, Zurich, October.

Reiss, C. L. (2001). *Risk identification and analysis: A guide.* Fairfax, VA: Public Entity Risk Institute.

Satyarno, I. (2009). *Socialization and training of earthquake-resistant house to the construction workers in Trimulyo Village, Jetis Sub District, Bantul District, Yogyakarta. From the Recovery Status Report: The Yogyakarta and Central Java Earthquake 2006.* International Recovery Platform Department of Architecture and Planning, UGM.

United Nations International Strategy for Disaster Reduction (UNISDR). (2005). *National Report of Japan on Disaster Reduction. World Conference on Disaster Reduction.* http://www.unisdr.org/eng/country-inform/reports/Japan-report.pdf.

5

Preparedness

Introduction

In the sixteenth century, Miguel de Cervantes Saavedra, author of *Don Quixote,* wrote, "Forewarned; Forearmed. To be prepared is half the victory." In terms of effective disaster management, his words could not ring more true. Even though mitigation measures are highly effective at reducing disaster risk, they cannot eliminate every threat to a community or country. When disasters strike, there may be little or no time to make any additional arrangements, to learn any new skills, or to acquire needed supplies. Disaster preparedness—defined as actions taken in advance of a disaster to ensure adequate response to its impacts, and the relief and recovery from its consequences—is performed to eliminate the need for any last-minute actions.

Many different organizations and individuals, including emergency response agencies, government officials, businesses, and citizens, conduct disaster preparedness activities. Each has a unique role to play and unique responsibilities to fulfill when disasters strike. The range of activities that constitute the preparedness component of the comprehensive emergency management cycle is expansive, and these actions are often the primary factors that determine whether or not actual response actions are successful.

This chapter presents an overview of disaster preparedness, followed by descriptions and discussions of the planning process, including Emergency Operations Plans (EOPs), exercises, training, equipment, statutory authority, warning, and public preparedness. A discussion of the media's role in disaster management is included as well.

Overview of Disaster Preparedness

The goals of disaster preparedness are know what to do in a disaster's aftermath, know how to do it, and be equipped with the right tools to do it effectively. This difficult process may take years before attaining satisfactory levels, and maintaining such levels is an ongoing effort.

Preparedness minimizes hazards' adverse effects through effective precautionary measures that ensure a timely, appropriate, and efficient organization and delivery of response and relief action. Responding to any disaster, especially a catastrophic event, is guaranteed to be unique, complex, and confusing.

Preparedness actions and activities can be divided according to recipient. The government component, which includes administration, emergency management, public health, and other services agencies, is one group. Individuals and businesses are the second group. Preparedness of the first group is normally defined and conducted through the creation and application of an EOP and bolstered by training and exercises. The basics of government preparedness actions are provided in the next section.

251

Government Preparedness

People in almost all nations have come to expect that their government will intervene in times of disaster and come to their aid. Likewise, many governments have assured their constituents that their response needs would be met should a disaster ever occur. Despite any image these governments may project regarding their ability to effectively govern and protect their people, the true test of their abilities is during times of disaster. Whether they pass that test is a matter of how well they have prepared themselves to respond.

The diverse range of government preparedness actions may be grouped into five general categories: planning, exercise, training, equipment, and statutory authority.

Planning

Emergency and disaster response planning at the government level is a necessary and involved process. In the event of a disaster, each government jurisdictional level will be expected or required to perform a range of tasks and functions in the lead up to its aftermath. Clearly, the onset of that disaster is not the ideal time to begin planning. Governments must know well in advance not only what they will need to do but also how they will do it, what equipment they use, and how others can and will assist them.

The most comprehensive methodology used to plan for disasters is the creation of a community or national EOP. These plans can be scaled up or down depending on the needs of the community and the particular disaster, and are able to accommodate the complex and diverse needs of a full range of disaster response and recovery actions.

The EOP

An EOP is a document that describes in intricate detail the people and agencies who will be involved in the response to hazard events (including disasters), the responsibilities and actions of these individuals and agencies, and when and where those responsibilities and actions will be called upon. It also describes how citizens and structures will be protected in the event of a disaster. It may catalog the equipment, facilities, and resources available within and outside the jurisdiction. EOPs are also referred to as contingency plans, continuity of operations plans, emergency response plans, and counter-disaster plans, although the functions of each remain largely similar to what was previously described.

EOPs are required at every level of government, from local to national. They also can be created for individual entities, such as schools, hospitals, prisons, or utilities. Plans can be integrated, which improves overall community response coordination. Beyond the national level, it is possible to create international EOPs, spanning countries, continents, and the entire globe, and because of the rising number of regional disaster events, the number of international plans has been increasing each year.

At each jurisdictional level where disaster planning is conducted, all players involved in the emergency response and recovery (the stakeholders) must be included, preferably from conception of the plan onward, to ensure that the resulting process and document are consistent, complete, and trouble-free.

EOPs not only define what is done at each organizational level, but also address under what circumstances each organizational level interacts, and how they will do so. It is important to note that EOPs are most effective when they are designed to be adaptable to the full range of hazards identified for the community.

The components of an effective emergency response plan include:

- Hazards risk analysis
- The basic plan
- Functional annexes
- Hazard-specific annexes

Before an EOP can be created, a *hazard risk analysis* must be performed. Different hazard types result in different consequences, so having a response mechanism that can accommodate the expected range of consequences is the wisest use of limited resources.

Through the hazard identification and description and the risk analysis and assessment processes, disaster managers will have discovered not only which hazards exist in the community but also how they affect the community, and will have prioritized them by need for treatment. Using this information, they likely will have addressed the mitigation of risk, as described in Chapter 4. The EOP follows this line of thinking.

The *basic plan*, also called the "base plan," is the main body of the document that describes emergency operations within the community or country. The main purpose of this document is to introduce and describe various concepts and policies, clarify individual and agency responsibilities, and delineate authority. The components of a Basic Emergency Operations Plan include:

- *The introductory material.* Found at the very beginning of the plan, it introduces the document, explains its need, and establishes credibility. It usually begins with a promulgation document, normally in the form of an open letter written and signed by the jurisdiction's most senior executive. This document provides confirmation that the plan is official and has been approved at the highest levels of government.

  The promulgation document may be accompanied by a signature page, which includes the most senior executive within each agency, department, or organization included in the body of the plan. The signature page provides a level of credibility because it shows that each involved organization not only participated in the plan's preparation but also that they agree to the role they will be required to play. An expanded signature section may include endorsements by key figures, giving the plan further credibility.

  A title page may be included to provide information about the document, including the names of those involved in its publication and the date and place of publication. A record of changes is also valuable. Change records, which include the dates of specific changes and what changes occur, are an effective form of version control among users. A distribution record, which outlines exactly who is provided with a copy of the plan, ensures that each time changes occur, the correct people are provided with an updated copy.

  A table of contents is included in the introductory section. The table of contents should include the material in the basic plan, as well as any graphs and charts for easy reference and any supplementary materials (such as annexes) that follow the basic plan. Finally, if necessary, there is a glossary of key terms and a list of acronyms.
- *Purpose.* Consists of one or more pages that clearly and concisely explain exactly what the plan is, why it was created, and what it does. Providing a brief explanation of each component of the plan is helpful, so that such explanatory information may be omitted from the main body of the document.

- *Situation and assumptions.* The situation section defines the plan's scope. It allows the reader or user to understand why and exactly for what the document is needed. The amount of information provided in this section is truly a factor of how much the users of the document would be expected to reasonably know. Commonly known information may be omitted, as may information that provides no benefit to the user in terms of disaster preparedness. Components of the situation section may include:
  - Geographical limit of the jurisdiction affected by the plan
  - Geographical, political, and demographic description of the affected area
  - Important, relevant information about the area, such as main population centers and utilities
  - Listing of the area's identified hazards, including their geographic range, likelihood, and consequences, as well as specific vulnerable populations and facilities
  - Special populations, such as the elderly, marginalized groups, children, disabled, and linguistically distinct
  - Maps and other useful facts and figures

  The assumptions section describes those details that the creators of the plan assume to be true, or that they believe would be true during the plan's activation. This section explains to readers and users that planning is performed without perfect information and that adjustments may need to be made if certain original assumptions are later discovered to be erroneous. Information stated in the assumptions section may range from the obvious (e.g., "Officials are aware that disasters may occur and that they shoulder specific responsibilities in the execution of the response plan developed for these disasters.") to conjecture ("A biological attack will involve a period of uncertainty and confusion, during which time it may not be apparent that an attack has occurred.").

- *Concept of operations.* The concept of operations section explains to the user how the planned disaster response will play out. Topics covered by the concept of operations section include what situations will initiate activation of the plan or a declaration of emergency, when and how an emergency operations center will be activated and staffed, what other general actions will be taken (and when and by whom), and additional logical, planned sequences and actions. Pre-disaster issues are covered in this section as well, including warning and evacuation.

  The concept of operations section is intended to give the reader a general overview of how response will be carried out. If more specific instruction is required, it will be covered under the "Annexes" section.

- *Organization and assignment of responsibilities.* This section of the plan describes and illustrates the actual organizational structure of the disaster management function of government. Organizational charts and other methods are often used for illustration. A detailed list follows of the actual organizational titles (roles) that will be involved in the response to a disaster (the roles are used, such as "Fire Chief," rather than the names of those that fill them, so that the plan need not be altered when there are changes in the people assigned to those roles). The actual responsibilities assigned to the person filling each role are listed, with information dictating how and when those responsibilities will be carried out (see Exhibit 5–1). In many cases, responsibilities require the involvement of several actors, and in such cases this section stipulates primary and supportive designations to clarify leadership. A chart or matrix is often included in this section that lists each responsibility or category of responsibilities on one axis and designates the primary and supportive roles along the other axis.

EXHIBIT 5–1: EXAMPLE OF RESPONSIBILITIES (SELECT) THAT MAY BE ASSIGNED IN AN EOP "ORGANIZATION AND ASSIGNED RESPONSIBILITIES" SECTION

Chief Executive Official (CEO)
- Sets policy for the emergency response organization
- Assumes responsibility for the overall response and recovery operations
- Authorizes the mitigation strategy for recovery
- Identifies by title or position the individuals responsible for serving as Incident Commander (IC), Emergency Operations Center (EOC) Manager, Health and Medical Coordinator, Communications Coordinator, Warning Coordinator, Public Information Officer (PIO), Evacuation Coordinator, Mass Care Coordinator, and Resource Manager
- Identifies by title or position the individuals assigned to work in the EOC during emergencies

Fire Department
- Manages fire department resources and directs fire department operations

Police Department
- Manages law enforcement resources and directs traffic control and law enforcement operations

Health and Medical Coordinator
- Coordinates the use of health and medical resources and personnel involved in providing medical assistance to disaster victims
- Meets with the heads of local public health, emergency medical (EMS), hospital, environmental health, mental health, and mortuary services, or their designees, to review and prepare emergency health and medical plans and ensure their practicality and interoperability. When appropriate, includes local representatives of professional societies and associations in these meetings to gain their members' understanding of and support for health and medical plans
- Meets with representatives of fire and police departments, emergency management agencies, military departments, state and federal agencies, and the ARC to discuss coordination of disaster plans

Public Works
- Manages public works resources and directs public works operations (e.g., water supply/treatment, road maintenance, trash/debris removal)
- Coordinates with private sector utilities (e.g., power and gas) on shutdown and service restoration
- Coordinates with private sector utilities and contractors for use of private sector resources in public works-related operations

Warning Coordinator
- Determines warning resource requirements
- Identifies warning system resources in the jurisdiction that are available to warn the public

(Continued)

EXHIBIT 5–1: EXAMPLE OF RESPONSIBILITIES (SELECT) THAT MAY BE ASSIGNED IN AN EOP "ORGANIZATION AND ASSIGNED RESPONSIBILITIES" SECTION (CONTINUED)

- Performs a survey to establish warning sites
- Identifies areas to be covered by fixed-site warning systems
- Develops procedures to warn areas not covered by existing warning systems
- Develops special warning systems for those with hearing and sight disabilities
- Develops means to give expedited warning to custodial institutions (e.g., nursing homes, schools, prisons)
- Coordinates warning requirements with the local Emergency Alert System (EAS) stations and other radio/TV stations in the jurisdiction
- Develops a chart of various warning systems, applicability of each to various hazards, and procedures for activating each
- Coordinates planning requirements with the EOC Manager

EOC Manager
- Manages the EOC as a physical facility (e.g., layout and setup), oversees its activation, and ensures it is staffed to support response organizations' needs
- Oversees the planning and development of procedures to accomplish the emergency communications function during emergency operations
- Ensures a sufficient number of personnel are assigned to the communications and information processing sections in the EOC
- Oversees the planning and development of the warning function
- Reviews and updates listings, including phone numbers of emergency response personnel to be notified of emergency situations
- Designates one or more facilities to serve as the jurisdiction's alternate EOC
- Ensures that communications, warning, and other necessary operations support equipment is readily available for use in the alternate EOC

Emergency Manager
- Coordinates with the Communications Coordinator, Warning Coordinator, PIO, Evacuation Coordinator, Health and Medical Coordinator, Resource Manager, and Mass Care Coordinator to ensure necessary planning considerations are included in the EOP
- Coordinates with the local chapter of the American Red Cross (ARC), Salvation Army, other public service nonprofit organizations, the School Superintendent, and so forth, as appropriate to identify a lead organization, if possible, and personnel to perform mass care operations jobs
- Coordinates volunteer support efforts to include the activities of volunteers from outside the jurisdiction and the assistance offered by unorganized volunteer and neighborhood groups within the jurisdiction
- Works with the PIO to develop emergency information packets and emergency instructions for the public
- Coordinates planning requirements with the emergency management staff in neighboring jurisdictions that have been identified as potentially hazard-free and have agreed to house evacuees in their mass care facilities

- Coordinates the provision of mass care needs for personnel performing medical duties during catastrophic emergencies
- Assists, as appropriate, the animal care and control agency staff's efforts to coordinate the preparedness actions needed to protect and care for animals during and following catastrophic emergencies; assists the Resource Manager as needed to prepare for response operations:
  - Convenes planning meetings for the function in consultation with (or on the advice of) the Resource Manager
  - Designates Emergency Management Agency staff to serve in key posts, as appropriate (whether the Resource Manager should be an emergency management official—given the emergency resources focus—or a Department of General Services person is left to the discretion of the jurisdiction)
- Advocates that mitigation concerns be addressed appropriately during response and recovery operations

---

Source: FEMA, 1996.

National plans, as well as many regional or local plans, also may list various government agencies that have been assigned responsibilities in line with their regular missions, and may describe the tasks and functions these agencies are expected to perform in the event of a disaster. For instance, the Ministry or Department of Transportation may be responsible for ensuring that all transportation routes are mitigated from a range of hazards and are quickly repaired in the aftermath of a disaster.

Generally, representatives from these agencies take an active role in the planning process and are signatories of the final plan. To be effective, the plan must outline the services expected of these agencies both before and after disasters occur, and also must detail how these agencies will cover the added expenses they will incur as a result of participation in the disaster response.

- *Administration and logistics.* The administration and logistics section outlines the jurisdiction's policies regarding general support and services and resource management required prior to and during the disaster response. If any agreements between jurisdictions, nations, or other organizational levels exist, they are referenced within this section. Other items that may be defined include:
  - Volunteer management
  - Record keeping
  - Reporting
  - Financial management and reimbursement for services and resources
  - Legal liabilities and protections
- *Plan development and logistics.* This section describes how the plan is or was developed, how it will be maintained, updated, and changed, and who will be responsible for those actions. A projected maintenance schedule is often included, detailing what kind of information will be checked for timeliness and accuracy, and what kinds of assessments (such as exercises) to base

changes on. Procedures for recording changes to ensure version control and distributing the updated plan may be defined as well. If a regimen of testing and exercising (see the next section) exists, it will be detailed within this section.

- *Authorities and references.* Any emergency operations plan must have a statutory authority upon which its operations are based. Without legal authority, many of the actions listed in the plan may not be possible. All actions must have a legal basis long before a disaster occurs, and the authorities section is a way to record the existence of those needed authorities.

  The references section provides the source information for much of the information found in the plan. Provided reference information allows for effective plan updating and maintenance, establishes further credibility to the materials, and allows users to expand upon the information as necessary. An accurate reference section can actually help to limit the overall size of the plan, as it can direct users to much of the nonemergency information that does not necessarily need to be called upon in the time-constrained aftermath of a disaster.

EOP base plans are often supplemented by *functional annexes* that provide much more highly detailed information about the operational needs of specific response mechanisms. These annexes go into much greater detail about who does what in fulfilling the many different functions in an emergency response. Annexes may cover any specific task or function that is conducted in the lead up to, response, or aftermath of the many different disaster types.

The planners must determine what functions need this extra treatment, as all jurisdictions have unique needs. Depending upon the type of activity, a significant amount of further study, research, and testing may be required, such as for evacuation planning.

For ease of understanding and clarity the organization of each annex may follow the basic organization used in the base plan, ensuring, however, that information is not unnecessarily repeated.

Various functions that may be covered by individual annexes in the plan (to be determined on a case-by-case basis) include:

- Direction and control
- Notification and warning
- Evacuation and/or shelter in place
- Communications
- Public works
- Public information
- Fire suppression
- Search and rescue
- Emergency medical services and mass care
- Mortuary services
- Security and perimeter control
- Inclusion of military resources
- Transportation
- Traffic control
- Relief

- Short- and long-term recovery
- Financial management
- International coordination
- Volunteer management
- Donations management
- Vulnerable populations
- Pet and animal response
- Catastrophic incident response (see Exhibit 5–2)

EXHIBIT 5–2: CATASTROPHIC DISASTER PLANNING

Several countries have begun placing more emphasis on catastrophic disaster planning, which is fundamentally different in concept than regular emergency and disaster planning. Catastrophic events are characterized by their acute, widespread, and complex consequences, each of which is capable of generating greater than typical response requirements. In the rare occurrence when such consequences manifest, there exists a much greater likelihood that national emergency management capacity will be unable to meet the response requirements. Moreover, because catastrophic events are not merely "bigger disasters," simply scaling up resources does not likely address these requirements. Catastrophic events can therefore be differentiated from more commonly occurring disasters and emergencies by a need for not only greater human and material resources, but also the requirement that planning complexities be addressed through a range of policy, procedural, and legal modifications, and that operational planning look beyond conventional planning practice.

What differentiates catastrophic planning is the approach it takes to response shortfalls. Catastrophic planning approaches large scale events in the context of specific points of failure, wherein standard national response and recovery capacities cannot meet assessed or actual needs. That is to say, standard EOPs will likely address many, if not most, of the required response functions called upon, but not all. It is, after all, those points of failure that make the event a catastrophe.

Where anticipated shortfalls are identified through conventional planning processes, it is through the enhanced collaborative efforts typified by catastrophic planning that alternate and external solutions are identified, adapted, and thus operationalized. Conventional planning shortfalls often result from one or more of the following:

- Insufficient or inappropriate response resources
- Inadequate or restrictive response policies, procedures, and statutory authorities
- Consequences that are regional or national in their effect (physical, financial, or psychological) on populations, the economy, the environment, or political institutions
- The inability to formulate a common operating picture

(*Continued*)

EXHIBIT 5–2: CATASTROPHIC DISASTER PLANNING (CONTINUED)

Catastrophic planning focuses efforts on the identification of factors that inhibit national response capacity, and seeks viable courses of action to address or circumvent such obstacles. Figure 5–1 illustrates the catastrophic planning threshold.

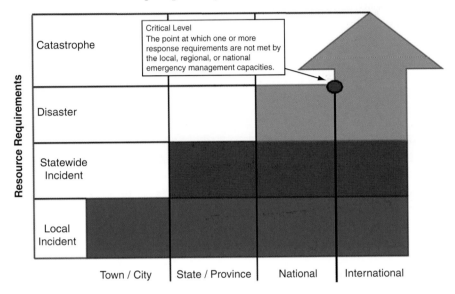

FIGURE 5–1 The Catastrophic Planning Threshold.

In most countries, the traditional planning paradigm uses the concept of sequential failure to plan for larger and larger scales of incidents, wherein response resources are supplemented by each subsequent organizational level of government. It is understood, however, that once the response has reached the point in which national-level resources have been deployed without success, the traditional planning paradigm breaks down. The national government is the last resort in such a planning paradigm, and as such there is no protocol to reach farther for needed resources. Plans of this type are limited by the normal operational policies, procedures, and legislation that assumes capacity is met. In a catastrophe, however, it may become incumbent upon the national government to take steps that would not normally be taken, including passage of new legislation, modification of current legislation, use of international resources, large-scale engagement of the private sector, and unusual deployment of national resources. These additional steps are addressed in a catastrophic planning process (CPP).

Catastrophic response must always be careful to recognize that not all areas of response capability will become overwhelmed. The challenge is in recognizing where failures will occur, how they will impact response, and where supplementary response resources may be found. Meanwhile, in those areas where there is no response shortfall, operations may continue as they normally would. Catastrophic planning tends to be scenario based for this reason, given that the type and scope of issues addressed by catastrophic planning will differ considerably depending on the incident.

EXHIBIT 5–3: EXAMPLES OF EOPS AVAILABLE ONLINE

- Kingston, Canada: www.cityofkingston.ca/residents/emergency/responseplan.asp
- Baltimore County, Maryland: www.baltimorecountymd.gov/
- Queensland, Australia: http://www.ag.gov.au/www/emaweb/emaweb.nsf/Page/Emergency Management Preparing for Emergencies Plans and Arrangements Australian Government Emergency Management Plans

---

Hazard-specific annexes contain operational information not covered in the basic plan and may include preparedness, response, and recovery actions. Building on information in the base plan, the hazard-specific annex may stipulate the risk information for individual hazards, including the geographic range, the population likely to be affected, and the season or time the disaster is most likely.

This annex will contain many of the same components required for the base plan, the difference is that the information here is hazard specific. Special detection and warning systems, evacuation routes, risk maps, preparedness and response issues, and other topics may be included. These annexes could be created for any hazard affecting the community, at the planners' discretion.

Exhibit 5–3 points to some EOP examples.

Exercise

A major part of the preparedness effort of a community or country's response capability is a regimen of exercises. Response exercises allow those involved in emergency and disaster response, as defined in the EOP, to practice their roles and responsibilities before an actual event occurs. Exercises not only prepare the individuals to carry out their duties but also help find problems in the plan in nonemergency situations. This allows for adequate time to address those problems, so unnecessary setbacks do not affect an actual response.

Exercises also serve a very important preparedness function: introducing individuals and agencies involved in response to each other. Response officials often do not formally meet in person until an actual disaster occurs. They may not know exactly what each other does during the response or even in their regular functions. Through predisaster introductions, officials are able to immediately call upon the right people in a time of need without having to second-guess whether the person is the appropriate resource.

A comprehensive exercise program is built upon the specific needs of the community or country for which the exercises are designed. It has four major components, and they are scheduled logically, from easy to difficult, basic to complex, to allow for incremental learning and experience. Each component of a comprehensive exercise program is listed and described in the following list.

1. *Drill.* A drill is a controlled, supervised method by which a single disaster management operation or function is practiced or tested. Most people are aware of drills, having practiced evacuation from their school classrooms as a child or from their workplace office as an adult. In relation to emergency and disaster response planning, drills are exercises that focus upon the individual building blocks of the EOP to perfect each of those components, such that full operation of the plan may run more smoothly.

Drills are most effective when they mimic real-life situations. For instance, if roadway clearance is being tested, the most effective drill format includes the controlled placement of debris or some other hazard in a roadway, followed by the actual deployment and use of the proper equipment to remove the debris. The amount of time required to plan and carry out a drill wholly depends upon the function or action being tested, as does the involvement of staff, and the location of the drill.

2. *Tabletop exercise.* A tabletop exercise is designed to allow disaster management officials to practice the full activation of the emergency response plan within the confines of a controlled, low-stress discussion scenario. The tabletop exercise follows a narrative hypothetical scenario predesigned to analyze a specific range of functions outlined in the EOP (such as a hazardous materials incident). Rather than requiring participants to actually perform their functions as defined in the plan, this exercise seeks to elicit a detailed dialog within which problems and weaknesses may be identified and addressed.

Tabletop exercises work because they remove stress and time limits from the situation. They gather officials who may not have known each other and allow them to understand what each will do during a disaster response. Officials often discover that their assumptions about the way situations will play out or how other officials might act are completely wrong.

Tabletop exercises are conducted by a facilitator, who begins by introducing the scenario and offering a brief narrative. Over the course of the exercise, the facilitator describes hypothetical actions and events and questions participants about what they would do at each juncture.

3. *Functional exercise.* The functional exercise tests and practices disaster managers' capabilities by simulating an event to which they must respond. Unlike a drill, which tests one function or activity, the functional exercise tests a full range of associated activities that together fulfill a greater overall response purpose.

The functional exercise is a step above the tabletop exercise in that it is time dependent, introduces stress to the scenario, and requires participants to actually act upon their roles and responsibilities rather than simply discuss what they would do. However, the functional exercise does not require a full activation of the emergency response plan, as it does not seek to test all plan components and participants. For instance, a fire department may wish to test how its members would respond to a chemical terrorist attack, carrying out all the tasks and functions as outlined in the EOP. Even though police, public health, and other officials would be involved in a real chemical attack, the functional exercise in this case would not include those players.

4. *Full-scale exercise.* The full-scale exercise is a scenario-based event that seeks to create an atmosphere closely mimicking an actual disaster. All players required to act during a real event, as outlined in the EOP, are involved in the full-scale exercise, working in real time and using all of the required equipment and procedures. Ideally, the full functional capacity of the response mechanism is tested.

Full-scale and functional exercises often use props, actors, and other tools to make the scenario as real as possible. For instance, for a wildfire scenario, a controlled fire may be set so responders can experience what they would most likely confront in a real event. A full-scale exercise tests all facets of the plan for accuracy and effectiveness. Both the full-scale and functional exercises are expensive, complex, and require months or years to plan.

Exhibit 5–4 provides an example of an emergency management exercise.

EXHIBIT 5–4: INDONESIA CONDUCTS BIRD FLU EXERCISE

In 2008, in the midst of an influenza epidemic that had at that time killed over 100 people world-wide (most in Southeast Asia), the Government of Indonesia conducted an exercise to prepare local and regional emergency responders to respond to outbreaks throughout the country. The scenario involved the detection of a case of bird flu, and a subsequent quarantine of related individuals, in a rural village. The World Health Organization, which coordinates emerging disease prevention and response, helped to coordinate and oversee the event.

The exercise lasted 3 full days, and involved 1000 people from 20 different institutions, including the military, the trade ministry, and the foreign ministry. Exercise play took place in multiple locations, including an airport and a hospital, in addition to the village where the supposed infection had occurred. The purpose of the exercise was to help relevant officials to learn how to prevent a single infection from spreading, which is key to limiting the epidemic nationally, and a pandemic at the global level. Because the exercise was full scale, everyone involved acted exactly as they would in an actual event, and used all of the equipment that would have been required—including hazardous materials suits and goggles, partitions inside the building to isolate the patient, and a full containment of the house where the infection had taken place.

Planning for the exercise took months to conduct, and quite a bit of money to plan. The same exercise scenario in either a poor village that was more remote or in a major city would prevent special problems that were not addressed in the exercise. One evaluator stated, "Here at least, houses had large backyards and were well spaced. If the pandemic starts in the densely packed alleyways of Java's big cities, it could be much harder to handle."

Source: Williamson, 2008.

Training

Training is the third component to government preparedness. It goes without saying that disaster response officials are more effective if they are trained to do their jobs. However, this statement must be taken one step further in disaster management, as response officials may place their lives in unnecessary and grave danger if they are not adequately trained in the particulars of specialized response. Untrained or insufficiently trained responders add to the possibility of a secondary emergency or disaster, and further strain response resources by diverting officials to manage responder rescue and injury care.

Disaster management training is not universally available. Even though first-response officials, namely, police, fire, and emergency medical services (EMS), are likely to have some basic standard of introductory training no matter where they are located, the specialized instruction required of disaster response is much more technical. Many developed nations have established centralized or regional training facilities to bring these skills to the local level. However, most countries still depend on outside training assistance or establish a small number of specially trained teams throughout the country that can be deployed to a disaster as necessary.

The following is a list of specialized training that falls outside the standard course of instruction generally required of fire, police, or EMS officials:

- Evacuation
- Mass care
- Mass fatalities management
- Debris management
- Flood-fighting operations
- Warning coordination
- Spontaneous volunteer management
- Hazardous materials
- Weapons of mass destruction
- Cyclonic storm response
- Urban and wilderness search and rescue
- Radiological response
- Crowd control
- Response to terrorist attacks
- Wildfire and wildland fire response

The following examples of nationally based academic and nonprofit training centers are given for further investigation:

- Asian Disaster Preparedness Center (Thailand): www.adpc.net
- Federal Emergency Management Agency Emergency Management Institute (United States): www.training.fema.gov/emiweb
- Emergency Management Australia Education and Training Program (Australia): www.ema.gov.au/www/emaweb/emaweb.nsf/Page/Education: http://www.publicsafety.gc.ca/prg/em/cemc/index-eng.aspx.
- Fire Services College (UK): www.fireservicecollege.ac.uk/
- Japan International Cooperation Agency (Japan): www.jica.go.jp/english/
- New Zealand Ministry of Civil Defence (New Zealand): www.mcdem.govt.nz/memwebsite.nsf
- Disaster Management Institute of Southern Africa (South Africa): www.disaster.co.za
- George Washington University Institute for Crisis, Disaster, and Risk Management (United States): http://www.gwu.edu/~icdrm/.

Equipment

The development of tools and other equipment to assist in disaster response and recovery has helped response agencies to drastically reduce the number of injuries and deaths and the amount of property damaged or destroyed as a result of disaster events. This equipment has also increased the effectiveness of response agencies by protecting the lives of the responders. Unfortunately, access to this equipment depends on available resources, so there exists great disparity throughout the world in terms of who has what equipment.

Opponents of advanced technology, as applied to disaster and emergency management equipment, contend that too much reliance on technologically advanced equipment is a mistake. These critics feel that responders will be worse off in the event of equipment failure than they might have been had they not depended so heavily on the technology in the first place. However, there are options available to emergency managers today that they would never have imagined possible just a few decades ago given the advancements that have been made in communications, sensing, and imagery technology (see Exhibit 5–5).

Fire suppression equipment is designed to limit the spread of fires affecting all forms of structures and vehicles, as well as land and sea areas. Fire suppression equipment ranges from hand-held devices to large vehicles. Equipment may include:

- Vehicles (trucks, tractors, boats, airplanes, helicopters)
- Devices (extinguishers, hose assemblies, imaging devices)
- Chemicals
- Access equipment (ladders, cranes, cutting and spreading tools)

EXHIBIT 5–5: TOKYO DISASTER ASSESSMENT NETWORK

The metropolitan Tokyo government has invested $12 million to develop an emergency information integration system that uses cellular phone technology to assess disaster damage and transmit imagery between the operations center and the field.

Using special mobile devices, firefighters and municipal government officials responsible for managing the disaster are able to provide geo-referenced pictures of disaster damage, which are immediately available at the EOC for operational planning purposes.

The images and associated assessment information can be displayed on screens 16 m wide and 3 m high, showing information about fires, structural collapse, injuries, fatalities, infrastructure damage, and other measures, throughout Tokyo's 23 wards and western cities. The system also integrates pictures and data from helicopters, increasing the accuracy of the common operating picture developed.

Following the Great Hanshin Earthquake in Kobe, the Japanese Government had a difficult time building a picture of disaster damages and identifying priority areas. The information this system helps to build can better enable response officials to understand overall damages rather than seeing bits and pieces. This guides operational planning, enabling the incident commander to dispatch rescue workers in the most effective way to prevent damage, such as fires, from spreading, and to save those most in need.

The biggest shortcoming of this system is its dependence on a steady connection between the field and the central system after an earthquake, which may not be possible given that cell phone disruptions are typical in the aftermath of a major disaster due to infrastructure damage or congestion.

Source: Teranishi, 2008.

Rescue equipment is designed to save the lives of humans or animals trapped or otherwise unable to extricate themselves from a dangerous situation. Rescue could be from a burning or damaged building, from floodwaters, or from burial under a mass movement (landslide, mudflow, avalanche), among other situations. Rescue equipment could include:

- Shoring and other support devices to stabilize collapsed buildings or mine shafts
- Vehicles and tools designed to extract victims from hard-to-reach locations (such as tree- or building tops, high elevations, swift water, or isolated harsh terrain)
- Digging, cutting, spreading, and other manipulation devices
- Imaging, listening, and locating devices (including specially trained animals)
- Specialized medical and emergency care devices (such as confined-space medical equipment)

Personal protective equipment (PPE; also called personnel protective equipment) is designed to protect responders from the life-threatening hazards they may face while performing their duties. Different forms of PPE may be acquired to protect responders from the following hazards:

- Extreme heat or cold
- Low or unsafe oxygen (including smoke, CO, and CO_2)
- Biological or chemical hazards
- Radiological hazards
- Blast or bullet protection
- Eye-injury hazards
- Medical pathogens
- Loud noises
- Presence of explosive gases
- Loss of consciousness (alarm to alert other responders that a colleague has lost consciousness)

Disasters involving *hazardous materials* require special response expertise and equipment to limit further injury to people, property, and the environment. Tens of thousands of HAZMAT incidents ranging in size occur each year throughout the world. The types of services performed by HAZMAT teams include site assessment, container evaluations, threat assessments, removal of victims, search and rescue, ventilation of toxic gases and smoke, identification of materials, evacuation, and safety monitoring. The released chemicals often must first be stabilized (especially if they are burning) and then contained and/or decontaminated. The surrounding area may be hazardous to responders' health because of airborne gases or caustic liquids or solids. Only specially trained and equipped responders can safely respond to HAZMAT incidents, which may include terrorist events involving WMDs (biological, chemical, radiological, or explosive devices). Equipment required for HAZMAT response could include:

- Specialized fire suppression gear
- Specialized PPE
- Containment equipment
- Neutralization equipment

- Cleanup equipment
- Decontamination equipment (for the environment, property, victims, and responders)

Disaster medical care goes far beyond regular emergency care. Disasters may involve a quantity of injured and dead that surpasses the capabilities of nondisaster scenarios. Hospitals can quickly become overwhelmed, and the abilities of medical practitioners spread thin. Specialized disaster medical care equipment helps to alleviate many of these stresses. This equipment may include:

- Mass-casualty victim transport vehicles
- Vehicles to transport medical officials to the disaster
- Mobile and field hospitals and morgues (see Figure 5–2)
- Stockpiled surge-capacity pharmaceuticals and other medical equipment in key locations

Command and control of disaster situations depend heavily upon the ability of responders to effectively communicate with each other via *communications systems*, with an established central command post or emergency operations center (EOC). Information is a key element in disaster response, and communications systems facilitate gathering and dispersing that information. Communications systems may involve the use of the following:

- Radios (conventional, trunked, and "ham")

FIGURE 5–2 The U.S. Coast Guard Floating Hospital *USNS Comfort* sailed to Haiti in January 2010 to provide medical assistance to victims of the earthquake. Local medical capacity was unprepared for the scale of injuries that had occurred. (Photo courtesy of Petty Officer 2nd Class Joshua Karstan, U.S. Department of Defense, 2007)

- Telephones (land line, cellular, and satellite)
- Personal digital assistants (PDAs)
- Video conferencing
- Facsimile machines
- E-mail

Public warning and alert systems have immense value to a disaster management system. They provide citizens with awareness of an impending hazard event before it occurs, allowing them to prepare themselves fully or even avoid the hazard altogether. Many people will not take preparedness measures for a hazard until the likelihood of catastrophe is certain, and for these people, the warning system may be the only difference between stocking up on needed supplies and protection and facing the disaster wholly unprepared.

Communication between the public and emergency responders allows the public to benefit from the responders' expertise and event-specific information. Responders, likewise, need to be able to receive information from the public to fully assess the disaster's response needs. Systems that allow the public to alert government response agencies are especially important in rural or isolated areas where notification would otherwise be difficult or impossible. Equipment involved may include:

- Public emergency reporting system ("9-1-1 system")
- Telephone-based public warning system ("reverse-9-1-1 system")
- Remote-activated emergency (weather) radios
- Sirens and public announcement (PA) systems
- Signs (electronic or conventional, stationary or moveable)
- Internet-based warning
- Disaster public information systems (to answer the flood of public inquiries during and in the aftermath of disasters that can flood communications lines and distract response resources)

Other emergency and *disaster response support equipment* is designed to facilitate one or more components of disaster response, as detailed in Chapter 6. This equipment may serve any of the following response functions:

- Disaster feeding
- Transportation (vehicles and temporary infrastructures, e.g., bridges)
- Storage, retrieval, and reporting of information
- Security and safety
- Environmental testing
- Shelter
- Imaging
- Damage and needs assessments

Statutory Authority

The final link in government emergency preparedness is statutory authority. Government response actions involve a diverse range of government officials and agencies interacting with the public and with businesses and operating on public and private land. There are often broad expenditures of funds, suspensions of normal government and private activities, and other major deviations from "normal." To ensure that all individuals and agencies involved in the emergency management system are able to carry out their duties, it is vitally important that the proper statutory authorities exist.

Statutory authorities ensure that emergency and disaster response agencies and functions are established, staffed, and receive regular funding. During emergencies, the costs of services and supplies can skyrocket and, without previously established laws defining where that money will come from and who may authorize it, confusion quickly ensues.

When government functions are disrupted in times of disaster, there can be situations in which leadership figures are unable or unwilling to take control. Alternatively, multiple figures may try to take control. Statutory authorities establish defined lines of control and succession. The EOP dictates the actions of specific authorities, and the statutory authorities give them the power to take those actions.

Agreements between neighboring communities and countries and between different jurisdictions within the same country require a legal framework before the onset of a disaster. Through these "mutual aid agreements," governments not only gain the benefit of the new partner's resources and expertise but also learn about those capabilities and form relationships with partners before a high-stress, time-constrained disaster scenario. Exhibit 5–6 provides an example of a regional mutual assistance agreement.

Statutory authorities are updated as required by new information or expanded needs. New and changing hazards can bring about changes in the emergency management system as a whole. For instance, in the aftermath of the September 11th terrorist attacks, the U.S. Congress passed and the president signed into law the Homeland Security Act of 2002, which was created to consolidate many of the emergency management- and security-related functions of the U.S. government under a single agency in response to a perception of increased terrorism risk.

Exhibit 5–7 lists some characteristics of successful emergency management organizations.

Public Preparedness

In the event of a disaster, it is assumed that response resources will be stretched to the limits of their capacity or even exceed their capacity during at least the first few hours of response. It is important that the public be prepared to provide for their own response needs in order to supplement these strained official resources.

Public preparedness can be considered actions taken to empower ordinary citizens to help themselves, their families, their neighbors, or complete strangers. To be effective, this effort must exceed simply raising awareness of a hazard. A prepared public must be given the skills that allow them to perform specialized actions such as search and rescue, first aid, or fire suppression.

In recent years, disaster managers have established more effective ways to increase public knowledge of disaster preparedness and response activities and to get the public to act upon that knowledge. Until recently, it was thought that the public was incapable of acting rationally in the face of disaster.

EXHIBIT 5–6: ASEAN AGREEMENT ON DISASTER MANAGEMENT AND EMERGENCY RESPONSE

In December of 2009, the 10 members of the Association of Southeast Asian Nations (ASEAN) ratified what is now the first binding regional mutual assistance compact. The goal of the project was to put an end to the *ad hoc* nature of hazard risk reduction and regional disaster response that was the norm, and which likely minimized the ability of countries to help each other in times of crises. The ASEAN Agreement on Disaster Management and Emergency Response (AADMER), which was first created in July 2005, requires a number of actions on the part of signatories, including:

- Drawing up a set of standard operating procedures for providing relief and recovery in the aftermath of a disaster
- Setting up early warning systems
- Identifying disaster risk areas
- Cooperating on technology and scientific research

AADMER greatly emphasizes disaster risk reduction, which is in alignment with the Hyogo Framework for Action. It also advocates a more proactive approach to dealing with disasters. The agreement is designed to bring together the ASEAN countries in addressing the disaster problem, which is more common and consequential in Asia than in any other region of the world. It also helps to normalize the varied capacities of the member countries, and provides a basis of collaboration on common problems including management of disaster risks and incorporating risk reduction and responsible recovery in overall development efforts. A 5-year AADMER strategy and program, spanning from 2010 to 2015, was developed by ASEAN members and international partners (including the UN International Strategy for Disaster Reduction, UNISDR; and the Asian Disaster Preparedness Centre; ADPC) and adopted in March 2010. This strategy outlines activities in four areas:

1. Risk assessment, early warning and monitoring
2. Emergency relief, prevention, and mitigation
3. Preparedness and response
4. Recovery, rehabilitation, and reconstruction

AADMER requires governments to work with civil society and NGOs on each of these topics. The cooperation of several key international NGOs, including Oxfam, Save the Children, Plan International, World Vision, Child Fund, Help Age, and Mercy Malaysia, was formalized by the agreement.

There are a number of challenges associated with this agreement. First, funding is voluntary, and at present the parent international association (ASEAN) does not have enough resources to maintain it without additional contributions. Second, there is no sanctions mechanism, and as such countries may not feel compelled to provide assistance when disasters occur. Third, the agreement is still regional in nature, and will need to be incorporated into the national laws of the participant countries to become effective. Last, the agreement will require the coordination and cooperation of agencies and offices that have not worked together in the past or that do not readily interact with each other at all.

Source: ASEAN Partnership Group (APG), 2010.

> ## EXHIBIT 5–7: THE 20 CHARACTERISTICS OF EFFECTIVE EMERGENCY MANAGEMENT ORGANIZATIONAL STRUCTURES
>
> The Public Entity Risk Institute, a nonprofit institute dedicated to researching the risk-based needs of public, private, and nonprofit organizations, developed a list of 20 characteristics common to emergency management agencies that were found to be successful in managing risk and the consequences of hazards.
>
> 1. Roles of elected officials defined
> 2. Strong and definitive lines of command in all phases of emergency management
> 3. Routine organizational structure similar to disaster organizational structure
> 4. Emergency management procedures are as close to routine operational procedures as possible
> 5. Good interpersonal relationships
> 6. Emergency management planning is an ongoing activity
> 7. All-hazard approach taken by emergency management agencies
> 8. Disaster prevention and mitigation practices
> 9. Motivation (incentives) provided for involvement in emergency management
> 10. Citizen involvement in emergency management
> 11. Strong coordination among participating agencies
> 12. Public/private cooperation
> 13. Multiple use of resources for both day-to-day and disaster operations
> 14. Public disaster information functions clearly defined
> 15. Ongoing monitoring for potential disasters
> 16. Internal alerting procedures
> 17. Ability to alert the public maximized
> 18. Active intergovernmental coordination
> 19. Ability to maintain comprehensive records during a disaster
> 20. Eligibility for (local, national, and international) funding considered
>
> Source: Public Entity Risk Institute (PERI), 2001.

Response officials feared the public would panic or would be unable to use preparedness information effectively. However, studies of actual postdisaster scenarios found that the public acts rationally and effectively, even when frightened or stressed. These studies highlight the need for governments and other agencies to help the public prepare.

During its International Decade of Natural Disaster Reduction, the UN introduced increasing disaster risk awareness among the more vulnerable populations as an important component of an effective risk reduction campaign. Today, through its International Strategy for Disaster Reduction, the UN has proclaimed that public disaster education is a key factor in reducing nations' vulnerability, and that governments are responsible for carrying out citizen training. Public preparedness is also one of four key objectives that guide the international strategy.

Public Education

Public education—also called risk communication, preparedness education, social marketing, and disaster education—is the backbone of any effective public preparedness effort. According to risk communication experts M. Granger Morgan, Baruch Fischhoff, Ann Bostrom, and Cynthia Atman, public education is "communication intended to supply laypeople with the information they need to make informed, independent judgments about risks to health, safety, and the environment" (Morgan et al., 2002). Creating messages that satisfy these high ideals requires extensive time, experience, and planning.

As was briefly touched upon in Chapter 4, public education efforts have three main goals:

1. Awareness of the hazard risk
2. Behavior change
   a. Predisaster risk reduction behavior
   b. Predisaster preparedness behavior
   c. Postdisaster response behavior
   d. Postdisaster recovery behavior
3. Warning

Public education, in both formal and informal capacities, seeks to provide risk-related information in the most effective way possible to a predetermined target audience. Morgan et al. (2002) pointed out that public education campaigns can help people to

1. Identify those risks that are large enough to warrant some of their very limited time and attention (for risks that are under personal control)
2. Identify the "best buys" in risk, which have significant compensating benefits for taking risks and no missed opportunities for cheaply reducing risk, or in which accepting a little more risk gains great benefits
3. Inform themselves and others around them about social risks that require participation or greater social consensus to bring about change or instigate mitigation measures

Public education, as it pertains to awareness, behavior, and warning, will be addressed next.

Awareness

The first step in educating the public about hazards and risks is correcting feelings of apathy toward preparedness, which are often based upon incorrect assumptions concerning personal need or the ability to affect one's fate. Correcting these feelings is best initiated by raising awareness about those hazards and risks. The actual occurrence of a disaster unfortunately is the most likely (and effective) means by which people are made aware of a particular hazard risk, but most disaster managers would prefer that the public be enlightened long before a disaster happens.

The process of raising awareness involves more than simply telling citizens what causes risk. Citizens must also be informed of how the risk affects them, why they are at risk, and where and when the hazard will likely strike. They must fully understand the risk as it applies to them and to the population as a whole in order to effectively absorb that information.

Hazard risks exist in many forms, as described in Chapters 2 and 3 and as experienced and perceived by individuals and communities. In a study performed by Morgan et al. (2002), citizens were asked to make lists of the risks that most concerned them. Their responses ranged from threats that would result in injury or death, such as accidents, disease, and crime to economic risks that would result in a financial loss, to "personal concern" type risks, such as "love-life" problems or problems in school or at work. Only 10% of the cited risks related to the "environmental" (natural) or technological hazards that result in disasters.

Morgan and his colleagues wrote:

> *Whereas professional risk experts devote many hours to considering rare and unusual hazards, most people do not share this preoccupation. With jobs, family, friends, and the other demands of daily living, their lives are filled with more immediate concerns. . . . The time that most people can devote to rare or unusual risks is usually very limited.*

Public education aimed at raising hazard risk awareness must be as accurate, trustworthy, and as effective as possible because, as this research showed, communicators face formidable social and psychological obstacles.

Public education communicators must be aware of how target audiences acquire their risk information, and then design their message within that framework. Many groups, especially the poor, gather much of their information through informal social networks rather than newspapers, government sources, or other formal communications methods. They may mistrust government and other "official" sources of information, and likely disregard messages framed within that context. Another group, transient populations (e.g., tourists), has a limited capacity and time frame to learn about a hazard because they are outside their normal social and physical environment. Through targeted educational material, such as hotel room placards and pamphlets, these populations have been quickly and effectively trained in preparedness measures ranging from fire to tsunami response. There are also many special needs populations in almost every community, including the elderly, young children, the disabled, and the illiterate. Each of these special populations must be approached in a manner that addresses their particular method of perception and learning. The section Obstacles to Effective Public Education and Preparedness, presented later in this chapter, expands upon this concept as it relates to developing countries, where public education can be the most challenging. Three categories dictate how the goals of public education can be reached (Morgan et al., 2002):

1. *Advice and answers.* "People who are poised, waiting to be told what to do, just need explicit instruction, summarizing the conclusions that they would reach if they had sufficient time and knowledge. It is not hard to imagine sometimes wanting a trusted doctor, lawyer, insurance agent, or investment counselor to spare us the details and tell us what we should do."
2. *Numbers.* "People often want to make choices themselves. Rather than instruction on how to choose, they want quantitative summaries of expert knowledge. For example, they may need to know the costs, probability of success, and probability of adverse side effects associated with alternative medical treatments. Having received such information, they can plug the values into their personal decision-making model and make the choice that makes most sense for their personal situations."
3. *Process and framing.* "In some cases, people need to know more than just a few numbers. They need to learn how a risk is created and how it can be controlled. That information allows them to monitor their own surrounding, identify risky situations, and devise appropriate responses. Such knowledge allows people to follow (and join) the public debate and be competent citizens. A risk communication effort that provides such information assumes that its audience is motivated to obtain such understanding and invest in the effort to gain it (when they believe that their efforts will be rewarded)."

Behavior Change

Once the public is made aware of a hazard, they are primed to receive information that will help them reduce their risk to that hazard, reducing their overall vulnerability. The actions that people can be instructed to take apply to four separate categories, depending on when they occur and for what purpose:

1. Predisaster risk reduction behavior
2. Predisaster preparedness behavior
3. Postdisaster response behavior
4. Postdisaster recovery behavior

Public education measures that address *predisaster risk reduction (mitigation) behavior* seek to instruct a population, which is already aware of the existence of a hazard risk, about the range of available options that can help reduce their individual and collective vulnerabilities to that risk. For instance, people living in areas where earthquakes are a problem could be shown how to secure their furniture to avoid injuries. Once informed about how their actions can affect their risk levels, people are more likely to act to improve their chances of avoiding disaster in the future.

Predisaster preparedness education attempts to inform the public about what they can do before a disaster happens. Actions include stockpiling certain materials; establishing individual, family, and community plans of action; and designating safe meeting places.

Education in *postdisaster response behavior* seeks to teach an informed public how to react in the midst and aftermath of a hazard event. For instance, the public must be instructed to recognize warnings and told what to do in response to those warnings, including the proper way to participate in an evacuation. This type of education also seeks to empower the public to provide first-response services to their families, friends, neighbors, and themselves, supplementing the assuredly overextended emergency management resources of their community. In nearly all disasters, it is the common citizen who provides the greatest amount of life-saving assistance to the wounded and not formal emergency management resources, whose actions come into play primarily after the critical first hour when the lives of the most severely injured have been saved.

Finally, education focused on *postdisaster recovery*, which tends to be provided only in the aftermath of a disaster, teaches the public how to rebuild their lives. This can include helping people to locate government, nonprofit, or international resources dedicated to relief and recovery, and how to provide those services for themselves.

Individuals and families can take general activities to prepare themselves for all hazards, but most hazard types have specific preparedness, response, and recovery actions that have been found to be most effective. Public educators must be ready and able to address the specific instructional behavior (see Exhibit 5–8).

Requirements of a Public Education Message

Numerous components of effective public education have been identified as vital to the success of an effective campaign. Morgan et al. (2002) concluded that effective public education requires authoritative and trustworthy sources. They added that if the communicators are perceived to personally gain

EXHIBIT 5–8: SOCIAL MARKETING

The concept of social marketing in public education is quickly gaining acceptance because of its potential in disaster management. A Novartis Foundation paper titled *The Social Marketing Concept* (Novartis Foundation, 1992) defines social marketing as "the design, implementation and control of programs aimed at increasing the acceptability of a social idea or practice in one or more groups of target adopters." Social marketing was introduced in 1971 by Philip Kotler and Gerald Zaltman and combines "traditional approaches to social change with commercial marketing and advertising techniques" (Novartis Foundation, 1992).

Social marketing borrows the lessons and methods perfected by the commercial sector to affect public behavior and learning. These lessons and practices include:

- Setting measurable objectives
- Doing market research
- Developing products and services that correspond to genuine needs
- Creating demand for them through advertising
- Marketing through a network of outlets at prices that make it possible to achieve the sales objectives

The primary difference between social and commercial marketing is related only to their content and objectives, not to the methods by which their goals are achieved. The Novartis authors contend that the social concept of marketing is somewhat more challenging than commercial marketing because, rather than influencing what people buy, it seeks to influence people's ideas and behaviors.

Social marketing expert Les Robinson has identified "a seven-step social marketing approach" that involves the following seven essential elements (Robinson, 1998):

1. *Knowledge (awareness).* "An obvious first step is that people must know there is a problem; know there is a practical, viable solution or alternative. This is important. People are practical—they will always demand clear, simple, feasible road maps before they start a journey to a strange place. And identify the personal costs of inaction and the benefits of action in concrete terms people can relate to (i.e., they 'own' the problem). An awareness campaign aims to harness people's judgment."

2. *Desire.* "Change involves *imagination.* People need to be able to visualize a different, desirable, future for themselves. This is different to being able to recognize rational benefits. Desire is an emotion, not a kind of knowledge. Advertising agencies understand this well— they stimulate raw emotions like lust, fear, envy, and greed in order to create desire. However, desire can also be created by evoking a future life which is more satisfying, healthy, attractive, and safe."

3. *Skills.* "Knowing what to do: Being able to easily visualize the steps required to reach the goal. This is not about emotion—it is purely rational (it is what we have rationality for). People learn skills best by *seeing* someone else do them. The best way to do this is to break the actions down into simple steps and use illustrations to make visualization easy. It's amazing how many social marketing campaigns forget this element."

(Continued)

EXHIBIT 5–8: SOCIAL MARKETING (CONTINUED)

4. *Optimism.* "The belief that success is probable or inevitable. Strong political or community leadership is probably an important ingredient of optimism. I can't over-emphasize optimism. [U.S. Environmental Protection Agency] research showed about 14% of the population is disabled from environmental action by their sense of isolation and powerlessness. If government and business are not leading by example, who can blame people for sensing their individual efforts may be futile?"

5. *Facilitation.* "Having outside support: People are busy with limited resources and few choices. They may need accessible services, infrastructure, and support networks that overcome practical obstacles to carrying out the action. If personal behavior change is blocked by real-world obstacles (and it usually is), then all the communications on earth will be ineffective. The role of an education strategy might therefore need to be expanded to involve the establishment of new services and infrastructure. This is why recycling has been successful—we now have simple, quick, low-cost collection services which make recycling easy."

6. *Stimulation.* "Having a kick-start: We are creatures of routine. Even with all the knowledge, desire, good will, and services in the world, there is still the inertia of habit to overcome. How can social marketers create moments that reach into our lives and compel us into wakefulness? When I think of the moments that have compelled me to act, they are of two kinds—either threatening or inspirational."

7. *Feedback and reinforcement.* "A host of voices, situations, and institutions daily compel us to act in undesirable, unhealthy, and antisocial ways. These forces don't disappear just because we've run a campaign. Effective social marketing is about continuous recruitment and reinforcement of messages—with regular communications that report back to people on the success of their efforts and the next steps that are expected of them. Many NGOs (CAA, Amnesty, Greenpeace, etc.) have [learned] this lesson and devote considerable resources to continuously feeding success stories and updates to their contributors, as well as new calls for support and action. We need to learn the same lesson and devote resources to celebrating people's successes."

from such preparedness, the public may be skeptical about their intentions. Dennis Mileti (1999) contended that several characteristics must be considered in creating messages:

- Amount of material
- Speed of presentation
- Number of arguments
- Repetition
- Style
- Clarity
- Ordering
- Forcefulness
- Specificity

- Consistency
- Accuracy
- Extremity of the position advocated

These characteristics are adjusted depending upon whether the communicators intend to attract attention or enhance the acceptance of their message (Mileti, 1999). Singer and Endreny (1993) claimed that, in order for a message to be considered comprehensive, it should include the annual mortality associated with the hazard (if known), the "spatial extent" of the hazard, the time frame associated with the hazard, and alternatives for mitigation.

Communicators must ensure that their messages are understood by their target audience (Morgan et al., 2002), which changes from community to community, depending on demographics. Mileti (1999) wrote, "Most hazard awareness and education programs have assumed a homogeneous 'public,' and have done little to tailor information materials to different groups." He adds that hazard awareness programs are more effective if they rely on multiple sources transmitting multiple messages through multiple outlets, and that radio and television are best at maintaining hazard awareness, while printed materials tend to provide more specific instructions.

The U.S. Centers for Disease Control and Prevention (CDC) state that community representatives must be involved in planning and developing public education campaigns to ensure community "buy-in." Public education activities must support other components of risk education and reduction activities, and the objectives for public action must be based on a realistic assessment of what the education method can be expected to contribute to actual preparedness and prevention (CDC, 1995).

Goals of a well-planned and public education effort include:

- Raising awareness
- Increasing knowledge
- Refuting myths and misconceptions
- Influencing attitudes and social norms
- Reinforcing knowledge, attitudes, and behaviors
- Suggesting and enabling action
- Illustrating the benefits of a behavior
- Increasing support and/or demand for services
- Helping to coalesce organizational relationships (CDC, 1995)

Methods of Public Education

The possible methods or "channels" by which disaster managers may educate the public are numerous and diverse. Feasibility and audience suitability are the key factors in choosing the appropriate method. Each method has inherent benefits and shortfalls, which must be weighed individually when planning a public education project. The various methods include:

- The mass media
  - Television (public service announcements, or PSAs, paid advertisements, editorials, press releases, interviews)

- Radio (live or prerecorded PSAs, call-in shows, interviews, announcements)
- Newspapers (news releases, editorials, letters to the editor, paid or donated advertisements)
- Magazines (educational story, paid or donated advertisements)
- Internet (press releases, online news media, posted educational materials, downloadable documents, online question submission utility)
- Within the community
    - Schools (courses, special events, distributed material, integrated coursework, games, coloring books, contests)
    - Businesses (advertisements, posters, endorsements, employee preparedness campaigns, inserts with utility mailings/phone books/shopping bags/paychecks, giveaway items, waiting room information, calendars) (see Figure 5–3)
    - Organizations (guest presenters, special course offerings)
    - Churches (pamphlets, events, community service projects)

FIGURE 5–3 Public education in the community: McDonalds Corporation donated the space and the printed materials for disaster education on their food tray liners in Tulsa, Oklahoma, as part of the Tulsa Mayor's Citizen Corps effort to reduce public risk. (From the Tulsa Mayor's Citizen Corps, 2003)

- Libraries (courses, topical discussions, guest speakers, informational tables or resource sections, pamphlets)
- Outdoors (advertisements, signs)
- Special events ("preparedness day," theater, information booths or tables, contests)
- Interpersonal social networks
  - One-on-one meetings
  - Informal social networks ("train the trainer" courses)
  - Within family networks (information distributed in school to bring home, video/DVD/ textbook lending or giveaway program)

Exhibit 5–9 illustrates a national-level public education campaign that included many of these channels and methods.

EXHIBIT 5–9: NEW ZEALAND "GET READY GET THRU" PUBLIC EDUCATION PROGRAM

In June 2006, New Zealand Civil Defense Minister Rick Barker launched a nationwide campaign that urged New Zealanders to "Get Ready Get Thru." The mass media campaign included radio, television, and print ads to encourage citizens of New Zealanders to prepare for disasters. The key messages to this campaign were listed on New Zealand's Department of Internal Affairs' Web page as:

- In a disaster, essential services will be disrupted.
- Emergency services and civil defense staff will be doing their job but help cannot get to everyone as quickly as they may need it.
- Each and every one of us needs to take responsibility to plan to look after those dependent on us.
- We need to take steps now to be prepared to look after ourselves for up to three days or more.

In addition to the mass media portion of the initiative, other public initiatives included:

- A school program titled "What's the Plan Stan?" was sent out to over 3000 primary and intermediate schools.
- Fifteen professional development workshops were held around the country and were attended by over 500 teachers and principals and civil defense staff.
- A Web site, www.getthru.govt.nz, was created to provide user-friendly information and advice for the public on what they should do to be prepared. The Web site also offers links to the nearest council so that people can easily access information specific to their region.

The agency also created a Public Education Toolbox (PEToolbox) to provide those tasked with developing public education programs for civil defense and emergency management groups with resources, such as templates, written materials, articles and media releases, communications strategies, a photo database, and examples of programs undertaken by others. The program includes an intensive evaluation component of quantitative benchmark research to understand current national levels of awareness, understanding, and preparedness. Finally, the program also became very involved with the promotion of the annual Disaster Preparedness Week.

Source: New Zealand National Public Education Program, www.getthru.govt.nz.

Warning

The final goal of disaster management public education is warning. Warnings are used primarily to help recipients understand that their risk situation has changed to one with increased or certain likelihood and to provide authoritative instruction on the appropriate action to take. Warnings differ from awareness in that they instruct recipients to take immediate action.

Warning systems and messages must be designed to reach the full range of possible recipients within their communities, no matter where people are or what time it is. Employing multiple systems, in partnership with various private and nonprofit entities, is often the only way to maximize population coverage. Examples of the various groups to consider in planning for hazard warnings include people:

- At home
- In school
- At work
- In public spaces
- In their cars
- Who are disabled
- Who speak different languages
- Who are uneducated or have little education
- Who are poor

Warnings must inform people of an impending hazard or disaster and must instruct them on what to do before, during, and after the hazard. They may include information on how citizens can get more information, such as a Web site, radio or TV station, or a phone number.

Public warnings are more than just a message. Warnings are built upon complex systems designed for the specifics of each hazard, population, and environment. Comprehensive warning systems seek to do most or all of the following, in order:

1. *Detect the presence of a hazard.* This step involves collecting data from a number of possible pre-established sensing and detection systems, including weather sensors, water flow sensors, seismicity and ground deformation sensors, air and water monitoring devices, and satellites.
2. *Assess the threat posed by that hazard.* All hazards include some variable component of risk likelihood, which changes through time as more information becomes available. The data collected from the sensing and detection systems allow disaster managers to update their assessments of the hazard and then consider how the community or country would be affected.
3. *Determine the population facing risk from that hazard.* The most effective warnings are those that target populations according to their risk, ensuring that those not at risk avoid taking unnecessary actions, which can get in the way of disaster managers. Targeted warnings also allow responders to focus their assistance on those people with the most pressing needs.
4. *Inform the population.* One of the most difficult decisions a disaster manager makes is whether to issue a warning. Many are afraid that the public will panic if they are told about a disaster or that they will accuse the disaster manager of "crying wolf" if the hazard does not materialize. However, researchers have found both these outcomes to be rare in actual practice. And if the disaster management agency has followed established guidelines on risk assessment, their decision on issuing a warning can only be regarded as responsible.

5. *Determine appropriate protective actions that may be taken.* Using their updated assessment of the situation, disaster managers must determine which protective actions the public should be instructed to take. For some hazards, such as chemical releases, the public may have been told about multiple, conflicting actions, such as both evacuation and sheltering in place (remaining at their indoor location, while sealing off the outside environment as much as possible).
6. *Direct the public to take those actions.* Through previous education efforts, the public should already be aware of the hazard and knowledgeable about the types of actions that may be required during a warning. Disaster managers must decide on the best course of action and relay that information to the public through previously established mechanisms. A warned public will seek information on what to do next, and it is important that a clear message is given to guide them.
7. *Support the actions taken by the public.* Actual response assets (such as police and fire officials, emergency management officials, volunteers, and other established responders) should assist the public in following any broadcasted instructions; for instance, facilitating evacuation efforts.

Warning systems are much more than technology and last-minute decisions. An effective warning system involves three distinct processes that are crucial so the public will actually take appropriate action. The three processes are

- *Planning.* During this first phase, disaster managers must consider what hazards allow for warnings, how and when the public will be warned, what the public can do in response to those warnings, what terminology will be used, and what authority and equipment is needed to issue the warnings. Warning plans can be integrated into community or national EOPs as a functional annex.
- *Public education.* The public will not automatically respond to a siren, announcement, or other form of warning just because the warning is given. Studies have shown that even with education about warnings, as few as 40% of recipients will take appropriate action. Without previous instruction on what to do, it can be assumed that even fewer would respond. Disaster managers must incorporate a full explanation of warnings into regular public disaster education campaigns, including what they will sound like, what they mean, where more information can be obtained, and the possible actions that will be taken in response.
- *Testing and evaluation.* Finally, as with official responders, testing and evaluation are necessary to ensure that recipients are not exposed to the action warning process for the first time during a disaster. Testing allows citizens to experience the warning in a low-stress environment and to hear the actual sound or wording of a warning when they are not anxious or scared. Testing also allows disaster managers to ensure that their assumptions about the system and its processes reflect what will actually take place during a real warning event. Evaluation of the warning system helps to ensure in advance that the system is as effective as it can be.

Many different words are used to describe the severity of a hazard warning. Confusion about these words may cause recipients to respond with either too much or too little action. Therefore, clarity and consistency are important. In general, the terminology used to describe warnings includes:

- *Warning.* The hazardous event is under way or is highly likely to occur soon. Generally, an immediate threat to life and/or property exists. The public should take immediate protective action.
- *Advisory.* Advisories, like warnings, are given for events that are currently occurring or are about to occur. Advisories apply to events that are less severe than warnings in terms of the expected

consequences to life and property. However, action to protect life and property are strongly recommended.

- *Watch*. Watches are issued when the likelihood of a hazardous event has increased significantly, but where and when the event will occur is uncertain. Watches are issued so that recipients may begin taking precautionary measures as far in advance as possible, even though there is a significant chance that the event may not materialize.

- *Outlook*. An outlook is a prediction of a hazardous event in the near future, based upon conditions that are beginning to look favorable for the onset of that event. Outlooks do not usually include action information or recommendations to prepare for the possible event.

- *Statement*. Statements are not warnings themselves, but are used to provide detailed follow-up information to warnings, advisories, or watches.

The Media as a Public Educator

The media play a significant role in disaster and emergency management, both before and after disasters occur. The media are well recognized for the invaluable service they consistently perform during the initial critical moments of a disaster when the emergency response efforts are mobilized. In these events, the media transmit warning messages and alerts and give instructions on where to evacuate, where to seek medical care and shelter, and where to go for more specific information (Mileti, 1999). In this sense, the media have assumed a tremendous disaster management responsibility. By providing vital information, the media's ability to educate people during times of disaster may be even more likely to save lives than many of the other emergency response components described in this text (Furman, 2002). For this reason, the emergency response community has embraced the media, recognizing that they will be the primary, if not the only, means of informing large numbers of potential victims (McCormick Tribune Foundation, 2002).

In regard to the preparedness phase of emergency management, the primary public education tasks assumed by the media include raising citizen awareness to the presence of an existing or future hazard and proving information to those citizens regarding prevention or protection (Burkhart, 1991). The effectiveness of the media as a conduit of educational information has been studied extensively, most notably in the area of public health. Many studies have shown a positive correlation between the use of the media and an increase in the promoted knowledge or behavior. A team of researchers working in Nigeria, for example, found that the promotion of family planning and clinic sites on local television played a significant role in the number of people utilizing those services (Piotrow et al., 1990). A study conducted in the United States extended these results to the industrialized world, finding that over 60% of Americans learn about cancer prevention from the media, while less than 20% do so from physicians (Nelken, 1987).

The behavioral modifications and preparatory measures taken by recipients as a result of media public education on natural and technological hazards have also been shown to be promising. Social scientists have gone as far as to claim that people use the media more than any other source to obtain hazard information (Walsh, 1996). Mitigation specialists at the Federal Emergency Management Agency (FEMA) claim that the media role in community and citizen preparedness is critical for the success of such efforts (FEMA, 1998). Personal preparedness is most likely to be undertaken by people attentive to the news media, although this tendency is usually accompanied by other behavioral characteristics, such as personal experience or expendable income. In this sense, media risk communication is seen to be an important *supplemental* component to official public preparedness communication (Burkhart, 1991; Mileti, 1999). Many factors determine how people view hazards, but for hazards that are extreme in consequence and rare in occurrence (like terrorism), the media are the *most* influential source of information (Singer & Endreny, 1993).

At the same time, some contest the view of the media as a successful risk communicator, with a handful of social scientists claiming that the media are ineffective or only moderately effective at informing the public about the risks they face. It has been theorized that there are "built-in, organizational, competitive and institutional biases" that prevent the media from informing citizens about hazards (Winston, 1985). Furthermore, these biases may be coupled with procedural standards that can make effective communication of risk difficult. For instance, the media often report on specific events, rather than longer term issues such as preparedness and mitigation. Additionally, they are more likely to describe the short-term consequences of disaster events rather than follow the event over the longer term. Widespread deficiencies in journalists' knowledge about hazards and disaster management are partly to blame, which makes them unable to transfer effective and useful knowledge to the public at large. Other studies conclude that restrictions of time and space prevent adequate knowledge transfer (Willis, 1997), and that the media's insistence on taking control of the selection and presentation of message format leads to a decrease in message effectiveness (Burkhart, 1991). Not all social scientists blame the media for inefficiencies, however. For instance, it has been found that public denial about risks gives them a false sense of protection, causing them to ignore media warnings unless they are direct victims (Raphael, 1986). Jerry Hauer of the New York City Office of Emergency Management feels that the emergency management community tends to exclude the media from training and drills due to fear that they will leak sensitive planning information or that their reports will cause mass panic, preventing the media from effectively informing the public (McCormick Tribune Foundation, 2002).

Regardless of their level of effectiveness, the media play a vital role in risk communication. For instance, while they often avoid contributing *solutions* to problems, they are effective at raising awareness about issues and communicating degrees of urgency (Willis, 1997).

One particular issue that must be examined when considering the media's ability to educate the public about risk is their ability to do so in a way that gives citizens an accurate perception of their personal vulnerability. In what is probably one of the earliest descriptions of the media's power to influence public risk perception and, likewise, preparedness and mitigative behavior, Walter Lippmann (1922) wrote in his acclaimed *Public Opinion*:

> We shall assume that what each man does is based not on direct and certain knowledge, but on pictures made by himself or given to him. If his atlas tells him that the world is flat he will not sail near what he believes to be the edge of our planet for fear of falling off.

Because the media's depiction of public health- and safety-related issues has either a direct or indirect effect on public behavior, they must be as accurate as possible in their presentation of such hazards (Willis, 1997). It is through perception that the public must judge their own risk and prepare themselves appropriately. It is important for the public not to understate risks, because they will likely not take the time and or money needed to adequately prepare themselves, but exaggerating the risk of a hazard can have drastic consequences, including stress-related health problems and financial and economic effects from business and tourism losses.

Thus far, research has found that the media tend to overstate the risk of hazards they focus on (which also tend to be those that are the least likely to occur) and understate commonly occurring hazards (Singer & Endreny, 1993). One study found that almost 80% of Americans feel that they are subject to more risk than their parents were 20 years ago, when evidence has shown that Americans today have a "competitive advantage in terms of disease, accidents, nutrition, medical care, and life expectancy," and that the media portrayal of risk is mainly to blame (Altheide, 2002). One reason this occurs is that they do not have the time or resources to ensure the accuracy of their reports beyond reasonable doubt.

Related to this concern is the concern that the public will become emotionally afraid of risks instead of aware of their dangers. This distinction is important because it determines the types of preparedness measures citizens take in response to the messages they receive and the rationality with which those actions are made. When people are presented with a risk, they are more likely to take preventive and preparatory measures if they are led to believe that the risk is a danger that can be managed than if it is one that they should fear (Bullock, 2003). Past research has found that increasing the levels of public fear can actually cause a decrease in public preparedness behavior (Mullis, 1998). Unfortunately, the very nature of media culture may promote and even amplify fear by attempting to draw viewers through entertainment and framing (Altheide, 2002; Willis, 1997).

Obstacles to Effective Public Education and Preparedness

Risk communication is recognized for its importance, as well as for the complex challenges associated with it. Although the World Bank claims that "awareness programs addressing existing hazards and physical and social vulnerabilities are often central to social risk reduction" (World Bank, 2002), the National Research Council (NRC) Committee on Risk Perception and Communication wrote, "risk messages are difficult to formulate in ways that are accurate, clear, and not misleading" (NRC, 1989).

Risk communicators working in developing countries have experienced project failure due to obstacles they did not plan for or could not overcome, ranging from internal and external political affairs to economic constraints to sociocultural issues. Even with the best-laid plans, the effectiveness of risk communication is likely to fall short of the communicator's expectations (Morgan et al., 2002). Therefore, it is vital that risk communicators be well prepared.

There are many reasons that risk communication so often misses its intended mark despite exhaustive planning, and in many cases such failures could have been prevented or minimized. Internal reasons for project failure can be budgetary shortfalls, performance problems, or schedule mishaps (Eisner, 2002). There can be many external obstacles as well, whether political, economic, or sociocultural, and they exist worldwide. Overcoming them is essential for maximizing the likelihood of success in risk communications efforts.

Successful risk communications tend to be highly situation-dependent. Practitioners who succeed in reaching target audiences with their intended messages effectively identified and mitigated for situational obstacles. Risk communicators working in developing countries may encounter obstacles not typically encountered in developed countries. If these obstacles are not considered in the planning stages, the communicators may face insurmountable problems in executing their project. Some obstacles that should be factored into risk communication projects in the developing world are reviewed in the following section.

Literacy and Education

According to a study conducted in 2000 by the United Nations Educational, Scientific, and Cultural Organization (UNESCO), there are an estimated 862 million illiterate adults throughout the world, about two-thirds of whom are women (UNESCO, 2002). The study indicates that developing countries have much higher illiteracy rates than developed countries. Over 90% of the world's illiterate adults reside in developing countries (UNESCO, 2000).

Illiteracy severely limits risk communication. A message can be distributed countless ways through written media, including leaflets, newspapers, billboards, and informational booklets. However, these tools are virtually ineffective if the target population is unable to read their messages.

Poor levels of education also can act as an obstacle to effective risk communication. If deprived of basic skills, for example, a person will be unlikely to understand the statistics included in risk communication or to completely understand the specific risk factors being explained (e.g., arsenic in water or biological means of spreading diseases). This barrier applies to formal risk education campaigns, such as for HIV/AIDS or nutrition, as well as to warnings and instructions included with consumer products.

A public health study (Swanson, 2000) in Honduras, where 30% of the population is illiterate, exemplifies the obstacles related to illiteracy and low education levels in risk communication. Clinics in rural areas, where the majority of the country's illiterate live, found that their patients had problems following the instructions for their medication. Doctors performing house calls discovered that many patients were either not taking their medication at all or doing so incorrectly, in many instances putting their health and lives in danger. The study revealed that due to illiteracy, patients visiting rural clinics were unable to understand the instructions explaining the use of their medication. Physicians had been giving oral instructions to the illiterate patients (who were unable to read the medicine bottles), but the instructions were often detailed and/or confusing. Further, many mothers were visiting the clinics with several children who required upwards of 15 different medications, each with its own instructions—a formidable memory task for anyone. By the time these patients arrived home, they were often unable to remember which directions applied to which medications, if they remembered any directions at all. In response, the clinics developed several measures to reduce this communication obstacle, such as relaying instructions directly to an adolescent in the family (who are typically more educated, less occupied with household duties, and more receptive to input from a physician) and using cartoon drawings to convey medical instructions.

Language

Language is an obvious obstacle to risk communication in both the developing and developed world. It would seem that simply learning the language of the target population would mitigate this issue, but the answer is not always that straightforward. In many countries, like Suriname in South America, for instance, several languages are spoken and each language has several dialects. There are "bush" tribes with populations under 10,000, such as the approximately 600 Carib Indians who speak Wayana (Danen.org, 2002). Many of these languages are unwritten, and few translators are usually available to assist in risk communication projects. This does not even account for local dialects, which can make a language unrecognizable between two villages of the same tribe.

There are more than 6000 recognized languages throughout the world, many disappearing as fast as others are evolving (Famighetti, 1998). It is a common misconception that the people of a nation will speak the "official" language of that particular country, and one that can easily lead to risk communicators not reaching target audiences. In Suriname, for example, the official language is Dutch, and schools are required to teach in Dutch. It would seem logical to assume that all Surinamer students therefore speak Dutch, but outside of the capital of Paramaribo this is not the case (Wikipedia .com, 2002). As a result, any Dutch-language risk education project designed to be included in regular classroom studies would likely fail. Even if the risk communicators were aware of this fact, and were able to establish the primary language of their target audience, it is possible that a great number of people would not be fluent enough in that language to understand anything but the most basic message.

Further, there may be particular abstractions and colloquialisms that cause common terms and phrases to have vastly different meanings among two speakers of the same language (Beebe, Beebe, & Redmond, 2000). Several humorous examples from the business world illustrate ways in which abstractions can severely distort a message. When General Motors introduced the Chevy Nova in South America, marketing agents were unaware that *no va* translated into Spanish as "it won't go." Surprisingly low car sales prompted GM to change the name of the car to Caribe, meaning "savage" in the Carib language of the West Indies. Ford had a similar problem in Brazil with its compact model, the Pinto, which identified the car in Brazilian Portuguese as "tiny male genitals." Ford quickly replaced all the Pinto nameplates with ones that read Corcel, meaning "horse." Parker Pen, marketing a ballpoint pen in Mexico, claimed that its product would not "leak in one's pocket and make them pregnant," because marketing executives had unwittingly used the Spanish adjective *embarasada,* which means "pregnant," not "embarrassed" (Confederation College, 2002).

These marketing mishaps are a headache for the companies involved and are costly in terms of product sales and reputation, but when the same misunderstandings occur in risk communication, the result can be counterproductive at best and deadly at worst. In the wake of Hurricane Mitch, the non-profit organization World Vision distributed powdered chlorine to many villages in Central America for purifying water. There was found to be widespread appropriate use of the chlorine in villages where Spanish was the primary language, but inquiries revealed that indigenous villagers (whose first language was not Spanish) were using the chemical to wash their clothes. Because the powdered chlorine was distributed to these populations without instructions in their native language, they were unable to properly utilize the preventive measure. In this instance, the primary outcome was many gastrointestinal illnesses that probably could have been avoided. But consequences could have been much worse if villagers had ingested the chlorine in deadly doses as a result of poor risk communication (Swanson, 2000).

Access to Technology and the Media

Risk communicators regularly employ the media to convey messages to a target audience. This is particularly true during sudden-onset disasters, where the media become the primary, if not only, source of communication between emergency response officials and the public. Recent events indicate the media-reliance trend is rapidly increasing, most notably regarding the "CNN effect"—the ability for disaster information to be broadcast throughout the world in just seconds or minutes (Livingston, 1997). Of course, this form of communication is only possible if the target audience has access to television, radio, newspaper, or the Internet. When access is substandard or nonexistent, risk communicators are presented with a formidable obstacle.

The Internet is digitally connecting the world's population at ever-increasing rates. It is estimated that over one billion people currently have access to the Internet (Internet World Stats, 2006). However, that access is not uniform, and the majority of the "connected" population lives within the borders of North America, Europe, and the Pacific Rim (Thompson, 2002). Of the 5.5 billion people who do not have access to the Internet, most live in the Middle East, Africa, South Asia, and Latin America. In this information age in which the Internet is gaining greater acceptance as a primary form of communication, many people are bound to be hopelessly left behind. Recognizing the dangers that can arise from such a great technology gap, the UN has initiated the United Nations Information Technology Service (UNITES) to help developing countries "benefit from the opportunities emerging from the digital revolution" (UNITES, 2002). Currently, however, the Internet is an ineffective medium for reaching many audiences.

Lack of access is an issue for older communications technologies as well, including radio, television, and telephone. These communications media, while more widespread than the Internet because of their institutionalization and financial and technical feasibility, are still unavailable to a great number of those living in developing countries. For example, it is estimated that three billion people have never made a telephone call (Mutume, 2002). Averaged across all developing countries, there are only 185 radios and 115 televisions per 1000 people, compared to 1005 radios and 524 televisions per 1000 people in developed countries (UNESCO, 2001). Newspaper readership levels follow these same trends.

While they may be the message vehicles of choice for risk communicators, researchers, and the media, these forms of communication may not be effective in developing countries. Therefore, it is important to identify and utilize alternate, nontechnical forms of risk communication.

Class Structure

Social scientists have focused considerable research upon community stratification (Cockerham, Lueschen, Kunz, & Spaeth, 1986). "Social stratification" refers to the way that certain societies' populations are divided into hierarchical groups based upon inequality. Every society has some form of social stratification, the United States included, but several countries formalize, institutionalize, and even legalize these divisions. Such "caste" systems, as they are called, often prevent crossing from a lower group to a higher one, or vice versa, effectively limiting access at each successive drop in class ranking (Norton, 2002). Apartheid in South Africa and the Indian caste system are two well-known examples, but many lesser known versions still exist throughout the world.

These institutionalized hierarchical systems have remained steadfast for centuries. Their effect has gone beyond the basic socioeconomic factors of wealth and power, creating a psychological "reality" that should not be underestimated by outsiders, who may not fully understand their influence. Emergency responders have encountered these issues during crisis events, when it would seem such barriers would temporarily cease to exist, and only cultural sensitivity and creativity have prevented secondary social crises. For instance, after a 7.7 magnitude earthquake struck in Gujarat, India, leaving near total destruction of buildings in much of the state, international response agencies arrived to assist the Indian government. They were quickly surprised to find that tent camps were divided by caste, and that the upper castes received relief aid before lower ones did (Associated Press, 2001). Not recognizing the existence of the caste system could easily have angered groups and caused civil unrest, but fully appeasing the caste system would virtually guarantee that the lowest castes would rarely, if ever, receive food or blankets. It took the creativity and organization of nongovernmental organizations (NGOs) and international organizations like the UNDP, who have had extensive experience working under similar conditions, to ensure that as many projects as possible worked effectively under such constraints.

Risk communicators attempting to effectively transfer their message to populations with such forms of class structures will face a formidable challenge. They will need an authoritative grasp of the history and culture of their target audience, much of which may not be formally recorded. They likely will encounter strong resistance unless they can find a diplomatic way to appease all groups while still achieving their stated goals. Furthermore, they will find resistance to change if the risk reduction message requires people to behave unlike traditional members of their caste (even if that behavior would reduce personal risk.)

Poverty or the Effects of Poverty

Poverty, as it influences behavior, access, and opportunity, is an obstacle to risk communicators in almost all countries. However, in developing countries, where poverty is pronounced and affects a large percentage of the population, these constraints will be even more pronounced. Poverty and disasters are intimately connected, as demonstrated by several UN and World Bank studies (UNDP, 1998). Poverty often causes disasters, as it forces poor populations to live under conditions that directly place them at great risk. In fact, the poor countries sustain 90% of all natural disaster events and, likewise, 90% of all disaster injuries and deaths (Boullé, 1999; ISDR, 2004).

In many developing nations, for example, illegal shantytowns crop up on unstable, contaminated, or other disaster-prone land surrounding major cities. The manner in which these shantytowns are built often makes them dangerous, for they foster deforestation, improper construction of drainage systems (if constructed at all), and unsanitary sewage disposal, among many other suboptimal conditions (IADB, 1999). The urban poor live under such precarious conditions because they have no other viable, easily identifiable alternatives. Their vulnerability to disasters is extreme, although little is done to mitigate this even in the face of extensive knowledge of the existing risks. Many who died during Hurricane Mitch were residents of shantytowns in drainage ditches, water runoff zones, or on steep inclines that were known to be unsafe for construction (BBC News, 1998).

People living in extreme poverty are often unwilling or unable to participate in conventional risk reduction measures that do not fully account for their poverty (IFRC, 2000). If risk communicators do not consider the economic means and monetary constraints of their audience, their message will surely fall upon deaf ears. Poor people do not live on unstable slopes because they do not know the risks; they do so because they are poor and cannot find alternate housing (Dawra, 2002). Simply informing them that they are at high risk from landslides will do little; nor will offering alternatives, unless those alternatives are 100% financially viable for the target population.

Cultural Understanding

Incorporating cultural context to risk communication can be very difficult. Risk communicators must fully understand the ways in which not only their words but also their actions, tone of voice, gestures, dress, and approach to discussion will influence the efficacy of their message. This "cultural sensitivity" to group-specific attributes must be observed in all countries, but generally to a greater degree in developing nations, where technology and globalization are not as pronounced (Akande, 2002). Ignoring this can result in a myriad of negative outcomes, from a communication breakdown to anger, insult, or an increase in risk.

Many African cultures have strong stigmas against discussions about sex. As a result, many HIV/AIDS programs have had a hard time getting people involved in their outreach efforts (Crosson, 2002). These strong cultural barriers have greatly contributed to the fact that Africans are contracting HIV at a rate that is not only much greater than in many other parts of the world, but is also only diminishing slightly, despite intensive risk-reduction programs (United Nations, 2001).

Cultural barriers are not impenetrable, however, if risk communicators avoid ethnocentrisms and utilize creative measures that accommodate local norms. For instance, a group of physicians working with Vietnamese and Ethiopian patients suffering from diabetes used culturally sensitive methods to encourage adherence to prescription instructions and dietary modifications. With a full understanding of cultural biases, they explained to patients that stigmas associated with amputations (a common effect of diabetes-related complications) were greater than stigmas associated with an illness requiring constant medication. The doctors created diets using food alternatives that were entirely within the regular range of choices for each cultural group. In addition, they tailored their education to reflect the cooking styles of each group, using measurements such as "a cupped hand of rice" instead of "8 ounces of rice." As a result, these physicians achieved an 87% compliance rate among their target audience (Lai, 2000).

Lack of Government Sponsorship

Effective risk communication is undoubtedly enhanced by the official support of a nation's government, even if that support is marginal. This enhancement is pronounced if there is great trust in the government agency or official that is championing the cause being communicated. Governments can show this support by performing actions ranging from making official statements of endorsement to passing laws requiring or prohibiting certain activities. However, if a nation's government does not support the public information message, their stance becomes a severe detriment for communicators. In extreme cases, when the government position is in complete opposition to that of the risk communicators, risky behaviors of the targeted group can even increase.

These methods have proven successful in many developing countries, illustrated by a decline in the spread of HIV/AIDS among sex workers in Thailand. A simple but comprehensive campaign aimed at convincing female prostitutes to use condoms resulted in almost complete compliance with the safety practice, and the number of new HIV/AIDS cases dropped dramatically (Cohen, 2002). In both these examples, the government echoed a message being broadcast by various actors, ranging from religious groups to international organizations.

Numerous foreign governments, nonprofit groups, and international organizations are working hard to educate Africans about both the means of transmission and prevention of HIV/AIDS. In Botswana, President Festus Mogae considers the fight against HIV/AIDS a top priority, and the government allocates a sizable portion of the budget to fund HIV/AIDS education programs. This strong government support has assisted risk communicators in teaching safer behavior (Secure the Future, 1999). Although the actual percentage of persons living with HIV/AIDS in Botswana is the highest in both Africa and the world, government-integrated education programs have curbed infection rates (UNAIDS, 2000). Infection rates have fallen dramatically in other African countries whose governments support HIV/AIDS education, such as Uganda, where infection rates among adults fell from 14% to less than 8% in under a decade (Africa Action, 2000).

However, in South Africa, the picture is much different. In South Africa, HIV/AIDS has reached epidemic proportions, far exceeding the mean levels of the rest of the continent (according to Avert,

2002, the Africa mean is 9.0%, and South Africa's is 20.1%). Since his election in 1999, President Thabo Mbeki has maintained that, contrary to billions of dollars' worth of research and conclusive findings by scientists in almost every region of the world, HIV does not cause AIDS (Russell, 2000). His message has not gone unheard, and it is having disastrous effects on groups working to prevent the spread of HIV/AIDS in South Africa. The Anglican bishop Peter Lee wrote to the African National Congress, stating, "Men in rural KwaZulu-Natal constantly said they did not need to change their sexual behavior because 'the big man'—President Mbeki—believed sex and HIV/AIDS were not linked" (Kindra, 2001). Even the South African Minister of Health denounced HIV as the cause of AIDS, and knocked the available anti-retroviral treatments as an ineffective "litmus test for a strong HIV/AIDS strategy" (Horton, 2000).

Conflicting Interests of "Big Business"

A sizable proportion of the risks people face is a product of industrial activities. This is especially true with processes requiring the use of hazardous materials. Mitigating such risks can incur heavy costs, and these costs rise considerably when minimum safety standards for production are set conservatively. Sovereign governments retain the authority to make regulatory decisions concerning risk levels imposed on populations, decisions that almost always are a compromise between ensuring public safety and allowing for the financial viability of (risk-creating) businesses. Not all governments enforce regulations to the same extent, as most industrial processes do not fall under international safety guidelines. Countries wishing to create a financial incentive for businesses willing to accept the moral trade-off of increased societal risk can enact more liberal policies concerning the use of hazardous materials in industrial processes (Karan, Bladen, & Wilson, 1986). These governments tend to downplay the risks caused by certain industries, even contradicting warnings made by risk communicators and the media, in order to protect their income-generating businesses. This practice poses a major challenge to attempts to educate the public.

Preferential treatment toward business is generally more pronounced in developing countries, where governments are often in debt and unable to adequately fund necessary social programs. All countries depend on the economic engines of industry, but developed countries tend to have stricter safety standards, enforced by government regulating agencies. This is not always the case in developing countries, and the situation is compounded by the reality that governments may be unwilling to establish disincentives for companies interested in investing in their country. This is not to say, however, that poor countries will always side with industry at the expense of safety. However, many people have suffered the effects of a disaster that could have been prevented had their government not colluded with a private company to hide societal risks, which is exactly what happened in Bhopal, India, in 1984.

By 1984, Union Carbide had been producing a powerful pesticide containing highly toxic methyl isocyanate at their Bhopal facility for several years. Production procedures had much lower safety standards than in an identical facility based in the United States, at a much lower cost to the company. It was well known by both Union Carbide and the Indian government that an accidental chemical release would result in a deadly gas cloud, possibly killing many people in the plant's immediate vicinity. In what appeared to be an attempt to prevent an alarmist uproar, which would threaten both the income and employment generated by Union Carbide, the local government downplayed the actual safety risk to the local population (CSB, 1999). Many illegal squatter settlements had sprung up around the plant over the years, well within what would be considered a proximity posing an extreme health risk. Even though Union Carbide and the Indian government were aware of these settlements, they did nothing to remove them. On December 24, 1984, 40 tons of poisonous gas was released in the middle of the night. Many people awoke, unable to breathe. Thousands panicked and fled their houses; hundreds died in the streets. Ironically, had residents been adequately educated in how to protect themselves in the case of an accidental release, they would have known to shut their windows and remain indoors until the cloud passed.

Although this case led to many "community right to know" laws in wealthier nations (CSB, 1999), governments continue to give excessive liberty to dangerous businesses in many poor countries. Risk communicators should find innovative ways to counteract false pretenses provided by government and business by working to change the political practices of government, alter the belief systems of the people, or a combination of both.

Hostile or Restrictive Governments

One of the greatest challenges for risk communicators can be access to their target populations. People of all countries face risks, and they have a fundamental right to be informed about those risks. However, when nations impose severe restrictions on speech, media, information, or movement, reaching at-risk groups using conventional methods may not be possible. Directly confronting these restrictions may place risk communicators at odds with the law or in harm's way. It is not hard to imagine how those trying to enter an oppressively ruled country for the purpose of public education could fall under government suspicion for attempted espionage or inciting civil unrest.

This last obstacle, while frustrating and at times dangerous, is not impossible to overcome. Often, it may simply be a problem of association or affiliation. A country is less likely to believe that the communicators are serving an ulterior motive if they are working under the representation of an international organization such as the UN or the Pan American Health Organization or with an international nonprofit organization like Catholic Relief Services. Groups representing an official organization or government agency may face difficulty in overcoming their political links, making it challenging to convince the host country government that both the government and their citizens will benefit from risk reduction programs these groups sponsor. While persistence and tactful diplomacy usually works best, this is not always the case.

When they assumed control of Afghanistan in 1996, the Taliban implemented a strict form of Islamic law that greatly conflicted with the widely accepted Universal Declaration of Human Rights (as established by the United Nations). Under Afghanistan's new legal system, women were severely restricted in their freedom of movement, their right to seek formal education, and their right to communicate with strangers. They were not allowed to perform any work outside the home (with the exception of health professionals), attend school (formal or informal, including home-based schooling), be in the presence of a radio or television, or move about in public without a male relative escort (RAWA, 2002). As a result, many women were not educated about their health risks and what they could do to prevent injury and disease. Under Taliban rule, only one hospital was designated for "maternity" issues (UNHCR, 2002), and there were no formal means of maternity-care training or treatment outside this one facility. In fact, many women who attempted to visit hospitals or clinics unaccompanied by a male relative, even in emergency situations, were threatened and often badly beaten by Taliban officials. A documented result was an increase in both infant mortality and maternal death from pregnancy-related issues (Kissling & Sippel, 2001). This environment was so hostile that even the United Nations Population Fund, a highly experienced international organization, was unable to perform "family planning" projects (Kissling & Sippel, 2001).

This case, and similar ones in countries like North Korea, China, Myanmar, and Somalia, illustrates the need for improving methods of countering obstacles in risk communications when working with restrictive governments. Access restrictions can even stem from the home country of the communicator, for example, due to bilateral political relationships, as is the case with the United States and Cuba. There are thousands of nonprofit, religious, and other NGOs that strive to perform humanitarian projects involving risk education in countries ruled by restrictive regimes, but there is no collective record of the methods they have found successful.

Conclusion

Preparedness must occur at both the government level and the individual level to reduce risk and vulnerability. Through the efforts of governments, NGOs, and the media, preparedness levels throughout the world are steadily increasing, despite the many obstacles that exist.

References

Africa Action. (2000). *Africa: HIV/AIDS update*. (July 5). www.africaaction.org/docs00/hiv0007.htm.

Akande, W. (2002). *The drawbacks of cultural globalization*. (November 10). www.globalpolicy.org/globaliz/cultural/2002/1110cult.htm.

Altheide, D. L. (2002). *Creating fear: News and the construction of crisis*. New York: Aldine de Gruyter.

ASEAN Partnership Group (APG). (2010). *The ASEAN Partnership Group: Civil Society Partnership in Action*. June 27. Presented at the ASEAN Defense Establishments and CSO Cooperation on Non-Traditional Security.

Associated Press. (2001). *Quake can't shake caste system*. www.amdavad.com/ecenter/newsc.htm.

Avert. (2002). *HIV & AIDS statistics in Africa: Estimated adults living with HIV/AIDS in Africa*. www.avert.org/subaadults.htm.

BBC News. (1998). *Hurricane aid arrives*. (November 8). http://news.bbc.co.uk/1/hi/world/americas/209580.stm.

Beebe, S. A., Beebe, S. J., & Redmond, M. V. (2000). *Interpersonal communication: Relating to others*. Scarborough, Ontario: Allyn and Bacon.

Boullé, P. (1999). *Prevention pays*. (October 13). www.unisdr.org/campaign/boullemessage.htm.

Bullock, J. (2003). *Interviews with the FEMA Chief of Staff*. Washington, DC.

Burkhart, F. N. (1991). *Media, emergency warnings, and citizen response*. Boulder, CO: Westview Press.

Centers for Disease Control and Prevention (CDC). (1995). *Guidelines for health education and risk reduction activities*. Atlanta, GA: CDC.

Chemical Safety and Hazard Investigation Board (CSB). (1999). *Bhopal disaster spurs U.S. industry, legislative action*. www.chemsafety.gov/lib/bhopal01.htm.

Cockerham, W., Lueschen, G., Kunz, G., & Spaeth, J. (1986). Social stratification and self-management of health. *Journal of Health and Social Behavior, 27*, 1–14.

Cohen, S. (2002). Flexible but comprehensive: Developing country HIV prevention efforts show promise. *The Guttmacher Report, 5*(4), October. www.guttmacher.org/pubs/tgr/05/4/gr050401.html.

Confederation College. (2002). *Doing business in the Americas.* http://www.courses.confederationc.on.ca/ge012/LectureHall/Session5/language.htm.

Crosson, L. (2002). *AIDS pandemic hits hardest in Africa* (November 5). www.alertnet.org.

Danen.org. (2002). *The languages of Suriname.* www.danen.org/travel/suriname/languages_of_suriname.shtml#lg.

Dawra, P. (2002). Boosting aid: US and business role critical. *Earth Times* (March 18).

Eisner, H. (2002). *Essentials of project and systems engineering management.* New York: Wiley.

Famighetti, R. (1998). *The world almanac and book of facts.* New York: St. Martin's Press.

Federal Emergency Management Agency (FEMA). (1996). *Guide for all hazards emergency operations planning: State and local guide.* www.fema.gov/pdf/rrr/slg101.pdf.

Federal Emergency Management Agency (FEMA). (1998). *Making your community disaster resistant: Project impact media partnership guide.* Washington, DC: Author.

Furman, M. (2002). Good information saves lives. In N. Ethiel (Ed.), *Terrorism: Informing the public.* Chicago: McCormick Tribune Foundation.

Horton, R. (2000). Mbeki defiant about South African HIV/AIDS strategy. *Lancet* (356), 225–232.

Inter-American Development Bank (IADB). (1999). *Reducing vulnerability to natural hazards. Consultative Group for the Reconstruction and Transformation of Central America.* Stockholm, May 25–28.

International Federation of Red Cross/Red Crescent Societies (IFRC). (2000). *Risk reduction.* Disaster Preparedness Training Programme. Geneva, June.

International Strategy for Disaster Reduction (ISDR). (2004). *Living with risk.* Geneva: The United Nations Inter-Agency Secretariat.

Internet World Stats.com. (2006). *Internet usage statistics: The big picture.* www.internetworldstats.com/stats.htm.

Joint United Nations Programme on HIV/AIDS (UNAIDS). (2000). *HIV/AIDS in Africa* (December). www.unaids.org/fact_sheets/files/FS_Afica.htm.

Karan, P., Bladen, W., & Wilson, J. (1986). Technological hazards in the third world. *Geographical Review, 76,* 195–208.

Kindra, J. (2001). Church fray over Mbeki's HIV/AIDS message. *Daily Mail and Guardian* (Johannesburg) (November 9).

Lai, K. V. (2000). *Multi-cultural diabetes education classes: Meeting the needs of the Vietnamese and Ethiopian Population.* Presentation at the University of Washington, Summer.

Lippman, W. (1922). *Public opinion.* New York: Harcourt.

Livingston, S. (1997). *Clarifying the CNN effect: An examination of media effects according to type of military intervention.* Cambridge, MA: Harvard University Press.

McCormick Tribune Foundation. (2002). *Terrorism: Informing the public*. In N. Ethiel (Ed.), *Cantigny Conference Series*. Chicago: McCormick Tribune Foundation.

Mileti, D. S. (1999). *Disasters by design*. Washington, DC: Joseph Henry Press.

Morgan, M. G., Fischhoff, B., Bostrom, A., & Atman, C. J. (2002). *Risk communication: A mental models approach*. Cambridge, UK: Cambridge University Press.

Mullis, J. P. (1998). Persuasive communication issues in disaster management. *Australian Journal of Emergency Management* (Autumn), 51–58.

Mutume, G. (2002). *Development: Information technology for whom?* (June 29). www.idea.int/2001_forum/feature_0629.htm.

National Disaster Education Coalition. (2004). *Talking about disasters: Guide for standard messages*. www.redcross.org/images/pdfs/code/earthquakes.pdf.

National Research Council (NRC), Committee on Risk Perception and Communication. (1989). *Improving risk communication*. Washington, DC: National Academies Press.

Nelken, D. (1987). *Selling science: How the press covers science and technology*. New York: W. H. Freeman.

Norton, G. (2002). *Caste and class. Introduction to sociology*. www.northern.wvnet.edu/~gnorton/soc125/soclec9.htm.

Novartis Foundation. (1992). *The social marketing concept*. Novartis Foundation for Sustainable Development. www.foundation.novartis.com/leprosy/social_marketing.htm.

Piotrow, P. T., Rimon, J. G., Winnard, K., Kincaid, D. L., Huntington, D., & Convisser, J. (1990). Mass media family planning promotion in three Nigerian cities. *Studies in Family Planning*, *21*(5), 265–274.

Public Entity Risk Institute (PERI). (2001). *Characteristics of effective emergency management organizational structures*. www.riskinstitute.org/ptrdocs/CharacteristicsofEffectiveEmergency.pdf.

Raphael, B. (1986). *When disaster strikes: How individuals and communities cope with catastrophes*. New York: Basic Books.

RAWA. (2002). Restrictions placed on women by the Taliban. *Islam for Today*. http://www.islamfortoday.com/afghanistanwomen4.htm.

Robinson, L. (1998). *A 7-step social marketing approach*. www.media.socialchange.net.au/strategy/.

Russell, S. (2000). Mbeki's HIV stand angers delegates/hundreds walk out on his speech. *San Francisco Chronicle* (July 10).

Secure the Future. (1999). *Speech by His Excellency, The President, Mr. Festus Mogae, the 6th of October 1999*. www.securethefuture.com/program/data/100699.html.

Singer, E., & Endreny, P. M. (1993). *Reporting on risk: How the mass media portray accidents, diseases, disasters, and other hazards*. New York: Russell Sage Foundation.

Swanson, J. (2000). Unnatural disasters. *Harvard International Review*, *22*(1), 32–35.

Teranishi, T. (2008). Tokyo to upgrade quake network. *The Asahi Shimbun* (January 31). http://www.asahi.com/english/Herald-asahi/TKY200801310080.html.

Thompson, B. (2002). *Why the poor need technology* (October 6). http://news.bbc.co.uk/1/hi/technology/2295447.stm.

United Nations. (2001). *An overview of the AIDS epidemic*. United Nations Special Session on HIV/AIDS. New York, June 25–27.

United Nations Development Programme (UNDP). (1998). *Linking relief to development*. Geneva: UNDP Rwanda.

United Nations Educational, Scientific, and Cultural Organization (UNESCO). (2000). *Estimated world illiteracy rates, by region and gender*. www.uis.unesco.org/en/stats/statistics/ed/g_%20all%20regions.jpg.

United Nations Educational, Scientific, and Cultural Organization (UNESCO). (2001). *World culture report: New media*. www.unesco.org/culture/worldreport/html_eng/graph2.shtml.

United Nations Educational, Scientific, and Cultural Organization (UNESCO). (2002). *Literacy as freedom*. http://portal .unesco.org/uis/ev.php?URL_ID=5063&URL_DO=DO_TOPIC&URL_ SECTION=201&reload=1036603423.

United Nations High Commissioner for Refugees (UNHCR). (2002). Afghanistan: Focus on maternal health care. *IRIN News* (January 28).

United Nations Information Technology Service (UNITES). (2002). Home page. www.unites.org.

Walsh, J. (1996). *True odds: How risk affects your everyday life*. Santa Monica, CA: Merritt Publishing.

Wikipedia.com. (2002). *Suriname*. www.wikipedia.org/wiki/Suriname.

Williamson, L. (2008). *Bird flu: Indonesia's trial run*. BBC News, April 29.

Willis, J. (1997). *Reporting on risks: The practice and ethics of health and safety communication*. Westport, CT: Praeger.

Winston, J. A. (1985). Science and the media: The boundaries of truth. *Health Affairs*, 6, 5–23.

World Bank. (2002). *Natural hazard risk management in the Caribbean*. Washington, DC: The World Bank, Latin America and the Caribbean Region. www.oas.org/cdmp/riskmatrix.

Appendix 5–1

Guidance on Creating a Public Education Campaign for Earthquakes

Earthquakes

Awareness Messages
Why talk about earthquakes?

Earthquakes strike suddenly, without warning. Earthquakes can occur at any time of the year and at any time of the day or night. On a yearly basis, 70 to 75 damaging earthquakes occur throughout the world. Estimates of losses from a future earthquake in the United States approach $200 billion.

Forty-five states and territories in the United States are at moderate to very high risk of earthquakes, and they are located in every region of the country. California has experienced the most frequent damaging earthquakes; however, Alaska has experienced the greatest number of large earthquakes—many of which caused little damage because of the area's low population density at the time.

In November 2002, a magnitude 7.9 earthquake in south-central Alaska ruptured the Denali Fault in the Alaska Mountain Range, about 90 miles (145 km) south of Fairbanks. Although this was the strongest earthquake ever recorded in the interior of Alaska, it caused no deaths and little damage to structures because the region was sparsely populated. In February 2001, the 6.8 magnitude Nisqually earthquake struck the Puget Sound area 12 miles (20 km) northeast of Olympia, Washington. Hundreds of people were injured and damages were estimated at more than $3.5 billion. In January 1994, the Los Angeles region of southern California was struck by a 6.7 magnitude earthquake centered in the San Fernando Valley town of Northridge. The Northridge earthquake killed 57 people, injured 9000, and displaced 20,000 from their homes. It was one of the costliest earthquakes in U.S. history, destroying or damaging thousands of buildings, collapsing freeway interchanges, and rupturing gas lines that exploded into fires.

The most widely felt sequence of earthquakes in the contiguous 48 states was along the New Madrid Fault in Missouri, where a 3 month long series of quakes from 1811 to 1812 included three with estimated magnitudes of 7.6, 7.7, and 7.9 on the Richter scale. These earthquakes were felt over the entire eastern United States, with Missouri, Tennessee, Kentucky, Indiana, Illinois, Ohio, Alabama, Arkansas, and Mississippi experiencing the strongest ground shaking.

Where Earthquakes Have Occurred in the Past, They Will Happen Again
What are earthquakes and what causes them?

An earthquake is a sudden, rapid shaking of the earth caused by the breaking and shifting of rock beneath the earth's surface. For hundreds of millions of years, the forces of plate tectonics have shaped the earth as the huge plates that form the surface move slowly over, under, past, and away from each other. Sometimes the movement is gradual. At other times, the plates are locked together, unable to release the accumulating energy as they bend or stretch. When the forces grow strong enough, the plates suddenly break free causing the ground to shake. Most earthquakes occur at the boundaries where two plates meet; however, some earthquakes occur in the middle of plates.

Aftershocks are smaller earthquakes that follow the main shock and can cause further damage to weakened buildings. Aftershocks can occur in the first hours, days, weeks, or even months after the quake. Some earthquakes are actually foreshocks that precede a larger earthquake.

Ground shaking from earthquakes can collapse buildings and bridges; disrupt gas, electric, and telephone service; and sometimes trigger landslides, avalanches, flash floods, fires, and huge, destructive, seismic sea waves called tsunamis. Buildings with foundations resting on unconsolidated landfill and other unstable soils are at increased risk of damage. Also, mobile homes and homes not attached to their foundations are at particular risk because they can be shaken off their foundations during an earthquake. When an earthquake occurs in a populated area, it may cause deaths and injuries and extensive property damage.

The Northridge, California, earthquake of January 17, 1994, struck a modern urban environment generally designed to withstand the forces of earthquakes. Its economic cost, nevertheless, was estimated at $20 billion. Fortunately, relatively few lives were lost. Exactly 1 year later, Kobe, Japan, a densely populated community less prepared for earthquakes than Northridge, was devastated by one of the costliest earthquakes ever to occur. Property losses were projected at $96 billion, and at least 5378 people were killed. These two earthquakes tested building codes and construction practices, as well as emergency preparedness and response procedures.

How can I protect myself in an earthquake?

Ground vibrations during an earthquake are seldom the direct cause of death or injury. Most earthquake-related injuries and deaths result from collapsing walls, flying glass, and falling objects caused by the ground shaking. It is extremely important for a person to move as little as possible to reach the place of safety he or she has identified, because most injuries occur when people try to move more than a few feet during the shaking.

Much of the damage caused by earthquakes is predictable and preventable. We must all work together in our communities to apply our knowledge to enact and enforce up-to-date building codes, retrofit older unsafe buildings, and avoid building in hazardous areas, such as those prone to landslides. We must also look for and eliminate hazards at home, where our children spend their days, and where we work. And we must learn and practice what to do if an earthquake occurs.

Action Messages
Be Prepared for an Earthquake

- Protect yourself

Core Action Messages

- Pick "safe places" in each room.
- Practice drop, cover, and hold on.

For general preparedness, every household should create and practice a Family Disaster Plan and assemble and maintain a Disaster Supplies Kit. In addition, every household should take earthquake-specific precautions and plan and practice what to do in the event of an earthquake.

If you are at risk from earthquakes, you should:

- Discuss with members of your household the possibility of earthquakes and what to do to stay safe if one occurs. Knowing how to respond will help reduce fear.

- Pick safe places in each room of your home and your office or school. A safe place could be under a piece of furniture, such as a sturdy table or desk, or against an interior wall away from windows, bookcases, or tall furniture that could fall on you. The shorter the distance to your safe place, the less likely it is that you will be injured by furnishings that become flying debris during the shaking. Injury statistics show that persons moving more than 5 feet (1.5 m) during an earthquake's shaking are the most likely to experience injury.

- Practice drop, cover, and hold on in each safe place. Drop to the floor, take cover under a sturdy piece of furniture, and hold on to a leg of the furniture. If suitable furniture is not nearby, sit on the floor next to an interior wall and cover your head and neck with your arms. Responding quickly in an earthquake may help protect you from injury. Practice drop, cover, and hold on at least twice a year.

- Keep a flashlight and sturdy shoes by each person's bed.

- Talk with your insurance agent about earthquake protection. Different areas have different requirements for earthquake protection. Study the locations of active faults, and, if you are at risk, consider purchasing earthquake insurance.

- Inform guests, babysitters, and caregivers of earthquake plans. Everyone in your home should know what to do if an earthquake occurs, even if you are not there at the time.

Protect Your Property
Core Action Messages

- Secure your home's structure and objects inside and outside.

  If you are at risk from earthquakes, you should:

- *Make sure your home is securely anchored to its foundation.* Depending on the type of construction and the materials used in building your home, you may need to have it bolted or secured in another way to its foundation. If you are not sure that your home is securely anchored, contact a professional contractor. Homes securely attached to their foundations are less likely to be severely damaged during earthquakes, while homes that are not are frequently ripped from their foundations and become uninhabitable.

- *Bolt and brace water heaters and gas appliances to wall studs.* If the water heater tips over, the gas line could break, causing a fire hazard, and the water line could rupture. The water heater may be your best source of drinkable water following an earthquake. Consider having a licensed professional install flexible fittings for gas and water pipes.

- *Bolt bookcases, china cabinets, and other tall furniture to wall studs.* Brace or anchor high or top-heavy objects. During an earthquake, these items can fall over, causing damage or injury.

- *Hang heavy items, such as pictures and mirrors, away from beds, couches, and anywhere people sleep or sit.* Earthquakes can knock things off walls, causing damage or injury.

- *Brace overhead light fixtures.* During earthquakes, overhead light fixtures are the most common items to fall, causing damage or injury.

- *Install strong latches or bolts on cabinets.* The contents of cabinets can shift during the shaking of an earthquake. Latches will prevent cabinets from opening and spilling out the contents. Place large or heavy objects on shelves near the floor.

- *Secure large items that might fall and break* (televisions, computers, etc.).
- *Store weed killers, pesticides, and flammable products securely in closed, latched metal cabinets.*
- *Evaluate animal facilities and places your pets like to hide in, to ensure that any hazardous substances or structures are dealt with.*
- *Consider having your building evaluated by a professional structural design engineer.* Ask about home repair and strengthening tips for exterior features, such as porches, front and back decks, sliding glass doors, canopies, carports, and garage doors. This is particularly important if there are signs of structural defects, such as foundation cracks. Earthquakes can turn cracks into ruptures and make smaller problems bigger. A professional can give you advice on how to reduce potential damage.
- *Follow local seismic building standards and land use codes* that regulate land use along fault lines, in areas of steep topography, and along shorelines. Some municipalities, counties, and states have enacted codes and standards to protect property and occupants in case of an earthquake. Learn about your area's codes before you begin construction.

What to Do During an Earthquake
Core Action Messages

- If inside when the shaking starts, move no more than a few steps and drop, cover, and hold on.
- If outside, find a clear spot and drop.

If you are inside when the shaking starts, you should:

- *Drop, cover, and hold on.* Move only a few steps to a nearby safe place. Most people injured in earthquakes move more than 5 feet (1.5 m) during the shaking.
- *If you are elderly or have a mobility impairment, remain where you are, bracing yourself in place.*
- *If you are in bed, stay there, hold on, and protect your head with a pillow.* You are less likely to be injured if you stay in bed. Broken glass on the floor can injure you.
- *Stay away from windows.* Windows can shatter with such force that you can be injured by flying glass even if you are several feet away.
- *Stay indoors until the shaking stops and you are sure it is safe to exit.* In buildings in the United States, you are safer if you stay where you are until the shaking stops. If you go outside, move quickly away from the building to prevent injury from falling debris.
- *Be aware that fire alarm and sprinkler systems frequently go off in buildings during an earthquake, even if there is no fire.* Check for and extinguish small fires, and exit via the stairs.
- *If you are in a coastal area, drop, cover, and hold on during an earthquake and then move immediately to higher ground when the shaking stops.* Tsunamis are often generated by earthquakes.

If you are outdoors when the shaking starts, you should:

- *Find a clear spot away from buildings, trees, streetlights, and power lines.*
- *Drop to the ground and stay there until the shaking stops.* Injuries can occur from falling trees, streetlights, power lines, and building debris.

- *If you are in a vehicle, pull over to a clear location, stop, and stay there with your seatbelt fastened until the shaking stops.* Trees, power lines, poles, street signs, overpasses, and other overhead items may fall during earthquakes. Stopping in a clear location will reduce your risk, and a hard-topped vehicle will help protect you from flying or falling objects. Once the shaking has stopped, proceed with caution. Avoid bridges or ramps that might have been damaged by the quake.

- *If you are in a mountainous area or near unstable slopes or cliffs, be alert for falling rocks and other debris* that could be loosened by the earthquake. Landslides are often triggered by earthquakes.

What to Do after an Earthquake
Core Action Messages

- Expect aftershocks.
- Check yourself and then others.
- Look for fires.

When the shaking stops, you should:

- *Expect aftershocks.* Each time you feel one, drop, cover, and hold on. Aftershocks frequently occur minutes, days, weeks, and even months following an earthquake.

- *Check yourself for injuries and get first aid if necessary before helping injured or trapped persons.*

- *Put on long pants, a long-sleeved shirt, sturdy shoes, and work gloves* to protect yourself from injury by broken objects.

- *Look quickly for damage in and around your home and get everyone out if your home is unsafe.* Aftershocks following earthquakes can cause further damage to unstable buildings. If your home has experienced damage, get out before aftershocks happen. Use the stairs, not an elevator.

- *Listen to a portable, battery-operated radio or television* for updated emergency information and instructions. If the electricity is out, this may be your main source of information. Local radio and television stations and local officials will provide the most appropriate advice for your particular situation.

- *Check the telephones in your home or workplace.* If a phone was knocked off its cradle during the shaking of the earthquake, hang it up. Allow 10 seconds or more for the line to reset. If the phone lines are undamaged, you should get a dial tone. Use a telephone or cell phone only to make a brief call to your Family Disaster Plan contact and to report life-threatening emergencies. Telephone lines and cellular equipment are frequently overwhelmed in disaster situations and need to be clear for emergency calls to get through. Cellular telephone equipment is subject to damage by quakes and cell phones may not be able to get a signal, but regular land line phones may work.

- *Look for and extinguish small fires.* Fire is the most common hazard following earthquakes. Fires followed the San Francisco earthquake of 1906 for 3 days, creating more damage than the earthquake.

- *Clean up spilled medications, bleach, gasoline, or other flammable liquids* immediately. Avoid the hazard of a chemical emergency.

- *Open closet and cabinet doors cautiously.* Contents may have shifted during the shaking and could fall, creating further damage or injury.

- *Help people who require special assistance*—infants, elderly people, those without transportation, large families who may need additional help in an emergency situation, people with disabilities, and the people who care for them.

- *Watch out for fallen power lines or broken gas lines,* and stay out of damaged areas. Hazards caused by earthquakes are often difficult to see, and you could be easily injured.

- *Watch animals closely.* Keep all your animals under your direct control. Pets may become disoriented, particularly if the disaster has affected scent markers that normally allow them to find their home. Pets may be able to escape from your house or your fence may be broken. Be aware of hazards at nose and paw level, particularly debris, spilled chemicals, fertilizers, and other substances that might seem to be dangerous to humans. In addition, the behavior of pets may change dramatically after an earthquake, becoming aggressive or defensive, so be aware of their well-being and take measures to protect them from hazards, including displaced wild animals, and to ensure the safety of other people and animals.

- *Stay out of damaged buildings.* Damaged buildings may be destroyed by aftershocks following the main quake.

- *If you were away from home, return only when authorities say it is safe. When you return home:*

  - Be alert for and observe official warnings.

  - Use extreme caution. Check for damages outside your home. Then, if the structure appears safe to enter, check for damages inside. Building damage may have occurred where you least expect it. Carefully watch every step you take. Get out of the building if you think it is in danger of collapsing. Do not smoke; smoking in confined areas can cause fires.

  - Examine walls, floors, doors, staircases, and windows.

  - Check for gas leaks. If you smell gas or hear a blowing or hissing noise, open a window and get everyone out quickly. Turn off the gas, using the outside main valve if you can, and call the gas company from a neighbor's home. If you turn off the gas for any reason, it must be turned back on by a professional.

  - Look for damage to the electrical system. If you see sparks or broken or frayed wires, or if you smell burning insulation, turn off the electricity at the main fuse box or circuit breaker. If you have to step in water to get to the fuse box or circuit breaker, call an electrician first for advice.

  - Check for damage to sewage and water lines. If you suspect sewage lines are damaged, avoid using the toilets and call a plumber. If water pipes are damaged, contact the water company and avoid using water from the tap. You can obtain safe water from undamaged water heaters or by melting ice cubes.

  - Watch for loose plaster, drywall, and ceilings that could fall.

Media and Community Education Ideas

- Ask your community to adopt up-to-date building codes. Building codes are the public's first line of defense against earthquakes. National model building codes are available to communities and states. These codes identify construction techniques for buildings that help them withstand earthquakes without collapsing and killing people. Codes are updated regularly to make use of information learned from recent damaging earthquakes, so adopting and enforcing up-to-date codes are essential.

- If your area is at risk from earthquakes, ask your local newspaper or radio or television station to
  - Present information about how to respond if an earthquake occurs.
  - Do a series on locating hazards in homes, workplaces, daycare centers, schools, etc.
  - Provide tips on how to conduct earthquake drills.
  - Run interviews with representatives of the gas, electric, and water companies about how individuals should prepare for an earthquake.

Help the reporters to localize the information by providing them with the local emergency telephone number for the fire, police, and emergency medical services departments (usually 9-1-1) and emergency numbers for the local utilities and hospitals. Also provide the business telephone numbers for the local emergency management office, local American Red Cross chapter, and state geological survey or department of natural resources.

Work with officials of the local fire, police, and emergency medical services departments; utilities; hospitals; emergency management office; and American Red Cross chapter to prepare and disseminate guidelines for people with mobility impairments about what to do if they have to evacuate.

Facts and Fiction

Fiction: During an earthquake, you should get into a doorway for protection.

Facts: In modern homes, doorways are no stronger than any other parts of the structure and usually have doors that will swing and can injure you. During an earthquake, you should get under a sturdy piece of furniture and hold on.

Fiction: During an earthquake, the earth cracks open and people, cars, and animals can fall into those cracks.

Facts: The earth does not crack open like the Grand Canyon. The earth moves and rumbles and, during that movement, small cracks can form. The usual displacements of the earth during an earthquake are caused by up-and-down movements, so shifts in the height of the soil are more likely than chasm-like cracks.

Fiction: Animals can sense earthquakes and give advance warning.

Facts: Animals may be able to sense the first low-frequency waves of an earthquake that occurs deep within the earth, but the damage-causing primary and secondary waves follow just seconds behind. Animals do not make good earthquake warning devices.

Fiction: Big earthquakes always happen in the early morning.

Facts: Several recent damaging earthquakes have occurred in the early morning, so many people believe that all big earthquakes happen then. In fact, earthquakes occur at all times of day. The 1933 Long Beach earthquake was at 5:54 p.m. and the 1940 Imperial Valley event was at 9:36 p.m. More recently, the 1989 Loma Prieta event was at 5:02 p.m.

Fiction: It's hot and dry—earthquake weather!

Facts: Many people believe that earthquakes are more common in certain kinds of weather. In fact, no correlation with weather has been found. Earthquakes begin many kilometers below the region affected by surface weather. People tend to notice earthquakes that fit the pattern and forget the ones that do not. In all regions of the world, "earthquake weather" is whatever type of weather prevailed at the time of the region's most memorable earthquake.

Fiction: Someday there will be beachfront property in Arizona.

Facts: The ocean is not a great hole into which California can fall, but is itself land at a somewhat lower elevation with water above it. The motion of plates will not make California sink—California is moving horizontally along the San Andreas Fault and up around the Transverse Ranges (coastal California mountains).

Fiction: We have good building codes so we must have good buildings.

Facts: The tragedy in Kobe, Japan, one year after the Northridge earthquake, painfully reminds us that the best building codes in the world do nothing for buildings built before that code was enacted. In many earthquake-prone areas of the United States, the building codes are out of date and therefore even new buildings are very vulnerable to severe earthquake damage. Fixing problems in older buildings—retrofitting—is the responsibility of the building's owner.

Fiction: Scientists can now predict earthquakes.

Facts: Scientists do not know how to predict earthquakes, and they do not expect to know how any time in the foreseeable future. However, based on scientific data, probabilities can be calculated for potential future earthquakes. For example, scientists estimate that during the next 30 years the probability of a major earthquake occurring is 67% in the San Francisco Bay area and 60% in southern California.

Source: From the National Disaster Education Coalition, 2004.

6

Response

Introduction

Through the processes of preparedness and mitigation, described in Chapters 4 and 5, individuals, communities, and countries work to reduce their hazard vulnerability and increase their resilience to disasters. Unfortunately, despite even the best-laid emergency plans, the most comprehensive preparedness programs, and the most effective mitigation programs, disasters will still strike, and they do every day of every year. When these hazards strike, individuals, communities, and countries must initiate disaster response, working within the confines of their limited funding, resources, ability, and time to prevent the onset of a catastrophe.

Ultimately, the scale of the disaster dictates the response. Individuals regularly experience emergencies that, in their perspective, are disastrous, such as house fires or car accidents. These events can easily overwhelm their individual capacities to respond, and local response resources such as the fire department or emergency medical units, if they exist, must be dispatched to manage the situation. Communities also experience events that are much larger than they are able to manage and require them to call upon their regional or central government for assistance. These are cases of national disaster. The largest events, however, are those catastrophes that overwhelm even national governments' capacities to respond. In these instances, it is contingent upon a global community of responders to quickly mobilize and assist the affected nation or nations in their disaster response efforts. These international disasters, as they are often called, are the most complex and significant challenges faced by the global emergency management community.

This chapter focuses on response as a disaster management function. The process by which international disasters are recognized, announced, and managed will also be addressed. Even though there are disaster management functions common to many disasters, each is unique, drawing upon several, or even all, of the tasks, processes, and systems described in this chapter.

What Is Response?

The response function of emergency management includes actions aimed at limiting injuries, loss of life, and damage to property and the environment that are taken before, during, and immediately after a hazard event. Response processes begin as soon as it becomes apparent that a hazard event is imminent and lasts until the emergency is declared to be over.

Response is by far the most complex of the four functions of emergency management, as it is conducted during periods of very high stress, in a highly time-constrained environment, and with limited information. During response, wavering confidence and unnecessary delay directly translate to tragedy and destruction.

The task of limiting injuries, loss of life, and further damage to property and the environment is diverse. Response includes not only those activities that directly address these immediate needs—such as first aid, search and rescue, and shelter—but also includes systems developed to coordinate and support such efforts. Response involves the rapid resumption of critical infrastructure (such as opening transportation routes, restoring communications and electricity, and ensuring food and clean water distribution) to allow recovery to take place, reduce further injury and loss of life, and speed the return to a normally functioning society.

Exercises and training may improve responders' skills, but many unknown variables unique to each hazard confound even the most well-planned response. Further, especially during response to disasters that are international in scope, many groups and individuals from all over the world suddenly converge upon the affected area, each with their own expectations, equipment, and mission.

Disaster response is centered upon information and coordination. Unique to each event are the participants, needs of the victims and the community, the timing and order of events, and the actions and processes employed. This section approaches the various functions and processes associated with response in a general sense, as they would apply to all hazards and all nations.

Response—The Emergency

Hazard events, regardless of whether they turn into disasters, are emergencies. They are situations in which the split-second thinking of both trained and untrained individuals must address conditions outside normal life. The emergencies continue until these extraordinary needs have ceased and the danger to life and property no longer persists.

Emergencies occur in three phases, with different response activities applying to each:

1. *Prehazard.* During this period of the emergency, the hazard event is impending and may even be inevitable. Recognition of the impending hazard event may or may not exist.
2. *The emergency: Hazard effects ongoing.* This period begins when the first damaging effects begin and extends until all damaging effects related to the hazard and all secondary hazards cease to exist. It may be measured in seconds for some hazards, such as lightning strikes or earthquakes. However, for others, such as floods, hurricanes, wildfires, or droughts, this phase can extend for hours, days, weeks, or even years. During this time, responders address the needs of people and property as well as the hazard effects.
3. *The emergency: Hazard effects have ceased.* During this final phase of the emergency, the hazard has exerted all of its influence, and negligible further damage is expected. Responders are no longer addressing hazard effects, so their efforts are dedicated to addressing victims' needs, managing the dead, and ensuring the safety of structures and the environment. The emergency still exists and the situation still has the potential to worsen, but the hazard or hazards that instigated the emergency are no longer present.

Recognition—Pre-disaster Actions

Response to a disaster begins as soon as the imminence of a hazard event is recognized by officials with the authority to commence the response effort (often designated in the Emergency Operations Plan, EOP). Recognition may occur via one or more routes, depending upon the hazard's characteristics and the available technology. Each disaster has specific indicators, and prior to the onset of the disaster, governments must have established means of detecting those indicators or received assurance of assistance from other governments with the ability to detect them.

While hazards such as wildfires, droughts, and cyclones may have a significant lead time (measured in hours, days, or even weeks), hazards like earthquakes can strike with almost no advance notice; that is, recognition does not occur until the actual event begins. Advances in technology continue to increase the amount of notice that disaster managers may have to issue a hazard warning. Although the availability of this technology is often limited to developed countries, international cooperation can expand its reach.

Unfortunately, technology is not a "silver bullet" solution, because a nation must be able to act on the information for it to be of any use. For instance, tsunami detection systems alerted the U.S. government of both the 2004 tsunami events in Asia and Africa and the 2009 tsunami events in the South Pacific. The U.S. government, in turn, alerted many of the countries and territories in the path of both of these events. However, most of these countries and territories lacked the procedures to quickly and effectively warn their populations and initiate evacuation to higher ground.

If recognition occurs in advance of the disaster, several pre disaster response processes are available to disaster managers. The specific actions that may be employed, which serve to limit the consequences of the hazard once it does arrive, depend upon the disaster's characteristics, the systems available to emergency managers, and the ability to communicate with a ready public. Although advance public education is not mandatory for proper functioning of pre-disaster actions, it significantly increases their effectiveness. The following three types of response actions may take place during the pre-disaster period:

- *Warning and evacuation.* If a warning system has been established, the public may have time to make last-minute preparations or evacuate away from the area, move into personal or established community shelters, or take other protective actions in advance of the hazard's arrival. As described in Chapters 4 and 5, for warnings to work effectively, the systems require the technology to detect the hazard and relay the warning, and the public must be trained to correctly translate and react to the issued warning. Although experience has shown that not everyone will evacuate or shelter themselves even in the most dangerous situations, protecting any significant portion of the population can drastically reduce overall vulnerability and make the post-disaster response easier.

- *Pre-positioning of resources and supplies.* Depending upon a country's size, responders, equipment, and supplies may be dispersed across a wide area prior to disaster recognition. Advance warning of the disaster allows officials to transport those supplies into the affected site before hazard conditions and consequences make such movement more difficult, dangerous, or even impossible. Pre-positioning of response supplies can also decrease the waiting time after the disaster begins for victims whose survival will depend on these items and services. To further simplify pre-positioning, many countries have created easily transportable disaster equipment kits for items such as pharmaceutical and medical supplies, food, clothing, and shelter. These kits can be stored in trailers, train cars, or moveable shipping crates (see Figure 6–1a and b).

- *Last-minute mitigation and preparedness measures.* Mitigation and preparedness are most effective when they are performed far in advance of a disaster. However, actions often may be taken in the few hours or days before a disaster occurs to further limit the hazard's consequences. For instance, before a flood, sandbags may be used to increase the height of levees or to create barriers around buildings and other structures. Windows and doors may be boarded up or

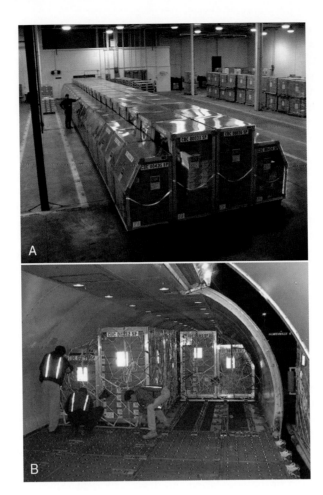

FIGURE 6–1 (a) and (b) U.S. Strategic National Stockpile "12-Hour Push Packages," designed for rapid transport within cargo planes to anywhere in the nation within 12 hours. (Photo courtesy of the U.S. Department of Health and Human Services)

shuttered before a windstorm. Vaccines and other prophylaxis may be used to minimize infection rates with epidemics. For many hazard types, the public may be reminded of stockpiling and other preparedness actions they still have time for (such as purchasing extra water, food, batteries, and candles).

In rare instances, most notably with intentional hazards and technological hazards, completely reducing or eliminating the likelihood of the event may be possible. By their very nature, these hazards are created by humans and thus are more likely to be corrected by humans, unlike natural hazard events, which are mostly unstoppable once recognition of the event occurs. For example, when the Y2K computer bug threatened systems failures around the world, many nations took measures to correct the problem before it materialized.

When pre-disaster hazard recognition is possible, it spurs existing local response resources into action, especially if appropriate tasks have been outlined previously in an EOP. If, based upon knowledge or experience, the hazard is predicted to cause widespread damage, regional or national governments be called in or may self-deploy to begin mobilizing response resources—including declaring a national disaster, if such a distinction is necessary according to legal requirements.

International aid is rarely deployed before a disaster occurs, and two reasons help to explain why. First, most governments prefer to maintain the image that they are able to manage the situation without outside assistance for as long as possible (and occasionally long after their abilities have been exceeded, as will be explained in Chapter 11). The affected country's government must invite international response agencies before these organizations may participate in any response, and because of governments' face-saving needs, they are unlikely to extend such invitations prior to a disaster actually striking. The second reason that international aid is rarely deployed in advance of a disaster is that international assistance is generally provided in proportion to the perceived seriousness of the disaster as well as to the perceived ability of the local government to manage those consequences. Most countries and organizations do not have stores of spare resources they can dedicate or deploy without absolute justification.

Recognition—Post-disaster

Once a hazard event begins and is recognized by response officials, response efforts may commence in earnest. Note, however, that the occurrence of a hazard emergency does not automatically translate to recognition. The affected are the most likely to be the first to know that a hazard has struck and a disaster event is in progress, especially with rapid-onset disasters such as flash floods and landslides. Local, regional, and national response agencies become aware of the disaster by means of first-hand experience, detection systems, and notification from others.

Reasons that emergencies may not be recognized immediately include:

- The scope of the unfolding event is underestimated, and insufficient response is mounted as a result.
- The hazard's initial effects are unrecognizable or undetectable, such as the spraying of a biological weapon in a public area.
- The hazard's initial effects are kept hidden from response officials.
- Disruptions of, inefficiencies in, or a lack of communications infrastructure prevents the affected from reporting an emergency in progress.
- Response officials are fully engaged in response to another hazard and are unable to receive information about a new, secondary hazard.

Once disaster response begins, the first priority is saving lives. This activity, which includes search and rescue, first aid, and evacuation, may continue for days or weeks, depending upon the disaster's type and severity (people have been rescued from rubble as long as 2 weeks after they were buried). As response resources are mobilized, additional functions will be added to the list in increasing priority, to include:

- Assessing the disaster
- Treating remaining hazard effects
- Providing water and food
- Shelter

- Fatality management
- Sanitation
- Security
- Social services
- Resumption of critical infrastructure
- Donations management
- Volunteer management

Search and Rescue

Many disasters result in victims being trapped under collapsed buildings, debris, or by moving water. Earthquakes, hurricanes, typhoons, storms, tornadoes, floods, dam failures, technological accidents, terrorist attacks, and hazardous materials releases, for example, all may result in the need for organized search and rescue. Search and rescue involves three distinct but interrelated actions: locating victims; extracting (rescuing) victims from whatever condition has trapped them; and providing initial medical first aid treatment to stabilize victims so that they may be transported to regular emergency medical practitioners.

Average citizens, victims' friends, family, and neighbors, perform the majority of search and rescue in the initial minutes and hours of a disaster. These people locate victims by listening for calls for help, watching for other signs of life, or using information to estimate where the trapped person may be (such as knowing that someone would have been at home at a certain time of day). It has been estimated that half of those rescued are rescued in the first 6 hours after a disaster happens (with only 50% of those who remain trapped beyond 6 hours surviving; BBC, 1999), so the contribution of ordinary citizens is significant. These untrained responders, operating without adequate equipment or expertise, often place themselves at great risk. But despite the incidence of rescuers being injured or killed, many more lives are saved than lost.

For more organized and technical search-and-rescue effort needs—where average, unequipped citizens are unable or unwilling to go—there are formal search-and-rescue teams. These teams train regularly and operate with a full cache of equipment, supplies, and animals. The teams may focus on general search and rescue or have specialty areas such as wilderness rescue, urban search and rescue, or swift water rescue. Their equipment, which includes medical equipment, rescue equipment (ropes, saws, drills, hammers, lumber), communications equipment (phones, radios, computers), technical support (cameras, heat and movement detectors), and logistics equipment (food, water, special clothing), greatly increases their ability to locate and save victims.

Many nations train, equip, and maintain search-and-rescue teams that are deployable anywhere in the world, with all of their equipment, at a moment's notice. These teams are able to perform several or all of the following tasks:

- Search collapsed buildings for victims and rescue them
- Locate and rescue victims buried in earth, snow, and other debris
- Rescue victims from swiftly moving or high water
- Locate and rescue victims from damaged or collapsed mines
- Locate and rescue victims lost in wilderness areas

- Provide emergency medical care to trapped victims
- Provide dogs trained to locate victims by sound or smell
- Assess and control gas, electric service, and hazardous materials
- Evaluate and stabilize damaged structures

One recognized setback to the deployment of search-and-rescue teams is that it often takes days before team members can begin searching for victims, despite the importance of their arrival very soon after the disaster has occurred. The governments of the affected countries cause the greatest delays. These governments may downplay the severity of the disaster from the outset (making recognition by search-and-rescue teams more difficult), can deny or delay the rapid passage of equipment through customs or borders, and can deny team members access to the affected area, for example. Despite these delays, team members often deploy anyway, knowing that there is always a chance that victims remain alive under debris or in confined spaces, even though significant time may have elapsed (see Exhibit 6–1).

More information on search and rescue can be found at:

- FEMA Search and Rescue: http://www.fema.gov/emergency/usr/
- U.S. National Association for Search and Rescue: www.nasar.org/nasar/
- Canada National Search and Rescue Secretariat: www.nss.gc.ca/site/index_e.asp
- South African Search and Rescue: www.sasar.gov.za/index.html
- Australia Search and Rescue: http://www.amsa.gov.au/search_and_rescue/

First Aid Medical Treatment

While accidents and emergencies commonly involve wounded people, the number of injured victims from disasters exceeds any amount considered normal. The number of victims may be so great that they completely overwhelm the capacity of local clinics or hospitals to care for them all (termed a *mass casualty event*). Disaster managers must find a way to quickly locate these injured victims, provide them with the first aid required to stabilize their condition, and transport them to a facility where they can receive the medical assistance necessary to save their lives.

Onsite first aid, like fire suppression, is a regular function familiar to local first responders. However, basic first aid practice assumptions can be completely undermined in a disaster's aftermath. Victims can quickly outnumber the medical technicians responding to the disaster scene. Supplies are

---

EXHIBIT 6–1: SEARCH AND RESCUE IN THE JANUARY 2010 HAITI EARTHQUAKE

Number of teams that deployed to Haiti: 62
Number of team members: Approximately 1800
Number of people rescued: 132
Number of days following the earthquake when the last survivor was rescued: 11
Estimated cost of all deployments: $10.8 million
Estimated cost of search and rescue per person rescued: $81,800

Source: Roberts, 2010.

rapidly depleted. Transportation to more adequate facilities, which is vital for the most severely wounded, may be delayed, obstructed, or simply impossible. And, even if the responders are able to move victims away from the disaster area, there may be nowhere to bring them, if other victims from throughout the greater disaster area occupy all nearby hospital beds.

One of the first steps that responders take to manage disaster first aid is triage. Triage is a system by which many victims are ranked according to the seriousness of their injuries, ensuring that the highest priority cases are transported to medical facilities before less serious ones. In essence, it is a needs assessment. By triaging patients, responders maximize their time and resources and prevent nonurgent cases from being double- or triple-checked unnecessarily.

Triage tagging involves marking patients with a symbol on their forehead or a color-coded tag. It is done primarily according to two established systems. The first, Simple Triage and Rapid Transport (START), is used when onsite medical resources are scarce and victims will be transported to more adequately staffed and prepared facilities. START tagging categories include:

- D—Deceased
- I—Immediate (victim needs advanced medical care within 1 hour)
- DEL—Delayed (victim needs medical care, but can wait until after I victim)
- M—Minor (victim can wait several hours before nonlife-threatening injuries are treated)

Advanced triage is the second system used when sufficient emergency medical care exists onsite. Advanced triage categories include:

- Black—Expectant (victims' injuries are so severe they are expected to die)
- Red—Immediate (victims are likely to survive their injuries, but only with immediate surgery or other life-saving treatment)
- Yellow—Observation (victims are injured and need emergency medical care, but current condition is stable; must be monitored for change in condition)
- Green—Wait (victims need medical care within several hours or even days, but will not die of their injuries if left untreated in the immediate future)
- White—Dismiss (victims need little more than minor first aid treatment or basic care not requiring a doctor)

When large numbers of injured victims are present, establishing field hospitals may be necessary. Field hospitals are temporary facilities constructed at or near the source of victims where surgical and other complex medical equipment and staff are available (see Figure 6–2). They can be set up from scratch inside large tents or undamaged buildings, relying on equipment and staff transported in from distant hospitals, for instance, or they can be constructed from "kits" designed especially for rapid deployment to disaster zones. Finally, transportable hospitals, such as the USNS *Comfort* pictured in Figure 5–1, may be brought in.

Evacuation

Before, during, or after a disaster occurs, it is often necessary to move populations away from the hazard and its consequences. This can reduce the effect of many disasters, whether natural, technological, or intentional, by simply removing potential victims from risk.

FIGURE 6–2 Field hospital established in the United States to treat the injured following Hurricane Francis in 2004. (Photo courtesy of FEMA/Andrea Booher)

Despite evacuation orders that come in advance of a disaster, many people refuse to evacuate or are unable to for a range or reasons (including poverty, disability, fear, or inability to receive or understand warning communications). Once the disaster begins and conditions worsen, however, these same people may still need to be evacuated, and they may even begin evacuating on their own in such a way as to place themselves at increased risk.

Evacuations are most effective when they are limited to only those areas facing risk. This could be a single building, a neighborhood, or a whole city or region. Once it has been deemed necessary, only government officials may order an evacuation. Fire or police officials may instigate and facilitate the evacuation of single buildings or neighborhoods, but, for larger jurisdictions, the call usually comes from the chief executive. Depending upon a nation's laws, these evacuations may be recommended or forced. Legal issues arise if statutory authority is not in place outlining how and when forced evacuations may be performed.

To be effective, evacuations must be facilitated. Evacuation routes able to convey evacuees all the way out of danger and to a safe destination should be predetermined according to hazard. Many people will need transportation, such as buses, boats, or trains, which must be resistant to the hazard's effects to be effective. Special needs populations, such as the elderly, the sick, children, the disabled, the illiterate, and others, should be pre-identified so that specific resources may be used to locate and extract them on an individual basis (many religious, community, or charitable groups organize this function).

Disaster Assessments

As soon as possible after the disaster has begun, response officials must begin collecting data, which is then formulated into information to facilitate the response. Responders must be able to know at any given time or at short intervals what is happening, where it is happening, what is needed, what is required to address those needs, and what resources are available. This data collection process, which is called *disaster assessment*, increases in difficulty and complexity with the size and scope of the disaster.

Disaster assessment efforts can be grouped into two general categories, defined by the type of data they seek:

1. *Situation assessment.* This assessment, also called a *damage assessment,* seeks to determine what has happened as a result of the hazard. Situation assessments can help determine the geographic scope of the disaster, and how it has affected people and structures. It is, in essence, a measure of the hazard's consequences. Data sought may include:
   - Area affected by the disaster (location and size—can be plotted onto a base map or described in words)
   - Number of people affected by the disaster
   - Number of injured (morbidity) and killed (mortality)
   - Types of injuries and illnesses
   - Description of the characteristics and condition of the affected
   - Description of the medical, health, nutritional, water, and sanitation situation
   - Ongoing or emerging hazards and hazard effects
   - Damage to infrastructure and critical facilities
   - Damage to residences and commercial structures
   - Damage to the agricultural and food distribution systems
   - Damage to the economic and social status of the affected area
   - Vulnerability of the affected population to ongoing disaster effects or to expected related or unrelated hazards
   - Current response effort in progress

2. *Needs assessment.* This assessment involves gathering data on the services, resources, and other assistance that will be required to address the disaster. It is used to determine what is needed to both save and sustain lives. Disaster managers may use a range of methods to conduct this assessment, which could include:
   - *Gathering of internal information.* This entails gathering and reporting all information known by staff or affiliates.
   - *Visual inspection.* This involves using various methods of observation, including satellite imagery, aerial flyovers, and drive or walkthrough surveying.
   - *Sample surveys.* Information gathered by interviewing representative segments of the affected population, usually by one of the following four methods:
     - *Simple random sampling.* Members of the population are selected purely at random.
     - *Systematic random sampling.* Members of the affected population are sampled according to a pre-set pattern, such as every fifth house, every tenth name on a list, etc.
     - *Stratified random sampling.* The affected population is first divided into demographic groups (strata), and then members of each strata are randomly selected for sampling.
     - *Cluster sampling.* Affected people are sampled in groups or clusters, arranged geographically within the affected area, representative of the different geographic areas affected by the disaster.

- *Sentinel surveillance.* Certain disaster characteristics or "early warning signs," which tend to be indicative of larger problems, are monitored and reported when found.
- *Detailed critical sector assessments by specialists.* Experts in various sectors, such as transportation, energy, health, or water supply, make targeted surveys of the infrastructure component for which they are specially trained.
- *Ongoing interviews.* People are designated to gather information on an ongoing basis to support updating the assessments.
- *Interviewing of informants.* Members of the affected population who are identified as being able to provide useful information regarding the situation and needs are contacted on a regular basis to report any findings they may have.

Appendix 6–1, found at the end of this chapter, provides an example of a checklist used to conduct assessments (in this case, by the U.S. Agency for International Development, Office of Foreign Disaster Assistance).

Reporting must be conducted in order for anything to be gained from the disaster assessment process. Effective reporting involves analyzing all of the collected data to create a clear and concise picture of what responders are dealing with. To increase its effectiveness, standardized formats, terminology, and collection systems have emerged throughout the disaster management world that, while not uniform across all agencies, offers greater ease of use by many recipients.

The overall assessment process is methodical. Several sequential steps are required if the information collected is to be of any use to responders; neglecting such an approach can result in incorrect or inaccurate information that ultimately may hurt response efforts (see Exhibit 6–2). The general process by which assessment and reporting are conducted entails the following:

1. *Planning.* In order to conduct assessments, a systematic approach must be taken throughout the process by which data are collected, analyzed, utilized, and reported. During planning, disaster managers decide what information is collected and how it is collected, with what instruments and by what staff, under what time frame, and in how much detail, among other factors.
2. *Data collection.* Data describing the disaster at hand is gathered using the methods mentioned earlier. This information must be verified to be true and relevant.
3. *Data analysis.* By looking at all of the information and pulling out what is important in terms of the response, including patterns, trends, problem areas, and critical activities, the data's usefulness emerges.
4. *Forecasting.* Using information collected over time, disaster managers must try to estimate how the disaster will progress, taking into account any response efforts that currently are under way. They must use this information to predict potential future problems so they can take advance action to prevent such problems before they start.
5. *Reporting.* The assessment is of no value unless it is distributed to those officials whose work depends on it. Systematic reporting allows all users to receive the information in a timely manner and ensures that everyone who needs updates receives them.
6. *Monitoring.* The emergency situation changes from minute to minute, so assessments are soon out of date. Periodic updates, scheduled at a pace that accommodates the speed of change (usually every 12 or 24 hours), increase the chances that everyone is acting on timely information.

EXHIBIT 6–2: INFLUENCE OF THE MEDIA ON THE ACCURACY OF INFORMATION

On January 1, 2007, Adam Air flight 574 disappeared along its course between Surabaya and Manado, both in Indonesia. Almost immediately, reports began to surface that the jet wreckage had been found in the mountains of Sulawesi and that twelve of the passengers had survived. The Indonesian media reported the following:

> Rescuers Tuesday found the smoldering wreckage of an Indonesian jetliner that went missing during a storm, and officials said 90 people were killed while the remaining 12 aboard survived. The Boeing 737 operated by local carrier Adam Air crashed in a mountainous region of Sulawesi island in the northeast of the sprawling archipelagic nation, said local police Chief Col. Genot Hariyanto. "The plane is destroyed and many bodies are around there," he said. Adam Air spokesman Hartono said 90 people were killed and that there were 12 survivors in Monday's crash. Their condition was not known, said Hartono, who goes by a single name. Rescue workers were at the crash site trying to evacuate survivors, officials said. (International Herald Tribune, 2007).

This prompted a major search-and-rescue operation to the reported site that included almost 800 people, but no plane debris could be found where the reports had come in. Later on January 2, the government of Indonesia announced that the reports were the result of rumors, and that the survivors were real, but had survived a ferry disaster that had also occurred in the previous week, not a plane crash. The reports stated,

> [Transport Minister Hatta Radjasa] blamed villagers for spreading rumors that the wreckage had been located. "It has not yet been found." The false news took a toll on the families of the 102 people aboard the Adam Air flight, many of whom had flown to Makassar near where the plane is believed to have gone down to find out more information about their loved ones. "Oh, what is happening to us?" said Dorce Sundalangi, whose daughter was on the flight, after hearing the report that the wreckage was found was based on rumors from villagers that reached the highest levels of government. "They had given us hope of seeing our beloved relatives ... but it was false hope," she said in an AP report. Capt. Hartono, a spokesman for Adam Air, told reporters earlier Tuesday that the rescue team found the site near the coastal village of Polewali, recovered 90 bodies, and found 12 survivors. That report was later disputed by transport minister Radjasa and other transportation officials. Setyo Rahardjo, the chairman of Indonesia's National Transport Safety Committee, blamed local police for spreading rumors that the wreckage and survivors of the crash had been located near Polewali village in western Sulawesi province. Aglionby said the false report was due to a combination of poor infrastructure in the region, and rescue workers sending out bad information. The lack of cell-phone networks has also hampered communications in the region, Aglionby added.
> Source: CNN, 2007.

The government resumed their search, and over one week later (on January 11), pieces of wreckage were found in the sea. It was not until January 21, however, that the black boxes were located. However, because they were at a depth of 2000 m, and no recovery resources existed in the region capable of reaching such depths before the boxes' batteries failed, they were never recovered.

Several different types of assessment reports, often called *situation reports,* may be used to broadcast the analyzed information to users. These reports are distinguished by what they contain, when they are released, and their level of detail. The following list explains several of the most common report types:

- *Flash report.* Also called an *SOS report,* this is designed for quick release. Its main purpose is to provide expanded recognition that the disaster has occurred, explain what is being done, and request assistance or report on expected assistance.

- *Initial assessment report.* This report may be the first assessment distributed or may follow the flash report, if one has been distributed. The initial assessment provides a more detailed description of the disaster's effect on the impact area and provides the condition of the affected population. Food, water, and other supply needs are identified, as are vulnerable populations that need the most urgent care. The local government's capacity to manage the disaster is described, and information to guide external assistance is proposed. Finally, any forecasts or expected issues are listed.

- *Interim report.* This builds upon information listed in the initial assessment or previous interim reports to relay changes in the situation and its needs. Disaster assessments are iterative and reported information needs to be updated every 12 hours, 24 hours, or longer, as is required or is feasible. Each interim report is merely a moment in time captured on paper that guides responders, not something that should be taken as flawless and complete information. Information in interim reports is not repeated unless required to illustrate changes.

- *Specialist/technical report.* This supplements the information in the initial or interim reports by providing information needed only by a particular person or small group within the greater body of responders.

- *Final report.* The final report is a summary, reporting the conclusion of response and recovery operations and describing the event, the response, and any lessons that were learned.

Reports are generally presented in a numbered, sectioned format that describes specific response tasks within separate sections. This format makes it easy for responders to find and use the information that pertains specifically to their needs, and all subsequent interim reports will display information related to those response functions in the same numbered category.

Examples of the category headings used in these reports include:

- Situation
- Background (a brief overview of original disaster or emergency situation, including the who, what, when, where of the event)
- Current situation (brief summary of what is in the report)
- Casualties and damages
  - Search and rescue
  - Evacuation
  - Protection
  - Shelter
  - Health and nutrition
  - Water and sanitation

- Communications
- Transportation
- Power
- Treating the hazard

Each hazard has its own mechanism by which it creates negative consequences. For instance, cyclonic storms wreak havoc on the human and built environment with high winds, heavy rains, and powerful storm surges, and earthquakes do so through violent ground movements. While some hazards unleash these effects over a very short time frame, others, including many secondary hazard effects, persist much longer.

Three types of hazard effects may occur, as identified during the hazard assessment process described in Chapter 2:

1. Effects that are over before any response activities may be initiated to treat them
2. Effects that persist, but for which no response actions exist that can limit or eliminate them
3. Effects that persist that may be limited or eliminated completely through existing response actions

For the first set—which includes effects such as the ground shaking associated with earthquakes, the energy release from a strike of lightning, and the damaging force of a landslide—responders only deal with the aftermath and any secondary hazards.

For the second set of effects—which include the strong winds of a cyclonic storm or periods of extreme heat or cold—responders can only take actions that protect themselves and the public from further injury. Over time, the effects will diminish, even though the emergency may continue.

The third and final group of hazard effects is those that responders are able to limit or eliminate. Using special equipment and training, responders reduce the existing hazard risk during the disaster by reducing the hazard's ability to exist at all. Although the range of disaster-causing hazards for which this is possible is narrow and the expense great, many developed countries (as well as many developing ones) have dedicated considerable resources to this group. Examples of response activities that may be performed to limit the ongoing effects of hazards include:

- Fire suppression
- Flood fighting
- Hazardous materials containment and decontamination
- Arrest of lava flows
- Snow and ice removal
- Epidemic public health efforts
- Law enforcement to curtail rioting or civil unrest

Provision of Water, Food, and Shelter

After disasters strike, people's homes may be destroyed or uninhabitable. Transportation routes and communication may be completely cut off, and whole regions may be completely isolated. Victims, however, must still drink, eat, and find shelter if they are to survive. As normal supply lines will likely be interrupted and victims' access to provisions limited or nonexistent, disaster management officials need to begin assisting them immediately.

Food, water, and shelter options must be located and acquired, and then somehow transported to the victims. Generally, two separate phases in the post-disaster response include this measure. The first phase is the short-term, immediate response. While systematic delivery of aid is optimal, the confusion that exists in the first hours and days of the disaster contributes to haphazard responder actions and decisions, with needs addressed as they are perceived. In the event that the disaster response moves into the second phase, the long-term provision of aid, camps of displaced people likely will be established to increase the efficiency of aid. The establishment of camps is described in the section entitled "Shelter."

Water

Although many other basic needs, such as clothing, shelter, and even food, may go unmet for one or more days at a disaster's onset, both people and animals need a constant supply of water in order to survive. Water is used for hydration (drinking), for hygiene, and for food preparation (cooking and cleanup).

During times of disaster, it is not uncommon for regular water sources to become interrupted or contaminated, leaving disaster victims without usable water. Even those who have stockpiled water could be left without it if they are forced to leave their homes in a hurry. Water needs are urgent and must be addressed very early in the disaster response. Without water, people will begin to fall ill, disease will quickly spread, and unrest will grow.

Using assessments, disaster managers must first determine the water needs of the affected population. They must find out if the needs are a result of displacement, damage to infrastructure, contamination, or a range of other problems. Managers must also determine how many victims are without water and where they are located. Finally, they must create an inventory of what water sources still exist, and which of those can be used to supply either drinking water or water for other uses.

Immediate water needs can be met through a range of methods, including:

- Trucking in water in tanker trucks, ships, railcars, or other large storage devices
- Transporting bottled or bagged water
- Locating and tapping unexploited water sources within the community
- Providing access to a functioning but restricted water source within the community
- Pumping water from a nearby source into the community
- Providing filters or other treatments to clean contaminated water (see Figure 6–3)
- Moving the population to another location where water is available

In a disaster's immediate aftermath, managers will make every effort to provide what water they can, even though the population needs will probably outweigh what they can feasibly supply from the outset. However, as the response begins to organize and assessments provide more information, disaster managers will need to begin a more technical analysis of the population needs for long-term aid. The following factors are commonly investigated as water relief is established:

1. *Needs*. Studies have determined the average amount of water needed by the individual victim, which can be used for planning purposes in disaster response. The actual needs of each individual will be unique and will depend upon such factors as the local climate, the availability

FIGURE 6–3 USAID Office of Foreign Disaster Assistance water purification unit that produced 78,000 liters of water per day for families affected by the January 2001 earthquake in India. (Photo courtesy of Michael Ernst, USAID/OFDA)

of sanitation facilities, religious and cultural customs, and food preferences, among other issues. The U.S. Agency for International Development (USAID) developed the following guidelines upon which water provision may be based:

- Drinking—3 to 4 liters per day
- Cooking and cleanup—2 to 3 liters per day
- Hygiene—6 to 7 liters per day
- Washing of clothes—4 to 6 liters per day
- Total water needs, per person, per day—15 to 20 liters
  The Sphere Project determined that 7.5 to 15 liters per day, per person, is sufficient.

2. *Source.* The chosen source of water plays a large part in determining how much water is available, how it may be extracted, and how much treatment must be applied to the water to make it safe for drinking. Sources that require the least technology for extraction (e.g., gravity flow rather than electric pumps) and the least amount of treatment are preferred. In general, groundwater sources are the cleanest. The three main sources of water are
   - Surface water (rivers, lakes, streams, ponds)
   - Groundwater (groundwater, springs, aquifers)
   - Rainwater

3. *Flow.* The amount of water that flows from a source will determine how many individuals may be associated with that source. For instance, if a tap has a flow of 10 liters of water per minute, no more than 300 people (with a total need of 4500–6000 liters per day) should depend upon that tap. Although the tap has a daily flow of 14,400 liters, people should only be expected to go to the source during daylight hours, the time lost between individuals using the tap is significant in sum, and higher dependence on the tap may lead to surges at certain times of the day.

4. *Quality.* The water that is provided must be healthy to drink. Many sources of groundwater appear to be clean because they are free from sediment, but they may contain harmful bacteria

(such as *E. coli*), viruses, or other pathogens that can cause diarrhea and other diseases. Regular testing must be performed to monitor any changes that may result from the heavy use of the single source. While water does not need to be 100% free from pathogens, certain pathogens must be avoided. It is believed that a large quantity of near-clean water is better than a small quantity of pure water. Water may be purified through the following means:

- *Storage.* Water that is left in a covered, protected container improves over time. This is because many pathogens have only a limited time before they must infect a host or die. It also allows for many of the larger, heavier, suspended pathogens and other impurities to settle out of the water, making it clearer. Storage cannot completely clean water, but it can improve its quality drastically.

- *Sand filtration.* Sand filters are specially designed containers through which water is passed before being stored or distributed. The sand filters clean the water by physically obstructing pathogens and other impurities as they pass through. A layer of algae and other live organisms forms on the top of the sand bed, feeding on the harmful bacteria in the water as it passes through.

- *Coagulation and flocculation.* Through the use of certain chemicals and organic compounds, impurities in the water can be caused to coagulate (join together), making it easier for them to either precipitate or be filtered out of the water.

- *Chemical treatment.* Water can be disinfected with commonly available chemicals, such as chlorine or iodine. Chemical treatment requires a certain amount of expertise, as too little chemical will not treat the water, while too much could make the water undrinkable or unhealthy. Chemical treatment can help ensure that water is not re-contaminated once brought home and stored by the disaster victim.

- *Boiling.* Boiling is highly effective at killing pathogens in water, but it is not always possible because the materials, such as metal pots, wood for fires, or electricity, may not be available. Also, while other forms of purification take place at the source, guaranteeing that disaster victims are provided with clean water from the start, boiling depends upon adherence to the process by individuals.

5. *Wait time.* The time available to disaster victims may be constrained by many concurrent needs. The time they have available to wait in a line for water is likely limited; therefore it is important that waiting is minimized as much as possible. Long wait times can be indicators of other problems, such as low water flow, too few water sources, and too many people using the same pump. Not addressing this issue could result in a lower amount of water used by each person; the desire to seek alternate, likely unsafe, water sources; and stress related to the reduced amount of time available to perform other needed tasks.

6. *Distance.* It is important that no victims need to travel too far to reach the water source. Many, if not all, will be without transportation and will need to carry a large volume of water by hand. Additionally, long distances directly translate to an increased burden on their limited time.

7. *Storage.* Individuals will need a way to store the water that they collect. Many people may have no possessions left or own nothing suitable for large amounts of water, and will need to be given containers to safely collect, transport, and store water. If using their own containers, these containers must be cleaned prior to use. Special needs populations, such as children, the elderly, or the disabled, should be equipped with appropriate containers for their abilities (e.g., containers with wheels). Families or households should have enough containers to transport at

least as much water as the family needs (15–20 liter containers per person) and an additional storage container at the house or shelter to store unused water when they return to the water source for more.

8. *Taste (palatability)*. Water must be palatable for people to be expected to drink it. Too much of a certain chemical (such as chlorine, iodine, or another chemical) or other minerals or materials, such as salt, may result in victims seeking other, less safe, although more palatable, water.

9. *Equity*. It is important that disaster managers setting up water sources for disaster victims understand the demographics of that population to ensure that all victims may use it, and that alternate options exist for those who may not. For instance, there may be situations in which men and women should not use the same pump. Other factors that could affect access include education, ethnicity, age, religion, health, physical ability, and social stratification.

People without water are likely to seek it wherever they can, even after more formal camps have been set up. In many cases, especially when flooding is present, water may be available in great quantity, but its quality is what causes the need for clean water. For this reason, it is of vital importance that any effort to provide water is conducted in concert with a public education campaign that informs victims about where to get water, the dangers of using unsafe water, and how to ensure that the water they are using is safe. They also must be told how to prevent contaminating those sources that remain available or that have been provided.

If plenty of untreated water is available but supplies of safe drinking water are not meeting current needs, then nondrinkable water may be recommended or required for anything other than cooking or drinking. Even brackish water or seawater may be used for bathing or washing dishes and clothes.

Water reserves should be created in large holding tanks as quickly as possible after a disaster. These reserves help to ensure distribution in case problems arise from other, established sources. Storage tanks already containing water may be brought in or they may be filled from sources established within the affected zone during periods when victims are not using them (such as late at night). Stored water has the added advantage that sedimentation can precipitate out, increasing the water's palatability.

Food

Like water, local stores of food will quickly be depleted in the aftermath of most large-scale disasters. Regular channels for acquiring food, whether subsistence farming, local markets, or some other means, will be severely disrupted or halted entirely. The normal means by which food is replenished from outside sources may be severely affected by the disaster, either directly (food production and distribution facilities hit) or indirectly (transportation routes blocked). Even if food is available within the affected area, many victims may not have the physical or economic means to acquire it. Thus, food provision to victims must begin very shortly after a disaster.

From the start, even before accurate assessments are performed, disaster managers must make every effort to supply food to the affected. Reaching people may be difficult, so creative methods of transport—including food drops—may be required before more dependable routes can be established. People will be desperate, and rioting or other violence is likely if food is not provided quickly.

Organized mass feeding cannot begin until accurate assessments have taken place. Those making the assessment must be aware of how many people are in need of food, how those people normally acquire their food (produce or purchase), and how those methods of acquisition have been affected. For some disasters, the shortage should only be expected in the short term (especially in wealthier nations), while for others, as is often the case with complex humanitarian emergencies, chronic food shortages will be expected to persist for weeks or even months.

Food aid must be formulated to suit the needs of the population being fed. The food must conform to local diets, preferably using local ingredients that are similar to or the same as what people would eat during nondisaster times. Many special needs populations, such as the sick, elderly, very young, and pregnant or lactating mothers, must have their nutritional needs addressed. The equipment used to transport, store, cook, and eat food must also conform to the needs of each of these groups for mass feeding to be effective.

Food storage is an important issue as well. Food stocks can become damaged by the weather, pillaged by looters or desperate victims, invaded by vermin, or spoiled. Storage areas, therefore, must be clean, dry, secure, and accessible to the various forms of transport that will be used to distribute food around the affected area.

There are two ways in which food may be distributed to disaster victims in the aftermath of a hazard: "wet" and "dry" distribution. Dry distribution, also called *ration distribution* or *take-home,* refers to the provision of uncooked ingredients, usually in bulk (e.g., a week's or month's worth of supplies), that victims take back to their homes or shelters to cook. The advantages of dry distribution are that victims can use only as much as they need at a time that is most convenient to them. Social units, such as families, are more likely to be able to eat together, which will likely benefit mental health and increased time available to perform other tasks (because of shorter time waiting in lines). However, dry distribution depends on ensuring that victims have proper cooking and eating utensils, as well as ample supplies of safe water. It also opens up the opportunity for the abuse of supplies, which may be hoarded or sold for a profit. Additionally, local markets may suffer from decreased demand.

Wet distribution involves providing victims with prepared meals, usually two or three times per day. To perform such a task, large-capacity, centralized cooking facilities (kitchens) must be located or established and stocked with adequate serving and eating utensils and staff. Wet distribution provides greater control of food stocks and increases the chance that meals are eaten regularly. However, victims lose a certain amount of independence and may need to skip meals if they have other pressing needs during meal times.

Public education is an important part of mass feeding, as most people will not be cooking or eating according to their normal routines or with their usual ingredients and, as result, may not be supplying themselves with the minimum basic nutritional requirements. They also are likely to be expending more energy and may be dealing with sick family members, and they may not know how to address those needs using the food they have been provided with. Finally, public health issues they do not normally confront, such as vermin, contamination, and disease, will need to be addressed to ensure that they do not harm themselves unwittingly through unsafe practices. Cooking fuel, such as wood or carbon (charcoal), may need to be provided with the food to ensure that families are able to prepare meals.

For long-term emergencies, in which food must be provided over a period of weeks or months, nutritional assessments may be necessary to ensure that widespread malnutrition within the population is not occurring. Research has found that it is suitable to perform the assessment on children between the ages of 1 to 5 years, as their condition is generally representative of the population at large. Measurements are taken either from a random representative sample of all victims or by measuring clusters of victims if victim distribution is not uniform (see the section Disaster Assessments). There are two primary methods by which malnutrition is measured for children under 5. The first method measures the victims' weight as a ratio to their height. This compares each victim (primarily children) to a normal child with the same height or length, and expresses his or her case as a percentage of normal. For instance, the average weight in kilograms of a child 1 meter in height is 15.6 kg. Therefore, a child weighing only 10.9 kg would have only 70% of the weight of a normal child (and would be considered severely malnourished). The second method is to measure the child's mid-upper-arm circumference (MUAC method). For normal children between the ages of 1 and 5, this measure will be almost uniform. This area of the arm loses circumference quickly when a child is malnourished; however, it is a fast way to measure for trends among populations. A child with an MUAC of less than 12.5 cm would be considered moderately to severely malnourished.

For certain members of the population, including pregnant or lactating mothers, severely sick or malnourished people, children, and the elderly, the general rations provided may not meet needs and supplemental feeding programs may need to be established. Supplemental programs are targeted and consist of foods with very high energy content or foods appropriate for the specific group (such as formula for babies whose mothers cannot breastfeed). For extreme cases of malnutrition in the overall population, blanket supplemental feeding programs are conducted.

Shelter

After food and water, the next vital need that responders must address is emergency shelter. Without shelter, survivors, the injured, and the well alike will soon become further victimized by the elements and by insecurity and psychological stress. For large, destructive events, like earthquakes, hurricanes, and floods, the number of people requiring shelter may be in the tens or hundreds of thousands.

Disaster managers will eventually need to assess whether the emergency shelter needs of the population will exist for the short or long term, but victims' immediate needs must be met in any way possible with what exists in the community (see Exhibit 6–3). The best choice for immediate shelter is public or private facilities within the community (which should have been identified before the disaster occurred) that were not damaged by the hazard. Common examples include covered stadiums, schools, auditoriums, warehouses, and airport hangars. Tent villages may be set up in the short term, but doing so greatly increases the chance that the displaced will later need to be moved if their shelter needs are long term. Long-term shelter needs require a more thorough assessment, as is described in the following section about setting up camps.

Various shelter options, and the period for which they are appropriate, include:

- Hosting by family, friends, or others within the community (short term)
- Placement in rental house or apartment, or in a hotel or motel (short term)
- Placement in suitable public or private structures, such as large halls, churches, warehouses, schools, covered sports stadiums, or theaters (short term)
- Placement in organized camps of tents or trailers, or other light housing options set up to accommodate victims' needs (short to medium term)
- Placement in sturdy but temporary newly constructed houses (medium to long term)

EXHIBIT 6-3: EMERGENCY, INTERIM, AND TRANSITIONAL HOUSING OPTIONS

Disaster managers faced with a homeless population need to decide in the immediate hours of response how to best house these individuals until permanent housing solutions can be provided. There are three categories of options, and the selection of one over another has far-reaching implications in terms of cost, feasibility, long-term success, privacy for occupants, and many other factors. These choices include:

- *Emergency Housing:* Typically provide an interim, safe haven until the situation stabilizes. Emergency housing is small in terms of space, provides little privacy or comfort, and may be nothing more than a tent camp or a converted structure (like a school gymnasium, for instance). Emergency housing is suitable for up to 60 days.
- *Interim (or Temporary) Housing:* Typically provides more of the comforts required to carry out a normal life until permanent housing can be provided. Occupants can live in the interim housing option for a year or longer, as it will have utilities and services provided.
- *Transitional Housing:* Transitional housing is a housing option wherein the emergency shelter can either be converted into permanent shelter, or can be disassembled into its base construction materials and used to build the permanent house. These are the most costly of the three options, but provide the most comfort and privacy for the recipient, and ultimately have the greatest success in moving victims to more permanent, sustainable housing solutions.

The United Nations guide "Shelter after Disaster: Strategies for Transitional Settlement and Reconstruction" provides a wealth of information about the different categories and options available to emergency managers and can be found at: http://www.sheltercentre.org/library/Shelter+After+Disaster.

As early on in the response as possible, disaster managers will decide whether they will need to establish long-term shelter options. Displaced people may need shelter for months if their home villages or cities were completely destroyed. In refugee situations, the average amount of time spent in a camp is 7 years (some Palestinian refugee camps set up over 50 years ago still exist today). The logistical requirements of these facilities, often referred to as *camps*, go far beyond what is typically seen at shelters or other short-term relief efforts. Camps, which are typically seen as a last-resort option, present disaster managers with a full range of problems that must be addressed if the facilities are to be sustainable, manageable, and beneficial to the people they are designed to assist.

The first issue in choosing a camp is site selection. Victims can be housed either onsite, where their former residence was located (also referred to as in situ), or off-site (also referred to as ex situ). In situ housing is always best, but often is not possible given lingering hazard effects such as flood waters, disaster debris, insecurity, or harsh climate. Off-site shelter decisions are equally difficult, as most sites suitable for mass-care shelter habitation have likely already been settled. Large, open spaces suitable for a dense population are rare, and any that are discovered need to be investigated as to why settlement has not yet occurred there. Because it is very difficult to change or move a site once the affected population has settled into it, it is important that a full assessment be made to ensure the site is appropriate. The following are the main considerations managers must address in choosing a site:

- *The social needs of the affected population.* Disaster managers may not immediately know victims' cultural, religious, and social attachments to the land. Victims may feel uncomfortable living on certain land. They may not want to venture too far away from the devastated area if they have strong cultural or social ties to it. In areas of political conflict or war, the site should be sufficiently far away to ensure the security of those who will be living in the camp.

- *Livelihoods.* People's means of financial gain can and most often are tied to place. Fisherfolk must live close to the water. Farmers must live on or near their farmland. Factory workers must be able to go to and return from the factory each day. Shelter efforts that fail to account for the loss of access to victims' livelihoods often result in victims returning back to their original place of residence, which in turn increases their risk to life and health and makes the overall response and recovery effort much more difficult to manage.

- *Access to water.* The displaced population will need to use significant amounts of water, so the site chosen should accommodate this need. The water supply should be available year round, and not depend upon weather or climatic patterns. In addition, there should be no threat of too much water at certain times of the year, which would result in flooding of the camp. Drainage, which is associated with the use of water resources by the displaced population, must be sufficient to ensure that wastewater can easily be transported away from the camp using natural or mechanical processes.

- *Space per person.* The selected site must be able to accommodate the number of displaced people who are slated to be located there. The World Health Organization established 30 square meters as the minimum amount of space that any person be allocated for long-term shelter. If the camp is to exist for longer than a year, it should be expected that the population would grow at a rate of at least 4% each year.

- *Accessibility of the camp.* The logistics of the camp will depend on a significant amount of transportation. The site should be in a place that can be reached by buses, trucks, and helicopters.

- *Environmental considerations.* The site should allow for safe, healthy operation. Sites that are subject to frequent natural or technological disasters are likely to create a second disaster for the displaced population. The environment should be resistant to the drivers of public health problems, such as mosquitoes, rodents, and flies. Sloping terrain is preferable because it allows for natural drainage. If at all possible, the site's climate should closely match what is considered normal by the population that will be living there, so that the conditions do not cause undue stress.

- *Soil and ground cover.* Certain soil conditions are unsuitable for human habitation, which may be why the site was available in the first place. The safety and success of latrines, for instance, depend upon the ability of the soil to contain human waste. Sandy or rocky soils will make subsistence gardening or farming impossible. Excessively dusty soils will cause health and other problems. Impermeable soils will result in flash flooding if heavy rains occur. Soil and environmental experts may need to be consulted about this factor before choosing a site.

- *Land rights.* Several problems can result if the land that is chosen is under private ownership or has been allocated by the government for grazing, mining, or other usage rights. The local population may resent the displaced people and may lash out or try to pressure them to leave. Cooperation with the surrounding, unaffected populations is vital to the success of the camp, so this factor must be investigated fully.

Once a site has been selected, the camp must be pre-planned to ensure that the population can function effectively after settlement. Like a small city, the camp will have infrastructure needs, which include:

- *The physical layout.* The physical layout of the camp, as with a normal city, will play an important role in the camp's success. A nondescript grid pattern is often used because it is easy to design (and map), easy to set up, and is the most efficient pattern for using every available space within the camp (see Figure 6–4). However, much practical experience has shown that the grid system is not ideal. It causes several problems for the population, including the loss of community identity, a higher incidence of communicable disease (due to very high population densities), inconsistencies in services and security (especially for those on the outer perimeter), and stress of the population, who are likely to find themselves lost and uncomfortable in the rectangular repeating pattern.

    A more appropriate layout is based upon decentralized "neighborhoods" that are distributed around more centralized facilities. Services are divided among those that can be decentralized to the neighborhoods (such as washing, bathing, education, health centers, or supplementary feeding stations) and those that are common to the camp as a whole (such as registration areas, administrative centers, and warehouses).

- *Shelter options.* Shelter is the primary reason that the displaced people are in the camp. When deciding on shelter options, camp planners must consider many factors including the type of material used, the structure style, who constructs the shelters, and the expected length of time

FIGURE 6–4 Grid pattern used in camp for internally displaced persons in Sierra Leone. (Photo courtesy of Sureka Khandagle, USAID/OFDA)

the structure will need to last. These shelters are where the displaced are likely to spend the most time, and therefore should be the most appropriate for the specific population being addressed. For that reason, housing that is most similar to how people live under normal conditions will be most widely accepted.

More than anything, shelters must be able to protect the inhabitants. The roof is the most important consideration, but the shelter must also be appropriate for the climate. For instance, it should allow for a fire or other heat source if cold is expected for any part of the year, it should be able to resist the weight of snow on the roof if heavy snow is probable, and it should resist wind pressure if the selected site is subject to heavy winds.

Many of the most successful sheltering projects were conducted by the displaced people themselves. When involved from the planning process, displaced people can communicate to planners the correct materials that should be acquired, can help to appropriately site the structures and divide the population into appropriate social groups, can build the structures to their liking, and will have more ownership of the project when it is finished (which, in turn, increases acceptance and satisfaction; see Figure 6–5).

- *Latrines.* Proper planning is necessary to ensure that people find latrines convenient and use them. Recommendations for the distance from any person to a latrine have been established as a minimum of 6 m and a maximum of 50 m. Improper placement will cause problems with use, and the latrines may be inaccessible by maintenance crews and may contaminate water sources. More information on latrines is found in the section Sanitation.

- *Water distribution.* The access points for water, as previously described, are a vital component in any response and relief operation. Important factors in the choice of water distribution include the number of people using any single access point and the amount of water provided.

- *Internal and external access routes.* Access to the camp and intracamp travel must be effective. It is important that roads and access ways are accessible year round, despite seasonal variations that may cause flooding or snow cover. To prevent accidents within the camp, separate roads for foot traffic and automobile traffic may be necessary along the most heavily traveled routes.

FIGURE 6–5 Shelters being constructed by displaced persons in a camp in Liberia, 2001. (Photo courtesy of Fiona Shanks, USAID/ OFDA)

- *Firebreaks.* Because of the population's high density and their dependence upon fires for cooking and heat, fire can be a major problem in camps. A fire in one shelter can quickly spread to nearby shelters. To limit the chance that an out-of-control fire will affect a large portion of the camp, planners can design firebreaks—large designated spaces between communities where no structures may be built—which will prevent rapid spreading. This space can be used for alternate activities, such as recreation or farming. Firebreaks are normally at least 50 m wide.

- *Administration and community services.* Camps, like regular communities, have many administrative and social requirements that must be addressed. Failure to plan these services and facilities into the layout of the camp from the outset could result in inefficient provision of services. Adequate space must be set aside for facilities housing various offices, meeting spaces, activity spaces, and other administrative functions. If there is any chance that the camp will expand, the central administrative facilities must have the ability to expand as well. Administrative and community services to consider include:

  - Check-in and administration buildings
  - Bathing and washing areas
  - Schools and training centers
  - Clinics, health care offices, and pharmacies
  - Food storage and distribution
  - Kitchens and feeding centers
  - Supplies storage (wood, blankets, clothes)
  - Vehicle and equipment storage (warehousing)
  - Tracing services
  - Daycare services
  - Religious centers
  - Waste storage or disposal
  - Markets
  - Cemeteries

The Web site www.refugeecamp.org provides information and photographs describing the construction of and life in the camps.

Health

Even in normal times, a population will need health facilities to manage illnesses and injuries. In times of disaster, those same injuries and illnesses exist and will likely increase. However, many of the facilities that normally manage health issues may be full, overtaxed, damaged, or nonexistent. Disaster managers thus must establish emergency health care operations to accommodate the health needs of the affected population.

As described earlier, the immediate health needs are likely to be emergency first aid. The population's injuries will be serious, possibly life threatening, and they will need stabilization and immediate medical treatment that may not be available locally because of a complete lack of services. However, as the disaster progresses and the emergencies are managed, other health care issues will need to be addressed; disease is the primary concern.

The level of health care that is established in the affected area will depend upon the condition of the affected population. This health assessment data is gathered as part of the overall disaster assessment process. Most countries and agencies use morbidity rates and the Crude Mortality Rate (CMR) as an indicator of the general health of the affected population.

The CMR is a measure of the number of people who die each day per 10,000 people. This figure does not tell responders what may be causing problems, but it provides them with greater awareness that one or more problems exist. What is important to disaster managers is how much greater than normal the CMR within the affected area has become. In most poor countries, the CMR of the total population is around 5 deaths per 10,000 people per day. For young children, the normal rate may be as high as 2 per 10,000.

The morbidity rate is somewhat harder to measure because, unlike deaths, detecting if a person is injured or sick may not be possible. Morbidity rates measure the frequency of various illnesses or injuries, often within specific demographic groups, and include measures of prevalence, incidence, and attack rates. Prevalence is a measure of the number of people who have a given condition at a given time, usually reported as a number per 1000 victims. Incidence is a measure of the probability that people without the condition will develop it during a specified period of time. Finally, the attack rate is an incidence rate given as a percentage.

Communicable diseases are commonly the most dangerous post-disaster threat. Exacerbated by the close quarters of victims, the lack of hygiene, poor water and food quality, deteriorating environmental conditions, and inadequate health care, communicable diseases can spread at rates many times higher than normal and greatly increase both mortality and morbidity. Diseases spread because of specific interactions between hosts (the victims), agents (the diseases), and the environment (the conditions that affect the potency of the disease, the ability to fight it, and the routes by which diseases are maintained and passed among victims). The greatest disease risks in the response and recovery phase of disasters are diarrheal diseases, acute respiratory infections, measles, and malaria.

The fundamental tasks necessary to prevent outbreaks from disease include:

- *Rapid assessment.* This involves identifying the communicable disease threats faced by the affected population, including those with epidemic potential, and defining the population's health status.

- *Prevention.* Communicable diseases may be prevented by maintaining healthy physical, environmental, and general living conditions.

- *Surveillance.* Rapid response to disease outbreaks is only possible if a strong disease surveillance system is set up and designed with an early warning mechanism to ensure the early reporting of cases and the monitoring of disease trends.

- *Outbreak control.* Ensuring that outbreaks are rapidly detected and controlled through adequate preparedness (i.e., stockpiles, standard treatment protocols, and staff training) and rapid response (i.e., confirmation, investigation, and implementation of control measures) can help to contain them and bring them under control.

- *Disease management.* Prompt diagnosis and treatment, with the help of trained staff using effective treatment and standard protocols at all health facilities, ensure that the ill are given the best chances for survival, limiting the risk of further transmission (WHO, 2005a).

Surveillance programs are established to detect signs that an outbreak of a disease is beginning or already exists among the population at large. Once victims are found infected with a particular disease, monitoring programs are established to watch those individuals and quickly detect spreading that originates from them. Eradication programs are set up after an outbreak is detected to control the outbreak and remove the agent from the population if possible. Immunization programs, which can be launched before or during an outbreak, help to increase the victims' resilience to specific forms of disease. Finally, behavior modification programs teach people how to avoid behaviors or actions that increase their risk of becoming sick. Disease prevention can only be effective if performed in concert with a sanitation program as described next.

Common diseases among disaster victims include:

- Respiratory infections
- Cholera
- Conjunctivitis
- Dengue fever
- Diarrheal diseases
- Diphtheria
- Tetanus
- Pertussis
- Intestinal parasites
- Lassa fever
- Leprosy
- Malaria
- Measles
- Meningitis
- Malnutrition (marasmus, kwashiorkor, scurvy, pellagra, anemia, beriberi)
- Polio
- Shigellosis
- Skin infections (scabies, impetigo)
- Tuberculosis
- Typhoid fever
- Typhus fever
- Yellow fever

Effective health care among disaster victims will include treatment and preventive care to stop outbreaks or other health problems before they become unmanageable. Public education is a major part of this effort, as the population is most effective at limiting disease when they do it themselves. Clinics should be established, with recommended coverage rates averaging around one per 5000 victims to ensure adequate care. Medical staff drawn from local resources and the various responders will be needed at rates of approximately 2 doctors and 10 nurses per 20,000 sick (USAID, 2005). Medical supplies will also be needed, including surgical and treatment tools and supplies, sterilization supplies and equipment, vaccines, and drugs.

Sanitation

The affected population's safety is dependent upon the ability of disaster managers to keep their living conditions relatively clean. From the emergency's onset, a considerable challenge will be achieving proper sanitation. There may be human and animal remains, hazardous materials pollution in the air, water, and on the ground, and debris may be significant and widely dispersed. If flooding exists, standing water will become a toxic soup of all of these materials in a very short time.

Humans also create waste through natural and social processes. By-products of food preparation, packaging, and human wastes (urine and feces) present a major health hazard if not removed properly. Not only are these removal systems often disrupted in a disaster's aftermath, but they may even reverse their course, spewing large amounts of waste back into the human environment. Victims, who may be crowded together in camps or in shelters, produce the same human waste, but in more concentrated quantities.

The following are the primary sanitation issues that must be addressed by disaster managers in the aftermath of a disaster:

- *Collection and disposal of human waste.* Many diseases that are most infectious among disaster victims, including those caused by bacteria, viruses, protozoa, and worms, are passed from the body in feces and urine. People cannot hold off from expelling feces and urine; unless they are provided with adequate sanitary facilities, excreta will soon become a public health hazard. Without sanitary facilities, victims will contaminate their water and shelter.

    Latrines are the most common solution to excreta disposal. Because of time constraints, two different types of systems normally are used. As soon as the emergency begins, viable short-term solutions must be sought. If public bathrooms are working, they must be identified, and an orderly system by which people may use them must be established. These facilities will also need to be cleaned regularly and stocked with any required materials (water, sanitary paper, etc.). Shallow trench latrines or pit latrines, which are quickly dug into the ground, are a second option, although they can only be used for a short time before they are exhausted.

    If the population will be sheltered for a considerable amount of time, more permanent disposal systems will need to be built, such as deep trench latrines. Public education to instruct people how to use and clean the latrines will be necessary. Any system must take into account the social customs of the population, including the toilet type (sitting or squatting), cleaning methods (paper or water), privacy, and segregation of sexes, among other issues.

- *Wastewater.* Significant amounts of wastewater are generated during cooking, washing, and bathing. In the absence of functioning infrastructure to manage this wastewater, disaster managers must devise a system that safely removes it from where victims reside. Failure to do so results in stagnant, unsanitary pools that become breeding grounds for mosquitoes.

    Generally, wastewater problems are managed by establishing special areas based on the land's topography and hydrology, selected both for their ability to ensure that wastewater is drained from the inhabited land and because the risk of contaminating drinking water sources is negligible.

- *Garbage.* Like wastewater, garbage generated by victims must be collected, stored, and disposed of on a regular basis to avoid negative public health consequences. In the absence of such systems, garbage quickly accumulates into a malodorous, unsightly habitat in which rodents and insects will thrive. Victims will often attempt to burn the garbage piles, creating more contamination, as well as secondary fire hazards.

  To manage garbage, families are often provided with collection points, such as barrels or half barrels, at a distance close enough to their shelter that use is convenient. Garbage collection from these established storage points must occur regularly, daily if possible, or people may cease to use them. Garbage disposal must be planned so it does not interfere with the victims' lives. It should be buried or burned far from any shelters, with special treatment given to any medical waste collected.

- *Dust.* Sites that shelter many victims can quickly become engulfed in dust. People congregating in a confined area quickly results in damage to dust-controlling ground vegetation, as does the construction associated with altering the landscape to accommodate people (building houses and roads). If left unmanaged, airborne dust can cause significant health problems among victims, contaminate food and water supplies, and damage electrical and mechanical equipment.

  By managing actions that result in destruction of ground vegetation, dust can be controlled. In areas where damage has already occurred, such as temporary roads that have been cut, spraying water or oil is effective at preventing dust from becoming airborne.

- *Vector control.* Insects and animals will thrive in post-disaster conditions if left unmanaged. The presence of garbage, wastewater, solid waste, corpses, and spoiled food all facilitate the breeding cycle of these disease-spreading creatures. Victims' close living quarters only exacerbates the problem.

  Failing to eliminate or control vectors may have catastrophic consequences. Mosquito-, louse-, and rodent-borne diseases will spiral out of control. Food and water stocks will quickly become contaminated and lost. The overall conditions within the shelter or camps will rapidly deteriorate until the problem is brought under control.

  The options available to disaster managers are diverse, but must be practiced in a manner that is appropriate for the existing conditions. Chemicals, for instance, while highly effective in killing vectors, can harm humans, contaminate food and water, and cause environmental harm if not used correctly. Additionally, resistance to chemicals and other treatments can arise, requiring a range of approaches. Soap and other implements of personal hygiene can be effective at controlling some vectors, but only if proper education is provided in concert. Proper sanitation measures (garbage removal, wastewater removal, and solid waste management) are highly effective. Repellents and mosquito nets are a good option if people can be convinced to use them and trained in their proper use.

  The most common vectors found in post-disaster conditions and the diseases they commonly transmit include (USAID, 2005):

  - Flies (eye infections, diarrhea)
  - Mosquitoes (malaria, filariasis, dengue fever, yellow fever, encephalitis)
  - Mites (scabies, scrub typhus)
  - Lice (epidemic typhus, relapsing fever)
  - Fleas (plague, endemic typhus)

- Ticks (relapsing fever, spotted fever)
- Rats (rat bite fever, leptospirosis, salmonellosis)
- *Fatality management.* Disasters result in a great many deaths worldwide each year. During the 1990s, the annual number averaged close to 62,000. In the 1970s, this number was more like 200,000. Unlike forms of death that are uniformly spread across time and place, such as chronic disease and automobile accidents, disaster deaths occur in clusters. An earthquake may kill 20,000 in seconds. A flood may drown thousands in just days. The 2004 tsunami is but one example of a single event that resulted in hundreds of thousands of deaths in mere hours.

  Because people die every day, communities have established methods by which the dead are collected, identified if need be, honored, and buried or cremated. Other than register the death, the government normally plays a very minor role in this process. During times of disaster, however, the number of dead may surge, and established systems of fatality management can be quickly overwhelmed, requiring outside assistance. In these times, it becomes the government's responsibility to manage fatalities (see Figure 6–6).

  Three factors contribute to human fatality during the emergency period of a disaster. First, direct injuries from the hazard's consequences result in both immediate death of some victims and subsequent death of other victims whose lives could not be saved. Second, the extraordinary conditions that arise as a direct result of the disaster, including a sudden lack of shelter, poor hygiene, deprivation of food and water, violence, and accidents, cause abnormally high mortality rates. And finally, those natural causes of death, such as chronic disease and old age, which would have occurred regardless of the disaster, continue.

  Although it is not an immediate priority like search and rescue, a system to manage the collection, storage, and burial of the dead must be established as soon as possible after the disaster begins. While there is wide dispute about whether or not bodies left in the open contribute to disease among the living (see Exhibit 6–4), they most certainly lead to distress among survivors and become a breeding ground for vectors. Management of the dead is a sensitive issue that must be approached with care. It is also an area in which incorrect

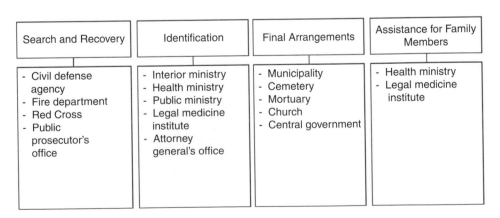

FIGURE 6–6 Fatality management tasks, and examples of agencies typically responsible for each. (From PAHO, 2004)

assumptions and myths, such as the actual danger corpses pose, can hamper responder efforts. The primary duties related to fatality management (see Exhibits 6–5 and 6–6) include:

- *Search and recovery of corpses.* Corpses may be buried under rubble, soil, sediment, snow, water, or other debris. Retrieving them may take days, weeks, or even months. The search area may range from a single building to whole cities to hundreds of square miles of land. Special teams with imaging equipment and animals trained in cadaver location may be used to locate the more difficult cases, but a majority of the bodies will be found as rescuers and responders canvass the disaster zone.

EXHIBIT 6–4: THE RISK RELATED TO CORPSES

Media reports that emerge in the immediate aftermath of high-fatality disasters almost always include some mention of the "disease risk" associated with dead bodies. However, the risk associated with corpses is more closely associated with contagious diseases, not with decomposition. Because most of those killed in disasters were the victims of trauma and otherwise healthy individuals, the likelihood that they also had some transmissible disease is very low. Even if they were infected with transmissible parasites or viruses, those parasites would also die soon after. Claude de Ville de Goyet, a former director of the Pan American Health Organization (PAHO), has stated for this reason that those with communicable diseases should be considered much less of a risk to others after they die than before. However, the fear instilled by the inaccurate media reports of a myriad of public and other officials very often leads to inappropriate cadaver disposal including mass burning or burial. This happened in Haiti after the January 2010 earthquake, and in many countries after the 2004 tsunami events. In 2009, the World Health Organization (WHO) published a guide to standardize the treatment and handling of dead bodies in disasters titled *Management of Dead Bodies After Disasters: A Field Manual for First Responders*. This guide can be found on the WHO Web site at http://www.paho.org/english/dd/ped/deadbodiesfieldmanual.htm.

Sources: Wenner, 2010; Cooper, 2010.

EXHIBIT 6–5: THE OBJECTIVES OF MEDICOLEGAL WORK

- Legally determine or pronounce death
- Recover the remains of the dead
- Establish identity of the dead
- Estimate the time of death
- Determine the cause of death
- Explain the possible circumstances of death
- Prepare the remains for final disposal
- Study the event to assist in prevention in the future

Source: PAHO, 2004.

EXHIBIT 6–6: RECOMMENDATIONS FOR THE MANAGEMENT OF THE DEAD AFTER NATURAL DISASTERS

The following recommendations are the result a study on the efforts to manage over 240,000 dead bodies after the 2004 Indian Ocean tsunami events:

Health Impacts
- The health risk to the general public of large numbers of dead bodies is negligible
- Drinking water must be treated to avoid possible diarrheal diseases
- Body handlers should follow universal precautions for blood and body fluids, wear gloves, and wash their hands

Body Storage
- Refrigerated containers provide the best storage, if available
- Temporary burial in trench graves can be used if refrigeration is not available

Body Identification
- Visual recognition or photographs of fresh bodies are the simplest forms of nonforensic identification and should be attempted after all natural disasters
- If resources and comparative data are available, simpler methods can be supplemented by forensic techniques (dental, fingerprint, and DNA analysis)

Body Disposal
- Communal graves may be necessary following large disasters
- Bodies should be buried in one layer to facilitate future exhumation
- Graves should be clearly marked

Coordination
- A named person/organization should have an agreed mandate to coordinate the management of dead bodies

Preparedness
- Mass fatality plans should be included in national and local disaster preparedness activities
- Systematic documentation about how the dead are managed in future disasters is needed to learn from them

Communications
- Close working with the media is needed to avoid misinformation and to promote the rights of the survivors to see their dead treated with dignity and respect

Source: Morgan et al. 2006.

- *Transportation of the bodies to a centralized facility.* As bodies are recovered, their characteristics, location, and condition must be recorded to assist later identification. In cases where a criminal investigation is likely, such as with terrorist attacks, this information will be crucial to investigators. A means by which the body can be associated with the written data, such as a hospital bracelet, is often used. The body must then be removed from the disaster site to an established area where the subsequent steps may take place unhindered. If possible, the bodies are wrapped in sealed bags and transported in refrigeration.

- *Examination and identification of the body.* A central fatality holding facility, or several regional holding facilities, is normally established. Here, medical experts can begin the process of photographing, describing, identifying, and preserving the victims. Identification almost always requires the help of family members, and a viewing area is usually established to facilitate this process.

- *Final disposal of the body.* After the victim has been positively identified, the body may be disposed of by the family or by the government. This may include burial or cremation. Myths that corpses lead to widespread disease among the living have resulted in the use of mass graves, sometimes even before definitive identification. However, unless the victim dies from a disease, a cadaver is unlikely to pose a major public health risk. For victims' psychological well-being, disaster managers should take every effort to ensure that proper body disposal, according to the religious and cultural beliefs of the region, are respected.

- Many individuals and groups are involved in the process of fatality management. For instance, religious institutions and other community interest groups are often very helpful in working with families to identify bodies and facilitate the final disposal process. Health personnel can perform autopsies and body preservation and preparation actions. First responders recover many of the bodies and transport them to the holding facility. Criminologists may be needed in terrorist or crime-based disasters. Morticians and gravediggers will surely be tapped to lend their specialties. Diplomats are required if a victim was from another country. A full support staff to supplement these efforts is needed as well.

Safety and Security

In the response period of a disaster, the entire social order of the affected area is disrupted. Police and fire officials who are not disaster victims are taxed to their organizational limits, focusing most or all of their time and resources on managing the hazard's consequences. However, many of the same security needs of the population remain during this period, and in many cases, they even increase. Emergency managers must be able to quickly ensure the safety and security of victims, people unaffected by the disaster but within the jurisdiction, and outside responders.

Looting is one of the most common security problems that follow major, disruptive disasters. Criminals become empowered by the lack of police presence and take advantage of the confusion to steal from businesses and homes. The threat of looting has been found to be a major factor contributing to the failure of some evacuation attempts.

Assaults on victims or on response and recovery officials may occur, at times to such a severe degree that response activities must be called off until security is resumed. In New Orleans, response officials had to suspend all search-and-rescue efforts for Hurricane Katrina after snipers fired upon rescuers in the air and on the ground (CNN, 2005). Like looting, post-disaster assaults are generally committed by opportunistic criminals, not the population at large.

Security is also an issue within shelters and resettlement camps. Victims' vulnerability is especially increased when they are removed or forced out of the protective environment of their home and are living in the high-density, close-quarters environment of the camps. Rapes, robberies, and assaults are common when proper preventative measures are not taken. Displaced persons can become victims not only of other displaced persons but also of people from outside the camp.

Domestic violence increases after disasters. Disaster victims face a complete loss of control over their personal lives and are exposed to extreme stress. Post-traumatic stress disorder occurs for many victims. Some will abuse their spouse, parent, or child. The World Health Organization found that child abuse after Hurricane Floyd increased fivefold in the affected areas (WHO, 2005b).

To ensure security, outside law enforcement resources often must be brought in to supplement what exists locally. Military police or other regional and national police resources usually have the training and expertise to limit looting and violence. Social and medical services will be needed to treat and counsel victims of assault, rape, and other violence.

The function of security also includes limiting access to areas where responders are working. Unsolicited volunteers, criminals, and others, who only hamper response efforts, must be kept out of the way of response operations. Perimeter control is performed by law enforcement officials as part of overall security operations. Many different systems have been developed to establish and maintain onsite credentialing of the hundreds, at times thousands, of response officials that may need to pass through the established security perimeters.

Critical Infrastructure Resumption

Infrastructure includes the basic facilities, services, and installations required for the functioning of a community or a society (*American Heritage Dictionary*, 2000). Since these facilities, services, and installations are spread throughout the community and country, they are normally impacted to some degree when disasters strike. Of the many components of a country's infrastructure, a select few are vital to both disaster response and to the overall safety and security of the affected population. These components are referred to as *critical infrastructure*.

While all infrastructure damaged or destroyed in the disaster will eventually require rebuilding or repair, critical infrastructure problems must be addressed in the short term, while the disaster response operation is ongoing (see Figure 6–7). The repair and reconstruction of critical infrastructure require not only specialized expertise but also equipment and parts that may not be easily obtained during the emergency period. However, without the benefit of certain infrastructure components, performing other response functions may be impossible. Examples of critical infrastructure components include:

- Transportation systems (land, sea, and air)
- Communication
- Electricity
- Gas and oil storage and transportation
- Water supply systems

FIGURE 6–7 Crews of specialists repair electrical transmission lines damaged during a tornado in 2004. (Photo courtesy of David Lawrence, Cindy Fay, and Rick Ewald, NOAA, 2004)

- Sanitation
- Emergency services
- Public health
- Continuity of government

Other forms of infrastructure, often not considered critical, are provided for comparison. Keep in mind that, for various reasons, a jurisdiction may consider any of the following to be critical and determine any of the above to be noncritical:

- Education
- Prisons
- Industrial capacity
- Information systems
- Mail system
- Public transportation
- Banking and finance
- Agriculture and food

Emergency Social Services

The psychological stresses that disaster victims face are extreme (see Exhibit 6–7). In an instant, often with little or no warning, people's entire lives are uprooted. They may have lost spouses, children, parents, or other family members or friends. They may have just found themselves homeless and jobless, with no apparent means to support their families. Without proper psychological care, victims may slip into depression.

EXHIBIT 6–7: POSSIBLE REACTIONS TO THE TRAUMA OF A DISASTER SITUATION, CONSIDERED NORMAL

Emotional Effects
- Shock
- Terror
- Irritability
- Blame
- Anger
- Guilt
- Grief or sadness
- Emotional numbing
- Helplessness
- Loss of pleasure derived from familiar activities
- Difficulty feeling happy
- Difficulty experiencing loving feelings

Cognitive Effects
- Impaired concentration
- Impaired decision-making ability
- Memory impairment
- Disbelief
- Confusion
- Nightmares
- Decreased self-esteem
- Decreased self-efficacy
- Self-blame
- Intrusive thoughts/memories
- Worry
- Dissociation (e.g., tunnel vision, dreamlike or "spacey" feeling)

Physical Effects
- Fatigue, exhaustion
- Insomnia
- Cardiovascular strain
- Startle response
- Hyperarousal
- Increased physical pain
- Reduced immune response
- Headaches
- Gastrointestinal upset
- Decreased appetite
- Decreased libido
- Vulnerability to illness

Interpersonal Effects
- Increased relational conflict
- Social withdrawal
- Reduced relational intimacy
- Alienation
- Impaired work performance
- Impaired school performance
- Decreased satisfaction
- Distrust
- Externalization of blame
- Externalization of vulnerability
- Feeling abandoned/rejected
- Over-protectiveness

Source: United States Department of Veterans' Affairs, n.d.

If severe, depression can have extreme consequences for disaster victims. Rates of suicide and violence tend to rise many times over what is normal for the affected population. Depressed victims may begin to neglect the tasks they depend on to survive, such as cooking, acquiring food and water, bathing, and maintaining adequate health care. Proper counseling services can limit these effects.

Disaster responders also need counseling services. They are exposed to the emotional pain and suffering associated with death, injury, and destruction as regular victims, and may even be victims themselves if they are from the affected area. Responders often have the added psychological pressure of feeling responsible for saving lives and protecting the community at a time when both tasks are extremely challenging.

Donations Management

Donations of all kinds are provided in the aftermath of large disasters. Individuals, governments, private and religious groups, and businesses all tend to give generously to disaster victims who may have lost everything they own. Without an effective mechanism to accept, catalog, inventory, store, and distribute those donations, however, their presence can actually create what is commonly called *the second disaster* (see Exhibit 6–8).

Cash donations tend to be the most appropriate, for a range of reasons. First, they allow disaster managers and relief coordinators to purchase from the depressed local economy the food, clothing, and building materials most appropriate for the disaster victims. Second, cash is available immediately, avoiding the delay related to shipping and sorting donated goods. Third, cash incurs no additional costs or logistical issues related to shipping and customs. Fourth, no storage space or other logistical needs arise, as occurs when goods are donated. Before cash can be accepted, systems must be in place to receive it, account for it, and distribute it in a transparent manner.

EXHIBIT 6–8: INAPPROPRIATE DISASTER DONATIONS

Poorly coordinated requests for disaster donations have on so many occasions led to far too much of one resource while others are left unmet—only because benevolent individuals, organizations, and governments were not informed about what was needed by victims. In one town in the United States, following a flood, over 100,000 toothbrushes were donated to meet the needs of 1400 victims—totaling 72 toothbrushes per person. Other examples of inappropriate donations that have been provided in this and other disasters include:

- 30,000 "tube top" shirts
- 40,000 pounds of cough drops
- Unmatched shoes
- Heavily-soiled clothing
- Jigsaw puzzles
- Hundreds of pairs of search dog "booties" (for only a few dozen dogs)
- Thousands of pairs of work boots
- Winter clothes (for a disaster in a tropical climate)

The problem with inappropriate donations is exacerbated when items are not accurately inventoried. After the Mexico City earthquake, for example, it took months to sort through scores of shipping containers of donated aid, most of which was burned given its inappropriate nature. This draws responders away from valuable tasks and leads to the increased suffering of victims and more hardships for the affected country.

Sources: Hogland, 2007.

Donations of goods can be beneficial if the proper systems have been established to ensure that the goods are donated in an appropriate, systematic way. Goods must:

- *Address the actual needs of the affected population.* For instance, winter coats do very little for disaster victims in the tropics. Disaster managers must be able to quickly assess needs and communicate those needs to the world community or to the community of response agencies that collects such donations (e.g., the International Red Cross and the Salvation Army). Managers must be aware that a single request can result in a deluge of donations. In the aftermath of the 2001 terrorist attacks in New York City, a donations manager mentioned on a radio station that search-and-rescue dogs needed protective booties. The operation was soon inundated with over 30,000 pairs of booties donated from around the world (Kim, 2004).

- *Be appropriate for the cultural setting into which they are donated.* When people have been victimized by a disaster, asking them to change their cultural clothing or food preferences to accommodate what has been donated only adds insult to injury. Victims need the comfort of what is normal to them, and food and clothing are one of the easiest ways to fulfill this need.

- *Be in good condition.* Some commonly donated goods in past disasters have included expired medications, spoiled food, and broken household goods. These items cause increased logistical problems for disaster managers who have wasted their valuable time inspecting the goods and must figure out how to safely dispose of them.

- *Be able to clear customs.* It may seem logical that governments would allow donated items to pass through their borders in times of disaster, but the opposite is very often the case. Without previously established agreements, disaster goods, including the equipment of search-and-rescue and other teams, may be held up so long that it is no longer needed by the time it is released. Perfectly good food has often spoiled while awaiting clearance. Even much needed donated blood has expired while held up for clearance (Kim, 1999). Emergency and donations managers must set up agreements with host governments to manage such materials before the disaster occurs to prevent such situations from occurring.

Donations management capabilities must be established early in the response process to ensure that appropriate, needed donations are collected and inappropriate donations are avoided. The official, agency, or team in charge of donations management must work closely with the media and with the various response and relief organizations to ensure that they all are operating under the same assumptions and in concert with each other. Coordination can avoid situations in which too much of one item is provided while another need goes unfulfilled. In appropriate situations, the UN can perform the Consolidated Appeals Process (CAP), under which all involved response agencies together form a single list of needed items and resources that is provided to the international community to ensure targeted, managed donations. This process is described in Chapter 10. In the aftermath of Hurricane Katrina in the United States (2005), the U.S. government released a defined list of items that were needed to the global community through embassies abroad (see Exhibit 6–9.) Items not found

---

EXHIBIT 6–9: ITEMS REQUESTED BY THE U.S. GOVERNMENT IN THE AFTERMATH OF HURRICANE KATRINA

- Cash
- Meals Ready to Eat (MREs)
- Water and ice
- Generators (large and small; 110 and 220 acceptable; 60 Hz required)
- Tarps and plastic sheeting
- Bedding (sheets and pillows)
- Medical supplies (first aid kits, bandages, crutches, wheelchairs, not pharmaceuticals)
- Comfort kits
- Baby formula and diapers
- Coolers
- Large tents
- Logistics crews
- Forklifts, pallets, and other shipping/logistical supplies
- Veterinarian supplies
- Cleaning supplies

Source: United States Department of State, 2005.

on this list were to be considered on a case-by-case basis. However, this incident highlighted another very important consideration with donations management, and that is the need for a system through which a government is able to accept, process, and use foreign aid. Because the U.S. government had never had to make such a large request for assistance, there was no agency previously tasked with such a responsibility, and as such there were no staff, no procedures, and no means of making a final decision on accepting or refusing such offers. In total, $854 million in cash and oil (to be sold for cash) were made, in addition to countless offers for in-kind assistance. The vast majority of this aid went uncollected, however, because the government could not handle the requests. Offers of food and medicine spoiled in ports awaiting processing. Communications devices that were desperately needed were declined and/or delayed. Two cruise ships were offered by Greece to be used as temporary housing, but confusion led to the offer being rescinded, and the U.S. government ended up leasing cruise ships for the same purpose at a cost of almost $250 million (Soloman & Spencer, 2007).

Volunteer Management

There is a heavy volunteer presence that emerges in the aftermath of a major disaster. While many non-governmental organizations (NGOs) and government groups maintain a cadre of trained and vetted volunteers, a much greater number of people with no previous association with emergency management other than a shared desire to help converge upon the disaster scene. Spontaneous volunteers—also called "convergent," "unaffiliated," or "walk-in" volunteers—are defined as those people who are not associated with any recognized disaster response agency, but who appear at the scene of a disaster (or who call a response center) eager to offer assistance. As a group, these volunteers possess a wide range of training, skills, and experience that cannot be overlooked by those managing the disaster response.

It is very difficult to narrowly define the spontaneous volunteer. Their only common trait is that they arrive unsolicited at the disaster scene. Researchers have identified six different convergent groups differing according to the motivating factor behind their convergence. These include:

1. Helpers—people who have come to help victims or responders in some way
2. Returnees—people who lived in the disaster-impacted area but who were evacuated
3. The anxious—people from outside the impacted area who are attempting to obtain information about family and friends
4. The curious—people who are motivated to come to the impacted site primarily to view the destruction left in the wake of the disaster
5. Fans or supporters—people who gather to display flags and banners encouraging and expressing gratitude to emergency workers
6. Exploiters—people who try to use the disaster for personal gain or profit

Of these groups, the helpers must be identified from among the larger population of convergent individuals, because they are the only group likely to offer any tangible support to the response and recovery effort. Oftentimes, the help of spontaneous volunteers is refused only because the organizations to which they present themselves are unprepared to utilize their assistance, or because they consider the volunteers' lack of disaster-specific training to be a liability to the organization's overall operation. These reactions are not completely unfounded, as it was found in several past disaster response efforts that poor management of spontaneous volunteers led to confusion, interference, and what has been termed a *disaster within the disaster* (see Exhibit 6–10). The last thing that any response

---

EXHIBIT 6–10: THE "DISASTER WITHIN THE DISASTER"

Volunteer convergence can be as much of a negative as a positive if volunteers get in the way of response efforts, or if they face increased risk by entering the disaster area (increasing the response requirements of the response organizations). In 2007, following a moderate earthquake in Japan, volunteers converged before volunteer management mechanisms could be established, and this second disaster almost occurred. In the early days of the disaster, the disaster volunteer center in the affected area (Niigata Prefecture) was almost immediately overwhelmed when over 1250 people appeared and began offering help. However, as there had only been 175 requests for help by response organizations, which would require only 40% of those who converged, the center had nothing for the remaining 60% of these individuals to do. Moreover, the large number of volunteers were causing transportation blockages and delays that impacted response and recovery efforts. Notices were eventually posted stating that volunteers were no longer needed and that they should find some other means to contribute.

Source: The Yomiuri Shimbun, 2007.

---

organization wants is for well-intentioned but inexperienced volunteers to hinder rather than help response and recovery operations.

Media coverage, and the graphic images of the destruction it transmits, spurs to action people living in neighboring areas and from the world community into action. Hundreds to thousands of people find themselves drawn to the disaster through compassion for the impacted population to offer assistance. It is contingent upon the donations manager to best catalog, organize, and utilize those resources to address the response and recovery needs of the disaster.

Spontaneous volunteers have become a vital player in the overall response and recovery efforts. The work that they do provides the recipient community with economic, logistical, and psychological benefits.

- *Economic benefits of spontaneous volunteers.* Volunteer efforts carry a tangible monetary value in terms of the reduction in actual labor costs that would be required in the absence of the volunteer. Volunteers also contribute financially by speeding up the overall recovery process. The faster a community is able to get up and running, the sooner residents will begin earning an income, businesses will return to operating status, and the community will stop incurring recovery costs.

- *Logistical benefits of spontaneous volunteers.* Events become disasters because a community is unable to manage the consequences on their own. By its very definition, a disaster is an event where additional manpower is desperately needed. It goes without mention, therefore, that the response and recovery operation that harnesses the efforts of the inevitable spontaneous volunteers rather than resists them enjoys a faster, more effective operation. Disaster victims have an immense need for community services, like counseling, shelter operations, relief supplies distribution, public information, and many other services that are overwhelming for response agencies but easily performed by volunteers. By allowing volunteer agencies and volunteers to not only perform these tasks but also oversee their administration, the traditional emergency response agencies have more time and resources to address their central missions.

- *Public perception.* When spontaneous volunteers are well received, properly managed, and fairly treated, they are effective and, for the most part, happy. Their efforts and their words have an incredible tendency to result in a more positive perception of how the overall response and recovery efforts are progressing. It is said that professional responders and trained, affiliated volunteers must maintain a "big picture" perspective and remain focused on their missions, while unaffiliated volunteers often have more time to meet the individual needs of survivors, to hold a hand, or to offer comfort and encouragement. These small individual actions are what spur the anecdotal stories upon which the media will latch.

Like the general public from where the spontaneous volunteers have come, their range of skills, talents, and interests is wildly diverse. Volunteers may have performed jobs or tasks at some point in their lives that have prepared them for some seemingly unrelated but very relevant response or recovery task. They may be certified in skills that are lacking in the strained official responder population. Or they may just be individuals willing to help in any way that they can. Disaster volunteer coordination is an essential function that falls squarely within the greater emergency management effort. Lessons learned from past disasters have shown that the coordination of spontaneous volunteers is best handled by traditional volunteer groups like the International Federation of Red Cross/Red Crescent Societies (IFRC).

Coordination

Coordination is a vital and immediate component of international disaster response because of the sheer numbers of agencies that quickly descend upon the impacted areas. It is common in larger disasters to see, in addition to the local, regional, and national government response agencies, several hundred local and international NGOs, each offering a particular skill or service. This massive conglomeration of resources presents a challenge for disaster management that has been compared to herding cats. While successful coordination and cooperation can and often does lead to many lives saved, much suffering alleviated, and the safe and efficient use of response resources, the common emergence of infighting, turf battles, and nonparticipation can lead to confusion, inefficient use or duplication of resources, and even greater disaster consequences.

Coordination has been found to be most effective when local government administrators, emergency managers, or chief executives of either the fire or police department maintain leadership at the most local level. These local response officials have the distinct advantage of being the most familiar with the affected area, including its people, geography, infrastructure, and important issues. However, unless they have had previous experience or training in large-scale disaster response, they will probably lack the ability to carry out the exceptionally challenging role of coordinator.

In those situations in which local coordination is impossible or is not authorized by statutory authority, it is preferable that the national government of the affected nation (or nations) assumes this role. National emergency management agencies are typically set up in this fashion in centralized government structures. In poor countries, however, especially those in which government authorities or abilities are weak or absolute changes in government personnel regularly occur, officials in charge may not be capable of performing this extreme leadership task.

The sad reality is that most of the world's poor countries will not be able to coordinate well during large-scale disasters, and most organizations and agencies that descend upon the disaster scene will not proactively coordinate with each other. If this is the case, coordination is left to the international community, and that role is normally (and most appropriately) assumed by the United Nations through the United Nations Office for the Coordination of Humanitarian Affairs (UNOCHA), United Nations Disaster Assessment and Coordination (UNDAC) team (as described in Chapter 10). Since 2009, the United Nations and the international community of responders have begun to prescribe to a coordination system based on response and recovery themes, which recognizes the divergence from regular command and control mechanisms that exist in national-level events, and break the large number of responders into thematic groups. These groups are called *clusters* (see Exhibit 6–11).

Coordination within a country is guided by a legal framework of statutory authority, as described in Chapter 5. At the international level, this framework is much less structured, and that can lead to confusion and a breakdown in coordination. The consequences of a poor international disaster management legal framework were highlighted in a 2006 press release by the IFRC. IFRC Secretary General Ibarahim Osman voiced frustration faced by many international organizations and

---

EXHIBIT 6–11: THE CLUSTER SYSTEM OF COORDINATION

In 2005, the UN conducted a review of global humanitarian response efforts, and found that coordination efforts could be increased in effectiveness through better coordination. The result of this review was the recommendation that UN agencies and partners adopt a system wherein humanitarian assistance efforts be grouped into themes, guided by one lead organization that was recognized among the responder community as such. From this effort, the UN Inter-Agency Standing Committee (IASC) first established nine groupings that were termed "Clusters." The clusters would each be made up of the different international, national, nongovernmental, private sector, and other organizations operating within that theme. Later, two more clusters were formed. The eleven clusters include:

1. Protection
2. Camp Coordination and Management
3. Water Sanitation and Hygiene
4. Health
5. Emergency Shelter
6. Nutrition
7. Emergency Telecommunications
8. Logistics
9. Early Recovery
10. Education
11. Agriculture

Each of these clusters is led by a designated agency. The first use of the cluster system occurred in Timor-Leste in March of 2009.

Source: UNMIT, 2010.

NGOs in stating that "[a]dequate legal preparedness is an essential tool in guaranteeing the speed and effectiveness of both domestic and international disaster response. However, before aid even reaches disaster-affected victims, providers of humanitarian relief often face a myriad of legal questions." There is a general sense among the international responder community that ad hoc response measures are adapted in each individual scenario, which undoubtedly leads to delays in assistance and subsequent death and suffering (Bernama, 2006). The IFRC initiated the International Disaster Response Laws (IDRL) project in 2001 to study, document, and improve international disaster response laws throughout the world.

It is important to note that any official coordination mechanism other than the host country government must be requested by that host government to have any legal authority to lead. Coordination is most effective if it is built around an organized, established structure. Many agencies and governments have begun to design coordination structures as part of their emergency and disaster planning operations. Although different terminology is used for various aspects of the system, the fundamental building blocks of an effective coordination system are fairly similar among most existing systems. The U.S.-based Incident Command System (ICS) will be presented to describe these structures of coordination.

The Incident Command System

The ICS was first developed over 30 years ago in California to address the growing problem with fighting wildfires. These large-scale events often involved resources from the local, state, and federal levels, and the challenge of coordination was seen as an ongoing problem. Issues that exist in multi-organizational disaster responses were recognized as the root of these coordination problems, which are universal to disaster responses anywhere in the world. These issues include:

- The use of nonstandard terminology among a diverse range of responding agencies
- A lack of capability to expand and contract the disaster response as required by the situation
- The existence of nonstandard and nonintegrated communications
- A lack of consolidated action (emergency operations) plans
- A lack of designated facilities
- Competing organizational structures
- Inconsistent or nonexistent information about the disaster
- Unclear designations of authority
- Competing objectives

The ICS was designed to be a model tool for the "command, control, and coordination" of a response and to provide a way to coordinate the efforts of individual agencies as they work toward the common goal of stabilizing the incident and protecting life, property, and the environment. The system was so effective in coordinating wildfire response that it was soon applied to other incidents, such as hazardous materials accidents, large structure fires, and even major disasters. Over time, the system was adopted by other states and then by other countries. Today, the ICS is the most widely used system of disaster event coordination in the world (International Forest Fire News, 2003).

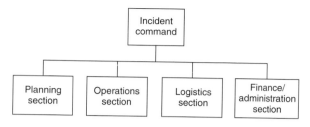

FIGURE 6–8 Incident Command System Organizational Chart. (From FEMA, n.d.)

The ICS is based upon a five-component model that includes (see Figure 6–8):

1. Command
2. Planning
3. Operations
4. Logistics
5. Finance and administration

- *Command.* The command function establishes the framework within which a single leader or committee can manage the overarching disaster response effort. The "Incident Commander" is responsible for directing the response activities that take place throughout the entire emergency incident. There is only one Incident Commander. However, as incidents grow in size and extend throughout many jurisdictions, the leadership authority of the single Incident Commander becomes insufficient, and expanding the command function becomes necessary. A Unified Command is then established, which allows for several Incident Commanders to operate together within a common command structure. Of this group, a single Incident Commander is normally singled out to lead the group as a "first among equals."

  The Unified Command allows for the establishment of a common set of incident objectives and strategies, without requiring local emergency response officials to give up authority, responsibility, or accountability within their individual jurisdictions. Within the command structure, representatives from all of the major agencies and organizations should be present, including the private and nonprofit agencies such as the Red Cross and local hospitals, so these organizations do not operate alongside but outside of the centralized command structure.

- *Planning.* The planning section of the ICS supports the disaster management effort by collecting, evaluating, disseminating, and using information about the development of the emergency and the status of all available agencies and resources. This section creates the action plan, often called the *Incident Action Plan* (IAP), by which the overall disaster response is managed. There are six primary activities performed by the planning section, including:

1. Collecting, evaluating, and displaying incident intelligence and information
2. Preparing and documenting IAPs
3. Conducting long-range and/or contingency planning
4. Developing plans for demobilization
5. Maintaining incident documentation
6. Tracking resources assigned to the incident

- *Operations.* The operations section is responsible for carrying out the response activities described in the IAP. This section coordinates and manages the activities taken by the responding agencies and officials that are directed at reducing the immediate hazard, protecting lives and property, and beginning the process of moving beyond the emergency into the recovery phase. The operations section manages the tactical fieldwork and assigns most of the resources used to respond to the incident. Within operations, separate functional sections are established to handle the various response needs, such as emergency services, law enforcement, and public works.

- *Logistics.* To be effective, all response agencies depend on a wide range of support and logistical factors that must be initiated as soon as they deploy. The engine of response includes personnel, animals, equipment, vehicles, and facilities, all of which will depend upon the acquisition, transport, and distribution of resources, the provision of food and water, and appropriate medical attention. The logistics section is responsible for providing these facilities, services, and materials, including the personnel to operate requested equipment for the incident and perform the various logistical tasks required. This section takes on increasing significance as the disaster response continues.

- *Finance and administration.* The finance and administration section, which does not exist in all ICSs, is responsible for tracking all costs associated with the response and beginning the process for reimbursement. The finance and administration section is especially important when the national governments have emergency funds in place that guarantee local and regional response agencies that their activities, supply use, and expenditures will be covered.

Command and coordination of disaster response and recovery activities is best facilitated from a centralized location, called an *Emergency Operations Center* (EOC). The EOC is normally established away from the disaster scene or in a safe part of the affected area if that area is exceptionally large, close to government offices. The EOC is a central command center through which all communications and information is gathered, processed, and distributed. For large-scale or widespread disasters, separate command posts may be set up throughout the affected area to manage the actual response operational activities.

The coordination mechanism described earlier portrays a best-case scenario, with systems established and exercised long before a disaster occurs, such that little or no confusion results. However, the mere presence of an ICS structure, even if imperfect, will likely increase the likelihood that the overall disaster response will be performed in a more organized and efficient manner.

The Disaster Declaration Process

The disaster declaration is a way for governments to acknowledge that response resources have become overwhelmed and to announce that additional assistance is required and, likewise, requested. The legal mechanisms established to guide how disaster declaration takes place depend upon the nation's form of government and the rules outlined in any established emergency operations planning. In general, however, the process adheres to the following pattern.

In countries of decentralized governing authority, where local responders have primary responsibility to respond to emergencies, the disaster declaration process takes a step-by-step approach. The affected local government will first attempt to manage the hazard consequences, until it reaches a point at which it is no longer able to do so effectively. This information is communicated to the local chief executive, who then decides whether to declare a disaster and appeal to the next level of government (usually a state, regional, or provincial leader) for assistance.

If the government executive to whom the appeal was made determines that assistance is warranted upon assessing the information, he will recognize the disaster declaration and dedicate response resources. If, however, he finds that those levels of resources are insufficient in managing the event's consequences, he will appeal to the national leadership for additional assistance. The national chief executive, usually the president or prime minister, must assess the situation using the provided information and decide whether the event merits characterization as a national disaster. If the situation is declared a national disaster, national government resources from various departments, agencies, or ministries will be dedicated to the disaster response as dictated in the national disaster plan. Additionally, any money from a dedicated disaster response fund will be freed up for spending on the various costs associated with the disaster response.

In the rare event that the disaster is so great in scope that it overwhelms even the national government's capacity, the chief executive may issue an international appeal for assistance. This appeal is either made through the nation's established diplomatic channels to mutual aid partners or through the UN Resident Representative posted in the country. In most cases, where the world community has recognized the disaster before a formal appeal for assistance, countries will offer various forms of assistance to the affected country or countries, consisting of cash, response and relief services, and supplies.

Recognition of the event by the world community is contingent upon the transfer of information and images. If other nations maintain diplomatic missions within the affected country, an immediate assessment of the disaster may be possible, although this is more difficult for events that occur far away from large cities (where embassies and consulates are not located). The primary means by which international recognition occurs, however, is through the news media. Because of the growing so-called CNN effect, in which information can now be relayed in real time from almost any point in the world in a matter of seconds, large-scale disasters rarely go unrecognized.

Conclusion

Response is the most visible disaster management function at the international level. Media images and video footage depicting disaster victims rescued by the international disaster response community are never in short supply. The response needs generated by disasters are complex and are heavily interconnected with the actions associated with preparedness, response, and recovery. However, for many countries, especially the poor nations of the world, the actions associated with disaster response may be the only actions that are taken to address the causative hazards. It is the ability of the responding agencies to carry out this function that most often determines how severely the affected area is impacted, and how quickly it can move on to recovery.

References

American Heritage Dictionary of the English Language. (2000). Boston: Houghton Mifflin.

BBC News. (1999). *The search for quake survivors* (August 19). http://news.bbc.co.uk/1/hi/world/europe/424834.stm.

Bernama. (2006). *Lack of international laws hampers disaster relief work.* Barnama.com, December 12.

CNN. (2007). Plane search resumes in Indonesia. *CNN World*, January 2.

CNN. (2005). *Relief workers confront "urban warfare."* September 1. www.cnn.com/2005/weather/09/01/Katrina.impact/.

Cooper, A. (2010). *Desperation grows: Mass grave found outside Port Au Prince.* CNN. January 16. http://www.cnn.com/2010/WORLD/americas/01/15/haiti.earthquake/index.html.

Federal Emergency Management Agency (FEMA). (2006). *The incident command system. NIMS basic. FEMA 501-8.* http://www.fema.gov/pdf/nims/NIMS_basic_incident_command_system.pdf.

Federal Emergency Management Agency (FEMA). (n.d.). *ICS 100 for Public works personnel.* Independent Study Course IS-100, Emergency Management Institute.

Hogland, N. (2007). *Donation dilemma is second disaster.* Disaster News Network. June 13; Interview with Oliver Davidson, USAID Response Director, March 2010.

International Forest Fire News. (2003). *Strategic paper: Incident command system.* Sydney, Australia: Outcomes of the International Wildland Fire Summit.

International Herald Tribune. (2007). *Indonesian jetliner found: 90 dead and 12 survivors, official says.* January 2. http://mathaba.net/news/?x=548070.

Kim, S. (2004). *Stop the booties* (August). www.fluxfactory.org/otr/kimtales.htm.

Kim, S. (1999). *Unwanted donations are "second disaster"* (April 5). www.disasternews.net/news/news.php?articleid=10.

Morgan, O., et al. (2006). Mass fatality management following the South Asian tsunami disaster: Case studies in Thailand, Indonesia, and Sri Lanka. *PLoS Medicine, 3*(6): e195. doi:10.1371/journal.pmed.0030195.

Pan American Health Organization (PAHO). (2004). Management of dead bodies in disaster situations. In *Disaster manuals and guidelines series,* No. 5. Washington, DC. www.paho.org/english/dd/ped/manejocadaveres.htm.

Roberts, D. (2010). A lesson from Haiti: Are search and rescue teams worth it? *Philanthropy Action,* February 26. http://www.philanthropyaction.com/nc/a_lesson_from_haiti_are_search_and_rescue_teams_worth_it/.

Soloman, J., & Spencer, H. (2007). Most Katrina aid from overseas went unclaimed. *The Washington Post,* April 29. http://www.washingtonpost.com/wp-dyn/content/article/2007/04/28/AR2007042801113.html.

The Yomiuri Shimbun. (2007). Quake-struck city overwhelmed by helpers. *The Daily Yomiuri,* July 22.

United States Agency for International Development (USAID). (2005). *Field operations guide for disaster assessment and response, Version 4.0.* Washington, DC: Office of Foreign Disaster Assistance.

United States Department of State. (2005). *Communication to U.S. embassies abroad regarding acceptance of offers of assistance following Hurricane Katrina.*

United States Department of Veterans' Affairs. (n.d.). *Effects of traumatic stress in a disaster situation.* www.ncptsd.va.gov/facts/disasters/fs_effects_disaster.html.

UNMIT. (2010). *The cluster system.* http://unmit.unmissions.org/Default.aspx?tabid=760.

Wenner, M. (2010). How to handle the dead in Haiti. *Popular Mechanics,* January 21. http://www.popularmechanics.com/science/health/4343222.

World Health Organization (WHO). (2005a). *Communicable disease control in emergencies: A field manual* (M. A. Connolly, Ed.). www.who.int/hac/techguidance/pht/communicable_diseases/Field_manual/en/.

World Health Organization (WHO). (2005b). *Violence and disasters.* Geneva: WHO, Department of Injuries and Violence Prevention.

Appendix 6–1

Sample of a Checklist to be Used for Assessments

Introduction

The following assessment checklists are intended to assist the Assessment Team in planning, formatting, and conducting a complete initial assessment. The answers to the checklist questions will provide the information needed to complete (disaster alerts). These assessment checklists are divided into major areas. They are meant to be as inclusive as possible of the types of questions that need to be answered in initial assessments of various disasters. To be answered completely, some of the questions would require extensive survey work, which the team may or may not have the capacity to perform. However, the information may already exist, and the task of the team may be only to gather assessment information assembled by others and evaluate the information for accuracy, timeliness, and completeness. An Assessment Team may also find it necessary to develop new or expanded questions to gather the required information for specific disasters.

1. *Victims/Displaced Population Profile*

a. **General Characteristics**

   i. Determine the approximate numbers and ages of men, women, adolescents, and children (ages 0–5, 6–14, 15 and older).

   ii. Identify ethnic/geographic origin (urban or rural).

      1. Sedentary or nomadic background?

      2. What is the average family/household size?

      3. How many households are headed by females?

      4. What are their customary skills?

      5. What is (are) the language(s) used?

      6. What is the customary basic diet?

      7. What is the customary shelter?

      8. What are the customary sanitation practices?

      9. What is the general distribution of socioeconomic statuses (poor, middle class, wealthy) in the population?

b. **Capacities**

   i. What percentage of male and female population is literate?

   ii. What emergency-related skills (e.g., health workers, individuals with logistics/organizational relief skills) are represented in the population that could be drawn on by relief organizations?

c. **Displaced Populations**

   i. Determine the approximate number of displaced people.

   ii. Determine their locations. Are they moving? To where? How many?

   iii. Determine how many are arriving per week. How many more could come?

   iv. Determine how they are arriving. Are they scattered individuals or families or clans, tribal, ethnic, or village groups? By what means are they traveling? How did those already there arrive? What is the average family size?

d. Physical Assets

    i. Determine what the displaced population has as personal property and what was lost as a result of the disaster.

    ii. Estimate the numbers and types of blankets needed (according to climatic conditions).

    iii. Identify what blankets are available in the country from personal, commercial, UN/PVO/NGO/IO, or government stocks. Determine the need for blankets from external sources.

    iv. Describe the clothing traditionally worn, by season and area.

    v. If clothing is needed, estimate the amount by age group and sex.

    vi. Describe normal heating/cooking practices.

    vii. Determine whether heating equipment and/or fuel is required.

    viii. Estimate the types and quantities of heating equipment and fuel needed over a specific time period.

    ix. Determine appropriate fuel storage and distribution mechanisms.

    x. Identify what fuel is available locally.

    xi. Identify what fuel is needed from external sources.

    xii. Determine if other personal effects, such as cooking utensils, soap, and small storage containers, are needed.

    xiii. If displaced persons (DPs) are arriving at a temporary settlement or camp, determine whether:

        1. The DPs brought any financial assets. Would those assets be convertible to local currency?

        2. Livestock were brought along.

        3. Shelter materials were brought along.

        4. Other possessions, such as cars, bicycles, or boats, were brought along.

2. Food

a. Baseline Data

    i. Describe the normal consumption pattern (food basket) of the affected population, any taboos, and acceptable substitutes.

    ii. Describe the normal food marketing system (including government involvement, imports, subsistence, and role of women).

    iii. Indicate what food aid programs exist, if any, and describe them.

    iv. Outline the indigenous food processing capacity.

b. Effect of the Event on Food

    i. Ascertain the disaster's effect on actual foodstocks and standing crops (damaged/destroyed).

    ii. Determine if access to food (e.g., roads, milling facilities) has been disrupted and, if so, how long will it likely remain disrupted.

    iii. Check market indicators of food shortages, such as:

        1. Absence or shortage of staple grains and other foods on the market.

        2. Price differential.

        3. Change in supplies on the market (e.g., an increase in meat supplies may indicate that people are selling animals to get money).

        4. Change in wholesale grain availability.

        5. Unusual public assembly at a warehouse or dockside when grain is being unloaded.

6. Changes in warehouse stocks.
7. Black market price changes or increase in black market activities.
8. Commercial import changes or proposed changes.
9. Sale of land, tools, draft animals, etc.
iv. Check nutritional indicators of food shortages by gender, such as:
  1. Signs of marasmus, kwashiorkor, or other signs of malnutrition.
  2. Increased illness among children.
  3. Change in diet (i.e., quantity, quality, type).
v. Check social indicators of food shortages, such as:
  1. Increased begging/fighting/prostitution.
  2. Migration from rural to urban areas.

c. **Food Availability**
  i. Determine how much food can be expected from future and/or specially planted, quick-maturing crops. Where in the production cycle was the affected area when the disaster struck? Is there any possibility for immediate local purchase?
  ii. Estimate the local government stocks on hand and those scheduled to arrive. Is borrowing of stocks on hand a possibility?
  iii. Estimate the local commercial stocks on hand and scheduled to arrive.
  iv. Estimate the local PVO/NGO/IO stocks on hand and scheduled to arrive. Is borrowing a possibility? Have standard procedures governing the transfer and use of commodities (Public Law 480, Title II) been considered?
  v. Estimate local personal stocks on hand and those scheduled to arrive.
  vi. Determine regional availabilities.
  vii. Canvass other donors to find out what they expect to contribute.
  viii. Estimate how much food aid would be required during specific time periods.

d. **Distribution Systems**
  i. Describe existing food aid distribution systems (e.g., government rationing, PVOs/NGOs/IOs).
  ii. Describe the effectiveness of the distribution system.
  iii. Describe the role of women in the distribution system.
  iv. Describe government marketing mechanisms.
  v. Judge the capacity of the above to expand/begin emergency aid. What is their record of accountability?
  vi. Describe potential alternatives.
  vii. Explain the country's (agency's) previous experience with mass feeding.
  viii. Determine the availability of facilities and materials, including fuel.
  ix. Determine whether repackaging facilities exist.
  x. Describe monitoring techniques at the various points of commodity transfer.
  xi. Describe targeting mechanisms required for vulnerable groups.

e. **Social and Market Impact of Food Aid**
  i. Analyze the likely price impact on normal food suppliers. Describe the suppliers.
  ii. Decide whether food aid would free cash and labor for other aspects of relief, or divert labor and create a dependent attitude.
  iii. Has a Bellmon Analysis been previously required and is that analysis still relevant? This analysis is required to determine that:

       1. Adequate storage facilities are available in the recipient country at the time when commodities are exported to prevent spoilage.
       2. Importing commodities will not be a disincentive to, or interfere with, domestic production or marketing.

  f. **Other**
    i. Research any legal impediments to importation of certain foods. Are there any current Genetically Modified Organism limitations and has customs been contacted?

3. Nutrition

  a. **Nutritional Status**
    i. Determine rate of moderate acute malnutrition.
    ii. Determine rate of severe acute malnutrition.
    iii. Determine how surveys were conducted.
      1. Methodology used, such as 30 by 30 cluster surveys, mid-upper arm circumference, weight for height/age, and height for age.
      2. Sample size.
      3. How sample was selected.
    iv. Determine if data are available from mother and child health clinics.
    v. Determine if data are available from existing supplementary feeding programs (SFPs), center-based therapeutic feeding programs (TFCs), or community-based therapeutic care (CTC) programs:
      1. When programs began.
      2. Number of children cared for.
      3. For TFCs and CTCs:
        a. Mortality, cure, default rate.
        b. Number of children with marasmus or kwashiorkor.
      4. For SFPs:
        a. Targeted or general distribution.
        b. Protection rate (e.g., families of children in SFPs receiving general food rations).
        c. Dry or wet ration distribution.
        d. Frequency of distribution.
    vi. If a food distribution program exists, identify:
      1. Targeted or general.
      2. Commodities.
      3. Ration and kilocalories per person per day.
      4. Method of distribution (daily/weekly/monthly).
      5. How long has the population been receiving this ration?
    vii. Ascertain the prior nutritional status of the affected population.
  b. **Public Health-Related Risk of Malnutrition**
    i. Identify disease outbreaks that may affect nutrition status (e.g., measles, acute diarrhea). Is there a risk that outbreaks will occur in the future?
    ii. Estimate the measles vaccination coverage of the population.
    iii. Are there apparent micronutrient deficiencies?
    iv. Estimate the vitamin A supplement coverage. Is vitamin provided in measles vaccinations?

v. Ascertain the CMR/under-5 mortality rate. What method was used to determine the rate?

vi. Identify factors that affect the energy requirements of the affected population or make them more vulnerable to malnutrition:

  1. Presence of persons with HIV/AIDS or tuberculosis (TB).
  2. Current or predicted decline in ambient air temperature (which can also increase the prevalence of acute respiratory infections).
  3. Have people been in water or wet clothes for long periods of time?

c. **Care-Related Risk of Malnutrition**

  i. Ascertain whether changes in work patterns (e.g., due to migration, displacement, or armed conflict) have altered household composition, roles, and responsibilities. Are there large numbers of separated children?

  ii. Determine whether the normal care environment has been disrupted (e.g., through displacement) or has altered access to water, food for children, secondary careers.

  iii. Describe normal infant feeding practices:

    1. Length of time mothers exclusively breastfeed their children.
    2. Whether mothers are bottle-feeding or using manufactured complementary foods.
    3. Is there an infrastructure that can support safe bottle feeding?

  iv. Determine whether evidence exists of donations of baby foods and milks, bottles and teats, or requests for donations.

  v. In pastoral communities, have the herds been away from young children for long? Has access to milk changed from normal?

  vi. Ascertain whether HIV/AIDS has affected caring practices at the household level.

d. **Food Access-Related Risk of Malnutrition**

  i. [reference to the Food section of the Field Operations Guide]

e. **Nutrition Interventions**

  i. Describe nutrition intervention or community-based support that existed before the disaster, and identify the groups involved (e.g., NGOs, religious groups, government or UN agencies).

  ii. Describe nutrition policies (past, ongoing, and lapsed), planned long-term nutrition responses, and programs being implemented or planned in response to the current situation.

  iii. Identify formal and informal local structures through which potential interventions could be channeled.

  iv. Describe the capacity of the Ministry of Health, religious organizations, HIV/AIDS community support groups, infant feeding support groups, or NGOs with a long- or short-term presence in the area.

  v. Determine the availability of food and describe the food pipeline.

  vi. Is the population likely to move (for pasture/assistance/work) in the near future?

4. *Health*

a. **Health and Demographic Information**

  i. Determine total population affected (include host population as well as displaced), including age (under 5 years), male and female ratio, average family size, and numbers of arrivals and departures per week in displaced populations (internally or refugees).

  ii. Identify vulnerable populations (numbers of female- or child-headed households, unaccompanied children, disabled, elderly, single women, pregnant and lactating women, etc.).

    iii. Establish CMR. The rate of death in the entire population for all diseases.

    iv. Establish under-5 mortality rate. The rate of death among children 59 months of age and younger.

    v. Obtain measles vaccination coverage for children between the ages of 6 and 59 months. (If coverage is less than 90%, plans should be made for a mass measles vaccination campaign that includes the administration of vitamin A to children ages 6 to 59 months. To protect the population from a measles epidemic, the coverage should be greater than 95%.)

    vi. Determine diarrhea incidence (bloody/nonbloody) in adults and children less than 5 years of age.

    vii. Establish incidence rates for other diseases of significant public health importance (cholera, yellow fever, dysentery, etc.). Ideally, the information should be disaggregated for adults and children under 5 years of age, although in emergencies it may be difficult to obtain. Identify and cite methods of diagnosis (clinical judgment, laboratory test, or other method).

    viii. Determine or estimate the incidence of major traumatic injuries requiring surgery or hospitalization (e.g., fractures, head injuries, internal injuries).

    ix. Identify incidence and trends of violence against women and children.

b. **HIV/AIDS**

    i. Assess baseline data for HIV/AIDS and risk factors for increasing transmission. Due to the HIV/AIDS pandemic and increasing evidence suggesting that transmission is increased in emergencies, efforts to prevent new transmissions must be started in the acute phase of an emergency.

    ii. Conduct a rapid risk and vulnerability assessment.

        1. Those at risk for HIV transmission are often context-specific but are essentially women, youth, drug addicts, and certain ethnic and religious groups that face discrimination.

        2. Assess the presence of groups considered "core transmitters," such as commercial sex workers and armed military and paramilitary personnel.

        3. Evaluate interactions among displaced and local populations and communities for the risk of HIV transmission.

        4. Ascertain the existing level of risk and specific factors that make the risk groups listed above more vulnerable to HIV/AIDS (e.g., trading sex for food).

        5. Existing baseline data may include:

            a. Voluntary blood donor testing.

            b. New TB cases.

            c. Trends of HIV/AIDS case surveillance reporting.

            d. Incidence and trends of sexually transmitted infections disaggregated by syndrome (male urethral discharge, genital ulcer disease, syphilis at antenatal clinics).

            e. Percent and trends of hospital bed occupancy of persons between 15 and 49 years of age.

            f. HIV/AIDS information for the displaced population areas of origin.

c. **Health System Capabilities**

    i. Determine the number, location, and condition of all health facilities and number of usable beds. Consider using a map for graphic representation during the assessment.

    ii. Determine the location and condition of all laboratory assets in country, including adequacy of equipment (microscopes) and supplies (reagents, gloves, slides, sharps containers, etc.). Determine laboratory capabilities for confirming major communicable diseases (malaria, cholera, shigellosis, meningitis, measles, yellow fever, and TB) and the testing of blood for transfusions for HIV/AIDS, hepatitis B, and if possible, hepatitis C and syphilis. Determine the effectiveness of lab referral systems.

iii. Identify available health personnel (doctors, nurses, community health workers, traditional birth attendants, midwives, lab technicians, etc.). Assess abilities and training needs.

iv. Determine the amount and types of medical supplies and drugs available locally or in-country.

v. Ascertain the availability of specialized medical care at appropriate hospitals for emergencies, such as severe trauma, life-threatening diseases, and comprehensive emergency obstetric care, and the availability of transportation to these hospitals.

vi. Determine the availability of referral mechanisms for transferring patients to specialized care.

vii. Determine the presence of systems to prevent and manage cases of gender violence.

d. **Local Health Programs**

i. Describe the following health programs (if present):

1. Diarrhea disease prevention and control (includes capacity of health facilities to treat dehydration from diarrhea, using oral rehydration therapy as well as capability to establish cholera treatment centers), adequacy and quality of water supply, and health education.

2. Reproductive health programs including prenatal, antenatal, deliveries, emergency obstetrical care (placental abruption, postpartum hemorrhage, ectopic pregnancy, obstructed labor, etc.), HIV/AIDS prevention (blood screening, use of universal infection control precautions, and condom availability), management of sexual violence, etc.

3. HIV/AIDS prevention and control (access to free condoms, relevant information, and education, linked with reproductive health and primary care facilities and programs).

4. TB prevention and control.

5. Malnutrition assessments (see the Nutrition section of this checklist).

6. Expanded program for immunizations.

   a. Determine routine immunization coverage rate (percent of children under age 5).

   b. Obtain dates of previous and/or proposed mass vaccination campaigns for measles, and possibly polio, if still present in the country. Assess whether vitamin A was given in the measles campaign. Determine if the host population and the displaced were included and the coverage rate.

   c. Assess capability of relief workers and/or local health personnel to begin or sustain an immunization program, including mass campaigns and routine immunization.

   d. Determine adequacy of coordination, logistics, infrastructure, cold chain (refrigerators/freezers/freezer packs), availability of vaccines and equipment (sharps containers, adequate supplies of syringes to prevent reuse, etc.).

7. Universal Infection Control Precaution Systems in health facilities and immunization campaigns to prevent transmission of HIV, hepatitis B, and other blood-borne infections in patients and health care workers.

e. **Health Information/Surveillance Systems**

i. Determine whether a health information system is in place to monitor the health of the affected population and provide disease surveillance:

1. Is a single authority responsible (e.g., the Ministry of Health) for its operation and data analysis?

2. How often is routine analysis done, and how are the results disseminated?

3. What proportion of the health facilities routinely send in health information reports and how often?
4. What diseases or health conditions are included in the system?
5. Are standardized case definitions used?
6. Is the system able to detect early outbreaks and provide a quick and effective response?

f. **Cultural and Social Health Factors**
   i. Describe nontraditional sources of health care (traditional healers, etc.).
   ii. Ascertain beliefs and traditions that could affect health care and delivery, such as food taboos during infancy and pregnancy, female genital mutilation, burial practices (special precautions needed for cholera and hemorrhagic fever deaths), blood-taking, injection, and patient isolation beliefs.
   iii. Describe the social structure and traditional leadership systems (e.g., determine if the displaced are grouped in their traditional villages and what type of social or political organization exists).
   iv. Discuss the presence of different ethnic groups/religions and their relationships.

g. **Environmental Health Factors**
   i. Determine the status and trend of climatic conditions of health interest, such as temperature, precipitation, flooding, etc. Obtain and cite relevant information from forecasts and local knowledge of weather conditions.
   ii. Identify significant topologic features that may influence access to health care (e.g., areas that flood during the rainy season causing landslides or preventing access to services, vector breeding habitat).
   iii. Identify water sources, and monitor quality, equitable access, and quantity.
   iv. Determine the local availability of materials for shelter and fuel.
   v. Determine whether existing shelter, water, and latrine locations and arrangements pose a safety or security risk to women and children.

5. *Water*

a. **Displaced Population Situation**
   i. Determine the number of liters of water available per person per day. Persons with HIV/AIDS and cholera may require extra water for drinking and hygiene.
   ii. Determine the source and quality of the water.
   iii. Determine how long the daily amount has been available.
   iv. Determine the evidence of water-related diseases.
   v. Determine the length of time users wait for water.
   vi. Determine whether safe and easy access to water is available for vulnerable groups, such as unaccompanied women and children or families affected by HIV/AIDS.
   vii. Determine the types of wells, transportation, and/or storage systems used.
   viii. Determine if problems exist with well repair/rehabilitation. Determine if equipment/expertise exists on site, is on order, or is available if needed.
   ix. Determine the availability of additional sources of safe water if required.
   x. Determine if problems exist with operation and maintenance of the emergency water system.
   xi. Determine the need for an engineering specialist to assist with evaluating requirements.

b. **Water System Disruption**
   i. Describe the types of systems and sources that existed before the disaster in the affected areas.
   ii. Specify how many people have been deprived of a functional water supply.
   iii. Determine who is in charge of the local water system(s) (e.g., community group, committee, national authority).
   iv. Determine whether the system is still functional or the requirements for repair.
   v. Determine the need for an engineering specialist to assist with evaluating requirements.

6. Sanitation

a. **Displaced Population Situation**
   i. Identify the sanitation problems caused by the disaster.
   ii. Determine the placement, number, and cleanliness of latrines.
   iii. Determine if cultural taboos are affecting the use of latrines.
   iv. Determine if there is an overall sanitation plan (including latrines, bathing areas, laundry sites, refuse pits, and drainage).
   v. Determine if safe access is available to latrines for women and girls.
   vi. Determine the evidence of fecal-oral transmitted diseases.
   vii. Determine the proximity of latrines and refuse areas to water sources, storage areas, distribution points, and food preparation areas.
   viii. Determine if a plan exists for hygiene education.
   ix. Determine if a plan exists for the collection and disposal of garbage and solid wastes.
   x. Determine if a plan exists for insect and rodent control.
   xi. Determine if a plan exists for the cremation or burial of the dead, and if precautions are needed for those who have died of cholera or hemorrhagic fever.
   xii. Determine the need for a specialist to assist with evaluating requirements.
b. **Nondisplaced Population Situation**
   i. Determine if sewage is collecting, or ponding, in or near settlement areas.
   ii. Determine if the sewerage system and the surface drainage system are still functioning.
   iii. Determine the adequacy of sewage disposal facilities in public buildings and other areas being used to temporarily shelter homeless people.
   iv. Determine if garbage and solid wastes are being collected.
   v. Determine the need for a specialist to assist with evaluating requirements.

7. Shelter and Settlements

a. **Establishing Context**
   i. The affected population
      1. Determine the area affected (e.g., portion of city, several villages, large area of a country).
      2. Are important terms (e.g., houses, dwelling units, households, families, homeless) defined clearly, *and* used consistently in any reporting documents generated?
      3. How many people lived in the affected area before the disaster or conflict?
      4. How many people comprised a typical household? On average, how many people lived per occupied dwelling unit before the disaster or conflict?

     5. What percentage of households owned their homes before the disaster or conflict?

     6. Did the affected community include groups of individuals who did not form typical households, such as unaccompanied children or particular minority groups with household sizes that were not considered typical?

     7. How did people earn a living before the disaster or conflict? What incomes did they have? What assets did households have? What was lost, and what remains? What household and livelihood support activities typically took place in and around the dwelling units of the affected population, and how did the resulting space provision and design reflect these activities?

  ii. Housing delivery system

     1. Who builds the housing?

     2. How is the housing built?

     3. How long does it take to build a typical dwelling unit?

     4. What materials are used?

     5. Where do the materials come from?

     6. What is the availability and cost of materials?

b. **Identifying Impacts, Resources, and Opportunities**

  i. Impacts

     1. What caused the housing damage? Is there likelihood that the cause of damage will be repeated in the foreseeable future? To what extent can the cause of damage be mitigated at reasonable cost?

     2. What is the degree of accessibility to the affected areas for assessment and possible delivery of relief supplies?

     3. How many households (and people) in the affected area sustained damage to their homes? What are the percentages of housing supply and population directly affected by disaster or conflict in affected areas?

     4. How many households are without any shelter or have inadequate shelter, and where are they? What does this number represent in terms of a percentage of total households in the affected area?

     5. Is the need for shelter temporary (a few weeks), or does a displaced population require shelter for an indeterminate time?

     6. Has a damage profile, which catalogs the varying degrees of housing damage from undamaged to destroyed, been developed? Estimate the number of private dwellings (single-family, attached, low-rise, and high-rise multiple family) and public buildings (schools, churches, hospitals) damaged or destroyed by city, village, or region. Determine the number of damaged dwellings that are habitable without immediate repair, habitable only after repair, and not habitable and must be destroyed.

     7. To what extent were nonhousing structures (e.g., shops, offices, and public buildings) also damaged? These structures might serve as resources for subsequent shelter provision, giving careful consideration to access to sanitation and water, and are also critical indicators of community well-being and security; therefore, the impact of disasters and conflicts on these structures should be documented.

     8. If relocation is necessary due to the nature of the disaster, what impacts might this cause on the local population? With resident populations in potential relocation areas?

ii. Resources
   1. What initial shelter solutions or materials have been provided to date by the affected households or other actors?
   2. Do affected families have friends and relatives who can provide assistance?
   3. What existing materials can be salvaged from the damaged site (if applicable) for use in the reconstruction of shelters?
   4. What are the typical building practices of the displaced and host populations, and what are the different materials that are used to provide the structural frame, roof, and external wall enclosures?
   5. What alternative design or materials solutions are potentially available and familiar or acceptable to the affected population? Would these materials meet cultural and disaster-resistance requirements?
   6. What are the types and quantities of building materials that the affected government can provide for the victims for temporary or permanent shelter? What are the types and quantities of materials needed from external sources for temporary or permanent shelter?
   7. What is the suitability (i.e., infrastructure support) of available sites for temporary and permanent shelters, including, where necessary, mass sheltering? Would environmental conditions impose constraints on temporary shelters or camps, such as all-season accessibility, proximity to sources of essential supplies (shelter materials, cooking fuel, water, etc.), soil, topography, drainage, and vegetation?
iii. Opportunities
   1. What local, national, and international organizations are present in affected areas? What are the capacities of these organizations, and what are they planning?
   2. What are the current material, financial, and human resources and constraints of the affected households and the community to meet some or all of their urgent shelter needs?
   3. What are the opportunities and constraints of the host population in accommodating displaced households in their own dwellings or on adjacent land?
   4. What are the opportunities and constraints of using existing, available, and unaffected buildings or structures to temporarily accommodate displaced households?
   5. What are the requirements and constraints of local authority regulations in formulating shelter solutions?
   6. What is the current provision of social facilities (health clinics, schools, places of worship, etc.), and what are the constraints and opportunities related to accessing these facilities?
   7. What are the organizational and planning issues of accommodating the displaced households in host communities or in temporary settlements?
   8. What are the environmental concerns in providing shelter assistance (e.g., access and sourcing shelter materials) and in supporting the displaced households (e.g., fuel, sanitation, waste disposal, grazing for animals if appropriate)?
   9. What opportunities are present for building local shelter/settlement provision and management capacities?
   10. How can women, youths, and older people be trained or assisted to participate in the building of their own shelters, and what are the constraints?
   11. What livelihood support opportunities can be provided through the sourcing of materials and the construction of shelter and settlement solutions?

12. How can the identified shelter solutions incorporate disaster prevention and mitigation concerns?
13. What is the topographical and environmental suitability of accessible vacant land to accommodate temporary settlements? What are the potential hazards and security vulnerabilities of available sites for temporary and permanent shelters?
14. What are the opportunities and constraints of current patterns of land ownership, land usage, drainage, and sanitation, and the availability of vacant land, in helping to meet urgent shelter needs?

8. Agriculture and Livestock

a. **Baseline Data**
   i. Describe crops grown in the affected area:
      1. Crop name.
      2. Average area planted (per data available).
      3. Average production (per data available).
      4. Planting season(s) (dates) and time to maturity.
      5. Are crops climate specific? If so, identify the climatic requirements.
      6. Are hybrid seeds being used in the area? If so, identify them.
      7. Are they cash or subsistence crops?
   ii. Describe domestic animals present in each affected area:
      1. Approximate number of animals in the area.
      2. Value of individual animals.
      3. Use of animals for food.
      4. Use of animals for work.
      5. Use of animals for cash production.
      6. Are bred stocks used in the area?
   iii. Describe the agricultural system:
      1. Main agriculturist in family units (male/female).
      2. Land-use systems.
      3. Agricultural labor system/land tenure.
      4. Crop preferences.
      5. Inputs.
      6. Seeds (reserved or purchases). Is treated seed used?
      7. Fertilizer.
      8. Machinery/tools.
      9. Pesticides.
      10. Storage (farm, government, private).
      11. Agribusiness facilities; processing of local or imported commodities.
   iv. Describe the local fishing industry.
b. **Effect of the Event on Agriculture**
   i. Ascertain the extent of damage to crop/fisheries by area, noting at what point in the production cycle the event occurred. State the source of the information.
   ii. Estimate the loss in production (tonnage/head) by crop/fisheries and by zone within the affected area. Is the output expected sufficient to cover consumption needs of the community (or household)? If not, how do families plan to meet those needs?

iii. Analyze whether losses will increase over time and state why or why not.

iv. Describe the damage to agricultural machinery.

v. Describe the damage to irrigation systems.

vi. Describe the damage to seed, fertilizer, and pesticide stocks.

vii. Describe the damage to fishing ponds, farms, and gear.

viii. For a drought, compare the current rainfall to the normal or recent past precipitation.

ix. Identify any unusual or untimely grazing changes.

x. Describe any threats from insects or disease that might follow the disaster.

xi. Describe the current terms of trade for rural farmers and livestock owners based on market information from rural areas (not major cities).

xii. Compare prices, availability, and quality of staple grains on rural markets with those of the last good year, as well as over the past several months. Indicate where the grain comes from (e.g., locally produced, imported from other regions or countries). Note availability of other commodities (e.g., vegetables, spices, oil).

xiii. Compare prices and condition of livestock on markets with those of the last good year, as well as over the past several months. How far are livestock owners traveling to sell their animals? Are buyers actively purchasing animals? Are signs of distress sales of animals evident? Talk with the sellers to determine why they are selling their animals, and look for camels, cows, and young calves on the market.

xiv. Analyze farmers' access to fields for planting, weeding, and harvesting (particularly in refugee situations). Is access assured during the entire agricultural cycle or will conflict or migration prevent harvest?

xv. Describe how fields are normally prepared for planting, and estimate community capacity to prepare land this year (labor, animal traction, etc.).

xvi. Identify start of next major planting season, what crops are commonly planted, and when seeds of these crops must be in farmers' hands to ensure that fields will be planted on time. Identify seed varieties that are suitable to the agro-ecological area and are known to farmers.

xvii. Analyze seed availability and access by rural farmers. If sufficient quantities or appropriate varieties are not available, describe the specific causes of shortage.

xviii. Estimate how much land was planted in the affected area during the most recent growing season, and compare this amount to average. Describe where farmers obtained seed for the previous season (if situation is ongoing and not a sudden disaster) and likelihood that farmers will be able to access the same source this season.

xix. Describe the availability of farming tools for individual households, and explain what hand tools could enhance productivity. Note local or regional sources of tools and whether tools were distributed for the previous season's planting.

xx. Examine other constraints (e.g., seed storage, soil fertility, water availability) that merit attention, and discuss how they can be addressed.

c. **Effect of the Event on Livestock**

i. Identify the primary livestock holdings in the area (e.g., camels, sheep, cattle, goats). Describe the local uses of livestock, the economic and cultural implications of these roles, and the extent to which livestock contributes to household food intake at different times of the year.

ii. Discuss the levels of livestock losses that are acceptable while still maintaining viable herds or flocks. Is increasing animal mortality evident? List the primary factors leading to animal deaths.

      iii. Describe the level of market access held by livestock owners and the ability of these owners to offtake animals from herds in difficult times.

      iv. Determine feed availability for animals, and the condition of pasture and water resources at home and along migration routes. Have migration routes changed significantly this year?

      v. Discuss relevant laws related to livestock slaughter or transport.

      vi. Ascertain the estimated duration and severity of the emergency, as well as the potential livestock losses. What is the estimated length of time needed to rebuild the pastoral economy?

      vii. Describe the regional and local animal health care systems, and determine what needs are met by these systems.

  d. Agricultural Production Capabilities

      i. Ascertain availability of inputs by type (e.g., seed, fertilizer, pesticides, tools, machinery, veterinary medicines, fishing boats, nets, breeding stock).

      ii. Estimate the local government stocks on hand and when they are scheduled to arrive.

      iii. Estimate the local commercial stocks on hand and when they are scheduled to arrive.

      iv. Estimate the local personal stocks on hand and when they are scheduled to arrive.

      v. Ask the victims how they plan to cope with losses.

      vi. Determine regional availabilities and elasticity of supplies.

      vii. Ascertain what other donors plan to supply.

      viii. Outline what further inputs would be required to restore minimum productivity.

      ix. Find out if repackaging facilities for seed, fertilizer, and pesticides exist.

      x. Identify distribution systems/technical infrastructure.

      xi. Outline host government (Ministry of Agriculture) operations in the affected area. Does it provide:

        1. Extension service?

        2. Crop storage/silos?

        3. Veterinary services?

        4. Irrigation services?

        5. Research facilities?

        6. Hybrid seed?

        7. Fertilizer?

        8. Other plants (fruit trees)?

        9. Pesticides?

  e. Other

      i. Describe any agricultural projects and inputs provided by foreign organizations or governments.

      ii. Describe the operations of rural or agricultural credit organizations, cooperatives, or credit-sharing organizations present in the affected area.

      iii. Judge the capacity of the above to incorporate rehabilitation disaster assistance.

9. Search and Rescue

  a. Determine how many collapsed structures in an urban area have been affected:

      i. What types?

      ii. Hospitals, multistory public housing units, schools?

b. **Identify buildings constructed of reinforced concrete or other materials that would leave voids where trapped victims could survive:**
   i. Apartment buildings.
   ii. Industrial buildings.
   iii. Office buildings.
   iv. Hazardous installations creating secondary risks.
c. **Determine the predominant building types and construction material:**
   i. Wattle and daub.
   ii. Masonry buildings (adobe, brick, concrete blocks, stone masonry).
   iii. Reinforced concrete structures (frames with brick infill, frames with load-bearing masonry walls, bearing walls, prefabricated structures).
   iv. Steel structures (multistory steel structures, steel frames in an enfilade arrangement with reinforced concrete).
   v. Timber structures.
   vi. Other.
   vii. Type of roof (reinforced concrete, steel, wood, grass, etc.).
d. **Determine the likelihood of finding survivors.**
e. **Describe the local search-and-rescue capacity, and whether international Urban Search and Rescue (USAR) teams are on the ground or have been requested.**
f. **Determine type of assistance needed:**
   i. Search with technical equipment and/or dogs.
   ii. Rescue with lifting, pulling, cutting, digging, and lighting equipment.
   iii. Medical to oversee and aid in victim extraction.
   iv. Special operations for removing hazardous materials, demolition, shoring of dangerous structures, or damage and emergency repair.

10. Logistics
a. **Airports**
   i. Identify the airport being assessed by:
      1. Name.
      2. Designator.
      3. Location.
      4. Elevation.
   ii. Describe the current condition of facilities.
   iii. Ascertain whether the airport is fully operational. Daylight hours only?
   iv. Furnish information on usable runway lengths and location(s).
   v. Determine whether taxiways, parking areas, and cargo handling areas are intact.
   vi. Establish whether runway and approach lights are operating.
   vii. Specify which navigational aids are operating.
   viii. Describe available communications facilities.
   ix. Determine whether the terminal building is operating.
   x. Check the availability and cost of aviation fuel.
   xi. Find out if facilities exist for mandatory aircrew rest.
   xii. Explore whether the cargo handling area can be lit for night cargo operations.

     xiii. Determine what cargo handling equipment is available, including fuel and operators:
1. Forklifts (number, capacity).
2. Scissors lift (capacity).
3. Cargo dollies (number).
4. Trucks with drivers and laborers for hand unloading.

    xiv. Determine what startup equipment is available, including fuel and operators.

     xv. Describe maintenance operations (facilities, personnel, hours).

    xvi. Outline what storage is available:
1. Covered?
2. At the airport? Off airport? How far?
3. Capacity and suitability for storage of foods or other perishables?

b. Civil Aviation

      i. Find out whether arrangements can be made for prompt overflight and landing clearances.

     ii. Ascertain that the air controller service is functioning.

    iii. Specify working hours for airport personnel.

    iv. Explore having "no objections" fees or "royalty" fees waived or paid locally.

     v. Find out if arrangements can be made to work around the clock, including customs.

    vi. Identify personnel to tally and document cargo when received and transshipped.

   vii. Ascertain that the host government will accept deliveries by means of military as well as civil aircraft.

  viii. Describe security arrangements.

    ix. Determine what repairs and/or auxiliary equipment would be needed to increase airport capacity. How soon can local authorities be expected to restore service?

     x. Determine if any local air carriers exist and what their availability and rates are.

c. Alternative Aircraft

      i. Identify any usable airports or suitable helicopter landing sites in the disaster zone.

     ii. Determine the local availability and cost of helicopters and/or fixed wing aircraft.

   iii. Estimate their capacity.

    iv. Identify the owners/agents.

     v. Determine the availability and cost of fuel.

d. Sea Ports

      i. Identify the port being assessed by:
1. Name and location.
2. Current description of the condition of the facilities.
3. Whether the port is fully operational. Daylight hours only?
4. Security fences/facilities.
5. Percentage of port losses reported.
6. Collection for port losses possible?

     ii. Determine whether the disaster has altered any of the following physical characteristics of the port:
1. Depth of approach channels.
2. Harbor.
3. Turning basin.
4. Alongside piers/wharves.
5. Availability of lighters.

     iii. Determine whether the disaster has blocked or damaged port facilities:
1. Locks.
2. Canals.
3. Piers/wharves.
4. Sheds.
5. Bridges.
6. Water/fuel storage facilities.
7. Communications facilities.
8. Customs facilities.

     iv. Describe the berths:
1. Number.
2. Length.
3. Draft alongside (high tide and low tide).
4. Served by rail? Road? Sheds? Lighters only?
5. Availability.

     v. Check the availability and cost of fuel. Outline what storage is available:
1. Determine what cargo handling equipment is available, including condition, fuel, and operators.
2. Heavy lift cranes (number, capacity).
3. Container and pallet handling (with port equipment? with ship's gear only?).

     vi. Outline what storage is available:
1. Covered?
2. Hardstand space?
3. Capacity?
4. Quality?
5. Security?

     vii. Find out if pilots, tugs, and line handlers are available.

     viii. Specify the working hours for the port.

     ix. Specify the working hours for customs.

     x. Determine whether arrangements can be made with the port and host-country authorities to obtain priority berthing for vessels delivering disaster relief shipments.

     xi. Identify an adequate number of personnel to tally and document cargo when received and transshipped.

     xii. Check the history of turnover time. What effect did the disaster have on turnover time?

     xiii. Determine what repairs and/or auxiliary equipment would be needed to increase the port's capacity. How soon can local authorities be expected to restore service?

e. Transfer Points

     i. Identify transfer points by location.

     ii. Determine whether surface transportation for cargo is available from airports and seaports:
1. Road?
2. Railroad?
3. Canal/river?

     iii. Estimate the capacity of transfer points, including handling.

     iv. Outline what storage is available.

     v. Describe security arrangements.

    vi. Identify an adequate number of personnel to receive and document cargo for transshipment.

f. **Trucking**

     i. Describe damage to the road network as it relates to the possibility of delivering relief supplies by truck.

    ii. Indicate any restrictions, such as weight, width, length, or height limitations at bridges, tunnels, etc.

   iii. Determine whether bypassing damaged sections of the road network is possible and what weight restrictions would apply.

   iv. Determine whether containers can be moved inland:

      1. 20- or 40-foot container sizes?

      2. To the disaster site or to a transfer point?

     v. Check the availability and cost of trucks owned by the government of the affected country.

    vi. Check the availability and cost of UN/PVO/NGO/IO-owned or -operated vehicles.

   vii. Check the availability and cost of commercial vehicles.

  viii. Determine the types, sizes, and number of commercial vehicles available.

    ix. Judge whether the relief program could or should contract for any of the above trucks. What would be the freight rates per ton? What about collection for losses?

     x. Ascertain that maintenance facilities and spare parts are available.

    xi. Outline measures to provide for security of cargo in transit.

   xii. Check the availability and cost of fuel.

g. **Railroads**

     i. Identify and locate any railroads in the disaster-stricken area. Assess their current condition.

    ii. Describe any damage to the electrical power system.

   iii. Identify any interdictions—damaged bridges and tracks, fallen trees, etc.

   iv. If moving shipments between counties, determine if tracks are compatible.

    v. Judge the reliability of the rail system.

    vi. Determine whether cars can be made available for relief shipments on a priority basis.

   vii. Determine the capacity and cost of rail shipments.

  viii. Outline security measures to protect cargo in transit.

h. **Warehousing**

     i. Identify undamaged or damaged but usable warehouses located in reasonable proximity to the disaster site.

    ii. Determine the capacity of these warehouses.

   iii. Determine their availability over a specific period of time.

   iv. Specify whether the warehouses are government-owned, UN/PVO/NGO/IO-owned, or privately owned.

    v. Determine whether they are staffed.

    vi. Determine the cost per square meter.

   vii. Assess the adequacy of the warehouses' construction:

      1. Ventilation?

      2. Lighting?

      3. Hard floor?

      4. Fireproofing?

      5. Loading docks?

      6. Condition of roof (check during day)?

   viii. Describe available loading/unloading equipment:

      1. Pallets.

      2. Forklifts and fuel.

   ix. Ascertain that adequate security exists:

      1. Perimeter fence.

      2. Lighting.

      3. Guards.

   x. Determine whether any refrigeration is available.

   xi. Determine whether sorting and repackaging facilities exist.

   xii. Determine whether fumigation is necessary and if the warehouse is available for food, medicines, etc.

   xiii. If assessing a functioning warehouse, determine:

      1. Accounting and recordkeeping procedures.

      2. Bin/stock cards on piles. (They must match the warehouse register.)

      3. Physical inventory checks at random intervals.

      4. Use of waybills.

      5. Stacking methods.

      6. Spacing system between rows.

      7. Cleanliness.

      8. Commodity handling system.

      9. Reconstitution of damaged goods.

     10. Prompt disposal of damaged goods.

     11. First in/first out system.

11. Infrastructure

   i. Determine the pre-disaster condition of the infrastructure.

   ii. Ascertain from the affected government the minimum needs for infrastructure recovery.

a. Communications

   i. Describe where the system's facilities are located.

   ii. Determine the broadcast/reception area or zone of influence (e.g., towns serviced by the system).

   iii. Identify the organization/firm responsible for operation and maintenance of the system. Is there a disaster response plan with identification of priority facilities, material supply, and priority screening of messages?

   iv. Obtain technical information, such as:

      1. Broadcast power.

      2. Operating frequencies, call signs.

      3. Relay/transmission points.

      4. Hours of operation.

      5. Standby power sources.

      6. Mobile capability.

    7. Repair/maintenance facilities, including capabilities of manufacturer's local agent.

    8. Language of transmission.

  v. Identify key personnel (owners, management, operations, maintenance).

  vi. Determine the degree of integration of military and civilian communications networks.

 vii. Note the source(s) of the above information.

viii. Determine which communications facilities exist that are operable or easily repaired and could be used to pass on assessment information and assist in coordination of lifesaving responses.

  ix. Identify the type of system assessed:

    1. Radio.

    2. Private ownership.

    3. Commercial.

    4. Broadcast.

    5. Two-way.

    6. Amateur.

    7. Citizens band.

    8. Public systems.

    9. Police.

   10. Armed forces.

   11. Government agencies. (Which ministries have communications facilities?)

   12. Telephone.

   13. Cable and wireless.

   14. Television.

   15. Newspaper.

   16. Other.

  x. Describe specific reasons why a system is not operating.

    1. Unavailability of:
- Personnel.
- Power.
- Fuel.
- Access to facilities.

    2. **Damage to system:**
- Broadcast/transmission equipment.
- Antennae.
- Buildings.
- Transmission lines.
- Relay facilities.
- Power source.
- Other.

    3. **Note source(s) of the above information.**

    4. **Outline options for restoring minimum essential services.**

5. Identify local/regional suppliers of communications equipment and materials available for repair. Check cost and availability.
6. Determine the local/regional availability of technical services available for repair.

b. Electric Power
   i. Describe the power system, including:
      1. Baseload facility.
      2. Peaking facility.
      3. Number of units.
      4. Fuel source.
      5. Plant controls.
      6. Output capability (specify voltage and cycle).
      7. Mobile plants.
      8. Other standby capability.
      9. Switching facilities.
      10. Transmission facilities.
      11. Distribution facilities (number of substations).
      12. Interconnections.
   ii. Inventory auxiliary equipment that may be available locally (e.g., from construction companies).
   iii. Determine why power is not available (i.e., at what point the system has been damaged).
   iv. Ascertain the condition of generating units.
   v. Check the integrity of the fuel system.
   vi. Determine whether towers, lines, and/or grounding lines are down.
   vii. Assess the condition of substations.
   viii. Outline the impact of power loss on key facilities, such as hospitals and water pumping stations.
   ix. Describe the options for restoring minimum essential services.
   x. Ascertain whether load shedding and/or switching to another grid can restore minimal services.
   xi. Identify local/regional suppliers of equipment and materials. Check the cost and availability.
   xii. Determine the local/regional availability of technical services available for repair.
c. **Community Water Supply and Wastewater Treatment/Disposal**
   i. Describe the preexisting systems:
      1. Water supply: sources, distribution system, pump stations, and treatment facilities.
      2. Wastewater treatment/disposal: sewer lines, pump stations, and treatment facilities.
   ii. Estimate the number of people who depend on the various water sources.
   iii. Determine why water, especially potable water, is not available. Determine what points in the system are nonfunctional or damaged.
   iv. Check the integrity and quality of the water sources.
   v. Assess the condition of water and wastewater treatment facilities and the condition of the distribution system. Are pump stations operational?
   vi. Determine whether water mains are broken. Are leaks in the sewer lines potentially contaminating the water supply?

vii. Outline the impact of water loss on key facilities and individual users. How quickly can the responsible ministries be expected to restore services?

viii. Describe options for restoring minimum essential services.

ix. Evaluate possible alternative water sources.

x. Identify local/regional suppliers of equipment and materials. Check cost and availability.

xi. Determine the local/regional availability of technical services for repair.

d. **Hydraulic Structures (Dams, Levees, Irrigation Canals, Hydropower Facilities)**

i. Describe the function of the facilities, their proximity to the stricken area, and possible effects resulting from the disaster.

ii. Identify the affected country organization that maintains and operates the facilities.

iii. Identify the suppliers, contractors, and/or donors who constructed the structures. What were the equipment and technical sources?

iv. Describe any damage to structures.

v. Check the stability of the structures and their appurtenances.

vi. Is there any significant water leak from structures, appurtenances, or surrounding ground?

vii. Identify any immediate or near-term safety risks (generating and control machinery, structural defects, power to operate gates, etc.). What are the risks to populations downstream associated with the failure of these structures and their appurtenances?

viii. Assess the condition of canals or downstream channels.

ix. Are there any obstructions to the outlet works that constitute a hazard to hydraulic structures?

x. Identify any changes in watershed conditions (e.g., new developments, deforestation, changes in the river course, new impoundments).

xi. Determine whether water is being contaminated.

xii. Evaluate the management of the facilities.

xiii. Determine whether storage and outflow quantities are being managed in accordance with reservoir operation rules and procedure.

xiv. Identify preparations for follow-on storm conditions. For example, can water in a reservoir be drained during an emergency? What will be impacts on downstream population?

xv. Describe the potential impacts of draining a reservoir on downstream areas and relief/response efforts (e.g., location of downstream population/settlements and infrastructure, depth at river crossings, condition of irrigation canals). Is there a need to impound water until downstream works can be repaired?

xvi. Outline the options for restoring minimum essential services and safety.

xvii. Outline the repair plans of the responsible affected country officials.

xviii. Check on any proposed assistance from the original donors of the facilities.

xix. Identify local/regional sources of equipment and technical expertise.

e. **Roads and Bridges**

i. Describe the road networks in the affected area by type.

ii. What is the load capacity of the bridges?

iii. Identify the responsible ministries and district offices and constraints on their operations.

iv. Describe any damage to the network.

v. Determine which segments are undamaged, which can be traveled on with delays, and which are impassable.

vi. Describe any damage by type:
1. Blockage by landslides, fallen trees, etc.
2. Embankments.
3. Drainage structures.
4. Bridges/tunnels.
5. Road surfaces.
vii. Identify alternate crossings and/or routes.
viii. Evaluate the importance of the road network to the relief effort and rehabilitation.
ix. Outline the options for restoring minimum essential service.
x. Determine which elements must be restored first.
xi. Describe the need for traffic control (police, military, other) on damaged or one-way segments.
xii. Determine how long the emergency repairs can accommodate relief traffic (size, weight, volume). Will emergency maintenance and fuel points be needed in remote areas?
xiii. Identify the affected country agencies and military and/or civilian forces that are available to make repairs. Do they have equipment, spare parts, and maintenance support?
xiv. Check whether local or expatriate construction companies can loan equipment and/or expertise.
xv. Check regional sources of equipment and/or expertise that are available for repair.
xvi. Ascertain that arrangements can be made for standby forces at damaged sections to keep roads open.

From USAID, 2005.

∷∷ 7
Recovery

Introduction

Disasters wreak havoc on the living, on built structures, and on the environment, but preparedness and mitigation reduce vulnerability to disasters, and response minimizes the loss of life and property. However, even with the best mitigation, preparedness, and response, there will almost always be some level of environmental damage, destruction of property and infrastructure, disruptions of social and economic systems, and other physical and psychological health consequences. The process by which all of these are rebuilt, reconstructed, repaired, and returned to a functional condition is called "recovery."

   This chapter explains what the recovery function is and what actions are taken to fulfill the recovery needs of communities affected by disasters.

Overview of Recovery

Disaster recovery is the emergency management function by which countries, communities, families, and individuals repair, reconstruct, or regain what has been lost as result of a disaster and, ideally, reduce the risk of similar catastrophe in the future. In a comprehensive emergency management system, which includes pre-disaster planning, mitigation, and preparedness actions, recovery actions may begin as early as during the planning processes and activities, long before a disaster occurs. Once the disaster strikes, planned and unplanned recovery actions are implemented and may extend for weeks, months, or even years.

   The actions associated with disaster recovery are the most diverse of all the disaster management functions. The range of individuals, organizations, and groups that are involved is also greater than in any other function (although these participants are much more loosely affiliated than in other disaster management functions). Because of the spectacular nature of disaster events and because disaster consequences affect so many peoples' lives, recovery generates the greatest amount of interest and attention from the world community as a whole. In relation to the other disaster management functions, it is by far the most costly. Disaster recovery is also the least studied and least organized of all of the disaster management functions, and therefore the most haphazardly performed.

   The most visible activity associated with the recovery function manifests at about the same time that formal emergency response measures are declared complete. Having taken the appropriate actions to save as many lives possible and having limited any further damage to the environment and to property, communities must face the long process to regain what was lost. But, as this chapter shows, recovery involves much more than simply replacing what once existed. It is a complex process, closely intertwined with the other three phases of emergency management, and requires great amounts of planning, coordination, and funding.

Actions and activities commonly performed in the recovery period of a disaster include:

- Ongoing communication with the public
- Provision of temporary housing or long-term shelter
- Assessment of damages and needs
- Demolition of damaged structures
- Clearance, removal, and disposal of debris
- Rehabilitation of infrastructure
- Inspection of damaged structures
- Repair of damaged structures
- New construction
- Social rehabilitation programs
- Creation of employment opportunities
- Reimbursement for property losses
- Rehabilitation of the injured
- Reassessment of hazard risk

The Effects of Disasters on Society

Disasters disrupt society in many ways. Most people are familiar with disaster statistics that relate to people killed and injured, buildings damaged and destroyed, and the monetary values of property loss. News media focus on images of destroyed homes, flooded streets, and downed trees, among other physical manifestations of the disaster. However, disaster consequences have a much greater effect on victims' overall quality of life than these statistics, pictures, and videos can show. This is because communities develop sociocultural mechanisms that allow them to function, and the countless individual components of these systems steadily become dependent on each other. Thus, the loss of any one component may affect many others.

When minor incidents occur in which people are killed or injured, buildings or infrastructure are destroyed, and lifelines are cut, components of society can break down on a small scale, but the community is likely to have the capacity to contain the loss and withstand any greater impact. During disasters, however, these damaging effects are spread across a much greater geographical range, affecting more people, more structures, more industries, and many more interconnected societal components. The secondary effects affect not only the disaster area but also can extend far beyond the actual physical range of the disaster and result in much wider logistical and economic impacts.

Examples of disaster consequences that disrupt the community and reduce the quality of life of individuals in that community include:

- A reduced ability to move or travel due to damaged or destroyed transportation infrastructure
- Interrupted educational opportunities due to damages to schools, loss or injury of teachers, student injuries, or inability to attend school because of added pressures of recovery

- Loss of cultural heritage, religious facilities, and communal resources
- Economic losses due to the loss of customers, employees, facilities, inventory, or utilities
- Communications difficulties due to infrastructure damage or loss
- Homelessness caused by housing and property losses
- Hunger and starvation due to breaks in the food supply chain that cause shortages and price increases
- Unemployment due to job cuts, damage to place of work, or conflicting recovery needs (loss of day care services, for instance)
- Loss of community tax base
- Environmental loss, damage, and pollution

The primary goal of the recovery process is to reverse these damaging effects and, in doing so, restore victims' lives. Clearly, this is a monumental task.

Pre-disaster Recovery Actions

Like response, recovery is a process that is performed within a time-constrained setting and on which victims' lives directly depend. To be performed well, recovery and response require special skills, equipment, resources, and personnel. Unlike response, however, disaster planning very rarely includes disaster recovery operations.

The recovery period follows the emergency phase of a disaster and is one in which confusion is likely to reign. There may be people displaced from their homes, business owners anxious to resume operations, and government offices that must restart service provision, among other pressures. As described in the following sections, to ensure that overall vulnerability is reduced, rebuilding without considering the disaster's effects as well as any new hazards is unwise and irresponsible. Unfortunately, decisions are often made with little or no planning or analysis, and opportunities for improvement can be lost.

In the planning process, described in previous chapters, disaster managers identify hazards, analyze risk, and determine ways to reduce those risks. In doing so, they gain a much greater understanding about how each of those hazards would affect the community if one were to strike. This information can be effective if used to plan the community's recovery from a disaster.

Pre-disaster planning—sometimes referred to as "Pre-Event Planning for Post-Event Recovery (PEPPER)—can reduce the risk of haphazard rebuilding. Although nobody can predict exactly how a disaster will affect a community, many processes are common to all disaster types (e.g., hurricanes), and they may be identified and studied in advance. Many decisions will have long-term repercussions and, as such, are better made in the relaxed, rational environment that only exists before the disaster occurs.

Examples of recovery decisions that may be made before a disaster include:

- The site selection for long-term temporary housing (which is often maintained for a period much longer than originally expected)
- The site selection for temporary business activity
- The site selection for the disposal of debris

- Contractors from around the country that could be called upon to assist in infrastructure and housing repair and reconstruction
- Coordination mechanisms, including leadership, membership, and information sharing
- Volunteer and donations management
- Mitigation measures and other hazard reduction actions that may be too expensive or unfeasible before a disaster, but may be more opportune if existing structures were damaged or destroyed (such as relocating power lines underground)

It has been postulated that disaster recovery based upon pre-disaster planning is much more organized, is more likely to result in community improvement, and is more likely to result in a reduction of future disaster losses. Because nobody knows for sure exactly how and where the disaster consequences will manifest themselves, recovery plans are hypothetical, focusing more on broad goals and ideals than on specific actions and procedures. For instance, they may include "Reduce vulnerability to electrical transmission wires" or "Revise building codes to address new seismicity estimates." During much of the actual recovery period, many decisions will require split-second action, with little or no time for analysis. A plan outlining overarching goals and objectives can help guide those decisions. Decisions made without considering these goals can drastically limit opportunities to rebuild the community to be more resilient and disaster resistant.

Through the hazard identification and analysis process, communities that have performed adequate hazards risk planning will have determined what consequences they should expect to occur. Using this information, they will have created a mitigation plan outlining the possible options for disaster risk reduction. In the post-disaster recovery period, when many decisions are made about construction and repair of structures, zoning of land, and new development, this mitigation plan can be used to ensure that proper action is taken to minimize risk. For example, if the community had explored strengthening building codes, those codes would be likely to pass in light of the recent disaster, and all new construction could be required to follow the new codes. Planners may find that many of the measures deemed unfundable or impossible before the disaster are now perfectly acceptable.

Short- and Long-Term Recovery

Recovery can be divided into two distinct phases, each with very different activities: short-term and long-term. The specific conditions and consequences surrounding the disaster aftermath, the capabilities of the affected government(s), and the capabilities and resources of the participating agencies all determine how quickly recovery can transition from the short- to the long-term phase.

The short-term recovery phase immediately follows the hazard event, beginning while emergency response operations are ongoing. Short-term recovery activities seek to stabilize the lives of the affected people in order to prepare them for the long road toward rebuilding their lives. These actions, which are often considered response actions or termed "relief," include the provision of temporary housing, distribution of emergency food and water, restoration of critical infrastructure, and clearance (but not removal or disposal) of debris. Short-term recovery actions tend to be temporary and often do not directly contribute to the community's actual long-term development. Short-term recovery operations also tend to be guided by response plans and are often uncoordinated.

Long-term recovery, on the other hand, does not begin in earnest until after the emergency phase of the disaster has ended. In long-term recovery, the community or country begins to rebuild and rehabilitate. For major disasters, it lasts for years. The economic renewal of a community or country may take even longer, making a return to pre-disaster conditions a challenge. In many cases, the community will need to be reinvented, accommodating the new information about the disaster while maintaining as much of its original culture and pre-disaster composure as possible. The greatest opportunities for projects addressing vulnerability reduction are possible during long-term recovery. More funding is dedicated to recovery than to any other emergency management phase (for a given disaster), and more players from all sectors are involved. Long-term recovery operations thus require a significant amount of coordination and planning if they are to be successful.

Components of Recovery—What Is Needed, and Where Does It Come From?

The long-lasting period of recovery following major disasters requires a tremendous supply of resources. Each resource category is dependent on the others, and thus a short supply of one resource could impact the others. Over time and with experience, the recovery function has become more practiced, more systematic, and better able to work toward the goal of setting the affected population back upon their own two feet, although that goal may not always be reached.

The following section details the general components of disaster response.

Planning

Although pre-disaster planning is logical, relatively easy to perform, and costs very little, most communities will likely have done little or nothing to directly prepare for recovery after a disaster. Post-disaster planning, as it is called, while entirely necessary, is performed in a much different environment from pre-disaster planning—one that is less favorable to success. Disaster managers in California addressing the aftermath of an earthquake described the differences between pre- and post-disaster recovery planning as follows:

- After a disaster, planning for rebuilding is a high-speed version of normal planning, as well as a dynamic cyclical process. Local communities faced with disaster recovery will not have the luxury of following normal procedures for development review and approval.

- After a disaster, planning for rebuilding is more sharply focused. This is not the time to begin a regional planning process.

- After a disaster, planning for rebuilding is more realistic. Planners must avoid raising false expectations by unrealistic planning schemes and, instead, strive to build public consensus behind appropriate redevelopment approaches. Comprehensive evaluation of funding sources for implementation is essential. (Spangle & Associates, 1991)

Most important when planning for recovery from a disaster is that as little construction or other action that could affect the long-term sustainability of the community is performed before being considered by the planning process. Several options can assist disaster managers with this, such as imposing a moratorium on new construction. However, the public and business owners place a lot of pressure on disaster managers and politicians to rebuild as quickly as possible. Demands will increase as victims grow impatient with temporary relief provisions (shelter, food, etc.) and businesses begin to fail. Recovery organizations add to this stress because of their workers' needs and donors' expectations to initiate and complete their projects as soon as possible. Without rapid and proper coordination mechanisms, many projects will begin on their own, irrespective of any central plans drawn to guide the recovery.

Several different activities may (and should) be initiated during the planning period. Many of these activities will already have begun due to their interconnectedness with response, such as the repair and recovery of critical infrastructure, the site selection for temporary housing, medical facilities and hospitals, the resumption of education, and the clearance of debris. William Spangle, author of several texts on post-disaster recovery, described two lessons that planners should consider during the planning process:

1. Planning and rebuilding can occur simultaneously; some rebuilding takes place before master plans are completed. Although building moratoria may be appropriate after a disaster, streamlined decision-making procedures for those land-use questions that can be resolved quickly might help demonstrate good faith on the part of local officials. As soon as possible, local officials need to determine areas of the community that can be rebuilt under existing plans and regulations and provide for rapid processing of permits for repairs and rebuilding in those areas. In the other, more problematic areas, clear procedures and time schedules for planning, making decisions, and getting information are needed. In this higher speed version of normal planning, decisions might be phased so that planning and rebuilding can proceed in tandem.
2. Defining urban expansion areas helps. After a disaster, planners usually have the information needed to plan for urban expansion while avoiding clearly unsafe ground. By quickly defining such areas, planners can speed up the relocation of people and businesses from heavily damaged areas that may be a long time in rebuilding. (Spangle & Associates, 1991)

Luckily, even if most disaster managers are facing the post-disaster recovery period without any recovery plans, they may not need to start from scratch (Patterson, 1999). Existing plans and regulations may be acceptable for many parts of the city, especially where buildings failed because they were not designed or built to modern codes (as opposed to having failed *despite* being up to code). Additionally, despite managers' best efforts to conduct planning as quickly as possible, some construction is likely to begin immediately. Existing building and development plans, zoning regulations, and land use regulations can all help to guide the fragmented groups of players involved.

Coordination

Coordination during the recovery phase is extremely difficult to achieve, but it is vital to successful accomplishment of its goals and, more important, in achieving reduced risk. Although a majority of the actual recovery actions taken are likely to occur at the local level, managed by local officials, regional or national coordination mechanisms will be required to ensure proper distribution of the many resources, technical assistance, internal and external financial assistance, and other special programs that will fuel the process. Recovery of major disasters is a patchwork of local level efforts feeding from and guided by larger, centralized resources.

The success of post-disaster recovery coordination depends on planners' ability to achieve wide representation within the coordination structure. For the recovery plans to address the community's demographic and sociocultural needs and preferences, all representative community groups must be involved including businesses, religious and civil society organizations, emergency managers, representatives from various government agencies, public advocacy groups, and the media. There may be considerable interaction between local and regional or national levels throughout the recovery process as well, so inclusion of these outside groups is vital. By involving all of these stakeholders, a highly organized recovery operation is possible that ensures lessons learned, best practices, and efficiency of labor are maximized. In the absence of full coordination and communications, recovery assistance likely will not be able to meet the needs at the local level (Patterson, 1999).

If structured correctly, the resulting coordination mechanism will become a central repository of information and assistance for all groups and individuals involved. The structure may be formed around an existing community group or government agency, or it may be a new representative committee. The committee may be elected, a public-private partnership, or any other appropriate format for the community or country it is serving. Officials who may be included in the recovery coordination structure include:

- Environmental officers
- Floodplain manager
- Building officials
- Rural and urban planners
- Zoning administrators
- Public works directors—city engineer
- Parks and recreation director
- Storm water manager
- Economic development officer
- Finance officer
- Transportation officer
- Housing department officer
- Regional planning organization or officer
- Local and regional emergency management (police, fire, EMS)
- Public information officer
- Chamber of commerce representatives
- Public and private utility representatives
- Neighborhood organizations
- Homeowners associations
- Religious or charitable organizations
- Social services agencies
- Red Cross/other nongovernmental organization (NGO) recovery officials
- Environmental organizations
- Private development and construction agencies

Statutory authority must be granted to this committee to ensure that they have adequate power to enforce their actions and recommendations. This group will perform many of the following functions:

- Collate damage and needs assessment data
- Guide and facilitate the recovery planning process
- Establish recovery and risk-reduction goals
- Centralize information on relief and recovery resources
- Minimize duplication, redundancy, or inefficiencies in services
- Gather and disseminate aid information for victims

In many developing countries, where the knowledge, experience, and expertise required to lead the planning and operation of recovery do not exist at any level of government, external coordination of technical assistance will be necessary. Generally, organizations such as the UN, which most likely already have had a relationship with the country's government, will assume such a role. The process by which this is done is described in greater detail in Chapter 10.

The disconnect that can exist in planning for and coordinating recovery often stems from inaccurate understandings of what is best for the individual communities. National officials, multilateral organization representatives, and national and international nonprofit agencies may all be working under assumptions that, albeit educated and informed, are incorrect in light of specific social and cultural conditions on the ground. Jim Rolfe and Neil Britton, of the Wellington, New Zealand Earthquake Commission and the Asian Development Bank (ADB), wrote, "The need for achieving consistency between a community's recovery and its long-term vision is perhaps one of the biggest reasons for placing management of the recovery process in the hands of local government" (Rolfe & Britton, 1995). The victims should be active participants in the recovery period, helping to define that local vision, outlining the overall recovery goals, and taking ownership of recovery projects, rather than being left on the sidelines to receive free handouts.

Information—The Damage Assessment

Before any effective recovery planning is possible, disaster managers must have access to accurate and timely damage assessment information. This will help identify the best strategy for employing available resources and setting action priorities. In the response phase, as described in Chapter 6, assessments are conducted to guide the various response activities needed. The information from those assessments is fully transferable for use in the recovery phase, as the information requirements are virtually identical.

Damage assessments can help planners identify the numbers and types of buildings damaged and destroyed as well as the spatial extent of the hazard consequences (land that was inundated, areas of strong seismic shaking, the location of failed slopes, the number and location of displaced people, and the loss of farmland, among other information dependent upon hazard type and intensity). During the recovery planning process, these assessments will act as the primary guide to determine areas that require attention and in what priority, and how to effectively distribute available resources.

Unfortunately, the assessments generated in the response phase will probably not contain *all* of the information recovery planners require, especially if they are intent on reducing future disaster risk. Further assessment will be necessary for these information needs, and that assessment will need to be performed by various subject experts as defined by the actual recovery needs. For instance, in many cases a more technical inspection of damaged buildings will need to be performed to determine which need to be demolished, which are repairable, and which can be re-occupied immediately. Also, in light of all the new, event-specific hazard and disaster information that will suddenly be available, experts dedicated to specific disaster impacts (such as geologists, meteorologists, or hydrologists) will be needed to create more accurate hazard risk maps. For instance, after an earthquake, new faults may be discovered, and better information about maximum ground-shaking potential for specific geographic regions may have been acquired. Planners can use this information to ensure that any reconstruction or repair fully incorporates those findings.

As was true in the response phase, recovery planners will need to periodically reassess the affected area to determine the pace of recovery. Using these assessments, resources may be reallocated and problems discovered before it is too late to correct them. With a strong coordination mechanism, maximizing the number of organizations participating in the coordination group, assessment will be much easier to conduct. In these cases, establishing a central information repository is desirable for collecting regular progress updates.

Money and Supplies

Unfortunately, without ample funding, very little may be done to help a disaster-struck region rebuild. Even with local and foreign volunteers and abundant donations of equipment and supplies, simply too many resources and services must be purchased. Financial investment in community reconstruction is necessary to complete each recovery goal, whether to repair and rebuild infrastructure, restart the economy, repair and reconstruct housing, or any other activity.

Responsibility for reconstruction costs is divided between various sectors of the community. The government is generally responsible for rebuilding public facilities and much of the infrastructure in the public domain. The private sector, including industries, individuals, and families, will lead the rebuilding of houses and businesses, helping to restore overall economic vitality. The public and private sectors will frequently work together and share reconstruction costs. For example, although an electric company is privately owned, a government-run water treatment plant may not be able to function until its access to power is returned. Likewise, private landowners may not be able to rebuild their houses if the government agency in charge of construction permits has not yet returned to servicing customers.

How quickly the affected country can organize financial and other types of resources will determine how quickly and how effectively that nation recovers from the disaster. A nation has several options for disaster response funding: insurance, government-based emergency relief funds, donations, loans, catastrophic bonds and weather derivatives, private development funding, incentives, and tax increases.

Insurance

If insurance was purchased prior to the disaster and the insurance industry is legitimate and able to sustain the disaster's financial impact, then settlements will be provided as defined in each customer's insurance policy. Insurance policies may cover a full range of losses, including building repair or reconstruction, replacement of building contents or other property, lost employment or business opportunities, and medical bills, among other costs. Individuals, businesses, and even public and non-profit entities may purchase insurance policies. Most relief programs require that insurance payments be exhausted on any given project before providing any other funding.

Unfortunately, insurance is not common in developing countries. The UN found that less than one-quarter of all disaster losses is covered by insurance (ISDR, 2005). There are a variety of reasons for this, including a lack of insurance offered, low understanding among the population of its benefits, premiums that are restrictive to tight budgets, and a lack of faith that companies will pay in the event of a disaster.

Government-Based Emergency Relief Funds (Reserve Funds)

Disasters place a heavy burden on all levels of governments: national, regional, and local. The government almost certainly will be required to pay for a wide range of relief expenses on top of the additional expenses incurred as a result of the response costs. Many governments have set aside in their budgets an emergency relief fund designed to allow for financial liquidity to cover anticipated expenses associated with disasters. Generally, these kinds of funds are created in the aftermath of a previous catastrophic disaster as a part of a more comprehensive statutory authority designed to increase overall disaster preparedness. Examples include:

- The Disaster Relief Fund (United States)
- FONDEN (Mexico)
- Disaster Financial Assistance Arrangements (Canada—see Exhibit 7–1)
- Sonderfonds Aufbauhilfe (Germany)
- National Calamity Fund (Philippines)
- National Calamity Contingency Fund (India)

EXHIBIT 7–1: THE CANADIAN "DISASTER FINANCIAL ASSISTANCE ARRANGEMENTS"

Overview

When response and recovery costs exceed what individual provinces or territories could reasonably be expected to bear on their own, the Disaster Financial Assistance Arrangements (DFAA) provide the Government of Canada with a fair and equitable means of assisting provincial and territorial governments.

Since the inception of the program in 1970, the Government of Canada has paid out more than $1.6 billion in post-disaster assistance to help provinces and territories offset the costs of response and of returning infrastructure and personal property to pre-disaster condition. Examples of payments include those for the 2003 British Columbia forest fires, the 1998 ice storm in Quebec and Ontario, and the 1997 Red River flood in Manitoba.

Roles and Responsibilities

The provincial or territorial government design, develop, and deliver disaster financial assistance, deciding the amounts and types of assistance that will be provided to those that have experienced losses. The Government of Canada places no restrictions on provincial or territorial governments in this regard—they are free to put in place the disaster financial assistance appropriate to the particular disaster and circumstances. Public Safety and Emergency Preparedness Canada (PSEPC) works closely with the province or territory to assess damage and review claims for reimbursement of eligible response and recovery costs. Other federal departments and agencies are sometimes asked to assist in determining what constitutes reasonable costs for recovery and restoration.

Eligibility and Reimbursement of Expenses

Through the DFAA, assistance is paid directly to the province or territory—not directly to the individuals or communities. The percentage of eligible costs reimbursed under the DFAA is determined by the cost-sharing formula outlined in the arrangements (a factor of the extent of damage and the population of the affected area). The Government of Canada may provide advance payments to provincial and territorial governments as the reconstruction of major infrastructure proceeds and funds are expended under the provincial/territorial disaster assistance program.

A province or territory may request Government of Canada disaster financial assistance when eligible expenditures exceed $1 per capita (based on provincial or territorial population). Payments are made after provincial/territorial expenditures have been audited.

Eligible expenses include, but are not limited to, rescue operations and restoring public works and infrastructure to their pre-disaster condition, as well as replacing or repairing basic, essential personal property of individuals, small businesses, and farmsteads. Examples of expenses that may be eligible for reimbursement include:

- Rescue, transportation, emergency food, shelter, and clothing
- Emergency provision of essential community services
- Security measures including the removal of valuable assets and hazardous materials from a threatened area
- Costs of measures taken in the immediate pre-disaster period intended to reduce the impact of the disaster
- Repairs to public buildings and related equipment
- Repairs to public infrastructure such as roads and bridges
- Removal of damaged structures constituting a threat to public safety
- Restoration, replacement, or repairs to an individual's dwelling (principal residence only)
- Restoration, replacement, or repairs to essential personal furnishings, appliances, and clothing
- Restoration of small businesses and farmsteads including buildings and equipment
- Costs of damage inspection, appraisal, and cleanup

Examples of expenses that would NOT be eligible for reimbursement:

- Repairs to a nonprimary dwelling (e.g., cottage, ski chalet, or hobby farm)
- Repairs that are eligible for reimbursement through insurance
- Costs that are covered in whole or in part by another government program (e.g., crop insurance)
- Normal operating expenses of a government department or agency
- Assistance to large businesses and crown corporations
- Loss of income and economic recovery
- Forest fire fighting

Source: Public Safety and Emergency Preparedness Canada, 2005.

One of the main advantages of emergency relief funds is that they are available immediately. Almost all other forms of funding require a waiting period, including donations from other national governments and insurance.

Many poor countries whose budgets are already stretched thin do not have the luxury of "setting aside" funding, and must find the money through some other means. Generally, this is performed through cutting or tapping into other government programs' funding. In many countries in which disasters are common and international relief assistance has been given, an attitude of "why reserve money for disaster relief if the international community is going to help us anyway" begins to form. Recent research has found that many of the poorest disaster-prone countries go as far as to concentrate their pre-disaster efforts upon maximizing their ability to garner post-disaster international aid (Miller & Keipi, 2005).

Ways do exist in which governments, both within the affected nation and abroad, can use current budgetary spending to supplement disaster recovery and place little or no additional pressure upon the current budget (i.e., not simply reallocating money within the budget). This is achieved through offering services that carry a monetary value but would have been utilized regardless of the disaster. For example, militaries often support relief efforts with their manpower, equipment, and/or supplies, with the operations falling within their general budget appropriations. Emergency foodstocks that may have been set aside throughout the country or the world may be available for transport to the affected region. Government employees may be able to set aside their regular duties in order to supplement the needs of the relief effort. Intelligence and other information-gathering agencies may be able to provide imagery and other data they gather as a regular part of their work.

Donations

The majority of relief effort funds often are philanthropic in origin. The world community as a whole is much better able to absorb the impacts of individual disasters than any single community (which is related to the concept of risk spreading, explained in Chapter 4). Even the United States, the world's richest nation, depended heavily on donated funds (measured in the billions of dollars) in the recovery for both the September 11th terrorist attacks in 2001 and Hurricane Katrina in 2005. The sources of donated funds are varied, and include:

- Other governments
- Multilateral organizations
- Nonprofit organizations (national and international)
- Businesses (national and international)
- Private citizens (national and international)
- Remittances (see Exhibit 7–2)

Goods and services, or "in-kind donations," are another common form of recovery support in place of or in addition to cash. Governments, organizations, or individuals may choose to send supplies, services, or manpower that they already possess in ample quantity to assist the affected region. In times of disaster, these supplies and services are desperately needed, as even the most well-funded governments may find themselves unable to acquire items such as tents, food, and

EXHIBIT 7–2: REMITTANCES AND DIASPORA BONDS IN DISASTERS

Remittances are funds sent home by citizens that live overseas. In many poor countries, remittances are measured in the billions of dollars, and in some cases can represent a sizeable portion of GDP. The incomes of individual households are drastically supplemented, and local economies depend on this money to function. In 2009, remittances amounted to over $55 billion in India, $21 billion in Mexico, and $17 billion in the Philippines. The $1.2 billion in remittances sent home to Laotian families represented over 34% of that country's GDP. When disasters happen, remittances can be instrumental in recovery, as was the case following the 2010 earthquake in Haiti. Following that event, remittances were expected to surge 20%. Prior to the quake, remittances already constituted between 25 and 50% of national income. A rise in remittances is common after disasters, but Haiti represented the first time the restoration of remittances services was seen as a critical part of disaster relief and response. The World Bank explored the role that a wealthy national diaspora living in the United States, Canada, France, and other countries continues to play in Haiti's recovery. The expected 20% increase amounts to an additional $360 million above normal levels, according to World Bank's Outlook for Remittance Flows 2010–2011. The diaspora officially sent $1.4 billion in remittances to Haiti in 2008, and unofficially may have sent as much as $2 billion. Much of the 2010 increase is likely to be from 200,000 undocumented workers granted "temporary protective status" to live and work legally in the United States for 18 months. If the temporary protective status is extended another 18 months, additional flows to Haiti could exceed $1 billion over three years. To capitalize on this support, the World Bank proposed Haiti issue reconstruction diaspora bonds to tap the wealth of the diaspora. This group is typically more willing than other foreign investors to lend money to the affected national government at a cheap rate, making socially relevant projects that offer a lower rate of return more affordable. In the past, diaspora bonds have been used by Israel and India to raise over $35 billion in development financing. Several countries—Ethiopia, Nepal, the Philippines, Rwanda, and Sri Lanka—are considering (or have issued) diaspora bonds recently to bridge financing gaps. By offering a reasonable interest rate (e.g., a 5% tax-free dollar interest rate), this option can attract a large number of investors. The bonds must, however, be implemented by a credible organization overseen by international agencies or observers. It was estimated that a diaspora bond sale could raise $200 million if 200,000 Haitians in the United States, Canada, and France were to invest $1000 each, and much higher amounts could be raised if bonds were open to friends of Haiti and guaranteed by multilateral or bilateral donors.

Source: World Bank Group, 2010.

building supplies; logistical needs such as flights, ships, and trucks to transport goods; or professional experts such as engineers, physicians, and public works contractors. Exhibit 7–3 details the humanitarian assistance donated by the U.S. government to the response and recovery following the 2001 earthquakes in El Salvador.

Figure 7–1 illustrates the flow of money from donors to recipients in the response and recovery to international disasters.

EXHIBIT 7–3: U.S. GOVERNMENT ASSISTANCE TO THE GOVERNMENT OF EL SALVADOR FOLLOWING THE EARTHQUAKES OF JANUARY 13 AND FEBRUARY 13, 2001

On January 13, 2001, at approximately 11:35 a.m. local time, an earthquake with a magnitude of 7.6 on the Richter scale and a depth of 60 km occurred off the coastline of El Salvador, about 105 km southwest of the town of San Miguel. A second earthquake struck El Salvador on February 13, 2001, at 8:22 a.m. local time with a magnitude of 6.6 on the Richter scale and a depth of about 13 km. The second earthquake's epicenter was located about 30 km east of San Salvador in San Pedro Nonualco in the department of La Paz. Both the January and February earthquakes were felt throughout El Salvador and in neighboring Guatemala and Honduras.

The National Emergency Committee for El Salvador (COEN) reported that as a result of both earthquakes, 1159 people died, 1,582,428 people were affected, 185,338 houses were damaged, and 149,528 houses were destroyed. In total, the Government of El Salvador (GOES) estimated that the cost of rebuilding damaged areas would be more than $2.8 billion.

The January Earthquake

On January 14, U.S. Ambassador Rose Likins declared a disaster due to the damage caused by the earthquake on January 13. USAID/OFDA responded by providing $25,000 to USAID/El Salvador for the purchase of tools, hard hats, gloves, goggles, flashlights, lighting, fuel, and related supplies or equipment required for the search and rescue activities.

At the time of the earthquake, three USAID/OFDA personnel were in San Salvador and immediately began liaising with the El Salvadoran Red Cross, COEN, the U.S. Embassy, and USAID/El Salvador to assess damages and relief needs and to begin to coordinate the USAID/OFDA response. On January 14, 11 additional USAID/OFDA personnel arrived in San Salvador to assist in the response effort. The USAID/DART also included a Miami-Dade Fire Rescue component, which assisted the GOES in developing site strategies for search and rescue activities, safety measures for rescue workers, security plans for search sites, and training on the construction of temporary shelters.

During the disaster response, USAID/OFDA conducted a total of six relief commodity airlifts to El Salvador. These airlifts included one prepackaged GO kit containing medical supplies to treat 1000 people for one week; 6008 hygiene kits, each with supplies sufficient for a family of five for two weeks; 3,600,000 sq. ft. of plastic sheeting; 2400 five-gallon water containers; and 1000 wool blankets. All of the relief commodities were consigned to COEN, except the medical supplies and plastic sheeting.

The medical supplies went directly to hospitals in the affected areas and the plastic sheeting to NGOs in support of their temporary shelter construction activities. In addition to the commodities that were airlifted to El Salvador, USAID/OFDA provided $215,000 through USAID/El Salvador for the local purchase and transport of relief supplies and for USAID/DART support.

To support temporary shelter needs in the affected areas, USAID/OFDA provided $4,787,000 in grants to the Cooperative Housing Foundation (CHF), CARE, and Samaritan's Purse to construct temporary shelters using plastic sheeting provided by USAID/OFDA. The three NGOs constructed a total of 13,061 temporary shelters for earthquake-affected families in the departments of Usulutan, La Libertad, and La Paz.

USAID/OFDA also provided plastic sheeting in support of SC/US's temporary shelter activities that were conducted through a partnership between SC/US and local Peace Corps volunteers who trained members of their communities on basic temporary shelter construction techniques.

USAID/OFDA funded the services of three Blackhawk and two Chinook helicopters and 46 support personnel provided by DOD's Southern Command (SOUTHCOM) in support of humanitarian relief missions from January 14 to 19. The total cost of SOUTHCOM's assistance was $450,000.

The February Earthquake

On February 13, a second disaster declaration was issued by U.S. Chargé d'Affaires Mark Boulware due to the damage caused by the February earthquake. USAID/OFDA provided $25,000 to USAID/El Salvador for the local purchase of emergency relief supplies.

A USAID/OFDA assessment team was deployed to El Salvador from February 13 to March 3 and coordinated relief efforts with the El Salvadoran Red Cross, COEN, the U.S. Embassy, and USAID/El Salvador. Based upon the assessment team's evaluation, USAID/OFDA provided $2,688,000 to USAID/El Salvador for grants to CHF, CARE, Samaritan's Purse, PCI, SC/US, and LWF for the construction of 8944 temporary shelters in the departments of Ahuachapan, Cuscatlan, La Paz, and San Vicente. These shelters also utilized USAID/OFDA plastic sheeting in the construction.

USAID/OFDA provided $730,000 for the local purchase of relief supplies, administrative support, the establishment of 18 temporary health posts, and the construction of 50 permanent houses for single mothers. USAID/OFDA funds also supported the temporary provision of potable water to three hospitals to meet interim needs until water tanks were installed. The relief supplies, consisting of 10,000 blankets, 10,000 mattresses, 14,000 five-gallon water containers, and 15,035 three-gallon water containers, were consigned to CARE, SC/US, and Samaritan's Purse for distribution to earthquake-affected families in the departments of Cuscatlan, La Paz, and San Vicente.

USAID/OFDA airlifted an additional 13,824,000 sq. ft. of plastic sheeting to El Salvador for consignment to local and international NGOs for the construction of emergency shelters following the February earthquake. The total cost of the plastic sheeting and other commodities airlifted by USAID/OFDA in response to the two earthquakes was more than $2.1 million, including transport.

In addition to the emergency relief assistance, USAID/OFDA provided $3 million and USAID/OTI provided $2 million to USAID/El Salvador as a portion of USAID/BHR's contribution to earthquake reconstruction activities. This assistance was part of the United States Government's (USG's) overall pledge of $110 million for a reconstruction program in El Salvador.

USAID/FFP contributed 1750 metric tons of emergency food commodities, valued at $926,100, to the World Food Programme (WFP). SOUTHCOM provided the services of one Chinook helicopter and two Blackhawk helicopters to respond to requests and priorities established by COEN and the El Salvadoran armed forces. The helicopters were in El Salvador from February 14 to 16 at a cost of $116,000.

Source: OFDA, 2001.

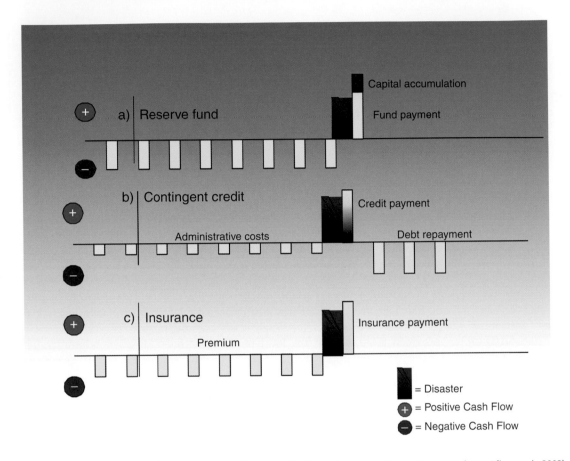

FIGURE 7–1 Illustration of expenditures and payouts for reserve funds, contingent credit, and insurance. (From Pflug et al., 2002)

Loans

Because most governments and communities will be unable to fully fund their recovery efforts through emergency funds and donations, it may be necessary to secure loans to cover what costs remain. There are a number of ways in which money can be borrowed by governments in times of emergency. The most common source of funding in developing countries are the International Financial Institutions (IFIs), detailed in Chapter 10. Private loans may have prohibitively high interest rates or may be difficult for the affected country to secure. Emergency loans from the IFIs, for which systematic processes have been developed, involve a much faster and easier approval process and may feature a delayed payment schedule and lower interest rates. Unfortunately, these emergency loans may be made on top of a heavy existing loan burden, so the affected government may eventually find itself cutting other programs to cover the future loan payments.

Another form of loan is "contingent credit." With this form of borrowing, governments pay creditors (usually private or international banks) a regular periodic fee that guarantees them the right to draw down emergency funds in the event of a disaster. The funds are pre-approved and rapidly disbursed to the affected government. With contingent credit, governments do not need to pay any interest or principal payments until after the funds are actually drawn down (as opposed to other loan forms, where these payments are likely to begin immediately upon approval of the loan). This loan form is most effective for countries with low risk for catastrophic disaster.

A third option for countries that already have loans for other development projects is "loan diversion." In loan diversion, money that has already been disbursed for other projects may be used to pay for post-disaster recovery expenses. The advantage of this option is that the country does not incur any additional debt as a result of the action. The disadvantage is that whatever development project the money was diverted from will probably not be completed on time, if at all.

It is important to note that loans present a unique opportunity in that the lender may impose restrictions on how the funds may be used. This is significant in that it can help to increase disaster resilience within the affected nation. For example, the World Bank may require that construction to rebuild damaged or destroyed hospitals adheres to the most current building codes and uses the most advanced mitigation technologies.

Many of the poorest nations affected by disasters are already so burdened with debt that they are unable to assume any additional loans. These countries, many of which expend a substantial percent of annual GDP on repaying international debt, literally have no room to expand their budgets. Despite the occurrence of the disaster, they are still liable for preexisting debt payments while they are trying to manage the current situation. The option of "debt relief" has been explored for countries facing this predicament; rather than have the international community supply these countries with more money, proponents of debt relief argue that it would make more sense to cancel or reduce their debts so the money earmarked for debt repayment could now be transferred to funding recovery. The counterargument is that many of these countries are in such grave debt in the first place because of corruption and poor financial management, which would only increase following debt relief, and the affected population would never enjoy the true benefits from relief measures.

Catastrophe Bonds and Weather Derivatives

Catastrophe (CAT) bonds are special high-return bonds issued before a disaster occurs. Some CAT bonds pay interest rates as high as 15%, which greatly exceeds most bonds on the international market. What makes a CAT bond relevant to disaster management is that the bond issuer may be freed from paying either the interest or the principal of the bond if the issuer suffers the consequences of a major disaster. Selling CAT bonds began in 1992, after Hurricane Andrew in the United States, when especially hard-hit insurance companies saw them as an option to spread risk across an even wider area (Kahn, 2004). International development banks and national governments have also begun to explore the CAT bond market, although not to any significant degree.

Weather derivatives are investment instruments that can be used to protect against adverse climate effects, such as extreme temperatures, heavy rainfall, or drought. An investor, who agrees to pay a claimed amount if a condition stipulated in the derivative occurs, buys the derivative. For instance, farmers can sell a derivative that covers their losses if lower than optimal rainfall results in low crop yields. Weather derivatives are related to insurance, but cover higher probability events than insurance usually does (Investopedia.com, n.d.). As with CAT bonds, the purchaser receives an agreed upon amount if no disaster befalls the entity selling the derivative.

Private Development Funding

Much of the disaster recovery burden will fall on the shoulders of private businesses and individuals. Those who have not been provided with insurance or recovery funds will have to spend their own money to repair or rebuild their home or business. Many who do receive funding are likely to receive it in the form of a loan, which they will ultimately be required to repay. These private expenditures are the greatest cause of economic hardship following disasters. Businesses may fail or be required to lay off employees to cover expenses, and citizens may have drastically reduced expendable income to inject into the local economy.

What is most difficult for recovery planners is ensuring that private expenditures for development funding, which are likely to be completely independent of any coordination mechanism, support disaster risk reduction. Unfortunately, most people will not understand or know how to reduce their future risk to similar hazards. And, even if they do understand how, it will be difficult to convince them to spend their already strained resources on mitigation measures that only increase the cost of rebuilding their lives. Public education and increased legal restrictions on minimum construction standards are often the only ways of reaching this goal.

Incentives

Local or regional governments often offer incentives for private development to speed up the rate at which private relief funding is applied and to attract external funding from other parts of the country, region, or world. A number of options are open to governments to lure private investment, all of which are based on the fact that demand for real estate will always exist among businesses and homeowners, and the competition between possible locations often boils down to the amenities each offers. By providing incentives such as tax breaks for homeowners, business and employees, tax-exempt bond financing, and other measures, businesses and individuals may be more likely to take a risk and invest in the affected area over other less risky areas with fewer financial incentives.

Tax Increases

It is possible to spread the cost of refinancing among the affected population, or across all of those affected or unaffected within the tax base, by increasing tax revenues to cover some of the recovery expenses. Unfortunately, many victims are likely to find themselves without any spare cash, so an increase in taxation is likely to be very unfavorable to them, and therefore, politically unattractive to those elected officials who would be responsible for passing the tax increase legislation.

Allocation of Relief Funds

How government emergency relief funds and supplies are disbursed is wholly dependent upon the affected government's preferences and abilities. In most cases, the national government will be given international funding in addition to whatever funding it has in reserve or has reappropriated. While some governments do allow funding to go directly to the victims to cover housing or other personal expenses, they may choose to keep the money at the government level to spend on large-scale projects. Alternatively, these funds may be disbursed as direct grants or as loans that must be repaid. In other cases, international funds will be given to international relief agencies operating in the affected zone, such as Feed the Children, CARE, or Médecins Sans Frontièrs (see Figure 7–2).

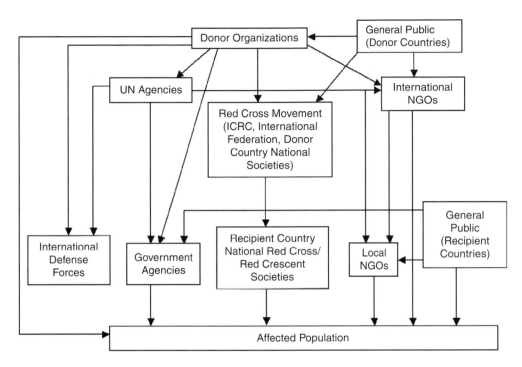

FIGURE 7–2 Common routes of relief and recovery funding from donors to recipients. (From Borton, 1996; Macrae, 2002)

Because international relief funding averages close to $10 billion each year, the potential for corruption exists and is relatively common (Willits-King & Harvey, 2005). The speed with which humanitarian relief must be provided often makes monitoring and auditing of funds more difficult than in more traditional development processes. For this reason, humanitarian aid is not often given directly to governments that are labeled as excessively corrupt by international groups like Transparency International, but rather to multilateral organizations or to the relief providers themselves.

Personnel

In the recovery period following a disaster, personnel needs for cleanup, repair, and development will be excessive. These range from unskilled or untrained laborers and volunteers to experts in technical fields relating to infrastructure, construction, planning, logistics, and specialized equipment. Without ample personnel, the community may find itself with enough funding and materials to rebuild but without the personnel to support the workload (see Exhibit 7–4).

The most important personnel source is the affected region itself. These individuals, whether personally affected by the disaster or not, have the most vested interest in the outcome of the recovery effort and are most in tune with the community's character. Many are likely to need immediate employment. As recovery efforts often require long-term commitments, locally hired workers are more likely to be able to commit to the full course of the reconstruction effort and are less likely to suffer from recovery and reconstruction "burnout." Using workers from the local economy has the added benefit of ensuring that more recovery funding stays within the community, which in turn helps to spur

EXHIBIT 7–4: TECHNICAL LABOR IN THE GREAT HANSHIN EARTHQUAKE RECOVERY

The Kobe earthquake caused significant damage to the infrastructure and transportation network in the affected areas. Extensive rail and roadway damage included the collapse of significant portions of three major freeway routes, damage to rail systems, and the collapse of Kobe's subway stations. There was also significant damage to the water, gas, and sewer systems, with over 1 million households losing access to related services. To address technical needs, the Japanese government created a formal organization through which human capital resources from all levels of the government were leveraged to plan for and implement recovery strategies. A committee comprising high-ranking officials (including members of the Japanese House of Representatives and leaders of affected jurisdictions and their staff) developed intergovernmental recovery strategies. In addition to those high-ranking officials, the committee also included working-level staff from national ministries to provide expertise for developing specific details to be included in the recovery plan. For example, staff from the Ministry of Transportation brought expertise on infrastructure replacement while those from the Kobe Chamber of Commerce and Industry contributed knowledge regarding economic recovery matters. According to a Japanese official involved in the recovery, this committee combined the political know-how from the top-level officials and interdisciplinary expertise from line-level bureaucrats to propose many recovery proposals that laid a foundation for the national government's approach to recovery. The Japanese government also leveraged human capital expertise through this committee to facilitate the implementation of recovery strategies. Upon the approval of certain recovery policies, working staff associated with the committee returned to their respective organizations to guide their home departments on how best to implement the strategies. A Japanese official involved in the committee said that this collaboration helped to ensure that disparate ministries understood and properly implemented the recovery strategies they helped to develop.

Source: GAO, 2009.

long-term economic recovery. Wages must be set competitively, but not set at a level so high as to draw workers out of other jobs, destabilizing any remaining balance in the local workforce (see Exhibit 7–5).

A second source of personnel is the many national and international nongovernmental agencies that assist in development and recovery. These groups provide funding, personnel, and expertise for any number of recovery components. For instance, Habitat for Humanity provided all needed materials and personnel to build over 5000 houses in Central America and the Caribbean after Hurricane Mitch.

Military forces, both local and from other countries, are often called upon to rebuild disaster-stricken areas. As disasters have become progressively more destructive, the military has been called upon for humanitarian assistance to a greater degree. The military can be ideal for such projects because of their sheer numbers, maneuverability, technical expertise, equipment, manageability, and relatively low cost.

Finally, private contractors from around the country and the world may be lured to work in the affected area. Local contractors will quickly find themselves overbooked. Technicians with equipment

---

EXHIBIT 7–5: FOOD FOR WORK AND CASH FOR WORK PROGRAMS

Food for work programs are recovery programs that provide food aid for victims in exchange for work on repair and reconstruction projects. The basic tenet of these programs is that victims are provided with a much needed resource (food), while the community directly benefits from the work that they conducted. When successful, these programs are effective in reducing the feeling among victims that they are merely begging for handouts, and they help recovery planners to increase the feeling among victims that they have an active stake in how their community recovers. Food aid programs must be designed so they do not benefit individuals in good health and physical condition over those who are unable to work, nor should they negatively impact local markets.

Like food for work programs, cash for work programs provide financial assistance to survivors of disaster events. These programs help to bridge the period between the disaster and the recovery of livelihoods when victims are able to begin earning an income in their former profession.

---

needed to repair infrastructure components, such as electrical lines, communications systems, or water pipes, will have much more work than they can handle. Therefore, outside assistance may need to be called on to speed up the pace of recovery (see Exhibit 7–6).

Types of Recovery

Countries and communities comprise diverse levels of organization, from the individual to the central government body. In a disaster's aftermath, a great many of these societal components probably will have sustained some form of injury, damage, or other negative consequence that collectively results in a greater need for recovery. Although the range of activities required to address these needs is as varied as if one were building the community from scratch, specific categories of assistance are common after almost all forms of disaster: public assistance, housing, economic recovery, and individual, family, and social recovery. Each category is described below.

Public Assistance

Public assistance recovery includes all aspects of recovery that fall within the public domain. Generally, these are the structures, systems, and services related to government. Because the government is ultimately responsible for its protection, the environment is also included in this category.

Disasters impact a government's operational capacity as a result of

- Damage or destruction of government facilities
- Loss or injury of government employees
- Loss of government files and other important information
- Lack of resources (e.g., electricity, water, communications)
- Political instability

EXHIBIT 7–6: CONTRACTOR-DRIVEN RECOVERY PROJECTS

The contractor-driven approach assigns the task of managing the overall reconstruction plan and efforts to a professional construction company. The company or companies select the design, construction materials, and expertise and labor (which are most often imported from outside the target community). The perceived benefits of such an approach are that it can bring about a very fast reconstruction with the least amount of effort expended on the part of the affected government or the victims. Through the work of a construction contractor, a large number of structures, typically with standard specifications, can be built quickly using staff with established technical expertise and skills. The benefits of such an option cannot be overlooked in the context of an affected community lacking the knowledge or capacity to rebuild their houses in a hazard-resistant manner, or where there is no enabling tradition of self-reliance. However, in the case of housing, most (about 95%) throughout the world are built with significant input of the owners.

Assessments of contractor-driven reconstruction programs have identified a number of associated drawbacks and risks. For instance, large-scale contracted construction tends to adopt a "one-size-fits-all" approach, which means that the specific needs of individual communities may not be met, and community character and culture may not be taken into consideration. These projects have also been found to be blind to the culture and preferences of recipients, and may include the use of materials that are poorly suited to the climate of the affected area, or are very difficult for the homeowners to replace in the future. Contractor-led projects are primarily driven by profit, and without proper oversight the quality of the finished product can be substandard if contractors attempt to increase their profit margins through the use of substandard materials and construction methods. As is true with government-driven recovery construction approaches, the use of contractors may promote a dependency relationship with recipients who could otherwise have learned valuable construction skills if given such leeway. Without adequate construction skills among recipients, the sustainability of projects is decreased.

The recovery in Gujarat, India, following the Bhuj Earthquake (2001) is an example where contractor labor was used heavily in recovery. On January 26, 2001, a magnitude 6.9 earthquake killed approximately 20,000 people and injured an additional 167,000. Over one million were rendered homeless; 7633 villages were affected and 450 villages were completely destroyed; and 344,000 houses were completely destroyed and 888,000 reported damaged. Many of the NGOs that became involved in housing reconstruction in Gujarat adopted a contractor-driven approach to manage their housing programs. In one instance, contractors were hired to rebuild victim's houses in situ. The program involved the reconstruction of 3000 homes. The contractor offered three different housing sizes, as determined by the plot size. For each of these sizes there were three or four different designs owners could choose from. A demonstration of models was provided in the village schools, allowing villagers to voice their input into the final selection. By allowing the victims to feel a part of the process, post-recovery owner satisfaction was greatly increased. Contractors were also able to utilize low-cost construction techniques, such as reusing old doors, window shutters, and frames that survived the earthquake. The program was not without its problems, of course. Some homeowners questioned the quality of the materials used. The program was also biased against communities that were less accessible, more spread out, or of lower income classes because contractors were reluctant to take on those projects. However, what is most significant is that, despite the individual satisfaction held by each homeowner, because no community-level consultations were made there was a loss of community character. A post-project assessment found that most people were happy that their new house was in the same location. In fact, several homeowners were able to upgrade their house through this program, which increased their satisfaction. However, it was found that there are inherent difficulties in controlling contractors, which can lead to poor construction quality. Even when a Village Committee was set up to supervise efforts, contractor supervision proved difficult. There were even occasions when the contractor designs were incompatible with the properties. This, and other related problems, were chiefly the result of contractors lacking sufficient contextual knowledge (e.g., geographic, socioeconomic, and agro-ecological).

Sources: Barenstein, 2005; Twigg, 2002; Oliver, 1987; and Housing Reconstruction After Conflict and Disaster 2003.

Reconstruction of government infrastructure and resumption of a government's operational capacity are vital to establishing a setting in which recovery is possible. Many actions that facilitate recovery functions require approval or assistance from government officials or facilities. The government's return to some level of operational effectiveness signals to victims that they will receive disaster assistance and that safety and security will be provided. In a complex humanitarian emergency, however, resumption of government may not be possible, especially if no accepted government exists.

In most countries, infrastructure is publicly owned and maintained. It is the government's responsibility, therefore, to fund and oversee its repair and reconstruction. When infrastructure components are privately owned, it still may fall upon the government to fund or support repair and reconstruction, as security and recovery of the affected area will depend heavily on such measures.

Many disasters produce a large quantity of debris, including trees, mud, rock, destroyed housing, damaged property and possessions, automobiles, boats, and other material. All of this material, much of which is cleared in the response phase, also must be removed and disposed of. Government agencies responsible for debris removal and disposal need to identify appropriate disposal sites based on estimates of the type and quantity of debris (taking into account the hazardous nature of certain types). Next, they must collect and clear the debris, which usually requires private contractors because regular garbage and debris clearance capacities will be quickly overwhelmed. Hurricanes and earthquakes, for example, regularly generate as much debris in a few hours as a municipality normally collects over 5 or more years.

Debris clearance must be coordinated with the public in order for it to be successful. Public education efforts that explain where debris may be left for collection, what may be disposed of, and when it will be collected will help facilitate the cleanup effort. Many houses and buildings will need to be demolished, adding to the total volume of debris that must be accommodated in the disposal sites. Much of the debris material, such as bricks, wood, and plastics, for example, are often recyclable for use in the reconstruction process. When proper planning includes sorting and recycling, the overall need for reconstruction resources can be greatly reduced.

Finally, it is the government's responsibility to address the recovery of the environment, which tends to suffer greatly during times of disaster. Much of the undeveloped environment falls under the government's ownership and care. As was noted in Chapter 6, the environment has many features that contribute to a community's resilience to certain hazards. For example, wetlands, mangrove swamps, and dunes all offer protection from hazards such as cyclonic storms, floods, and severe weather storms. These environmental features may be destroyed during a disaster and require rebuilding to ensure that their protection is regained. Failure to address these losses will result in an increase in future risk.

Pollution is another common consequence of disasters. Hazardous materials will have been released from a variety of sources (e.g., flooded cars, damaged holding tanks, leaking pipes) and may now pose a great threat to people, animals, agriculture, and the environment. Floods may have polluted groundwater, wells, and bathing sites. Mud may be contaminated with fuels, bacteria, and chemicals. The air may have toxic particulates, vapors, and smoke. It will be contingent upon the government to monitor the land, air, and water and treat any pollutants discovered to be at unacceptable levels.

The Housing Sector

Housing throughout the affected area will exhibit differing levels of damage and destruction due to its composition, location, elevation, and proximity to the hazard, among other factors. The government's first priority will be to supply housing inspectors, who can determine which structures are capable of repair, which must be demolished, and which require no work at all. There likely will not be enough locally trained and hired inspectors to quickly perform this task, so outside assistance will be required immediately.

The actual cost of housing repair and reconstruction ultimately falls on the homeowners if governments or NGOs cannot subsidize or fully reimburse these expenses. Many victims will lack the financial resources to rebuild, and will therefore need to turn to outside assistance. Unfortunately, this assistance is not always available, and there have been situations, such as after the 1985 earthquake in Mexico City, in which victims were still without permanent housing almost 15 years after the disaster occurred.

Housing reconstruction is most successful when it is performed by or with input from the recipient population. Housing constructed by resources from within the community, as opposed to external contractors, tends to cost less and is more acceptable to the recipients. It also ensures that relief funding and locally secured funds remain within the local economy (see Exhibit 7–7).

Victims who are able to reconstruct immediately will want to begin as soon as possible. Although the speed at which they are able to commence will impact morale, planners must ensure that vulnerabilities are not repeated. To manage this problem, planners must quickly identify which areas are able to begin reconstruction without significant re-engineering and which require further evaluation. This will reduce dependence on temporary housing and provide a "sense of progress while other housing rebuilding issues are deliberated" (Patterson, 1999). For those areas that require further evaluation and analysis, a construction moratorium may be imposed and building permits denied. Using information gained through these further evaluations, the government can require mitigation measures to reduce future risk, such as measures that call for raising houses above flood levels or strengthening them from wind or shaking. While incorporating hazard-resistant design into construction plans is important, it is equally important that the resulting house is not built in a way that is culturally unacceptable to the recipient.

For areas where the risk of rebuilding is too great, it is best that the homeowners abandon their plans and seek alternative sites to construct their new homes. Forcing these people from their land may

EXHIBIT 7–7: OWNER-DRIVEN HOUSING RECONSTRUCTION

The primary advantages of owner inclusion in the reconstruction process include:

- Lower project costs
- Higher rates of satisfaction
- Earlier occupancy (even before the structure is completed in some instances)
- Higher occupancy rates

In owner-driven implementation, the recipients can drive the selection of building materials and design, which allows them to incorporate their preferences and requirements as needed. The self-help nature of the approach can also restore community pride and address some of the psychosocial impacts that have occurred. Finally, in the case of cash for work programs, it can help to keep many community members (including housing recipients) employed during the recovery phase. With adequate financial and technical assistance, self-built houses are likely to be more sustainable. People, if given an option, tend to choose building materials and techniques that are familiar to them. Accordingly, they may be in a better position to provide for future additions and repairs. Finally an owner-driven approach may contribute to preserve the local cultural heritage and vernacular housing style, which is instrumental for the preservation of a community's cultural identity. Relative to the devastating experience of a disaster, it is important to give people some sense of continuity. There are obvious risks associated with an implementation approach that places a significant amount of responsibility in the hands of owners. For instance, a minimum degree of knowledge about project management and technical knowledge required to enable the project to progress from commencement to completion must exist. More vulnerable communities may not have the knowledge or the time to handle what is required. Disaster victims as a general class typically lack the time between facilitating other areas of recovery and addressing their primary livelihood concerns to conduct an effort as comprehensive as the construction of a house (including supervision). If traditional construction design and practice are the sources of risk, and owners are intent on rebuilding in the same manner, this approach can actually preserve high levels of risk. Finally, in urban settings where buildings are multistory (low- and high-rise) structures, the complexity involved in project implementation will be much too great to hand over wholesale to victims.

Owner-driven reconstruction was relied upon heavily in the aftermath of the Pakistan earthquake (2005). The event destroyed or damaged 600,000 houses across 30,000 square kilometers of land, leaving 3.5 million homeless in over 4000 villages. To address the monumental task of rebuilding housing infrastructure, the Government of Pakistan funded a $2 billion program that put the task of rebuilding in the hands of the owners. Families were provided with $2800 if their house was destroyed, and $1200 if it only required repairs. Funds were disbursed in installments, with each successive payment dependent upon an inspection that verified the application of hazard-resistant construction methods and materials. The government worked closely with the United Nations, the World Bank (and other International Financial Institutions), the military of Pakistan, and scores of NGOs operating in the area, to develop a program of technical assistance that would ensure aid recipients were able to carry out the home-building and repair projects in a way to prevent repeat failures in a future seismic event. For the most highly skilled needs, such as steel work

(Continued)

EXHIBIT 7–7: OWNER-DRIVEN HOUSING RECONSTRUCTION (CONTINUED)

and specialty masonry, training was provided to local contractors and artisans who could better meet those needs. This approach led to the loss of some funding when donors were unwilling to support a donor-driven support, but it is felt by those involved that the reduction in construction costs, and the long-term benefit of a trained and empowered population, more than made up for the losses.

Source: UN-HABITAT, 2007.

---

be legally impossible, so incentive programs must be created. The most popular are housing buyout schemes, where homeowners in a highly risk-prone area are given fair market value for their homes. As the new property owner, the government can reserve the risk-prone area for parks or other nonstructure-dependent uses.

In informal settlements, which are common on the outskirts of cities in developing countries, it may be difficult for victims to prove ownership of the land or show title for a damaged or destroyed house. Most informal settlements exist because the land was originally left undeveloped due to an existing hazard risk. In a disaster's aftermath, governments have a unique opportunity and ample assistance to move entire populations out of these high-risk areas into safer zones with supplied public housing and access to resources. The section Special Considerations in Recovery at the end of this chapter expands on this issue.

Economic Recovery

Disasters place pressure on local, national, and, in the largest disasters, international economies. Lost resources, lost production, lost jobs, lost business opportunities, and heavy government expenditures all contribute to economic downturns that must be stabilized and then reversed.

Individual local economies are sustained by a unique set of drivers, which might include tourism, mining, manufacturing, crafts, services, agriculture, or education. Communities grow around and become dependent on the success of these industries, and their citizens acquire skill sets and training tailored to them. Support and service industries, such as transportation, communications, public relations, and shipping, will have developed around these core industries as well. Thus, economic recovery must begin with the recovery of these local economic drivers.

Revitalizing the local economy must be a priority for recovery planners. It is vital that local businesses return to full capacity, especially in the immediate recovery period when significant amounts of recovery funding are injected into the affected area (see Exhibit 7–8). If local businesses are unable to capitalize on that funding, outside contractors are sure to step in and reap the monetary benefits. The ultimate consequence of such an outcome will be that the injected cash is not used to support the local economy.

If large amounts of funding and investment have been collected in the early periods of recovery, it may be possible to revitalize the economy by improving previously existing business infrastructure. Almost all damaged or destroyed infrastructure components, such as communications, facilities, Internet access, and equipment, can and should be rebuilt to the most modern standards, so the

---

EXHIBIT 7–8: IMPACTS ON LOCAL MARKETS

The selection of materials to support reconstruction almost always impacts local markets, although there are a number of factors that determine whether this impact is positive or negative. When local materials are chosen, the local economy can benefit greatly from the injection of income. However, if supply is unable to meet demand, prices will skyrocket causing what is known as a positive demand shock, and subsequently, an increase in construction costs. If foreign materials are chosen, the local markets may become marginalized and eventually see their inventory become irrelevant. Conversely, the use of foreign materials can help to ensure that overharvesting of local resources, leading to environmental damages, does not occur.

In the aftermath of the earthquake and tsunami in Aceh, Indonesia (2004), the cost of construction materials on the local market quickly rose. Steel, cement, bricks, wood, sand, aggregate, and stone all became scarce, and thus expensive, given that they were needed not only in housing but also in the reconstruction of infrastructure. Moreover, there existed the possibility of the local population turning to scarce wood resources in the Sumatran forests. Uplink Banda Aceh, an NGO involved in housing reconstruction, mobilized a logistics team that worked to ship construction materials of the same kind and quality from elsewhere in Indonesia (including Jakarta and Southern Sumatra) to reduce prices and help the local merchants restock their supplies. Local suppliers participated by letting the organization use their warehouse space. The organization was able to reduce the construction costs across the 3000 houses they built by millions of dollars without having to rely on materials that would not be available locally once the effort was concluded, and did little to impact the income of the local sources of such materials.

Source: ByPeople, 2005.

---

overall economic potential is greater than pre-disaster conditions. Preexisting problems that may have prevented economic expansion, such as a lack of useable industrial or office space or poor transportation options, may be easier to resolve in the post-disaster climate (Spangle & Associates, 1991).

How well a community recovers tends to directly follow how well that community was doing economically before the disaster occurred. Businesses that had previously enjoyed success are much more likely to have the reserves to carry them through the difficult period of recovery than businesses that were operating on the brink of bankruptcy even before the disaster occurred. Successful communities are more likely to have the levels of civic pride and cohesion necessary to collectively move forward and even exceed pre-disaster prosperity levels, while communities that had been failing will only deteriorate further (Spangle & Associates, 1991).

Unemployment is a common disaster consequence. Job loss comes as a double blow to victims, who must not only dip into any savings they may have to support their families in the short term but also attempt to recoup their home and property losses. Unemployed victims are more likely to depend on handouts rather than purchase items from the local market, which may further slow the local economy. And without adequate jobs, psychological stresses and depression quickly increase. Fortunately, boosting employment in the affected region can address each of these needs, allowing for victims to regain their sense of independence and pride while injecting much needed money into the damaged local economy. Because most of the initial recovery needs, such as demolition and debris clearance, are labor intensive, this process can begin almost immediately.

The quality of recovery planning and coordination will affect employment in several ways. First, only efficient provision of recovery services, including the distribution of relief (e.g., goods and water) will allow residents time to dedicate to a job. Poor relief distribution that requires victims to wait in line for hours or travel long distances prevents them from being able to take advantage of job opportunities. Second, victims must be provided with the means to accept jobs that are created, including any needed training, transportation, or application assistance. Employers must consider the extra commitments that victims may have outside of work, such as rebuilding their homes, ensuring their children attend school or have adequate daycare, or attending medical appointments.

Many businesses affected by the disaster will ultimately fail, resulting in a loss of long-term jobs. This is especially true with small businesses. Statistics in the United States have shown that 25% of small businesses forced to close as a result of a disaster never reopen and 40–60% will close permanently within 2 years of the disaster. Recovery funding can address this problem and, in doing so, retain jobs that would otherwise be lost. Microcredit and "start-up" business grant schemes have been found to be successful after disasters in many countries for helping small businesses to stay in business and helping new businesses get off to a stronger start.

Individual, Family, and Social Recovery

A community's recovery is closely tied to the physical and mental health of its individuals, families, and social groups. Even if every building, infrastructure component, and house is repaired, the community will continue to suffer unless its social needs are addressed. While this need exists after any disaster, the degree of need grows incrementally with the number of injured and killed. Social recovery from complex humanitarian emergencies, where a full breakdown in security is also likely to have occurred, often requires considerable attention.

Regardless of the level of injury or loss sustained, all people in the affected area will face a certain amount of emotional distress and anxiety. Disasters are stressful and troubling because they force people to confront their vulnerabilities and may shatter any assumptions people have had about their ability to avoid catastrophe. Those who are injured; lose family members or friends; or lose a job, home, or property experience this to an even greater degree. Their lives are disrupted and dislocated, and their future may suddenly seem very uncertain. Research has shown that children are especially susceptible to emotional distress.

The emotional pain, suffering, and loss during and following disasters can lead to psychosocial problems, including post-traumatic stress disorder in the most severe cases (detailed in Exhibit 7–9). Victims coping with the aftermath of a disaster exhibit a wide range of reactions, most of which are normal given the circumstances. Most of these victims (including first responders) will fail to consider themselves in need of mental health services and therefore are unlikely to request them. Both a cadre of counselors and a community outreach program must be established to ensure that help is available and that victims know why and how to get help.

Physical disability is another problem exacerbated by disasters. First, disaster-related injuries cause an increased need for physical rehabilitation over the affected communities normally handled. Second, those with prior disabilities will find themselves at a great disadvantage when the social

EXHIBIT 7–9: POST-TRAUMATIC STRESS DISORDER

What Is Post-Traumatic Stress Disorder?

Post-traumatic stress disorder (PTSD) is a psychiatric disorder that can occur after witnessing life-threatening events such as military combat, natural disasters, terrorist incidents, serious accidents, or violent personal assaults like rape. People who suffer from PTSD often relive the experience through nightmares and flashbacks, have difficulty sleeping, and feel detached or estranged, and these symptoms can be severe enough and last long enough to significantly impair the person's daily life.

PTSD is marked by clear biological changes as well as psychological symptoms. It is complicated by the fact that it frequently occurs in conjunction with related disorders such as depression, substance abuse, problems of memory and cognition, and other problems of physical and mental health. The disorder is also associated with impairment of the person's ability to function in social or family life, including occupational instability, marital problems and divorces, family discord, and difficulties in parenting.

How Does PTSD Develop?

Most people who are exposed to a traumatic, stressful event experience some of the symptoms of PTSD in the days and weeks following exposure. Available data suggest that about 8% of men and 20% of women go on to develop PTSD, and roughly 30% of these individuals develop a chronic form that persists throughout their lifetimes.

The course of chronic PTSD usually involves periods of symptom increase followed by remission or decrease, although some individuals may experience symptoms that are unremitting and severe. Some older veterans, who report a lifetime of only mild symptoms, experience significant increases in symptoms following retirement, severe medical illness involving themselves or their spouses, or reminders of their military service (such as reunions or media broadcasts of the anniversaries of war events).

How Is PTSD Assessed?

In recent years, a great deal of research has been aimed at developing and testing reliable assessment tools. It is generally thought that the best way to diagnose PTSD—or any psychiatric disorder—is to combine findings from structured interviews and questionnaires with physiological assessments. A multi-method approach especially helps address concerns that some patients might be either denying or exaggerating their symptoms.

Who Is Most Likely to Develop PTSD?

1. Those who experience greater stressor magnitude and intensity, unpredictability, uncontrollability, sexual (as opposed to nonsexual) victimization, real or perceived responsibility, and betrayal
2. Those with prior vulnerability factors such as genetics, early age of onset and longer lasting childhood trauma, lack of functional social support, and concurrent stressful life events

(Continued)

EXHIBIT 7–9: POST-TRAUMATIC STRESS DISORDER (CONTINUED)

3. Those who report greater perceived threat or danger, suffering, upset, terror, and horror or fear
4. Those with a social environment that produces shame, guilt, stigmatization, or self-hatred

What Are the Consequences Associated with PTSD?

PTSD is associated with a number of distinctive neurobiological and physiological changes. It may be associated with stable neurobiological alterations in both the central and autonomic nervous systems, such as altered brainwave activity, decreased volume of the hippocampus, and abnormal activation of the amygdala. Both the hippocampus and the amygdala are involved in the processing and integration of memory. The amygdala has also been found to be involved in coordinating the body's fear response.

Psycho-physiological alterations associated with PTSD include hyperarousal of the sympathetic nervous system, increased sensitivity of the startle reflex, and sleep abnormalities.

People with PTSD tend to have abnormal levels of key hormones involved in the body's response to stress. Thyroid function also seems to be enhanced in people with PTSD. Some studies have shown that cortisol levels in those with PTSD are lower than normal and epinephrine and norepinephrine levels are higher than normal. People with PTSD also continue to produce higher than normal levels of natural opiates after the trauma has passed. An important finding is that the neurohormonal changes seen in PTSD are distinct from, and actually opposite to, those seen in major depression. This distinctive profile associated with PTSD is also seen in individuals who have both PTSD and depression.

PTSD is associated with the increased likelihood of co-occurring psychiatric disorders. In a large-scale study, 88% of men and 79% of women with PTSD met criteria for another psychiatric disorder. The co-occurring disorders most prevalent for men with PTSD were alcohol abuse or dependence (51.9%), major depressive episodes (47.9%), conduct disorders (43.3%), and drug abuse and dependence (34.5%). The disorders most frequently comorbid (occurring together) with PTSD among women were major depressive disorders (48.5%), simple phobias (29%), social phobias (28.4%), and alcohol abuse/dependence (27.9%).

PTSD also significantly impacts psychosocial functioning, independent of comorbid conditions. For instance, Vietnam veterans with PTSD were found to have profound and pervasive problems in their daily lives. These included problems in family and other interpersonal relationships, problems with employment, and involvement with the criminal justice system.

Headaches, gastrointestinal complaints, immune system problems, dizziness, chest pain, and discomfort in other parts of the body are common in people with PTSD. Often, medical doctors treat the symptoms without being aware that they stem from PTSD.

How Is PTSD Treated?

PTSD is treated by a variety of forms of psychotherapy and drug therapy. There is no definitive treatment, and no cure, but some treatments appear to be quite promising, especially cognitive-behavioral therapy, group therapy, and exposure therapy. Exposure therapy involves having the patient repeatedly relive the frightening experience under controlled conditions to help him or her work through the trauma. Studies have also shown that medications help ease associated symptoms of depression and anxiety and help with sleep. The most widely used drug treatments for PTSD are the selective serotonin reuptake inhibitors, such as Prozac and Zoloft. At present, cognitive-behavioral therapy appears to be somewhat more effective than drug therapy. However, it would be premature to conclude that drug therapy is less effective overall since drug trials for PTSD are at a very early stage. Drug therapy appears to be highly effective for some individuals and is helpful for many more. In addition, the recent findings on the biological changes associated with PTSD have spurred new research into drugs that target these biological changes, which may lead to much increased efficacy.

Source: National Center for PTSD, n.d.

and physical infrastructure upon which they depend is damaged or destroyed. The following list details ways in which disasters may affect the physically injured and disabled (adapted from WHO, 2005):

- For victims with existing disabilities:
  - In comparison to their nondisabled peers, persons with disabilities can be more at risk of disasters.
  - Many people with disabilities lose their assistive devices, such as artificial limbs, crutches, hearing aids, and eyeglasses.
  - Persons with disabilities can have greater difficulty accessing basic needs, including water, food, shelter, latrines, and health care services.
  - Rehabilitation infrastructure may suffer damage or destruction and rehabilitation personnel, including primary caregivers, may be killed, injured, or diverted to other tasks.
- For victims with injuries and/or newly acquired disabilities:
  - Untreated or inadequately treated fractures and infected wounds may lead to severe and long-lasting disabilities.
  - Referral of victims to appropriate health facilities may become difficult or impossible.
  - A scarcity of locally available health and rehabilitation personnel to deal with the "new generation" of people with disabilities may exist.
  - Those who are injured will be at a distinct disadvantage in receiving aid and recovery assistance compared to their noninjured peers, and may be at greater risk of developing mental health issues.

Cultural Recovery

After disasters, communities often find that their cultural heritage has been devastated or completely destroyed. Historic buildings and other structures, art, items of clothing, and landmarks may have been lost. The loss of these cultural components may result in a loss of identity for the community, who are now residing and functioning in buildings that do not address their cultural needs, customs, or preferences. They may be wearing donated clothing that is not normal for them, and eating food they are not used to.

Cultural recovery must come from within the community, although outside assistance may be able to facilitate it. Festivals and observances must be restarted as soon as possible. A return to normal dress and food must take place. Preserving and repairing historic structures that are salvageable, as well as collecting building materials from those destroyed, can signal to victims that their community spirit has been retained. These structures will often become the centerpieces around which social recovery is achieved. All external recovery officials must recognize, respect, and even celebrate local cultural and associated customs. Doing so will help not only to speed up the community's social recovery but will also ensure that the community is able to accept their community in its recovered state.

Education

It is often said that the youth are a community's future. This cliché takes on new meaning when a community is faced with repairing a damaged or destroyed education infrastructure. Schools may be unusable; teachers may have been injured, killed, displaced, or have conflicting responsibilities; educational materials may have been lost or destroyed; and students may have been relocated far away from their schools.

According to Article 26 of the Universal Declaration of Human Rights adopted by the UN in 1948, everyone has a right to education. This right is not suspended during times of disaster. In fact, the need for education goes even further in times of disaster. Schools may be the best way to ensure that children remain safe. They are the most effective way to teach children new skills that are necessary in the post-disaster period, such as hygiene and safety. Schools help to free up parents so that they can either go to their job or attend to other relief needs. Finally, children are most likely to feel a sense of normalcy and therefore stay mentally healthy if they are given the chance to participate in something as familiar as school.

Governments have a responsibility to help provide temporary facilities, educators, and materials during the short term and to rebuild permanent facilities for the long term. Many nonprofit and multilateral agencies specialize in providing disaster education while long-term facilities are designed and constructed. Disasters may provide an opportunity for education to be modernized and otherwise improved, as there will be the chance to review and update the curriculum, to incorporate modern technology and practice into school design, and to provide occupational training to teachers.

Special Considerations in Recovery

Resisting the Urge to Return to "Normal"

The greatest obstacle that disaster managers face in the recovery phase is the community's urge to rebuild and return to its pre-disaster status—often referred to by victims as "normal." This sentiment will first emerge in the short-term phase as a drive to prove that, despite its consequences, the disaster did not defeat the victimized communities. Then, in the long-term recovery phase, as victims continue to live in a state of reduced quality of life (usually as a result of temporary housing, dependence on aid, and/or lost income, among other factors), they will want to return to their old life as quickly as possible simply to put an end to the inconveniences they are experiencing.

This overarching public sentiment will create tremendous pressure for disaster managers. The public outcry will be echoed, and even amplified, by the news media, which will focus on the most extreme cases of victim discomfort and state that disaster recovery is taking too long. Businesses that are losing valuable opportunities soon will join the chorus of disapproval. Pressure will begin to build on the shoulders of politicians at all government levels, who will respond by placing additional demands on the disaster managers.

Many people victimized by disasters feel that the answer to the recovery problem is simple—replace what was destroyed. The "lightning never strikes twice" mentality may tell them that they no longer need to worry, since the disaster finally occurred. However, the fact that the hazard event did occur and that a disaster did result is evidence that the community as previously existed was ill-prepared. Therefore, simply rebuilding to pre-disaster specifications would only retain any preexisting vulnerabilities the disaster exposed.

Recognizing That Recovery Is an Opportunity in Disguise

Despite the misery, destruction, and disruption disasters cause, it is often said that the recovery period presents an opportunity in disguise. This relates not only to the chance of increasing community resilience to future disasters but also to economic revitalization, urban improvement, rezoning, modernization, and many other areas. The spectacular nature of a disaster's aftermath, the wide scope of elements affected, and the attention and need placed upon recovery and reconstruction present a real opportunity to create a better, more resilient, and more successful community—an opportunity that would rarely exist otherwise. However, as was mentioned earlier, the pressure to rebuild as quickly as possible makes such an opportunity difficult to exploit.

During the pre-disaster period, the community may have analyzed their risk and even come up with a broad range of mitigation options. Due to expense or feasibility problems, they may have discarded many of these options. After a disaster, conditions change considerably. Budgets may swell with relief funding. Buildings that required very expensive retrofitting may have been destroyed, allowing for much cheaper "mitigation through design" to be performed. Residents of high-risk areas where housing should never have been built in the first place and subsequently was destroyed by the disaster may be more easily convinced to relocate or may be prevented from rebuilding. Unknown risks from unmapped or poorly understood hazards will now be easier to incorporate into development plans and thus avoid.

The post-disaster period can be one of the best times for a community to enhance its risk- and disaster-related statutory authority. During the recovery period, when the disaster is still confronting victims or is fresh in their memory, leaders will enjoy much greater success in enacting legislation and policy decisions that help the community to increase resilience and decrease vulnerabilities. The community may be willing to agree to new building code, zoning, and environmental policies that might result in higher building costs or taxes during this period, when the proverbial window of opportunity is "open."

Throughout the recovery process, recovery planners must be sure to align any recovery efforts with the community's needs and goals. This also is true for new opportunities. Communities may have already been planning improvements before the disaster occurred. In communities that developed with little or no planning, recovery can provide the rare opportunity to apply lessons learned on a grand scale, creating an end product that is much more conducive to the community's social and commercial activities and needs. Planners who allow community members to guide themselves through recovery and reconstruction will likely find a great deal of acceptance, enthusiasm, and success.

Examples of changes to community design that can reduce hazard vulnerability and be made in the recovery period include:

- Redistribute emergency resources (fire, police, emergency medical)
- Rezone to account for new hazard information
- Adjust building codes and ensure that all repairs and reconstruction are made to code
- Restrict building within zones of greatest risk (e.g., in the floodplain, on unstable ground, below landslide risk zones)
- Create natural fire breaks
- Design adequate evacuation routes
- Construct public buildings that can double as shelters
- Reduce population density
- Widen primary roads to alleviate pressure (for evacuation or emergency response)
- Address problems related to informal settlements in high-risk zones

Disaster managers and recovery planners can only capitalize on opportunities to reduce risk and improve the community if they are able to recognize their value and exploit them quickly. Examples include:

- The public, media, and government are likely to be much more receptive to information detailing disaster prevention, regardless of whether they were directly impacted themselves. The chance for policy, spending, and action on disaster mitigation and prevention measures is never as great as in the immediate aftermath of a disaster. The community, for the short term at least, will be very aware of their vulnerability and will be more likely to take action to reduce it than at any other time.
- The consequences of disasters initiate certain aspects of construction and community revitalization projects that previously may have been decided against or delayed due to cost or for other reasons. For instance, many old buildings slated for replacement may be destroyed or damaged beyond repair. Old infrastructure, which had been in need of updating, may be completely destroyed (such as aboveground power lines, old roads and bridges, or water and sewer pipes).
- The immediacy of victim needs will essentially "force" community leaders and other stakeholders to make difficult decisions about development that otherwise may have taken years to settle. This includes decisions related to disaster mitigation, such as buying out or relocating structures in the floodplain or building a new emergency management facility.
- More accurate hazard information becomes available from a variety of academic and professional sources that otherwise might not have been interested in the region. These experts will likely conduct their assessments with their own funding, but share results among planners.
- Technical assistance provided by the various national and international relief agencies that respond to the disaster will allow for more accurate assessments, and will increase the chance that newly constructed building stock and infrastructure will adequately handle future disaster events.
- Financial assistance, whether from government, private, or international sources, may be available to fund construction to a level of safety that might not be possible using regular, local funds.

- Land use regulations may help to prevent reconstruction on areas that previously had been found unsafe but upon which structures had already been built and could not legally be removed.
- Damaged or destroyed infrastructure, such as roads, utilities, or government buildings, may be rebuilt in safer locations, and with modern hazard-resistant design (NHRAIC, 2001).

Disaster managers and recovery planners must have the ability to recognize what is possible regarding risk reduction and must quickly apply these new lessons learned to the overall recovery guidance they develop. The Natural Hazards Research and Application Information Center (NHRAIC, 2001) reports that the ideal disaster recovery process is one in which the community proactively manages:

- Recovery and redevelopment decisions to balance competing interests so constituents are treated equitably and long-term community benefits are not sacrificed for short-term individual gains
- Multiple financial resources to achieve broad-based community support for holistic recovery activities
- Reconstruction and redevelopment opportunities to enhance economic and community vitality
- Environmental and natural resource opportunities to enhance natural functions and maximize community benefits
- Exposure to risk to a level that is less than what it was before the disaster

As mentioned, the recovery period is not limited to risk reduction alone. This period presents a perfect opportunity to right past wrongs; to fix existing problems; to rejuvenate old, failing, and dilapidated infrastructure and neighborhoods; and to inspire the community to take action like never before. Other quality of life issues that may be addressed include:

- Improving housing stock, increasing the safety of affordable housing, and increasing the overall value of property in the community
- Increasing the efficiency of transportation routes and traffic flow
- Increasing the quality of available health care within the community
- Greater public involvement in community planning and development
- Rebuilding schools, government buildings, utilities, and other facilities within the community to accommodate changes that have occurred since those facilities were first constructed
- Creating new green spaces by preventing reconstruction in high-risk areas, creating new areas for recreation and public enjoyment
- Reducing unemployment, at least in the short term, by hiring victims to participate in the reconstruction effort, and revitalizing the community through development so long-term unemployment is reduced as well
- Improving the quality of education, including facilities, staff training, curriculum, equipment, and student materials

For more examples of ways in which the quality of life of the community or country can be improved in the recovery period of a disaster, see Exhibit 7–10. For obstacles to recovery, see Exhibit 7–11.

EXHIBIT 7–10: RECOVERY STRATEGIES FOR ENHANCING QUALITY OF LIFE

Enhancing quality of life can start during disaster recovery. A community can start with the *situations* that exist after a disaster and pick and choose among the *options* for improving its quality of life and among the implementation *tools* available to help pursue each of those options to develop *strategies* that are specially tailored to its own needs. The situations and options listed below are not exhaustive; rather, they are meant to give an idea of the range of possibilities. Likewise, these sample strategies suggest ways in which some options and disaster-induced situations could be combined to help a community improve its quality of life.

Situation: Damaged transportation facilities
Recovery strategies to enhance quality of life:

- Rebuild to increase mobility. Circulation patterns should allow efficient and safe movement between home, work, and recreation, as well as effective evacuation. Rebuilding efforts should not threaten neighborhood integrity, historic and cultural resources, or environmental quality.
- Allow for alternative modes of transit such as walking and cycling. Create connecting paths and greenways for pedestrians and cyclists, with some common nodes for social interaction.
- Beautify the parking lots of public facilities. Upgrade outdoor parking lot facilities to integrate greening concepts and improve aesthetics. Community residents can be asked to compete in design competitions or tree planting and tree maintenance programs.
- Rebuild to enhance capacity. Increase the ability to bring people into a business district, and to move goods in and out of a community.
- Rebuild to improve functionality. Create a different circulation pattern; create and/or expand transit.
- Undo past mistakes and support redevelopment. Demolish an unneeded overhead freeway to re-establish a stronger urban pattern as a key element of economic revitalization of a district.
- Rebuild to promote more sustainable transportation systems. Change land use to promote higher density, mixed uses, and/or concentrated development in support of less auto-dependent transportation systems.
- Ask: Where are roadways and bridges being built? Will moving a road displace a neighborhood?
- Rebuild to improve resistance to damage. Older transportation facilities can be upgraded to more modern standards that make them more resistant to damage from floods, earthquakes, and other risks.
- Relocate, where feasible. In some cases, transportation facilities could be relocated or rerouted around hazard-prone areas.
- Reduce adverse impacts caused by transportation facilities. For example, certain roads and highways can act as dams during periods of flooding, obstructing the flow of runoff or floodwaters.
- Examine the impact of such facilities on encouraging development in hazard-prone locations. For instance, widening roads may actually stimulate additional development in risky areas.

Situation: Damaged public facilities
Recovery strategies to enhance quality of life:

- Make public facilities less vulnerable to future hazards. Move public facilities out of known hazard zones but first study the impact of their new locations on future growth and transportation patterns in the community.
- Enhance educational opportunities by rebuilding or upgrading schools. Repairs, modernization, and upgrades should focus not only on structural safety but also on energy efficiency.
- Enhance public facilities and access to them by designing or redesigning schools to be magnets for recreation, sports, and meetings. Ensure that schools have recreational facilities and meeting rooms to host sports tournaments and other activities.
- Rebuild to transform/expand school facilities in support of economic strategies.
- Upgrade public spaces to support economic revitalization. Create new sidewalks and street furniture and plant street trees to create a downtown "civic living room" to enhance the pedestrian experience and increase commercial activity.
- Locate new public uses into a damaged area. Establish a community college branch in a downtown area to expand activity and population. Establish a community center for displaced families and others to meet social goals and create higher activity levels in support of economic goals.
- Rebuild key economic facilities to improve economic and environmental functionality. Rebuild a port facility with state-of-the-art characteristics resulting in greater capacity, reduced energy consumption, restoration of environmental features, enhanced pollution controls, and disaster-resilient design.
- Ask: What are the impacts of redevelopment decisions on vulnerable populations? Does a setback mean the loss of land?
- Protect against future damage by making such facilities more resistant to damage. For example, elevate buildings above the flood height or build a berm to help keep out floodwaters.
- Relocate to a less vulnerable area.
- Avoid building new public facilities in hazard-prone areas.

Situation: Damaged utilities
Recovery strategies to enhance quality of life:

- Relocate critical facilities and equipment out of known hazard zones or retrofit the facilities so that hardship and disruption of services are avoided.
- Create new infrastructure that supports economic growth while incorporating sustainable features. Rebuild a damaged telecommunications system for increased capacity; establish storm water systems where none existed; increase capacities of water, wastewater, or power facilities to meet future economic needs; use disaster-resilient designs.
- Form partnerships with utility companies to upgrade the system. Add fiber optics or other advanced technologies in infrastructure when it is rebuilt.
- Safeguard power lines from damage by fallen trees by putting the lines underground.

(Continued)

EXHIBIT 7–10: RECOVERY STRATEGIES FOR ENHANCING QUALITY OF LIFE (CONTINUED)

- Move water or gas lines out of harm's way. For example, re-route utility lines around earthquake fault zones or floodplains.
- Protect existing facilities from damage, for example, by constructing berms around sewage treatment facilities located in floodplains.
- When planning to install new lines, identify the location of hazard-prone areas and try to avoid them.
- Build redundancy into the system. For example, be able to shift water or wastewater treatment capacity to treatment plants not located in hazard-prone areas.
- Develop plans to contain and treat spills from existing gas or wastewater treatment lines that may be damaged by natural disasters.

Situation: Damaged housing

Recovery strategies to enhance quality of life:

- Create disaster-resilient, affordable housing. Rezone parts of the community for affordable housing.
- Inventory damaged housing that has a history of abandonment and tax delinquency. Consider buyouts of these properties to eliminate eyesores and to reduce potential negative impacts on property values and potential health threats.
- Move toward energy-efficient buildings. Provide education forums and advice for home and business owners on techniques and funding sources to replace aging, damaged heating and cooling equipment with the latest techniques and equipment to lower costs.
- Provide public spaces for social interaction and recreation. Buy out homes in known danger zones and utilize the space as parkland, community gardens, or other public open spaces that will promote social interaction and recreation for all residents.
- Upgrade building codes so that new construction will be done to a higher standard.
- Create new housing opportunities to support area redevelopment. Establish new housing stock in a rebuilding area to support neighborhood-serving businesses.
- Create new housing stock to serve specialized needs in the economy.
- Create housing to attract or retain businesses. Establish housing near job centers and in keeping with the housing needs and preferences of workers.
- Improve neighborhoods to attract or retain businesses. Establish new schools or parks to improve neighborhood vitality. Upgrade housing that was not damaged but could benefit from higher levels of mitigation or quality.
- Relocate housing out of hazard zones. Create new public attractions such as parks and recreation facilities in flood-prone areas to mitigate a hazard and attract people into a business district.
- Ask: Has the community replaced a devastated section of housing (e.g., trailers) with the same, vulnerable housing?
- Ask: Is overcrowding resulting?
- Buy out or relocate damage-prone properties. Acquiring or relocating homes or businesses located in hazard-prone areas, particularly structures that have been damaged repetitively,

can help reduce the public costs of disasters, which include emergency services, evacuation, emergency shelters, debris removal, and the loss of tax revenues.

- Acquire vacant, hazard-prone property. Buying vacant property and prohibiting its development permanently reduce the risk of damage to those properties while providing additional open space, wildlife habitat, and recreation areas.
- Rebuild according to modern building codes; upgrade the local code if necessary. Typically, older buildings not built to modern standards are the ones that suffer the most from natural disasters. When rebuilding, make sure that structures comply with modern building codes that specify how to make buildings more resistant to damage from hurricanes, floods, wildfires, wind, or earthquakes. Educate builders about hazard-resistant provisions in the codes.

Situation: Damaged commercial/industrial facilities
Recovery strategies to enhance quality of life:

- Maintain employment opportunities and minimize economic disruption.
- Rebuild commercial buildings with enhanced business supporting features. Rebuild retail buildings to have increased floor-to-ceiling ratios, window/display area, and better floor layouts.
- Create interim commercial facilities. Build temporary retail spaces consolidating multiple businesses in shared facilities.
- Establish and/or improve mitigation features. Rebuild commercial/industrial facilities in flood-prone areas with elevated electrical elements and ability to seal water out in floods.

Situation: Environmental damage
Recovery strategies to enhance quality of life:

- Create or enhance natural resources and environmental features.
- Restore damaged environmental features in ways that support other economic goals. Consider adding improved public pedestrian access along the coastline to encourage tourism while repairing coastal erosion damage.
- Integrate natural features into business district recovery. Upgrade damaged river levees with improved walkway connections and linkages with a downtown commercial area.
- Establish new tourism opportunities based on interest in understanding natural systems. For instance, create an "earthquake park" focused around dramatic examples of faulting, liquefaction, or landslides.
- Establish memorials or tributes. Memorialize people or events in new green areas.
- Relocate and prohibit land use activities that are not safe for hazard-prone areas, including animal waste lagoons, animal production facilities, septic systems, hazardous waste facilities, junkyards, and sewage treatment plants.
- Maintain and restore mitigation functions of the natural environment. The natural environment can help mitigate the impacts of natural hazards. For example, wetlands and floodplains slow down and absorb excess water during storms and then slowly release the

(Continued)

EXHIBIT 7–10: RECOVERY STRATEGIES FOR ENHANCING QUALITY OF LIFE (CONTINUED)

stored water, thus reducing flooding downstream. Similarly, dunes help protect inland areas from the onslaught of storm-driven waves, and dense forests on steep slopes can reduce the risk of landslides.

- Protecting natural areas keeps people and buildings out of the path of natural hazards and maintains the natural capacity of the environment to attenuate disasters. In addition, protecting natural areas serves other purposes, such as preserving open space and wildlife habitat.

Situation: Disruption of health and safety

Recovery strategies to enhance quality of life:

- Use the opportunity to identify gaps in family services, social services, and health care facilities and ensure that emergency plans have defined strategies and policies for short- and long-term sheltering for residents with special needs.
- Create or update the community's inventory of housing locations of most vulnerable populations for evacuation and rescue purposes. Create maps that show locations of different population segments and their potential vulnerability to future hazards.
- Consider whether the staff in the health and social service sectors is representative of the wider community, especially with regard to spoken languages.
- Relocate and reuse medical facilities to support economic as well as health objectives. Relocate a damaged hospital while repairing and reusing the previous structure for mixed-use housing, commercial, or office uses.

Source: NHRAIC, 2001.

Ensuring Equity in Recovery

In studying how communities recover from disasters, it has been discovered that in the vast majority of situations the poor will bear a greater brunt of the disaster consequences and face much greater difficulty recovering than the wealthy. This is not much of a surprise, considering the resources available to the wealthy to ensure that risk is reduced before the disaster. For instance, the wealthy are much more likely to have purchased insurance, to have used disaster-resistant construction, to live in lower risk neighborhoods, and/or to be educated in how to reduce risk and acquire recovery benefits if needed.

In the recovery period, it will be contingent upon disaster managers and recovery planners to ensure that disaster recovery assistance is distributed equitably, and that opportunities are spread evenly throughout the community. Planners must take an active role in this effort, as the wealthy often have the means and know-how to receive their share of what is available, while the poor are much more likely to lack these qualities, preventing them from accessing all available assistance benefits.

Inequity in recovery goods and services is not limited to inequities in wealth, however. Cultural beliefs and practices may place certain groups at a disadvantage. Racism, caste systems, and bigotry can cause groups to suffer disproportionately. The disaster providers themselves may contribute to these discrepancies if they knowingly or unknowingly follow the cultural or other beliefs that cause them.

EXHIBIT 7–11: NINE OBSTACLES TO HOLISTIC RECOVERY

There are lots of obstacles to a successful recovery. Although they will not necessarily prevent recovery, they can slow the process down, and create sidetracks for the unaware. If they are ignored they can become barriers to achieving success.

The degree of damage inflicted upon the community. Decisions on whether to repair or replace buildings, and the processes by which each of these actions is conducted, will determine how disaster risk reduction is achieved. When facilities require full replacement, there are often more alternatives to correct poor decisions in the past than there would be if only slight repairs are needed.

Rules, regulations, and policies. Many times, disaster relief funding is provided contingent upon several rules. It will often be the planners' duty to work within the limits of those rules to maximize recovery potential. The rules, regulations, and policies that often accompany funding can alter priorities, limit opportunities, and curtail creative solutions.

Other "money" issues, such as property rights, development, insurance, land use, and substandard housing. These broadly connected issues can affect how and when communities make recovery decisions. For example, after a flood, a community may identify an opportunity to enhance economic development, natural resource protection, and the quality of life by limiting redevelopment in certain areas. The idea of establishing a riverfront park that combines flood loss reduction with a pedestrian/bicycle corridor and public access for picnicking, fishing, and boating is becoming commonplace. But communities are often surprised to discover that many owners of flooded homes not only want to return to their riverfront vistas, but also intend to take the opportunity to replace the structures with larger, more modern units. In other cases, damaged flood-prone property often represents the least desirable housing in the community due to its location, repetitive damage, and decreasing property values. Here, otherwise unaffected property owners may choose to "fight" any redevelopment plan, arguing that government should not help those that knowingly chose that risk to begin with.

The propensity to strive for "a return to normal." Proposed post-disaster changes in land use, building codes, densities, infrastructure, property ownership, and redevelopment plans always take time. This is often seen as an unnecessary delay in what otherwise would be a recovery "back to normal," and can be an obstacle to utilizing recovery opportunities for community improvement. It is at this point that the concept of pre-disaster planning for post-disaster redevelopment makes the most sense to everyone involved. People say, "If we'd only figured this out *before* the disaster, it would be so easy to rebuild and recover to an improved state—but now, since this all takes so long, maybe we'd be better off if we just put things back the way they were. Then we can look at making plans for recovering from the next disaster if we still want to."

A lack of awareness of what the true redevelopment possibilities are. People are not aware of how other communities have made substantial community improvements by using a disaster to initiate the process. Others are more concerned with their own personal world than with the "bigger picture" of community betterment, and it is difficult to change their primary focus without significant preplanning, coordination, leadership, political will, and some vision of an improved future.

(Continued)

EXHIBIT 7–11: NINE OBSTACLES TO HOLISTIC RECOVERY (CONTINUED)

The immediate change in the roles and procedures of local government officials. Post-disaster government roles, procedures, and priorities change, often requiring different mixes of skills from those to which officials are accustomed. Job functions change, workloads increase dramatically, and the work involves new players, new terminology, and even new structures, such as will likely be outlined in disaster response and recovery plans. Additionally, public scrutiny and political pressure reach new plateaus as local officials try to maintain the day-to-day functions that government normally provides. Confidence in government may be eroded during times of recovery as well, especially if the response was considered inadequate or slow, and such sentiment can be detrimental when planners attempt to guide risk reduction in private redevelopment.

Searching for the extraordinary solution to what appears to be an extraordinary problem. Most "extraordinary problems" are actually problems that governments deal with routinely: picking up debris, conducting building inspections, planning, permitting new development, managing grants and loans, and providing public information. The situation becomes extraordinary only because all these functions are happening at the same time, and with greater demands. Communities need to break down the problems into those that they are already accustomed to resolving, and then use the standard procedures to do so. Otherwise, the search for the extraordinary solution will only slow them down.

The lack of systematic communication between decision makers, various departments and agencies, and stakeholders. Communities can develop a mechanism that ensures that the principles of sustainability are incorporated into each and every decision faced every day by communities. There needs to be a comprehensive, ongoing, systematic series of checkpoints at which every decision is weighed against its impact on hazard vulnerability, economic vitality, environmental preservation, quality of life, and social justice. Unless this occurs, few decisions are analyzed to the extent that their direct and indirect consequences can be foreseen.

The lack of political will to "do the right thing." Addressing the needs of those impacted by disaster and determining methods to prevent a recurrence are often goals unintentionally sacrificed for the lack of appropriate support. When public decisions are swayed by the immediacy of constituent needs, preexisting conditions are often re-established. Local leaders must define a vision of the future, provide the direction to get there, and establish the priorities to make it happen. They must develop and create a will that is infectious among community politicians and constituents alike. Disaster recovery managers must juxtapose short-term and long-term community needs against the "quick and easy fix" or the perceived rights of select property owners. They must protect the health, safety, and welfare of the community from the desires, power, and influence of those who promote shortsighted solutions. They need to foster personal and community responsibility for recovery decisions that will affect their community for years to come.

Source: NHRAIC, 2001.

Examples of situations where inequity in recovery can occur include the following:

- Although the rich may be able to afford to rebuild according to new standards and regulations, the poor may not be able to afford the higher construction costs.

- The poor may not have the time to wait in line for goods and services or have access to information about available goods and services.

- Racism, poverty, or other social discriminations may prevent groups from access to goods and services. Locally hired disaster relief and recovery employees may discriminate against victims and give preferential treatment to some groups over others.

- Newly built communities may require higher rents, property values, or property taxes, such that the displaced can no longer afford to live where they did before.

- Certain groups, such as single women, the elderly, or the disabled, may be subject to cultural norms that prevent them from accessing goods and services.

Planners must be aware of the causes of inequity in order to prevent such practices. Simply hiring or working with a member of the local population is not enough to prevent these activities, because this local representative may believe in the views that cause the inequality. Only a wide, representational participatory process can ensure that relief and recovery resources are spread equitably across the affected population. The following groups tend to be particularly susceptible to inequity in relief (NHRAIC, 2001):

- *Low-income households.* How much money people have influences what type of housing they live in, whether they can engage in mitigation actions, and how long they take to recover. Income is probably the most difficult challenge to address because it is not based solely on an individual but is influenced by the larger economy, the availability of jobs, educational opportunity, and much more. Expenses also vary by location: rural places are cheaper to live in but have fewer job opportunities, whereas urban areas may be exceptionally costly, even for renters.

- *Single parents.* Single parents tend to have lower incomes and greater constraints placed upon their time. These constraints often restrict the family's access to many community recovery activities and resources.

- *Medically dependent (physical and psychological) or disabled.* People who rely on certain types of machinery (ranging from life support to oxygen) are often unable to participate in many recovery programs or access relief, increasing their risk. The mentally ill may experience increased fear and confusion due to increased stress or inability to access needed medication or treatment. In their altered mental state, they may be helpless and unable to access recovery assistance. The disabled are often marginalized in relief efforts when systems of relief distribution do not accommodate their special needs. For instance, shelters may not be built with ramps, limiting the movement of wheelchair-bound victims.

- *Language minority and illiterate.* Countries often have many languages but operate in a chosen or established "official language." Relief and reconstruction activities and information may all be conducted in that official language, or in a common international language such as English or Spanish. Those who are unable to speak that language will be at a disadvantage regarding warnings, relief information, instructions, and other factors (such as job opportunities). The same problem exists for the illiterate, who will not be able to benefit from any printed material describing benefits or providing instructions, or fill out application forms or register for assistance.

- *Elderly.* The elderly may be overlooked in considering holistic recovery because of the stereotypical notion that they are burdens and not producers for a community. They may experience difficulty with bureaucratic regulations after a disaster, not qualify for loans, or become disabled as a result of the event itself.

- *Homeless and street children.* The most rapidly growing homeless group is families. Little is known about what happens to them after disasters, although some researchers have found that familiar places (doorways, traditional shelters) are often ruined or permanently altered, further displacing the homeless. After housing stock is depleted by disaster, the homeless get pushed farther back in the line for a place to live. Although some homeless persons may find temporary shelter in disaster facilities, they typically go back to the streets when the facilities close.

- *The marginally housed.* People in informal settlements or living in doubled, tripled, or greater occupancy in a building may find themselves unable to benefit from relief and recovery because of their inability to prove residence.

- *Immigrants.* Residents without legal status or those with legal status but newly arrived in the country often face a complex array of obstacles, including language barriers, bureaucratic rules and regulations, fear of military assistance, fear of deportation, and not being included in long-term recovery efforts. Lack of respect for religious customs can also contribute to social inequities. Recent immigrants from the Middle East, for example, may follow religious norms of modesty and separation of the sexes that usually are not accommodated in emergency shelters and may influence who participates in community activities.

- *Transients, newcomers, and tourists.* People who pass through, stay temporarily, or have recently arrived in a community may not hear warnings, know where to take shelter, or have resources immediately available to them. Communities must plan to reduce the vulnerability of this population, particularly in communities with large tourism industries.

- *Isolated households, farms, and ranches.* Families living in remote and/or rural areas often face great difficulty receiving information about relief assistance or acquiring the actual assistance and supplies. Farmers and ranchers may face continued stock mortality after an event and may find themselves caring not only for themselves and their family but also for their animals that need food, water, and medical treatment.

- *Racial and ethnic minorities.* An extensive review of research studies on race, ethnicity, and disasters found that minorities experienced longer recoveries due to lower incomes, savings, and insurance; experienced differences in access to insurance; and used aid and relief organizations differently from what was expected by the predominantly Anglo emergency management sector (Fothergill et al., 1999). Lower class members within formal or informal caste systems have also been shown to be affected by disaster relief and recovery operations, even when efforts to circumvent class issues are conducted. Recovery organizations must be certain that they have a strong grasp of these culturally based issues and are able to plan accordingly.

- *Children.* Society tends to be adult-oriented. Children are completely dependent upon adults for their safety and security, as well as for their feeding, care, and education. Many relief and recovery systems assume that children will be cared for by the parents and neglect to directly consider their needs. However, the care system for many children breaks down during disasters, and they are left to fend for themselves in a system that does not account for their needs. Involving children and teenagers in community recovery activities and planning not only helps to ensure they receive adequate services and care but also facilitates healing and promotes lifelong civic participation.

- *Lesbian and gay households.* Little is known about homosexual families after disasters other than to speculate that the hostility they experience every day may be exacerbated. Some groups and organizations may deter aid because of a person's sexual orientation. It may not be safe for a local teacher, for example, to be open about her sexual orientation even if her lifetime partner was killed or injured in the disaster.

- *Battered women.* Incidents of relationship violence may increase after disasters. Certainly, shelters report higher numbers of and increased inabilities to deal with post-traumatic stress.

- *Future generations.* It goes without saying that the people of the future are not able to voice their needs and desires in today's communities. But the components and characteristics of social and intergenerational equity rest on "not precluding a future generation's opportunity for satisfying lives by exhausting resources in the present generation (Mileti, 1999)."

Moving the Whole Community

On a number of occasions, it has been determined in a disaster's aftermath that the only viable option for reducing future disaster risk was to relocate the entire community. Examples of cities that have been moved in the past and are doing fine today include:

- Chernobyl, Ukraine—nuclear accident (1986)
- Wurang and Babi Islands, Indonesia—earthquake and tsunami (1992)
- Valdez, Alaska—earthquake (1967)
- Valmeyer, Mississippi—flood (1993)
- Gediz, Turkey—earthquake (1970)
- Dagara, India—earthquake (2001)
- Kiruna, Sweden—land subsidence (ongoing; see Exhibit 7–12)

EXHIBIT 7–12: RELOCATION OF KIRUNA

The town of Kiruna lies in the extreme north of Sweden. The area has been inhabited for thousands of years, but it was an advance in iron mining technology that resulted in the creation of an organized community. Kiruna, which was founded in 1900 with a population under 250, blossomed to over 25,000 in the mid-1970s as demand for iron ore increased. Kiruna also enjoyed a healthy income from tourism, given the 300,000 people that visit the area each year to see the northern geography and to visit the famous Ice Hotel. However, the ongoing mining operations have begun to take an environmental toll on the community. Underground extraction, which began in the 1960s, has left expansive voids directly under the inhabited parts of the community, compromising the stability of the soil. This has resulted in cracks and slumps on the surface, and bit by bit entire sections of town are collapsing into the voids below. Rather than end the mining—which is the lifeblood of the community and a major source of the world's iron resources—a decision was made in 2004 to relocate the town and its remaining 18,000 residences elsewhere to avoid the damages associated with increased land subsidence as mining continues.

Source: Abrahams, 2009.

Such a measure may seem like an appealing solution in any situation in which a catastrophic disaster has occurred and it is expected to recur. However, moving an entire community is a complicated undertaking. The following lists several reasons why this measure is so rarely employed:

- It is extremely difficult to locate safer sites within close proximity to the original community.
- Substantial infrastructure may still be intact or repairable.
- The cost to relocate is usually higher than the cost to rebuild.
- People have strong attachments to a specific location and refuse to move.
- It may be difficult or impossible to recreate livelihoods in the new location.

Conclusion

Disaster recovery is almost always a long and arduous process that is more often measured in decades than in months or years. As this chapter described, communities may never recover if not provided proper assistance. Fortunately, with pre-disaster preparedness measures and ample post-disaster international assistance, even countries that experience the most catastrophic damages can enjoy some level of recovery. Those that recover and reduce the original hazard risk may even find themselves stronger as a result.

References

Abrahams, T. (2009). The city that had to move. *Wired,* May 26. http://www.wired.co.uk/wired-magazine/archive/2009/05/features/the-city-they-had-to-move?page=all.

Barenstein, J. (2005). *A comparative analysis of six housing reconstruction approaches in post-earthquake Gujarat.* Scuola Universitaria Profesionale della Svizzera Italiana. http://www.odi.org.uk/hpg/meetings/SUPSI.pdf.

Borton, J. (1996). *An account of coordination mechanisms for humanitarian assistance during the international response to the 1994 crisis in Rwanda.* Tokyo: Advanced Development Management Program, Institute of Comparative Culture, Sophia University.

ByPeople. (2005). *Housing in Asia.* Newsletter of the Asian Coalition for Housing Rights, No. 16 (August).

GAO. (2009). *Disaster recovery: Experiences from past disasters offer insights for effective collaboration after catastrophic events.* GAO Report 09-811.

Housing Reconstruction After Conflict and Disaster. (2003). *Humanitarian Practice Network*, No. 43 (December). http://www.odihpn.org/documents/networkpaper043.pdf.

International Strategy for Disaster Reduction (ISDR). (2005). *Living with risk: A global view of disaster reduction initiatives.* Geneva: The United Nations.

Kahn, J. (2004). CAT bonds provide shelter from disaster. *New York Times* (September 19), Section 3, Page 5.

Macrae, J. (2002). *The new humanitarianisms: A review of global trends in humanitarian action.* London: Overseas Development Institute.

Mileti, D. (1999). *Disasters by design: A reassessment of natural hazards in the United States*. Washington, DC: Joseph Henry Press.

Miller, S., & Keipi, K. (2005). *Strategies and financial instruments for disaster risk management in Latin American and the Caribbean*. Washington, DC: Inter-American Development Bank.

Natural Hazards Research and Application Information Center (NHRAIC). (2001). *Holistic disaster recovery: Ideas for building local sustainability after a natural disaster*. University of Colorado and the Public Entity Risk Institute. www.colorado.edu/hazards/holistic_recovery/.

Oliver, P. (1987). Cultural aspects of housing in seismic areas. In: *Earthen and low strength masonry buildings in seismic areas. Conference Proceedings*, Ankara, Turkey; Barakat, Sultan: METU, 2003.

Patterson, J. (1999). *A review of the literature and programs on local recovery from disaster*. Fairfax, VA: Public Entity Risk Institute.

Pflug, G., Mechler, R., Saldana, S., Warner, K., & Bayer, J. (2002). *The IIASA model for evaluating ex ante risk management*. Presentation at the 2nd Meeting of the Disaster Network of the Inter-American Development Bank, Regional Policy Dialogue, Washington, DC, May 23–24.

Public Safety and Emergency Preparedness Canada. (2005). *Disaster financial assistance arrangements*. Fact sheet. www.psepc.gc.ca/prg/em/dfaa/index-en.asp.

Rolfe, J., & Britton, N. (1995). Organisation, government and legislation: Who coordinates recovery? In *Wellington after the quake: The challenge of rebuilding cities*. Wellington, NZ: Wellington Earthquake Commission and the Centre for Advanced Engineering.

Spangle, W., & Associates, Inc. (1991). *Rebuilding after earthquakes: Lessons from planners*. Portola Valley, CA: Author.

Twigg, J. (2002). *Technology, post-disaster housing reconstruction and livelihood security*, Benfield Hazard Research Center, Working Paper 15. http://www.abuhrc.org/Publications/Working%20Paper%2015.pdf.

UN-HABITAT. (2007). Twenty First Session of the Governing Council, 16–20 April, Nairobi, Kenya. In *Field report: Building back better in Pakistan*. http://irp.onlinesolutionsltd.net/assets/submissions/200909010544_pakistanearthquakeshelterunhabitat2007.pdf.

U.S. Office of Foreign Disaster Assistance (OFDA). (2001). *FY 2001 annual report*. United States Agency for International Development (USAID). www.usaid.gov/our_work/humanitarian_assistance/disaster_assistance/publications/annual_reports/index.html.

Willits-King, B., & Harvey, P. (2005). *Managing the risks of corruption in humanitarian relief operations*. UK Department of International Development. Overseas Development Institute. www.odi.org.uk/hpg.papers/corruption_dfid_disclaimer_added.pdf.

World Bank Group. (2010). *Haiti remittances key to earthquake recovery*, 2007; IFAD, 2007. http://www.ifad.org/remittances/maps/brochure.pdf.

World Health Organization (WHO). (2005). *Disasters, disability, and rehabilitation*. Geneva: Department of Injuries and Violence Prevention.

Participants: Governmental Disaster Management Agencies

Introduction

Citizens throughout the world look to their governments—elected or not, nationally, regionally, or locally based—to provide safety and security. Chapter 1 described how communities and governments have developed systems and structures to fulfill this responsibility as it pertains to disaster management, utilizing mitigation, preparedness, response, and recovery. The success with which governments are able to perform these functions determines to what extent they can reduce hazard risk for their citizens.

In general, the evolution of emergency management capacity in any country begins with the most pressing need—response. Response, at least in the short term, is distinguished among the four emergency management functions as having the greatest immediate potential for saving lives and for being the most time-sensitive. Even in the smallest village, spontaneous response mechanisms will arise as a result of people's survival instinct and collective community concern. Almost all nations have at least a limited emergency response capacity that presumably can address the most common hazard risks affecting their citizens. Unfortunately, outside of the industrialized world, very few nations have developed the capacity to address the more comprehensive needs of hazard and risk management. Whether through sheer negligence, ignorance, or conflicting priorities, many developing countries take little or no emergency planning and preparedness actions, disregard recognized mitigation opportunities, and take no measures to consider how they would recover from major events. What ultimately results is an elementary and, thus, inadequate emergency management capacity that is quickly overcome by even minor disaster events.

Thanks to international advocacy and the actions of the United Nations, national government development agencies', and many nongovernmental organizations' (NGOs), recognition of the importance of mitigation, preparedness, and recovery planning is rapidly growing. Both rich and poor countries are working hard to increase their ability to reduce their hazard risk before emergencies begin and are educating their citizens to take action on the personal level. National governments are even partnering to increase their collective hazard risk reduction potential. But, as shown by events like the December 26, 2004, tsunami in Asia, the 2005 Hurricane Katrina in the United States, and most notably, the 2010 earthquake in Haiti, there is still a long way to go before governments, rich or poor, have fully tackled the emergency management problem.

This chapter explores governmental emergency management structures from two very different vantage points. First, it will explain how government emergency management agencies address disasters within their own borders, and how they ensure their citizens' safety and security. Several of the many ways in which this capacity may be structured within individual countries will also be detailed. Second, it will look at the tools and processes through which governments lend assistance to each other in times of need; in other words, the point at which disasters become international.

Governmental Emergency Management Structures

The systems and tools that governments have available to address hazard risks in their communities are relatively universal throughout the world. Although each country's emergency management organizations and systems have developed independently from a variety of sources, vast institutional sharing between countries has created an overall standardization of types of emergency management organizations, most notably in the area of first response. Additionally, globalization has facilitated the standardization of practices, protocols, and equipment used by emergency management organizations.

This section defines and details the various components of emergency management systems that exist in most countries of the world. Although certain factors—wealth, technical expertise, government type, and specific risk profile—contribute to defining how agencies are organized and equipped, their fundamental missions are almost identical. These agencies include:

- Fire departments
- Law enforcement agencies
- Emergency management (civil protection) agencies
- Emergency medical services
- The military

A range of other peripheral organizations and agencies also participate in emergency management activities to a varying degree, and these are discussed at the end of this section.

Emergency Management Participants

Fire Departments

Fire departments (also known as the "fire brigade" or "fire service") are the most common emergency management structure in local communities throughout the world. This makes perfect sense, because fire is the most common hazard communities face on a daily basis (FEMA, 2004). The earliest fire suppression services were singular in function, but over time, many nations' fire departments have expanded their abilities to address a wider range of both regular and rare hazards including:

- Fire suppression (structural, brushfire, wildfire, hazardous material fire)
- Fire and arson investigation
- Rescue (urban, swift water, wilderness, cave, airborne, alpine, dive, crack and crevice)
- Vehicle extraction
- Warning issuance

- Terrorism (actual or threatened) response
- Hazardous materials response and cleanup
- Fire and structural safety inspections
- Permits
- Prevention
- Training
- Public relations
- Disaster response coordination
- Emergency medical services
- Emergency management

Fire departments may be organized at the local, regional (e.g., county or province), or national levels. How a fire department is structured often depends on whether the fire service personnel are paid and the type of existing government. The three kinds of fire department organizational levels, and examples of countries employing each type, are provided below:

- Local organizational structure (Canada, Germany, United States)
- Regional organizational structure (Australia, UK)
- National organizational structure (Spain, France, Hong Kong)

Fire departments' needs are driven by both community risk and funding access. The following factors determine fire risk likelihood: individual cooking and heating practices; outdoor burning practices; housing materials and design; population density; industrial activities; climate; vegetation; availability of water; and topography. Funding sources and levels differ from country to country, but rarely exist at levels sufficient to fully address recognized fire risk and meet all of a fire department's needs, including:

- *Personnel.* A fire department depends on an available staff of dedicated, trained employees. Fire departments may be all volunteer, part paid, or fully paid. Most countries do not have paid volunteer fire services outside of larger urban centers because of light demand for emergency services. Most firefighters work part time, often reporting to work only when called in for emergencies. In the United States, for example, over 70% of firefighters work on a volunteer basis (U.S. Department of Labor, 2004). In cities, however, the number of emergency events is much greater and more involved training is required to address the variety of emergencies seen on a regular basis, so full-time, paid fire departments are the norm.
- *Training.* To be effective, firefighters must be trained to address the community's recognized hazards. Many governments operate regional or national training centers to ensure a national standard of proficiency, though the majority of firefighters trains locally. Web sites of various national firefighter academies include:
  - Australia (Queensland): www.fire.qld.gov.au/about/training.asp
  - UK: www.fireservicecollege.ac.uk/
  - United States: www.usfa.fema.gov/training/nfa/

- *Equipment.* Fire departments depend on a wide range of basic and technical equipment to conduct fire suppression, rescue, emergency medical, and other services. The primary categories of equipment used by fire departments include:
  - *Apparatus.* A fire apparatus is a vehicle specially designed for the firefighters' needs. There are several different categories of fire apparatuses, including the fire engine, that are designed to pump water: a fire truck, which fights fires but does not contain onboard water; a ladder truck, which allows access above fires or to high-rise structures; a snorkel truck, which raises hoses high above fires; a floodlight truck, which provides illumination for nighttime emergencies; a search-and-rescue truck; a paramedic (medical) truck; a command vehicle; a hazardous material response truck; a mobile laboratory; and an equipment (mostly hoses) transport vehicle.
  - *Firefighting equipment.* In addition to the apparatus, firefighters depend on a full range of equipment to suppress fires. This equipment includes extinguishers, axes, hooks, ladders, chemical suppressants, breathing apparatus, emergency alarms, and illumination.
  - *Personal protective equipment (PPE).* Firefighters must regularly enter very hazardous environments. Several types of PPE have been developed to protect them. They can be used to protect against extreme temperatures (high or low); a lack of oxygen; smoke; chemical, biological, or radiological hazards; noise; or caustic liquids.
  - *Rescue equipment.* A major part of most firefighters' duties includes rescue from vehicles, structures, water, and other wilderness or outdoor locations. Rescue equipment includes cutting tools, spreading tools, impact tools, ladders, ropes, harnesses, shoring equipment, and illumination.
- *Communications.* Effective fire departments rely upon three different forms of communication. The first is the emergency notification system, which enables the public to inform the fire department of an emergency. The most common system is an emergency telephone number, so the public can dial a simple, well-publicized number to quickly reach emergency services. In Europe this number is 1-1-2 (Exhibit 8–1); in Canada and the United States it is 9-1-1. (See Appendix 8–1 for a list of emergency numbers from around the world.) Unfortunately, these systems can be costly to establish and maintain, so many poor cities and countries are unable to utilize this efficient emergency management resource. The second communications system is the use of radios, which allow responders to talk to each other and to their command center. The third system is one that allows responders to communicate with the public. This may be as simple as a megaphone or as complex as a reverse emergency telephone system or a system of radios that can be remotely activated by fire department officials.
- *Facilities.* Fire department facilities are strategically placed buildings where personnel and equipment are located until called on to respond to an emergency. Fire department equipment requires a considerable amount of maintenance and cleaning, as well as safe storage, and the facility must be designed to accommodate these needs. The facility's location will determine response times to various points throughout the community, and its selection must take into consideration point-to-point travel impediments such as topographical or hydrological obstacles.
- *Information.* Fire department information needs are extensive and range from notification to assessment of risk and damages to demographic and settlement change within the community. The utility of this information depends on the quality of the source, which may be poor in many developing countries.

EXHIBIT 8–1: EUROPE'S 112 EMERGENCY NUMBER (2010 FACT SHEET)

Why 112?

As European citizens travel more often to other countries of the European Union (EU), for business or holidays, a single emergency number throughout the EU is of great value. Citizens no longer need to remember several emergency numbers, but only 112. Some Member States (Denmark, Finland, the Netherlands, Portugal, Romania, Malta, and Sweden) have introduced 112 as their main emergency number, while in most Member States, 112 operates alongside national emergency numbers.

What happens when you call 112?

People calling 112 are connected to an operator. Depending on the national civil protection system, the operator will either deal with the request directly or transfer it to the appropriate emergency service (ambulance, fire brigade, police, etc.). In many cases, operators are able to answer in more than one language. Each Member State is responsible for the organization of its own emergency services, including the response to 112 and to national emergency calls.

What are the EU rules on 112?

The 2002 EU rules require that 112 is available from fixed and mobile phones free of charge, that calls are appropriately answered and handled, that information on the location of the caller is made available to emergency services, and that EU countries inform citizens of 112. The EU telecoms rules of December 2009 strengthened the 112 provisions by requiring quicker provision of caller location information, extending 112 access obligations for certain VoIP providers, prompting to raise awareness of travelers, and improving access to 112 for people with disabilities. Moreover, the Roaming Regulation of July 2009 provided that citizens should receive information about 112 by short message service (SMS) when they travel across the EU.

Who has heard about 112?

A survey published in February 2010 showed that nine out of ten EU citizens found it useful to have a single emergency number everywhere in the EU. However, two-thirds of respondents to the survey believed that people are not adequately informed about 112, which is a call for further action by national authorities. Even where people recognize 112 as a national emergency number, three out of four are not aware they can call this number from anywhere in the EU. In the Czech Republic, Luxembourg, Poland, Slovakia, and Finland, more than half of the population know about 112. However, Italy, Greece, and the UK continue to have the lowest awareness levels in the EU and less than 10% of citizens know about 112. There was a modest increase of awareness at the EU level compared to the previous year—from 24% in 2009 to 25% in 2010. In Belgium Slovakia, Poland, Latvia, and Hungary citizens are significantly more aware of 112 as the EU-wide emergency number than in 2009. In February 2009, the European Commission, the European Parliament, and the Council declared 11 February the European 112 Day to spread the word about the single emergency number. The European 112 Day will be celebrated each year with the organization of awareness raising and networking activities. On 11 February 2010, the European 112 Day was celebrated throughout the EU with different activities, including the release of a 112 anthem in Romania and the distribution of a 112 eBook at schools in Slovakia.

(Continued)

EXHIBIT 8–1: EUROPE'S 112 EMERGENCY NUMBER (2010 FACT SHEET) (CONTINUED)

The role of the European Commission

The European Commission monitors the functioning of 112 in Member States and will take legal action if necessary. For instance, it launched legal action against Italy as the emergency centers are not yet able to determine the location of the person calling 112 from mobile phones. The Commission is also co-financing projects such as REACH112, which aims at implementing new ways of accessing emergency services, particularly for disabled users. It is also supporting e-Call, which is an in-car technology that can call the emergency services in case of an accident, using 112 to send accident data, including the car's location. The Commission will continue to play an active role in promoting 112 and outlining best practices. It has launched a Web site in six languages, which includes an interactive quiz for children, to inform citizens about 112 and to encourage best practices among the 27 EU Member States.

Source: European Commission, 2010.

- *Authority.* Fire department officials need the statutory authority to prevent and respond to fires. Fire officials may be given the power to close down businesses that do not comply with accepted fire codes or to refuse occupancy to public or private structures that have not been constructed to fire safety standards. Firefighters may need to impose restrictions on movement or facilitate evacuations, both of which require preexisting statutory authority.

Law Enforcement

Police departments (or "constabularies") are government-sanctioned entities responsible for maintaining law and order within the community. Police (and other law enforcement departments) are often part of the emergency management function at the local level. Although crime fighting is the police's primary responsibility, they are often an integral component of a community's emergency response system. Law enforcement emergency management responsibilities may include:

- Disaster scene security (see Figure 8–1)
- Warning issuance
- Security at critical facilities
- Search and rescue
- Crime fighting
- Crowd control
- Traffic control
- Bomb removal and disposal
- Assessment
- Investigations

FIGURE 8–1 Poor scene security, such as occurred at this 2007 Bangkok, Thailand, hotel fire, can place many civilians at needless risk and can hinder the access of emergency responders.

Although police departments are often centralized and managed at the national government level (as in France), many governments (especially federalized systems, such as in the United States) maintain local police forces. Still others, such as Canada, maintain a mix of organizational police forces (the Royal Canadian Mounted Police have national jurisdiction, while three provinces and several cities maintain their own local forces). In centralized systems, police officers may be based within their local communities or assigned to communities other than their own.

Police forces have traditionally enjoyed more secure and greater funding than other first-response officials, including the fire and emergency medical departments.

Emergency Management (Civil Protection)

Emergency management performs mitigation, preparedness, response and recovery planning, and coordination for large-scale events. The field of emergency management was practically non-existent until the civil defense days of the 1950s, when the governments of many industrialized countries began to make formal preparations for nuclear war. These systems, often called "Civil Protection," helped to prepare communities by building shelters, educating the public, and training first responders.

Over time, offices of civil protection began to address other catastrophic hazards. A few agencies even began to assume response and recovery coordination functions. Today, most countries maintain some form of civil protection or emergency management office at the central government level, which addresses mitigation of and preparedness for major disasters. Several of these national-level offices have developed the capacity to offer response and recovery assistance to disasters as well, usually in a supportive fashion rather than leading the response. All smaller, more routine emergency events are usually left to police, fire, and emergency medical responders designated to a specific area.

At the local and regional levels, the fire department or the police department handles emergency management planning and coordination, although many major cities have created government offices dedicated to emergency management practice. The field of emergency management has experienced tremendous "professionalization" in the past two decades, as practitioners have gone from having little formal education to earning specialized master's and doctorate degrees in the field.

Emergency Medical Services

Emergency medical services, often called "EMS" or "ambulance service," is a specialized form of medical care performed at the scene of the disaster or emergency event. EMS personnel (or emergency medical technicians; EMTs) are highly trained professionals who offer medical assistance greatly exceeding basic first aid. EMTs stabilize victims for transport to a hospital where better equipment and conditions are present.

Although many police and fire officials are trained to provide first aid and medical assistance, EMS organizations are usually trained and equipped to go beyond the basics, and may even be certified to perform invasive procedures or to administer a range of drugs. Two levels of care may be offered by EMS agencies: basic life support (BLS; usually noninvasive) and advanced life support (ALS; certified to perform invasive procedures).

Nations' EMS systems differ in their level of training, availability of funding, and quality of equipment. A further difference is the general mode of operation the organizations assume in response to emergency events. Two general philosophies guide the actions EMS officials take when they encounter a victim in the field and, likewise, guide their levels of training and equipment. These two philosophies are known as:

- *Stay and play (pre-hospital advanced life support)*. In this form of treatment, EMTs provide as much medical assistance as possible to stabilize and treat victims before transporting them to the appropriate facility. Vehicles and teams are heavily equipped with much of what would be found in a hospital emergency room to limit the amount of time between the event and when victims receive medical care.
- *Scoop and run*. Agencies that employ "scoop and run" treatment try to get victims to the hospital or other medical facility as quickly as possible. They believe that the victims' best chance of survival depends on reaching an emergency room within 1 hour of the actual accident. The goal is to have victims in transit to the hospitals within 10 minutes of their arrival.

In most countries, EMS services are private and charge victims a fee for their services. They may be publicly funded and associated with a hospital or a fire department, or be an independent public service. The vast majority of EMS officials are volunteers.

The Military

Almost every country includes the military in their overall disaster management planning and operations process. Although most democratic governments hesitate to utilize their military resources to address domestic issues, these national defensive forces are best suited in many ways to meet the needs required when responding to disasters. They have secure budgets; specialized equipment and a trained and quickly deployable workforce; are self-sufficient; and have a highly organized, hierarchical structure (see Exhibit 8–2).

The connection between the military and emergency management goes beyond mere coincidence or convenience for many countries. As will be described in greater detail in the section Organizational Structures, many modern emergency management structures that exist today are still rooted in civil defense. Emergency management grew out of a defensive need, and the military has been involved throughout the course of that evolutionary process. As such, their status as a valuable resource is widely recognized and often seen as the ultimate last resort.

Nations' primary concern when involving military assets in disaster response is that of authority. Military forces work with a command structure that can be at odds with the chain of command outlined in most emergency response plans. Military training optimizes behavior appropriate in hostile, foreign environments, so civilian–military interface during disasters can quickly become contentious if the proper mechanisms and training are not in place to guide such action and prevent conflict.

The University of Wisconsin's Disaster Management Center (1987) has identified several issues that must be addressed when disaster response involves the armed forces:

1. Military resources are best suited for high-intensity, short-term assignments. Military departments often will be unwilling to dedicate their forces for extended periods because of conflicting defense-related activities.
2. The military is likely to adapt disaster response and recovery needs to fit more closely with its own training, abilities, and operations. Actions that may be more appropriate but are not a normal function of the military (such as building temporary housing, as opposed to creating a tent city) are likely to be disregarded in favor of the actions that the military is most well-suited to perform.
3. Emergency managers may be unable to maintain control of the situation if military commanders begin to guide forces according to their own agenda (rather than that of the emergency

---

EXHIBIT 8–2: BRAZILIAN MILITARY DEPLOYED TO LEAD DENGUE EPIDEMIC FIGHT

In 2008, the government of Brazil deployed the army in Rio de Janeiro to combat a dengue fever outbreak when confusion arose about who was in charge of managing the emergency domestically. At the point that the military was deployed, more than 45,000 had contracted the disease, a rate of contraction several times the annual average. The military was able to quickly set up three military field hospitals in centralized locations in Rio, which almost immediately eased the shortage of hospital beds that had persisted and relieved the pressure placed on emergency rooms packed with dengue victims.

Source: Associated Press, 2008.

management agency). The military may be unwilling to take certain orders and, likewise, may be unwilling to participate in a consensus-based process.

4. In countries where military personnel have a reputation for corruption or abuse of power, or have not had adequate training in humanitarian operations, disaster victims may be unreceptive, distrustful, or fearful of them, which may lead to response inefficiencies or secondary disasters (see Exhibit 8–3).

EXHIBIT 8–3: 2004 TSUNAMI GIVES ACEH (INDONESIA) TROOPS NEW ROLE

In the Indonesian province of Aceh, military personnel start their days on the parade ground, preparing for action. Each soldier has a rifle slung across his back. But the rubber boots and facemasks are not exactly standard military issue. These men are not planning an offensive strike, but leading the cleanup operation in the wake of the earthquake and tsunami that devastated this region on December 26, 2004.

And even for these battle-hardened troops—more used to fighting separatist Acehnese rebels than carrying out aid work—it is a harrowing task. Sergeant Joko Songkono was out on patrol when the earthquake hit. His truck was almost turned over by the force of the tremor, but he survived. Many of his friends were not so lucky. Like most of the soldiers in Aceh, Joko Songkono was sent to the province to fight separatist rebels from the Free Aceh Movement (Gam), but he has spent most of the past three weeks collecting dead bodies. "Even now the rebels are still a threat. They have bases in the hills over there. We need to be careful—they are still around," he said. "Our mission was to fight the rebels, not to do humanitarian work. I never expected to be doing this," he said.

The latest phase of what has been a long-running separatist conflict in Aceh began in May 2003, when an internationally backed peace process fell apart. The fighting since then has been brutal, and both sides have committed abuses. Indonesian soldiers are feared and mistrusted by local people in Aceh—an image that the military is now trying to change. One soldier, Renaldi, his camouflage uniform spattered with dirt, said he was proud of the work he was doing to clear wreckage from a school. "Now we're helping people directly. I hope this disaster will bring us closer to the locals," he said.

So could this catastrophe be a chance for the military to improve its image? Opinions seem to be divided.

"I've changed my opinion of the army," one woman said. "Before things were bad because of the fighting. But now we see that the soldiers have come forward to help Aceh." But other Acehnese are more skeptical. "It's all just the same, there's no change at all," one man said. "They just walk about the city, but still shops are being looted all the time. It's like the soldiers are just pretending." Cynicism runs deep in this traumatized province. Before the earthquake struck, Aceh was virtually cut off from the outside world. The Indonesian military was in control and it did not want outsiders scrutinizing the way it conducted its war with the rebels.

But now, the air is filled with the noise of helicopters flown in by foreign troops. On the ground, foreign aid workers and journalists roam areas which used to be off limits. Indonesian soldiers may be at the forefront of humanitarian operations for now, but many local people are already wondering what will happen when the eyes of the world finally turn away.

Source: Harvey, 2005.

In countries where a complex humanitarian emergency is unfolding due to internal conflict or where a natural disaster has occurred in the midst of an active war, the military's involvement in the response may be either positive or negative. If the affected population is considered the enemy, the military may take action to prevent humanitarian assistance from reaching them. This is especially true in situations of genocide or ethnic cleansing, because any humanitarian assistance would fundamentally oppose the belligerent goals of that military force. The UN Office for the Coordination of Humanitarian Affairs writes:

> *The suffering inflicted on innocent civilians is aggravated by restrictions on humanitarian access. Indeed, humanitarian access to aid-dependent civilian populations is often restricted or denied altogether as a political bargaining chip and means of imposing even greater suffering on civilians. There is an increasing need to re-examine approaches to security of humanitarian activities in light of the changing environment. The targeting of aid workers, which is often planned and deliberate, closes humanitarian space and jeopardizes relief programmes. In twenty current conflict zones, humanitarian access is restricted, condemning civilian populations to protracted and unmitigated suffering. The risks for civilians are exacerbated even further by the proliferation of small arms and light weapons and their illicit sale or supply to armed groups or militias via porous borders and lax regulations, combined with the attractive economies of war that control of rich natural resources offers. (UNOCHA, 2005)*

However, if the military is willing to cooperate in the humanitarian efforts, especially in situations of cross-border conflict, they may be the only source of much needed physical protection for humanitarian workers, in addition to the source of information about dangerous territory. More information on civil–military cooperation will be provided in Chapter 9.

Other Resources

A full range of players work alongside the traditional disaster management agencies discussed earlier. The ability or appropriateness of these actors to participate in the process is closely connected to the individual characteristics of each community. Governments use a range of titles to describe these departments, many of which perform the same or similar activities despite differences in nomenclature. These offices may exist at the local, regional, or national levels.

These other resources include:

- *Department (Ministry) of Public Works.* This department often has responsibility for publicly owned utilities. It may be involved in decreasing utility companies' vulnerability to disasters, preparing citizens for accidents that involve utilities (e.g., loss of services, secondary negative consequences if the utilities were damaged), responding to incidents that affect the utilities, or helping to rebuild infrastructure after a disaster. Because of its regular use of tractors and other heavy machinery, public works is often involved in post-disaster debris clearance, cleanup, and disposal.

- *Transportation Department (Ministry) or Authority.* Transportation routes are often adversely affected in disasters. They are also depended upon heavily for evacuation, mobilization, and other response activities. Transportation authorities may be called upon to ensure transportation viability before and after disasters strike and/or to repair damaged transportation infrastructure.

- *Department (Ministry) of Public Health.* This agency may be involved in disasters generated by biological pathogens or chemical agents, or ones that involve illness as a secondary effect. The public health department monitors public health before disasters to allow for early intervention and prevents disasters through education and regulatory mechanisms. During disasters, it works alongside responders to reduce the incidence of illness and injury and responds to epidemics. In mass casualty incidents, which are those that exceed the local or regional capacity to respond to victims' health and medical needs, this department may be called upon to assist in accommodating the increase in service demand.

- *Building or Housing Department (Ministry) or Authority.* The building or housing department may be involved in any or all of the four emergency management phases. Before disasters occur, this department may work to reduce risk by conducting building safety or passing regulations that guide building occupancy limits and use. During the emergency phase of a disaster, this department may be involved in providing emergency shelter and housing or relocating people whose homes are damaged or destroyed. Finally, in the recovery phase, the building or housing department will likely be heavily involved in the reconstruction or repair of damaged and destroyed housing infrastructure.

- *Office of the Coroner.* Most communities will have an office of the coroner, which becomes integral in the response phase of the disaster. Employees from the coroner's office may assist in the process of collecting, safely storing, identifying, and disposing of victim's bodies or body parts. The coroner is also involved in notifying next of kin when a death has occurred and issuing death certificates, which may be required before certain forms of aid may be received. In the pre-disaster phase, coroners are involved in planning for mass-fatality events, and may have specific responsibilities and authorities as outlined in the Emergency Response Plan.

- *Department (Ministry) of the Environment.* The department that handles environmental issues may be involved in both pre- and post-disaster activities. Before disasters occur, this department may be involved in activities to monitor environmental health, including monitoring the degradation of disaster reduction environmental features such as dunes, forests, and wetlands. This department is also integral to the monitoring of air and water quality and pollution on land, each of which becomes an acute issue in the emergency period of a disaster when it may present a health hazard. Finally, this department may assist during the reconstruction period by helping to guide the use of environmental practices that increase disaster resilience. In countries where flooding is a problem, this department is likely to be heavily involved in management of the floodplain.

- *Department (Ministry) of Public Affairs.* This department is the public face and voice of government. In the pre-disaster phase, it may work closely with the public to provide risk-reduction education and other materials. This department may also be involved in both pre- and post-disaster emergency warnings, and is likely to be the agency that informs the public about what has happened, what they can do to protect themselves, how they may seek assistance, and where they can acquire recovery resources.

- *Department (Ministry) of Development.* This department is most likely to be involved in the recovery phase, offering guidance and assistance as the affected areas recover. If external development agencies are involved, this department will help to coordinate activities and may work to ensure that recovery actions will reduce overall hazard risk.

- *Department (Ministry) of Education.* In the pre-disaster phase, the department of education is often involved in developing disaster-related curriculum and guides exercises and drills to prepare students, teachers, and administrators for emergency procedures that may be necessary if a sudden-onset disaster occurs when children are in school. In the disaster aftermath, this department will work to help children return to school as quickly as possible, whether to their own school or to an alternate one, and will help to guide the reconstruction or repair of damaged facilities.

- *Department (Ministry) of Energy.* Nations have become highly dependent on their energy resources. In the aftermath of a disaster, when energy resources may be in short supply or damaged by the hazard's consequences, the Department of Energy may be involved in acquiring and transporting emergency energy reserves and in repairing the energy infrastructure. It may also be involved in assessing damages to the energy infrastructure. Before disasters occur, this department may be called on to strengthen energy infrastructure and resources against the impacts of hazard events.

- *Department (Ministry) of Agriculture, Forests, Fisheries, and Food.* This department may assume many roles in both the pre- and post-disaster phases, depending on its regularly assigned responsibilities. In the pre-disaster phase, it may be responsible for monitoring food safety and food supply. It may be involved in surveillance of animal or crop epidemics and manage them before a food-related disaster occurs. It also may provide assistance to farmers and other workers in the food industry to help them mitigate or prepare for various hazard consequences. In the post-disaster phase, this department may be intimately involved in the distribution of food resources. Disasters, especially floods, can destroy millions of hectares of agricultural land, which ultimately affects both the food supply and the economy. In the recovery phase, this department may work closely with farmers or fishermen to help them to rebuild.

- *Department (Ministry) of Public Safety.* This office conducts activities aimed at increasing public preparedness in the pre-disaster phase through public education and other means. Following disasters, this department may be involved in helping to ensure the safety and security of the affected areas, working with the police or other law enforcement agencies.

- *Department (Ministry) of Civil Defense.* In many countries in which the emergency management function is vested within a department of civil defense, officials from this department will be involved in the coordination of all four phases of emergency management.

- *Department (Ministry) of the Interior or Home Affairs.* In many countries, the emergency management infrastructure at the national level falls within the national department or ministry of the interior, or home affairs, as it is often called. This department, which maintains general responsibility for the country's domestic well-being, will likely be very involved in the coordination and dedication of disaster response and recovery resources. In the pre-disaster phase, it may be involved in many preparedness and mitigation activities, including emergency management, guidance of emergency management planning, and hazard risk reduction.

- *Department (Ministry) of Labor.* Many people are unemployed following a disaster, either because their place of employment has been damaged or destroyed, insufficient demand for the service or task that they conducted before the disaster, or a whole range of other reasons. In a disaster's aftermath, the Department of Labor may work to help the unemployed find jobs via job creation programs, job training, or other technical assistance.

- *Department (Ministry) of Communications.* Communications systems are vital to all phases of emergency management. These systems may be heavily damaged by a disaster's consequences, and this department may be called on to assess damages and to restore the communications infrastructure quickly. During the emergency phase of the disaster, information exchange is intimately linked to responders' ability to quickly and effectively communicate, and the communications department will be critical in facilitating such exchanges despite any disaster consequences. In the recovery phase, this office may be responsible for rebuilding and improving damaged or destroyed communications infrastructure.

- *Department (Ministry) of Foreign Affairs, State, or the Exterior.* When governments request assistance from the international community, they will likely engage other countries through the department that normally handles international relations.

- *Office of the lead government executive.* This official and the staff will inevitably become heavily involved in the response to and recovery from disasters. With respect to emergency management, whether this official is the president, the prime minister, the governor, the mayor, the administrator, the commissioner, or the bearer of another title will be defined by that nation's emergency management statutory authority. In a highly centralized system, it may be the president of that country, while in decentralized systems, the lead emergency manager is usually a local or regional official. These officials are normally tasked with declaring a state of emergency and may also be involved in guiding the response activities that follow (as defined by the Emergency Operations Plan, if one exists). Another key member of the office of the lead government executive is the city manager, who is likely to be involved in all aspects of reconstruction.

Government executives must always be given their due respect and consideration for the jurisdictional authority they maintain over an affected area. All emergency response agencies ultimately report to them unless directed otherwise. This is less common, but these officials also may be involved in pre-disaster activities (mitigation and preparedness), especially if these activities involve large amounts of funding or if politically charged, as large mitigation and preparedness projects often fail without the support of the chief executive.

Organizational Structures

Agencies and individuals involved in international emergency management efforts will encounter a full range of national and local government structures with whom they will have to interface and cooperate. There is no overarching style when it comes to emergency management, and therefore no single approach that any agency can use. Each government and each emergency management structure will require a unique management approach that suits the specific organizational framework in the country being assisted. Except for an absolute failure or erosion of the affected nation's governmental capacity (such as during a complex humanitarian emergency, CHE), all agencies must remember that the supporting external emergency management agency will be required to work under the direction and authority of the national government and, likewise, within the bounds of their institutional framework.

While it is impossible to predict exactly how each government will perform and what they will expect, there are general structures for which specific interfaces are likely and may reasonably be expected. Often, the ultimate determinant regarding the type of structure employed within each country is the form of government in power (ranging from autocratic totalitarianism to a democratic republic). Many other influential factors help to define not only what type of framework exists but how effective it is and what functions it addresses, including risk profile, social structure, risk perception, level of development, wealth, access to technical expertise, and where within the structure of government the emergency management agency has been placed (which will be discussed later in this section).

In attempting to understand how the organizational framework of emergency management has developed throughout the world, it is important to remember that the concept of comprehensive emergency management is relatively new. Historically, as described in Chapter 1, very little has been done to address risk reduction, with any formalized emergency management structures focusing solely on emergency response. It was not until well into the twentieth century that the intrinsic value of comprehensive emergency management was recognized on a global scale, and risk reduction and more formalized emergency planning emerged.

In the past, most nations left the responsibility for managing the consequences of emergencies and disasters on the shoulders of local government. For the most part, these communities had little power or resource backing to fully assess their risks, and therefore prepared only for those events they were aware of because of previous experience (such as fires or annual floods). If they had the means, they would develop the capacity to target these hazards through designing or purchasing equipment and training responders. With only isolated exceptions, very little action was taken to reduce the likelihood or consequence components of these hazards before they struck.

Local communities became adept at handling common, everyday hazards. However, in any situation that went beyond these simple events, the local government was quickly overwhelmed. With no formal national framework, higher levels of government could do little other than provide funding, equipment, technical assistance, or manpower during recovery. Because only during the past few decades has the value of mitigation and preparedness come to light, governments did not normally dedicate funds to these practices. Those that did allocated funds only to those areas that had already sustained disaster damage, as there were few ways to determine risk other than historical incidence. The resulting pattern was one in which communities were unable to adequately prepare for a disaster until a disaster had occurred.

During World War II and the Cold War era, several national governments (including the United Kingdom, Canada, Australia, the United States, and the Soviet Union) perceived what they believed to be a significant risk of nuclear or other attack. In a move that was seen as addressing a national security concern rather than one of public safety, several of these nations set out to prepare their citizens for this singular hazard. National civil protection agencies were established to instruct local and regional governments in the importance and methodology of building community shelters, to provide public preparedness education (see Figure 8–2), to conduct air-raid exercises, and to create squads of medical and other response crews, among other activities. The civil protection organizations created during this time are seen as the root of many of the more advanced emergency management organizations that exist today.

The perceived risk from these threats began to dissipate during the 1970s and 1980s. At the same time, several governments in the industrialized world began to notice a sharp increase in the human and financial cost consequences of disasters and began seeking ways to reduce risk before disasters happened. Recognizing that an effective framework existed at all levels of government, many of these

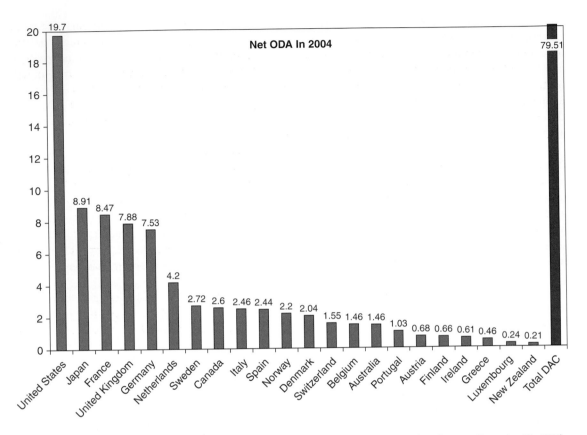

Net ODA In 2004

FIGURE 8–2 Duck and cover civil defense drills of the 1950s. (From City of Grand Forks, North Dakota on November 21, 1951)

nations, including those mentioned previously, began to pass legislation expanding the role of the civil defense organizations such that their responsibilities would include all hazards.

Outside of the industrialized world, very little was done to address emergency management on a national level. Developing countries had little or no organized emergency management capacity at the local level due to lack of resources, and this reality continues today. Only the largest towns and cities in these nations tend to develop an emergency response capacity; even there, equipment is often outdated, insufficient for recognized needs, and in poor condition. Little funding is available to pay full-time first responders, and responders often lack even the most fundamental training required to safely and efficiently manage emergency and disaster situations.

By the 1990s, many developed countries had made significant advancements in their emergency management structures at the national and the local levels, and the result was clearly illustrated in the trend of disaster deaths disproportionately moving to developing countries (see Figure 1–10). To reverse this trend, the UN named the 1990s the International Decade for Natural Disaster Reduction. During this decade, the UN worked with member countries to design institutional emergency management frameworks and to introduce the basic concepts of hazards risk management and risk reduction. Their goal was to transfer the post-disaster response focus in those countries to that of comprehensive pre- and post-disaster emergency management.

In 1994, during the World Conference on Natural Disaster Reduction, developing countries lacking any organized disaster management capacity presented action plans for developing a formalized emergency management structure. This meeting culminated with the famous Yokohama Strategy and Plan of Action for a Safer World (see Exhibit 8–4). Most of these countries subsequently took legislative action to establish a separate agency within their central government structure dedicated expressly to addressing hazard risk. Unfortunately, many countries have found it difficult to extend this effort much further because any effective emergency management function must have three things: an ample budget, an appropriately sized and trained staff, and statutory authority.

There is one major exception to this pattern of emergency management development in developing countries. Several developing countries were struck by major disasters during this decade that significantly strained their economies and reversed many years of development. These countries, which needed to borrow significant amounts of funding from international financial institutions and required assistance from countless emergency management experts, were rebuilt in a manner that promoted the importance of disaster risk reduction and were motivated to take the necessary legislative actions to strengthen their emergency management capacity at the national and local levels. This happened in many countries in Central America devastated by Hurricane Mitch and also in the Ukraine following the Chernobyl nuclear accident.

The evolution of emergency management within a country is a process that can move in a circular fashion. It begins with forming elementary response mechanisms at the local level, inspired through mutual concern and civic involvement. Next, the national government is called on or is inspired to accommodate for the lack of a comprehensive risk reduction mechanism (mitigation, preparedness, response, and recovery) by developing capacity at the national level. And, finally, as resources and expertise permit, this central authority works over time to develop communities' capacity to perform all these tasks at the local level.

If a government structure is so centralized that there is virtually no local capacity to build upon, it may be impossible for local communities to ever fully assume any emergency management responsibilities. This is especially true in authoritarian regimes, which resist transferring power to the local level because that is seen as surrendering central government control. Otherwise, and often through the guidance of the UN and other development agencies, most governments are able to gradually transfer these skills and assets to the local level, where they are most effective. The most successful emergency management systems are those in which local emergency management agencies maintain operational control of all phases of emergency management with regional and national authorities only intervening in a supportive role and never assuming any leadership control. Many countries do not yet have the institutional capacity at the local level to assume these responsibilities, but the UN and other development agencies are working to help these nations gradually develop such capacity.

The following section describes the various frameworks that support emergency management throughout the world. External agencies performing international emergency management, whether response, recovery, or mitigation and preparedness, must be able to identify and cooperate with each type of emergency management structures.

Locally Based Structures

There is a saying that "all disasters are local." Nobody knows a community's needs, capacities, and risks as well as the community members. When disasters do strike, the victims are friends, neighbors, employees, colleagues, and families. Damaged and destroyed structures are community buildings,

EXHIBIT 8–4: ACTIVITIES TASKED TO COMMUNITY AND NATIONAL GOVERNMENTS THROUGH THE 1994 YOKOHAMA STRATEGY AND PLAN OF ACTION FOR A SAFER WORLD

1. Express the political commitment to reduce their vulnerability, through declaration, legislation, policy decisions, and action at the highest level, which would require the progressive implementation of disaster assessment and reduction plans at the national and community levels
2. Encourage continued mobilization of domestic resources for disaster reduction activities
3. Develop a risk assessment program and emergency plans focusing efforts on disaster preparedness, response and mitigation, and design projects for subregional, regional, and international cooperation, as appropriate
4. Develop documented comprehensive national disaster management plans with emphasis on disaster reduction
5. As appropriate, establish and/or strengthen National Committees for the Decade or clearly identified bodies charged with the promotion and coordination of disaster reduction actions
6. Take measures to upgrade the resistance of important infrastructure and lifelines
7. Give due consideration to the role of local authorities in the enforcement of safety standards and rules and strengthen the institutional capacities for natural disaster management at all levels
8. Consider making use of support from NGOs for improved disaster reduction at the local level;
9. Incorporate disaster reduction prevention or mitigation in socioeconomic development planning based on the assessment of the risk
10. Consider the possibility of incorporating in their developmental plans the conducting of environmental impact assessments with a view to disaster reduction
11. Clearly identify specific disaster prevention needs which could use the knowledge or expertise that may be available from other countries or from the UN system, for instance, through training programs designed to enhance human resources
12. Endeavour to document all disasters
13. Incorporate cost-effective technologies in reduction programs, including forecasting and warning systems
14. Establish and implement educational and information programs aimed at generating general public awareness, with special emphasis on policymakers and major groups to ensure support for, and effectiveness of, disaster reduction programs
15. Enroll the media as a contributing sector in awareness raising, education, and opinion building to increase recognition of the potential of disaster reduction to save human lives and protect property;
16. Set targets that specify how many distinct disaster scenarios can reasonably be given systematic attention by the end of the decade
17. Stimulate genuine community involvement and empowerment of women and other socially disadvantaged groups at all stages of disaster management programs to facilitate capacity building, which is an essential precondition for reducing vulnerability of communities to natural disasters
18. Aim at the application of traditional knowledge, practices, and values of local communities for disaster reduction, recognizing these traditional coping mechanisms as a valuable contribution to the empowerment of local communities and the enabling of their spontaneous cooperation in all disaster reduction programs.

Source: IDNDR, 1994.

schools, markets, and homes. Although the consequences of a hazard may affect a whole region, a whole nation, or even several nations, the individual losses have profound effects at the local community level.

Emergencies occur every day in almost every community. The vast majority are minor, involving few victims and minimal property, and are considered routine by the responding agencies or individuals. Although local governments differ considerably regarding their emergency management capacity, each community maintains a minimum capacity proportional to its risk complexity and need. In small towns and villages, where populations are much smaller and where fires and other accidents rarely occur, it might not make sense to have a fully equipped fire department idly waiting for weeks on end; even in developed countries, rural communities may have no dedicated emergency services of their own. On the other hand, a minimum of tens of thousands of fire, police, and emergency medical technicians may be necessary in large cities to meet the emergency needs of millions of residents.

Many governments that have developed strong multitiered emergency management systems have recognized the value of a prepared, equipped, and trained local emergency management capability, and have worked to support that capacity through funding, technical assistance, and operational support in times of disaster. Their response agencies, including fire departments, police departments, emergency medical services, and offices of emergency management, are staffed by local officials (even if their administrative framework is national).

Local emergency management agencies are most effective when they conduct the full range of emergency management functions, including pre- and post-disaster activities. Mitigation and preparedness activities tend to enjoy the greatest impact when they are conducted locally, as these practices require a significant amount of local knowledge, input, and dedication to be accurate or effective.

When local response agencies become overwhelmed, regional or national resources may be brought in to assist in response and recovery. Even then, these functions are often most effectively performed when a local executive remains in command of all resources dedicated to the disaster.

Locally based response agencies may involve several or all of the following:

- Fire department
- Police department
- Emergency medical services
- Office of emergency management
- Emergency call center

Countries that utilize locally focused emergency management (regardless of the existence of regional or national organizations) include Brazil, New Zealand, Switzerland, the United Kingdom, and the United States.

Regionally Based Structures

Local government authority is regionally based in several countries. Countries may be subdivided into a whole range of administrative and political divisions, including counties, parishes, cantons, territories, districts, provinces, and states. How much authority and administrative power are granted to government officials at each level is primarily a factor of the form of the country's national government.

In those countries with a federal or federated system of government, the primary power structure is one of decentralization. Regional governments within these systems have broad discretionary power to make laws, spend resources, and impose restrictions or requirements on communities. In some of these systems (e.g., the United States) the regional (state) level government extends primary emergency management authority to local authorities. This is not always the case, however. In Australia, the regional government retains the authoritative base of comprehensive emergency management.

In these cases, many first-response agencies, including the fire and police departments, are likely to be organized, funded, and dispatched from the regional level. Local officials have very little decision-making power over actions taken in any of the four emergency management phases. They also have very little or no control over the actions of the emergency management agencies.

In many large countries, regional emergency management structures have emerged even when the administrative base of emergency management has been granted to the local government agencies. These regional offices usually focus on policy setting, funding, and direction, rather than actually taking operational measures in response to or in preparation for disasters. Functions commonly assumed by these regional offices include:

- Setting standards for emergency management based upon recognized needs within the region, and monitoring adherence to those standards
- Providing grants for funding projects that enhance local agency response, mitigation, preparedness, and/or recovery capacity
- Establishing programs that address the training and other technical assistance needs of local agencies, including developing regionally based training academies
- Maintaining specialized teams of responders or specialized equipment that is deployable throughout the administrative region in times of need

When they exist in concert with local agencies, regional agencies may be called in when local resources are overwhelmed. Regional agencies may either provide the assistance themselves or coordinate a response that involves resources from neighboring jurisdictions. Many regional governments have at their disposal dedicated military, police, or other similar assets that may be brought in to assist the affected local populations. Belarus, France, and Germany are three examples of countries with regionally based emergency management structures.

Nationally Based Structures

Largely as a result of UN efforts, almost all countries have developed an office at the national government level that manages emergency situations. These offices are not uniform, and differ most in the following:

- Where within the national government they are situated
- What authority (statutory or otherwise) they have to manage, assume responsibility for, or assist in disaster response
- The size of their budget (including the ability to acquire funds in response to unforeseen emergencies)
- How well trained their staff is in the practice of emergency management
- What assets they may bring to bear in the event of an emergency

Nationally based structures are most effective when their role is purely supportive, leaving the actual decision making to local or regional government authorities. Few national government–based emergency management structures have the staff or budget to effectively address the particular needs of every community in their country. National government authorities are not direct community stakeholders and therefore do not have the same knowledge or concern for the community's safety as local officials do and are not likely to promote important risk-reduction preparedness and mitigation measures with the same enthusiasm or effectiveness. Further, experience shows that when emergency management authority and funding are controlled at the highest levels of government, the local ability to respond quickly and effectively in the face of disaster becomes severely impeded by both bureaucracy and reduced capacity.

Even though they are not suited for the day-to-day emergency management activities of every community, national government emergency management structures are necessary. For instance, national government emergency management agencies are the best places to:

- Provide emergency management priorities, standards, direction, and goals to guide local emergency managers
- Provide training and expertise in the field of emergency management
- Provide funding to support mitigation, preparedness, response, and recovery
- Provide technical support, in the form of imagery, information, assessment, early warning, and engineering
- Assist in the coordination and facilitation of external assistance, whether from within or outside of the country
- Organize and facilitate hazard-based insurance programs that may not be offered by private insurance providers
- Provide specialized assets, which could include urban search-and-rescue (USAR) teams; hazardous materials detection, containment, cleanup, and decontamination; heavy lifting and debris removal equipment; and infrastructure repair teams and equipment

Examples of international offices of emergency management include:

- Emergency Management Australia: www.ema.gov.au/
- Public Safety and Emergency Preparedness Canada: www.publicsafety.gc.ca/index-eng.aspx
- Belarus Ministry of Emergency Situations: http://www.rescue01.gov.by/eng/
- Dominican Republic Office of Civil Defense: www.defensacivil.gov.do/
- Japan Fire and Disaster Management Agency: www.fdma.go.jp/en/
- Mexico System of Civil Protection: www.proteccioncivil.gob.mx
- New Zealand Ministry of Civil Defence & Emergency Management: www.mcdem.govt.nz/memwebsite.nsf
- Panama Civil Protection: http://www.sinaproc.gob.pa/
- Civil Protection Switzerland: http://www.bevoelkerungsschutz.admin.ch/
- United Arab Emirates National Emergency and Crisis Management Authority (NCEMA): http://www.cemc.ae/subindex.aspx?Id=104&Lid=1

- UK Civil Contingencies Secretariat: www.cabinetoffice.gov.uk/ukresilience.aspx
- U.S. Federal Emergency Management Agency: www.fema.gov

One of the most important factors in determining both the focus of the national emergency management function and its level of funding and authority is where that function is located within the overall government structure. In a best-case scenario, the emergency management structure is its own department, ministry, or agency, reporting directly to the most senior executive in the country. However, in most countries, the emergency management function lies buried below one or more bureaucratic organizational levels. This may be because of how the government perceives emergency management in relation to other government functions, such as the U.S. government locating FEMA within the Department of Homeland Security, or it may be a sign that there is not enough institutional support for emergency management to give it a high status in government. Examples of where emergency management functions are located within national government structures can be found in Exhibit 8–5.

No Capacity or No Recognized Government Exists

Under certain circumstances, there may be no national government emergency management structure with which external agencies may interface in their efforts to offer assistance (see Exhibit 8–6). When this occurs because a government has not established a national emergency capacity but maintains most other regular government services, it is often possible to establish a working relationship and offer support through another function of government equipped to serve as an intermediary. However, in situations where absolutely no government capacity exists, either because of ongoing or recently ended conflict, because a disaster has completely obliterated all national government capacity, or because the existing government is unable to offer any useful assistance, an external improvised coordination framework must be established. Under these circumstances, the UN most often assumes the role of coordinator. How this is done will be explained in greater detail in Chapter 10. Exhibit 8–7 lists some decentralized and centralized governments.

EXHIBIT 8–5: LIBERIA NATIONAL EMERGENCY MANAGEMENT CAPACITY

The Government of Liberia announced in 2007 that its national-level emergency management agency, the National Disaster Relief Commission, exists in name only. The entity was all but eliminated during that nation's 1990 civil war, and no successful efforts have been made to reinstate it. The primary obstacle is the lack of resources and the lack of individuals trained in disaster monitoring, recognition, mitigation, response, or recovery. There is also no equipment (including vehicles) left. The absence of a functioning government relief agency came to the forefront in 2007 when floods and storm surge caused housing loss and displaced hundreds of people in and around Monrovia. At that time, the Liberian Red Cross Society, not the government, managed the disaster response from the beginning. A lack of a government capacity also means no adequate warning, nor any network to coordinate trained disaster workers. In the absence of a national disaster response capacity, the Liberian government established ad hoc teams for assessment missions after floods and other disasters.

Source: All Africa, 2007.

EXHIBIT 8–6: PLACEMENT OF VARIOUS NATIONAL EMERGENCY MANAGEMENT FUNCTIONS

- Albania: Ministry of Internal Affairs
- Algeria: Ministry of the Interior
- Austria: Federal Ministry of the Interior
- Azerbaijan: Ministry of Defense
- Bahrain: Interior Ministry
- Belarus: Ministry of Emergency Situations
- Belgium: Ministry of the Interior
- Benin: Ministry of the Interior, Security and Territorial Administration
- Bolivia: Ministry of Defense
- Brazil: Ministry of National Integration
- Burkina Faso: Ministry of Territorial Administration and Decentralization
- Canada: Department of National Defense
- Cape Verde: Ministry of Defense
- Central African Republic: Fire Brigade Battalion of Central Africa
- Chad: Ministry of the Interior
- China: Ministry of Civil Affairs
- Colombia: Committee led by the President of the Republic
- Cote d'Ivoire: Spread among several ministries
- Croatia: Ministry of the Interior
- Cyprus: Ministry of the Interior
- Czech Republic: Ministry of the Interior
- Denmark: Ministry of Interior and Health
- Democratic Republic of the Congo: Ministry of the Interior
- Djibouti: Ministry of the Interior and Decentralization
- Ecuador: National Civil Defense Directorate
- Egypt: Ministry of the Interior
- Estonia: Spread among several ministries
- Ethiopia: Disaster Prevention & Preparedness Commission
- Finland: Ministry of the Interior
- France: Ministry of the Interior
- Gabon: Ministry of the Interior
- Georgia: Ministry of Internal Affairs
- Germany: Federal Ministry of the Interior
- Ghana: Ministry of the Interior
- Greece: Ministry of Interior Public Administration and Decentralization
- Guatemala: National Committee for the Reduction of Natural or Man-Made Disasters (CONRED)
- Guyana: Civil Defense Commission (Office of the President)
- Haiti: Spread among several ministries
- Hungary: Ministry of the Interior
- Iceland: Minister of Justice
- India: Ministry of Home Affairs

(Continued)

EXHIBIT 8–6: PLACEMENT OF VARIOUS NATIONAL EMERGENCY MANAGEMENT FUNCTIONS (CONTINUED)

- Indonesia: Ministry of Home Affairs
- Iran: Ministry of the Interior
- Iraq: Transition Government (formerly Ministry of the Interior)
- Ireland: Department of Defense
- Isle of Man: Ministry of Home Affairs
- Japan: Ministry of Internal Affairs and Communications
- Jordan: Ministry of the Interior
- Kazakhstan: Spread among several ministries
- Kiribati: Ministry of Home Affairs and Rural Development
- Laos: Ministry of Labor and Social Welfare
- Latvia: Ministry of the Interior
- Lebanon: Ministry of the Interior
- Liberia: Ministry of National Defense
- Libya: Ministry of the Interior
- Lithuania: Ministry of National Defense
- Luxembourg: Ministry of the Interior
- Malawi: No formal national structure—there exists a Commissioner for Disaster Preparedness, Relief, and Rehabilitation in the Office of the President
- Maldives: Ministry of Home Affairs
- Mali: Ministry of Security and Civil Defense
- Malta: Minister of Home Affairs
- Mauritania: Ministry of the Interior, Post, and Communications
- Moldova: State Department of Emergency Situations
- Monaco: Ministry of State
- Mongolia: Spread among several ministries
- Morocco: Ministry of the Interior
- Myanmar (Burma): Ministry of Home and Religious Affairs
- Namibia: Inter-ministerial Committee operating under the Office of the Prime Minister
- Nepal: Ministry of Home Affairs
- Netherlands: Ministry of Home Affairs
- New Zealand: Ministry of Civil Defense
- Niger: Ministry of the Interior
- Norway: Spread among several ministries
- Oman: Sultanate of Oman Police
- Pakistan: Ministry of the Interior
- Panama: Ministry of Interior and Justice
- Papua New Guinea: Spread among several ministries
- Paraguay: Ministry of the Interior
- Philippines: Ministry of Defense
- Poland: Spread among several ministries
- Portugal: Ministry of the Interior
- Qatar: Ministry of the Interior

- Romania: Ministry of the Interior
- Russian Federation: Ministry for Civil Defense
- St. Lucia: Spread among several ministries
- Saudi Arabia: Ministry of the Interior
- Senegal: Interior Ministry
- Singapore: Ministry of Home Affairs
- Slovakia: Ministry of Interior
- Slovenia: Ministry of Defense
- South Africa: Spread among several ministries
- Spain: Ministry of the Interior
- Sri Lanka: Ministry of Social Affairs and Housing Development
- Swaziland: There is an ad hoc committee within the Deputy Prime Minister's Office
- Sweden: Ministry of Defense
- Switzerland: Federal Department of Defense
- Thailand: Ministry of the Interior
- The Former Yugoslav Republic of Macedonia: Ministry of Defense
- Togo: Ministry of the Interior and Security
- Trinidad and Tobago: Ministry of National Security
- Tunisia: Ministry of the Interior
- Turkey: Ministry of the Interior
- Ukraine: Ministry of Ukraine of Emergencies and Affairs of Population Protection from the Consequences of Chernobyl Catastrophe
- United Arab Emirates: Directorate General of Civil Defense
- United Kingdom: Cabinet Office
- United States: Department of Homeland Security
- Venezuela: Spread among several ministries
- Yemen: Ministry of the Interior
- Zambia: National Disaster Management Committee, Office of the Vice President
- Zimbabwe: Minister of Local Government and National Housing

Bilateral Disaster Management Assistance

International development assistance is an ongoing activity involving many national government donors and an even greater number of recipients. The value of international development assistance grows each year, with a record high in 2004 of over $78 billion (see Figure 8–3). A significant portion goes to activities rooted in emergency management, many of which have been described in previous chapters. Through the support of the UN and many regional organizations and the work of individual governments and nongovernmental agencies, development focuses more and more closely on global disaster risk reduction. Many mitigation and preparedness activities are considered "dual-benefit solutions," serving two or more goals, such as building a school using modern disaster-resistant design and concurrently creating a community shelter. This makes it difficult to separate the amount of funding spent on disaster management activities from overall development assistance (ODA) figures. However, post-disaster support is much easier to distinguish and track.

EXHIBIT 8–7: LIST OF DECENTRALIZED AND CENTRALIZED GOVERNMENTS THROUGHOUT THE WORLD

Decentralized (Federal) Systems

Argentina, Australia, Austria, Bosnia and Herzegovina, Brazil, Canada, Comoros, Ethiopia, Germany, India, Mexico, Micronesia, Nigeria, Pakistan, Russia, Serbia and Montenegro, Switzerland, United States, Venezuela

Centralized (Unitary) States

Afghanistan, Albania, Algeria, Andorra, Angola, Antigua and Barbuda, Armenia, Azerbaijan, Bahamas, Bahrain, Bangladesh, Barbados, Belarus, Belize, Benin, Bhutan, Bolivia, Botswana, Brunei, Bulgaria, Burkina Faso, Burundi, Cambodia, Cameroon, Cape Verde, Central African Republic, Chad, Chile, China, Colombia, Congo, Costa Rica, Cote d'Ivoire, Croatia, Cuba, Cyprus, Czech Republic, Denmark, Djibouti, Dominica, Dominican Republic, East Timor, Ecuador, Egypt, El Salvador, Equatorial Guinea, Eritrea, Estonia, Fiji Islands, Finland, France, Gabon, Gambia, Georgia, Ghana, Greece, Granada, Guatemala, Guinea, Guinea-Bissau, Guyana, Haiti, Honduras, Hungary, Iceland, Indonesia, Iran, Iraq, Ireland, Israel, Italy, Jamaica, Japan, Jordan, Kazakhstan, Kenya, Kiribati, Kuwait, Kyrgyzstan, Laos, Latvia, Lebanon, Lesotho, Liberia, Libya, Liechtenstein, Lithuania, Luxembourg, Macedonia, Madagascar, Malawi, Maldives, Mali, Malta, Marshall Islands, Mauritania, Mauritius, Moldova, Monaco, Mongolia, Morocco, Mozambique, Myanmar, Namibia, Nauru, Nepal, Netherlands, New Zealand, Nicaragua, Niger, North Korea, Norway, Oman, Pakistan, Palau, Panama, Papua New Guinea, Paraguay, Peru, Philippines, Poland, Portugal, Qatar, Romania, Rwanda, Saint Kitts and Nevis, Saint Lucia, Saint Vincent and the Grenadines, Samoa, San Marino, Sao Tome and Principe, Saudi Arabia, Senegal, Seychelles, Sierra Leone, Singapore, Slovakia, Slovenia, Solomon Islands, Somalia, South Africa, South Korea, Sri Lanka, Sudan, Suriname, Swaziland, Sweden, Syria, Taiwan, Tajikistan, Thailand, Togo, Tonga, Trinidad and Tobago, Tunisia, Turkey, Turkmenistan, Tuvalu, Uganda, Ukraine, United Kingdom, Uruguay, Uzbekistan, Vanuatu, Vatican City, Vietnam, Yemen, Zambia, Zimbabwe

---

When disasters become international in scope, unaffected national governments often join the assortment of players providing assistance to the affected nations. Their options for assistance range from direct cash donations to sending equipment and teams for any of the many tasks related to preparedness, mitigation, response, and recovery. While it is true that almost any government may be able to contribute cash (even the impoverished nation of Sri Lanka, devastated by the 2004 tsunami disaster, pledged $25,000 to the U.S. government following Hurricane Katrina in 2005), a number of national governments are in the position to provide much more.

The many governments that provide international humanitarian assistance and whose disaster management capacity is well developed and regularly maintained may have much to offer to fulfill response and recovery needs. Their disaster management assets may be able to deploy throughout the world almost as easily as within their own territory and with little advance warning. Such assistance may be the fulfillment of a pre-established mutual assistance agreement or an opportunity for the responders to practice their skills in a real-world scenario (see Exhibit 8–8).

When reporting the amount of money a government spends on humanitarian assistance, it is important to consider how those monetary values are calculated. While a percentage of that amount

USD billion

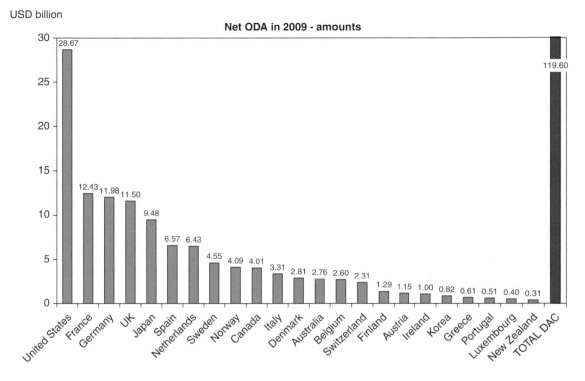

FIGURE 8–3 Overseas development assistance (ODA) from the Organisation for Economic Cooperation and Development (OECD) Development Assistance Committee (DAC) member countries, 2009. (From OECD, 2010)

EXHIBIT 8–8: CROSS-BORDER HUMANITARIAN ASSISTANCE CONTRACT BETWEEN CANADA AND THE UNITED STATES

A 2007 agreement simplified the process of cross-border emergency management between the United States and Canada. The International Emergency Management Assistance Memorandum provides the legal framework for assistance and covers issues such as training, liability, and the licensing of professionals, such as physicians, to work in each country from the other. The primary purpose of the agreement is to reduce bureaucracy that often delays aid in times of emergency. The vital need for such an agreement emerged in 1998 when an ice storm devastated parts of the northeastern United States and southern Canada and cross-border assistance was required. The memorandum recognizes the licenses of both countries' medical and health professionals, and can help to ensure that physicians or other health care workers can easily enter the other country. Under certain circumstances it would make responders eligible for reimbursement by the affected country's government.

Source: Ring, 2007.

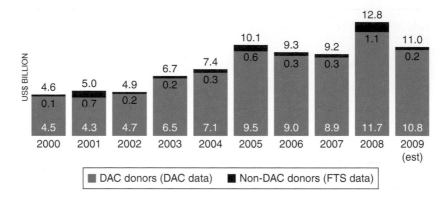

FIGURE 8–4 Bilateral humanitarian assistance from the OECD DAC countries, 2000–2009 (estimated). (From Development Initiatives, 2010; www.devinit.org)

is likely to be in the form of direct cash transfers, the majority will be measured as a value of goods or services provided. Every transport flight, tent, and food ration has a set value, and each amount is added to the total calculated amount of assistance provided. Figures 8–4 to 8–6 illustrate trends in donor giving over time and show the amount of giving by country in the latest year of record. Many developed countries, most notably the United States, are criticized because, despite giving much more in absolute dollar amounts than other countries, their giving as a percentage of annual national income is lower. A counterargument is that private citizens in many of these countries (the United States included) give a much higher percentage of their personal wealth to humanitarian and development assistance. (For more information about humanitarian assistance related to these figures, see www.devinit.org.)

In pure dollar figures, the greatest amount of bilateral humanitarian aid is provided to meet the needs of CHEs, where an absolute lack of all services and complete dependence of the population on

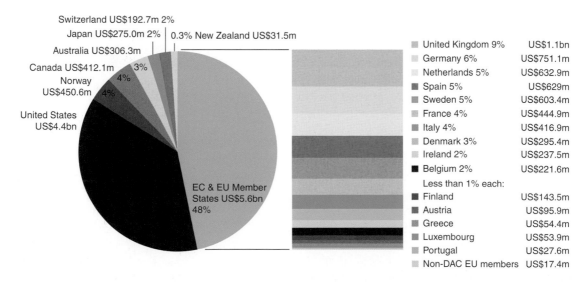

FIGURE 8–5 Total humanitarian assistance by donor, 2008. (From Development Initiatives, 2010, www.devinit.org)

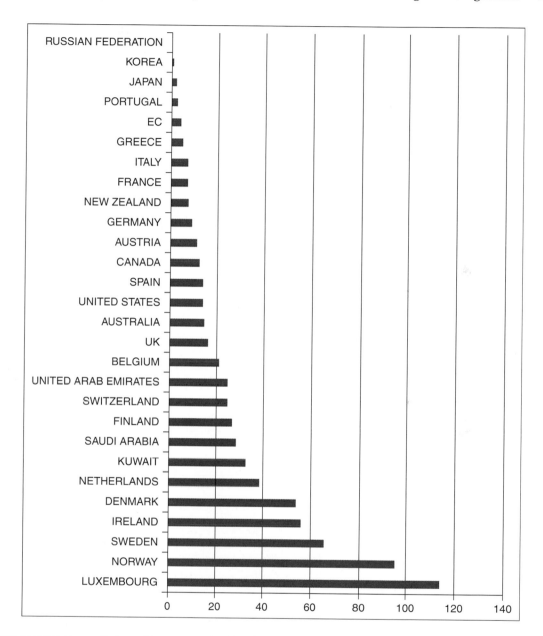

FIGURE 8–6 Total humanitarian assistance per capita, 2008. (From Development Initiatives, 2010; www.devinit.org)

assistance exists. Table 8–1 lists the top 10 recipients in 2003 of humanitarian assistance from the Development Assistance Committee (DAC) of the Organisation for Economic Cooperation and Development (OECD), each of which is listed because of an ongoing CHE. Figure 8–7 shows the amount of funding over $1 million provided for humanitarian assistance in response to all natural disasters in 2004. Aid for only one of these events exceeds $100 million.

Table 8–1   Top 10 Recipients of Humanitarian Assistance from OECD
DAC Countries, 2008

Country	Humanitarian Assistance in 2008 ($m)
Sudan	1,419.1
Palestine/OPT	884.3
Afghanistan	871.8
Ethiopia	829.6
Somalia	566.7
Democratic Republic of the Congo (DRC)	547.1
Myanmar	427.7
Iraq	382.1
Zimbabwe	335.1
Kenya	304.1

Source: Development Initiatives, 2010.

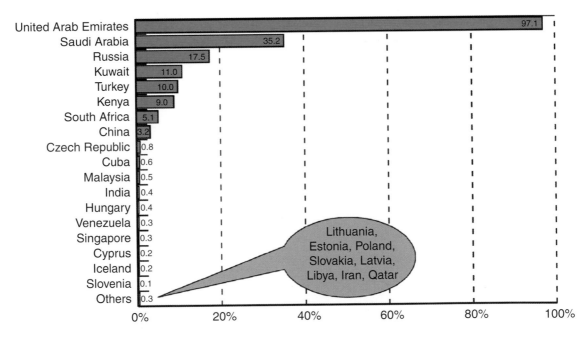

FIGURE 8–7 Natural disasters for which over $1 million in international humanitarian aid was provided, 2004. (From Development Initiatives, 2005)

Of course, the 22 OECD DAC countries are not the only ones that contribute to international humanitarian assistance. Between 2002 and 2004, 61 other countries provided humanitarian assistance in some form, although the majority of the total amount was provided in the form of a very few large donations. Figure 8–8 illustrates the amount that many of these non-OECD DAC countries donated in 2004.

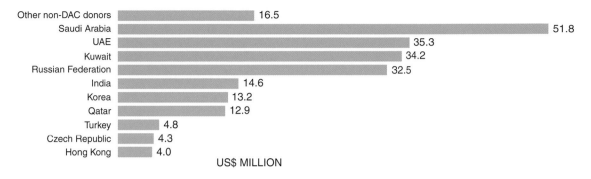

FIGURE 8–8 Top ten non-OECD DAC donors, 2009. (From Development Initiatives, 2010; www.devinit.org)

How Governments Provide Assistance

These previously mentioned figures (8–4 to 8–8) and the table (8–1) detailing bilateral government humanitarian assistance portray only the value of the assistance. In reality, direct cash donations are a small percentage of the actual assistance included in those numbers. National governments provide assistance in myriad ways, depending on the disaster type, the needs of the recipient government, and the capacity of the donor. These donations may come in the form of consumable products, equipment, building materials, transportation, labor, technical assistance, or debt relief. Table 8–2, compiled by the UN, lists the various donation sectors.

Donor governments provide this funding in a range of ways other than a direct handover of cash or provision of supplies. The UN often is the central recipient of donated funds, goods, and services

Table 8–2   Types of Humanitarian Assistance Provided by Sector, 2009

Donor	Commitments/Contributions (USD)	% Of Grand Total
Food	4,497,287,093	40.4%
Multi-sector	1,654,022,925	14.9%
Health	1,012,681,345	9.1%
Coordination and support services	764,448,209	6.9%
Sector not yet specified	706,037,786	6.3%
Sanitation and non-food items	507,312,249	4.6%
Water and sanitation	454,122,796	4.1%
Agriculture	396,805,940	3.6%
Protection/human rights/rule of law	388,461,333	3.5%
Economic recovery and infrastructure	374,512,729	3.4%
Mine action	198,267,755	1.8%
Education	171,622,342	1.5%
Security (of staff and operation)	8,671,506	0.1%
Grand total, USD	**11,134,254,008**	**100%**

Source: UNOCHA, 2010.

through the Consolidated Appeals Process (CAP) described in Chapter 10. Assistance may be provided through a regional multilateral organization, such as the Organization of American States or the African Union, which may coordinate the response to one or more of the affected countries within its field of influence. Finally, governments may donate directly to NGOs that in turn provide the services or deliver the goods required to carry out the disaster response and recovery.

Types of Bilateral Assistance

Monetary Assistance

Monetary assistance is the easiest, and often the most needed, form of assistance in a disaster's aftermath. It requires the least amount of effort for the donor nation and can help offset much of the cost of response efforts and supplies, as well as repair and reconstruction expenditures, which can be staggering and add up to a significant percentage of a country's annual income. (See Chapter 7 for more on this issue, and see Exhibit 8–9.)

As described earlier, donor governments offering cash to affected nations have a range of ways to deliver this form of assistance. If the recipient country has a recognized and strong government known to be relatively free from corruption and found to be able to carry out the necessary tasks involved in response and recovery, the funds may be given directly to the recipient government. However, this is not always the wisest or most efficient choice.

In countries where the UN has a strong presence and history of development work, one of the UN agencies (the UN Office for the Coordination of Humanitarian Affairs or the UN Development Programme) usually assumes the coordination role and manages the collection and disbursement of donated funds. Multilateral regional organizations may play the same role.

Finally, many nations give their humanitarian assistance cash donation directly to the NGOs, whether local or international, that will carry out the humanitarian work in the affected country. These organizations are described in more detail in Chapter 9.

Bilateral loans are another option for governments that do not wish or cannot afford to give grants without repayment obligations. Although affected nations borrow money from international financial institutions (IFIs) in a disaster's aftermath, this option might not be available or it may not cover enough of the nation's financial needs. In these situations, other nations will often step in to provide for these shortfalls (usually at a higher interest rate than might be possible with the IFIs).

Equipment/Supplies

A second common form of bilateral disaster assistance is donated equipment or supplies. In times of disaster, many items are needed in much greater numbers than during nonemergency times, and local supplies are quickly exhausted. Examples include:

- Food
- Water
- Medical tools and supplies
- Vaccines

EXHIBIT 8–9: U.S. OFFICE OF FOREIGN DISASTER ASSISTANCE PROVIDES BILATERAL DISASTER RELIEF FUNDING TO FACILITATE CYCLONE AND CHE RESPONSE AND RECOVERY IN MADAGASCAR (2009)

On January 20, 2009, Tropical Cyclone Fanele struck the west coast of Madagascar with winds of more than 90 mph. Heavy rains and flooding damaged homes, infrastructure, and agriculture in the western, southwestern, and central regions of the country, particularly in the Menabe Region. The cyclone affected approximately 40,400 people, displaced 4000 individuals, and killed 10 others, according to the U.N. and the Government of Madagascar (GoM) National Office for Natural Disasters Preparedness (BNGRC). In addition, U.S. Embassy staff reported that the cyclone damaged 3000 hectares of agricultural land and disrupted the ground transportation network in many communities throughout the affected areas.

On April 6, Tropical Storm Jade made landfall in northeastern Madagascar with winds of more than 70 mph and moved along the east coast before returning to sea on April 7. Heavy rains and flooding damaged houses, infrastructure, roads, and crops along Madagascar's east coast, particularly in the Sava, Vavatenina, and Atsinanana regions. According to the Office for the Coordination of Humanitarian Affairs (OCHA), the storm affected approximately 60,800 people, displaced more than 4000 individuals, and killed 15 others. In addition, OCHA reported that the storm damaged more than 41,000 hectares of agricultural land, particularly rice fields, resulting in acute food shortages. The BNGRC indicated that political unrest had reduced GoM response capacity, as evidenced by the suspension of national radio broadcasts and the looting of emergency supplies and food in some affected areas.

On February 3, 2009, the U.S. Ambassador to Madagascar declared a disaster due to the effects of Tropical Cyclone Fanele and in anticipation of additional seasonal cyclones and storms. In response to Tropical Cyclone Fanele, OFDA provided $30,000 for the distribution of 167 rolls of OFDA-supplied plastic sheeting, benefiting more than 8200 cyclone-affected people. In response to Tropical Storm Jade, OFDA provided more than $860,000 for emergency food assistance through food-for-work programs, agricultural inputs and instruction, reparation of damaged irrigation systems and rice paddies, and restoration of damaged roads.

Beginning in January 2009, politically motivated violence killed more than 150 people and injured approximately 1000 others. The crisis also affected vulnerable urban populations through increased unemployment, rising food prices due to shortages brought on by looting and hoarding, and limited government support for public sanitation and social services. According to an assessment conducted by U.N. agencies and NGOs, more than 50,000 people in the Madagascar capital of Antananarivo lost employment due to the deteriorating socioeconomic situation. In addition, the GoM BNGRC reported that unseasonably poor rainfall had resulted in severe food insecurity in 31 communes in the Androy and Anosy regions of southern Madagascar. Households in affected areas had begun employing coping strategies, including selling livestock or other assets, to purchase food. On March 25, the U.S. Ambassador declared a disaster due to the impact of the complex emergency, and OFDA in response provided $50,000 for an assessment of urban and rural food insecurity and an additional $177,502 in funding for emergency agriculture and food security activities to benefit drought-affected populations in Androy, Anosy, and Atsemo Andrefana regions.

Source: OFDA, 2010.

- Pharmaceuticals
- Clothing
- Housing materials/tents
- Plastic sheeting
- Blankets
- Cooking/cleaning/water storage/hygiene supplies
- Fuel
- Ice
- School supplies

Certain types of equipment are also needed in much greater supply for response actions and for recovery. Donor governments often send experts to operate the equipment during the emergency period of the disaster and train citizens of the affected nation to operate the equipment so that it can be left behind for reconstruction efforts. Examples of equipment commonly lent or donated in the response and recovery to disasters include:

- Short-range transportation equipment (helicopters, trucks, tankers)
- Long-range transportation equipment (airlifts, charter flights)
- Moving/loading equipment (forklifts, cranes, tractors)
- Generators
- Refrigerators
- Utility repair equipment
- Field hospitals/morgues
- Water purification equipment
- Water pumps (see Figure 8–9)

Expertise

Experts are needed in post-disaster settings to save lives, limit property damage, and reconstruct the affected community. While much of this expertise is directly associated with emergency and disaster management, some skills and talents are used in nondisaster times but are in greater demand in the mass casualty, mass damage setting of disaster response and in the construction and planning needs of the recovery phase (see Exhibit 8–10).

In the emergency phase that immediately follows many sudden-onset disasters, the most celebrated and well-known group of experts that respond to disasters worldwide are the search-and-rescue teams (see Figure 8–10). Following earthquakes in which many buildings have collapsed, or following many landslides in populated areas, the affected government may lack adequate resources to reach all survivors in the critical first hours and days when chances for survival are greatest. The assistance of these international teams has been instrumental in saving many lives that otherwise might have been lost. Search-and-rescue teams, described in detail in Chapter 6, are active in dozens of countries throughout the world, and can deploy around the world, with all of their equipment, within 12 to 24 hours.

FIGURE 8–9 U.S. military personnel unload a diesel-powered water pump flown in by a Russian AN-124 Condor aircraft to Naval Air Station Joint Reserve Base New Orleans, LA, September 12, 2005, in support of Hurricane Katrina relief efforts. The water pump was used to help pump out the water from New Orleans left over from Hurricane Katrina. (From U.S. Navy photo by Photographer's Mate 2nd Class Dawn C. Morrison)

Other expertise provided by national governments in a disaster's aftermath include teams specializing in the following:

- Medical response
- Public health
- Transport and heavy lifting
- Engineering
- Mass feeding
- Coordination support
- Utility repair and reconstruction
- Security (usually military)
- Damage and needs assessment
- Mortuary affairs

EXHIBIT 8–10: INTERNATIONAL DISASTER MANAGEMENT RESOURCES OF THE DANISH EMERGENCY MANAGEMENT AGENCY (DEMA)

Search-and-rescue unit

This unit is deployed in earthquakes, landslides, flooding, and other natural disasters. Contains advanced electronic search and listening equipment; canine search teams; heavy breakthrough tools; and advanced winch gear for rescue operations from tall, collapsed buildings or mountain slopes. This unit is furnished with satellite equipment and GPS for communication and work in deserted areas. A medical team accompanies the search-and-rescue (SAR) team.

Management and communication module

This unit is deployed for the support of the UN and other organizations in disaster coordination tasks at natural or man-made disasters. Contains computer equipment, including PCs and printers and networks for handling large amounts of data. There are mobile phones and satellite telephones, which can also transmit electronic mail and fax.

Telephone networks can be established from portable local telephones. Via satellite they have direct access to worldwide databases, the Internet, and to DEMA or its partners. The module also has radio stations for both short- and long-wave transmissions of electronic mail and voice calls.

Transport module

This unit is deployed for the transport of emergency relief to victims of famines, civil war, or other crises. This module is particularly useful in difficult terrain and consists of 18-ton four-wheel-drive trucks, a complete repair workshop and spares, workshop vehicles for the repair of immobilized trucks, and four-wheel-drive escort vehicles with protection gear against Anti-Personnel mines, as well as washing and maintenance facilities.

Logistics module

This unit is deployed when establishing large relief supply stocks. This module contains storage tents—Rubb Halls—each with a storage capacity of 550 m^2. The module also has forklift trucks, telescope loaders, four-wheel-drive Toyota pick-ups, and other equipment for handling large amounts of food, accommodation equipment, and other relief deliveries.

Camp module

Units dispatched to disaster areas are self-supplying through the use of a camp module. It works as an office for the unit's management and administration and contains accommodation as well as recreational and eating facilities for the units. The camp module comprises the following elements: sleeping and day facilities for up to 100 people; kitchen and eating facilities with a large cooling and freezing capacity; toilets and showers; recreation and welfare facilities; its own supply of drinking water and electricity; and its own logistic and supply unit for local transport, fuel, food, spare parts, and maintenance. The camp module functions as a small town, with heating and air conditioning enabling it to function optimally in cold winters and hot summers as well as in tropical climates.

Environment and chemical module

DEMA can render support in cases of environmental disasters; monitoring and cleaning at nuclear, biological, and chemical disasters; water transport for wilderness fires; pumping of large amounts of water in flooding; and water cleaning and drinking water supply in case of contamination or in desert areas.

Supply module

In addition to its own trucks on 24-hour call, DEMA cooperates with various suppliers, enabling the agency to pack and ship off equipment units and supplies by truck, ship, or aircraft at a few hours' notice.

Training and counseling module

Know-how and training are available for the many different areas of relevance to international disaster situations. In addition to courses in fire and rescue service, various professional groups are trained in basic international work to fill positions as support staff, managers and administrators, technicians, and disaster management.

Emergency Mobile Hospital

The Danish Emergency Mobile Hospital is a unique modular medical facility that can be configured to accommodate different types of medical needs. The 72-bed Emergency Mobile Hospital, equipped with two operating theaters, is entirely self-contained. It can be deployed for natural disasters, as well as extended relief operations. A core staff of Danish doctors, nurses, and volunteer specialists support the facilities, augmented by local medical staff in most cases. The hospital is operated by the Emergency Management Organization of Greater Copenhagen, and has previously been deployed in Bosnia in 1993–1996 and Gujarat, India, after the 2001 earthquake. In August of 2002 it commenced operations in Kabul, Afghanistan, on behalf of UNFPA.

Human resources

Staff available for international tasks can be emergency management officers with expertise in the areas of disaster management, logistics, and administration; middle managers with experience in a broad range of disaster-related areas; and conscripts with experience in practical tasks. Finally, human resources can be staffed from the municipal rescue services that can be available on short notice through cooperation agreements. In special situations, DEMA cooperates with external specialists.

Source: DEMA, 2003.

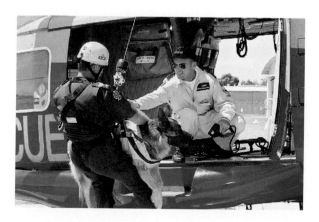

FIGURE 8–10 Australian search-and-rescue team. (From South Australian State Emergency Service (SA SAS) and Trevor Arnold, photographer, SA SAS Noarlunga Unit, 2005)

Types of National Government Agencies Involved in International Disaster Management

Any national government may have several agencies involved in international emergency and disaster management efforts. Many agencies have a specific focus or expertise to assist in humanitarian efforts or to help another nation reduce its hazard risk, either before or after a disaster occurs. This section details the most common types of national agencies involved in international disaster management.

Overseas Diplomatic Missions (Embassies and Consulates)

Often, a donor country's first contact with an affected country is through their embassy in that country. Sometimes the embassies or consulates are directly affected by the consequences of a disaster. Embassies provide assessment of the situation on the ground to their government, and the donor government may extend its offer of humanitarian assistance to the affected government through its ambassador. Embassies assist citizens of their own countries who are traveling or living in the affected country. They also assist in the logistics and coordination of donated goods and services. In many cases, high-ranking political figures from the donor country will make a humanitarian visit to the affected country, and the embassy staff organizes these visits.

International Development Agencies

Many developed countries have been involved in international assistance for decades. Although disaster management and risk reduction have never been the primary focus of these agencies, many governments have come to realize that their projects would enjoy much more sustainable outcomes if they could account for the various risk factors affecting the recipient country, and that disasters very often impeded and even reversed development in poor countries. More and more, disaster resilience has come to be viewed as a component of a nation's overall development (see Chapter 1).

Development agencies have several options to help poor nations decrease their hazard risk. These options fall primarily under the emergency management functions of mitigation, preparedness, and recovery:

- Projects addressing issues that are not disaster related per se but include the condition that a full hazard assessment be performed and that the project design fully address disaster resilience enhancement based on the assessment's findings
- Funding for projects that directly address specific mitigation and preparedness needs, such as developing early warning systems, strengthening building stock and infrastructure, and educating the public about actions to reduce their personal risk
- Technical assistance and funding to national and local governments to help develop disaster management frameworks and increased capacity
- Post-disaster recovery assistance requiring that any reconstruction must directly address hazard risk reduction

Examples of international development agencies that incorporate disaster management into their development activities include:

- United States Agency for International Development (USAID): www.usaid.gov
- British Department for International Development (DFID): www.dfid.gov.uk/
- Canada International Development Agency (CIDA): www.acdi-cida.gc.ca/index-e.htm
- Australian Agency for International Development (AusAID): www.ausaid.gov.au/
- Swedish International Development Cooperation Agency (SIDA): www.sida.se/
- New Zealand International Aid and Development Agency (NZAID): www.nzaid.govt.nz/

In most cases, a country's international development agency has the lead responsibility for their government's response to an international disaster. Designated offices of humanitarian assistance within these agencies, such as the USAID Office of Foreign Disaster Assistance (OFDA), respond to appeals for aid from affected countries. These international development agencies normally have a pre-established working relationship with either the affected nation's government or the UN and other nongovernmental and international organizations working in the country. Exhibit 8–11 is provided as an example of how international development agencies operate in this area.

National Disaster Management Agencies

Governments can also offer assistance to disaster-affected countries through their national disaster management agencies. As with international development agencies, national disaster management agencies may offer assistance in any of the four phases of emergency management. Their exact role depends on their country's statutory authority guiding who has jurisdiction for providing international assistance.

In general, national disaster management agencies do not provide as much assistance as development agencies. They may provide operational assistance in the form of specialized teams (such as search-and-rescue, emergency medical, assessment, and other teams) during disaster response. But they primarily offer technical assistance to help other countries establish their national disaster management capability during the mitigation and preparedness phases (see Exhibit 8–12).

Other Government Agencies Involved in International Disaster Management

In addition to those agencies with a direct link to international disaster management, a number of government entities, while not primarily focused on disaster or emergency management, have various skills and expertise that could assist in any of the four disaster management components. The international collaboration between the departments and ministries of public health of the nations threatened and affected by the SARS and avian influenza viruses is one example, as is the increased cooperation between allied governments' intelligence agencies aimed at limiting terrorism. Through international cooperation, many of these government agencies regularly provide technical assistance to their counterparts in other national governments. They also support disaster response efforts in their own countries and abroad. Exhibit 8–13 discusses this international cooperation in more detail.

EXHIBIT 8–11: U.S. GOVERNMENT INTERNATIONAL DISASTER MANAGEMENT ASSISTANCE

The Office of U.S. Foreign Disaster Assistance (USAID/OFDA) is responsible for providing humanitarian assistance in response to international crises and disasters. The USAID Administrator is designated as the President's Special Coordinator for International Disaster Assistance and USAID/OFDA assists in the coordination of this assistance. USAID/OFDA is part of the Bureau for Democracy, Conflict, and Humanitarian Assistance. Figure 8–11(a) illustrates where OFDA falls within the USAID organizational structure.

USAID/OFDA is organized into three divisions, under the management of the Office of the Director, shown in Figure 8–11(b).

- The Disaster Response and Mitigation (DRM) division is responsible for coordinating with other organizations for the provision of relief supplies and humanitarian assistance. DRM also devises, coordinates, and implements program strategies for the application of science and technology to prevention, mitigation, and national and international preparedness initiatives for a variety of natural and man-caused disaster situations.
- The Operations (OPS) division develops and manages logistical, operational, and technical support for disaster responses. OPS maintains readiness to respond to emergencies through several mechanisms, including managing Urban Search and Rescue (USAR) Teams, Disaster Assistance Response Teams (USAID/DART), and Washington-based Response Management Teams (RMT).
- The Program Support (PS) division provides programmatic and administrative support, including budget and financial services, procurement planning, contracts and grants administration, general administrative support, and communication support for both USAID/OFDA and its field offices.

USAID/OFDA provides humanitarian assistance in response to a declaration of a foreign disaster made by the U.S. Ambassador or the U.S. Department of State. Once an event or situation is determined to require U.S. government assistance, USAID/OFDA can immediately provide up to $50,000 to the U.S. Embassy or USAID Mission to purchase relief supplies locally or to give a contribution to a relief organization in the affected country. USAID/OFDA can also send relief commodities, such as plastic sheeting, tents, blankets, and water purification units, from its five stockpiles in Guam, Honduras, Italy, Maryland (U.S.), and the United Arab Emirates, as well as from a smaller cache in Florida. Increasingly, USAID/OFDA deploys short- or long-term field personnel to countries where disasters are occurring or threaten to occur, and in some cases, dispatches a Disaster Assistance Response Team (DART) to assess the damages and recommend the level of assistance that should be provided by the U.S. government.

OFDA developed the Technical Assistance Group (TAG) to increase its capabilities in planning and programming. TAGs consist of scientists and specialists in agriculture and food security, emergency and public health, water and sanitation, geoscience, climate, urban planning, contingency planning, cartography, and so on. TAGs work with DARTS in response, as well as USAID development missions, in preparation and mitigation for future disasters.

A large percentage of USAID/OFDA's assistance goes to disaster relief and rehabilitation projects managed by NGOs (including U.S. private voluntary organizations [PVOs] registered with USAID), U.N. organizations, and international organizations.... Relief projects include airlifting supplies to affected populations in remote locations, managing primary health care and supplementary feeding centers, and providing shelter materials to disaster evacuees and displaced persons.

A rehabilitation project might immunize dislocated populations against disease, provide seeds and tools to farmers who have been adversely affected by disasters, drill water wells, or rehabilitate water systems in drought-stricken countries. USAID/OFDA carefully monitors the organizations implementing these projects to ensure that resources are used wisely and to determine if the project needs to be adapted to changing conditions. The goal of each project is to meet the humanitarian needs of the affected population, with the aim of returning the beneficiaries to self-sufficiency.

USAID/OFDA also oversees a portfolio of mitigation projects designed to reduce the impact of disasters on victims and economic assets in disaster-prone countries. USAID/OFDA has invested in a number of programs in partnership with the U.S. Geological Survey (USGS), the Pan American Health Organization (PAHO), the Asian Disaster Preparedness Center, the World Environment Center, and other offices within USAID. These programs not only enhance a country's capacity to manage its own disasters and hazards, but they also promote the transfer of technology, goods, and services between the United States and the host country. USAID/OFDA mitigation-related programs range from investing in drought early warning systems that can possibly head off a famine to training local relief workers to manage the response to a disaster more effectively. USAID/OFDA is increasingly investing in programs designed to prevent, mitigate, prepare, and plan for complex emergencies.

USAID/OFDA is not the only USAID office that provides humanitarian aid to foreign countries. The U.S. Office of Food for Peace (USAID/FFP) provides food aid donations to cooperating sponsors (NGOs, cooperatives, the World Food Programme, and other IOs) to address both emergency food needs (targeting vulnerable, food-insecure populations affected by natural disasters, civil conflict, and other crises) and food security development activities. The USAID Office of Transition Initiatives (USAID/OTI) is the office responsible for providing assistance to countries that are in a stage of transition from crisis to recovery. Its assistance is designed to facilitate the transition to peace and democracy by aiding in the demobilization of combatants or developing democratic governance and media structures within the affected country. Other parts of USAID, such as the regional bureaus, provide development aid, which often complements humanitarian relief programs or can be regarded as disaster rehabilitation or reconstruction assistance.

Other major providers of U.S. government foreign humanitarian assistance include the U.S. Department of Agriculture (USDA), the U.S. Department of State's Bureau of Population, Refugees, and Migration (State/PRM), and the U.S. Department of Defense's Office of Stability Operations (DoD/SO). Food aid that is administered by the USDA has often been used for emergency feeding programs in countries experiencing food shortages due to drought and civil strife. USDA also provides international food assistance through the McGovern-Dole International Food for Education and Child Nutrition program and the Food for Progress program. State/PRM provides multilateral grants to international relief organizations in response to refugee emergency appeals and contributes to the regular program budgets of organizations such as the U.N. High Commissioner for Refugees (UNHCR) and the International Committee of the Red Cross (ICRC). DoD/SO, in collaboration with USAID/OFDA, coordinates with other DoD offices to direct the utilization of DoD assets for humanitarian assistance overseas. The USGS, the Centers for Disease Control and Prevention (CDC), the U.S. Forest Service (USFS), the National Oceanic and Atmospheric Administration (NOAA), and the Environmental Protection Agency (EPA) also provide technical assistance, in coordination with USAID/OFDA, in response to disasters and potential hazards overseas. See Figure 8-11A and B.

Source: OFDA, 2004.

EXHIBIT 8–12: U.S. FEDERAL EMERGENCY MANAGEMENT AGENCY POST-HURRICANE MITCH ASSISTANCE IN CENTRAL AMERICA AND THE CARIBBEAN

Following the devastation in Central America caused by Hurricane Mitch, the U.S. Federal Emergency Management Agency (FEMA) became involved in sharing many of its emergency management principles with Honduras, El Salvador, Nicaragua, Guatemala, Haiti, and the Dominican Republic through various development projects. FEMA's involvement came only after an agreement between it and USAID, following passage of a law in the U.S. Congress that directed FEMA's participation in the reconstruction efforts in Central America and the Caribbean and provided FEMA with $3 million over 2 years.

FEMA's involvement in the reconstruction efforts involved work at all levels of government. At the local level, FEMA conducted pilot versions of its risk reduction program Project Impact: Building Disaster-Resistant Communities in each affected country. In-country assistance by NGOs trained in Project Impact strategies as well as visits from U.S. experts served to implement Project Impact initiatives. At the national government level, technical assistance was provided by sharing FEMA's experience in the planning and execution of emergency management functions. This included the establishment of a national emergency plan, emergency operations centers, state and local partnerships, and capacity building for each country.

Whereas the specific projects that emerged varied between countries, FEMA's major goals were to help enhance the role, authority, and capabilities of each country's emergency management agencies; analyze and refine national emergency management plans coordinating the activities of the different agencies in each national government; design efficient emergency operations centers capable of processing the information received from the new equipment; and initiate the pilot projects.

Through its disaster management university, FEMA helped to train emergency management executives from the six affected countries as well as representatives from NGOs. The training allowed FEMA to efficiently provide these countries with direct access to its knowledge base and its emergency management experts. It also allowed the country representatives to further refine their goals and the methods of achieving them, and gave them an opportunity to continue to work with their neighbors to share their experiences and lessons learned.

Source: ISDR, 2001.

Military Resources

Military resources may be involved in international disaster or humanitarian missions for many different reasons. It often is argued that nobody is better equipped to handle disasters than the military because of their wide assortment of heavy equipment, enormous reserve of trained personnel, and common culture of discipline and mission-oriented standard operation. However, some believe that the military is a war agency, not a humanitarian assistance agency, and that these two organizational ideals are too fundamentally and diametrically opposed in practice to allow for effective military involvement.

Apart from fighting wars, military resources traditionally were only used in peacekeeping operations. But it is becoming more and more common for governments to lend their military resources, including troops, equipment, and information, to assist a nation or nations affected by a major

EXHIBIT 8–13: U.S. WEATHER SERVICE HELPS TUNISIA UPDATE FORECASTING ABILITIES

Scientists from the U.S. National Weather Service (NWS) and the National Institute of Meteorology (NIM) in Tunisia are working together to modernize weather forecasting and services in the North African country, whose regions range from the Mediterranean in the northwest to the Sahara Desert in the south. The collaboration—made possible by a June 2004 science and technology agreement between the United States and Tunisia—began in April of 2005, when scientists from the NWS, part of the National Oceanic and Atmospheric Administration (NOAA), traveled to Tunisia for a workshop on hydrometeorological data collection and forecasting. Hydrometeorology is a branch of meteorology that deals with the occurrence, motion, and changes in water (rain, snow) in the atmosphere.

"The primary purpose of the workshop was to talk about what the National Institute of Meteorology does and how it goes about its operations," said Robert Jubach, project coordinator for the NWS International Activities Office. It was also a fact-finding mission, he said, to learn what the Tunisian Weather Service does and to learn more about its capacities and interests. "We got to know them and they got to know us," he said in an interview.

The meetings emphasized the NIM institutional structure, the Tunisian agency's vision for the future, NWS meteorological and hydrologic forecasting technologies that could be transferred to and applied in Tunisia, NWS technical assistance areas, and potential collaborations. Severe weather, flooding, locust swarms, and tornadoes prompted the Tunisians to modernize their weather system. In November 2004, a rare but powerful tornado swept through Kelibia, Tunisia, killing 12 people and causing extensive destruction.

"Tunisia has a strong climate gradient," Jubach said. "In the north part on the Mediterranean it's not wet but they get ample rainfall, and in the southern part you're in the Sahara. In a very short distance of several hundred miles you go from a very green fertile area and dry out as you head south. Each region has unique issues."

In the semi-arid area between the desert and the Mediterranean, heavy rainfall can cause flooding, and the desert and semi-arid areas have problems with locusts. In a locust attack, up to 80 million insects may descend over a square kilometer and can devour twice their weight in crops in a day. "Locusts wreak havoc on agriculture," Jubach said, "and weather plays an important role because locusts only come out of the ground under certain humidity and temperature conditions." After the locusts come out of the ground, they hover in the air at a certain altitude until they get the scent of plants and feed, so winds are also important, he said. Accurate weather forecasts can help target locust spraying, which can only be done when the locusts are on the ground.

"We talked quite a bit about how we could work together to help them with their weather prediction models, to be able to more accurately predict the right weather conditions for locusts," Jubach said. One of the technologies critical for forecasting severe weather events is weather radar. "Weather radars cover almost every square mile of the United States," Jubach said. The Tunisians would like to upgrade their weather radar and add more radars throughout the country. "A lot of heavy rain falls toward the south in the semi-arid regions," he said. "They're worried about flooding and radar would help them with that."

Workshop discussions also included remote sensing capabilities and satellites. During the workshop, scientists described the modernization of NWS over the last 10 years—consolidating

(Continued)

EXHIBIT 8–13: U.S. WEATHER SERVICE HELPS TUNISIA UPDATE FORECASTING ABILITIES (CONTINUED)

weather forecast offices, automating the collection of weather data, and installing modern weather radars. The NWS has helped other countries modernize aspects of their weather services—flood forecasting and warning capabilities in Mexico, an early warning system for severe weather in Central America, hydrometeorological services in Russia, and disaster-management capabilities in India, as well as others.

The next step, Jubach said, is to complete a bilateral agreement with the Tunisians under the main science and technology agreement signed in June 2004. After the agreement is signed, work can begin. "I think a long-term goal is to work with them on weather forecast modeling improvements overall," he said. "They've asked if we could send a visiting scientist there to work with them on the weather forecast model."

Source: Pellerin, 2005.

---

disaster. This government entity is very well trained and equipped to work in the high-intensity and high-stress environment of a disaster's aftermath and recovery. Military assistance may include providing food, technical assessment, medical treatment, transportation logistics, assistance with a refugee crisis, search and rescue, stabilization of infrastructure, security, sheltering, or engineering, among many other tasks (see Exhibit 8–14).

The U.S. Military

The U.S. military is frequently involved in natural and technological disaster and CHE relief efforts. Military assistance is normally requested by USAID OFDA through the U.S. Department of Defense (DoD) Office of Political/Military Affairs. U.S. military participation in international disaster response is carried out by organized operations, termed "foreign humanitarian assistance" (FHA) or "humanitarian assistance operations" (HAO). The chain of command for military operations begins with the president of the United States and the Secretary of Defense, collectively referred to as the "National Command Authority" (NCA). The NCA, which directs all functions of the U.S. military, is advised by the Joint Chiefs of Staff of the Army, Navy, Air Force, and Marines (see Exhibit 8–15). The entire military force is divided into six geographic areas of responsibility (AORs) and four functional commands, as follows:

- Africa Command (AFRICOM): Stuttgart, Germany headquarters
- European Command (EUCOM): Stuttgart, Germany headquarters
- Pacific Command (PACOM): Honolulu, HI headquarters
- Central Command (CENTCOM): Tampa, FL headquarters
- Southern Command (SOUTHCOM): Miami, FL headquarters
- Northern Command (NORTHCOM): Colorado Springs, CO headquarters
- Joint Forces Command (USJFCOM): Concerned with military transformation and advancement; Norfolk, VA

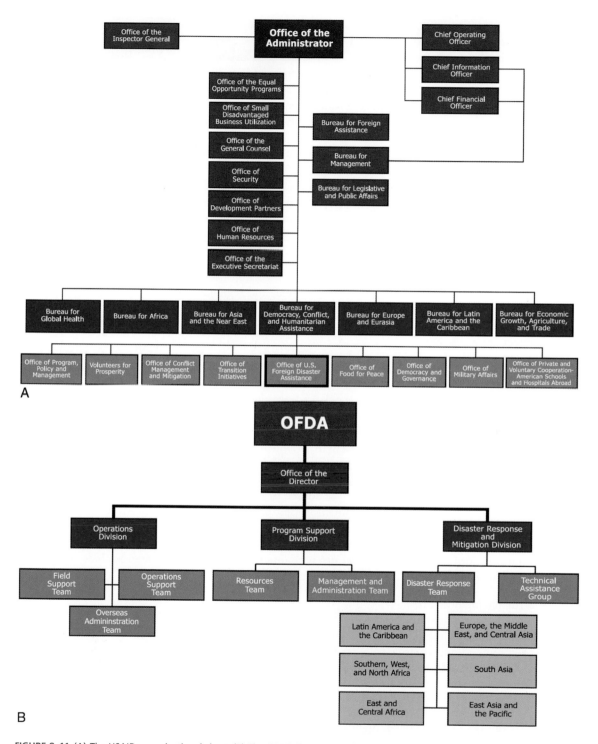

FIGURE 8–11 (A) The USAID organizational chart. (B) The USAID/OFDA organizational chart. (From OFDA, 2010)

EXHIBIT 8–14: CANADIAN MILITARY INVOLVEMENT IN INTERNATIONAL DISASTER MANAGEMENT OPERATIONS

The Canadian government has consistently demonstrated strong support for humanitarian assistance and disaster-relief operations throughout the world. Nationally and internationally, the Canadian Forces (CF) unit has deployed to disaster-stricken regions to conduct humanitarian relief operations. International missions since 1990 include relief operations in Rwanda, Haiti, Honduras, and Turkey.

In 1994, the CF deployed two field ambulances to Rwanda to provide medical relief to the refugees suffering from the many ill effects of the conflict in that country. Despite the best efforts of all concerned, the relief effort arrived after the peak of a cholera epidemic that brought great suffering. This experience convinced the Canadian government of the need to create a rapid-response capability to provide effective humanitarian aid. The concept of the CF Disaster Assistance Response Team (DART) was born.

The DART is a military organization designed to deploy rapidly anywhere in the world to crises ranging from natural disasters to complex humanitarian emergencies. The DART:

- Responds rapidly, in conjunction with national and regional governments and nongovernmental agencies, to stabilize the primary effects of an emergency or disaster
- Provides purified drinking water and medical aid to help prevent the rapid onset of secondary effects of a disaster
- Gains time for the deployment of national and international humanitarian aid to facilitate long-term recovery in a disaster-stricken community

Comprising about 200 CF personnel ready to deploy quickly to conduct emergency relief operations for up to 40 days, the DART can either enhance emergency relief efforts or bridge the gap until members of the international community arrive to provide long-term help. The DART is designed to deploy only to permissive environments; that is, locations where it will not encounter any organized resistance or threat.

For international missions, the DART can be activated by a request from either an individual country or from the UN. Regardless of the source of the request, the final decision to deploy the DART rests with the Canadian government, based on advice from Foreign Affairs Canada, the Department of National Defense, and the Canadian International Development Agency.

In a UN operation, the DART is required to coordinate its work with the UN-appointed humanitarian coordinator. It also cooperates with international agencies onsite to achieve the maximum positive impact. The DART serves four critical needs in emergencies:

- Primary medical care
- Production of safe drinking water
- A limited specialist engineer capability
- A command and control structure that allows for effective communications between the DART, the host nation, and the other agencies involved in the relief effort, including international organizations, NGOs, and UN aid agencies

The DART is composed of highly trained military personnel drawn mostly from Land Force units. It comprises the following main elements:

- **DART Headquarters,** consisting of about 45 personnel drawn mainly from the Canadian Forces Joint Headquarters and the Canadian Forces Joint Signal Regiment, both based in Kingston, Ontario. DART Headquarters is responsible for command and control in theater, and for the strategic-level liaison required to determine and coordinate the DART's humanitarian response with the governments of Canada and the host nation, and officials of international organizations and NGOs operating in the theater.
- A logistics **platoon** of about 20 personnel, responsible for the logistical support services essential to sustaining DART, such as maintenance, transport and movements control, supply, procurement and contracting, and food services.
- The **headquarters of the various DART subunits** deployed on the mission, each comprising about nine personnel, to coordinate onsite tasking priorities and provide a command capability for split operations when required. These headquarters provide the day-to-day command and control of the following DART subunits:
  - An **engineer troop** of about 37 personnel, including both field and construction engineers. The field engineer element consists of a water supply section, a field engineer section, and a heavy equipment section. The construction engineer element provides limited construction and utility services. The engineer troop produces bulk and bagged water from its Canadian-built Reverse Osmosis Water Purification Unit (ROWPU), which can produce purified drinking water for use by medical services and for distribution to disaster victims. Once it has completed the DART camp—an austere facility—the engineer troop can take on other tasks in support of the host nation and humanitarian aid agencies.
  - A **medical platoon** of approximately 40 personnel is able to provide support to area hospitals or to operate a small medical aid station, a tented facility capable of providing care for 200 to 250 outpatients and 10 in-patients per day, depending on the requirements of the mission. The medical aid station currently includes a laboratory, a pharmacy, limited obstetrics services, and rehydration and preventive medicine sections; it has no surgical or trauma care capabilities. The medical platoon provides treatment of minor injuries, disease control, and routine health care services to relieve the host nation's medical facilities of these responsibilities.
  - A **defense and security platoon** of about 45 personnel to provide camp security and general support for DART operations.

Following the earthquake-generated tsunamis that devastated coastal regions of Southeast Asia on December 26, 2004, Canada sent an interdepartmental reconnaissance team to assess the requirement for assistance to the region. Using commercial aircraft, the team left Ottawa for Colombo, Sri Lanka, on December 30. The team was comprised of an 11-member CF advance party—mostly from the Disaster Assistance Response Team—three representatives from Foreign Affairs Canada, two from the Canadian International Development Agency, and one from the Public Health Agency.

The aim of the CF members on the reconnaissance team was to assess the potential requirement for military assistance to the humanitarian effort while staying within the Government of Canada guidelines on civil–military coordination and humanitarian action.

(Continued)

EXHIBIT 8–14: CANADIAN MILITARY INVOLVEMENT IN INTERNATIONAL DISASTER MANAGEMENT OPERATIONS (CONTINUED)

On January 2, 2005, the Prime Minister announced the imminent deployment of the DART, pending receipt of the final recommendation from the deployed reconnaissance team. The recommendation was delivered that same day. The following day, the Minister of National Defense announced the DART would begin deploying to the Ampara region of Sri Lanka. Ampara, a district of approximately 600,000 people, was one of the districts worst affected by the tsunamis, with an estimated 10,400 people killed. Approximately 180,000 people have been displaced, and damage to hospital infrastructure and water supplies is significant.

A 21-member advance party deployed to Sri Lanka via commercial aircraft on January 4 and 5. Five chartered Antonov-124 flights were used to carry the DART's equipment. DART personnel deployed on two CF CC-150 Polaris flights. The first group of 137 personnel left on January 6, and the second group of 33 personnel departed on January 9.

The DART moved into the Ampara region on January 10 with tents, food, and four water purification systems capable of producing 150,000 to 200,000 liters of water per day. The water purification units and medical platoon supported local hospitals until normal services could be restored. The DART set up its main camp at a former sugar factory located about 6 km south of Ampara, which allowed the DART to bring assistance to several nearby communities simultaneously.

Source: Canadian National Defense, 2005.

EXHIBIT 8–15: U.S. NAVY FLEET DEDICATED TO HUMANITARIAN ASSISTANCE

In April of 2008, the U.S. Navy created the "4th Fleet," consisting of ships, aircraft, and submarines. This fleet, which operates in the Caribbean and Central and South America, is headquartered in Florida, and is dedicated (in part) to allowing the Navy to respond more quickly to natural disasters and emergencies requiring humanitarian relief. The U.S. Navy's new maritime strategy elevated disaster relief and humanitarian operations to the same level as combat operations, and the service's amphibious warfare ships have the shallow draft that allows them to enter the region's ports. They also have the capacity to carry large quantities of medical supplies.

The hospital ship *Comfort*, which is part of the 4th fleet, is often seen participating in humanitarian responses throughout the world when coastal countries are affected. Navy ships can be positioned nearby when a hurricane is approaching landfall and can move in almost immediately to provide medical care and deliver food and shelter.

Source: Grant, 2008.

- Strategic Command (USSTRATCOM): Charged with space operations, information operations, missile defense, command and control, intelligence, surveillance, and reconnaissance; Omaha, NE headquarters
- Special Operations Command (SOCOM): In command of special operations, including Special Forces, Civil Affairs, and Psychological Operations; Tampa, FL headquarters
- Transportation Command (TRANSCOM): Provides management for all air/sea/land transportation; Scott Air Force Base, IL headquarters

Assistance may be provided in the form of physical or technical support, such as logistics, transportation, communications, relief distribution, security, or emergency medicine. In natural or man-made emergencies that do not involve conflict, the military's role is to provide support, not leadership, to the affected national government and the overall relief community.

The military is known for its self-contained operational abilities, arriving on the scene with everything it needs. Once in country, it works under the strict guidelines of force protection (enforced security of all military and civilian personnel, equipment, and facilities associated with its mission) and Rules of Engagement (ROE, a structured, pre-established guideline of "circumstances and limitations under which the military will initiate or continue combat engagement"; Aid Workers Network, n.d.). The ROE dictates military action in both peacekeeping and disaster operations.

If a particular command unit is tasked with assisting a relief operation, it may deploy a humanitarian assistance survey team (HAST) to assess what the military is best suited to address. These assessments tend to focus on different issues than those handled by humanitarian-based organizations, such as the UN or OFDA, because the military operates differently. HAST concentrates on the military support and logistical requirements related to the deployment of its troops. Following the HAST assessment, a joint task force (JTF) is established to handle the management and coordination of military personnel activities, with a JTF Commander designated as the onsite officer in charge of the operation; however, if an operation involves only one branch of the military or is minimal, a JTF may not be needed.

One of the main roles of the JTF is to establish a civil military operations center (CMOC). This center coordinates military support with all others involved in the response and/or recovery. The CMOC mobilizes requests for assistance from OFDA, the UN, NGOs, and the host government. All intermilitary planning is conducted through this center, including operations involving cargo transportation and food logistics. This center is the primary node of information exchange to and from the JTF. In recent years, CMOCs have taken on expanded responsibility, including the re-establishment of government and civil society and the repair or rehabilitation of critical infrastructure.

Conclusion

Responsibility for disaster management ultimately rests with the local and national governments of the affected country or countries. Citizens expect their governments to provide both pre- and post-disaster assistance, regardless of the disaster's cause. But all too often, local and national governments are unable to manage the preparedness, mitigation, response, and recovery needs of large-scale disasters, and must turn to other governments for assistance. As this chapter explained, the mechanisms by which governments participate in international disaster management are diverse. Unfortunately, this support is not always sufficient. But where government assistance leaves off, multilateral and NGOs pick up. Chapters 9 and 10 will detail international disaster management support by these entities.

References

Aid Workers Network. (n.d.). *Working with the military in the field.* www.aidworkers.net/management/military/military.html.

All Africa. (2007). *Liberia: national disaster relief agency inoperable for years.* AllAfrica.Com. September 12; Sungbeh, Tewroh-Wehtoe. 2010. Liberia Can Learn from the Haitian Tragedy. TheLiberianDialogue.Org. January 30.

Associated Press. (2008). *Brazil army enters battle against dengue.* April 1.

Canadian National Defense. (2005). *Canadian forces disaster assistance response team background.* January 10. www.forces.gc.ca/site/newsroom/view_news_e.asp?id=301.

Danish Emergency Management Agency (DEMA). (2003). *DEMA's international capacity.* www.baredskabsstyrelsen.dk/demaint/engelsk%20version.pdf.

Developmental Initiatives. (2010). *GHA Report 2010.* UK. http://www.globalhumanitarianassistance.org/report/gha-report-2010.

Development Initiatives. (2005). *Humanitarian assistance update, 2004–2005.* Somerset, UK: Global Humanitarian Assistance Report Series.

European Commission. (2010). *112: Your lifeline in the EU. EC Fact sheet.* http://ec.europa.eu/information_society/doc/factsheets/044-112-bluerev-en.pdf.

Federal Emergency Management Agency (FEMA). (2004). *Emergency management guide for business and industry.* www.fema.gov/library/biz3.shtm.

Grant, G. (2008). *Navy forms fleet to serve Western Hemisphere.* Government Executive. April 30.

Harvey, R. (2005). *Tsunami gives Aceh troops new role* (January 21). news.bbc.co.uk/2/bi/asia-pacific/4194773.stm.

International Decade for Natural Disaster Reduction (IDNDR). (1994). *Yokohama Strategy and plan of action for a safer world.* World Conference on Natural Disaster Reduction. Yokohama, Japan, May 23–27.

International Strategy for Disaster Reduction (ISDR). (2001). *Activities of the Federal Emergency Management Agency in Central America and the Caribbean.* www.crid.or.cr/crid/CD_EIRD_informa/no2_2001/pagina15.htm.

OECD. (2010). Development aid rose in 2009 and most donors will meet 2010 aid targets. Development Cooperation Directorate. OECD Website. http://www.oecd.org/document/11/0,3343,en_2649_3447_1_1_1_1_1,000.html.

Pellerin. (2005). U.S. Weather Service helps Tunisia develop forecasting abilities. *Washington File* (May 19).

Ring, W. (2007). *Congress makes it easier for cross-border emergency cooperation.* The Associated Press. December 18.

Santa Clara County Fire Department. (2010). *International "911" and emergency numbers.* www.sccfd.org/travel.html.

United Nations Office for the Coordination of Humanitarian Affairs (UNOCHA). (2005). *Humanitarian affairs.* http://ochaonline.un.org/webpage.asp?Nav=_humanissues_en&Site=_humanissues.

UNOCHA. (2010). *UNOCHA Annual Report (2009).* http://ochaonline.un.org/Portals/0/2010/Reports/OCHA%20AR2009_Hi%20Res_Final.pdf.

USAID. (2010). Most recent disaster declaration: Cyclone 03-17-2010. USAID Disaster Assistance. http://www.usaid.gov/our_work/humanitarian_assistance/disaster_assistance/countries/madagascar/template/index.html

United States Department of Labor. (2004). *Firefighting occupations*. Washington, DC: Bureau of Labor Statistics.

United States Office of Foreign Disaster Assistance (OFDA). (2004). *OFDA annual report FY 2003*. Washington, DC: USAID.

University of Wisconsin's Disaster Management Center. (1987). *Disaster preparedness*. Course C280-BB04, Disaster Management Center.

Appendix 8–1

Emergency Numbers of the World

Country or Region	EMS	Fire	Police
Afghanistan		No national system	
Albania	17	18	19
Algeria	21606666	14	17
American Samoa	911	911	911
Andorra	118	118	110
Angola	118	118	110
Anguilla	911	911	911
Antarctica	911	911	911
Antigua & Barbuda	999/911	999/911	999/911
Argentina	107	100	101
Armenia	103	—	—
Aruba	911	911	911
Ascension Island	6000	911	6666
Australia	000 (112 on mobile)	000 (112 on mobile)	000 (112 on mobile)
Austria	112/122	112/122	112/122
Azerbaijan (Baku)	03	01	02
Azores	112	—	—
Bahamas	911	911	911
Bahrain	999	999	999
Bali	112	118	118
Bangladesh (Dhaka)	199	9 555 555	866 551-3
Barbados	511	311	211
Belgium	112	112	112
Belarus	103	101	102
Belize	911	911	911
Benin		No national system	
Bermuda	911	911	911
Bhutan	110	112	113
Bolivia (La Paz)	118	—	110
Bonaire	911	911	911
Borneo (Sabah)	999	—	—
Bosnia-Herzegovina	124	123	122

(*Continued*)

Emergency Numbers of the World—Continued

Country or Region	EMS	Fire	Police
Botswana	997/911	997/911	997/911
Brazil	192	193	190
Bosnia	94	93	92
British Virgin Islands	999	999	999
Brunei	991	995	993
Bulgaria	150	160	166
Burkina Faso		No national system	
Burma/Myanmar	999	999	999
Burundi		No national system	
Cambodia (Phnom Penh)	119	118	117
Cameroon		No national system	
Canada (AB, MB, NB, NS, ON, PE, QU)	999	911	999
Canada (BC, NF, SK)	911 (only in major cities)	911 (only in major cities)	911 (only in major cities)
Canada (NT)		3 dig + 2222	3 dig + 1111
Canada (NU)		Local only	
Canada (YK)	3 dig + 3333	3 dig + 2222	3 dig + 5555
Canary Islands	112	112	112
Cape Verde	130	131	132
Cayman Islands	911	911	911
Central African Republic		No national system	
Chad		18	17
Chile	131	132	133
China	999/120 (Beijing)	119	110
Christmas Island	000	000	000
Colombia	112/123 (land & mobile)	112/123 (land & mobile)	112/123 (land & mobile)
Comoros Islands		No national system	
Congo		No national system	
Cook Islands	998	996	999
Costa Rica	911	911	911
Côte d'Ivoire	110	111	170
Croatia	94/112	93/112	92
Cuba	26811	26811	26811
Curaçao	112	114	444444
Cyprus	112	112	112
Czech Republic	112/155	112/150	112/158
Congo		No national system	
Denmark	112	112	112
Djibouti	351351	18	17
Dominica	999	999	999

Emergency Numbers of the World—Continued

Country or Region	EMS	Fire	Police
Dominican Republic	911	911	911
East Timor	112	112	112
Easter Island	100-215	100-264	100-244
Ecuador	131	—	101
Egypt	123	180	112
El Salvador	911	911	911
England	112/999	112/999	112/999
Equatorial Guinea		No national system	
Eritrea		No national system	
Estonia	112	112	112
Ethiopia	92	93	91
Faeroe Islands	112	112	112
Falkland Islands	999	999	999
Fiji	911	9170	911
Finland	112	112	112
France	112/15	112/18	112/17
French Guiana	112/15	112/18	112/17
Gabon	1300-1399	18	1730
Gaborone	997/991	998	999
Gambia	16	18	17
Georgia	022	022	022
Germany	112	112	112
Ghana	193	192	191
Gibraltar	999	999	999
Greece	112/166	112/199	112/100
Greenland	—	113	—
Grenada	434	112	911
Guadeloupe	18	18	17
Guam	911	911	911
Guatemala	123	123	110
Guernsey	999	999	999
Guinea Bissau		No national system	
Guinea Republic		No national system	
Guyana	912	913	911
Haiti	118	—	114
Honduras	195/37 8654	198	119
Hong Kong	999/112 (mobile)	999/112 (mobile)	999/112 (mobile)
Hungary	112/105	112/107	112/104
Iceland	112	112	112
India	102	101	100
Indonesia	118/119	113	110
Iran	115	125	110

(Continued)

Emergency Numbers of the World—Continued

Country or Region	EMS	Fire	Police
Iraq		No national system	
Ireland, Republic of	112/999	112/999	112/999
Israel	101	102	100
Italy	118/112	115/112	113/112
Jamaica	110	110	119
Japan	119	119	110
Jersey	999	999	999
Jordan	191	193	192
Kazakhstan	03	03	03
Kenya	999	999	999
Kiribati	994	—	—
Kosovo	991	991	991
Korea (North)		No national system	
Korea (South)	119	119	112
Kuwait	112	112	112
Kyrgyzstan	103	103	103
Laos		No national system	
Latvia	03/112	01/112	02/112
Lebanon	140	175	112
Lesotho	121	122	123/124
Liberia	911 (mobile only)	911 (mobile only)	911 (mobile only)
Libya	193	193	193
Liechtenstein	112	112	112
Lithuania	112	112	112
Luxembourg	112	112	112/113
Macau	999/318	999/318	999/318
Macedonia	193	192	193
Madagascar		No national system	
Madeira	112	112	112
Malawi	998	999	997
Malaysia	999	994	999
Maldives Republic	102	999	119
Mali	15	17	18
Malta	112	112	112
Marianas Island	911	—	—
Marshall Islands	625411	—	6258666
Martinique	15	18	17
Mauritania	—	118	117
Mauritius	999	999	999
Mayotte	15	—	—

Emergency Numbers of the World—Continued

Country or Region	EMS	Fire	Police
Menorca	112	112	112/091
Mexico	066/060/080	066/060/080	066/060/080
Micronesia		No national system	
Moldavia	903	901	902
Monaco	112	112	112
Mongolia	103	101	102
Montserrat	911	—	999
Morocco	15	15	19
Mozambique	117	198	119
Myanmar	199	199	199
Namibia	2032276	2032270	1011
Nauru		No national system	
Nepal		101	100/103
Netherlands	112	112	112
Netherlands Antilles	112	112	112
New Caledonia	18	18	17
New Zealand	111	111	111
Nicaragua	128	115/911	118
Niger		No national system	
Nigeria	199	199	199
Niue	999	999	999
Norfolk Islands	000	000	000
Northern Ireland	112/999	112/999	112/999
Norway	113	110	112
Oman	9999	9999	9999
Pakistan	115	16	15
Palau	911	911	911
Palestine	101	101	100
Panama	911	911	911
Papua New Guinea (Port Moresby)		110 (cities)	000 (cities)
Paraguay	911	911	911
Peru		116	105
Philippines	117	117	117
Pitcairn Islands		No telephone system	
Poland	112/997	112/999	112/998
Portugal	112	112 (115 for forest fires)	112
Puerto Rico	911	911	911
Qatar	999	999	999

(*Continued*)

Emergency Numbers of the World—Continued

Country or Region	EMS	Fire	Police
Réunion	15/112	18	17
Romania	112	112	112
Russia	112	112	112
Russian Federation	03/911/112	01/911/112	02/911/112
Rwanda	—	—	112
Saba	912		5994 63237
Sabah (Borneo)	999	999	999
Samoa	999	999	999
San Marino	118	115	113
São Tomé and Principe		No national system	
Sarawak	999	994	999
Saudi Arabia	997	998	999
Scotland	112/999	112/999	112/999
Sicily, Isles of	999	999	999
Senegal	—	No national system	
Serbia	112	112	112
Seychelles	999	999	999
Sierra Leone	999	019	999
Singapore	995	995	999
Slovak Republic (Slovakia)	155	150	158
Slovenia	112	112	113
Solomon Islands	999	999	999
Somalia		No national system	
South Africa	10177	10177	10111
South Africa (Cape Town)	107	107	107
S. Georgia Islands/S. Sandwich Islands	—	No telephone system	
Spain	112	112	112
Sri Lanka	110	111	118/119
St. Eustatius	140	140	140
St. Helena	911	911	911
St. Kitts & Nevis	911	911	911
St. Lucia	999/911	999/911	999/911
St. Maarten	911/542-2111	911/120	911/542-2111
St. Pierre & Miquelon	15	18	17
St. Vincent & the Grenadines	999/911	999/911	999/911
Sudan	—	—	112
Suriname	115	115	115
Swaziland		No national system	
Sweden	112	112	112
Switzerland	112/144	112/118	112/117

Emergency Numbers of the World—Continued

Country or Region	EMS	Fire	Police
Syria	110	113	112
Tahiti (French Polynesia)	15	—	—
Taiwan	119	119	110
Tajikistan	03	—	—
Tanzania	112/999	112/999	112/999
Thailand	1669	199	191
Tibet		Unknown	
Togo	—	—	101
Tonga	911	911	911
Trinidad & Tobago	990	990	999
Tunisia	190	198	197
Turkey	110	155	112
Turkmenistan	03	03	03
Turks and Caicos Islands	999/911	999/911	999/911
Tuvalu/Ellice Islands	911	911	911
Uganda	112 (mobile)/ 999 (fixed)	112 (mobile)/999 (fixed)	112 (mobile)/999 (fixed)
Ukraine	112	112	112
United Arab Emirates (Abu Dhabi)	998/999	998/999	998/999
UK	112/999	112/999	112/999
United States	911	911	911
Uruguay	911	911	911
U.S. Virgin Islands	911	911	911
Uzbekistan	03	03	03
Vanuatu	112	112	112
Vatican City	113	115	112
Venezuela	171	171	171
Vietnam	05	08	03
Wake Island		No telephone system	
Western Sahara	150		
Western Samoa	999	999	999
Yemen	191	191	194
Yugoslavia (Serbia & Montenegro)	94	—	—
Zambia	999/112 mobile	993/112 mobile	999/112 mobile
Zimbabwe	994/999	993/999	995/999

Source: Adapted from International "911 and Emergency Numbers," Santa Clara County Fire Department, 2010.

9

Participants: Nongovernmental Organizations (Including the Private Sector and Academia)

Introduction

A nongovernmental organization (NGO) is an organization independent of the government whose primary mission is not commercial, but focuses on social, cultural, environmental, educational, and other types of issues. These organizations often work locally and internationally in the field of development. There are hundreds of thousands of NGOs worldwide.

With the increasing recognition of the plight of disaster victims and the vulnerability of nations, the number of NGOs focusing on international humanitarian relief and development has grown exponentially. These organizations have asserted their position as a primary component of disaster response and recovery through the vital role they have assumed in filling the many gaps left unattended by national and multilateral organizations. NGOs have significantly improved the ability of national and international relief agencies to address the victims' needs with their diverse range of skills and supplies. Outdated stereotypes of NGOs as made up of idealists who merely interfere with the "official" responders have been replaced by a collective and genuine appreciation for their invaluable and irreplaceable capability and professionalism. Some larger NGOs, like the International Federation of Red Cross/Red Crescent Societies (IFRC), have established an international presence similar to that of the United Nations, which has allowed them to develop strong local institutional partnerships and a capacity to provide immediate and highly effective response services.

As a group, NGOs tackle an incredibly wide range of response and recovery needs. Individually, they tend to address single needs or sets of related needs around which they have focused and refined their abilities. Their organizational structure may be adapted to best address those needs in as short a time and with as little administrative cost as possible. These organizations overall have enjoyed such great success in performing their humanitarian assistance tasks that major humanitarian aid organizations such as USAID/OFDA, AusAID, and the UN now provide a majority of their relief assistance by directly funding the responding NGOs, rather than doing the same work using their own staff and resources. Through their focus and dedication, NGOs have been able to greatly improve upon the governments' ability to address specific humanitarian tasks, and in doing so have greatly improved the success of international disaster management.

In any large-scale, internationally recognized disaster, it is not uncommon to see hundreds of individual NGOs working side by side to address the needs of the affected population. These organizations are the workhorses of response, rapidly assessing and addressing the needs of the hundreds, thousands, or even millions of victims affected by the disaster before the resources of the affected government arrive. After most other responders, government or otherwise, have concluded their actions at the disaster scene, the same NGO community remains working for years and decades to help the affected communities and countries rebuild what was lost and reduce future disaster vulnerability.

This chapter discusses the various types of NGOs involved in international disaster management, and describes the kinds of activities they often perform throughout the four phases of the disaster management cycle. Their operations, including the funding they receive, the ways they coordinate, and how they interact with the military, will be addressed. Various "standards of conduct" by which NGOs have come to operate will be presented. The role of the private sector and academia in disaster management will be addressed as well. Finally, two examples of successful disaster management-focused NGOs will be provided.

Who Are the NGOs?

In the field of disaster management, NGOs are commonly defined as nonprofit, civilian-based, staffed organizations that depend on outside sources of funding and materials (including funding from governments) to carry out a humanitarian-based mission and associated goals in a target population. Individually, they tend to perform unique tasks, while collectively addressing all facets of predisaster development and postdisaster response and recovery. The majority of NGOs that work in development and disaster management are small, although the most well known, such as the Red Cross and Catholic Relief Services, are very large.

NGOs in the field of disaster management and humanitarian assistance tend to have two defining characteristics. First, their members generally have a common background, whether religious, technical (doctors or engineers, for instance), national, regional, or otherwise. Second, they have a defined mission that guides their actions, such as to build housing, address medical needs, provide counseling, build wells, and so forth. Their area of operations—where they perform their work—may be global, regional, or national. And within each community, one or more "local" NGOs may be willing to respond to a disaster, even if their primary purpose is other than disaster management.

Several classifications of humanitarian-based NGOs are described in the following list. These broad definitions are widely accepted among the international relief community and, while not every organization will neatly fit into one of these categories, they have become part of the standardized disaster response nomenclature:

- *Nongovernmental organization (NGO).* The general term for an organization made up of private citizens, with no affiliation with a government of any nation other than support from government sources in the form of financial or in-kind contributions. These groups are motivated by greatly varying factors, ranging from religious beliefs to humanitarian values. NGOs are considered "national" if they work in one country, "international" if they are based out of one country but work in more than four countries, and "multinational" if they have partner organizations in several countries. Oxfam and the IFRC are examples of multinational NGOs. NGOs can be further defined according to their functionality: religious groups, such as the Catholic Church; interest groups, such as Rotary International; residents' organizations; occupational organizations; educational organizations; and so on.

- *Private voluntary organization (PVO).* An organization that is nonprofit, tax-exempt, and receives at least a part of its funding from private donor sources. PVOs also receive some degree of voluntary contributions in the form of cash, work, or in-kind gifts. This classification is steadily being grouped together under the more general NGO classification. It should be mentioned that although all PVOs are NGOs, the opposite is not true.

- *International organization (IO).* An organization with global presence and influence. The Union of International Organizations lists over 50,000 international organizations in their online registry (UIO, 2005). Although both the UN and the International Committee of the Red Cross (ICRC) are IOs, only the ICRC is an NGO. International law provides a legal framework under which these organizations function.

- *Donor agencies.* Private, national, or regional organizations whose mission is to provide the financial and material resources for humanitarian relief and subsequent rehabilitation. These donated resources may go to NGOs, national governments, or private citizens. Examples of donor agencies are USAID, the European Community Humanitarian Organization (ECHO), and the World Bank.

- *Coordinating organizations.* NGO associations that coordinate the activities of tens to hundreds of preregistered member organizations to ensure response with maximized impact. They can decrease the amount of overlap and help distribute need to the greatest range of victims. They also can analyze immediate needs assessments and recommend which member organizations would be most effective to respond. Examples of coordinating organizations include InterAction and the International Council for Voluntary Agencies (ICVA).

Although these organizations differ in many ways, they can be characterized by several traits they share almost without exception:

1. *They value their independence and neutrality.* Especially in situations of civil conflict or government oppression, being perceived as independent is vital to both safety and success. Employees of an NGO could become targets if they are associated with an enemy group. They may be denied access to victims located in territory under the control of a certain faction. And finally, the victims may refuse assistance due to fear of government or other influence. NGOs thus often are unwilling to cooperate with government and military organizations when conflict exists. They also are unwilling to share assessment and other information gathered through their work at the field level—including reporting observed war crimes to international tribunals—for fear that this would be seen as assisting one group over another. A perception of independence has other advantages outside of conflict situations. For instance, in disaster situations where an affected national government does not want to be perceived as needing the assistance of other national governments, they may be willing to accept the help of autonomous bodies.
2. *Their organizational structure tends to be decentralized.* NGOs will often carry out their work without any binding or definitive hierarchy, succeeding in their actions through field-level management. Ground-level units or teams are given much more flexibility and decision-making power than military and government organizations, which primarily use the opposite approach.
3. *They are committed.* NGOs have been called the "arms and legs of disaster response" (ICDF, 2004). They deploy to disaster and conflict zones with great speed and efficiency, risking

life and limb to provide humanitarian assistance. NGOs are involved not only in short-term disaster relief but also in the long-term recovery efforts, which may follow for months, years, or even decades—long after most other organizations have given up.

4. *They are highly practice-oriented.* As is true in many ways with military resources, NGOs are very "operational" in nature. However, teams tend to improvise in the field as necessary and provide onsite training as part of their regular procedures. They rarely use field guides to direct their work, relying instead on the individual experience of employees and volunteers. (CDMHA, n.d.)

Because NGOs depend on outside funding for their operations, they must spend a significant amount of effort on public relations, fundraising, and outreach. For this reason, locating detailed information about these organizations can easily be done by accessing their Web sites. The various coordinating agencies, of which many NGOs are members, maintain contact lists of associated NGOs. The following lists some Web sites that provide NGO listings and contact information:

- InterAction: http://www.interaction.org/member-directory-all
- Aid Matrix: http://www.aidmatrix.org/Partners/ngopartners.htm
- Relief Web: http://www.reliefweb.int/rw/rwc.nsf/doc202?OpenForm
- NGO Voice: http://www.ngovoice.org/index.php?page=121
- Alert Net: http://www.alertnet.org/member_directory.htm
- International Council for Voluntary Organizations: http://www.icva.ch/members.html
- One World: http://us.oneworld.net/organizations/nonprofitpartners/directory

What Do They Do?

NGOs that focus on disaster management provide a great many required resources and services. For instance, NGOs are well regarded for their information-gathering abilities, which are used to create and verify damage and needs assessments. Rather than try to address all aspects of disaster management, they focus their efforts upon individual skill sets or technical services—such as the medical abilities of Médicins sans Frontières (MSF, or Doctors Without Borders) or Oxfam's ability to address nutritional needs—providing a much higher level of service than otherwise would be available and increasing the overall effectiveness of response and recovery. Through their sheer numbers, NGOs allow for a greater capability to reach a larger population in less time. The amount of financial support that is dedicated to disasters through these NGOs' fundraising efforts greatly increases the amount of humanitarian work that is performed.

Disaster management is an ever-improving science, growing in efficiency and efficacy through the shared knowledge base augmented by each successive disaster response. One of the most notable changes over the past several decades that continues today is the increasing dependence of governments and multilateral organizations on NGOs to execute much of the actual humanitarian work. These same organizations that not long ago were regarded as obstacles are now being entrusted with the bulk of the funding that allows for response, relief, reconstruction, and recovery. The result is that NGOs have begun to develop an enormous institutional base of educated, experienced staff, located in all parts of the world that are seen in many ways as the authorities in the functions they perform.

Governments often no longer need to dedicate and transport specialized teams of response and recovery officials, because they are confident that NGOs will provide equal or even better levels of quality.

The primary goal of NGOs involved in disaster management and humanitarian operations is to reduce victims' pain and suffering. How they do this depends on their mission, goals, and focus. Some NGOs may provide food, while others may provide shelter or medical assistance. All of these actions can be grouped into four overarching objectives:

1. Reduce the crude mortality rate observed among disaster victims
2. Reduce or minimize the incidence of disease and disability, while stabilizing public health conditions
3. Assist in the reconstruction and repair of infrastructure that has been damaged or destroyed
4. Protect displaced populations, and provide for their safe return once the emergency has passed (Frandsen, 2002).

Examples of areas in which NGOs focus their efforts include:

- Agriculture
- Animal rescue and care
- Clothing
- Community development
- Coordination of NGO action
- Cultural preservation
- Disarmament
- Disaster mitigation, preparedness, and education
- Early childhood and adult education
- Emergency response
- Food provision and nutrition
- Health education
- Housing repair and reconstruction
- Human rights
- Immediate shelter and mass care camp administration
- Microfinance
- Peace building/conflict resolution
- Protection of the environment
- Providing for the special needs of vulnerable groups (children, seniors, women)
- Psychological counseling
- Refugee and internally displaced persons care
- Safe water provision
- Sanitation
- Short- and long-term medical assistance
- Victim security and safety

Because development and disaster management are so closely linked, as was described in Chapter 1 and will be further addressed in Chapter 11, many NGOs operate in developing countries irrespective of the presence of a disaster. Although smaller NGOs do not always deploy to a disaster scene until after they have been alerted to the need, a great many organizations invariably will long have had a presence in the affected country by the time the disaster strikes. They thus have trust established with the people and government of that country, and they hold a unique understanding of the specific problems of the affected population, as well as how best to address them. They are also able to commence their operational work almost immediately and with little or no additional, site-specific employee training. They are familiar with cultures, languages, governance structures, economies, social networks, climates, and geographies. The Red Cross, for example, has operating chapters in almost every country of the world, and has built strong partnerships with many local and national agencies that may lead the response to a crisis. By the time their services are called on in response to a disaster, they may have all the personnel, equipment, and resources in place to begin work without hesitation.

NGO disaster management work, like all other disaster management work, falls under the four functions of the emergency management spectrum: preparedness, mitigation, response, and recovery. Governments and multilateral organizations almost always provide the greatest amount of operational and financial support to achieve the "pre-disaster" activities of preparedness and mitigation. While many "development NGOs"—those that have a long-standing presence in the country before the disaster occurs—do address mitigation and disaster management capacity through their overall efforts, it is rarely central to their mission. On the other hand, NGOs play a very large part in the response and long-term recovery from disaster events in all nations, rich or poor.

Some NGOs' organizational efforts and actions focus almost entirely on the disaster's short-term response needs. Involvement may include actual emergency response activities equivalent to or in support of those performed by local fire, police, emergency medical, and emergency management agencies (as described in previous chapters), or they may offer comfort to victims by providing much needed food, water, clothing, and shelter. One of their greatest strengths is that they do not suffer from bureaucracy so they are able to deploy on very short notice. They may have pre-established teams, as well as caches of equipment and supplies, all of which are on standby 24 hours per day (many NGOs operate in the affected area within 12 hours' notice alongside the local first responders, long before donor government and other responders have arrived). Once the emergency phase of the disaster is over, most NGO volunteers and employees will return home, often to a full-time job that they temporarily vacated. Examples of organizations in this category include:

- Doctors Without Borders (Médecins sans Frontières)
- Doctors of the World (Médecins du Monde)
- International Medical Corps
- Mercy Corps
- Air-Serv International

In contrast to these rapid-deployment, rapid-return organizations are the development organizations that address the actual recovery and longer term reconstruction needs, including the preexisting vulnerability issues. Rather than provide for victims' individual needs, they tend to work on enhancing the community's overall capacity to provide these services for themselves. For instance, they will help a community rebuild a hospital, rather than offer medical care. In cases of complex humanitarian emergencies (CHEs), involving refugees and internally displaced persons, the agencies will work with these people to help them survive while displaced, and then provide them with the skills and resources necessary to reintegrate into an independent life after the emergency phase has ended. These NGOs have a deep institutional knowledge and understanding of the customs, language, politics, and other general characteristics of a society, making their operations more finely tuned to the special needs of the affected area. They may also have an infrastructure already in place before the disaster occurs from which to launch relief and recovery operations. Because of their development mission, however, these organizations may be unable to offer much in the form of short-term response assistance. Examples of this kind of organization include:

- Habitat for Humanity (see Figure 9–1)
- Health Volunteers Overseas
- Heifer International
- World Learning
- Synergos

There are some organizations that blur these lines, supporting both long- and short-term activities in disaster response. Large organizations that have been working in the country or community for a long time will, as previously mentioned, maintain a strong and established presence. Likewise, they have the infrastructure and knowledge necessary to either put other projects on hold to address

FIGURE 9–1 Relief and reconstruction efforts of NGOs like Habitat for Humanity supplement (and in many cases they exceed) the efforts of governments.

emergency needs or to add response activities to their regular range of services. These organizations have an intrinsic ability to gather timely and accurate assessment data on both the local population and the condition of the existing response and recovery systems, upon which data almost all other response actions will hinge. The numerous external response agencies that descend on a disaster scene, including other NGOs, often heavily rely on this expertise and knowledge to launch their own disaster response more effectively. Examples within this category of NGO include:

- International Federation of Red Cross and Red Crescent Societies
- Adventist Development and Relief Agency
- AmeriCares
- Concern Worldwide
- Latter-Day Saint Charities
- Relief International

Appendix 9–2 lists many of the NGOs that responded to (and continue to respond to) the 2010 earthquake in Haiti. Appendix 9–3 lists many of the academic and professional disaster management institutions that exist.

NGO Operations

Funding

Unlike governments and businesses, which have a fairly constant flow of money, NGOs must either conduct fundraising campaigns or apply for competitive grants to sustain their mission and activities. Each organization is unique in how it supports its financial requirements. For instance, NGOs that focus on emergency response activities may have few opportunities apart from defined emergencies to apply for grants or funding to support their emergency management-related work because governments, multilateral organizations, and private donors do not perceive an imminent need. These organizations may operate on very low administrative budgets at such times to compensate. The development organizations, on the other hand, whose activities are ongoing regardless of the presence of a disaster, must constantly seek grants and solicit funds—and request supplemental funds to address the increased demands resulting from the added disaster responsibilities.

Most organizations other than the larger, more established NGOs must quickly raise funds for response or recovery activities. Although they may be able to manage a few weeks or even months of operation by tapping into funding reserves, they must soon either generate funding from private or public donors or cease operations entirely. Wide recognition of the plight of the affected countries is key to the success of these organizations, because only through public knowledge of the disaster can they effectively tap into a philanthropic funding base. The expansion of media coverage has definitely helped in this regard, but NGOs must still campaign to raise awareness about the specific needs of the affected population they serve.

Several sources of funding exist for humanitarian and development NGOs. The United States Agency for International Development (USAID), most notably its Office of Foreign Disaster Assistance (OFDA), provides a significant amount of the funding used to support primarily U.S.-based NGOs in disaster response and recovery operations. Other important sources of funding include the various

Organisation for Economic Cooperation and Development (OECD) countries described in Chapter 8 and the UN through its various operational offices. NGOs also receive support in the form of in-kind assistance, such as equipment, supplies, and food aid. Many NGOs have pre-established relationships with corporations or other organizations (trade, religious, civic, etc.) that can quickly mobilize extensive resources. The various forms of funding that NGOs may tap into include:

- Philanthropic giving from private citizens (cash or in-kind)
- Corporate ongoing or one-time support (cash or in-kind)
- Religious organizations
- Civic organizations
- Government contracts
- Government grants
- International organization contracts
- International organization grants

NGOs compete to secure grants, contracts, or other funding for disaster management work using various proposal systems, defined by each donor agency. These agencies may solicit a request for proposals (RFP) from agencies that can perform highly specific humanitarian work to address pre-assessed needs. Depending on the size and scope of the emergency and the work required, an individual donor may choose to fund one NGO to perform all the necessary work or fund several to perform various tasks. Due to the time constraints of humanitarian emergency work, the bidding process is compressed and fast-paced, requiring NGOs to produce proposals in much less time than in other fields. Funded NGOs may perform all of the work themselves or may subcontract out specific tasks to other (often smaller) NGOs (local, national, or international) as required and allowed by their grant proposal or contract.

Coordination

Coordination is vital to every emergency situation. Disaster response and relief organizations and agencies working in concert clearly provide a greater sum benefit than they could working on their own. This applies to NGO agencies just as much as any other type—if not more. For years, the NGO community has resisted widespread coordination for many reasons, including fear of external control, their territorial nature concerning their mission objectives and goals, and a desire to avoid the bureaucracy that often accompanies formal coordination mechanisms. However, this trend has reversed in the past two decades.

NGOs are under no obligation to work with each other or with any other organization involved in response and recovery. However, many have recognized that they can benefit significantly from each other's expertise, equipment, information, access, and skills to further their own mission and goals, and have realized that they are likely to surpass these benchmarks if they successfully coordinate their actions. NGOs have found that they can share valuable resources, such as vehicles; air transport; supply transport; office and warehouse space; and information on dangers, damages, and needs, and benefit from the information and logistical support of the governmental resources responding to the disaster. Additionally, the very nature of their funding—from national governments and the international organizations—often *requires* that they coordinate their actions on cooperative projects and tasks to cut costs and increase capacity. Coordination is now an important topic of development study and of NGO non-emergency collaborative industry efforts (such as meetings and conventions).

There are several forms of coordination and, likewise, several mechanisms that have developed to accommodate these needs. NGOs must often coordinate with other NGOs and with local, national, or international government response and recovery organizations or military resources operating in the affected area. This coordination could range from the very informal, including teleconferences or meetings in temporary headquarters, to established systems that exist solely to monitor NGO activity and centralize information and resources. The coordination mechanism may originate within the NGO community or may be an office established by the affected government, an outside donor government, or an international organization such as the UN.

Depending on the disaster's size, onset speed, and scope, the range of agencies involved in response, and the emergency management capacity, NGOs may coordinate under several different locations, mechanisms, and situations. These include, but are not limited to,

- Local/national government emergency operations center
- Formal NGO coordination mechanisms established, maintained, and populated by only NGOs participating in the humanitarian response
- NGO field coordination meetings (formal or informal)
- Conference calls and teleconferences
- Designated coordination Web sites
- NGO-established permanent or temporary offices or operations centers
- UN-established coordination mechanism such as a UN Inter-Agency Standing Committee (IASC) or the UN Clusters (see Exhibit 6–11)
- Civil–military operations center (CMOC; see Chapter 8)
- Humanitarian information center (HIC) (see Exhibit 9–1)

EXHIBIT 9–1: HUMANITARIAN INFORMATION CENTERS

HICs support the coordination of humanitarian assistance through the provision of information products and services. The HIC supports the decision-making process at headquarters and field level by contributing to the creation of a common framework for information management within the humanitarian community.

Background

Accurate and timely information is crucial to the effective provision of humanitarian assistance. HICs aim to ensure that individuals and organizations at field and strategic levels have access to the benefits of information management tools to assess, plan, implement, and monitor humanitarian assistance. HICs are an interorganizational resource, reporting to the Humanitarian/Resident Coordinator, whose products and services are available to the entire humanitarian community. HICs provide surge capacity to the humanitarian community, particularly to the coordination function, usually (but not exclusively) in the context of complex emergencies.

Role of the HIC
- A space where the humanitarian community can share and access information resources to improve the planning and delivery of humanitarian assistance
- A provider of information products and services that enable the humanitarian community to deliver assistance more effectively, following principles of good practice in information management
- A focal point for data collection, analysis, and dissemination in support of the provision of humanitarian assistance, developing and supporting data standards
- A facilitator for initiatives and activities related to information management in the field, particularly in collaboration between other humanitarian actors in support of existing coordination structures
- An advocate for a culture of information-sharing in the humanitarian community, generating awareness of good practice and making it possible for agencies to develop common standards and practices in the field

Characteristics of the HIC
- A common resource of the humanitarian community
- An integral part of the coordination structure, seeking to avoid duplicating existing initiatives and maximizing resources
- Must work in partnership with specialized agencies to support, if required, sector-specific work
- Must be demand driven and must serve operational and strategic needs and seek feedback from users to ensure that products and services meet the needs of customers and adapt those outputs accordingly
- Must be service-oriented, open-access projects that create a link between technical staff and nontechnical users
- Should encourage participation by local, national, and international actors
- Along with its partners will develop a phase-out and transition strategy from the onset of its operation to link with reconstruction, rehabilitation, and development activities

Activities of the HIC
The HIC's work may include, but will not be limited to, the following activities:

- Provide orientation material to humanitarian actors, in written, graphic, and/or verbal form
- Provide a range of information services such as maps, contacts lists, meetings, schedules, etc.
- Develop and promote standards to facilitate data and information sharing
- Collect and maintain data on who's doing what where in the humanitarian community
- Collect, maintain, and make available a range of data sets from all sources, processing and disseminating this data as appropriate to support humanitarian operations
- Collect and maintain data for a Survey of Surveys to develop a master list of assessments planned, under way, and completed by all partner agencies
- Establish document management and archive facilities for the storage and retrieval of relevant documentation relating to the emergency and the humanitarian response

(Continued)

EXHIBIT 9–1: HUMANITARIAN INFORMATION CENTERS (CONTINUED)

- Develop and deploy Geographic Information Systems in key humanitarian sectors
- Create a framework and strategy for information management in the field, liaising with other organizations
- Advise other organizations on information management issues
- Provide technical support to improve the information management capacity of the humanitarian community, including working with key partner organizations
- Provide physical space for the humanitarian community (include meeting space, mailboxes, noticeboards, and connectivity for humanitarian actors)
- Engage with local actors to support and develop existing information infrastructures

Source: HumanitarianInfo.org, 2005.

- Onsite operations coordination center (OSOCC), created to assist the local authorities of the affected country with managing the disaster, particularly coordinating international search and rescue teams. The OSOCC can be established by the first international search-and-rescue (SAR) teams to arrive in cooperation with national authorities, or by resources mobilized by the International Search and Rescue Advisory Group (INSARAG) Secretariat in Office for the Coordination of Humanitarian Affairs–Geneva and the United Nations Disaster Assessment and Coordination (UNDAC) team. The OSOCC will assess the need for and use of international resources and provide support to the affected country by managing operations and logistical support for international SAR teams and registering their operational capabilities. The OSOCC provides a platform for national and international relief agencies to exchange information and coordinate their activities. In the OSOCC, international relief teams are registered and are provided with basic information about the situation, operations of national authorities, and logistics arrangements.

- Humanitarian assistance coordination center (HACC), usually created by a military organization participating in the humanitarian assistance operation. It assists with interagency coordination and planning, providing the critical link between the military commander, other government agencies, and nongovernmental, international, and regional organizations that may participate in a humanitarian assistance operation at the strategic level.

- Humanitarian operations center (HOC), an interagency policy-making body that coordinates the overall relief strategy among all participants in a large foreign humanitarian assistance operation. It is normally established under the direction of the affected country's government, the UN, or a U.S. government agency during a unilateral U.S. operation. The humanitarian operations center should consist of representatives from the affected country, embassies or consulates, military forces, the UN, NGOs, international organizations, and other major players in the operation.

- Civil–military coordination center (CMCC), located inside the military operational compound for planning, coordinating, and conducting civil–military operations. In principle, it is accessible only to designated key representatives of the civil authorities and the heads of civilian agencies such as UNHCR, United Nations High Commissioner for Human Rights, UN International Organization for Migration, UNDP, ICRC, and Red Crescent that are involved in planning, conducting, and coordinating the humanitarian operation.

- Civil–military information center (CIMIC), equivalent to a U.S. CMOC, but established outside the designated military compound. It is essentially a humanitarian assistance coordination center, providing information about and coordination of plans and joint projects with civilian agencies, civil authorities, contractors, and the local population. A CIMIC will usually provide civilian authorities, IOs, NGOs, UN agencies, and the civilian population with information on the prevailing operational situation and plans and minor/major projects, either planned or ongoing.

Despite the advances in coordination among the responding NGOs and the other responding agencies, there is often a lack of cooperation between the local and international NGOs operating within the disaster response. In several humanitarian emergencies, two entirely separate NGO coordination mechanisms have developed—one for local NGOs and one for international NGOs—rather than one single coordination mechanism to address the needs of all NGOs involved. Fortunately, this is not always the case, and there are several recognized examples of effective NGO coordination mechanisms, including:

- Committee for Coordination of Services to Displaced Persons in Thailand (CCSDPT)
- NGO Coordination Committee in Iraq (NCCI)
- NGO Coordinating Committee for Northern Iraq (NCCNI)
- NGO Coordination Committee for the Maharashtra flood relief efforts (India)
- Coordination Committee of the Women NGOs (Bam, Iran earthquake)

NGOs also maintain permanent associations that serve as coordination mechanisms both outside of and during disaster operations. These permanent associations primarily enable member NGOs to share ideas and lessons learned, and act as a collective advocacy body that pools the influence of all members. They provide much of the funding for, or even conduct, research aimed at improving overall NGO participation and coordination in global humanitarian efforts. Examples of NGO associations include:

- InterAction
- International Council of Volunteer Agencies (ICVA)
- International Network of NGOs for Emergency and Development (INNED)
- Steering Committee for Humanitarian Response (SCHR)
- Voluntary Organizations in Cooperation in Emergencies (VOICE)
- Dóchas—The Irish Association of Non-governmental Development Organizations

NGO/Military Cooperation

Over time, the military (from the affected country and outside donor countries) and NGOs have emerged as the two most significant operational humanitarian response participants. These organizations are conceptually and idealistically very different, presenting a formidable coordination challenge. Their organizational structures are very different (centralized vs. decentralized), as are their operations (top-down vs. bottom-up), and length of commitment (short-term vs. long-term). As international disaster management has become more complex, these two important players are interacting and cooperating to an ever-increasing degree for the mutual benefit of both.

NGOs traditionally have resisted direct cooperation with military organizations. First and foremost, NGOs have feared that such cooperation would compromise the core values that allow them to perform their work, including the perception of impartiality (neutrality) and independence. They believe it is vital that the host population view their actions as entirely independent of any government or military interference, securing both the acceptance of their actions and the safety of their employees. Second, NGOs have a long-standing fear that military organizations will attempt to take over the humanitarian operation, impeding or preventing them from serving their target populations. Finally, some NGOs simply are biased against working with the military, whether based on ideological or political differences, negative past experiences, or, specifically in reference to CHEs, the perception that military organizations are ultimately to blame for the disaster.

On the other hand, many NGOs have recognized that there are valuable resources and services that only the military can offer, each of which can be used to increase the NGO's ability to achieve its humanitarian goals. For instance, the military is often the only source of heavy equipment to transport response and recovery supplies and materials, as well as NGO employees, to the affected areas. The military also has the technological resources to generate more broad-reaching damage assessment data (e.g., satellite and aerial imagery), and can offer highly specialized technical and logistical assistance. In particular, NGOs rely on their advanced mobile communications capacity in situations where infrastructure is damaged or destroyed. Finally (and in many cases, most significantly), the military can offer protection from violence. Besides actual physical protection, they have highly specific information on mines and dangerous territory. Though protection is often required in CHEs, this need has become more widespread in recent years as attacks on NGO personnel have increased (see Exhibit 9–2). In both the 2004 Asian earthquake and tsunami events in Aceh Province, Indonesia, and the 2005 Asian earthquake

---

EXHIBIT 9–2: CHRONOLOGY OF HUMANITARIAN AID WORKERS KILLED IN 2008

Date	Country	Explanation
1/7/2008	Somalia	Isse Abdulkadir Haji, an employee of the Zam Zam Foundation, was shot dead in Yaaqshiid district of Mogadishu by unknown gunmen.
1/28/2008	Somalia	Damien Lehalle, Victor Okumu, and Billan, all from MSF Netherlands, were killed after their car was hit by an IED in Kismayo.
2/13/2008	Somalia	A WFP contract convoy leader was shot dead at an illegal checkpoint near Bu aale.
2/25/2008	Pakistan	Gunmen opened fire on the Plan International office in Mansehra, killing four, including three Pakistani staff members. Another two were badly hurt.
2/28/2008	Afghanistan	Aid workers Cyd Mizell and Muhammad Hadi were killed in Afghanistan. The pair had been kidnapped by armed men in Kandahar while they traveled to work in the morning.
3/3/2008	Nepal	Six foreigners and four Nepalese were among seven UN staff and three crew members who died when a UN helicopter crashed in Ramechhap district, eastern Nepal.

3/12/2008	Somalia	An MSF Spain employee died after armed men opened fire on an MSF vehicle and several other nearby vehicles. The likely target of the attack was the TGF District Commissioner of Balcad.
3/15/2008	Pakistan	A Turkish aid worker involved in earthquake relief was killed in a bomb blast at a popular Italian restaurant in Islamabad.
3/24/2008	Sudan	A driver with WFP was killed while transporting food.
4/4/2008	Chad	Ramadan Djom, a driver of Save the Children UK, was killed during a carjacking.
4/7/2008	Sudan	Hamid Dafaalla, 47, the driver of a WFP-contracted truck, and his assistant were shot and killed by unknown assailants after delivering humanitarian food supplies.
4/14/2008	Somalia	Four teachers from the Hiran Community Education Project school in Beletweyne were killed during an al-Shabab attack on the town. Daud Hassan Ali and Rehana Ahmed were British nationals while Gilford Koech and Andrew Kibet were Kenyan.
4/21/2008	Sudan	Mohammed Makki El Rasheed, 58, a worker for a WFP-contracted trucking firm, was shot and killed on a main transport route between North and South Darfur.
4/30/2008	Sudan	Three armed men gained entry into the Save the Children's truck compound in Geneina. The gunmen shot Abdalla Hamid multiple times before they fled the compound in a Save the Children vehicle.
5/1/2008	Chad	Pascal Marlinge, the country director for Save the Children, was shot by bandits after they stopped his three-vehicle convoy.
5/7/2008	Kenya	Gunmen shot dead 37-year-old Zimbabwean Silence Chirara outside a UN compound in Lokichoggio, north of Nairobi, near the border with southern Sudan. He was ambushed while driving a clearly marked UN vehicle.
5/7/2008	Somalia	A WFP truck driver was shot by militiamen who stopped a convoy of 12 WFP-contracted trucks at an illegal checkpoint 30 km north of Galkayo.
5/8/2008	West Bank/ Gaza	Wafa Shaker El-Daghma, a school teacher serving with the United Nations Relief and Works Agency for Palestine Refugees (UNRWA), was killed at her home in Gaza in an operation conducted by the Israel Defense Forces.
5/14/2008	Iraq	A demining NGO employee was killed in a demining accident.
5/17/2008	Somalia	The director of the Somali aid organization Horn Relief was killed by masked gunmen as he arrived at his house in Kismayo.
6/10/2008	Pakistan	Three workers with the Pakistani humanitarian organization RISE were killed and two sustained injuries when their vehicle plunged into a ravine while negotiating a turn near Hungrai. The three employees were identified as driver Mohammad Pervaiz, Zaiba Shehnaz, and Babar Lateef.

(*Continued*)

EXHIBIT 9–2: CHRONOLOGY OF HUMANITARIAN AID WORKERS KILLED IN 2008 (CONTINUED)

6/11/2008	Somalia	Mohammed Abdulle Mahdi, the head of the Woman and Child Care Association (WOCCA) in Beletweyne, was killed by unidentified gunmen in Somalia. The gunmen opened fire on Mahdi's car as he was traveling through the Suqbad neighborhood of Mogadishu. Mahdi's driver was also killed in the incident.
6/12/2008	Somalia	A WFP-contracted driver was killed while transporting food aid to Bay and Bakool.
6/19/2008	Afghanistan	Unidentified armed men stormed a medical clinic run by Merlin in Kunduz. Dr. Sayid Masoom, the clinic head, and Mohammad Ewazewaz, the unarmed duty guard for the clinic, were fatally shot in the attack.
6/22/2008	Somalia	Mohamed Hassan Kulmiye, a peace activist with the Center for Research and Development, was shot in the head several times by unidentified gunmen.
6/27/2008	Sudan	Muzamil Ramadan Sida, 28, the Ugandan driver of a WFP-contracted truck, was shot and killed by unidentified assailants in an ambush on the Juba-Yei road in southern Sudan.
6/30/2008	Tanzania	Darren Stratti, an Australian aid worker helping build a village for orphans in northern Tanzania, was shot by burglars in a robbery attempt. He later succumbed to his wounds. Mr. Stratti worked for foodwatershelter, a small NGO set up to work in developing countries, building the villages that provide education, health, and social facilities for women, children, and orphans.
7/3/2008	Afghanistan	Three Afghan aid workers employed by an international NGO were reportedly killed in a Coalition Force (CF) air strike in Nuristan. Another staff member was wounded in the incident.
7/6/2008	Somalia	Osman Ali Ahmed, 48, head of the United Nations Development Programme (UNDP) office in Mogadishu, was assassinated by gunmen as he returned home from evening prayers. The gunmen shot him six times at close range. His younger brother was also fatally wounded in the incident.
7/7/2008	Somalia	In southern Somalia, gunmen shot and killed a WFP-contracted driver. Ahmed Saali was killed in fighting between convoy escorts and militiamen at a checkpoint in the Lower Shabelle region on Monday.
7/9/2008	Somalia	Ali Jama Bihi, a local peace activist, was killed by two gunmen as he left the local Mosque after morning prayers.
7/11/2008	Somalia	Gunmen shot and killed Mohamed Muhamoud Qeyre, the deputy head of Mogadishu-based, German-funded Daryeel Bulsho Guud (DBG). DBG reported that he had been gunned down as he was performing ablutions at a Mosque at Elasha Biyaha, Mogadishu.

7/13/2008	Somalia	A WFP contractor was killed by local authorities at a food warehouse in Buale after a confrontation in which they demanded a USD 30.00 tax per aid vehicle.
7/14/2008	Somalia	Safhan Moalim Muktar, the director of the South Somalia Youth Organization, was killed and his car was stolen.
8/6/2008	Somalia	Abdikadir Yusuf Kariye, head of an orphanage in Lafole near Mogadishu, was shot dead by unidentified attackers. Kariye had received death threats after organizing demonstrations to protest the killing of aid workers in Somalia.
8/12/2008	Somalia	Adan Quresh, a staff member of World Vision International, was killed in the crossfire as fighting broke out between armed groups in Wajid, southern Somalia.
8/13/2008	Afghanistan	Four International Rescue Committee aid workers were killed in an ambush in Logar Province in Afghanistan. They include three international staff members, all women—a British-Canadian, a Canadian, a Trinidadian-American—and an Afghan driver. Another Afghan driver was critically wounded. They were traveling to Kabul in a clearly marked International Rescue Committee vehicle when they came under fire. The staff members were identified as: Mohammad Aimal, 25, of Kabul; Nicole Dial, 30, a dual citizen of Trinidad and the United States; Jacqueline (Jackie) Kirk, Ph.D., 40, of Outrement, Quebec, a dual citizen of Canada and the United Kingdom; and Shirley Case, 30, of Williams Lake, British Columbia.
8/15/2008	Somalia	Abdulkadir Diad Mohamed, a Somali who joined WFP in June as an administration and finance assistant, was abducted and then shot dead after he tried to escape. His driver, who was not a WFP employee, was also killed.
8/27/2008	Afghanistan	Authorities identified a body as Kazuya Ito, a Japanese engineer who was seized by gunmen a day earlier in Nangarhar province. Kazuya Ito worked for Peshawar-kai.
9/1/2008	Congo, Dem. Rep.	Seven UN staff are among the 17 killed when an AirServ plane carrying humanitarian supplies crashes into a mountain 15 km northeast of Bukavu airport. The UN identified the victims as a Canadian member of the UN Development Programme (UNDP), an Indian who worked for the Office for the Coordination of Humanitarian Aid, two members of Médecins sans Frontiéres, one from France and one from the Republic of Congo. The other thirteen were citizens of the DRC. Two were employees of AirServ and were the crew. Four were with the UNDP and another four were civil servants, while the last three worked for Handicap International.

(Continued)

EXHIBIT 9–2: CHRONOLOGY OF HUMANITARIAN AID WORKERS KILLED IN 2008 (CONTINUED)

9/7/2008	Sudan	There was a fatal road traffic accident on the Juba Torit road around Liria (about 60 km southeast of Juba). One UNHCR national staff and one international NGO national staff were killed in the accident. In addition, one international staff member was injured.
9/14/2008	Afghanistan	Two Afghan doctors working for WHO and traveling in a clearly marked UN vehicle were targeted by a suicide bomber. Both doctors were killed.
9/23/2008	Somalia	Muslim extremists from the al Shabab group fighting the transitional government on September 23 sliced the head off of Mansuur Mohammed, 25, a World Food Programme (WFP) worker, before horrified onlookers from the Manyafulka village, 10 km (6 miles) from Baidoa.
10/6/2008	Somalia	A RCIED detonated in close proximity to a UN vehicle carrying UN staff members from Marka airstrip to town. A driver was killed and an international staff member wounded.
10/17/2008	Somalia	Gunmen killed WFP staffer Abdinasir Adan Muse, who was murdered as he left a local mosque after evening prayers. The incident occurred in Merka, about 80 km southwest of Mogadishu.
10/19/2008	Somalia	Unidentified gunmen killed Muktar Mohammed Hassan, a local man working for UNICEF, in the southern Hudur town.
10/20/2008	Afghanistan	Gayle Williams, a British aid worker with SERVE, was killed by two Taliban gunmen while she walked to work in Kabul. The Taliban falsely accused Gayle of spreading Christian propaganda.
10/25/2008	Somalia	Gunman shot dead Duniya Sheik Dauda, an employee of Iida, as she returned from work at the organization in the central Somali town of Gurilel. Iida campaigns for women's rights and against female genital mutilation.
10/29/2008	Somalia	Mohammed Geele, a local security adviser, and Hashi Sayid, a driver for the United Nations Office for Project Services (UNOPS), were killed in a suicide car bombing against the UNDP compound in Hargeisa, northern Somalia. Six staff members were also injured, two of them seriously.
11/8/2008	Somalia	Gunmen shot dead a Somali aid worker in southern Somalia. Mohamud Mohamed Osman Sakow of Mercy Corps was assassinated while walking to his house in Jamame, north of Kismayu.
11/12/2008	Pakistan	Stephen Vance, an aid worker in a USAID-funded project, was murdered by gunmen suspected of being associated with the Pakistani Taliban. Stephen and his driver were shot while leaving his home in the upscale University town area of Peshawar.

11/21/2008	Congo, Dem. Rep.	Munyiragi Didace Namujimbo, a national staff member in the United Nations Mission in the Democratic Republic of Congo (MONUC) working as a journalist with Radio Okapi, was shot and killed in Bukavu.
11/26/2008	Afghanistan	Belqis Mazloomyar—a UNHCR contract worker, women's rights activist, and community worker—was killed by unknown gunmen in Surkh Rod district of Nangarhar province in eastern Afghanistan. She was shot during a local shura meeting at Lower Sheikh Mesri, a temporary settlement for returnees. The identity of the perpetrators and their motives remain unclear.
11/28/2008	Sri Lanka	An aid worker with the Norwegian Refugee Council (NRC) was killed by unidentified gunmen in Batticaloa. A. Vigneswaran was shot and killed after the gunmen forced him from his house.
11/30/2008	Afghanistan	Mohamad Shar was killed when a suicide bomber attacked a passing vehicle. Shar had been working for Christian Children's Fund (CCF) for 18 months.
12/11/2008	Congo, Dem. Rep.	Seguin Tshisekedi was shot dead by unknown assailants a short distance from his home in the city center of Bukavu, Democratic Republic of Congo. According to the IRC, Mr. Tshisekedi had worked for IRC as a data entry assistant since 2003.
12/13/2008	Somalia	A Somali security guard working for ICRC was killed in a shooting incident in Mogadishu. An ICRC staff member and a driver were apparently temporarily detained by TFG police but were later released.
12/15/2008	Congo, Dem. Rep.	Gunmen shot and killed a Congolese aid worker from an Italian aid group in eastern Congo. Boduin Ntamenya was killed and his driver, Ciza Deo Gratias, was seriously wounded when their vehicle was ambushed in the town of Burayi 5 km south of Rutshuru. Both men worked for the Voluntary Association for International Service (AVSI), an Italian NGO operating in eastern Congo.
12/17/2008	Myanmar	A Thai aid worker with the Pattanarak Foundation was killed in a car accident in Burma. Mong Aye, 30, died of head injuries after the truck he was riding in had an accident about 12 km west of Three Pagodas town. Four other staff members from the Pattanarak Foundation were unharmed.
12/23/2008	Sri Lanka	Unidentified gunmen shot and killed a driver with the International Committee of the Red Cross (ICRC) in Jaffna, Sri Lanka. Sivasundaralingam Gangatharan, 32, was killed near the ICRC office after stepping down from the bus he was taking to work.
12/30/2008	West Bank/ Gaza	Two UNRWA staff members died as a result of the conflict in Gaza.

Source: Patronus Analytical, 2010. www.patronusanalytical.com.

in Kashmir, humanitarian assistance was required in areas of ongoing fighting, illustrating the importance of military protection in international disaster management.

In turn, the military is coming to accept the value of their NGO counterparts, recognizing that NGOs are not uninformed, ineffective "do-gooders" that merely interfere without actually performing any useful service, but quite the opposite. Besides their vital role in providing humanitarian assistance to the affected population, NGOs have unique access to the affected individuals themselves. The military is often unable to or prevented from making local assessments, which are required to develop true needs assessments and status reports. NGO workers tend to be much more trusted by victims, and are therefore better positioned to perform the kind of face-to-face interaction required to assess the situation on the ground and meet individual needs. NGOs also have the specific training to address disaster victims' less tangible needs, including mental health issues and public education to prevent secondary public health disasters. A good example of the synergy that has developed between military and NGO participants is the internally displaced persons (IDP) or refugee camp—the military is best suited to build it quickly, while the NGOs are better at administrating.

Several militaries, including the U.S., Canadian, and members of the North Atlantic Treaty Organization (NATO), have developed formal coordination mechanisms within which cooperation with NGOs may be carried out more systematically (and, hopefully, more effectively). Examples of these coordination mechanisms, as described previously, include the CMOCs, CIMICs, HACCs, and CMCCs. These systems are by no means perfect, however, because the NGOs and military groups have no obligation to cooperate with each other, and they often have different and conflicting goals and priorities. Some NGO advocacy groups have gone as far as to say that these military coordination mechanisms are designed only to accommodate the needs of the military partners, not of the NGOs. Coordination mechanisms do serve a useful purpose, as they allow for a much higher level of cooperation than is possible in their absence.

Standards of Conduct

Unlike governments and multilateral organizations, NGOs are accountable only to themselves and their donors. As mentioned, they have no obligation to coordinate with other NGOs or with official government responders. Further, they are subject only to the laws of the affected countries in terms of what they can and cannot do. Such independence influences NGO humanitarian response operations in both positive and negative ways.

In the early years of international disaster management, when each successive disaster resulted in the creation of and participation by new NGOs, a great deal of competition existed among the NGOs. International disaster management as a practice was still in its formative stages, and very little coordination of activities was attempted. Because these NGOs were often resource poor, operating on shoestring budgets and reaching only small pockets of need, government responders regarded their actions as benevolent, small-scale operations that merited little scrutiny. The NGOs had almost no professional foundation to guide their actions or professional associations to share their experiences and ideas. As a result, certain services and resources were duplicated, while other needs remained unmet.

Beginning in the 1980s and 1990s, NGOs significantly expanded their role in international disaster management and in the amount of funding they brought to the scene. As often occurs with rapid, unchecked growth, some instances of corruption and misuse of funds, among other problems, tarnished the reputation of the industry as a whole. Donors, whose generous philanthropic contributions the NGOs depended on, began losing confidence in the ability of the NGOs to carry out their mission. Meanwhile, the lack of coordination and effective management among the NGOs put the victims at risk as well.

Recognizing the need for self-discipline and organization, several NGOs set out to create codes of conduct and standards of service to regulate and guide their actions in humanitarian response. In 1994, eight of the largest NGOs involved in humanitarian response—the International Federation of Red Cross and Red Crescent Societies, Caritas Internationalis, Catholic Relief Services, International Save the Children Alliance, Lutheran World Federation, Oxfam, the World Council of Churches, and the International Committee of the Red Cross—developed "The Code of Conduct" and agreed to abide by its policies. This code formalized the actions of the growing number of NGOs involved in humanitarian assistance. They then extended the Code to serve as a general guideline to be followed by all organizations involved in international disaster management (IFRC, 2005a).

The Code was written to address the actions of any NGO, no matter its size, background, or affiliation, or whether its scope was local, national, or international. It mentions "10 Points of Principle" that NGOs may apply to their humanitarian work (see Exhibit 9–3). The Code helps to guide successful working relationships between NGOs and the other actors commonly engaged in disaster response and recovery operations. Today, there are over 350 signatories of this self-regulating code.

EXHIBIT 9–3: THE CODE OF CONDUCT

1. **The humanitarian imperative comes first.**
   The right to receive humanitarian assistance, and to offer it, is a fundamental humanitarian principle which should be enjoyed by all citizens of all countries. As members of the international community, we recognize our obligation to provide humanitarian assistance wherever it is needed. Hence the need for unimpeded access to affected populations is of fundamental importance in exercising that responsibility. The prime motivation of our response to disaster is to alleviate human suffering among those least able to withstand the stress caused by disaster. When we give humanitarian aid it is not a partisan or political act and should not be viewed as such.

2. **Aid is given regardless of the race, creed, or nationality of the recipients and without adverse distinction of any kind. Aid priorities are calculated on the basis of need alone.**
   Wherever possible, we will base the provision of relief aid upon a thorough assessment of the needs of the disaster victims and the local capacities already in place to meet those needs. Within the entirety of our programs, we will reflect considerations of proportionality. Human suffering must be alleviated whenever it is found; life is as precious in one part of a country as another. Thus, our provision of aid will reflect the degree of suffering it seeks to alleviate. In implementing this approach, we recognize the crucial role played by women in disaster-prone communities and will ensure that this role is supported, not diminished, by our aid programs. The implementation of such a universal, impartial, and independent policy can only be effective if we and our partners have access to the necessary resources to provide for such equitable relief, and have equal access to all disaster victims.

3. **Aid will not be used to further a particular political or religious standpoint.**
   Humanitarian aid will be given according to the need of individuals, families, and communities. Notwithstanding the right of nongovernmental humanitarian agencies (NGHAs) to espouse particular political or religious opinions, we affirm that assistance will

(Continued)

EXHIBIT 9–3: THE CODE OF CONDUCT (CONTINUED)

not be dependent on the adherence of the recipients to those opinions. We will not tie the promise, delivery, or distribution of assistance to the embracing or acceptance of a particular political or religious creed.

4. **We shall endeavor not to act as instruments of government foreign policy.**
   NGHAs are agencies that act independently from governments. We therefore formulate our own policies and implementation strategies and do not seek to implement the policy of any government, except insofar as it coincides with our own independent policy. We will never knowingly—or through negligence—allow ourselves, or our employees, to be used to gather information of a political, military, or economically sensitive nature for governments or other bodies that may serve purposes other than those that are strictly humanitarian, nor will we act as instruments of foreign policy of donor governments. We will use the assistance we receive to respond to needs and this assistance should not be driven by the need to dispose of donor commodity surpluses, nor by the political interest of any particular donor. We value and promote the voluntary giving of labor and finances by concerned individuals to support our work and recognize the independence of action promoted by such voluntary motivation. In order to protect our independence we will seek to avoid dependence upon a single funding source.

5. **We shall respect culture and custom.**
   We will endeavor to respect the culture, structures, and customs of the communities and countries we are working in.

6. **We shall attempt to build disaster response on local capacities.**
   All people and communities—even in disaster—possess capacities as well as vulnerabilities. Where possible, we will strengthen these capacities by employing local staff, purchasing local materials, and trading with local companies. Where possible, we will work through local NGHAs as partners in planning and implementation, and cooperate with local government structures where appropriate. We will place a high priority on the proper coordination of our emergency responses. This is best done within the countries concerned by those most directly involved in the relief operations, and should include representatives of the relevant UN bodies.

7. **Ways shall be found to involve program beneficiaries in the management of relief aid.**
   Disaster response assistance should never be imposed upon the beneficiaries. Effective relief and lasting rehabilitation can best be achieved where the intended beneficiaries are involved in the design, management, and implementation of the assistance program. We will strive to achieve full community participation in our relief and rehabilitation programs.

8. **Relief aid must strive to reduce future vulnerabilities to disaster as well as meet basic needs.**
   All relief actions affect the prospects for long-term development, either in a positive or a negative fashion. Recognizing this, we will strive to implement relief programs that actively reduce the beneficiaries' vulnerability to future disasters and help create sustainable lifestyles. We will pay particular attention to environmental concerns in the design and management of relief programs. We will also endeavor to minimize the negative impact of humanitarian assistance, seeking to avoid long-term beneficiary dependence upon external aid.

9. **We hold ourselves accountable to both those we seek to assist and those from whom we accept resources.**

   We often act as an institutional link in the partnership between those who wish to assist and those who need assistance during disasters. We therefore hold ourselves accountable to both constituencies. All our dealings with donors and beneficiaries shall reflect an attitude of openness and transparency. We recognize the need to report on our activities, both from a financial perspective and the perspective of effectiveness. We recognize the obligation to ensure appropriate monitoring of aid distributions and to carry out regular assessments of the impact of disaster assistance. We will also seek to report, in an open fashion, upon the impact of our work, and the factors limiting or enhancing that impact. Our programs will be based upon high standards of professionalism and expertise in order to minimize the wasting of valuable resources.

10. **In our information, publicity, and advertising activities, we shall recognize disaster victims as dignified humans, not hopeless objects.**

    Respect for the disaster victim as an equal partner in action should never be lost. In our public information we shall portray an objective image of the disaster situation where the capacities and aspirations of disaster victims are highlighted, and not just their vulnerabilities and fears. While we will cooperate with the media in order to enhance public response, we will not allow external or internal demands for publicity to take precedence over the principle of maximizing overall relief assistance. We will avoid competing with other disaster response agencies for media coverage in situations where such coverage may be to the detriment of the service provided to the beneficiaries or to the security of our staff or the beneficiaries.

Source: IFRC, 2005.

While the Code of Conduct prescribed general, overarching guidelines to direct the action of NGOs, it still left open to interpretation what constituted acceptable care and action in responding to the needs of disaster victims. There was no system by which NGOs could hold each other accountable for the *quality* of assistance provided, or allow them to gauge the effectiveness and fairness of their actions. As it stood, victims could receive a range of service quality, ranging from excellent to wholly ineffective.

To address the need for an improvement in both the effectiveness and accountability of NGOs operating in disaster response, a group of NGOs came together in 1997 and developed the *Sphere Project Humanitarian Charter and Minimum Standards in Disaster Response* handbook. This guide, which has since been revised, expanded, and updated with input from thousands of representatives from over 400 NGOs, UN agencies, and academic institutions, was created to serve as a guideline for all NGOs working in the field of humanitarian assistance. It has been made available to all interested NGOs or other organizations or individuals on the Sphere Project Web site (www.sphereproject.org). The handbook addresses the standards by which humanitarian organizations can conduct operations in eight sectors:

- Water supply and sanitation
- Nutrition
- Food aid

- Shelter
- Health services
- Food security
- Process standards
- Participation
  - Assessment
  - Response
  - Targeting
  - Monitoring
  - Evaluation
  - Staff competencies and management
- Cross-cutting issues
  - Children
  - Older people
  - Disabled people
  - Gender
  - Protection
  - HIV/AIDS
  - The environment

Taken together, the Humanitarian Charter and the Minimum Standards create an operational framework for accountability in disaster assistance efforts. They have received wide endorsement by the most prominent humanitarian aid agencies, and are regularly referenced in the management of actual disasters. While these two initiatives are the most widely recognized and accepted standards and conduct codes developed by NGOs, there are other collaborative agreements that include:

- Active Learning Network for Accountability and Performance in Humanitarian Action (www.alnap.org/)
- Oxfam Code of Conduct for NGOs (www.oxfam.org)
- People In Aid Code of Good Practice (http://www.peopleinaid.org/code/)
- Projet Qualité (http://www.projetqualite-sn.org/)
- Synergie Qualité Project (www.coordinationsud.org/)
- The Humanitarian Accountability Project (www.hapinternational.org/en/)

The Role of the Private Sector

Businesses have a major role to play in overall disaster management—one that they have only recently begun to recognize. As a large and influential component in every community, their ability to prepare for and recover from disasters plays a major, defining part in determining a community's resilience. Businesses are more than physical structures—they represent jobs, community income, vitality, and identity. In times of disaster, businesses are exposed to the damaging consequences of hazards just like any other component of society. If they are unable to withstand these impacts and survive the disaster, the whole community's economic and social recovery could be difficult, or even impossible.

To a growing degree, businesses have begun to subscribe to the self-preservation practice of business continuity planning (BCP). BCP is defined as the process by which companies of any size design plans and procedures to ensure that their critical business functions are maintained during emergencies or disasters, whether internal or external. Statistically, 20–30% of businesses suffer major disruptions each year. Any disruption will adversely impact a business, most notably those functioning on the brink of survival, a condition that is true of most small businesses, especially those in developing countries. Following disasters, businesses often have insufficient time to respond to the needs of customers, creditors, and suppliers, while also trying to recover from physical damages and possible human losses. Recovery time and cost can be significantly reduced by preparing before a disaster happens and training employees in how to respond. Especially for small businesses, this planning may be the only difference between surviving and going under.

Businesses control a significant amount of the nation's infrastructure in many countries, particularly electrical, water treatment, and communications systems, as well as public transportation networks. Following a disaster, both response and recovery success depend on their ability to quickly and effectively repair damaged infrastructure. If the disaster is particularly devastating, governments and international organizations must contribute to this effort, providing heavy equipment, manpower, and financial assistance.

All businesses, regardless of whether they control critical infrastructure or are corner markets, play an important role in their community. Whole communities have been uprooted when employers were unable to reopen, leaving residents with no means of income and the local government with no revenue or resources. Businesses are the source of vital goods, such as food, gasoline, banking, and construction supplies. Until these services return, the quality of life in the affected region suffers. If the affected businesses are regional or national suppliers or customers, the disaster's economic impacts can extend far beyond the directly affected area. The consequences of the September 11, 2001, terrorist attacks in New York City and Washington, D.C. extended across the globe, with effects being felt in nearly every country when air travel and tourism fell significantly.

Businesses also play an active role in disaster management activities that extend beyond the company property. Many companies, especially large multinational corporations, increase their philanthropic giving in the aftermath of a disaster (see Exhibit 9–4) providing in-kind donations of their products (such as heavy lifting equipment, medical supplies, and food), as well as direct cash donations. Service industries applicable to response and recovery may provide assistance in the form of supply or human transport, technical assistance, medical and engineering expertise, search and rescue (as with the mining industry), and many other services. Businesses further increase community resilience by providing first aid and other response education for their employees, which serves as a community resource for the many hours each day that these employees are outside their offices. Examples of private sector organizations that often partake in disaster response efforts include:

- Hospitals (privately owned)
- Ambulance companies
- Private search-and-rescue teams
- Veterinarians
- Private hazardous materials teams
- Poison control centers

EXHIBIT 9–4: PRIVATE SECTOR DISASTER RECOVERY ASSISTANCE IN ASIA

Two years after the Asian tsunami struck, communications giant Nokia announced that it was launching several community recovery projects to help young people in India, Sri Lanka, and Indonesia with training and new skills. The initiative helps young people to find jobs or set up small businesses, which in turn builds long-term livelihoods for themselves and their families. In addition to immediate disaster relief funding Nokia provided to the region in December of 2004 when the event occurred, it pledged €2.5 million for longer term recovery for this project.

Nokia works with the NGOs International Youth Foundation and Grameen Foundation. Projects are specially tailored to meet the needs of the target country. For example:

- **India**—Young people are offered training in business enterprise and life development skills, through courses focusing on community mobilization, problem solving, and negotiation skills. The training encourages them to take an active role in their communities and the decision-making process within their villages.
- **Sri Lanka**—Training is provided to allow immediate employment opportunities. Besides management and business skills such as tourism management, accounting, and sales, vocational programs such as sewing, weaving, and carpentry are provided for longer term livelihood sustainability.
- **Indonesia**—Young people with limited education affected by the tsunami are able to sign up for training courses and apprenticeships where they will learn more about how to work and build careers within small business and financial management.
- **Thailand**—Nokia began a program of training schemes and support for young people in Thailand in 2005. Courses are available in a range of areas including boat construction, boat motor and motorcycle repair, and apprenticeship courses in various aspects of the hotel industry.

Source: Government Technology Emergency Management, 2006.

- Private utilities' emergency response units
- Private funeral businesses
- News media outlets

One particular program noted for its success in involving businesses in comprehensive disaster management was a U.S. government initiative called Project Impact: Building a Disaster Resistant Community. Under Project Impact, private businesses assumed an active role in increasing disaster resilience at the local level. Through private/public partnerships, the project created a more comprehensive approach to emergency management by bringing all community stakeholders together into a single planning structure for disaster risk reduction. Businesses accepted their responsibility as members of the community, recognizing that a more resilient community worked in their favor by increasing the chance that they would survive a disaster event. Project Impact was discontinued in 2001, although several Project Impact communities maintain the program using local funds:

- Evansville, IN (www.vanderburghgov.org/home/index.asp?page=1023)
- Tulsa, OK (www.tulsapartners.org/)

Unfortunately, businesses are also a major source of hazard and disaster. A majority of the man-made disasters that occur each year, many of which result in fatalities and significant injury, are the result of business negligence or malevolence. The Union Carbide accident in Bhopal, India, was the direct cause of at least 3000 deaths. Examples such as this illustrate the preventive and mitigative responsibility that many businesses must assume in light of their community's overall risk profile.

As is true with the NGOs, the private sector has sought to explore the creation of humanitarian response standards of conduct. During the World Economic Forum (WEF) annual meeting in Davos, Switzerland (2007), over 800 private sector representatives discussed their involvement in emergency relief and considered adoption of draft "Guiding Principles" developed by the WEF and humanitarian agencies. The principles, which draw on codes of conduct developed by the UNIASC, insist that corporations involved in humanitarian relief do the following:

- Coordinate with mainstream humanitarian actors
- Distinguish commercial from philanthropic operations
- Be accurate and truthful in public relations activities
- Train standby staff in humanitarian principles
- Be clear about the real value of their contributions

Corporations are also urged to consider cash donations to humanitarian relief, including through the Central Emergency Revolving Fund (CERF), even though big business generally contributes in-kind goods and services in emergencies. The Humanitarian Relief Initiative (HRI) of the WEF was launched in 2006 to "develop public-private partnerships that match the core competencies of the private sector with the priority needs of the global humanitarian community in advance of humanitarian crises" (WEF, 2006). The emphasis of the initiative is on better preparedness and clear terms of engagement for the private sector in the event of crisis (All Africa, 2007).

The Role of Academia

Academia, universities and independent research institutions, has played an integral role in advancing emergency management as a profession. Their work has contributed to the reduction of hazard risks through a deeper understanding of the threats hazards pose and the actions that may mitigate them. Furthermore, academia has fostered greater institutional knowledge transfer, thus improving emergency management practices and applications.

Working with the UN and other multilateral organizations, universities are helping to create a "culture of disaster prevention" (Blanchard, 2004). Their research tracks disaster events and analyzes the consequences, helping disaster management organizations learn from their mistakes and capitalize on their successes. As a result, academic institutions have become the central repositories for hazards and disaster knowledge. This knowledge can be distributed through the Internet among an ever-expanding audience.

In addition to the many emergency- and disaster management–specific programs that have appeared in universities throughout the world, other traditional disciplines have sought to address the issue:

- Engineering (structural mitigation design)
- Geology (earthquake prediction)
- Meteorology (cyclonic storm forecasting)

- Sociology (risk perception and disaster behavior)
- Medicine (mass-casualty disaster response protocols)
- Public health (epidemic recognition and control)
- Political science (emergency management institutional framework design)
- Development studies (sustainability through disaster resilience)
- Computer science (hazard and disaster imagery)
- Public affairs (risk and disaster communications)

See Appendix 9–3 for a list of academic and professional institutions that focus on disaster management.

Conclusion

The vast NGO community has revolutionized management of international disasters. From their diverse predisaster development and public education projects to their response and recovery actions, they work with dedication and conviction. The humanitarian NGOs have elevated their disaster management role from supplemental to central. The capacity and influence that the International Federation of the Red Cross and Red Crescent Societies has assumed, including their inclusion in many nations' internal disaster management structures and their leadership in international disaster response and recovery operations, are indicative of the direction the entire NGO sector will be taking in the future. Without NGOs, international disaster management as we know it would not be possible. The private and academic sectors also have begun to recognize their role in international disaster management, and are working to limit vulnerabilities by performing business continuity planning and conducting valuable disaster-related research.

References

All Africa. (2007). *WEF considers new approach to private sector humanitarian response.* January 31.

Blanchard, B. W. (2004). *HiEd briefing for course developers.* www7.nationalacademies.org/guirr/Blanchard.ppt.

Frandsen, G. (2002). *A guide to NGOs.* Washington, DC: Center for Disaster and Humanitarian Assistance Medicine, Department of Defense.

Government Technology Emergency Management. (2006). *New initiatives launched to help young people affected by the Asian tsunami rebuild their lives.* http://www.govtech.com/dc/articles/103040.

Humanitarianinfo.org. (2005). *Humanitarian information centers.* www.humanitarianinfo.org/abouthics.html.

IFRC. (2010). *Chile: Earthquake. Emergency appeal MDRCL006.* http://www.ifrc.org/docs/appeals/10/MDRCL006REV.pdf.

InterAction. (2005). *Earthquake and tsunamis in South Asia: Inter-Action members respond to those affected in South Asia.* www.interaction.org/sasia/index.html#Uni.

InterAction. (2010). *InterAction members respond to the earthquake in Haiti.* www.interaction.org/crisis-list/earthquake-haiti.

International Cooperation and Development Fund (ICDF). (2004). *Collaboration between NGOs and the government on humanitarian aid.* www.icdf.org.tw/pdf/20041016international%20NGO%20and%20USAID%20_final_.pdf.

International Federation of Red Cross & Red Crescent Societies (IFRC). (2005). www.ifrc.org.

International Federation of Red Cross/Red Crescent Societies (IFRC). (2005b). *Federation appeals: Number of appeals since 1919.*

Patronus Analytical. (2010). www.patronusanalytical.com.

Union of International Organizations (UIO). (2005). UIO Web site. www.uia.org.

World Economic Forum (WEF). (2006). *Humanitarian relief initiative.* http://www.weforum.org/en/initiatives/HumanitarianReliefInitiative/index.htm.

Appendix 9–1

Profile of an NGO: The IFRC

The International Federation of Red Cross and Red Crescent Societies

The International Red Cross and Red Crescent Movement (www.redcross.int) is comprised of three distinct but interrelated components:

- *International Committee of the Red Cross (ICRC).* The ICRC is an impartial, neutral, and independent organization with a humanitarian mission to protect the lives and dignity of victims of war and internal violence and to provide them with assistance. It directs and coordinates the international relief activities conducted by the Movement in situations of conflict. It also endeavors to prevent suffering by promoting and strengthening humanitarian law and universal humanitarian principles. Established in 1863, the ICRC is the foundation of the International Red Cross and Red Crescent Movement.

- *Red Cross and Red Crescent Societies.* These Societies embody the work and principles of the International Red Cross and Red Crescent Movement in 181 countries around the world. National Societies act as auxiliaries to the public authorities of their own countries in the humanitarian field and provide a range of services, including disaster relief, health, and social programs. During wartime, National Societies assist the affected civilian population and support the army medical services where appropriate.

- *International Federation of Red Cross and Red Crescent Societies (IFRC).* The IFRC works on the basis of the Principles of the Red Cross and Red Crescent Movement to inspire, facilitate, and promote all humanitarian activities carried out by its member National Societies to improve the situation of the most vulnerable people. Founded in 1919, the Federation directs and coordinates international assistance of the Movement to victims of natural and technological disasters, to refugees, and in health emergencies. It acts as the official representative of its member Societies in the international field. It promotes cooperation between National Societies and works to strengthen their capacity to carry out effective disaster preparedness, health, and social programs.

The ICRC, National Societies, and the IFRC are independent bodies. Each has its own individual status and exercises no authority over the others. Like the UN, the IFRC has a presence in most countries throughout the world and as such is poised to assist in the event of a disaster. Volunteers are continually trained and engaged at the most local levels, providing a solid knowledge base before the organization's services are needed. Cooperation among the bodies through the federation provides an enormous pool of people and funds from which to draw when local resources are exhausted.

History

In 1859, Henry Dunant came up with the concept of the Red Cross, following a particularly brutal battle he witnessed in Italy. Bringing together a group of locals, Dunant began providing the wounded with medical assistance, food aid, and ongoing relief. After returning to his native Switzerland, he led a campaign to form the International Committee for Relief of the Wounded. He succeeded in 1863, and by World War I, the organization had mobilized millions. His initiative eventually evolved into the ICRC. The Committee, recognized best by their symbol of a red cross on a white background, is now the standard provider of neutral wartime medical care for wounded combatants and civilians.

The IFRC was founded in 1919 following World War I. After World War I, U.S. Red Cross War Committee President Henry Davison proposed the creation of a League of Red Cross Societies, so that the expertise of the countless volunteers from the wartime efforts of the ICRC could be garnered for peacetime activities. Originally this new organization was called the League of Red Cross Societies, but it changed its name to the League of Red Cross and Red Crescent Societies in 1983, and then to the IFRC in 1991. Today the IFRC is the world's largest humanitarian organization, with 181 member societies, a Secretariat in Geneva, and more than 60 delegations dispersed throughout the world.

IFRC Mission and Role

The IFRC does not discriminate on the basis of nationality, race, religious belief, class, or political opinions. The Federation's mission is "to improve the lives of vulnerable people by mobilizing the power of humanity." The IFRC considers vulnerable people to be "those who are at greatest risk from situations that threaten their survival, or their capacity to live with an acceptable level of social and economic security and human dignity." This can include victims of natural disasters, victims of poverty brought about by socioeconomic crises, refugees, and victims of health emergencies.

The IFRC combines relief operations to assist victims of disasters with development work to strengthen the capacities of its member National Societies. Their work focuses on four core areas:

- Promoting humanitarian values
- Disaster response
- Disaster preparedness
- Health and community care

The National Societies, present in almost every country in the world, cooperate to give the IFRC greater power to develop capacities and assist those most in need. Their community-based format allows the IFRC to reach the most local levels of society. National Societies act as auxiliaries to the public authorities of their own countries in the humanitarian field and provide a range of services, including disaster relief, health and social programs, and assistance to victims of war. Together, the

National Societies have 97 million members and volunteers and 300,000 employees, assisting some 233 million beneficiaries each year. National Society programs and services address both immediate and long-term needs:

- Emergency shelter, food, and medicine
- Water and sanitation
- Restoring family contact for disaster victims
- Disaster preparedness
- Community-based health and care
- First aid training and activities
- Control and prevention of diseases
- HIV/AIDS prevention
- Blood donor recruitment, collection, and supply
- Youth and volunteer activities

A list of all National Societies and their contact information, including e-mail addresses and Web sites (where available), can be found on the IFRC Web site (www.ifrc.org/ADDRESS/directory.asp).

The Secretariat in Geneva coordinates and mobilizes relief assistance for international emergencies, promotes cooperation between National Societies, and represents these National Societies in the international field. Field delegations assist and advise National Societies with relief operations and development programs and encourage regional cooperation. While the Secretariat is responsible for the day-to-day running of the Federation, the decisions on its direction and policy are made by governing bodies. These bodies define a framework of purpose, policies, goals, and programs, and provide a mechanism for accountability and compliance.

The General Assembly is the highest decision-making body of the Federation. It meets every two years and comprises representatives from all member National Societies. It met last in Seoul, Korea, in November 2005. A Governing Board gathers between general assemblies, meeting twice a year with the authority to make certain decisions.

The IFRC works through its National Societies and with the ICRC, but it also collaborates with many other organizations to carry out its work more effectively. Since 1994, the Federation has had Observer status with the UN General Assembly, giving it the opportunity to take part in international debates at the highest level and access to negotiations and deliberations within the structures of almost all international organizations. In addition, the Federation has utilized its international legal personality to build working agreements with a wide range of international partners, focusing on the priorities it has set in its "Strategy 2010":

- *Promotion of fundamental principles and humanitarian values.* National Societies have traditionally worked to spread knowledge of the Fundamental Principles and international humanitarian law. To facilitate the dissemination and the understanding of the principles and values, at the international level the Federation has developed working relations with other organizations, such as the International Olympic Committee, UN Children's Fund, the Office of the UN High Commissioner for Human Rights, UN volunteers, the UN Population Fund, UNAIDS, and many others.

- *Disaster response.* The Federation collaborates with international bodies and many NGOs and intergovernmental organizations to improve the effectiveness of its assistance and to help establish standards and procedures for its humanitarian work. Partners include ECHO and members of the IASC, such as the UN Office for the Coordination of Humanitarian Affairs (OCHA), the UN High Commissioner for Refugees (UNHCR), the World Health Organization (WHO), the World Food Programme (WFP), and UNICEF. Collaborative work with OCHA is a key element in the furtherance of the Federation's International Disaster Response Law project (IDRL). The Federation, together with ICRC, is one of the standing invitees of the IASC, which brings together all the major agencies involved in emergency response.

- *Disaster preparedness.* The IFRC aims to ensure that assistance is not only for immediate relief but that it also contributes to sustainable development. This includes capacity building in infrastructure and nonstructure sectors for disaster reduction and mitigation. The Federation, together with the Netherlands Red Cross, works closely with the UN Inter-Agency Secretariat of the International Strategy for Disaster Reduction (ISDR), the UN Environment Program, the ProVention Consortium, the Asian Disaster Preparedness Center, and others.

- *Health and care in the community.* The Federation continues to build partnerships with regional and international institutions to address global health issues and to build on National Societies' comparative advantages and capacity to complement their national and local efforts. The International Partnership against AIDS in Africa and the WHO-led "Stop TB" and "Roll Back Malaria" campaigns will be used as frameworks for joint experiences in pilot countries. The Federation also has formal agreements with several organizations for cooperation, such as with the Joint UN Programme on HIV/AIDS, WHO's Eastern Mediterranean Regional Office, WHO's South-East Asia Regional Office, the Pan American Health Organization, UN Population Fund, as well as organizations like GNP+ and the OPEC Fund. The Federation's Observer status with the UN General Assembly has resulted in active cooperation with many other relevant organizations, such as the UN Office on Drugs and Crime (UNODC).

The Seven Fundamental Principles

Proclaimed in Vienna in 1965, the seven Fundamental Principles bond together the National Red Cross and Red Crescent Societies, the International Committee of the Red Cross, and the International Federation of the Red Cross and Red Crescent Societies. They guarantee the continuity of the Red Cross/Red Crescent Movement and its humanitarian work:

- *Humanity.* The International Red Cross and Red Crescent Movement, born of a desire to bring assistance without discrimination to the wounded on the battlefield, endeavors, in its international and national capacities, to prevent and alleviate human suffering wherever it may be found. Its purpose is to protect life and health and to ensure respect for human beings. It promotes mutual understanding, friendship, cooperation, and lasting peace among all peoples.

- *Impartiality.* It makes no discrimination as to nationality, race, religious beliefs, class, or political opinions. It endeavors to relieve the suffering of individuals, being guided solely by their needs, and to give priority to the most urgent cases of distress.

- *Neutrality.* To continue to enjoy the confidence of all, the Movement may not take sides in hostilities or engage at any time in controversies of a political, racial, religious, or ideological nature.

- *Independence.* The Movement is independent. The National Societies, while auxiliaries in the humanitarian services of their governments and subject to the laws of their respective countries, must always maintain their autonomy so that they may be able at all times to act in accordance with the principles of the Movement.

- *Voluntary service.* It is a voluntary relief movement, not prompted in any manner by desire for gain.

- *Unity.* There can be only one Red Cross or one Red Crescent Society in any one country. It must be open to all. It must carry on its humanitarian work throughout its territory.

- *Universality.* The International Red Cross and Red Crescent Movement is worldwide, and all Societies have equal status and share equal responsibilities and duties in helping each other.

The Federation's Approach to Disaster Preparedness: Being Proactive

Readiness to reduce the impact of disasters and, where possible, predict and even prevent disasters from occurring is central to the work of the IFRC and its member Societies. Mitigation programs developed with vulnerable groups that complement national development strategies are the most effective at lessening a disaster's impact while at the same time raising the capacities of at-risk groups. The organization has identified the following four approaches to achieve their goals:

1. Reducing the vulnerability of households and communities in disaster-prone areas and improving their ability to cope with the effects of disasters
2. Strengthening the capacities of National Societies in disaster preparedness and postdisaster response
3. Determining a role and mandate for National Societies in national disaster plans
4. Establishing regional networks of National Societies that will strengthen the Federation's collective impact in disaster preparedness and response at the international level

Disaster Response

The IFRC is well placed to assist victims of disasters thanks to its network of National Societies. Almost every country in the world has a Red Cross or Red Crescent Society, each with branches and trained volunteers at the community level. Cooperation among these societies provides additional capacity, solidarity, and financial and human resources to the Federation and its members. The response system is based on the right of National Societies to request support from the Secretariat during a crisis. The Secretariat's role is that of coordinator; it launches international appeals to raise funds for the relief operations, and then mobilizes personnel and relief goods. Through its regional and country field offices, the Federation can also provide managerial, technical, and administrative expertise to National Societies. On average, the Federation launches 30 new emergency appeals each year as disasters strike, and supports smaller operations from its disaster relief emergency fund.

With increasing needs and decreasing resources in many disaster-prone countries, the Federation finds its National Societies engaged well beyond the initial response into long periods of rehabilitation and reconstruction work. This work is also supported by the Federation, as it plays an important role in decreasing people's vulnerability and strengthens their coping capacities.

Emergency Response Units

In 1994, following a spate of notably severe disasters and humanitarian emergencies (i.e., the Armenian earthquake, the Gulf War Kurdish refugee problem, and the African Great Lakes Region crisis), the IFRC began to develop an Emergency Response Unit (ERU) program to increase disaster response efficiency and efficacy. ERUs are made up of preestablished supplies, equipment, and personnel, and act as a quick-response unit trained and prepared to handle a wide range of disaster scenarios. This concept, similar to the UNDP Emergency Response Division (ERD), has already proved effective in making the IFRC response mechanism faster and better, with successful deployments to Hurricane Mitch in Honduras and the Gujarat, India, earthquake in 2001. Upon completion of their response mission, the teams remain in country to train locals in water and sanitation issues, thus further ensuring the sustainability of their efforts. ERU teams are most effective in large-scale, sudden-onset, and remote disasters.

ERUs are now a crucial part of the IFRC's disaster response and their integrated disaster management programming (which deals with emergency response, preparedness, and recovery/rehabilitation). The IFRC is responsible for the coordination, technical monitoring, and evaluation of ERU deployments. Together with the various ERU National Societies, the IFRC ERU focal point and technical advisors have developed standard operating procedures and technical specifications for the different ERUs. Regular consultative ERU working group meetings are held to further refine standards and rapid response mechanisms.

Field Assessment and Coordination Teams

Depending on the complexity of the required response, one or more Field Assessment and Coordination Teams (FACTs) may be deployed to assist a local chapter in determining event support needs. The teams, which are deployable to any location with only 12–24 hours' notice, consist of Red Cross/Red Crescent disaster managers from throughout the IFRC, who bring with them skills in relief, logistics, health, nutrition, public health, epidemiology, water and sanitation, finance, administration, and psychological support.

In the case of a humanitarian emergency, the National Society in the affected country may request assistance from the IFRC. In such cases, FACT members around the world are alerted using automated systems requesting availability within 12–24 hours. A team is organized by the Operations Support Department in consultation with the Regional Department at the Secretariat and is deployed immediately to the disaster area. The FACT team works with counterparts from the local National Society, members of Regional Disaster Response Teams (RDRT), members of the IFRC regional and/or country delegation, and the ICRC.

These teams work in conjunction with local counterparts and host government representatives to assess the situation and determine the IFRC response. An international appeal for assistance is then drafted and launched by the Secretariat in Geneva. These teams stay in country to coordinate the initiation of relief activities. Once the effort has stabilized and has become locally manageable, the FACT cedes its control to the local Red Cross headquarters.

Disaster Relief Emergency Fund

The IFRC Disaster Relief Emergency Fund (DREF) represents a pool of money for immediate emergency response funding. The fund is managed by the IFRC Secretariat Disaster Management and Coordination Division and is a valuable part of the organization's overall disaster response capacity. Financial assistance is allocated through the DREF as follows:

- DREF funds are sought through a Federation annual appeal.
- Contributions against the DREF appeal are received from National Societies and other sources.
- The DREF is an un-earmarked fund with allocations provided on a recoverable basis. It allows immediate release of funds and start of emergency operations prior to any donor response to emergency appeals.
- The majority of funds are used to start operations in major disasters. Up to 30% of the available funds may provide support to small-scale or less visible emergencies, as well as to forgotten disasters where emergency appeals are either not appropriate or donor interest is not forthcoming, but the Red Cross and Red Crescent response to specific humanitarian needs is required.
- Requests for DREF allocations are reviewed on a case-by-case basis. Allocations to start operations in major disasters do not exceed 15% of an emergency appeal or 2 million Swiss francs.
- Allocation reimbursements are made from contributions received against relevant emergency appeals.
- Minor emergencies are often fully funded by DREF. The Federation increasingly encourages National Societies, through its information bulletins, to cover the cost and thus facilitate the recovery of funds.
- Standard program support recovery (PSR) of 6.5% is applied, as the same Secretariat services are required as for any other operation.

The IFRC is committed to maintaining the DREF at the target level of 10 million Swiss francs to be able to respond to the increasing number of emergency requests. Upon request, a maximum of 500,000 Swiss francs annually can be allocated from DREF for disaster/emergency preparedness activities in disaster-prone countries.

IFRC Disaster Preparedness Policy

Central to the IFRC's disaster preparedness policy is maintaining a readiness to predict and where possible prevent disasters, reduce their impact, and respond to and cope with their consequences at international, national, and local levels. With this in mind, the IFRC believes that the following measures are key to development:

- A reduction in household and community vulnerability in disaster-prone areas and improvement of their ability to cope with the effects of disasters

- Strengthening of the capacities of National Societies in disaster preparedness and post-disaster response
- Determination of a National Society role and mandate in national disaster plans
- Establishment of regional networks of National Societies that will strengthen the Federation's collective impact in disaster preparedness and response at the international level

This policy applies to all types of disaster preparedness activities at local, national, regional, and international levels, whether carried out by a branch of a National Society, an individual National Society, or by the International Federation.

The IFRC proclaims that it and each National Society will:

- Recognize that disaster preparedness should be one of the primary activities of the International Federation and each National Society
- Recognize disaster preparedness as an effective link between emergency response, rehabilitation, and development programs
- Recognize the Red Cross/Red Crescent role in disaster preparedness as complementary to government
- Advocate the need for and effectiveness of disaster preparedness with government, donors, NGOs, and the public as needed
- Strengthen the organizational structures at international, national, and local levels, as required for effective disaster preparedness
- Improve coordination by promoting better cooperation and partnerships between National Societies, ICRC, governments, NGOs, and other disaster response agencies at local, national, regional, and international levels
- Identify those persons, communities, and households most at risk to disaster
- Raise awareness of disaster hazards through public education
- Improve the ability of vulnerable communities to cope with disasters through community-based disaster preparedness strategies that build on existing structures, practices, skills, and coping mechanisms
- Strive to provide the financial, material, and human resources required to carry out appropriate and sustainable disaster preparedness activities

IFRC Emergency Response Policy

The IFRC emergency response policy states that the Red Cross and Red Crescent must be able to act in all life-threatening situations regardless of the scope of the emergency, and that its actions must be governed by the same policy regardless of the size and level of the response. To do this, the IFRC proclaims that it and each National Society will:

- Seek to assist the most vulnerable people in emergencies to protect life and health and to ensure respect for the individual through assisting those most affected in obtaining adequate access to basic life support needs, which include at a minimum:

- Adequate safe water and sanitation
- Adequate food
- Adequate healthcare, including psychological support
- Adequate shelter

- Recognize the Red Cross/Red Crescent role as auxiliary to government in humanitarian services
- Undertake emergency response according to the Fundamental Principles of the Red Cross and Red Crescent and apply the principles and spirit of the Code of Conduct for the International Red Cross and Red Crescent Movement and NGOs in disaster relief
- Work within the competence of the Operating National Society
- Base their actions on appropriate disaster preparedness programming and planning
- Work toward self-reliance and sustainability of programming by both the Operating National Society and the assisted population
- Continue until the acute threat to life and health has abated
- Maximize the strategic advantage of the IFRC by "working as a Federation" to mobilize all appropriate resources

IFRC operations depend upon four primary resources, including:

- *Financial resources.* The primary tool for IFRC emergency response fundraising is the Emergency Appeal. The National Society of the affected country launches national Appeals. International Appeals are launched by the Federation Secretariat.
- *Human resources.* Recognizing the vital role of human resources in emergency operations, the IFRC ensures the proper identification, placement, retention, development, support, administration, and management of suitably qualified, trained, and experienced personnel.
- *Information resources.* Data and information are key resources in emergency response. The IFRC has committed to making the Red Cross and Red Crescent a reliable and timely source of disaster-related information. Information systems have been and continue to be designed and implemented to maximize:
  - The speed, efficiency, and effectiveness of emergency response
  - The security and safety of beneficiaries, staff, volunteers, and fixed assets
  - The timeliness, accuracy, and clarity of reporting and accountability systems
  - The involvement of beneficiaries and local organizations
- *Physical resources.* IFRC policy dictates that the need for physical resources is well defined, that quality standards are ensured, that delivery is timely, that stocks are adequately maintained, and that distribution is controlled. Physical assets not used in the emergency response program or surplus to operational requirements as the program scales down are deployed to support other emergency programs whenever possible. The impact of local purchase upon the local economy and well-being of the population is always assessed to ensure that such actions do not cause undue harm. Program officials are always urged to refrain from creating duplicate infrastructures when existing National Society or commercial enterprises can provide the necessary support.

IFRC Recovery and Rehabilitation Policy

Once emergency needs have been met following a disaster and the initial crisis is over, the affected populations and communities may still be in a state of heightened vulnerability. The country and the National Society, from branch to national level, may have been weakened by the disaster. It is in these situations that post-emergency rehabilitation programs should be considered. IFRC action for recovery and rehabilitation, including all National Society and IFRC assistance targeted to disaster-affected communities in the post-emergency phase of disaster response, is designed to reduce immediate vulnerability to disaster or to address the root causes of those vulnerabilities. It also includes action taken specifically to rebuild and strengthen the capacity of the disaster-affected National Society. The IFRC proclaims that it and each National Society will:

- Undertake rehabilitation activities with the active participation of the community in the planning and implementation of the activities on the basis of a timely and thorough assessment of unmet needs and available response capacity
- Engage in active dialog with local authorities over the priorities and focus of rehabilitation
- Prioritize community services
- Enhance capacity building
- Consider gender and environment factors
- Effectively coordinate rehabilitation activities
- Coordinate with national and local authorities and other agencies
- Develop advocacy for disaster mitigation
- Develop an exit strategy

See Table 9–1 for a list of Red Cross humanitarian beneficiaries by region from 1998 to 2004, and see Table 9–2 and Exhibit 9–5 for more information on specific appeals.

Table 9–1   Red Cross Humanitarian Assistance Beneficiaries by Region, 1998–2004

Target Benefit Region	1998	1999	2000	2001	2002	2003	2004
Middle East and North Africa	160,000	500,000	2,578,000	2,508,000	2,359,800	4,458,000	6,487,856
Europe	6,798,500	6,583,000	4,657,700	4,555,500	5,055,221	1,424,000	2,088,512
Americas	480,434	818,880	2,936,300	958,000	522,150	231,000	1,379,600
Asia Pacific	7,709,000	14,529,200	17,351,000	15,818,959	17,675,581	30,834,000	22,965,492
Africa	4,350,920	7,682,500	8,910,500	10,481,375	27,457,614	31,415,500	10,787,491
Multi-region	—	—	14,000,000	2,133,500	5,900,000	—	
Grand Total	**19,498,854**	**30,113,580**	**50,433,500**	**36,455,334**	**58,970,366**	**68,362,500**	**43,708,951**

Source: IFRC, 2005.

Table 9–2   IFRC Appeals, 1919–2005

Country	Number of Appeals
Afghanistan	30
Africa	7
Albania	11
Algeria	23
Americas	13
Angola	19
Antigua and Barbuda	1
Argentina	10
Armenia	5
Asia	6
Asia and Pacific	3
Australia	1
Austria	3
Azerbaijan	5
Bahamas	3
Bangladesh	42
Belarus	1
Belgium	3
Belize	2
Benin	10
Bolivia	17
Bosnia and Herzegovina	11
Botswana	7
Brazil	3
Bulgaria	9
Burkina Faso	12
Burkina Faso, Mali, Mauritania, Niger	1
Burundi	11
Cambodia	23
Cameroon	4
Cape Verde	7
Caribbean	21
Caucasus	10
Central Africa	20
Central African Republic	11
Central America	13
Central Asia	14
Central Europe	20
Chad	12
Chernobyl region	13
Chile	6

(Continued)

Table 9–2   IFRC Appeals, 1919–2005 Continued

Country	Number of Appeals
China	24
Colombia	9
Comoros	2
Congo Republic	13
Costa Rica	7
Côte d'Ivoire	5
Croatia	2
Cuba	14
D.R. Congo	14
Djibouti	5
Dominica	1
Dominican Republic	4
DPR Korea	16
East Africa	25
East Asia	8
East Timor	5
Eastern Europe	16
Ecuador	8
Egypt	5
El Salvador	6
Equatorial Guinea	1
Eritrea	12
Ethiopia	35
Europe	1
Fed. States of Micronesia	1
Fiji	10
Finland	1
France	5
FYR Macedonia	4
Gabon	3
Gambia	10
Georgia	7
Germany	2
Ghana	8
Global	79
Great Britain	5
Greece	17
Guatemala	9
Guinea	11
Guinea Bissau	4
Guyana	2
Haiti	26
Honduras	17

Table 9–2   Continued

Country	Number of Appeals
Horn of Africa	1
Hungary	5
Iceland	1
India	48
Indian Ocean	2
Indonesia	26
Iran	36
Iraq	20
Israel	1
Italy	9
Jamaica	2
Japan	3
Jordan	6
Kazakhstan	3
Kenya	28
Korea Rep.	11
Kuwait	2
Laos	8
Lebanon	17
Lesotho	6
Liberia	7
Libya	1
Liechtenstein	1
Madagascar	12
Malawi	21
Malaysia	5
Mali	8
Mano River region	2
Mauritania	17
Mauritius	1
Mexico	8
Middle East	1
Middle East, North Africa	41
Moldova	2
Mongolia	11
Morocco	20
Mozambique	25
Multiple regions	5
Myanmar (Burma)	27
Namibia	7
Nepal	30
Netherlands	4
New Zealand	1

(Continued)

Table 9–2   IFRC Appeals, 1919–2005 Continued

Country	Number of Appeals
Nicaragua	13
Niger	11
Nigeria	11
Nigeria subregion	2
North Africa	1
Norway	1
Pacific	13
Pakistan	47
Panama	3
Papua New Guinea	20
Paraguay	9
Persian Gulf region	1
Peru	19
Philippines	28
Poland	7
Portugal	7
Romania	6
Russian Federation	21
Rwanda	22
Sahel	5
Sao Tome and Principe	4
Senegal	14
Serbia, Montenegro, Kosovo	3
Sierra Leone	9
Solomon Islands	1
Somalia	28
South Africa	4
South America	13
South Asia	12
Southeast Asia	14
Southern Africa	21
Spain	4
Sri Lanka	35
Sudan	42
Swaziland	8
Syria	8
Taiwan	1
Tajikistan	12
Tanzania	18
Thailand	5
Togo	7

Table 9–2   Continued

Country	Number of Appeals
Tonga	1
Trinidad and Tobago	1
Tunisia	9
Turkey	35
Uganda	20
Ukraine	1
Uruguay	1
Uzbekistan	1
Vanuatu	2
Venezuela	2
Vietnam	37
West Africa	36
Western Samoa	1
Yemen	19
Yugoslavia	25
Zambia	13
Zimbabwe	12
Grand Total	**2120**

Source: IFRC, 2005b.

EXHIBIT 9–5: IFRC APPEAL NUMBER MDRCL006: JANUARY 27, 2010, EARTHQUAKE IN CHILE

Emergency appeal number MDRCL006
Appeal Date: March 2, 2010

This Preliminary Emergency Appeal seeks CHF 7m (USD 6.4m or EUR 4.7m) in cash, kind, or services to support the Chilean Red Cross to assist some 15,000 families (75,000 people) for 6 months. The operation will be completed by 2 September 2010. A Final Report will be made available by 2 December 2010 (3 months after the end of the operation).

CHF 300,000 (USD 279,350 or EUR 204,989) was allocated from the Federation's Disaster Relief Emergency Fund (DREF) on 27 February 2010 to support the Chilean Red Cross (CRC) to initiate the response and deliver immediate relief items for 3000 families. Un-earmarked funds to repay DREF are encouraged.

Summary

On 27 February 2010, at approximately 3.35 a.m. local time, an earthquake of magnitude 8.8 struck the country of Chile. The epicenter was located 63 km southeast of Cauquenes in the region of Maule (406 km south from Santiago). As a consequence, the tsunami generated affected a

(Continued)

EXHIBIT 9–5: IFRC APPEAL NUMBER MDRCL006 (CONTINUED)

coastal strip of more than 500 km. There have been more than 128 aftershocks causing extensive damage throughout the region. Reports indicate over 700 deaths. Approximately 1.5 million people have been affected and thousands have lost their homes and livelihoods.

This Preliminary Emergency Appeal responds to a request from the CRC, and focuses on providing support for an appropriate and timely response in delivering assistance in the sectors of emergency health (field hospitals), relief, water and sanitation, emergency shelter, and early recovery.

The situation

The 8.8 magnitude earthquake that hit on 27 February resulted in a death toll of approximately 708 people and this is expected to rise. This was one of the most powerful earthquakes in decades to strike Chile causing destruction in isolated towns. Waves generated by the tsunami swept into the port town of Talcahuano in the region of Bio-Bio, causing serious damage to port facilities and lifting fishing boats out of the water. A tsunami warning was issued for more than 50 countries around Latin America and Asia and Pacific. The tsunami warnings have now been suspended. The region is continuing to experience aftershocks—more than 120 have occurred since the earthquake. People are still missing in a number of communities in the worst-hit central region of Chile (Maule and Bio-Bio), which remained largely cut off by mangled highways and fallen telephone lines. There is a shortage of water and food, worsening the effects of the disaster. Power cuts have slowed relief efforts; nevertheless government authorities are doing everything possible to assist the most vulnerable people. Public services (electrical and communications) were interrupted in the area of Conception and Valparaiso, but have now been partially reinstalled.

The Government of Chile has declared 6 of 15 regions "catastrophe zones." The six affected regions are Bio-Bio, Maule, Valparaiso, Metropolitana, Libertador O'Higgins, and Araucania. The government declared a state of emergency in the regions of Maule (septima región del Maule) and Bio-Bio (octava región del Bio-Bio), the region of La Araucania (novena región de la Araucania), the region of Metropolitan Santiago, and the region of Valparaiso (quinta región de Valparaiso). The town of Concepción is reportedly the most affected area. Looting activities have been reported in the Concepción area and the government has ordered a nighttime curfew between 9 p.m. and 6 a.m. The earthquake's major impact was on infrastructure. An estimated 500,000 homes have been seriously damaged and some 1.5 million people are affected. It is believed that adobe structure homes will be the most affected and that indigenous populations are at most risk.

The following table shows details by region:

Region	Casualties	Missing people
Valparaiso	16	8
Metropolitana	36	5
O'Higgins	46	2
Maule	541	4
Bio-Bio	64	No reports
La Araucania	5	No reports
TOTAL	**708**	**19**

Source: IFRC, 2010.

Current status of ports, airports, and border crossings

Port	Region	Damages	Operational
San Antonio (main port)	Valparaiso	Structural damages	Yes
Talcahuano	Bio-Bio	Collapsed docks	No
San Vicente	O'Higgins	Partially destroyed	No
Muelle Schuster	Los Rios	Collapsed dock	N/A

The airport in Concepción has been damaged but is opening again for commercial flights and is already open for cargo flights. The Santiago airport remains closed due to damages in the terminal building. The Civil Aeronautics Direction of Chile is studying the best approach to open emergency installations in the next 48 hours to receive national and international flights.

The border crossings of Puerto Montt and La Araucania are functioning normally while the border of Los Libertadores is only allowing the transit of trucks. The rest of the borders are closed as a security measure.

Government actions

Chile is a country with very well-organized institutions that function well. The newly elected President will be sworn in following 11 days; however, the head of the National Office of Emergencies and Information (Oficina Nacional de Emergencias e Información; ONEMI) will remain as the leader of the response.

The ONEMI deployed response units to the most affected regions of Valparaiso, O'Higgins, Maule, and Bio-Bio and has carried out aerial and land assessments with the assistance of the Army and police authorities in the coastal zone of Maule to evaluate areas that have not been accessed and that may be seriously affected. Relief items have been dispatched to the island of Juan Fernandez to assist the people affected. At the same time, logistical support is being deployed to the regions of Maule, Bio-Bio, Valparaiso, and O'Higgins.

ONEMI is the lead government agency responsible for managing and coordinating the first response to the emergency. Search and rescue activities are being carried out and collective centers have been opened in schools. In the Metropolitana region, there are five establishments housing people who lost their homes. ONEMI has started to distribute basic food items and generators in the southern region; the most affected. Additionally, the government started to set up field hospitals in Curico, Talca, and Concepción to provide medical assistance to the most affected.

Water units have been mobilized as well as special machines for debris clearing. Search-and-rescue specialists from the Fire Department and search-and-rescue (SAR) teams have been deployed to the affected areas.

The Chilean Ministry of Health (MoH) has activated an Emergency Committee to coordinate the response in the health sector. The MoH informs that hospitals have been severely damaged in the cities of Putaendo (Valparaiso region), Curico, Licanten, Hualañé, Talca, and Parral (Maule region). Patients in these facilities are being transferred to alternative public and private clinics. Other hospitals have sustained damages in Chillan, Los Angeles (Bio-Bio region), Angol, and Temuco (Araucania region).

(*Continued*)

EXHIBIT 9–5: IFRC APPEAL NUMBER MDRCL006 (CONTINUED)

Due to magnitude of this disaster the government has requested international assistance in several sectors:

- Four field hospitals
- Tents
- Electric generators
- Water (distribution is the major problem)
- Telecommunication equipment

Coordination and partnerships

The CRC is participating in coordination meetings with ONEMI and other governmental authorities including the MoH. The CRC acts as an auxiliary to all public services, responsible for intervention in the event of disasters in conjunction with bodies such as ONEMI, the fire department, and health services. During emergencies, the National Society coordinates with ONEMI to provide assistance when required.

The International Federation's Pan American Disaster Response Unit (PADRU) has been in communication with the CRC and the IFRC Regional Representative who arrived in Chile on Sunday, February 28, to provide support to the CRC. The CRC and the IFRC Regional Representative participated in a high-level meeting with the Chilean President and other authorities. The CRC and the IFRC Regional Representative also participated in an air assessment which took place on March 1 to better assess the level of damages in the most affected areas, including Curicó, Talca, and the zone most affected by the tsunami. Information alerts have been issued for FACT, ERU, and RIT teams. In addition, an ERU alert was issued for health and water and sanitation support. The Federation has deployed a team of five people to Chile (via Argentina) to provide technical support in damage assessments, health, relief, and information management to the National Society.

The Federation has been in touch with the ICRC in order to coordinate activities and activate the Restoring of Family Links (RFL) service to assist the affected families.

In addition, several humanitarian agencies including Telecommunications without Borders (TSF), the European Union's European Commission Humanitarian Aid Department (ECHO), the Swiss Cooperation (COSUDE), and OCHA have teams ready to be deployed to provide support to the national response and to partners in the country. Several National Societies have also pledged support to assist in initial response activities.

Red Cross and Red Crescent action

Since the onset of the emergency the CRC National Relief Department activated response mechanisms and set up a special office to centralize and coordinate the response. The CRC National Intervention Teams (NITs) and CRC volunteers have been alerted and are involved in response activities. Furthermore, the CRC relief director is coordinating with ONEMIA, which is dedicated to prevention, organization, and coordination in natural disaster situations as well as in information provision. The affected region in Bio-Bio has 29 branches and there are 14 CRC branches in the region of Maule. The CRC informs PADRU that they are constantly monitoring the situation and that communication is very limited, and it has not been possible to communicate with affected regional branches.

To date, CRC headquarters has mobilized approximately 120 volunteers; the number of volunteers from other branches is still unknown since there is no stable communication network. On February 28, the CRC distributed 300 hygiene kits and 300 blankets from its headquarters warehouse, and in coordination with the ONEMI, delivered these by air cargo to the region of Bio-Bio. More distributions are planned for tomorrow, March 2.

The main activities carried out to date are

- Collection of humanitarian aid in coordination with the ONEMI
- Damage assessments
- Aerial assessments in the affected regions
- Collection of funds
- Preparation of food kits to be distributed in the affected regions
- Organization of a donation campaign (launched on March 1).
- Restoring of Family Links

The CRC has previous experience in natural disasters and has taken an active role in this response. Its role as an auxiliary to the State is recognized and accepted by the authorities. The CRC has opened a bank account to obtain funds and has called upon the population to donate blood to supply the hospital demand in the assistance network. The CRC has launched a national donation campaign that will focus only on cash donations. The CRC communications department was reinforced to attend to the media and will be responsible for all communications.

The needs

The National Office for Emergencies and Information is leading the overall response of the government, and cooperation with the CRC is strong. Based on the information available at the moment, the immediate needs identified are SAR activities, emergency health, provision of water, emergency shelter, logistics, and telecommunications. The capacity of the National Society needs to be strengthened and the affected branches need to be reconstructed (the Talagante branch in the Metropolitan area is being demolished). Once initial official assessments are obtained, further needs will be identified. The International Federation through its zone office in Panama is in close contact with the CRC in this regard.

The proposed operation

The operation will provide support to the National Society in the delivery of immediate assistance for 15,000 families in the sectors of relief (3000 families), emergency shelter, public health in emergencies and water, sanitation, and hygiene promotion. Early recovery needs will be assessed and implemented together with the CRC, the affected communities and key local, national, and international stakeholders. The DREF funds have enabled the CRC to mobilize personnel and initiate initial response and relief activities.

Assessments are still being undertaken, and more detailed information will become available shortly. Based on this, objectives may be included or expanded, as relevant to the operation.

(Continued)

EXHIBIT 9–5: IFRC APPEAL NUMBER MDRCL006 (CONTINUED)

Relief distributions (basic nonfood items)

 Objective: 3000 families affected by the earthquake will have benefited from the distribution of nonfood items in order to help them recover from the earthquakes.

- Expected results: Approximately 15,000 people see their basic needs met by receiving essential nonfood items.
- Activities planned:
  - Conduct rapid emergency needs and capacity assessments.
  - Develop beneficiary targeting strategy and registration system to deliver intended assistance.
  - Distribute relief supplies and control supply movements from point of dispatch to end user.
  - Monitor and evaluate the relief activities and provide reporting on relief distributions.
  - Develop an exit strategy.

Emergency shelter

 Objective: Ensure that the most affected families have a healthy and safe emergency shelter to help preserve their physical and mental well-being, human dignity, and prevent the further deterioration of the humanitarian situation.

- Expected results: Families have adequate shelter that assists them in returning to their daily lives.
- Activities planned:
  - Conduct rapid emergency needs and capacity assessments.
  - Develop community and beneficiary targeting strategy in coordination with local authorities.
  - Assess the extent of the shelter needs and preferred shelter solutions.
  - Provide appropriate emergency shelter solutions, such as tents, tarpaulins, and shelter kits, integrated with water and sanitation activities.
  - Develop awareness raising activities on safe shelter and Disaster Risk Reduction (DRR) in coordination with CRC and local authorities.

Emergency health, water, sanitation, and hygiene promotion

 Objective 1: The affected communitie' health and water and sanitation needs and capacities are understood and well-targeted.

 Objective 2: The affected communities will benefit from curative care through deployment of needed field health and water and sanitation facilities and hardware.

 Objective 3: The affected communities and people in shelters will benefit from health and hygiene promotion for disease prevention.

- Expected results: Up to 10,000 families have received adequate emergency health care.
- Activities planned:

- For objective 1:
  - Conduct rapid health and water and sanitation emergency needs and capacity assessments
  - Develop a community and beneficiary targeting strategy in coordination with local authorities.
  - Assess the extent of the water and sanitation and hygiene promotion needs and preferred solutions.
  - Design a plan of action for health and water and sanitation for the immediate relief and early recovery phase.
- For objective 2:
  - Provision of basic first aid by CRC volunteers.
  - Identification of need and location of field hospital and other health facilities.
  - As identified, deployment of health ERUs or other needed field health capacities.
  - As identified, deployment of water and sanitation hardware and assets needed.
- For objective 3:
  - Mobilization of volunteer water, sanitation, and health teams.
  - Identification of beneficiaries.
  - Training workshops in health, water, sanitation, and hygiene promotion for volunteers.
- General:
  - Coordination with health authorities and other partners.
  - Planning and implementation of longer term health program including Community Based Health and First Aid (CBHFA), Epidemic Control for Volunteers (ECV), and others, according to needs of CRC.
  - Psychosocial support assessment and activities will be determined and implemented according to identified need.

Early recovery

Early recovery needs will be assessed, planned, and implemented together with the affected communities and key local, national, and international stakeholders. The initial team deployed from PADRU will initiate the detailed assessment process with the CRC to identify opportunities for early recovery interventions targeting the restoration of livelihoods and permanent shelter.

Options including a small unconditional cash transfer program for food can be considered.

Logistics

A coordinator from the Regional Logistics Unit (RLU) has the primary tasks of providing additional logistics capacity on the ground with the aim to

- Assess logistics infrastructure, set up an efficient logistics system and identify the best supply chain to support the operation.
- Carry out receipt of relief goods shipped by air and sea and arrange transportation to distribution points.
- Liaise and coordinate with other key actors to ensure best uses of all information.

(*Continued*)

EXHIBIT 9–5: IFRC APPEAL NUMBER MDRCL006 (CONTINUED)

Communications—Advocacy and public information

The steady flow of timely and accurate information between those working in the field and other major stakeholders will support the program objectives of this emergency appeal; increase the profile, funding, and other support for the CRC and the Federation; and provide a platform on which to advocate in the interests of vulnerable populations. In close collaboration with the operation, those affected by this emergency will be provided with information to support their relief and recovery. Donors and National Societies will receive information and materials they can use to promote this operation and communications initiatives will help to build the information and public relations capacity of the host National Society for future emergencies. Key aspects of the relief and recovery operation including its achievements, challenges, donor support, and beneficiary needs will be consistently promoted in all relevant media channels and supported through regular and timely media relations. An information officer from PADRU has been deployed to Chile to support the National Society with the media. A detailed communications plan of action is forthcoming.

Capacity of the National Society

The CRC has developed community disaster prevention education programs, in collaboration with municipalities and has participated together with the Bolivian and Peruvian Red Cross Societies in the formulation of a regional disaster preparedness and response plan. The National Society's main focus of activities is health, especially in the area of blood donation, first aid, mother and child health, and the elderly. It has trained emergency health volunteers throughout the country. The CRC has main branches in 13 regions of the country.

Capacity of the Federation

The Zone Office in the Americas including PADRU and the Regional Representation for the Southern Cone is providing support to the National Society in the response and is carrying out actions such as the deployment of a first-response team and organizing the provision of initial relief items; it will also assist in the development of Plans of Action, the provision of logistics services and human resources as needed.

Appeal budget summary

Relief needs

Shelter	2,300,000
Construction materials	150,000
Clothing and textiles	200,000
Food	0
Seeds and plants	0
Water and sanitation	750,000
Medical and first aid	750,000
Teaching materials	0
Utensils and tools	100,000
Other supplies and services	40,000
Total relief needs	4,290,000

Capital equipment

Land and buildings	0
Vehicles purchase	100,000
Computers and telecom equipment	50,000
Office/household furniture and equipment	100,000
Medical equipment	50,000
Other machinery and equipment	20,000

Transport, storage, and vehicles

Storage—warehouse	0
Distribution and monitoring	500,000
Transport and vehicles costs	100,000

Personnel

International staff	50,000
Regionally deployed staff	200,000
National staff	150,000
National society staff	400,000
Consultants	0

Workshops and training

Workshops and training	75,000

General expenses

Travel	60,000
Information and public relations	180,000
Office running costs	50,000
Communication costs	100,000
Professional fees	0
Financial charges	15,000
Other general expenses (evaluation)	50,000

Program support

Program support (PSR)	454,652
Total operational needs	2,704,652
Total appeal budget (cash and kind)	**6,994,652**

Source: IFRC, 2010. http://www.ifrc.org/docs/appeals/10/MDRCL006REV.pdf.

Appendix 9–2
NGOs Involved in the January 12, 2010, Earthquake in Haiti Response and Recovery Operations as of August 1, 2010

Action Against Hunger

Action Against Hunger/ACF-International mobilized an emergency response following the earthquake in Haiti. The organization provided clean water for survivors in Port-au-Prince and surrounding areas and delivered emergency services in nutrition, sanitation, and hygiene. ACF filled more than 20 large bladder tanks with clean water each day in affected areas of Port-au-Prince and Leogane; distributed high-protein biscuits and hygiene kits to thousands of vulnerable families in displacement camps; established emergency shelter for pregnant and lactating women; and provided urgent nutrition, medical, water, and sanitation support in Gonaives health centers.

Actionaid

ActionAid supported relief efforts focused on providing psychosocial support, protection and access to clean water, food, sanitation, and shelter. ActionAid Haiti was the first agency to visit the town of Marianni and distribute food and medicine to many of the 9000 who were made homeless.

Adventist Development and Relief Agency

ADRA put more than $1 million in aid, personnel, and assets on the ground in Haiti to meet the immediate needs of survivors and distribute over 1 million meals. ADRA provided more than 200,000 people a day with clean drinking water. Daily, ADRA's inflatable clinics provided treatment for more than 1000 people. ADRA also provided temporary shelter materials, hygiene kits, and tens of thousands of pounds of medical equipment and supplies to support local hospitals.

African Methodist Episcopal Church Service and Development Agency

AME-SADA provided humanitarian relief and care onsite through its system of local clinics and microcredit operations.

Air Serv International

Air Serv International coordinated and assisted with small aircraft and crews for immediate deployment in support of the Haiti earthquake response—charter flights to and from Haiti for people and supplies, dedicated aircraft for short-term or open-ended in-country use.

America's Development Foundation

America's Development Foundation (ADF) provided urgently needed food, water, shelter, and other resources to earthquake victims in orphanages, schools, IDP camps, and communities including peasants in rural mountain regions. The provision of food included 20,000 beneficiaries in 46 camps in Petit Goave. Also, ADF provided emergency shelter materials and worked toward building transitional shelters for thousands of earthquake victims in both urban and rural mountain regions of Petit Goave.

American Friends Service Committee

The American Friends Service Committee worked with partners to deliver food in three neighborhoods in Port-au-Prince. Ground staff coordinated work with partners and prepared the infrastructure for long-term work in Port-au-Prince. AFSC also provided funds for emergency shelter supplies and shipping medical equipment to mobile medical teams.

American Jewish Joint Distribution Committee

JDC moved swiftly to coordinate relief efforts with its network of Israeli, American, and other local partners on the ground, focusing on the provision of critical food, water, and medical aid to local residents.

American Jewish World Service

AJWS created the Haiti Earthquake Relief Fund to send immediate emergency aid to communities affected by this disaster. Particular focus is being placed on aiding populations in the crisis zone that have not already been targeted for large-scale relief, such as poor and rural areas outside Port-au-Prince. AJWS's long-standing partnerships in the region enabled them to send funding directly to grantees in hard-hit areas that have the knowledge and capacity to spend the money effectively where it is most immediately needed.

American Red Cross

The American Red Cross met urgent needs for earthquake survivors in Haiti, with more than $67 million spent in support of response efforts. More than 40 staff members were on the ground distributing essential relief supplies, supporting logistics, disaster assessments, communications, recovery, shelter, and market analysis. An additional 70 volunteers served as Creole translators aboard the USNS *Comfort*. The American Red Cross provided relief supplies, such as hygiene kits, buckets, mosquito nets, and kitchen sets for 100,000 people. Besides immediate response, the American Red Cross is working on long-term recovery assistance, such as restarting the local market economy and addressing housing needs.

American Refugee Committee International

ARC formed partnerships with local NGOs and international NGOs to distribute food items, nonfood items, and relief supplies in Port-au-Prince, and to provide support and emergency supplies to medical clinics on the border with the Dominican Republic that received injured from earthquake-affected areas. ARC implemented long-term recovery activities in the areas of temporary emergency shelter, WASH (Water, Sanitation, and Hygiene), health care, and protection.

AmeriCares

AmeriCares delivered lifesaving medicines, medical supplies, bottled water, and other aid to Haiti and the Dominican Republic. AmeriCares worked with health care partners to distribute medical assistance to earthquake survivors, and supplied volunteer medical teams with medicines and supplies to provide medical treatment and surgery. AmeriCares emergency relief teams prepared and coordinated the delivery and distribution of additional shipments of emergency medical assistance.

AmericasRelief Team

ART collaborated with a large number of corporations and international NGOs to stage a substantial amount of humanitarian aid for shipment once it became permissible for the private sector to ship and fly the commodities to Haiti.

Ananda Marga Universal Relief Team

AMURT organized medical clinics, ready-to-eat food distributions, and child-friendly trauma evacuation centers in several locations in Port-au-Prince. Their projects and offices in Northern Haiti supported the influx of refugees from the city. Their teams continue to participate in long-term development and disaster relief programs.

B'nai B'rith International Response

B'nai B'rith funded emergency relief teams from Israel's Humanitarian Organizations coordinated by IsraAID.

Baptist World Aid

BWA worked in Haiti with its member bodies and international medical teams. Longer term relief and rehabilitation plans are being formulated to be able to continue to assist Haiti. BWA member bodies from North America coordinated response efforts with shipments, response teams of volunteers, and medical supplies.

Brother's Brother Foundation

BBF worked with partner organization Food for the Poor to send requested medical relief supplies to those in need in Haiti.

Buddhist Tzu Chi Foundation

Tzu Chi launched an immediate emergency response targeting most affected areas of Port-au-Prince and displaced populations in the neighboring areas focused on food, clothing, and health assistance to the community members with unmet needs. Tzu Chi assessed needs for housing settlement and school education.

CARE

CARE has more than 100 staff members in Haiti and continues to grow their staff. Contributions supported immediate emergency operations including getting desperately needed food and water to the Haitian people as well as longer term rehabilitation and recovery efforts. CARE reached tens of thousands of people through its distribution of food, water purification packets, jerry cans, hygiene kits, mattresses, and blankets and provided access to water through installation of water bladders and water tankers. CARE planned to reach a total of 60,000 beneficiaries during the first 3 months through its water sanitation and hygiene, shelter, and nonfood items programs.

Catholic Relief Service

CRS and its Caritas partners have stepped up relief efforts in Port-au-Prince and surrounding areas, delivering food and water to hundreds of thousands and providing medical care to thousands more. A CRS team also worked to get St. Francois de Sales Hospital in Port-au-Prince up and running within days of the disaster. Volunteer medical teams performed up to 200 critical operations per week. As the rainy season loomed, CRS stepped up efforts to build temporary shelter and stem the outbreak of disease that results from a lack of clean water and poor hygiene.

CHF International

CHF cleared rubble from major roads and retrieved government records from major Haitian government ministries, through a partnership with Caterpillar and through cash-for-work teams working throughout Port-au-Prince. CHF had over 400 Haitian workers in Petit Goave cleaning the city. CHF started its pilot transitional shelter project in advance of a large program offering temporary homes to thousands of Haitians. CHF continues infrastructure rehabilitation and job creation programs in Cap Haitien, Gonaives, and St. Marc.

ChildFund International

ChildFund International partnered with the Christian Blind Mission (CBM), an organization that has been working in Haiti for 30 years, by meeting the needs of people with disabilities. ChildFund is especially concerned with child protection and keeping children at the center of recovery efforts and rebuilding, particularly with universal access. ChildFund sent staff to Haiti to assist CBM and local partners to establish child-centered spaces for disabled and injured children.

Christian Blind Mission

CBM mobilized an emergency team in support of partners; two of which are hospitals. Direct support was provided to injured persons and persons with disabilities. CBM is partnering with ChildFund to ensure children with disabilities, who are particularly vulnerable in crisis situations, are supported. Major efforts will come in recovery and transition to development as we focus on ensuring that people with disabilities have access to services and are included in development.

Christian Reformed World Relief Committee

CRWRC relief managers joined staff in Port-au-Prince on January 16 and set up logistics in Santo Domingo. CRWRC distributed water, food, and medical aid. Initial aid included water purification units and rice, cornmeal, and beans. First surgical aid, with MTI, arrived January 14; an orthopedic team arrived January 18. CRWRC set up response in Leogane, working with Haitian partner, PWOFOD, to coordinate relief.

Church World Service

CWS pre-positioned emergency supplies began to be distributed to survivors in Port-au-Prince within 24 hours of the earthquake. CWS, its Haitian partners, and the CWS-supported ACT Alliance worked together to provide emergency kits, blankets, food, water, tents, and psychosocial assistance. On behalf of the ACT Alliance, CWS, and its Dominican partners, CWS coordinated the transport of continuing material aid shipments through the Dominican Republic into Haiti. In addition to meeting needs in the capital and other heavily affected communities, CWS focused on the needs of at-risk children and people with disabilities and long-term food sustainability.

CONCERN Worldwide

Concern Worldwide's immediate emergency relief response included daily distributions of food, water, and medical supplies; providing urgently needed tents and other shelter materials to displaced families; providing emergency health services in 10 outpatient centers to screen and treat children for severe malnutrition; and give supplementary food and counseling to mothers and pregnant women. They also built temporary latrines, established education programs and offered psychosocial support for children living in temporary camps, and set up cash-for-work programs to provide urgently needed income and stability to women and other vulnerable earthquake survivors.

Counterpart International

Counterpart International coordinated an immediate lift of pharmaceuticals valued at over $500,000, including anesthetics, antibiotics, and other essential medications. Counterpart also prepared shipments of hygiene supplies, first aid kits, basic supplies for infants, and foodstocks. As these supplies arrived, Counterpart worked with ground partners to distribute these items and to begin the process of long-term recovery.

Direct Relief International

DRI committed $1 million in aid for the response and coordinated with its other in-country partners and colleague organizations. Emergency aid was offered to all partners in Haiti to support their response to the quake. Two shipping containers of medical material were sent to Port-au-Prince. The 40- and 20-foot containers, containing over $420,000 of essential medicines, supplies, and nutritionals, were destined for St. Damien Children's Hospital.

Episcopal Relief & Development

Episcopal Relief & Development reached out to its Haitian partners in an effort to determine the extent of the damage and coordinate a swift response. The agency disbursed emergency relief funds to the Diocese of Haiti to help them meet immediate needs such as providing food, shelter, and water, and supports their ongoing recovery as they rebuild their ministries.

Food for the Hungry

FH is concentrated its work in Siloe, Bellevue la Montagne, Kenscoff, and Aux Cadets (with a total population of around 100,000), working closely with international and local. FH also purchased 600 water filtration systems for distribution. It coordinated food aid and NFI distribution to target areas, as well as medical supplies to hospitals and clinics. Program setup and implementation for trauma recovery (including protection and psychosocial care), cash-for-work, and hygiene education were developed. FH also had a 16-member medical team on the ground providing assistance to local hospitals.

Friends of ACTED

ACTED launched a primary emergency response targeting the most affected areas of Port-au-Prince and neighboring areas. It focused on water and sanitation, food assistance, emergency shelter, and the health and protection of the most vulnerable community members such as women and children. ACTED also secured a donation of 1000 shelter kits from ShelterBox.

Friends of the World Food Programme

WFP delivered 2.6 million rations, the equivalent of nearly 8 million meals, to nearly 400,000 people, in the initial days of the emergency. WFP aimed to reach 100,000 people each day as the operation scaled up. The agency targeted orphanages and hospitals to reach the most vulnerable as a matter of priority. This was one of the most complex operations WFP ever launched because Haiti's entire supply chain infrastructure was devastated.

Giving Children Hope

Giving Children Hope air-freighted 47,000 pounds of disaster relief to Haiti in partnership with Virgin America. Efforts also included sending $1 million worth of pharmaceuticals to help with infection and disease. GCHope sent two teams that hand-delivered over 1000 pounds of aid. These teams helped with distribution and administered aid to a refugee camp and several orphanages in the country. GCHope partnered with World Emergency relief by providing them medical supplies and food for their Haiti relief efforts.

Global Links

Global Links worked with national and international health authorities to identify short- and long-term needs for medical materials in response to the disaster. Global Links collaborated with the Pan American Health Organization/World Health Organization (PAHO/WHO) and other partners to develop a long-term recovery and medical assistance program for water, food, shelter, and sanitation.

Habitat for Humanity

Habitat for Humanity has set a goal of providing housing solutions to 50,000 earthquake-affected families in Haiti—about a quarter of a million people—over the next 5 years. In the initial stage, the organization provided emergency shelter kits to 10,000 households. An aggressive building program was planned to include transitional shelter and construction of small core houses. Habitat implemented its recovery project through Habitat Resource Centers that provide technical assistance and support to restoration of the construction sector as well as direct housing production.

Handicap International

After the earthquake hit, Handicap International's team provided emergency aid to those affected, particularly amputees, of whom there are now more than 2000 according to their estimates. They have also prepared a long-term response, including the production and fitting of temporary artificial limbs and later, permanent prostheses. HI distributed humanitarian aid with the 45 World Food Program trucks they manage and another 10 trucks from the Dominican Republic. WHO appointed Handicap International and Christian Blind Mission to lead a subgroup on disability that coordinates assistance for Haitians suffering from traumatic injuries leading to disability.

Hands On Disaster Response

HODR launched Project Leogane to assist the devastated community of Leogane, Haiti, which was 90% destroyed by the earthquake. HODR coordinated volunteers to provide "hands on" response and recovery assistance to affected residents, in collaboration with the community and local government. HODR coordinated spontaneous volunteers following the disaster.

Heart to Heart

Heart to Heart International sent medical aid and medical volunteers in support of local relief efforts surrounding the major earthquake that struck Haiti on January 12, 2010.

Heartland Alliance

Heartland Alliance for Human Needs & Human Rights sent a team of staff and volunteers to establish long-term services for survivors. Their initial assessment allowed critical time for mobilizing resources that were needed once emergency rescue efforts waned. With their expertise in community-based health care, mental health, and trauma recovery, Heartland Alliance provided long-term mental health services to first-responder relief workers (local and international), to Haitian communities experiencing severe destruction, to Haitian children with severe trauma, and to internally displaced populations experiencing trauma.

Heifer International

Heifer International worked with its in-country team in Haiti to assess conditions on the ground and to plan and prepare a program of rehabilitative work with current partner project families as well as implementation of Heifer's core livestock, agricultural core sustainability programming to help rebuild, long term, people's lives and livelihoods. Heifer has worked in Haiti for more than 10 years and currently works with more than 16,000 families in Haiti, providing gifts of livestock, seeds, trees, and training to help them become self-reliant.

HelpAge USA

HelpAge USA launched a Haiti Emergency Response Fund to assist the 800,000 older people who are the most at-risk during a disaster of this magnitude. Operations focused primarily on search and rescue, followed by the provision of food, water, shelter, and medical attention.

Holt International Children's Service

Holt International established a childcare center 40 miles north of Port-au-Prince and a family preservation program for more than 100 families. Holt staff in Haiti assessed the needs of children and families in their programs and provided additional support to additional families affected.

Humane Society International

Humane Society International sent veterinary experts to vaccinate, treat injuries, and rescue animals affected by the disaster.

Information Management and Mine Action Program

iMMAP received funding from the U.S. Centers for Disease Control and Prevention (CDC) to support CDC and United Nations response and coordination activities in Haiti. iMMAP deployed a team of disaster response experts at the request of UNOCHA and CDC.

International Medical Corps

International Medical Corps' Emergency Response Team focused on providing lifesaving medical care and relief to earthquake survivors.

International Orthodox Christian Charity

IOCC mobilized its disaster response team and coordinated with partners to monitor and respond to emerging needs in Haiti. IOCC provided emergency relief to those affected by the earthquake.

International Relief and Development

IRD mobilized an emergency response team to Haiti in Port-au-Prince and the surrounding areas. IRD focused on the provision of emergency commodities, such as water, sanitation kits, hygiene kits, and shelter materials.

International Relief Team

IRT deployed emergency medical teams, each consisting of four ER physicians and one ER nurse. Teams assess medical needs and provide service. IRT also worked with suppliers to provide substantial material aid to earthquake victims.

International Rescue Committee

The IRC deployed a team of veteran first responders to deliver urgent assistance in Haiti. It worked with partners to set up healing, recreational, interim education, and family tracing programs for children and provide them with food and water. IRC repaired, re-equipped, and re-supplied health clinics run by local partners and restored clean water and sanitation at the centers. They initiated programs to protect women and girls from sexual violence and responded to needs of survivors. A cash-for-work program was launched aimed at clearing rubble, making repairs, and giving Haitians money to buy needed items.

Islamic Relief

Islamic Relief USA launched an appeal for the victims of the quake and coordinated a massive shipment of aid to the island nation.

Jesuit Refugee Service/USA

JRS distributed food and nonfood emergency assistance to 16,000 people at eight locations in Port-au-Prince and to displaced Haitians at three locations on the Haiti-Dominican border. It supported two international surgical teams, providing emergency services to earthquake survivors. In the United States JRS/USA collected cash donations for relief, and undertook advocacy to improve the American and international response to the crisis.

Life for Relief and Development

Life for Relief and Development sent aid to Haiti immediately after the earthquake occurred, and provided food, water, temporary shelter, hygiene kits, and medical aid to victims in the earthquake-affected areas.

Lutheran World Relief

LWR raised over $7 million for relief and development efforts after the earthquake and worked with partners on the ground to provide food, water, sanitation, and shelter both in the capital of Port-au-Prince and in rural communities affected by mass migration. LWR shipped and committed over $2.2 million worth of material resources including health kits, quilts, layettes, school kits, tarps, and tents. LWR also implemented a long-term response that focused on agricultural rehabilitation and rural livelihoods.

Management Sciences for Health

MSH staff in Haiti provided immediate care to victims and distributed kits of medicines and other medical supplies from existing stock in their project warehouses to 16 hospitals and 14 clinical sites in Port-au-Prince.

MAP International

MAP International sent over $2 million in medical assistance to Haiti, including 15 containers with 20 pallets of supplies.

Medical Emergency Relief International

Merlin's emergency response team worked with Haitians and other international agencies to meet the most urgent needs: water, sanitation, shelter, disease prevention, and restoration of basic health services. The main elements of Merlin's Haiti emergency response were distribution of aid materials and equipment, support to local health staff, and training community members to help protect public health.

Medical Teams International

Medical Teams International sent more than 60 volunteer medical professionals to work in the areas of Leogane, Carrefour, and Port-au-Prince in Haiti. Volunteer teams treated more than 10,000 people and conducted more than 50 mobile medical clinics. They airlifted and shipped in medicines and supplies valued at $3.5 million. Medical teams worked to prevent and treat disease in the temporary shelter camps, ensuring that people receiving medical care from their teams also had access to clean water, sanitation, shelter, and proper nutrition.

Mercy Corps

Mercy Corps conducted cash-for-work programs in Port-au-Prince that employed upward of 7000 earthquake survivors to clear rubble, clean wells, and more to help improve the city's damaged infrastructure. Mercy Corps addressed water and sanitation as well as distributing shelter materials to displaced families in makeshift camps and food to those camps. The agency also began the Comfort for Kids program to help Haitian children overcome the emotional trauma of the earthquake.

Operation Blessing

OB provided emergency food, water, and medical relief to thousands in Haiti. Teams worked with IsraAID to provide emergency medical care at relief camps; installed water treatment plants and delivered critical medical supplies and equipment to aid Dr. Paul Farmer's Partners in Health, hospitals, and relief camps; started daily feeding programs for children; coordinated with the U.S. Navy to ship more than 290 tons of OB relief supplies such as bottled water and baby food; provided logistical support and transportation of supplies with Mission Aviation Fellowship; and deployed an OB El Salvador medical team to help treat Haitian victims evacuated to hospitals along the Haiti/Dominican Republic border.

Operation USA

Operation USA sent eight planeloads of emergency supplies to partner agencies. These shipments ($4.3 million) included electric generators, portable lights, medications, shelter materials, and water resources equipment. Commitments have been made to rebuild schools in Jacmel and Port-au-Prince, to provide livelihood grants to re-launch economic activity and employ teenagers. The recovery phase will focus on aid to clinics, hospitals, and schools as well as water and sanitation.

Oxfam America

Oxfam delivered water and provided sanitation facilities to earthquake survivors living in camps in Port-au-Prince and in other hard-hit towns. Oxfam prepared and distributed emergency shelter materials (plastic sheeting and rope) to 4000 families (20,000 people). Family kits containing soap, toothbrushes and paste, and other personal items were distributed to 10,000 people. Oxfam conducted cash-for-work programs that provided income in exchange for work on community projects like building latrines and preparing aid materials for distribution.

Pan America Development Foundation

PADF provided immediate emergency relief and support through the provision of food, water, tools, and basic necessities.

Physicians for Peace

Provided training and education services for health care providers of Haiti's disabled as well as long-term assistance and rehabilitation for amputees and the disabled. PFP accepted donations of new and used prosthetics, wheelchairs, crutches, and canes.

Plan USA

Thousands of tents, family kits, and vast amounts of food and water supplies were provided by Plan USA. They implemented major water and sanitation projects as well as cash-for-work programs to provide locals with income while they participated in the renewal of their own communities. Plan Haiti was asked by the Ministry of Education to help develop a program focused on psychosocial support for parents, teachers, and students affected by the crisis. Plan International committed $28 million to the response.

Plant with Purpose

The PwP staff of 40 worked to provide relief in 41 communities impacted by the earthquake. The team is rebuilding roads to isolated communities and providing urgently needed vehicles and expertise to care for injured and displaced persons. PwP worked with community leaders in Leogane, Grand Goave, and Petit Goave to coordinate relief efforts.

Presbyterian Disaster Assistance/Hunger Program

Presbyterian Disaster Assistance humanitarian relief efforts focused on search-and-rescue and medical attention for those injured by the earthquake, along with food distribution for the survivors. Funds were also used to provide water and sanitation engineers and equipment to construct water purification systems. Resources for building latrines were provided.

Project C.U.R.E.

PROJECT C.U.R.E. worked with the U.S. Military Southern Command, American Airlines, Catholic Relief Services, Partners in Health, and several other humanitarian organizations onsite in Haiti to deliver desperately needed medical relief to earthquake survivors in Haiti.

Project Concern International

In its first month of response PCI provided immediate assistance to more than 60,000 survivors of the January 12 earthquake. In partnership with AmeriCares and others, PCI helped distribute $6 million of medicines and emergency supplies to local health facilities, and delivered lifesaving food, water, and nonfood items to some of the hardest hit neighborhoods. PCI is continuing to work in close collaboration with partner organizations and the governments of the United States and Haiti to improve the lives of more than 215,000 people through integrated interventions in protection, economic recovery, water and sanitation, health, and shelter.

Relief International

RI carried out rapid damage and needs assessments, and provided immediate emergency response in the form of food and nonfood items, and sector-specific responses in health, education, and temporary shelter. Longer term assistance included livelihoods, cash for work, and local capacity development for disaster risk reduction.

Salvation Army World Service

The Salvation Army mobilized two emergency response teams that included doctors and nurses. A container with food and water to serve 1,000,000 people was sent early in the response. SA also sent 1000 temporary shelters (tents). Medical supplies were shipped in along with doctors and nurses trained to provide emotional and spiritual counseling to family victims. New teams were deployed on a weekly basis.

Save the Children

Save the Children identified areas of immediate priority as addressing shelter, health, water, sanitation, child protection needs, and the restoration of education for children.

Solidarity Center

Solidarity Center sent support to its Haitian partners through a union-to-union effort that provides short-term emergency aid and builds toward long-term reconstruction and strengthening of Haiti's labor movement. Donations enabled SC to purchase and transport regular truckloads of food, water, first aid supplies, medicine, and other critical items. The Solidarity Center joined with Dominican unions to respond to specific requests of Haitian unions as they progressed in relocating members, better assessed needs, and moved toward reconstruction.

Stop Hunger Now

Stop Hunger Now coordinated relief efforts with partners in Haiti by organizing shipments of meals and financial support.

Unitarian Universalist Service Committee

UUSC sent an assessment mission to Haiti to meet with survivors and grassroots organizations and develop a mid- and long-term strategy for helping to rebuild lives. Survivors with significant unmet needs including orphaned children, women merchants and street vendors, newly displaced Haitians fanning out to the countryside, and amputees who will need to develop longer-term rehabilitation, were assisted.

United Methodist Committee on Relief

Following the January 12 earthquake, UMCOR re-established operations in Haiti and instituted a 5-year plan to support the rebuilding of Haiti, which includes three phases: emergency, recovery, and rehabilitation. The emergency phase addressed immediate needs such as food, clean water and sanitation, temporary shelter, and emotional and spiritual support. During the recovery phase, UMCOR will build housing, schools, and clinics; restore agriculture; and create income-generating opportunities. During the rehabilitation phase, assistance for physical reconstruction, economic development, and rebuilding of health, education, and other systems will be offered.

United Way Worldwide

Donations to the United Way Worldwide Disaster Fund worked toward Haiti's long-term recovery, and worked to meet the needs of Haitians affected by the disaster who relocated to the United States and throughout the Caribbean. United Way worked with Haitian community networks to determine the most pressing long-term recovery needs. It focuses on education, income, and health, helping to re-establish the educational and health infrastructure of Haitian communities, and to work to improve the income-earning potential of Haitian families.

U.S. Committee for Refugees and Immigrants

The USCRI partnered with Haitian-run organizations to ensure that help reaches the most vulnerable survivors. It also promoted human rights monitoring in camps.

U.S. Fund for UNICEF

UNICEF focused on protecting and assisting children. Its emergency relief efforts in Haiti included saving children's lives by making sure lifesaving supplies reached children in need. UNICEF was also the UN's designated lead agency for coordinating relief efforts in water and sanitation, child protection, education, and nutrition.

World Concern

World Concern provided assistance with water supplies, shelter, blankets, distribution of food, and long-term needs such as job training, education, and loans and home construction, among other projects.

World Hope International

World Hope International launched an emergency response program that mobilized its strong capacity on the ground in the most severely impacted areas of Haiti. Ten different communities were identified as sites for distribution of food, water, other supplies, and basic medical care. WHI is working on the reconstruction of destroyed facilities such as schools, clinics, churches, and an orphanage in Leogane. They have also launched "day camps" for children whose schools were destroyed, and to assist in the cleanup of affected areas.

World Neighbors

World Neighbors worked in the areas north of Port-au-Prince to address declining food production, malnutrition, ill health, and environmental degradation.

World Relief

World Relief staff and partners worked with King's Hospital, a 300-bed hospital in Port-au-Prince, to provide surgeries and medical care to the critically injured. Food items and emergency supplies were distributed through the hospital and local churches, and hot meals were provided to up to 15,000 victims per day. Activities included drilling wells and improving sanitation.

World Vision

World Vision supplied families in Port-au-Prince with rations of water, food, and other emergency items including hygiene kits, tarps, blankets, and water containers. It set up mobile clinics and provided urgently needed medical supplies to hospitals. Children were a main focus of World Vision's response, and they created child-friendly spaces in camps and provided psychological care. An operations center on the border at Jimani worked to help support the influx of displaced Haitians in that area.

Source: InterAction, 2010.

Appendix 9-3
Academic and Professional Disaster Management Institutions

American Association of Wind Engineering, USA—www.aawe.org

American Avalanche Association, USA—http://www.avalanche.org

American College of Emergency Physicians, Section on Disaster Medicine, USA—www.acep
.org

American Psychological Association, Disaster Response Network, USA—www.apa.org

Arkansas Center for Earthquake Education and Technology Transfer, USA—http://quake.ualr
  .edu
Asian Disaster Preparedness Center (ADPC), Thailand—www.adpc.net/
Asian Disaster Reduction Center, Japan—www.adrc.or.jp
Benfield Hazard Research Centre, UK—www.benfieldhrc.org
California Specialized Training Institute (CSTI), USA—www.csti.ca.gov
Canadian Center for Emergency Preparedness (CCEP), Canada—www.ccep.ca
Cascadia Region Earthquake Work Group (CREW), USA—www.crew.org
Center for Disaster Management, Turkey—www.cendim.boun.edu.tr
Center for Disaster Research and Education, Millersville University, USA—http://www
  .millersville.edu/cdre/
Center for Earthquake Research and Information (CERI), University of Memphis, USA—http://
  www.ceri.memphis.edu/
Center for Earthquake Studies, Southeast Missouri State University, USA—www2.semo.edu/ces
Center for Hazards and Risk Research, Columbia University, USA—www.ldeo.columbia.edu/
  CHRR/
Center for Public Health and Disasters, USA—www.ph.ucla.edu/cphdr/
Center for Technology, Environment, and Development (CENTED), Clark University, USA—
  www.clarku.edu/departments/marsh
Center of Excellence in Disaster Management and Humanitarian Assistance, USA—http://coe-
  dmha.org/
Central United States Earthquake Consortium (CUSEC), USA—www.cusec.org
Centre for Disaster Management, India—www.yashada.org/centre/cdm.htm
Centre for Disaster Studies, James Cook University, Australia—http://www.jcu.edu.au/cds/
Centre for Environmental Strategy, UK—www.surrey.ac.uk/CES/
Centre for Research on Epidemiology of Disasters, Belgium—www.cred.be/
Climatic Research Unit, UK—www.cru.uea.ac.uk
Consortium of Universities for Research in Earthquake Engineering (CUREE), USA—www
  .curee.org
Cooperative Institute for Research in Environmental Sciences (CIRES), University of Colorado,
  Boulder, USA—http://cires.colorado.edu/
Cooperative Institute for Research in the Atmosphere (CIRA), Colorado State University,
  USA—www.cira.colostate.edu
Disaster Management Center (DMC), University of Wisconsin, USA—http://dmc.engr.wisc.edu
Disaster Mental Health Institute, University of South Dakota, USA—www.usd.edu/dmhi/
Disaster Mitigation for Sustainable Livelihoods Programme (DiMP), South Africa—www.egs
  .uct.ac.za/dimp
Disaster Mitigation Institute, India—www.southasiadisasters.net
Disaster Preparedness & Emergency Response Association (DERA), USA—www.disasters.org
Disaster Preparedness Resource Centre, Canada—www.chs.ubc.ca/
Disaster Prevention Research Institute (DPRI), Japan—www.dpri.kyoto-u.ac.jp
Disaster Recovery Information Exchange (DRIE), Canada—www.drie.org
Disaster Recovery Institute International (DRII), USA—www.drii.org
Disaster Research Center (DRC), University of Delaware, USA—www.udel.edu/DRC/
Disaster Research Unit, Germany—www.kfs.uni-kiel.de/impr.html

Earthquake Disaster Mitigation Research Center, Japan—www.edm.bosai.go.jp/english/default
.htm

Earthquake Engineering Research Institute (EERI), USA—www.eeri.org

Earthquake Hazard Centre, New Zealand—www.ehc.arch.vuw.ac.nz

Emergencies Research Center, Greece—www.erc.gr

Emergency Administration and Planning, University of North Texas, USA—http://pacs.unt.edu/
public-administration/

Emergency Health Services Department, University of Maryland Baltimore County, USA—
http://ehs.umbc.edu/

Emergency Management Australia Institute (EMAI), Australia—www.ema.gov.au

Environmental Change Institute, UK—www.eci.ox.ac.uk

European Centre for Disaster Medicine, Italy—www.omniway.sm/cemec/

Flood Hazard Research Centre (FHRC), UK—www.fhrc.mdx.ac.uk/

Global Earthquake Safety Initiative, USA—www.geohaz.org/project/gesi.html

Global Fire Monitoring Center (GFMC), Germany—www.uni-freiburg.de/fireglobe

Global Volcanism Program, USA—www.volcano.si.edu

Hazards Reduction & Recovery Center, Texas A&M University, USA—http://archone.tamu.edu/
hrrc

Hazards & Vulnerability Research Institute, University of South Carolina, USA—http://webra
.cas.sc.edu/hvri/

Humanitarian Practice Network, UK—www.odihpn.org

Hydrologic Research Center (HRC), USA—www.hrc-lab.org/

Incorporated Research Institutions for Seismology (IRIS), USA—www.iris.edu

Institute for Business and Home Safety (IBHS), USA—www.ibhs.org

Institute for Catastrophic Loss Reduction, Canada—www.iclr.org

Institute for Crisis, Disaster, and Risk Management (ICDRM), George Washington University,
USA—www.gwu.edu/~icdrm/

International Center for Urban Safety Engineering/International Center for Disaster Mitigation
Engineering (ICUS/INCEDE), Japan—http://icus-incede.iis.u-tokyo.ac.jp/

International Hurricane Center (IHC), Florida International University, USA—www.ihc.fiu .edu/

International Institute of Earthquake Engineering and Seismology (IIEES), Iran—www.iiees
.ac.ir

International Recovery Platform—www.recoveryplatform.org

International Society for the Prevention and Mitigation of Natural Hazards, UK—www
.umanitoba/ca/institutes/natural_resources/naturalhazards/home.htm

Pacific Tsunami Warning Center, USA—It is now the Pacific Tsunami warning center: www.
weather.gov/ptwc/

John A. Blume Earthquake Engineering Center, Stanford University, USA—http://blume
.stanford.edu

Louisiana State Hurricane Center, USA—http://hurricane.lsu.edu

Mid-America Earthquake Center (MAE), USA—http://mae.crr.uiuc.edu/

Multidisciplinary Center for Earthquake Engineering Research (MCEER), University at Buffalo,
USA—http://mceer.buffalo.edu

National Center for Atmospheric Research (NCAR), Environmental and Societal Impacts Group
(ESIG), USA—www.isse.ucar.edu

National Drought Mitigation Center, University of Nebraska, USA—http://drought.unl.edu

National Institute for Urban Search and Rescue (NI/USR), USA—www.niusr.org

National Institute of Building Sciences (NIBS), USA—www.nibs.org

National Lightning Safety Institute (NLSI), USA—www.lightningsafety.com

National Research Institute for Earth Science and Disaster Prevention (NIED), Japan—http://www.bosai.go.jp/e/index.html

Natural Hazards Research and Applications Information Center (NHRAIC), University of Colorado, Boulder, USA—www.colorado.edu/hazards

Natural Hazards Research Centre, New Zealand—www.nhrc.canterbury.ac.nz/

Oregon Natural Hazards Workshop, University of Oregon, USA—http://darkwing.uoregon .edu/~onhw

Overseas Development Institute (ODI), Humanitarian Policy Group, UK—www.odi.org.uk/hpg/index.html

Pacific Disaster Center (PDC), USA—www.pdc.org

Pacific Earthquake Engineering Research (PEER) Center and National Information Service for Earthquake Engineering (NISSE), University of California, USA—http://peer.berkeley.edu/

Pacific Marine Environmental Laboratory (PMEL), USA—www.pmel.noaa.gov/

Program for the Study of Developed Shorelines, Duke University, USA—www.nicholas.duke .edu/psds

ProVention Consortium, Switzerland—www.proventionconsortium.org/

Public Entity Risk Institute (PERI), USA—www.riskinstitute.org

Research Center for Disaster Management, Guatemala—www.uvg.edu.gt

Society for Risk Analysis (SRA), USA—www.sra.org/

Southern California Earthquake Center (SCEC), USA—www.scec.org/

The James and Marilyn Lovell Center for Environmental Geography and Hazards Research, Texas State University, USA—www.geo.txstate.edu/lovell

The Tornado Project, USA—www.tornadoproject.com/

Tsunami Society, USA—www.tsunami.org

University of Geneva, Section of Geosciences and Environment, Switzerland—www.unige.ch/hazards

Urban and Regional Information Systems Association (URISA), USA—www.urisa.org

World Association for Disaster and Emergency Medicine (WADEM), USA—http://wadem .medicine.wisc.edu/

World Institute for Disaster Risk Management, USA—www.drmonline.net

World Seismic Safety Initiative (WSSI), Singapore—www.wssi.org/

10

Participants: Multilateral Organizations and International Financial Institutions

Introduction

A multilateral organization is an organization composed of the central governments of sovereign nations. Member States come together under a charter of rules and responsibilities they have drawn up and agreed upon. Multilateral organizations may be regionally based (e.g., the European Union [EU]), organized around a common issue or function (e.g., the North Atlantic Treaty Organization [NATO] or the Organization of the Petroleum Exporting Countries [OPEC]), or globally based (e.g., the United Nations [UN]). Like sovereign states, they are recognized as having an established legal status under international law. The UN is the most well known and largest of all of the multilateral organizations because its membership is drawn from nearly every nation, and because it covers a wide range of issues.

The first international organization to address the topic of disaster management was the International Relief Union (IRU), which was founded in Italy in 1921 and later integrated into the League of Nations, which then became the UN. Since that time, a number of international organizations have addressed disaster management as a part of their general operation.

International financial institutions (IFIs) are international banks composed of sovereign Member States. They use public money from the Member States to provide technical and financial support for developing countries. IFIs were first developed to help restore peace in the wake of conflict, but their mission and purpose has expanded greatly. Today, IFIs seek to provide development and emergency assistance to stabilize local and world economies. As part of this mission, IFIs have become heavily involved in the reconstruction of nations affected by large-scale disasters and in funding mitigation and preparedness measures that prevent recurrent disasters.

This chapter discusses the various forms of multilateral organizations involved in international disaster management. The UN and its individual offices, agencies, and organizations working in mitigation, preparedness, response, or recovery are also described, followed by a description of other multilateral organizations, including NATO, the EU, the Organization of American States, and the Southern African Development Community, among others. Finally, the international financial institutions that fund much of the world's development, as well as recovery from disasters of all kinds, are addressed. Although this chapter touches upon some issues required in managing complex humanitarian emergencies (CHEs), it does not address the peacekeeping and peacemaking operations of the UN or any other international organization.

The United Nations

Background

The UN was established in 1945, when representatives from 51 countries converged in San Francisco to establish the UN Charter as a commitment to preserve peace in the aftermath of World War II. Later that year, the Charter was ratified by the five permanent members, China, France, the Soviet Union, the United Kingdom, and the United States, as well as several other countries. Today, 192 countries are members of the UN, and the Charter (which is similar to a sovereign state's constitution and establishes the rights and responsibilities of Member States) continues to be amended to reflect the changing needs of world politics.

The UN is not a government body, nor does it write laws; however, Member States can use the UN to resolve conflict and create international policy. While the UN cannot force a sovereign country to comply with its decisions or actions, the organization's global stature and collaborative nature give weight to its resolutions.

The UN has six main organs. Five of these—the General Assembly, the Security Council, the Economic and Social Council, the Trusteeship Council, and the Secretariat—are based in New York City at the UN Headquarters. The sixth, the International Court of Justice, is located at The Hague in the Netherlands. The UN also maintains operational and program offices throughout the world (see Figure 10–1). Through these major bodies and their associated programs, the UN has established a presence in most countries and has fostered partnerships with Member State governments.

The General Assembly

All of the UN Member States are represented in the General Assembly, which is considered a "parliament of nations" that meets to address issues of global significance. Each Member State is given a single vote, with key issues decided by two-thirds majority (less significant matters are decided by simple majority). As mentioned earlier, the General Assembly cannot force its decisions on a sovereign state, although they generally receive wide support. The Assembly holds regular sessions from September to December, and special/emergency sessions may be called at any time. When not in session, the Assembly's work is carried out by its six main committees, other subsidiary bodies, and the Secretariat.

The Security Council

The UN Security Council's primary responsibility is maintaining international peace and security in accordance with the UN Charter. This council, which convenes at will, consists of 15 members, five of which (China, France, the Russian Federation, the United Kingdom, and the United States) are permanent members. All UN Member States are obligated to carry out the Council's decisions. Decisions require nine affirmative votes, including all five votes of the permanent members. When the Council considers threats to international peace, it first explores peaceful settlement options. If fighting is under way, the Council will attempt to secure a cease-fire, and it may send a peacekeeping mission to help the parties maintain the truce and keep opposing forces apart. The Council can take measures to enforce

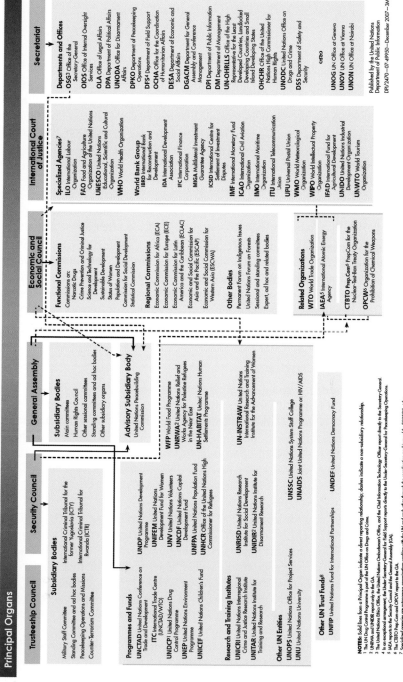

FIGURE 10-1 UN organizational chart. (From UN, 2010)

its decisions, such as imposing economic sanctions or arms embargoes. On rare occasions, the Council has authorized Member States to use "all necessary means," including collective military action, to see that its decisions are carried out. These are referred to as "peacemaking operations."

The Economic and Social Council

The Economic and Social Council is the central mechanism by which international economic and social issues are addressed and by which policy recommendations are created. It also consults with nongovernmental organizations (NGOs) to create and maintain working partnerships between the UN and civil society. The Council has 54 members, elected by the General Assembly for 3-year terms. It meets throughout the year, but its main session is held in July, during which major economic, social, and humanitarian issues are discussed. The Council has several subsidiary bodies that regularly meet to address issues such as human rights, social development, the status of women, crime prevention, narcotic drugs, and environmental protection.

The Trusteeship Council

The Trusteeship Council originally provided international supervision for 11 trust territories adminis-tered by seven Member States and ensured that adequate steps were taken to prepare the territories for self-government or independence. By 1994, all trust territories had attained self-government or inde-pendence. Its work completed, the Trusteeship Council now consists of the five permanent members of the Security Council. It has amended its rules of procedure to allow it to meet as and when the occa-sion may require.

The International Court of Justice

The International Court of Justice, also known as the World Court, is the UN's main judicial organ. The World Court consists of 15 judges elected jointly by the General Assembly and the Security Coun-cil. It serves to settle disputes between countries. Participation is voluntary, but when a state agrees to participate, it must comply with the Court's decision. The Court also provides advisory opinions to the General Assembly and the Security Council upon request.

The Secretariat

The Secretariat carries out the day-to-day work of the UN as directed by the General Assembly, the Security Council, and the other organs. At its head is the Secretary General, who provides overall administrative guidance. The Secretariat is made up of various departments and offices and maintains a total staff of about 40,000 people throughout the world. Duty stations include the UN Headquarters in New York, offices in Geneva, Vienna, and Nairobi, as well as other locations.

The Secretariat's functions are diverse, ranging from "administering peacekeeping operations to mediating international disputes, from surveying economic and social trends and problems to prepar-ing studies on human rights and sustainable development" (United Nations, 2004a). The Secretariat staffs also work to publicize the UN's work through the world media and to organize conferences on issues of global concern. Secretariat staffs are considered international civil servants and answer only to the UN for their activities.

The UN System

The system known as the UN includes many integrated and related offices and agencies that work around the world. There are independent organizations known as "specialized agencies" linked to the UN through cooperative agreements. These agencies are autonomous bodies created by intergovernmental agreement. They maintain broad international responsibilities in economic, social, cultural, educational, health, and related fields. Additionally, a number of UN offices, programs, and funds work to improve the economic and social condition of people around the world. These agencies report directly to the General Assembly or to the Economic and Social Council (see Figure 10–1). Each organization has its own governing body, budget, and secretariat. Together with the UN bodies previously listed, they are known as the UN family or the UN system.

UN Role in Disaster Management

The UN is the organization most involved in the mitigation, preparedness, response, and recovery of disasters around the world. It is considered the best equipped to do so because of its strong relationships with most countries, especially developing countries, where such assistance is most needed. Through its many offices, agencies, and programs, it helps nations to reduce hazard vulnerability by increasing the capacity of their institutions and their citizens. The UN is one of the first organizations to mobilize when disasters strike, and it remains in the affected countries during the recovery period for many years.

When a disaster occurs, the UN responds immediately and on an ongoing basis with relief aid such as food, water, shelter, medical assistance, and logistical support. The UN Office of the Coordination of Humanitarian Affairs (UNOCHA) Emergency Relief Coordinator heads UN response to emergency situations. The coordinator works with a committee of several UN humanitarian agencies, including the UN Children's Fund (UNICEF), the UN Development Programme (UNDP), the World Food Programme (WFP), the UN High Commissioner for Refugees (UNHCR), and other associates as needed, depending on the problems specific to the event.

The UN promotes prevention and mitigation activities through development projects. Long before disasters strike, the UN works with governments, organizations, and citizens to address disaster risk-reduction measures by ensuring that appropriate measures are included in development activities. The UN has helped to map risk throughout the world and has assisted national governments in creating the institutional frameworks to reduce or respond to those risks. By encouraging the building of early warning systems and monitoring and forecasting routines, the UN is boosting local and regional preparedness capacity. At the end of the International Decade for Natural Disaster Reduction (which strove to shift from disaster–response-oriented projects to disaster mitigation), the UN adopted its International Strategy for Disaster Reduction to promote disaster reduction and risk mitigation as part of its central mission. This initiative seeks to promote global resilience to the effects of natural hazards and reduce human, economic, and social losses by

- Increasing public awareness
- Obtaining commitment from public authorities
- Stimulating interdisciplinary and intersectoral partnership and expanding risk-reduction networking at all levels
- Enhancing scientific research on the causes of natural disasters and the effects of natural hazards and related technological and environmental disasters on societies

These strategies are carried out through UN Country Offices and local governments in the most vulnerable communities. Mitigation and preparedness strategies are implemented at all levels of society via public awareness campaigns, commitment from public authorities, cooperation and communication between various government and nongovernmental sectors, and technical knowledge transfer.

Because the UN is such a complex organization, it can be difficult to illustrate the myriad ways in which it addresses disaster management other than to describe the role of each organization and agency in this area.

The General Assembly

The UN General Assembly does not partake in any operational disaster management activities. However, as the main deliberative organ of the UN, it is responsible for launching many influential and effective disaster management programs that are carried out by the various UN offices and by the UN Member State governments. Examples include the endorsement of the UNDP Capacity for Disaster Reduction Initiative (CADRI) and the launching of the International Decade for Natural Disaster Reduction and its subsequent International Strategy for Disaster Reduction. The General Assembly is also responsible for organizing and reorganizing the UN system to maximize its disaster management capabilities, as in 1997 under the UN Program for Reform (1997), which created the Office for the Coordination of Humanitarian Affairs (OCHA; see the next section).

The Secretariat

Within the UN Secretariat are several departments and offices that address pre- and post-disaster management activities. These include the Office for the Coordination of Humanitarian Affairs, the Inter-Agency Standing Committee (IASC), the Executive Committee on Humanitarian Affairs, and the Department of Economic and Social Affairs (DESA).

The UN Office for the Coordination of Humanitarian Affairs

OCHA's mandate is to ensure that the relief provided is effective, not to provide effective relief. (UNDAC, 2000)

UN Resolution 46/182, adopted in December 1991 by the UN General Assembly, was passed to bolster the UN's ability to respond to disasters of all types (including CHEs), and sought to improve how the UN addresses humanitarian operations at the field level. Before 1991, the UN Disaster Relief Coordinator managed natural disasters, and special representatives of the UN Secretary General coordinated CHEs. This resolution merged these two roles to create the Emergency Relief Coordinator (ERC).

The Department of Humanitarian Affairs was created soon after, with the ERC elevated to the status of Under Secretary General for Humanitarian Affairs. The IASC, the Consolidated Appeals Process (CAP), and the Central Emergency Response Fund also were created to increase the humanitarian assistance abilities of the ERC.

The UNOCHA replaced the Department of Humanitarian Affairs under the UN Secretary General's Program for Reform in 1998. It was established to accommodate the needs of victims of disasters and emergencies. Its specific role in disaster management is to coordinate assistance provided by the UN system in emergencies that exceed the capacity and mandate of any individual agency. OCHA response to disasters can be categorized under three main groupings:

1. Coordinating the international humanitarian response
2. Providing support and policy development to the humanitarian community
3. Advocating for humanitarian issues to ensure that the overall direction of relief reflects the general needs of recovery and peace building

OCHA operations are carried out by a staff of approximately 1980 people in New York, Geneva, and in the field (see Figure 10–2). OCHA's 2010 budget was $239,109,637, of which only slightly more than 5% was from the regular UN budget. The remaining 95% is from "extra-budgetary resources," which is primarily donations from Member States and donor organizations.

As head of OCHA, the Under Secretary General for Humanitarian Affairs/UN Emergency Relief Coordinator is responsible for the coordination of UN response efforts through the IASC, which consists of UN and outside humanitarian organization leaders, and analyzes crisis scenarios to formulate joint responses that maximize effectiveness and minimize overlap. The ERC works to deploy appropriate personnel from throughout the UN to assist UN resident coordinators and lead agencies to increase onsite coordination. In March of 2007, the Secretary General appointed John Holmes of the United Kingdom to replace Mr. Jan Egeland of Norway as Under Secretary General for Humanitarian Affairs/UN Emergency Relief Coordinator.

OCHA's Disaster Response System monitors the onset of natural and technological disasters. This system includes training assessment teams before disasters strike, as well as conducting post-disaster evaluations. When a disaster is identified, OCHA activates a response and generates a situation report to provide the international response community with detailed information (including damage assessment, actions taken, needs assessment, and current assistance provided). If necessary, OCHA may then deploy a UN Disaster Assessment and Coordination (UNDAC) team to assist relief activity coordination and assess damages and needs.

If a disaster appears inevitable or is already significant, the ERC in consultation with IASC may designate a humanitarian coordinator (HC), who becomes the most senior UN humanitarian official on the ground for the emergency. The HC is directly accountable to the ERC, increasing the likelihood that the humanitarian assistance provided is quick, effective, and well coordinated. The HC appointment generally signals that the event merits a long-term humanitarian presence. These criteria used by the ERC in deciding whether to appoint an HC are based upon recognition of a need for

- Intensive and extensive political management, mediation, and coordination to enable the delivery of humanitarian response, including negotiated access to affected populations
- Massive humanitarian assistance requiring action by a range of participants beyond a single national authority
- A high degree of external political support, often from the UN Security Council

An OnSite Operations Coordination Center (OSOCC) may be set up in the field to assist local first-response teams to coordinate the often overwhelming number of responding agencies. Finally, OCHA can set up communications capabilities if they have been damaged or do not exist at an adequate level, as required by the UN responding agencies. OCHA generally concludes its responsibilities when the operation moves from response to recovery.

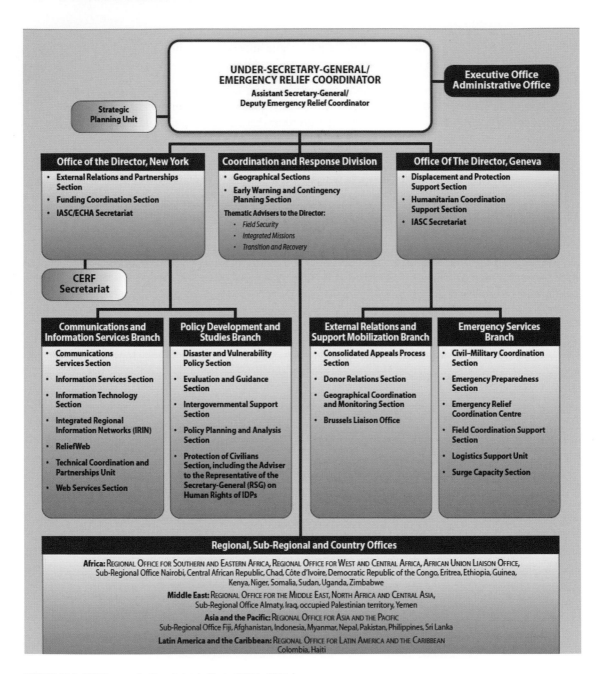

FIGURE 10-2 OCHA organizational chart. (From OCHA, 2010a)

Overall, OCHA coordinates humanitarian affairs to maximize response and recovery operations and minimize duplications and inefficiencies through established structures and policies set forth by the IASC (adapted from OCHA, 2005):

- *Developing common strategies.* OCHA recognizes that humanitarian assistance is most effective when the actors involved define common priorities, share goals, agree on tactics, and jointly monitor progress. OCHA works with both internal and external partners to develop a common humanitarian action plan and to establish clear divisions of responsibility.

- *Assessing situations and needs.* Throughout a crisis, OCHA is responsible for identifying overall humanitarian needs, developing a realistic plan of action for meeting these needs (avoiding duplication), and monitoring progress. It must adjust its response if necessary and analyze any resulting changes. Ongoing analysis of political, social, economic, and military environments and assessing humanitarian needs help response and recovery agencies to better understand disasters' causes and impacts.

- *Convening coordination forums.* In its role as coordinator, OCHA holds a wide range of meetings to bring together the various disaster management players for planning and information exchange. These meetings help the participants to more accurately analyze the overall status of humanitarian relief efforts as well as network and share lessons learned/best practices.

- *Mobilizing resources.* Through the CAP, OCHA is able to raise humanitarian assistance funds cost-effectively. Allocation of funds has been found to be more efficient within this centralized system.

- *Addressing common problems.* Because every crisis is unique, both new and old problems are bound to arise. These issues may affect several agencies and NGOs but might also exist outside of any particular agency's mandate. As coordinator, OCHA analyzes and addresses problems common to humanitarian actors, such as negotiating with warring parties to gain access to civilians in need or working with UN security officials to support preparedness and response measures in changing security situations.

- *Administering coordination mechanisms and tools.* OCHA, and the UN in general, have several tools with which they can better address the humanitarian needs of disaster victims. These include the IASC; rapid-response tools, such as the UN Disaster Assessment and Coordination Teams and the International Search and Rescue Advisory Group; and smaller forums such as the Geographic Information Support Team. OCHA also assists with civil–military cooperation, ensuring a more efficient use of military and civil defense assets in humanitarian operations.

The Field Coordination Support Unit in Geneva manages the human, technical, and logistical resources OCHA uses. These resources are primarily provided by the Danish and Norwegian Refugee Councils, the Danish Emergency Management Agency, the Swedish Rescue Services Agency, and the Emergency Logistics Management Team of the United Kingdom Overseas Development Administration.

The Emergency Relief Coordinator

The Under Secretary General for Humanitarian Affairs/Emergency Relief Coordinator advises the UN Secretary General on disaster-related issues, chairs the Executive Committee on Humanitarian Affairs (ECHA), and leads the IASC. The coordinator is assisted by a deputy, who holds the position of

Deputy Emergency Relief Coordinator (DERC) and is responsible for key coordination, policy, and management issues.

The IASC

The IASC was established in 1992 under UN Resolution 46/182. It serves as a platform within which the broad range of UN and non-UN humanitarian partners (including UN humanitarian agencies, the International Organization for Migration, three consortia of major international NGOs, and the Red Cross movement) may come together to address the humanitarian needs resulting from a disaster. The IASC's primary role is to formulate humanitarian policy that ensures a coordinated and effective response to all kinds of disaster and emergency situations. The primary objectives of the IASC are to (OCHA, 2005)

- Develop and agree on system-wide humanitarian policies
- Allocate responsibilities among agencies in humanitarian programs
- Develop and agree on a common ethical framework for all humanitarian activities
- Advocate common humanitarian principles to parties outside the IASC
- Identify areas where gaps in mandates or lack of operational capacity exist
- Resolve disputes or disagreement about and between humanitarian agencies on system-wide humanitarian issues

  IASC members (both full members and standing invitees) include:

- Food and Agriculture Organization
- InterAction
- International Committee of the Red Cross (ICRC)
- International Council of Voluntary Agencies
- International Federation of Red Cross and Red Crescent Societies (IFRC)
- International Organization for Migration
- Office for the Coordination of Humanitarian Affairs
- Office of the High Commissioner for Human Rights
- Office of the Special Representative of the Secretary General on Internally Displaced Persons
- Steering Committee for Humanitarian Response
- The World Bank
- United Nations Children's Fund
- United Nations Development Fund
- United Nations High Commissioner for Refugees
- United Nations Development Programme
- United Nations Population Fund
- World Food Programme
- World Health Organization

The Executive Committee on Humanitarian Affairs

The Executive Committee on Humanitarian Affairs (ECHA) was created by the UN Secretary General to enhance coordination among UN agencies working on humanitarian affairs issues. ECHA meets on a monthly basis in New York to add a political and peacekeeping dimension to humanitarian consultations. Its members include:

- United Nations Development Program
- United Nations Children's Fund
- United Nations High Commission for Refugees
- World Food Programme
- Office of the High Commissioner for Human Rights
- Department of Peace-keeping Operations
- Department of Political Affairs
- United Nations Relief and Works Agency for Palestine Refugees in the Near East
- Office of the Special Representative of the Secretary General for Children and Armed Conflicts
- World Health Organization
- Food and Agriculture Organization

The OCHA Donor Relations Section

The OCHA Donor Relations Section (DRS), separated from the CAP in 2003, is the focal point for all relations with donors, particularly for funding-related issues. DRS advises the senior management team on policy issues related to interaction with donors and resource mobilization. In addition, it plays a key role in facilitating the interaction of all OCHA entities with donors, both at headquarters and in the field level.

The Coordination and Response Division

The Coordination and Response Division (CRD) was created in 2004 by joining the former New York–based Humanitarian Emergency Branch and the Geneva-based Response Coordination Branch. CRD is responsible for providing disaster-related direction, guidance, and support to the ERC, the UN Resident/Humanitarian Coordinators, and OCHA's field offices (including the deployment of extra personnel as necessary or emergency cash grants).

The OCHA Emergency Services Branch

Based in Geneva, the OCHA Emergency Services Board (ESB) was created to expedite the provision of international humanitarian assistance. ESB develops, mobilizes, and coordinates the deployment of OCHA's international rapid response "toolkit"—the expertise, systems, and services that aim to improve humanitarian assistance in support of disaster-afflicted countries. ESB's humanitarian response activities include the coordination of disaster response and assessment (UNDAC; see in the following section), the setting of international urban search and rescue standards (INSARAG; see in the following section), and the establishment of OSOCCs. ESB supports OCHA field offices through the following:

- Surge capacity and standby partnerships
- Military and civil liaison and mobilization of military and civil defense assets
- Dispatch of relief supplies and specialized assistance in environmental emergencies
- Dissemination of disaster-related information by means of ReliefWeb, the Central Register of Disaster Management Capacities, and the Virtual OnSite Operations Coordination Center.

Within the ESB are four separate sections, established to manage particular aspects of disaster response:

1. Field Coordination Support Section
2. Civil Military Coordination Section
3. Logistics Support Unit
4. Environmental Emergencies Section

- The *Field Coordination Support Section* (FCSS) was established within ESB in 1996 to support national governments and the UN Resident Coordinators in developing, preparing, and maintaining "standby capacity" for rapid deployment to sudden-onset emergencies to conduct rapid needs assessments and coordination. FCSS manages several programs and offices to improve international disaster coordination and cooperation, including:
- *The United Nations Disaster Assessment and Coordination (UNDAC) team.* The UNDAC team is made up of disaster management specialists selected and funded by the governments of UN Member States, OCHA, UNDP, and operational humanitarian UN agencies (such as WFP, UNICEF, and WHO). It provides rapid needs assessments and supports national authorities and the UN Resident Coordinator in organizing international relief. UNDAC teams are on permanent standby status so that they can deploy within hours.
- *The International Search and Rescue Advisory Group (INSARAG).* INSARAG is an intergovernmental network within the UN that manages urban search-and-rescue (USAR) and related disaster-response issues. It promotes information exchange, defines international USAR standards, and develops methodologies for international cooperation and coordination in earthquake response.
- *The Virtual OnSite Operations Coordination Centre (Virtual OSOCC).* The Internet has made it possible for humanitarian relief agencies to share and exchange disaster information continuously and simultaneously, and between any locations where Internet access can be obtained. The Virtual OSOCC is a central repository of information maintained by OCHA that facilitates this exchange of information with NGOs and responding governments. The information is stored on an interactive Web-based database, where users can comment on existing information and discuss issues of concern with other stakeholders.
- *The Surge Capacity Project (including the Emergency Response Roster).* OCHA's Surge Capacity Project seeks to ensure that OCHA always has the means and resources to rapidly mobilize and deploy staff and materials to address the needs of countries affected by sudden-onset emergencies. The Emergency Response Roster (ERR), which became active in June 2002, aims to

rapidly deploy OCHA staff to sudden-onset emergencies to conduct assessments and establish initial coordination mechanisms. Staff included in the ERR are deployable within 48 hours of a request for their services through a deployment methodology based on the UNDAC model. Staff serve on the roster for 2 months at a time.

Established by the IASC in 1995, The *Civil Military Coordination Section (CMCS),* previously entitled Military and Civil Defense Unit (MCDU), is the focal point for the efficient mobilization of Military and Civil Defense Assets for use in humanitarian emergencies and for liaison with governments, international organizations, regional organizations, and military–civil defense establishments deploying these assets. It also coordinates UN agency participation, and participates in major military exercises comprising significant humanitarian scenarios. This section is responsible for the overall management of the OCHA Central Register of Disaster Management Capacities, with specific maintenance of the MCDA Directory of Military and Civil Defense Assets and expertise. CMCS acts as a facilitator and secretariat to the development of documents involving the broad international humanitarian community and is custodian of the "Oslo" and "MCDA" Guidelines detailing the use of MCDA in support of UN humanitarian operations in natural, technological, and environmental disasters and complex emergencies, respectively.

The *Logistics Support Unit* (LSU) manages stocks of basic relief items that can be dispatched immediately to disaster- or emergency-stricken areas. The stockpile, which is located at the UN Humanitarian Response Depot in Brindisi, Italy, includes nonfood, nonmedical relief items (such as shelter, water purification and distribution systems, and household items) donated by UN member governments. The LSU is also involved in other logistical challenges, such as designing contingency plans for the rapid deployment of emergency relief flights and providing interface on logistical matters with other humanitarian agencies (such as WFP, WHO, UNHCR, IFRC, and ICRC). The LSU participates in the operation of a UN Joint Logistics Center (see Exhibit 10–1) and has cosponsored an effort to adopt a UN-wide system for tracking relief supplies and common procedures for air operations. Finally, the LSU contributes information related to stockpiles and customs facilitation agreements (which helps speed up the delivery of relief items).

The *Environmental Emergencies Section*, or the Joint UN Environmental Programme (UNEP)/ OCHA Environment Unit, serves as the integrated UN emergency response mechanism that provides international assistance to countries experiencing environmental disasters and emergencies. This joint unit can rapidly mobilize and coordinate emergency assistance and response resources to countries facing environmental emergencies and natural disasters with significant environmental impacts. The unit performs several key functions geared toward facilitating rapid and coordinated disaster response:

- *Monitoring.* The unit performs continuous monitoring and ongoing communication with an international network of contacts and permanent monitoring of news services and Web sites for early notification of environmental occurrences.
- *Notification.* When disasters strike, the unit alerts the international community and issues Information and Situation Reports to a comprehensive list of worldwide contacts.
- *Brokerage.* The unit is able to quickly establish contact between the affected country and donor governments ready and willing to assist and provide needed response resources.
- *Information clearinghouse.* The unit serves as an effective focal point to ensure information on chemicals, maps, and satellite images from donor sources and institutions are channeled to relevant authorities in the affected country.

EXHIBIT 10–1: THE UN JOINT LOGISTICS CENTER

The UN Joint Logistics Center (UNJLC) is an interagency facility reporting to the Humanitarian Coordinator within a CHE, and overall to the IASC. Its mandate is to coordinate and optimize the logistics capabilities of humanitarian organizations in large-scale emergencies. UNJLC operates under the direction of the World Food Programme (WFP), which is responsible for the administrative and financial management of the UNJLC. The UNJLC is funded from voluntary contributions channeled through the WFP.

The need to establish the UNJLC was realized during the humanitarian response to the 1996 Eastern Zaire crisis, which demanded intensified coordination and pooling of logistics assets among UNHCR, WFP, and UNICEF. This interagency logistics coordination model was applied on subsequent UNJLC interventions in Somalia, Kosovo, East Timor, Mozambique, India, and Afghanistan. In March 2002, the Inter-Agency Standing Committee Working Group institutionalized the UNJLC concept as a UN humanitarian response mechanism. The UNJLC core unit was established in Rome.

In a major disaster with substantial humanitarian multisector involvement during the immediate relief phase, the UN agencies involved may decide that establishing a JLC would contribute to the rapid response, better coordination, and improved efficiency of humanitarian operations. A standby capacity will be developed for facilitating, if required, the UNJLC's timely activation and deployment in the field. The UNJLC will support the UN agencies and possibly other humanitarian organizations that operate in the same crisis area. The capacity includes the option to establish satellite JLC at critical locations in the affected area to offer logistics support on a reduced scale.

Upon UNJLC activation, agencies will establish a Deployment Requirements Assessment (DRA) Team to carry out a quick evaluation of the logistics situation and determine the requirements to deploy the UNJLC in the crisis area. This DRA Team will work closely with the humanitarian authorities and, if deployed, with the UNDAC Team. It will take all necessary measures for installing the UNJLC and draft Ad Hoc Terms of Reference for endorsement by the relevant humanitarian authorities. In case of peacekeeping operations or in a complex environment, the UNJLC activation will be coordinated with the Department of Peacekeeping Operations or the relevant military entities.

UNJLC Role and Scope of Activities

- The role of the UNJLC will be to optimize and complement the logistics capabilities of cooperating agencies within a well-defined crisis area for the benefit of the ongoing humanitarian operation.
- The UNJLC will provide logistics support at operational planning, coordination, and monitoring levels. Unless specified otherwise, the UN agencies and other humanitarian bodies established in the area will continue to exercise their normal responsibilities. As a result, the UNJLC will not be involved in policy and establishment of humanitarian needs and priorities.
- Responsibilities will be defined as per the requirements on a case-by-case basis but will, in principle, be limited to logistic activities between the points of entry and distribution in the crisis area. Detailed responsibilities would be

- Collecting, analyzing, and disseminating logistics information relevant to the ongoing humanitarian operation
- Scheduling the movement of humanitarian cargo and relief workers within the crisis area, using commonly available transport assets
- Managing the import, receipt, dispatch, and tracking of nonassigned food and nonfood relief commodities
- Upon specific request, making detailed assessments of roads, bridges, airports, ports, and other logistics infrastructure and recommending actions for repair and reconstruction
- The scope of the UNJLC activities may vary with the type of emergency, the scale of involvement of the cooperating partners, and the humanitarian needs. In general terms, the UNJLC would:
  - Serve as an information platform for supporting humanitarian logistics operations
  - Upon specific request, coordinate the use of available warehouse capacity
  - Coordinate the influx of strategic humanitarian airlift into the crisis area
  - Serve as an information platform for recommending the most efficient modes of transportation
  - Identify logistical bottlenecks and propose satisfactory solutions or alternatives
  - Serve as the focal point for coordinating facilitation measures with local authorities for importing, transporting, and distributing relief commodities into the country
  - Provide reliable information regarding the logistics capacity in meeting the prioritization of targets
  - Be the focal point to coordinate humanitarian logistics operations with the local emergency management authorities or, in a peacekeeping or complex environment, with the Department of Peace Keeping Operations or the relevant military entities

Source: UNJLC, 2005.

- *Mobilization of assistance.* The unit mobilizes assistance from the international donor community when requested by affected countries.
- *Assessment.* The unit can dispatch international experts to assess an emergency's impacts and to make impartial and independent recommendations about response, cleanup, remediation, and rehabilitation.
- *Financial assistance.* In certain circumstances, the unit can release OCHA emergency cash grants of up to $50,000 to meet immediate emergency response needs.

OCHA Preparedness and Mitigation Measures

Although OCHA's efforts primarily focus on coordinating humanitarian emergency response, the agency also serves a risk-reduction function. For instance, OCHA representatives work with operational humanitarian agencies to develop common policies aimed at improving how the humanitarian response network prepares for and responds to disasters. It also works to promote preparedness and mitigation efforts in Member States to decrease vulnerability. CRD and ESB work closely with the UN Development Programme, other UN programs as necessary, and outside organizations on various projects and activities to increase working relationships with national governments and apply lessons learned from completed disaster responses.

OCHA's Geneva offices are continually monitoring geologic and meteorological conditions, as well as major news services, for early recognition or notification of emerging disasters. Working with UN resident coordinators, country teams, and regional disaster response advisers, OCHA maintains close contact with disaster-prone countries in advance of and during disaster events. OCHA's Regional Disaster Response Advisers work with national governments to provide technical, strategic, and training assistance. They also provide this assistance to other UN agencies and regional organizations to improve international disaster management capacity.

OCHA Information Tools and Services

Clearly, information is key to disaster management, and information must be timely and accurate to be useful. This is especially true in the case of early warning and disaster prevention initiatives. OCHA maintains several information management activities in support of its humanitarian efforts, and provides systems to collect, analyze, disseminate, and exchange information. These functions are performed jointly by the Early Warning and Contingency Planning Unit, the ReliefWeb project, the Field Information Support Project, and the Integrated Regional Information Networks.

Department of Economic and Social Affairs

Department of Economic and Social Affairs (DESA) is another component within the Secretariat that addresses disaster management, primarily regarding predisaster capacity building. DESA addresses a full range of issues under three general areas:

- It compiles, generates, and analyzes a wide range of economic, social, and environmental data and information from which Member States draw to review common problems and evaluate policy options.

- It facilitates the negotiations of Member States in many intergovernmental bodies on joint courses of action to address ongoing or emerging global challenges.

- It advises national governments on translating UN-developed policy frameworks into country-level programs and, through technical assistance, helps build national capacities.

This final area is where DESA addresses disaster management activities within its Division for Sustainable Development. As part of this effort, DESA launched a plan of action during the 2002 World Summit on Sustainable Development in Johannesburg, South Africa, that included commitments to disaster and vulnerability reduction. See Exhibit 10–2 for more information on this plan of action.

The UN Center for Regional Development (UNCRD) is another component of DESA that addresses disaster management issues. Through its headquarters in Nagoya, Japan, and its regional offices in Nairobi, Kenya, and Bogotá, Colombia, UNCRD supports training and research on regional development issues and facilitates information dissemination and exchange. UNCRD maintains a

EXHIBIT 10–2: CHAPTER IV, SECTION 37 OF THE JOHANNESBURG PLAN OF IMPLEMENTATION

An integrated, multihazard, inclusive approach to address vulnerability, risk assessment, and disaster management, including prevention, mitigation, preparedness, response, and recovery, is an essential element of a safer world in the twenty-first century. Actions are required at all levels to

a. Strengthen the role of the International Strategy for Disaster Reduction and encourage the international community to provide the necessary financial resources to its Trust Fund

b. Support the establishment of effective regional, subregional, and national strategies and scientific and technical institutional support for disaster management

c. Strengthen the institutional capacities of countries and promote international joint observation and research, through improved surface-based monitoring and increased use of satellite data, dissemination of technical and scientific knowledge, and the provision of assistance to vulnerable countries

d. Reduce the risks of flooding and drought in vulnerable countries by promoting wetland and watershed protection and restoration, improved land-use planning, improving and applying more widely techniques and methodologies for assessing the potential adverse effects of climate change on wetlands and, as appropriate, assisting countries that are particularly vulnerable to those effects

e. Improve techniques and methodologies for assessing the effects of climate change, and encourage the continuing assessment of those adverse effects by the Intergovernmental Panel on Climate Change

f. Encourage the dissemination and use of traditional and indigenous knowledge to mitigate the impact of disasters and promote community-based disaster management planning by local authorities, including through training activities and raising public awareness

g. Support the ongoing voluntary contribution of, as appropriate, NGOs, the scientific community, and other partners in the management of natural disasters according to agreed, relevant guidelines

h. Develop and strengthen early warning systems and information networks in disaster management, consistent with the International Strategy for Disaster Reduction

i. Develop and strengthen capacity at all levels to collect and disseminate scientific and technical information, including the improvement of early warning systems for predicting extreme weather events, especially El Niño/La Niña, through the provision of assistance to institutions devoted to addressing such events, including the International Center for the Study of the El Niño phenomenon

j. Promote cooperation for the prevention and mitigation of, preparedness for, response to, and recovery from major technological and other disasters with an adverse impact on the environment in order to enhance the capabilities of affected countries to cope with such situations

Source: UNDESA, 2004.

Disaster Management Planning Office in Hyogo, Japan, that researches and develops community-based, sustainable projects for disaster management planning and capacity-building in developing countries. The Hyogo office also runs the Global Earthquake Safety Initiative, designed to improve risk recognition and reduction in 21 cities around the world.

The Regional Commissions

Five regional economic commissions are within the Economic and Social Council. The secretariats of these regional commissions are part of the UN Secretariat and perform many of the same functions (including the disaster management functions listed earlier). The five commissions promote greater economic cooperation in the world and augment economic and social development. As part of their mission, they initiate and manage projects that focus on disaster management. While their projects primarily deal with disaster preparedness and mitigation, they also work in regions that have been affected by a disaster to ensure that economic and social recovery involves adequate consideration of risk reduction measures. The five regional commissions are

- The Economic and Social Commission for Asia and the Pacific (ESCAP)—www.unescap.org
- The Economic Commission for Latin America and the Caribbean (ECLAC)—www.eclac.cl/
- The Economic Commission for Europe (ECE)—www.unece.org/
- The Economic Commission for Africa (ECA)—www.uneca.org/
- The Economic and Social Commission for Western Asia (ESCWA—www.escwa.org.lb

UN Agencies and Programs

The UN Development Programme

In response periods of disasters, the UNDP sees that development does not cease during emergencies. If relief efforts are to contribute to lasting solutions, sustainable human development must continue to be vigorously supported, complementing emergency action with new curative initiatives that can help prevent a lapse into crisis. (The UN General Assembly, 56th Session)

The UNDP was established in 1965 during the UN Decade of Development to conduct investigations into private investment in developing countries, to explore the natural resources of those countries, and to train the local population in development activities (such as mining and manufacturing). As the concept and practice of development expanded, the UNDP assumed much greater responsibilities in host countries and in the UN as a whole.

The UNDP was not originally considered an agency on the forefront of international disaster management and humanitarian emergencies because, while it addressed national capacities, it did not focus specifically on the emergency *response* systems (previously considered to be the focal point of disaster management). However, as mitigation and preparedness received their due merit, the UNDP gained increased recognition for its vital risk reduction role.

Capacity building has always been central to the UNDP's mission in terms of empowering host countries to be better able to address issues of national importance, eventually without foreign assistance. International disaster management gained greater attention as more disasters affected larger populations and caused greater financial impacts. Developing nations, where the UNDP worked, faced the greatest inability to prepare and/or respond to these disasters, largely as a result of the development trends described in Chapter 1. UNDP's projects have shifted toward activities that indirectly fulfill mitigation and preparedness roles. For instance, projects seeking to strengthen government institutions also improve those institutions' capacities to respond with appropriate and effective policy, power, and leadership in the wake of a disaster.

The UNDP now recognizes that disaster management must be viewed as integral to their mission in the developing world, as well as to civil conflict and CHE scenarios. As excerpts from the UNDP mission show, there are implicit similarities between UNDP ideals and those of agencies whose goals specifically aim to mitigate and manage humanitarian emergencies (UNDP, n.d.(a)). For instance:

- [The UNDP] is committed to the principle that development is inseparable from the quest for peace and human security and that the UN must be a strong force for development as well as peace.

- UNDP's mission is to help countries in their efforts to achieve sustainable human development by assisting them to build their capacity to design and carry out development programs in poverty eradication, employment creation and sustainable livelihoods, the empowerment of women, and the protection and regeneration of the environment, giving first priority to poverty eradication.

- UNDP strives to be an effective development partner for the UN relief agencies, working to sustain livelihoods while they seek to sustain lives. It acts to help countries prepare for, avoid, and manage complex emergencies and disasters.

- UNDP supports [development] cooperation by actively promoting the exchange of experience among developing countries.

The UNDP links disaster vulnerability to a lack of or weak infrastructure, poor environmental policy, land misuse, and growing populations in disaster-prone areas. When disasters occur, a country's national development, which the UNDP serves to promote, can be set back years, if not decades. Even small- to medium-size disasters in the least developed countries can "have a cumulative impact on already fragile household economies and can be as significant in total losses as the major and internationally recognized disasters" (SARPN, n.d.). It is the UNDP's objective to "achieve a sustainable reduction in disaster risks and the protection of development gains, reduce the loss of life and livelihoods due to disasters, and ensure that disaster recovery serves to consolidate sustainable human development" (UNDP, n.d.(b)).

In 1995, as part of the UN's changing approach to humanitarian relief, the Emergency Response Division (ERD) was created within the UNDP, augmenting the organization's role in disaster response. Additionally, 5% of UNDP budgeted resources were allocated for quick response actions in special development situations by ERD teams, thus drastically reducing bureaucratic delays. The ERD was designed to create a collaborative framework among the national government, UN agencies, donors, and NGOs that will immediately respond to disasters, provide communication and travel to disaster management staff, and distribute relief supplies and equipment. It also deploys to disaster-affected countries for 30 days to create a detailed response plan on which the UNDP response will be based.

In 1997, under the UN Programme for Reform, the mitigation and preparedness responsibilities of the OCHA Emergency Relief Coordinator were formally transferred to the UNDP. In response, the UNDP created the Disaster Reduction and Recovery Programme (DRRP) within the ERD. Soon after, the UNDP again reorganized, creating a Bureau of Crisis Prevention and Recovery (BCPR) with an overarching mission of addressing a range of nonresponse-related issues:

- Natural disaster reduction
- Recovery
- Mine action
- Conflict prevention and peace building
- Justice and security sector reform
- Small arms and demobilization

BCPR helps UNDP country offices prepare to activate and provide faster and more effective disaster response and recovery. It also works to ensure that UNDP plays an active role in the transition between relief and development.

UNDP's disaster management activities focus primarily on the development-related aspects of risk and vulnerability and on capacity-building technical assistance in all four phases of emergency management. It emphasizes:

1. Incorporating long-term risk reduction and preparedness measures in normal development planning and programs, including support for specific mitigation measures where required
2. Assisting in the planning and implementation of postdisaster rehabilitation and reconstruction, including defining new development strategies that incorporate risk-reduction measures relevant to the affected area
3. Reviewing the impact of large settlements of refugees or displaced persons on development, and seeking ways to incorporate the refugees and displaced persons in development strategies
4. Providing technical assistance to the authorities managing major emergency assistance operations of extended duration (especially in relation to displaced persons and the possibilities for achieving durable solutions in such cases)

UNDP has created the Disaster Reduction Unit (DRU) within BCPR, which includes a team of seven Geneva-based professionals and four regional disaster reduction advisors located in Bangkok, Nairobi, New Delhi, and Panama. DRU works to reduce disaster risk and increase sustainable recovery in countries where UNDP operates. It strengthens national and regional capacities by ensuring that new development projects consider known hazard risks, that disaster impacts are mitigated and development gains are protected, and that risk reduction is factored into disaster recovery. DRU provides the UNDP Country Offices with technical assistance and financial support for the design and implementation of disaster reduction strategies and capacity-building programs to carry out these goals. DRU focuses their support to developing countries in the following areas:

- Increasing capacity for disaster risk reduction
- Mainstreaming disaster risk reduction into development
- Increasing investment in disaster risk reduction

The UNDP Recovery Unit

Following conflict, crises, and disasters, countries must transition from response to recovery. Many countries are unable to manage the difficult and widespread needs of recovery on their own, as they may have experienced widespread loss of infrastructure and services. Displaced persons and refugees may have little to return to, and economies may be damaged or destroyed. The Recovery Unit (under the BCPR) operates during the period when the response or relief phase of the disaster has ended but recovery has not fully commenced (sometimes referred to as the "early recovery period").

The Recovery Unit addresses problems normally encountered in this postcrisis period through its Transition Recovery Programme. This program works to restore government and community capacities to rebuild and recover to prevent a return to a crisis situation. Sustainable risk reduction as a component of recovery is central to this mission. The UNDP has recognized that local expertise in risk management and reduction may not be available, and that the technical assistance they provide may be the only option these communities have to increase their resilience to future disasters. This program has proved effective in many recovery operations, including Cambodia after three decades of civil war, Afghanistan after the 2001 conflict, and Gujarat, India, after the 2001 earthquake. Specific activities of the UNDP Recovery Unit include:

- Performing early assessments of recovery needs and designing integrated recovery frameworks
- Planning and assistance in area-based development and local governance programs
- Developing comprehensive reintegration programs for former IDPs, returning refugees, and ex-combatants
- Supporting economic recovery both at the local and national levels
- Supporting in-country capacity building, UN system coordination, resource mobilization, and partnerships

To meet these recovery priorities, five support services have been developed within the Recovery Unit to assist the UNDP Country Offices and other UNDP/UN agencies to identify areas where BCPR and the Recovery Unit can provide assistance. These support services include:

- *Early assessment of recovery needs and the design of integrated recovery frameworks.* This includes assessing development losses caused by conflict or natural disaster, the need for socioeconomic and institutional recovery, identification of local partners, and the need for capacity building and technical assistance.

- *Planning and assistance in area-based development and local governance programs.* Area-based development and local governance programs play key roles in recovery from conflict because they tailor emergency, recovery, and development issues across a country area by area, based on differing needs and opportunities. Area-based development helps bring together different actors at the operational level, promoting enhanced coordination, coherence, and impact at field level. Area-based development is often seen as the core mechanism that most benefits reintegration.

- *Developing comprehensive reintegration programs for IDPs, returning refugees, and ex-combatants.* Internal displacement, returning refugees, and demobilized former combatants create a huge need for in-country capacity building on different levels. Protection and security become serious issues, and efforts to sustainably reintegrate these populations into their host communities are critical. The Recovery Unit provides expertise on reintegration of IDPs, returnees, and ex-combatants, including capacity building benefiting both the returnees and formerly displaced as well as their host communities through activities such as income generation, vocational training, and other revitalization activities.

- *Supporting economic recovery and revitalization.* One main characteristic of disasters and conflict is their devastating impact on the local and national economies. Livelihoods are destroyed through insecurity, unpredictability, market collapse, loss of assets, and rampant inflation. For recovery to achieve success, these issues need to be well understood from the outset and addressed accordingly.

- *Supporting capacity building, coordination, resource mobilization, and partnerships.* Protracted conflict and extreme disasters tend to create political stressors that temporarily exceed the capacities of UN Country Offices and other NGO partners. However, many recovery needs must be addressed right away to ensure that recovery sets out on a sustainable course. The Recovery Unit offers several services to accommodate the needs of this intense phase through the provision of surge capacity and short- to medium-term staff, assistance in resource mobilization within specific fundraising and coordination frameworks (such as the CAP), and partnership building.

When required to assist in recovery operations, the Recovery Unit may deploy a special Transition Recovery Team (TRT) to supplement UNDP operations in the affected country. These teams' focus varies according to specific needs. For instance, when neighboring countries have interlinked problems (such as cross-border reintegration of ex-combatants and displaced persons), the TRT may support a subregional approach to recovery.

It is important to note that the UNDP has no primary role in the middle of a CHE peacekeeping response, only a supportive one in helping to harmonize development with relief. During recovery and reconstruction, together with others, they take the lead.

In addition to the previously mentioned roles and responsibilities, the UNDP leads several interagency working groups. One such group (which consists of representatives from the WFP, WHO, the Food and Agriculture Organization (FAO), the UN Populations Fund, and UNICEF) develops principles and guidelines to incorporate disaster risk into the Common Country Assessment and the UN Development Assistance Framework. The International Strategy for Disaster Reduction Working Group on Risk, Vulnerability, and Disaster Impact Assessment sets guidelines for social impact assessments. UNDP also coordinates a Disaster Management Training Programme in Central America, runs the conference "The Use of Microfinance and Micro-Credit for the Poor in Recovery and Disaster Reduction," and has created a program to elaborate financial instruments to enable the poor to manage disaster risks.

The UNDP has several reasons for its success in fulfilling its roles in the mitigation, preparedness, and recovery for natural and man-made disasters. First, as a permanent in-country office with close ties to most government agencies, activities related to coordination and planning, monitoring, and training are simply an extension of ongoing relationships. The UNDP works in the country before, during, and long after the crisis. It is able to harness vast, first-hand knowledge about the situations leading up to a crisis and the capacity of the government and civil institutions to handle a crisis, and can analyze what weaknesses must be addressed by the responding aid agencies. In addition, its neutrality dispels fears of political bias.

Second, the UNDP functions as a coordinating body of the UN agencies concerned with development, so when crisis situations appear, there is an established, stable platform from which it may lead. From this leadership vantage, it can (theoretically) assist in stabilizing incoming relief programs of other responding UN bodies, such as the WFP, UNICEF, the Department of Humanitarian Affairs, and the UNHCR. Once the emergency phase of the disaster has ended and OCHA prepares to leave, UNDP is in a prime position to facilitate the transition from response efforts to long-term recovery.

And third, the UNDP has experience dealing with donors, from foreign governments or development banks, and therefore can handle the outpouring of aid that usually results during the relief and recovery period of a disaster. This contributes greatly to reducing levels of corruption and increasing the cost-effectiveness of generated funds. In several recent events, the UNDP has established formalized funds to handle large donor contributions, which have been used for long-term, postdisaster reconstruction efforts (see Exhibits 10–3 and 10–4).

EXHIBIT 10–3: UNDP IN SRI LANKA — A CHE RESPONSE AND RECOVERY OPERATION

On May 19, 2009, the government of Sri Lanka declared military victory over the rebel Liberation Tigers of Tamil Eelam, formally ending a decades-long armed conflict. In the wake of the war, UNDP demonstrated that developing and building on strong partnerships is key to ensuring a fast and well-targeted response. An estimated 300,000 IDPs gathered in camps during the first half of 2009. Many of them lacked basic documentation, making it difficult to access basic services and prove claims to land and assets. UNDP assisted the registrar general to establish a temporary office inside one of the largest camps with capacity to process 50 birth and marriage certificates per day, complemented by additional staffing capacity in Colombo to handle the increased number of document requests. Between July and December the camp office processed close to 10,000 requests, prioritizing those from children who needed identification to sit for national school exams. UNDP also supported mine action coordination and management. Survey and clearance activities advanced rapidly, and by the end of 2009 a total of 879 square kilometers of land had been released for resettlement. This allowed the pace of returns and resettlements to increase exponentially in the fourth quarter of 2009, with over 150,000 IDPs returning or resettling. In the Eastern Province, FAO, ILO, WFP, UNHCR, and UNDP continued to champion the "delivering as one" approach to support community-based recovery and contribute to the stability of returnees in selected divisions of the East. As the funding conduit, UNDP was in charge of the overall coordination of project implementation while also directly implementing small-scale infrastructure construction such as roads, wells, and community centers (which provided a space for cooperatives and trading groups to come together). The selection of target communities was informed through village profile maps and data generated by UNHCR, while WFP provided 6 months of food supply rations until the foundations for agricultural self-reliance and food security for resettled families were laid. UNDP also launched a new initiative in 2009 to foster partnerships between Sri Lanka's manufacturers and resettled communities. UNDP, with its presence in the field, played a catalytic role, identifying the resettled communities, facilitating meetings with the large consumer companies, securing fair and long-term contracts, and supporting training as well as supply of equipment to improve production. Through this project 450 farming and fishing families in the North and the East have secured income for the next 2 to 3 years.

Source: UNDP, 2010.

EXHIBIT 10–4: ROLE OF UNDP IN BANGLADESH AFTER CYCLONE AILA, 2009

On May 25, 2009, Cyclone Aila hit southern Bangladesh, resulting in widespread tidal flooding and the destruction of large parts of the region's protective embankment network. Economic losses were estimated at $106 million and more than 29,000 families were affected in Satkhira, the district that had also suffered the most from Cyclone Sidr in 2007. Many of the affected were still recovering from the impact of the earlier disaster. The government of Bangladesh provided emergency relief and planned for the reconstruction of the damaged embankment network, but many of the most vulnerable families have been unable to return to their homes, which remain submerged.

With funding from the UNDP Bureau of Crisis Prevention and Recovery (BCPR), a livelihoods focused early recovery program was developed, covering all villages in the worst affected part of Satkhira. The program included a cash-for-work component that built upon self-recovery efforts of affected families. This resulted in the creation of an estimated 37,400 work days devoted to road repair and ground elevation. The program also included support for the restoration of essential community infrastructure; support to local small enterprises through working capital grants for carpentry tools, sewing machines, and tea stall equipment; and assistance for home-based income-generating activities, such as vegetable cultivation, crab fattening, handicrafts, poultry rearing, and fish drying. This effort benefited over 4000 families.

Source: UNDP, 2010.

When a major disaster operation requires extended efforts, the UNDP may accept and administer special extra-budgetary contributions to provide the national government with both technical and material assistance, in coordination with OCHA and other agencies involved in the UN Disaster Management Team (DMT). An example of such assistance includes the establishment and administration of a UN DMT Emergency Information and Coordination (EIC) Support Unit. Special grants of up to $1.1 million also may be provided, allocated from the Special Programme Resources funds for technical assistance to postdisaster recovery efforts following natural disasters. See Exhibit 10–5 for information about the UNDP Capacity for Disaster Reduction Initiative.

UNICEF

Like most major UN agencies, UNICEF (formerly known as the United Nations International Children's Emergency Fund) was established in the aftermath of World War II. Its original mandate was to aid children suffering in postwar Europe, but this mission has been expanded to address the needs of women and children throughout the world. UNICEF is mandated by the General Assembly to advocate for children's rights, to ensure that each child receives at least the minimum requirements for survival, and to increase children's opportunities for a successful future. Under the Convention on the Rights of the Child (CRC), a treaty adopted by 191 countries, the UNHCR holds broad-reaching legal authority to carry out its mission.

As of late 2010, UNICEF maintained country offices in 190 different nations. This is probably its greatest asset in terms of the agency's disaster management capacity. Preparedness and mitigation for disasters among its target groups is a priority, with programs able to address both local-level action

---

EXHIBIT 10–5: THE UN CAPACITY FOR DISASTER REDUCTION INITIATIVE (CADRI)

CADRI was created in 2007 as a joint program of the UNDP Bureau for Crisis Prevention and Recovery (UNDP/BCPR), the United Nations Office for the Coordination of Humanitarian Affairs (UNOCHA), and the secretariat of the International Strategy for Disaster Reduction (ISDR). Recognizing that capacity development is a cross-cutting activity for disaster risk reduction, as stipulated in the Hyogo Framework (HF), CADRI's creation is designed to support all five priorities of the HF. CADRI was formally launched by the three organizations at the recent Global Platform for Disaster Risk Reduction Meeting, June 2007, Geneva.

CADRI succeeds the UN Disaster Management Training Programme (DMTP), a global learning initiative, which trained United Nations, government, and civil society professionals between 1991 and 2006. DMTP is widely known for its pioneering work in developing high-quality resource materials on a wide range of disaster management and training topics. More than 20 trainers' guides and modules were developed and translated.

CADRI's design builds upon the success and lessons learned from the DMTP and reflects the significant evolution in the training and learning field since the start of the DMTP, particularly regarding advances in technology for networking and learning purposes. CADRI's design also reflects the critical role that the UN system plays at the national level in supporting government's efforts to advance disaster risk reduction. In the context of the UN's increasingly important role, CADRI provides capacity enhancement services to both the UN system at the country level as well as governments. These include learning and training services and capacity development services to support governments to establish the foundation for advancing risk reduction.

Source: CADRI, 2010.

---

and national-level capacity building. In keeping with the recommendations laid out by the Yokohama Strategy and Plan of Action for a Safer World, UNICEF incorporates disaster reduction into its national development plans. It also considers natural hazard vulnerability and capacity assessments when determining overall development needs to be addressed by UN country teams.

Through public education campaigns, UNICEF works to increase public hazard awareness and knowledge and participation in disaster management activities. UNICEF country offices include activities that address these predisaster needs in their regular projects. For example, they develop education materials required for both children and adults and then design Web sites so educators and program directors can access or download these materials for use in their communities.

In situations of disaster or armed conflict, UNICEF is well poised to serve as an immediate aid provider to its specific target groups. Its rapid-response capacity is important because vulnerable groups are often the most marginalized in terms of aid received. UNICEF works to ensure that children have access to education, health care, safety, and protected child rights. In the response and recovery periods of humanitarian emergencies, these roles expand according to victims' needs. (In countries where UNICEF has not yet established a permanent presence, the form of aid is virtually the same; however, the timing and delivery are affected, and reconstruction is not nearly as comprehensive.)

The UNICEF Office of Emergency Programmes (EMOPS), which has offices in New York and Geneva, maintains overall responsibility for coordinating UNICEF's emergency management activities.

EMOPS works closely with the UNICEF Programme Division, managing the UNICEF Emergency Programme Fund (EPF; see the following section) and ensuring close interagency coordination with other participating humanitarian organizations. In this role, UNICEF is also in the position to act as coordinator in specific areas in which it is viewed as the sector leader. For instance, UNICEF was tasked with leading the international humanitarian response in the areas of water and sanitation, child protection, and education for the 2004 Asia tsunami and earthquake response (in Aceh province alone, over 250 agencies addressed water and sanitation issues). UNICEF maintains that humanitarian assistance should include programs aimed specifically for child victims. Its relief projects generally provide immunizations, water and sanitation, nutrition, education, and health resources. Women are recipients of this aid as well because UNICEF considers women to be vital in the care of children (see Exhibit 10–6).

EXHIBIT 10–6: UNICEF OPERATIONS IN THE OCCUPIED PALESTINIAN TERRITORY, 2009

By the end of the 3 weeks of fighting in early 2009 in Gaza, 350 children had been killed and 1600 injured, and much of Gaza's infrastructure, including schools, health facilities, and vital infrastructure for water and sanitation, had been damaged.

UNICEF was on hand to provide humanitarian support. It led the collective efforts of UN agencies on the ground to restore education, provide emergency water supplies and sanitation, maintain nutritional standards, and protect children from further harm.

From the early days, UNICEF made sure that first aid and emergency medical kits, essential drugs, and water purification tablets flowed into Gaza. Emergency education supplies such as classroom tents and School-in-a-Box kits maintained some sense of continuity and normalcy for children. UNICEF and its partners were able to reach more than 200,000 school-age children.

UNICEF raised global awareness of the harm being done to children through extensive media coverage and advocacy. Attention was also raised by the visits of the Special Representative of the Secretary-General for Children and Armed Conflict, Radhika Coomaraswamy—who called for the protection of children—and UNICEF Executive Director Ann M. Veneman, as well as Goodwill Ambassadors Mia Farrow and Mahmoud Kabil.

UNICEF also extended psychosocial services, including in-depth counseling and structured recreational activities, across Gaza. Training reinforced the capacities of psychosocial workers to protect children and help them heal. Radio programs and 200,000 leaflets designed for children warned of the risks of mines and unexploded ordnance left behind.

UNICEF water tankers ensured a steady supply of clean drinking water to 135 schools with 110,000 students, while desalination units were installed to rid water of dangerous concentrations of chlorides and nitrates. To thwart the risk of acute malnutrition, UNICEF worked through 53 health clinics for mothers and children to offer supplements of micronutrients and fortified food.

The quality and supply of teaching materials were improved through UNICEF's provision of math and science teaching kits. Programs for vulnerable adolescents concentrated on supporting remedial learning, relieving stress, and providing life skills-based education and opportunities to engage in civic activities. Through UNICEF's systematic advocacy with partner organizations, almost half the attendees were girls.

Source: UNICEF, 2010.

To facilitate an immediate response to an emergency situation, UNICEF is authorized to divert up to $50,000 from country program resources to address immediate needs. If the disaster is so great it affects existing UNICEF programs operating in the country, the UNICEF representative can shift these programs' resources once permission is received from the national government and UNICEF Headquarters. UNICEF also maintains a $25 million global EPF, which provides funding for initial emergency response activities.

The World Food Programme

The WFP is the UN agency tasked with addressing hunger-related emergencies. It was created in 1961 by a resolution adopted by the UN General Assembly and the UN FAO. Today, the program operates in 73 countries and maintains eight regional offices. In the year 2009 alone, the WFP provided 4.6 million metric tons of food aid to 101.8 million people in 75 countries through its relief programs. Over the course of its existence, the WFP has provided more than 60 million metric tons of food to countries worldwide.

Since 2000, the WFP has been an active member of the Inter-Agency Task Force on Disaster Reduction (IATF/DR; see the following section). WFP has identified mitigation as one of its five priority action areas, focusing on reducing the impact of natural hazards on food security, especially for the vulnerable. WFP has established a steering committee for disaster mitigation to help its offices integrate these activities into regular development programs. Examples of mitigation projects that focus on food security include water harvesting in Sudan (to address drought), the creation of grain stores and access roads in Tanzania, and the creation of early warning and vulnerability mapping worldwide.

Because food is a necessity for human survival and is considered a vital component of development, a lack of food is, in and of itself, an emergency situation. The WFP works throughout the world to assist the poor who do not have sufficient food so they can survive "to break the cycle of hunger and poverty." Hunger crises are rampant—more than 1 billion people across the globe receive less than the minimum standard requirement of food for healthy survival. Hunger may exist on its own, or it may be a secondary effect of other hazards such as drought, famine, and displacement.

The WFP constantly monitors the world's food security situation through its international Food Aid Information System (FAIS). Using this system, WFP tracks the flow of food aid around the world (including emergency food aid) and provides the humanitarian community with an accurate inventory and assessment of emergency foodstock quantities and locations. This database also includes relevant information that would be needed in times of emergency, such as anticipated delivery schedules and the condition and capabilities of international ports.

In rapid-onset events such as natural disasters, the WFP is a major player in the response to the immediate nutritional needs of the victims. Food is transported to the affected location and delivered to storage and distribution centers (see Figure 10–3). The distribution is carried out according to pre-established needs assessments performed by OCHA and the UNDP. The WFP distributes food through contracted NGOs that have the vast experience and technical skills to plan and implement transportation, storage, and distribution. The principal partners in planning and implementation are the host governments (who must request the WFP aid, unless the situation is a CHE without an established government, in which case the UN Secretary General makes the request). The WFP works closely with all responding UN agencies to coordinate an effective and broad-reaching response because food requirements are so closely linked to every other vital need of disaster victims (see Exhibit 10–7).

During the reconstruction phase of a disaster, the WFP often must continue food distribution. Rehabilitation projects are implemented to foster increased local development, including the provision

FIGURE 10–3 Rice donated by Japan is loaded by the World Food Programme onto 72 WFP trucks to feed survivors of the 2004 Asia tsunami and earthquake events. (From Skullard, 2005; WFP, 2005)

of food aid to families, who as a result will have extra money to use in rebuilding their lives, and food-for-work programs, which break the chains of reliance on aid as well as provide an incentive to rebuild communities.

WFP administers the International Emergency Food Reserve (IEFR), which is designed to store a minimum of 500,000 tons of cereals. IEFR also manages separate resources provided by donors to address long-term operations such as CHEs. The program annually reserves $15 million from its general resources for emergency assistance, in addition to $30 million for long-term emergency assistance. The Immediate Response Account is a cash account established within the IEFR for rapid purchase and delivery of food in emergency situations. These resources are bought from local markets whenever possible, and taken from regional or international sources if necessary, ensuring their arrival before food aid that moves through regular channels.

The World Health Organization

WHO was proposed during the original meetings to establish the UN system in San Francisco in 1945. In 1946, at the United Health Conference in New York, the WHO constitution was approved, and it was signed on April 7, 1946 (World Health Day). WHO proved its value by responding to a cholera epidemic in Egypt months before the epidemic was officially recognized.

EXHIBIT 10–7: WFP DISASTER RESPONSE SYSTEM

WFP response begins at the request of the affected country's government.

1. Emergency Assessment teams are sent in to ask the key questions: How much food aid is needed for how many beneficiaries, and for how long? And how can the food be delivered to the hungry?
2. Equipped with the answers, WFP draws up an Emergency Operation (EMOP), including a plan of action and a budget. The EMOP lists who will receive food aid, what rations are required, the type of transport WFP will use, and which humanitarian corridors lead to the crisis zone.
3. WFP launches an Appeal to the international community for funds and food aid. The agency relies entirely on voluntary contributions to finance its operations, with donations made in cash, food, or services. Governments are the biggest single source of funding. More than 60 governments support WFP's worldwide operations.
4. As funds and food start to flow, WFP's logistics team works to bridge the gap between the donors and the hungry. In 2004, the agency delivered 5.1 million tons of food aid by air, land, and sea.

Ships carry the largest WFP cargo, their holds filled to the brim with 50,000 tons or more of grain, cans of cooking oil, and canned food; the agency has 40 ships on the high seas every day, frequently rerouting vessels to get food quickly to crisis zones. In extreme environments, WFP also uses the skies to reach the hungry, airlifting or airdropping food directly into disaster zones. Before the aid can reach its country of destination, logistics experts often need to upgrade ports and secure warehouses. Trucks usually make the final link in WFP's food chain, transporting food aid along the rough roads that lead to the hungry. Where roads are impassable or nonexistent, WFP relies on less conventional forms of transport: donkeys in the Andes, speedboats in the Mozambique floods, camels in Sudan, and elephants in Nepal. At this stage, local community leaders work closely with WFP to ensure rations reach the people who need it most: pregnant mothers, children, and the elderly.

Source: WFP, 2005.

WHO serves as the central authority on sanitation and health issues throughout the world. It works with national governments to develop medical and health care capabilities and assist in the suppression of epidemics. WHO supports research on disease eradication and provides expertise when requested. It provides training and technical support and develops standards for medical care. WHO became a member of the IATR/DF in 2002, and continues to assist local and national governments as well as regional government associations with health-related disaster mitigation and preparedness issues. It does this primarily by providing education and technical assistance to government public health officials about early detection, containment, and treatment of disease and the creation of public health contingency plans. WHO activities address primary hazards, such as epidemics (e.g., avian influenza, malaria, dengue fever, SARS, and swine flu), and the secondary health hazards that accompany most major disasters. Through their Web site and collaboration with various academic institutions, WHO has also worked to advance public health disaster mitigation and preparedness research and information exchange.

The WHO Director-General is a member of the IASC and the IASC Working Group. In those capacities, the WHO recommends policy options to resolve the more technical and strategic challenges of day-to-day emergency operations in the field. To incorporate public health considerations in UN interagency contingency planning and preparedness activities, the WHO also participates in the IASC Taskforce on Preparedness and Contingency Planning.

The WHO Health Action in Crisis (HAC) department was designed to "reduce avoidable loss of life, burden of disease and disability in crises" (WHO, n.d.). In the event of a disaster, WHO responds in several ways to address victims' health and safety. Most important, it provides ongoing monitoring of diseases traditionally observed within the unsanitary conditions of disaster aftermath. WHO also provides technical assistance to responding agencies and host governments establishing disaster medical capabilities and serves as a source of expertise. It assesses the needs of public health supplies and expertise, and appeals for this assistance from its partners and donor governments. The key functions of HAC in times of crises are

- Measure health-related problems, and promptly assess health needs of populations affected by crises, identifying priority causes of disease and death
- Support Member States in coordinating action for health
- Ensure that critical gaps in health response are rapidly identified and filled
- Revitalize and build capacity of health systems for preparedness and response

When other government or NGO agencies cannot meet the public health needs of the affected population, WHO's mobile response teams bring together expertise in epidemics, logistics, security coordination, and management, collaborating with UN agencies participating in response and recovery. WHO has several bilateral agreements with other UN agencies and NGOs (including the Red Cross/Red Crescent Movement) and coordinates the Inter-Agency Medical/Health Task Force (IMTF), an informal forum that provides guidance on technical and operational health challenges in humanitarian crises. HAC secures funding for its humanitarian action through three primary sources:

1. The regular budget, which is approved by the World Health Assembly biannually
2. General voluntary contributions to WHO; donors spell out a share for emergency activities in their funding agreements or lists of priority allocations
3. Broadly or specifically earmarked voluntary contributions for the Voluntary Fund for Health Promotion for Catastrophes and Disasters

Since its inception, six regional offices have been established. These offices focus on the health issues in each region:

- Regional Office for Africa
- Pan American Health Organization
- Regional Office for South-East Asia
- Regional Office for Europe
- Regional Office for Eastern Mediterranean
- Regional Office for the Western Pacific

Food and Agriculture Organization

The FAO was established as a UN agency in 1945 in Quebec City, Canada. The organization's mandate is to "raise levels of nutrition, improve agricultural productivity, better the lives of rural populations and contribute to the growth of the world economy" (FAO, 2006). It provides capacity-building assistance to communities that need to increase their food output potential. In 2000, FAO pledged to help current and future generations achieve food security by 2015. With headquarters in Rome, Italy, FAO maintains five regional, five subregional, and 80 country offices, each of which works with UN member countries and other partners to coordinate various activities, including disaster management.

FAO is a member of the Inter-Agency Task Force on Disaster Reduction. The 1996 World Food Summit mandated FAO to assist UN member countries in developing national food security, vulnerability information, and specialized mapping systems to cut worldwide malnutrition in half by 2015. A key component of this strategy is strengthening the capacity of communities and local institutions to prepare for natural hazards and respond to food emergencies during disasters and crises. This objective focuses on

- Strengthening disaster preparedness and mitigation against the impact of emergencies that affect food security and the productive capacities of rural populations
- Forecasting and providing early warning of adverse conditions in the food and agricultural sectors and of impending food emergencies
- Strengthening programs for agricultural relief and rehabilitation and facilitating the transition from emergency relief to reconstruction and development in food and agriculture
- Strengthening local capacities and coping mechanisms by guiding the choice of agricultural practices, technologies, and support services to reduce vulnerability and enhance resilience

Within FAO, the Emergency Coordination Group is the organizational mechanism for the overall coordination of emergency and disaster reduction issues. This group has strengthened FAO's capacity to address disaster preparedness, mitigation, relief, and rehabilitation together with member countries and partners in a more integrated way through:

- Preparation of a disaster management database
- Development of a guide for emergency needs assessment and guidance on management of food and agricultural emergencies
- Development of strategies and capacity building for drought mitigation

FAO also maintains a Web site of disaster reduction information through its World Agricultural Information Center. This center has garnered international support through a Global Information and Early Warning System that monitors food supply and demand around the world, provides information on crop prospects, and gives early warning on imminent food crises. FAO also works to help countries adopt sustainable agricultural and other land-use practices. Its land and water development division has helped to reverse land loss, thus increasing disaster resilience, by promoting the development of disaster-resistant agro-ecosystems and the sound use of land and water resources.

In times of disaster, the Emergency Operations and Rehabilitation Division helps communities recover. While other agencies, such as WFP, address immediate food needs by providing the actual food aid to victims, FAO provides assistance to restore local food production and reduce dependency on food aid.

The FAO's first action following disasters, in partnership with WFP, is to send missions to the affected areas to assess crops and food supply status. The Emergency Operations Service of the Emergency Operations and Rehabilitation Division leads these missions, sending FAO experts to consult with farmers, herders, fisheries, and local authorities to gather disaster and recovery data. Using their assessment, FAO designs an emergency agricultural relief and rehabilitation program and mobilizes the funds necessary for its implementation. The Emergency Operations and Rehabilitation Division distributes material assets, such as seeds, fertilizer, fishing equipment, livestock, and farm tools. In a CHE, FAO helps affected communities bolster overall resources and restore and strengthen agricultural assets to make them less vulnerable to future shocks. For example, FAO has been working in regions outside government authority in the Sudan to conduct community-based training of animal health workers aimed at keeping their livestock—a vital part of local livelihoods—from dying.

When a disaster occurs, the Emergency Operations and Rehabilitation Division of FAO establishes an emergency agriculture coordination unit consisting of a team of technical experts from a wide range of fields (including crop and livestock specialists). This field-level team provides information and advice to other humanitarian organizations and government agencies involved in emergency agricultural assistance in the affected area. FAO coordination units also facilitate operational information exchange, reducing duplications of and eliminating gaps in assistance.

FAO's primary beneficiaries include:

- Subsistence farmers
- Pastoralists and livestock producers
- Artisan "fisherfolk"
- Refugees and internally displaced people
- Ex-combatants
- Households headed by women or children and/or afflicted by HIV/AIDS

The Special Emergency Programmes Service (TCES), also within the Emergency Operations and Rehabilitation Division, is responsible for the effective implementation of specially designed emergency programs. These programs require particular attention due to the political and security context surrounding their interventions and the complexity of the institutional setup. TCES was responsible for FAO's intervention in the framework of the Oil for Food Program in Iraq and FAO's emergency and early rehabilitation activities in the West Bank and Gaza Strip.

The Rehabilitation and Humanitarian Policies Unit (TCER) is the final component of the Emergency Operations and Rehabilitation Division. TCER is responsible for making recommendations regarding disaster preparedness, postemergency, and rehabilitation initiatives. The Unit coordinates FAO's position on humanitarian policies and ensures that FAO addresses the gap between emergency assistance and development. TCER also liaises with other UN entities dealing with humanitarian matters.

The FAO's disaster- and emergency-related projects are funded by contributions from governmental agencies, NGOs, other UN agencies, and by the FAO Technical Cooperation Programme (TCP). Each year, approximately 75% of FAO emergency funds are raised through the CAP. FAO expenditure on emergency efforts has grown significantly during the past few years, indicative of the greater role the organization has assumed in disaster management. Current emergency-related projects include:

- Improved food security for HIV/AIDS-affected households in Africa's Great Lakes Region
- Rehabilitation of destroyed greenhouses in the West Bank and Gaza Strip

- Land-tenure management in Angola
- Emergency agricultural assistance to food-insecure female-headed households in Tajikistan
- Consolidation of peace through the restoration of productive capacities of returnee and host communities in conflict-affected areas in Sudan
- Rehabilitation of irrigation systems in Afghanistan
- Rehabilitation of farm-to-market roads in the Democratic Republic of the Congo

UN High Commissioner for Refugees

The position of UNHCR was created by the General Assembly in 1950 to provide protection and assistance to refugees. The agency was given a 3-year mandate to resettle 1.2 million European World War II refugees. Today, UNHCR is one of the world's principal humanitarian agencies, operating through the efforts of 6006 personnel and addressing the needs of 36.5 million people in 126 countries.

UNHCR promotes international refugee agreements and monitors government compliance with international refugee law. UNHCR programs begin primarily in response to an actual or an impending humanitarian emergency. In complex humanitarian disasters and in natural and other disasters that occur in areas of conflict, there is a great likelihood that refugees and IDPs will ultimately result. The organization's staffs work in the field to provide protection to refugees and displaced persons and minimize the threat of violence many refugees are subject to, even in countries of asylum. The organization seeks sustainable solutions to refugee and IDP issues by helping victims repatriate to their homeland (if conditions warrant), integrate in countries of asylum, or resettle in third world countries. UNHCR also assists people who have been granted protection on a group basis or on purely humanitarian grounds, but who have not been formally recognized as refugees.

UNHCR works to avert crises by anticipating and preventing huge population movements from recognized global areas of concern ("trouble spots"). One method is to establish an international monitoring presence to confront problems before conflict breaks out. For example, UNHCR mobilized a "preventive deployment" to five former Soviet republics in Central Asia experiencing serious internal tensions following independence. UNHCR also promotes regional initiatives and provides general technical assistance to governments and NGOs addressing refugee issues.

In times of emergency, UNHCR offers victims legal protection and material help. The organization ensures that basic needs are met, such as food, water, shelter, sanitation, and medical care. It coordinates the provision and delivery of items to refugee and IDP populations, designating specific projects for women, children, and the elderly, who comprise 80% of a "normal" refugee population. The blue plastic sheeting UNHCR uses to construct tents and roofing has become a common and recognizable sight in international news.

UNHCR maintains an Emergency Preparedness and Response Section (EPRS), which has five emergency preparedness and response officers (EPRO) who remain on call to lead emergency response teams into affected areas. The EPROs may be supported by a range of other UNHCR human resources, including:

- Emergency administrative officers and emergency administrative assistants, for quickly establishing field offices
- The 130 members of the Emergency Roster, which includes staff with diverse expertise and experience, are posted throughout the world and are available for rapid emergency deployment

- Staff (by existing arrangement) from the Danish Refugee Council, the Norwegian Refugee Council, and UN volunteers to provide specialized officials on short notice as needed (more than 500 people are available at any given time)

- Individuals registered on a roster of "external consultant technicians," who are specialized in various fields often required during refugee and IDP emergencies (including health, water, sanitation, logistics, and shelter)

- Select NGOs that have been identified as capable of rapid deployment to implement assistance in sectors of need (e.g., health, sanitation, logistics, and social services)

The staff mentioned in the previous list may be supported under an agreement with the Swedish Rescue Services Agency, which is prepared to establish a base camp and office in affected areas within 48 hours' notice. Other supplies and resources, such as vehicles, communications equipment, computers, personal field kits, and prepackaged office kits are maintained for rapid deployment to support field staff.

UNHCR maintains stockpiles of relief aid, including prefabricated warehouses, blankets, kitchen sets, water storage and purification equipment, and plastic sheeting. These are stored in regional warehouses or may be obtained on short notice from established vendors that guarantee rapid delivery. UNHCR also maintains agreements with stockpiles outside the UN system from which they may access items, such as the Swedish Rescue Board and various NGOs.

UNHCR developed a Quick Impact Project (QIP) initiative. QIPs are designed to bridge the gap between emergency assistance provided to refugees and people returning home and longer term development aid undertaken by other agencies. These small-scale programs are geared toward rebuilding schools and clinics, road repair, and bridge and well construction.

UNHCR is funded almost entirely by voluntary contributions from governments, intergovernmental organizations, corporations, and individuals. It receives a limited subsidy of less than 2% of the UN budget for administrative costs and accepts "in-kind" contributions, including tents, medicines, trucks, and air transportation. As the number of persons protected by or of concern by UNHCR jumped to a record high of 36,464,241 in 2009, its budget rose accordingly to $1.754 billion (see Figure 10–4).

Although UNHCR does not often become involved in natural disaster response, rather focusing on areas of conflict, its expertise and assistance were required in the aftermath of the October 2005 earthquake that severely impacted South Asia. During the response phase of this disaster, UNHCR provided 12 flights loaded with supplies from its global and regional stockpiles and contributed 15,145 family tents, 220,000 blankets, 69,000 plastic sheets, and thousands of jerry cans, kitchen sets, stoves, and lanterns. The aid items were drawn from its existing warehouses in Pakistan and Afghanistan, as well as other locations throughout the world. Due to the earthquake, roads used to access 45,000 Afghan refugees affected by the earthquake were severely damaged, but UNHCR was able to quickly assess damages and needs and meet those needs through their existing networks (UNHCR, 2005).

UN Disaster Management Team

In the event of a large-scale disaster, the UN may form a DMT in the affected country. If the disaster clearly falls within the competence and mandate of a specific UN agency, that organization will normally take the lead, with the UN DMT serving as the forum for discussing how other agencies will work to support that lead agency.

FIGURE 10–4 UNHCR-supported refugees in Sudan upon their return from Ethiopia. (From Coseac, Arsenie, October 12, 2008)

The UN DMT is convened and chaired by the UN Resident Coordinator and is comprised of country-level representatives of FAO, UNDP, OCHA, UNICEF, WFP, WHO, and, where present, UNHCR. Specific disaster conditions may merit participation by other UN agencies. The leader of the UNDAC team, assigned by OCHA, automatically becomes a member of the UN DMT. A UNDP official called the Disaster Focal Point Officer often serves as the UN DMT secretary, but the team is free to choose another person if necessary. UNDP is also responsible for providing a venue for the team and any basic administrative support needs.

The UN DMT's primary purpose is to ensure that in the event of a disaster, the UN is able to mobilize and carry out a prompt, effective, and concerted response at the country level. The team is tasked with coordinating all disaster-related activities, technical advice, and material assistance provided by UN agencies, as well as taking steps to avoid wasteful duplication or competition for resources by UN agencies. The UN DMT interfaces with the receiving government's national emergency management team, from which a representative may, where practical, be included in the UN DMT.

Central Emergency Response Fund

The Central Emergency Response Fund (CERF) was created in 1991 through UN General Assembly Resolution 46/182 to allow for faster operational action by UN agencies. The Fund, which was originally called the Central Emergency Revolving Fund, but renamed in 2005 under resolution 60/124, is administered on behalf of the UN Secretary General by the Emergency Relief Coordinator. During times of disaster, CERF provides agencies involved in the humanitarian response with a constant source of funding to cover their activities. Its purpose is to shorten the amount of time between the recognition of needs and the disbursement of funding. Agencies that have received pledges from donors but have not yet received actual funds, or agencies that expect to receive funds from other sources in the near future, can borrow equivalent amounts of cash, interest free, through CERF.

Voluntary contributions of 120 donor nations and 27 nongovernmental entities have raised almost $2 billion since the inception of CERF, of which $1.6 billion has been allocated in the form of grants. The program's goal is to have $500 million replenished annually (see Table 10–1 for a full list of donors). At the outset, CERF was designed only for CHEs, but in 2001 the General Assembly voted to expand CERF to cover all types of disaster situations. Up to two-thirds of the CERF can be allocated to rapid response with the other one-third devoted to addressing underfunded emergencies (see Exhibit 10–8).

Table 10–1   CERF Donor Contributions as of January 1, 2010

Country	Pledges and Contributions (US$)
United Kingdom	$364,933,003
Netherlands	$285,068,964
Sweden	$259,454,320
Norway	$241,193,303
Canada	$168,185,892
Spain	$165,754,141
Ireland	$98,083,022
Germany	$63,500,346
Denmark	$45,740,645
Australia	$44,684,600
Finland	$36,905,545
Switzerland	$29,017,279
Luxembourg	$27,822,901
United States of America	$25,000,000
Belgium	$23,707,347
Republic of Korea	$14,500,000
Qatar	$12,150,000
Japan	$10,669,083
Italy	$8,621,295
France	$4,798,946
New Zealand	$3,762,700
India	$3,000,000
Austria	$2,308,032
China	$2,000,000
Russian Federation	$2,000,000
Portugal	$1,399,385
Greece	$1,379,138
Poland	$1,360,000
Iceland	$1,319,861
Turkey	$1,300,000
South Africa	$1,197,138

Table 10–1   Continued

Country	Pledges and Contributions (US$)
Liechtenstein	$899,970
Czech Republic	$531,706
Indonesia	$525,000
Mexico	$500,000
Saudi Arabia	$500,000
Monaco	$491,608
Romania	$430,625
Brazil	$429,985
Estonia	$350,558
Kuwait	$350,000
Malaysia	$350,000
Kazakhstan	$250,000
Slovenia	$247,371
Andorra	$162,179
Chile	$150,000
Nigeria	$100,000
Trinidad & Tobago	$100,000
Pakistan	$93,967
Argentina	$90,000
Hungary	$84,088
Croatia	$83,000
Egypt	$75,000
Ecuador	$60,000
Israel	$60,000
San Marino	$54,413
Bahamas	$50,000
Brunei Darussalam	$50,000
United Arab Emirates	$50,000
Sri Lanka	$49,982
Algeria	$40,000
Azerbaijan	$40,000
Thailand	$40,000
Bulgaria	$34,966
Philippines	$30,390
Cyprus	$30,000
Oman	$30,000
Singapore	$30,000
Antigua & Barbuda	$25,000
Morocco	$25,000
Peru	$25,000
Lithuania	$20,845

(*Continued*)

Table 10–1   CERF Donor Contributions as of January 1, 2010 (Continued)

Country	Pledges and Contributions (US$)
Armenia	$20,000
Colombia	$20,000
Latvia	$20,000
Myanmar	$20,000
Kenya	$19,895
Bangladesh	$15,000
Ghana	$15,000
Montenegro	$12,475
Grenada	$10,000
Guatemala	$10,000
Jamaica	$10,000
Malta	$10,000
Moldova	$10,000
Mongolia	$10,000
Slovakia	$10,000
Syrian Arab Republic	$10,000
Viet Nam	$10,000
Djibouti	$8000
Albania	$6500
Haiti	$6480
Lebanon	$6000
Bosnia and Herzegovina	$5000
Botswana	$5000
Mozambique	$5000
Tunisia	$5000
Venezuela	$5000
Guyana	$4913
Mauritania	$3844
Afghanistan	$3039
Lao People's Democratic Republic	$3000
Bhutan	$2960
Republic of Congo	$2256
El Salvador	$2000
The former Yugoslav Republic of Macedonia	$2000
Madagascar	$2000
Maldives	$2000
Samoa	$2000
Benin	$1500
Timor-Leste	$1200
Namibia	$1000
St. Lucia	$1000
Tuvalu	$1000

EXHIBIT 10–8: CERF SUPPORTS UN ACTION IN EL SALVADOR, 2009

In November 2009, Hurricane Ida battered El Salvador, killing at least 80 people. Heavy rainfall caused landslides and flooding in seven of the country's 14 departments, affecting 120,000 people. Homes were destroyed, livestock and poultry killed, irrigation systems damaged, and crops of coffee, sugar cane, and red beans were lost. Estimates of the damage were put at $240 million, or 1.1% of the country's GDP.

In the immediate aftermath of the hurricane, the greatest needs were in camp management, food assistance, and water and sanitation. While some UN agencies were able to use existing cash reserves, additional resources were required urgently. As soon as a Flash Appeal was launched, CERF responded with an allocation of $2.5 million to kick-start programs for camp management, food assistance, health, water and sanitation, shelter, protection, and agriculture. The initial CERF contribution proved vital in encouraging further contributions through other channels as donors became aware of the needs and the impact of the response.

Results:

- $423,000 in CERF funding made it possible for WFP to provide enough food aid for 47,000 people staying in temporary shelters.
- CERF funds allowed UNICEF and WHO to provide drinking water, chemical latrines, and chlorine tablets at an early stage, helping reduce the risk of infection and disease for 120,000 people.
- CERF funds enabled a common housing model for emergency shelter to be agreed on quickly and implemented by partners in the Shelter Cluster.
- Even after other contributions arrived, CERF allocations accounted for 37% of all funding received for the Flash Appeal.

Source: CERF, 2010.

CERF has a grant component of $450 million and a loan component of $50 million. The following illustrates how CERF funds are used by a UN organization during an emergency:

1. The lending agency submits a request for an advance to the ERC, which includes a descriptive justification on the project or activities to be funded. If a future pledge for funding has been promised by a donor or if the agency has other means for repaying the loan, this information is included in the request.
2. An OCHA officer reviews the request. If it is accepted (statistics show that the majority are accepted), the ERC informs the agency and sets out the loan use and repayment terms.
3. Disbursement usually occurs within 72 hours. Payment is made through an internal UN "voucher."
4. Loans must be repaid within 6 months.

This entire process is conducted at OCHA's New York office. Figure 10–5 illustrates patterns of use by the various UN agencies.

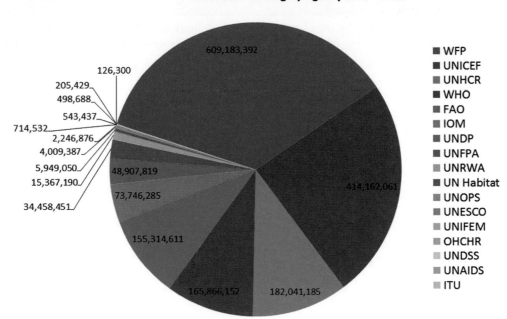

FIGURE 10–5 Use of CERF by UN agency, 2006–2010. (From ochaonline.un.org/CERF/CERF Figures/)

The Consolidated Appeals Process

The CAP, which began in 1991, allows humanitarian aid organizations to plan, implement, and monitor their activities. These organizations can work together to produce a Common Humanitarian Action Plan (CHAP; see the following section) and an appeal for a specific disaster or crisis, which they present to the international community and donors.

The CAP fosters closer cooperation between governments, donors, aid agencies, and many other types of humanitarian organizations. It allows agencies to demand greater protection and better access to vulnerable populations, and to work more effectively with governments and other actors. The CAP is initiated in three types of situations:

1. When there is an acute humanitarian need caused by a conflict or a natural disaster
2. When the government is either unable or unwilling to address the humanitarian need
3. When a single agency cannot cover all the needs

The CAP is led by the HC, who triggers the interagency appeal and collaborates with the IASC Country Team at the local level and the ERC at headquarters. Participants in the process include:

- *IASC*. Although all team members are encouraged to participate in CHAP development, some members may make appeals for funding outside of the UN and its CAP (as is often the case with the Red Cross).

- *Donors*. Donors participate in CHAP development by committing to "Good Humanitarian Donorship principles."
- *Host government(s)*. The CAP is best prepared in consultation with the host government, particularly the ministries the UN operational agencies are working with on a day-to-day basis.
- *Affected population(s)*. Whenever possible, it is always advantageous to include the affected populations' perspective into relief and recovery planning.

A Consolidated Appeal (CA) is a fundraising document prepared by several agencies working to outline annual financing requirements for implementing a CHAP. Although governments cannot request funding through the CA, NGOs can make a request as long as their proposed project goals are in line with CHAP priorities. The CA is usually prepared by the HCs in September or October, and then launched globally by the UN Secretary General at the Donor's Conference held each November. The CA lasts as long as is necessary for funding purposes, usually a year or more. The sectors that may be considered by the CA include:

- Agriculture
- Coordination and support services
- Economic recovery and infrastructure
- Education
- Family shelter and nonfood items
- Food
- Health
- Mine action
- Multisector
- Protection/human rights/rule of law
- Security
- Water and sanitation

The process for filing a CA is as follows:

1. At the onset of the emergency, a Situation Report is issued (can cover from day 1 to week 2).
2. In the meantime, a Flash Appeal may be prepared and launched (covers week 2 to month 6).
3. Finally, a CA may be issued.

If the situation and needs in the field change, a revision to any part of an appeal can be issued at any time. Additionally, projects can be added, removed, or modified within the appeal at any time.

Approximately 80% of CAP and Flash Appeal funding comes from a small group of wealthy nations, including Canada, the European Community Humanitarian Office (ECHO) and the European Commission, Germany, Japan, the Netherlands, Norway, Sweden, the United Kingdom, and the United States. In high-profile events, private donors may constitute a large percentage of donations, such as occurred in the case of the 2004 tsunami disaster in Asia.

The CHAP is a strategic plan developed by agencies working together at the field level that assesses needs in an emergency and coordinates response. It acts as the foundation for a CA, and includes the following information:

1. Common analysis of the context for humanitarian assistance
2. Needs assessment
3. Best, worst, and most likely scenarios
4. Identification of roles and responsibilities (who does what and where)
5. Clear statement of long-term objectives and goals
6. Framework for monitoring strategy and revising as necessary

A Flash Appeal is a special kind of CA, designed for structuring a coordinated humanitarian response for the first 3 to 6 months of an emergency. Whenever a crisis or natural disaster occurs, the UN HC may issue a Flash Appeal in consultation with all stakeholders involved in the humanitarian response (including the affected government). It is normally issued between the second and fourth weeks of the response and provides a concise overview of urgent lifesaving needs. It may also include early recovery projects if they can be implemented within the appeal's time frame.

Since 1992, over 330 Consolidated and Flash Appeals have been launched, collectively raising over $42 billion for NGOs, International Organization for Migration (IOM), and UN agencies (see Exhibit 10–9).

Other UN Agencies Involved in Disaster Response

In addition to the UN agencies discussed earlier, which tend to be the primary agencies involved in all forms of disaster management, a handful of organizations provide more focused assistance as deemed necessary in most disasters that require international participation. As illustrated earlier in Figure 10–5, which details UN assistance to the various countries affected by the December 2004 Asian tsunami and earthquake events, a different mix of UN assistance is needed in each country, even within the same international disaster scenario. Several of these organizations are detailed in the following list.

- *International Labour Organization (ILO)*. Works with the affected population to address issues related to employment, including job creation, skills training, employment services, small business assistance, and other functions (see Exhibit 10–10; www.ilo.org).
- *International Organization for Migration (IOM)*. Provides rapid humanitarian aid to displaced populations by supplying emergency shelter, transporting relief materials, and assisting in medical evacuations. Stabilizes populations through the provision of short-term community and microenterprise development programs. IOM also actively supports governments in the reconstruction and rehabilitation of affected communities by being the lead service provider of
  - Transitional shelters
  - Health care services
  - Countertrafficking activities
  - Psychosocial activities
  - Capacity building for disaster
  - Transportation and logistics
  - Registration and information management of affected populations
- Finally, IOM returns and reintegrates both IDPs and demobilized combatants (see www.iom.int).

EXHIBIT 10–9: CAP MID-YEAR APPEAL — JUNE 14, 2010

The revised appeals are now seeking a total of $9.5 billion to help 53 million people in 34 countries. Funding is now at 48%, leaving $4.9 billion still needed. "Maintaining humanitarian aid budgets this year in the face of recession and pressure on budgets has been a real achievement by many donors," John Holmes, United Nations Under-Secretary-General for Humanitarian Affairs and Emergency Relief Coordinator, said. "I urge them to keep up this effort to ensure that people struck by disaster or conflict receive the help they desperately need for the rest of the year," he added.

The original appeals for 2010, launched in November 2009, sought $7.1 billion, which has now risen to $9.5 billion with new crises, including the earthquake in Haiti, plus deterioration in some existing crises, including the Sahel and the Central African Republic. In the Sahel, food insecurity and malnutrition are increasing because of drought and crop failure, particularly in Niger and western Chad. In Niger, acute malnutrition among children is now well above emergency levels. The number of people in severe need of food in the country has almost doubled compared to the number originally planned. In Chad, the number of people in urgent need of help has more than doubled. In the Central African Republic, where the appeal has received only 35% of requirements so far, the amount of funding needed has increased by 28% because the overall humanitarian situation has deteriorated, leaving increasing numbers of people in need.

One key finding in the review is that funding levels this year have dropped slightly compared to recent years but not as deeply as feared, considering the global economic recession. The major donations to Haiti following the earthquake in January seem to have affected funding for other crises, but again only slightly.

In total, funding for appeals at this juncture amounts to $4.5 billion, compared to $4.6 billion at mid-2009. This total is, however, influenced by funding from private sources after the earthquake in Haiti, of which $278 million has gone to projects in the Haiti humanitarian appeal, accounting for almost one-third of the appeal's funding to date. The Haiti appeal itself has been fully reviewed but remains at around $1.5 billion for the year, with 64% of this so far met.

The review also found a wide variation in appeal coverage, with appeals receiving anywhere between 31 and 64% of the funding required. Funding from CERF, now the seventh largest source of aid to appeals, has helped to balance such disparities, but only up to a certain point.

Source: UN News Center, 2010.

- *International Telecommunications Union (ITU).* Concerned with increasing the role of telecommunications in disaster situations (see www.itu.int).

- *World Meteorological Organization (WMO).* The specialized UN agency for meteorology, operational hydrology, and related geophysical sciences. WMO plays a leading role in international efforts to monitor and protect the environment. For instance, in collaboration with UN agencies and the National Meteorological and Hydrological Services, WMO supports the implementation of relevant conventions such as the UN Framework Convention on Climate Change, the International Convention to Combat Desertification, and the Vienna Convention on

EXHIBIT 10–10: ILO PRESS RELEASE — "SOME 1.1 MILLION JOBS MAY HAVE BEEN LOST IN PAKISTAN DUE TO QUAKE"

More than 1.1 million jobs may have been lost as a result of the south Asian earthquake that devastated parts of Pakistan, the International Labour Office (ILO) said today, adding that productive and labor-intensive job creation programs are urgently needed to lift millions of people out of poverty that has been aggravated by quake damage.

"Reports of widespread destruction show that the livelihoods of millions of people are threatened or have been destroyed," said ILO Director-General Juan Somavia. "As humanitarian and reconstruction efforts proceed, we must begin working immediately to ensure that initiatives are established to monitor and create decent and productive employment and rebuild peoples' livelihoods."

An initial assessment conducted in the days following the south Asian earthquake on October 8 indicated that it caused the widespread destruction of most infrastructure and shops in the affected towns in the region — including the North West Frontier Province (NWFP) and Pakistan-administered Kashmir, with heavy loss of livestock and agricultural implements required for income generation in the rural areas. The assessment added that residents of the badly afflicted parts of Pakistan would require "substantial support to rebuild their income-generating prospects."

Compounding the devastation was the fact that the areas affected are among the poorest in Pakistan, the ILO said. The ILO estimates that total employment in the affected areas was around 2.4 million at the time of the disaster and that over 2 million of these workers and their families were living below the poverty line of less than $2 per person per day before the disaster struck.

Prior to the earthquake, each employed person in the region also supported on average more than two additional dependents, the ILO said, adding, "This means that the 1.1 million workers who lost their employment not only provided their own livelihoods, but also the livelihoods of an additional 2.4 million people, over half of whom were estimated to be under the age of 15."

"Reviving the rural economy where most people in the affected areas live and work is both urgent and challenging," the initial assessment said. "Prior to the earthquake, over 1.4 million workers in the area were engaged in agricultural activities, an estimated 40% or more of whom are now without work. Livestock which provides essential dairy products and the animal power to cultivate the land has also suffered badly."

The ILO assessment also noted that while the medium- and small-sized towns in the area that provided jobs and incomes to almost one-third of the population lie in ruins, the informal economy where most people worked in the urban areas had also been destroyed. Rebuilding the minimum of assets to revive the urban informal economy requires urgent support, the ILO said.

In total, the ILO estimates that around 730,000 workers were employed in the service sector (many in the informal economy), while 230,000 worked in industry (comprised of construction, manufacturing, utilities, and mining). Taken together, more than half of these workers have likely lost one of their primary sources of income.

To meet the needs of the population in the afflicted areas, the ILO urged that programs aimed at generating new employment and other income-producing opportunities be incorporated into the rehabilitation and reconstruction programs that will need to be immediately undertaken following the relief efforts now under way.

These would include employment support services to provide both information and short-term training for the jobs that will be generated through the reconstruction effort; financial and institutional support to rebuild small businesses and income-generating assets in both the rural and urban areas; channeling of financial support from the outside world, including remittances from overseas toward meeting urgently needed basic services; and the creation of institutional mechanisms to ensure that this happens.

"Rebuilding the basic infrastructure—roads, utility services, schools and hospitals—can create employment," Mr. Somavia said. "This means ensuring that decent and productive yet labor-intensive methods are utilized."

Such programs would include:

- Identifying and registering the affected population who have lost their livelihoods
- Recording and classifying job seekers and allocating workers to reconstruction efforts in need of skilled labor
- Developing local capacities to implement emergency employment services
- Linking unemployed people with available work opportunities
- Assisting in restoring the capacity of local government to provide basic services needed by the population and to coordinate rebuilding efforts during both emergency and postemergency phases
- Assisting in the rehabilitation and reconstruction of public infrastructure with focus on employment-intensive approaches to maximize job opportunities for local population
- Providing short-term skills training for men and women from severely affected households to be able to be engaged in the reconstruction effort
- Providing skills training and microbusiness management training to regenerate immediately needed employment and livelihood opportunities for severely affected households

Proposals covering all these elements have been included in a $272 million flash appeal launched by the UN.

The ILO also cautioned that the earthquake could aggravate the already vulnerable position of children, many of whom may be left orphaned, homeless, and out of school in the wake of the disaster, and force them to seek alternative forms of support. In addition, women and youth in the region have traditionally found it particularly difficult to find decent employment opportunities and to secure a life outside of poverty. Without immediate help, poverty among these groups will grow, leaving thousands more young people and women with little hope for the future, the assessment report said.

"Working in the aftermath of this earthquake is not going to be easy," Mr. Somavia said. "These are proud people who have over generations fought against the region's difficult terrain to earn for themselves and their families a better living. Much of their hard-won assets have been destroyed. What is needed urgently is to monitor and support the creation of decent jobs and livelihoods in the future. The ILO stands ready to play its part in a global effort, along with the national authorities, to assist families and communities in rehabilitating the region, rebuilding lives, and restoring hope."

Source: ILO, 2005.

the Protection of the Ozone Layer and its Protocols and Amendments. In the specific case of weather-, climate-, and water-related hazards, which account for nearly 90% of all natural disasters, WMO's programs provide advance warnings to help save lives and reduce damage to property and the environment. WMO also contributes to reducing the impacts of man-made disasters, such as those associated with chemical and nuclear accidents, forest fires, and volcanic ash. Several of WMO's scientific and technical programs related to disaster management include:

- *The WMO World Weather Watch Programme.* Coordinates the preparation and distribution of weather, climate, and hydrological data, analyses, and forecast products to all nations.

- *The WMO Tropical Cyclone Programme.* Promotes the establishment of national and regionally coordinated systems to ensure effective preparedness so that the loss of life and damage caused by tropical cyclones and associated phenomena are reduced to a minimum.

- *The WMO Public Weather Services Programme.* Supports national meteorological and hydrological services in disaster reduction planning by providing routine forecasts and information to enhance nations' social and economic well-being.

- *The World Climate Programme.* Provides an authoritative international scientific voice on climate, climate variations, and climate change. It has provided advanced climate database management systems to many countries, with applications in several areas of disaster mitigation, especially drought.

- *The WMO World Weather Research Programme.* Aims to develop improved and cost-effective techniques for forecasting high-impact weather and promote their applications among countries.

- *The Hydrology and Water Resources Programme.* Assists the national hydrological services of member countries to assess risk and forecast water-related hazards, particularly major floods and droughts (see www.wmo.ch/).

- *Joint United Nations Programme on HIV/AIDS (UNAIDS).* The mission of UNAIDS is to lead, strengthen, and support an expanded response to HIV and AIDS, including preventing the transmission of HIV, providing care and support to those already living with the virus, reducing the vulnerability of individuals and communities to HIV, and alleviating the impact of the epidemic. In times of humanitarian crisis, whether natural, man-made, or conflict-related, UNAIDS works with victims to protect them from the kinds of violence and activity that spreads HIV. In 2001, the UN General Assembly held a special session on HIV/AIDS and declared that the UN would, through UNAIDS:

  develop and begin to implement national strategies that incorporate HIV/AIDS awareness, prevention, care, and treatment elements into programs or actions that respond to emergency situations, recognizing that populations destabilized by armed conflict, humanitarian emergencies, and natural disasters, including refugees, internally displaced persons, and in particular, women and children, are at increased risk of exposure to HIV infection; and, where appropriate, factor HIV/AIDS components into international assistance programs. (PAHO, n.d.; see www.unaids.org)

- *United Nations Population Fund (UNFPA).* UNFPA works to "promote the right of all individuals to develop to their fullest potential" (UNFPA, n.d.) by providing access for all people, especially women, to information and services on reproductive health, including family planning and sexual health, with the goal of helping them to make informed and voluntary choices and decisions. During humanitarian crises, there is often a demand for reproductive health services even though distribution and health care systems have broken down. UNFPA works closely with its humanitarian relief partners to support early and effective action to meet the reproductive health needs of refugees, IDPs, and others caught in crisis situations. Supply shortages compound health risks in already dangerous situations and are a major obstacle to reproductive health in emergencies. Existing supplies may fall far short of demand when large numbers of people move into a safer location. Supplies, equipment, and medicine are organized and stored by UNFPA for immediate distribution when an earthquake, flood, violent conflict, or other crisis arises. A rapid-response fund enables UNFPA to mount a quick response to emergencies, especially in the initial stages. Supplies are packaged in 12 different emergency reproductive health kits. Once an emergency situation stabilizes, the procurement of reproductive health materials becomes a regular part of a more comprehensive healthcare program (see www.unfpa.org).

- *United Nations Human Settlement Programme (UN-HABITAT).* UN-HABITAT is mandated by the UN General Assembly to "promote socially and environmentally sustainable towns and cities with the goal of providing adequate shelter for all" (UN-HABITAT, 2003). UN-HABITAT is mandated through the Habitat Agenda (a global settlement plan adopted in June 1996 by the international community) to take the lead in mitigation, response, and postdisaster rehabilitation capabilities in human settlements. The Habitat Agenda clearly outlines the link between human settlement development and vulnerability to disasters. In addition, it emphasizes the need for coordination and close partnerships with national and local governments, as well as civil society. Finally, the Habitat Agenda recognizes the strong impact disasters have on women, and affirms the need for women's active involvement in disaster management. These steering principles underpin all normative and operational activities of the UN-Habitat Disaster Management Programme (DMP). DMP operates under the Disaster, Postconflict and Safety Section (DPCSS), Urban Development Branch. It was created to marshal the resources of UN-HABITAT and other international agencies to provide local government, civil society, and the private sector with practical strategies for mitigating and recovering from conflicts and natural disasters in the context of human settlements. Specific areas of attention include:
  - Protecting and rehabilitating housing, infrastructure, and public facilities
  - Providing technical and policy support to humanitarian agencies before and after crisis in the context of human settlements
  - Building partnerships and providing complementary expertise in resettlement of displaced persons and refugees
  - Restoring local social structures through settlement development
  - Rehabilitating local government structures and empowering civil society
  - Land and settlements planning and management for disaster prevention
- UN-HABITAT has created a new section (DPCSS) to address the increasing demand from countries for technical support, policy tools, and field operational capacity in disaster prevention, mitigation, and rehabilitation of human settlements and issues related to urban safety. The risk and disaster management program was established to strengthen UN-HABITAT's abilities to deliver technical cooperation and capacity-building services. The focus is on direct

country support, with the objective of helping human settlements reduce their vulnerability and better manage the effects of disasters and conflict. It provides support to national governments, local authorities, and communities in close cooperation with technical cooperation units and other specialized programs. Specific program activities deliver direct support to national and local partners through:

- Technical advisory missions responding to requests by governments and external support agencies
- Execution of assessments in disaster-prone countries and postconflict situations
- Identification, design, technical support, and follow-up of operational projects in response to country requests
- Participation in donor consultations for the provision of external support to disaster-affected countries
- Assessment of global and regional expressions of need related to hazardous conditions or disaster risks and human settlements management, including the design and implementation of global and regional projects (see www.unhabitat.org)

- *United Nations Environmental Program (UNEP)*. UNEP is the UN agency focused on the protection of the environment and wise use of natural spaces. UNEP has several divisions that address global emergency and disaster management needs, such as the Division of Early Warning and Assessment, the Postconflict Assessment Unit, the Collaborating Center on Water and Environment, and the Global Reporting Initiative. Together, these offices provide the UN system with a comprehensive environmental monitoring and hazard safety capability. In particular, UNEP's Division of Technology, Industry, and Economics has a designated disaster management function. The goal of its International Environmental Technology Center (IETC) disaster management efforts is to strengthen the relationships between environmental management and disaster preparedness. IETC's objectives are to

  - Identify the causes and effects of disaster with specific reference to the environment
  - Develop environment management strategies that will help reduce the vulnerability of high-risk communities to disasters
  - Mainstream environmental management practices for disaster mitigation within the overall perspective of poverty alleviation
  - Implement pilot projects and demonstrations of effective strategies in developing countries

- One of the key themes that IETC focuses upon is disaster debris and waste management strategies.

UNEP maintains a program called Awareness and Preparedness for Emergencies at a Local Level (APELL), which is based out of the UNEP Industry and Environment Office in Paris. It serves as a tool for disaster prevention and preparedness and raises public awareness of the need to reduce environmental emergencies and damage. It seeks to minimize the occurrence and harmful effects of technological accidents and emergencies resulting from human activity or as the consequence of natural disasters, particularly in developing countries (see www.unep.org/).

- *United Nations Educational, Scientific, and Cultural Organization (UNESCO)*. UNESCO's goal is to contribute to the peace and security of the world through education, science, and culture.

UNESCO has been involved in disaster management for decades. This organization advocates for the need for a shift in emphasis from relief and emergency response to prevention and increased preparedness and education of potentially affected populations. It strongly supports the design and dissemination of mitigation measures, as well as public education and awareness. UNESCO works to increase the role of academic and research sectors in creating risk and vulnerability reduction measures, and supports existing and new institutions through financial and material support. UNESCO proclaims that their function regarding disaster management is

to promote a better understanding of the distribution in time and space of natural hazards and of their intensity, to set up reliable early warning systems, to devise rational land-use plans, to secure the adoption of suitable building design, to protect educational buildings and cultural monuments, to strengthen environmental protection for the prevention of natural disasters, to enhance preparedness and public awareness through education and training communication and information, to foster post-disaster investigation, recovery and rehabilitation, to promote studies on the social perception of risks. (UNESCO, 2004; www.unesco.org)

- *United Nations Development Fund for Women (UNIFEM).* UNIFEM provides financial and technical assistance to innovative programs and strategies to foster women's empowerment and gender equality. During times of disaster, UNIFEM helps to provide for the unique needs that women normally experience as a vulnerable population (see Exhibit 10–11 see www.unifem.org).

- *United Nations Institute for Training and Research (UNITAR).* UNITAR was created to provide training and research within the UN system, with the goal of increasing the effectiveness of all UN programs. In recent years, more of these efforts have focused upon the four phases of disaster management, addressing many related topics such as climate change, hazardous materials and pollution, land use, and biodiversity (see www.unitar.org).

EXHIBIT 10–11: UNIFEM PRESS RELEASE—"ASIAN TSUNAMI: UNIFEM CALLS FOR GREATER ROLE OF WOMEN IN RECOVERY AND RECONSTRUCTION EFFORTS"

Women survivors of the tsunami that struck in December 2004 are demanding a greater role in the recovery and reconstruction efforts under way in the affected countries. For years at the forefront of survival strategies that sustained their families and communities during conflict, women assumed critical roles in the tsunami emergency response effort, taking in relatives and children orphaned by the tsunami, offering care and support within camps and shelters for grieving survivors, and participating in aid and health care distribution and evacuation of the dead. As tsunami-affected communities transition from the emergency to the reconstruction phase, however, women's participation is lacking in the planning and implementation of recovery and rebuilding processes.

    In two of the severely affected areas, Aceh, Indonesia, and Sri Lanka, UNIFEM and its local partners have been working to mobilize women's networks to identify the needs and concerns of women survivors and ensure that a gender perspective is incorporated in reconstruction processes. Two major women's meetings, one in Aceh and the other in Colombo, Sri Lanka, have taken place in the last 2 months, gathering hundreds of women to discuss their concerns and articulate their role in the recovery and rebuilding phase. The meetings follow on visits by Noeleen Heyzer, executive

(Continued)

EXHIBIT 10–11: UNIFEM PRESS RELEASE—"ASIAN TSUNAMI (CONTINUED)

director of the UN Development Fund for Women (UNIFEM), to Aceh and Sri Lanka to hold consultations with various women's groups at the grassroots level in preparation for the meetings.

"Women must be at the heart of the recovery process. For decades, they have been the lifeline of their communities, leading survival systems and mutual-aid networks, including among the internally displaced and refugee communities. Women are not just victims, they are survivors, and they need to be part of the solution," she said. "The reweaving of the social fabric of life is the foundation for reconstruction and a necessary part of the healing process. It is women, in their families and their communities, who are playing this role."

According to Heyzer, women on the ground identified four critical issues: the urgent need to re-establish livelihoods; the issue of land titles and ownership, including inheritance rights, particularly in the case of children who lost their entire family; the creation of adequate settlements and housing, and the lack of gender sensitivity in the planning and management of temporary barracks; and the need for more opportunities for women to interact with local and national authorities and participate in decision making to engage with the reconstruction process.

Recommendations put forward at the meetings are being submitted at the highest policy levels with the support of UNIFEM and other partners. At the same time, women's groups are being supported to undertake advocacy activities, to ensure that their voices are heard at local and national decision-making levels, especially in critical policy decisions affecting livelihoods, land rights, shelter, and recovery.

Sri Lankan women stressed the need to address access to recovery programs — in many instances, although they received relief supplies in the form of goods, they were not able to get access to recovery grants since these were only provided to men as heads of households. Without cash to start over, it would be difficult for them to rebuild their livelihoods. Many also complained of a lack of access to information, and the threat of losing land or property rights given the loss of deeds and personal documents during the tsunami. In the eastern part of Sri Lanka, women are particularly concerned that customary laws that give women equal rights to land and inheritance may be lost in the new legal regime being designed.

In Aceh, women put at the top of their list of recommendations the re-establishing of Balai Inong, or "women's house." Before the tsunami, every village in Aceh had a Balai Inong where women could meet to network, convene, and work together on projects. According to the women, starting up these women's houses in villages again would be an effective way to ensure that women's concerns were being heard, while also providing a safe space for women to grieve, share experiences, and develop skills to sustain their livelihoods.

Based on the priorities and concerns identified by women, UNIFEM is concentrating its efforts in the tsunami-affected areas on leadership, livelihoods, and protection. Activities include identifying the specific needs of women, and female-headed households in particular, and advocating for an adequate response to these within the reconstruction process; supporting women's organizations in their efforts to engage in the reconstruction process; and building the capacity of partners to include a gender perspective in program design and implementation by national authorities, the UN system, international NGOs, and multilateral and bilateral organizations.

Source: UNIFEM, 2005.

The UN International Strategy for Disaster Reduction

The international community, through the efforts of the UN, named the 1990s the International Decade for Natural Disaster Reduction to increase awareness of the importance of risk reduction. Following the positive advances by the UN and member governments during this time, the UN General Assembly voted to further their successes by creating the International Strategy for Disaster Reduction (ISDR).

ISDR helps nations and organizations design communities to be "disaster resilient" by espousing the idea that disaster reduction must be fully interlinked with development. ISDR seeks to reduce disasters' human, social, economic, and environmental toll that plagues rich and poor countries. To achieve these goals, the ISDR promotes four objectives as tools toward reaching "disaster reduction for all":

- *Increase public awareness about risk, vulnerability, and disaster reduction.* The more people, regional organizations, governments, NGOs, UN entities, representatives of civil society, and others know about risk, vulnerability, and how to manage the impacts of natural hazards, the more disaster reduction measures will be implemented in all sectors of society.

- *Obtain commitment from public authorities to implement disaster reduction policies and actions.* The more decision makers at all levels commit themselves to disaster reduction policies and actions, the sooner communities vulnerable to natural disasters will benefit from applied disaster reduction policies and actions. This requires, in part, a grassroots approach where communities at risk are fully informed and participate in risk management initiatives.

- *Stimulate interdisciplinary and intersectoral partnerships, including the expansion of risk-reduction networks.* The more disaster reduction entities share information on their research and practices, the more the global body of knowledge and experience will progress. By sharing a common purpose and through collaborative efforts, the world's nations will be more resilient to natural hazards impacts.

- *Improve scientific knowledge about disaster reduction.* The more we know about the causes and consequences of natural hazards and related technological and environmental disasters on societies, the better prepared we are to reduce risks. Bringing the scientific community and policymakers together allows them to contribute to and complement each other's work (UNISDR, 2001).

The ISDR works with many different UN agencies and outside organizations, as administered by the IATF/DR and the Inter-Agency Secretariat of the ISDR (UN/ISDR; see Figures 10–6 to 10–8). These two bodies were formed by the UN General Assembly through UN Resolutions 54/219 and 56/195 to implement ISDR.

Inter-Agency Task Force for Disaster Reduction (IATF/DR)

The IATF/DR is the principal body for the development of disaster reduction policy. The Task Force is led by the UN Under Secretary General for Humanitarian Affairs and is composed of representatives from 25 UN, international, regional, and civil society organizations. Task force working groups bring together specialists and organizations to address issues relevant to disaster management, such as climate change, early warning, vulnerability, and risk analysis, among many others. In 2005, the IATR/DR task force working groups included Climate and Disasters (chaired by WMO); Early

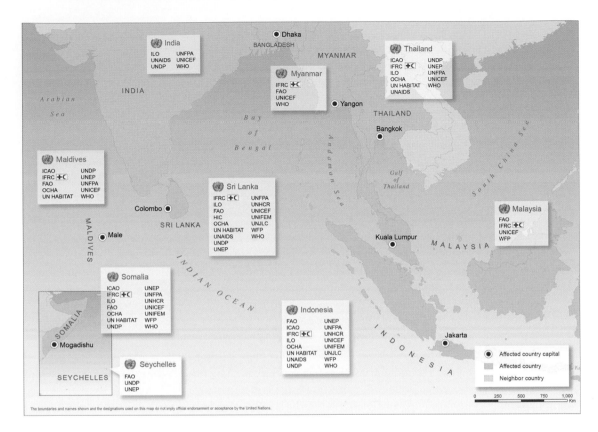

FIGURE 10–6 UN assistance to countries affected by the December 2004 Asian tsunami and earthquake events. (From ReliefWeb, 2005)

Warning (chaired by UNEP); Risk, Vulnerability, and Impact Assessment (chaired by UNDP); and Wildland Fires (chaired by the Global Fire Monitoring Center, Freiburg, Germany). The mandated functions of IATF/DR are

- To serve as the main forum within the UN system for devising strategies and policies for the reduction of natural hazards
- To identify gaps in disaster reduction policies and programs and recommend remedial action
- To ensure complementarities of action by agencies involved in disaster reduction
- To provide policy guidance to the ISDR Secretariat
- To convene ad hoc meetings of experts on issues related to disaster reduction

The Inter-Agency Secretariat of the ISDR

The UN/ISDR serves as the UN system's focal point for disaster reduction activities in the socioeconomic, humanitarian, and development fields, as well as supporting policy integration (Figure 10-8). It functions as a clearinghouse for disaster reduction information, campaigns to raise hazard awareness, and

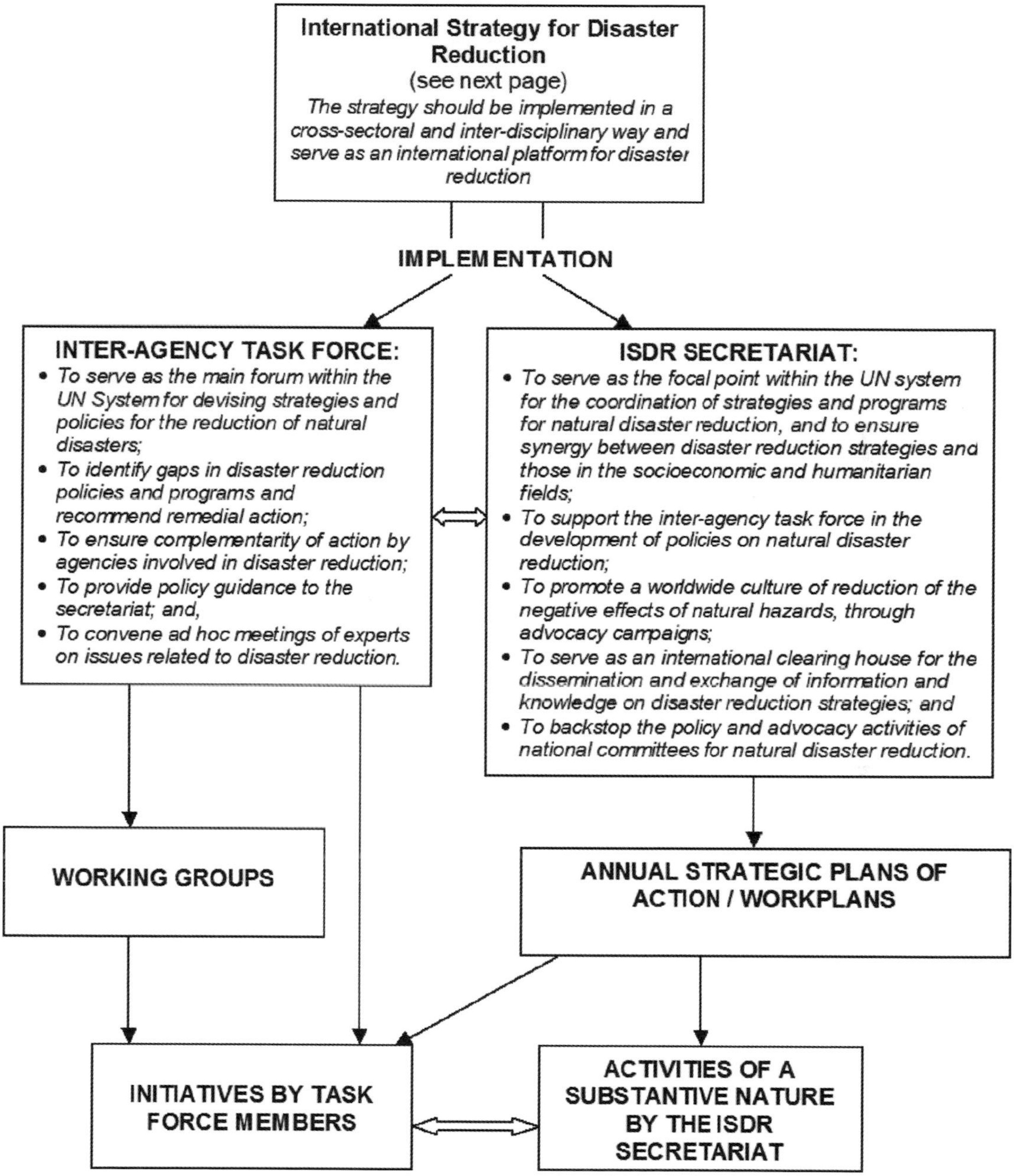

FIGURE 10–7 Overall structure of the ISDR. (From UNISDR, 2001)

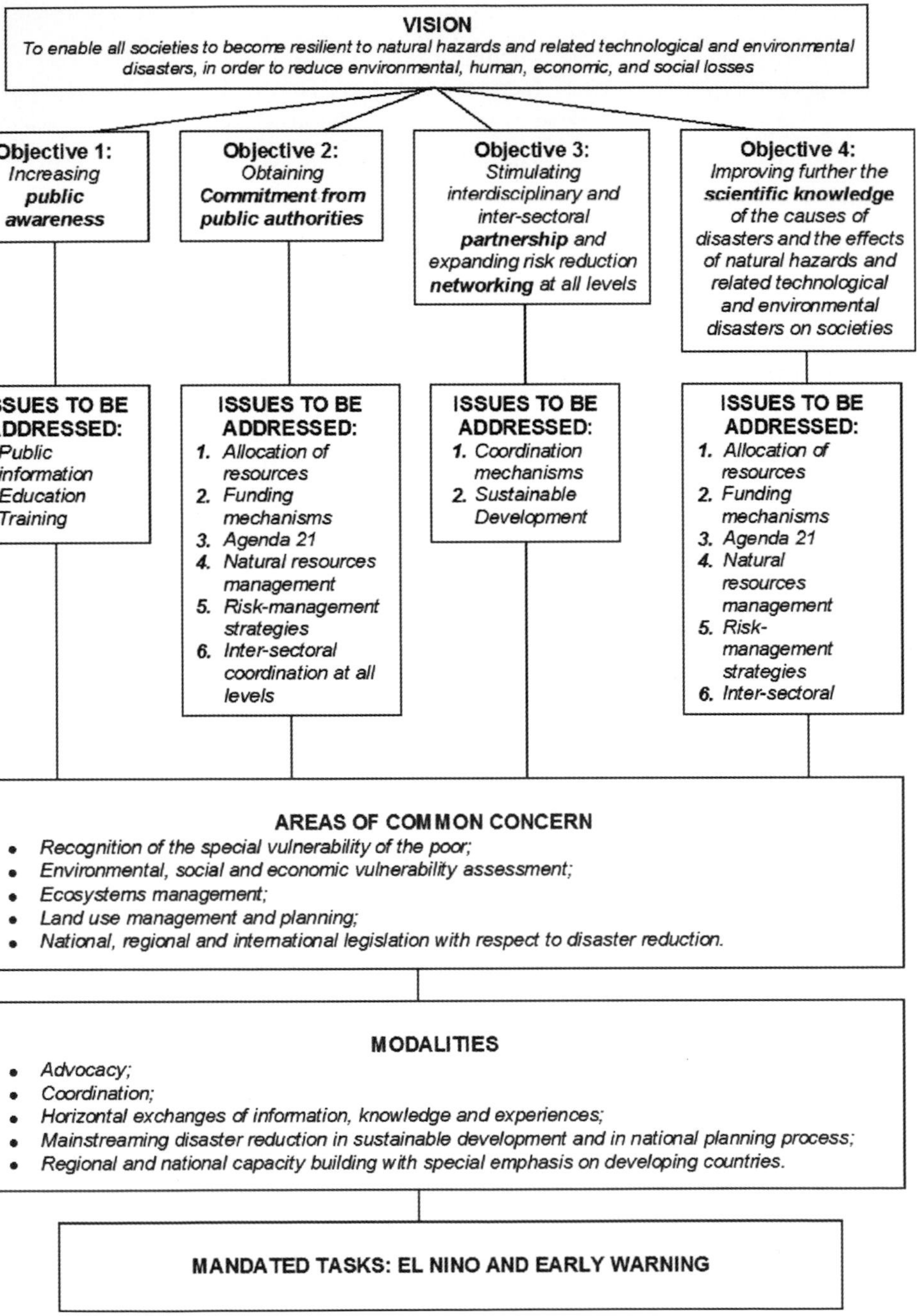

VISION
To enable all societies to become resilient to natural hazards and related technological and environmental disasters, in order to reduce environmental, human, economic, and social losses

Objective 1:
Increasing **public awareness**

Objective 2:
Obtaining **Commitment from public authorities**

Objective 3:
Stimulating interdisciplinary and inter-sectoral **partnership** and expanding risk reduction **networking** at all levels

Objective 4:
Improving further the **scientific knowledge** of the causes of disasters and the effects of natural hazards and related technological and environmental disasters on societies

ISSUES TO BE ADDRESSED:
1. Public information
2. Education
3. Training

ISSUES TO BE ADDRESSED:
1. Allocation of resources
2. Funding mechanisms
3. Agenda 21
4. Natural resources management
5. Risk-management strategies
6. Inter-sectoral coordination at all levels

ISSUES TO BE ADDRESSED:
1. Coordination mechanisms
2. Sustainable Development

ISSUES TO BE ADDRESSED:
1. Allocation of resources
2. Funding mechanisms
3. Agenda 21
4. Natural resources management
5. Risk-management strategies
6. Inter-sectoral

AREAS OF COMMON CONCERN
- Recognition of the special vulnerability of the poor;
- Environmental, social and economic vulnerability assessment;
- Ecosystems management;
- Land use management and planning;
- National, regional and international legislation with respect to disaster reduction.

MODALITIES
- Advocacy;
- Coordination;
- Horizontal exchanges of information, knowledge and experiences;
- Mainstreaming disaster reduction in sustainable development and in national planning process;
- Regional and national capacity building with special emphasis on developing countries.

MANDATED TASKS: EL NINO AND EARLY WARNING

FIGURE 10–8 Detail of the ISDR. (From UNISDR, 2001)

produces articles, journals, and other publications and promotional materials related to disaster reduction. The functions and responsibilities of UN/ISDR are

- To serve as the focal point within the UN system for the coordination of strategies and programs for natural disaster reduction, and to ensure synergy between disaster reduction strategies and those in the socioeconomic and humanitarian fields
- To support the interagency task force in the development of policies on natural disaster reduction
- To promote a worldwide culture of reduction of the negative effects of natural hazards, through advocacy campaigns
- To serve as an international clearinghouse for the dissemination and exchange of information and knowledge on disaster reduction strategies
- To support the policy and advocacy activities of national committees for natural disaster reduction.

Regional International Organizations

The UN is the only global international organization of its kind. It is not, however, the only governing organization made up of several national governments. Many of the world's regions have pooled their collective resources and services to create large, influential organizations.

Like the UN, these organizations address issues of regional and global importance, many of which focus on or peripherally address disaster management. In times of disaster, both within and outside of their regions of concern, they bring much of the same financial, technical, and equipment resources discussed throughout this book. This section identifies and briefly describes the largest of these organizations.

North Atlantic Treaty Organization

NATO is an alliance of 28 countries from North America and Europe formed by a treaty signed April 4, 1949. Its fundamental goal is safeguarding its members' freedom and security using political and military means. Over the years, NATO has taken on an increasing role in international disaster management and peacekeeping missions.

NATO maintains a military force made up of member countries' troops. Although they work in concert, troops always remain under the control of their home nation's government. NATO has helped to end violent conflicts in Bosnia, Kosovo, and the Former Yugoslav Republic of Macedonia.

NATO's disaster and crisis management activities, which extend beyond its typical military operations, are geared toward protecting populations. As part of the worldwide civil protection drive described in Chapter 8, NATO began developing measures to protect member nation citizens from nuclear attack as early as the 1950s. As elsewhere, NATO member countries soon realized that these capabilities could be used effectively during disasters induced by floods, earthquakes, or technological incidents and during humanitarian disasters.

NATO's first involvement in disaster operations came in 1953, following devastating floods in northern Europe. In 1958, it established detailed procedures for the coordination of assistance between NATO member countries in case of disasters. These procedures remained in place and provided the basis for NATO's civil emergency planning in subsequent years. In 1998, NATO established the Euro-Atlantic Disaster Response Coordination Center to coordinate aid provided by member and partner countries to a disaster-stricken area in a member or partner country. It also established a Euro-Atlantic Disaster Response Unit, which is a nonstanding, multinational mix of national civil and military elements volunteered by member or partner countries for deployment to disaster areas.

Civil emergency planning has become a key facet of NATO involvement in crisis management. In recent years, NATO has assisted flood-devastated Albania, Czech Republic, Hungary, Romania, and Ukraine, supported the UNHCR in Kosovo, sent aid to earthquake-stricken Turkey, helped to fight fires in the former Yugoslav Republic of Macedonia and in Portugal, and supported Ukraine and Moldova after extreme weather conditions destroyed power transmission capabilities. NATO has taken an active role in the response to the 2005 South Asia earthquake, as described in Exhibit 10–12. NATO also regularly conducts civil emergency planning exercises.

EXHIBIT 10–12: NATO RESPONSE TO THE 2005 EARTHQUAKE IN PAKISTAN

The devastating October 2005 earthquake in Pakistan is estimated to have killed 80,000 people and left up to three million without food or shelter just before the onset of the harsh Himalayan winter. On October 11, 2005, in response to a request from Pakistan, NATO launched an operation to assist in the urgent relief effort.

NATO airlifted supplies donated by NATO member and partner countries as well as the UNHCR via two air bridges from Germany and Turkey; 168 flights delivered almost 3500 tons of relief supplies. The supplies provided included thousands of tents, stoves, and blankets necessary to protect the survivors from the cold. In addition, NATO deployed engineers and medical units from the NATO Response Force to assist in the relief effort. The first teams arrived on October 29, 2005.

In just 3 months of operations, NATO achieved the following:

- NATO's air bridges flew almost 3500 tons of aid to Pakistan with 168 flights. These flights carried in nearly 18,000 tents, 505,000 blankets, nearly 17,000 stoves/heaters, more than 31,500 mattresses, 49,800 sleeping bags, tons of medical supplies, and more.
- NATO's field hospital treated approximately 4890 patients and conducted 160 major surgeries. Mobile medical units treated approximately 3424 patients in the remote mountain villages; they also contributed significantly to the WHO immunization program that has helped to prevent the outbreak of disease.
- In the cities of Arja and Bagh, NATO engineers repaired nearly 60 km of roads and removed over 41,500 cubic meters of debris, enabling the flow of aid, commerce, and humanitarian assistance to the inhabitants of the valley. Nine school and health structures were completed and 13 tent schools erected. The engineers distributed 267 cubic meters of drinking water and upgraded a permanent spring water distribution and storage system to serve up to 8400 persons per day.
- NATO engineers also supported the Pakistani Army in Operation Winter Race, by constructing 110 multipurpose shelters for the population living in the mountains.

- NATO helicopters transported more than 1750 tons of relief goods to remote mountain villages and evacuated over 7650 disaster victims.
- NATO set up an aviation fuel farm in Abbottabad, which carried out about 1000 refueling missions for civilian and military helicopters.

During the mission approximately 1000 engineers and supporting staff, as well as 200 medical personnel, worked in Pakistan.

NATO was part of a very large effort aimed at providing disaster relief in Pakistan. The Pakistani Army provided the bulk of the response, with the support of NATO, the UN, and other international organizations and several individual countries.

The evolution of NATO's assistance

On October 10, NATO received from Pakistan a request for assistance in dealing with the aftermath of the October 8 earthquake. The next day, the North Atlantic Council approved a major air operation to bring supplies from NATO and Partner countries to Pakistan.

The airlift began on October 13 and the first tons of supplies arrived in Pakistan on October 14. On October 19, NATO opened a second air bridge from Incirlik, Turkey, to deliver large quantities of tents, blankets, and stoves donated by the UNHCR.

On October 21, in response to a further request from Pakistan, NATO agreed to deploy engineers and medical personnel from the NATO Response Force to Pakistan to further assist in the relief effort. A NATO headquarters was deployed to Pakistan on October 24 to liaise with Pakistani authorities and pave the way for the incoming troops. The first troops, the advance elements of the medical team, began arriving on October 29, and immediately began treating hundreds of people a day.

Engineering teams followed and began working in the area around Bagh in support of Pakistani efforts to repair roads and build shelters and medical facilities. NATO engineers also supported the Pakistani Army in Operation Winter Race, by constructing multipurpose shelters for the population living in the mountains.

On November 9, NATO opened a sophisticated 60-bed field hospital, which provided a wide range of care including complex surgical procedures. On the same day, heavy-lift transport helicopters assigned to NATO for the operation began flying and delivering supplies to remote mountain villages and evacuating victims. NATO also set up an aviation fuel farm in Abbottabad, which carried out refueling for civilian and military helicopters, which were essential to the relief effort.

On October 27, Foreign Secretary of Pakistan Tariq Osman Hyder addressed a meeting of the Euro-Atlantic Partnership Council at NATO Headquarters in Brussels, asking for further assistance. He said that NATO could provide continued airlift, funds, logistic and airspace management, mobile fuel tanks, spare parts for helicopters and tactical aircraft, command and control, and winterized tents and sleeping bags. That same day, NATO's Euro-Atlantic Disaster Response Coordination Center (EADRCC) received an urgent request from the UNHCR for the transport of additional shelter and relief items stored in Turkey to Pakistan before the winter sets in.

NATO's relief mission came to an end, on schedule, on February 1, 2006. NATO's short-term relief mission was based on the following five elements:

(Continued)

EXHIBIT 10–12: NATO RESPONSE TO THE 2005 EARTHQUAKE IN PAKISTAN (CONTINUED)

1. Coordination of donations from NATO and partner countries through the EADRCC in Brussels
2. The air bridge from Turkey and Germany for the transport of relief goods to Pakistan
3. Five helicopters operating in the earthquake-affected area for the transport of supplies to remote mountain villages and evacuation of victims
4. Medical support with a field hospital and mobile medical teams in the area of Bagh
5. Engineer support operating in the area around Bagh in support of Pakistani efforts for the repair of roads and building of shelters, schools, and medical facilities

The NATO Land Component in Pakistan was led by the Spanish and headquartered in Arja. It included:

- A headquarters element in Arja
- Two light engineer units in the Bagh district (one Spanish and one Polish)
- An Italian engineer unit with heavy construction equipment
- A unit of British engineers specialized in high-altitude relief work
- A multinational team of medics operating the NATO field hospital, including staff for inpatient and outpatient care, as well as mobile medical teams in the area of Bagh—led by the Dutch Army including Czech, French, Portuguese, and British personnel
- Four water purification teams (one Spanish, three Lithuanian)
- Two civil–military cooperation teams from Slovenia and France.

The NATO Air Component in Pakistan came from the French Air Defense and Operation Command and included:

- A German helicopter detachment
- Luxembourg rescue helicopter
- A French ground handling team
- A fuel farm operated by a French unit at Abbottabad

The NATO HQ in Pakistan was comprised of personnel from NATO's Joint Force Command Lisbon, augmented by staff from NATO's Supreme Headquarters Allied Powers Europe (SHAPE). In total about 1000 NATO engineers and supporting staff, as well as 200 medical personnel, worked in Pakistan during the operation.

Source: NATO, 2010.

The European Union

The roots of the European Union date back to May 1950, when six European countries (Belgium, Germany, France, Italy, Luxembourg, and the Netherlands) joined to collaborate on the coal and steel industries. Today, following four rounds of reform and expansion, the EU represents 25 Member States and is about to allow several other eastern and southern European countries to join. The EU considers itself to be a "family of democratic European countries, committed to working together for peace and prosperity" (Europa, n.d.). Like the UN, it is not a government, nor does it have any authority over its members; it is an organization established for increased regional cooperation.

The EU Environmental Department addresses regional cooperation on disaster management (civil protection) activities. Its overall objective is to improve levels of protection for people, the environment, property, and cultural heritage in the event of major disasters inside or outside of the EU. Through mutual cooperation, EU members have agreed to (EU, 2005):

- Support and supplement efforts at national, regional, and local levels regarding disaster prevention, preparedness of those responsible for civil protection, and intervention in the event of disaster
- Establish a framework for effective and rapid cooperation between national civil protection services when mutual assistance is needed
- Set up and implement training programs for intervention and coordination teams as well as for assessment experts, including joint courses and exchange systems among different Member States
- Enhance the coherence of actions undertaken at the international level in the field of civil protection, especially in the context of cooperation with the candidate Central European countries in view of enlargement and with the partners in the Mediterranean region
- Contribute to public information in view of increasing the level of self-protection of European citizens
- Collect and disseminate validated emergency information
- Pool information on national civil protection capabilities, military, and medical resources
- Ensure efficient information sharing between the Commission and the competent authorities in the Member States
- Facilitate the rapid mobilization of intervention teams, experts, and other resources on request in the event of major emergencies to alleviate the effects of a disaster during the first days
- Offer technical support, including satellite images
- Share lessons learned from interventions
- Grant financial assistance via the Solidarity Fund (see Exhibit 10–13).

EXHIBIT 10–13: THE EU SOLIDARITY FUND

Established by the EU Council Regulation on November 11, 2002, the main purpose of the Fund is to grant financial assistance to help EU Member States and Candidate Countries who are hit by a major disaster and faced with serious repercussions regarding living conditions, the natural environment, or the economy in one or more regions of the affected country. The total amount that can be mobilized in a given year is 1 billion. Items and actions that are considered eligible for compensation under the Solidarity Fund Regulation are those necessary to address the emergency situation, including operations and equipment necessary to combat the disaster, action to restore infrastructure to working order, and rescue services, among others.

Source: Europa, 2006.

The EU developed two mechanisms to facilitate cooperation between Member States and increase civil protection structures: the Community Action Programme and the Community Civil Protection Mechanism.

The Community Action Programme supports and supplements Member States' national, regional, and local efforts to protect citizens, property, and the environment in the event of a disaster. It also facilitates cooperation, exchange, and mutual assistance between Member States. It supports major projects, workshops, and training courses in the field of prevention, preparedness, and response to natural and man-made disasters at land and at sea.

The Community Civil Protection Mechanism pools the civil protection capabilities of the 30 participating states (the EU-27 core members plus Iceland, Liechtenstein, and Norway). It may be called on by a country overwhelmed by a disaster that requires immediate assistance. The Community Civil Protection Mechanism's purpose is twofold. First, it facilitates and supports disaster management assistance to disaster-affected countries. The Monitoring and Information Center (MIC) is at its heart, giving countries access to a common platform for mutual aid assistance. Any country affected by a major disaster—within or outside the Union—can request assistance through the MIC. The MIC immediately forwards the request to participating states, which then decide whether they will offer assistance. The MIC has been called a "one-stop shop for assistance," because it reduces the burden on states requesting aid. The MIC can mobilize (within a few hours) small teams of experts to assess specific needs, to coordinate assistance operations, and to liaise with authorities and other international organizations. It also acts as an information center, collecting validated information throughout the emergency and disseminating regular updates to all participating countries.

Second, the Community Civil Protection Mechanism enhances preparedness. Using a database of national civil protection capabilities, experts and team leaders are invited to participate in a comprehensive disaster management training program that includes training courses, exercises, and an expert exchange program. A Common Emergency Communication and Information System is being developed to ensure efficient and secure information sharing between the MIC and the national contact points.

Since inception, the Community Civil Protection Mechanism has provided disaster management assistance for many disasters. The Community Civil Protection Mechanism allows disaster managers from across Europe to meet regularly, exchange views, and learn from one another's best practices to contribute to advancement in the EU community's disaster-response strategies.

The EU addresses humanitarian affairs through its European Commission Humanitarian Aid Department. ECHO was established in 1992 to provide fast and effective emergency assistance and relief to victims of natural disasters or armed conflict outside the EU. In 2009, ECHO funded humanitarian aid in over 70 countries, totaling over $1.2 billion. Its annual grants cover emergency aid, food aid, and aid to refugees and displaced persons. ECHO also performs the following disaster-related services:

- Conducts feasibility studies for its humanitarian operations
- Monitors humanitarian projects and sets up coordination arrangements
- Promotes and coordinates disaster prevention measures by training specialists, strengthening institutions, and running pilot microprojects
- Provides partners with technical assistance
- Raises public awareness about humanitarian issues in Europe and elsewhere
- Finances network and training study initiatives in the humanitarian field

To provide formalized mitigation and preparedness assistance, ECHO launched its disaster preparedness program, Disaster Preparedness ECHO (DIPECHO), in 1996. DIPECHO attempts to reduce population vulnerability in disaster-prone regions. Between 1996 and 2009, DIPECHO provided more than $235 million for hundreds of projects worldwide. DIPECHO-funded projects are implemented by aid agencies working in the region of concern, and support training, capacity building, awareness raising, and early warning projects as well the organization of relief services.

ECHO disaster preparedness efforts, however, extend beyond DIPECHO. Many of ECHO's major humanitarian financing decisions, for example, include disaster preparedness or prevention as an objective. Even postdisaster emergency responses can seek to reduce future risk. Examples of ECHO risk-reduction activities include livestock shelters built after extreme cold snaps to protect against further herd depletion (Peru); training and equipping of community-based fire brigades in forest fire risk zones (Indonesia); cholera preparedness and health information (Malawi); and antirust measures to prevent water pollution and protect pipes from the effects of volcanic ash (Ecuador).

Organization of American States

The Organization of American States (OAS) was established in 1948 by 21 nations located in North, Central, and South America and the Caribbean to strengthen cooperation and advance common interests in the Western Hemisphere. The OAS Charter affirmed the commitment of these nations to common goals and to their respect for each nation's sovereignty. Today, all 35 independent countries of the region have ratified the Charter and belong to the organization, although the government of Cuba was excluded from participation from 1962 to 2009, and has not rejoined since its ban was lifted.

The OAS is heavily involved in disaster mitigation and preparedness to reduce hazard risk in the region. The vast majority of these projects is carried out via the Office for Sustainable Development and Environment (OSDE), which supports individual and multicountry activities in several intersecting areas:

- Supporting the management of transboundary water resources
- Improving information for decision making in biological diversity
- Establishing land-tenure reform and property rights
- Supporting the exchange of best practices and technical information in environmental law and enforcement, renewable energy, water management, and biodiversity
- Improving management systems to reduce the impacts of natural disasters
- Understanding climate-related vulnerabilities affecting small island states

  Several projects illustrate the range of activities in mitigation and preparedness carried out by OAS:

- The Natural Hazards Project lends support to Member States to assess their vulnerability to natural hazards and to mitigate the effects of disasters. Its activities include technical assistance, training and technology transfer through intervention in development planning, and project formulation. Among its current areas of interest are floods, school buildings, and transportation corridors.
- Completed in 1999, the Caribbean Disaster Mitigation Project was a joint effort with USAID to establish sustainable public/private disaster mitigation mechanisms that measurably lessen loss of life, reduce potential damage, and shorten the disaster recovery period.

- In response to Hurricane Georges damage, the Hurricane Georges Reconstruction and Recovery in the Eastern Caribbean Project, targeting Antigua and Barbuda and St. Kitts and Nevis, was developed by OAS and several partners. OSDE implemented the disaster mitigation capacity-building component of the project, under the title Post-Georges Disaster Mitigation (PGDM). The PGDM included four primary objectives:

  1. Develop national hazard mitigation policies and plans
  2. Strengthen building practices
  3. Strengthen national emergency shelter policies and programs
  4. Support public information programs on hazard mitigation

- The OAS and the Caribbean Disaster Emergency Response Agency created the Caribbean Hazard Mitigation Capacity Building Program. The 3-year program assisted countries in the Caribbean region to develop comprehensive, national hazard vulnerability reduction policies and associated implementation programs, and develop and implement safer-building training and certificate programs.

- The National Research and Development Foundation created the Hurricane-Resistant Home Improvement Program with assistance from OAS to offer hurricane-resistant home improvement options to low-income families. This program trains local builders in safer construction, offers small loans to families wishing to upgrade their homes, and provides the services of a trained building inspector who approves materials to be purchased and checks minimum standards.

In addition to the OSDE, the OAS addresses disasters through its Inter-American Committee for Natural Disaster Reduction (IACNDR). IACNDR is the main forum of the OAS and the Inter-American System for analyzing policies and strategies aimed at natural disaster reduction in the context of sustainable development. The OAS General Assembly established the IACNDR to strengthen its role in natural disaster reduction and emergency preparedness.

Southern African Development Community

The Southern African Development Community (SADC) began in 1980, when a loose alliance of nine southern African states formed (then known as the Southern African Development Coordination Conference; SADCC). The organization's aim was to coordinate development projects to decrease economic dependence on South Africa. In 1992, it shifted from a "coordination conference" to a development community, known as the SADC. SADC Member States are Angola, Botswana, the Democratic Republic of Congo, Lesotho, Malawi, Mauritius, Mozambique, Namibia, South Africa, Swaziland, United Republic of Tanzania, Zambia, and Zimbabwe.

SADC's primary mission is to help define regional priorities, facilitate integration, assist in mobilizing resources, and maximize regional development. It approaches problems and national priorities through regional cooperation and action. Several SADC programs address the region's safety and security, primarily through risk-reduction mechanisms that include disaster preparedness and mitigation. The following are some examples of SADC disaster-related programs:

- Food, Agriculture, and Natural Resources Directorate
- Regional Early Warning Unit
- Regional Remote Sensing Unit

Coordination Center for Natural Disaster Prevention in Central America

The Coordination Center for Natural Disaster Prevention in Central America (CEPREDENAC) was established in 1988 as a coordination center to strengthen the Central American region's ability to reduce their population's vulnerability to natural disasters. In May 1995, CEPREDENAC became an official organization to foster regional cooperation among the governments of Costa Rica, El Salvador, Guatemala, Honduras, Nicaragua, and Panama. The organization's headquarters are in Panama City.

Since its founding, CEPREDENAC has coordinated several international assistance projects and provided significant disaster management-related technical assistance to its members. It currently is managing the coordination of three projects financed by Sweden, Germany, and Norway:

- Strengthening of Local Structures for Disaster Mitigation (Fortalecimiento de Estructuras Locales Para la Mitigación de Desastres—FEMID). A regional program supported by Germany to strengthen local capacity to mitigate disasters' impacts
- Strengthening Local Structures and Early Alert Systems (Reforzamiento de Estructuras Locales y Sistemas de Alerta Temprana—RELSAT). A program supported by Sweden that focuses on development of CEPREDENAC and its affiliated institutions and seeks to increase CEPREDENAC's ability to manage disaster management projects
- Reduction of Natural Disasters in Central America, Earthquake Preparedness, and Hazard Mitigation (Mitigación del Riesgo Sísmico y Preparativos para Terremotos—RESIS). A project supported by Norway to strengthen seismological institutions and national projects, including seismic microzonation and risk analysis

Caribbean Disaster Emergency Response Agency

The Caribbean Disaster Emergency Response Agency (CDERA) is an intergovernmental agency established in September 1991 by an agreement of the Caribbean Community governments to address the region's disaster management needs. There are presently 16 participating states within CDERA: Anguilla, Antigua and Barbuda, Bahamas, Barbados, Belize, British Virgin Islands, Dominica, Grenada, Guyana, Jamaica, Montserrat, St. Kitts and Nevis, Saint Lucia, St. Vincent and the Grenadines, Trinidad and Tobago, and Turks and Caicos. CDERA is comprised of the following components:

- The Coordinating Unit, which is the CDERA Secretariat, headquartered in Barbados
- Sixteen National Disaster Organizations, one in each participating state
- A Board of Directors, comprising the 16 National Disaster Coordinators (the head of each National Disaster Organization)
- A Council, which is the supreme policy-making body, made up of the government heads of each member nation that meets annually to review the agency's work, approve its work program and budget, and make any other major policy decisions required

CDERA activities focus on the four phases of emergency management, and involve all sectors of society:

- Training for disaster management personnel
- Development of model training courses and products

- Institutional assistance for disaster management organizations
- Development of model disaster legislation for adaptation and adoption by participating states
- Development of model policies and guidelines for use in emergencies
- Contingency planning assistance
- Resource mobilization for strengthening disaster management programs in participating states
- Improving emergency telecommunications and warning systems
- Development of disaster information and communication systems
- Education and public awareness
- Establishment of a CDERA Web site to allow information dissemination

A participating state may request disaster response assistance once its capabilities have been overwhelmed. CDERA solicits and coordinates the assistance offered by other governments, organizations, and individuals, both within and outside the region. This is CDERA's primary function. Other functions include:

- Securing, collating, and channeling disaster information to interested governmental organizations and NGOs as needed
- Mitigating disaster consequences affecting participating states
- Establishing and maintaining sustainable disaster response capabilities among participating states
- Mobilizing and coordinating disaster relief from governmental organizations and NGOs for affected participating states

International Financial Institutions

IFIs provide loans for development and financial cooperation throughout the world. They exist to ensure financial and market stability and to increase political balance. These institutions are made up of Member States arranged on a global or regional basis that work together to provide financial services to national governments through direct loans or projects.

In a disaster's aftermath, nations with low capital reserves often request increased or additional emergency loans to fund the expensive task of reconstruction and rehabilitation. Without IFIs, most developing nations would not have the means to recover. Several of the largest IFIs, including the World Bank; one of its subsidiaries, the International Monetary Fund (IMF); the Asian Development Bank; and the Inter-American Development Bank are detailed below.

The World Bank

The World Bank was created in 1944 to rebuild Europe after World War II. In 1947, France received the first World Bank loan of $250 million for postwar reconstruction. Financial reconstruction assistance has been provided regularly since that time in response to countless natural disasters and humanitarian emergencies.

Today, the World Bank is one of the largest sources of development assistance. In the 2009 fiscal year, it provided more than $58.8 billion in loans, breaking all previous lending records for the organization. The World Bank is owned collectively by 187 countries and is based in Washington, DC. It comprises several institutions referred to as the World Bank Group (WBG):

- International Bank for Reconstruction and Development
- International Development Association
- International Finance Corporation
- Multilateral Investment Guarantee Agency
- International Center for Settlement of Investment Disputes

The World Bank's overall goal is to reduce poverty, specifically, to "individually help each developing country onto a path of stable, sustainable, and equitable growth, [focusing on] helping the poorest people and the poorest countries" (Source Watch, n.d.). As disasters and CHEs take a greater and greater toll on the economic stability of many financially struggling countries, the World Bank is taking on a more central role in mitigation and reconstruction.

Developing nations, which are more likely to have weak disaster mitigation or preparedness capacity and therefore little or no affordable access to disaster insurance, often sustain a total financial loss. In the period of rehabilitation that follows the disaster, loans are essential to the success of programs and vital to any level of sustainability or increased disaster resistance. The World Bank lends assistance at several points along this cycle.

First, for regular financial assistance, the World Bank ensures that borrowed funds are applied to projects that give mitigation a central role during the planning phase. It utilizes its privilege as financial advisor to guide planners, who otherwise might forego mitigation measures in an effort to stretch the loaned capital as far as possible. Ensuring that mitigation is addressed increases systems of prediction and risk analysis in projects funded by the World Bank.

Once a disaster occurs, the World Bank may be called on for help. Because it is not a relief agency, it will not take on any role in the initial response; however, it works to restore damaged and destroyed infrastructure and restart production capabilities. A World Bank team may assist with initial impact assessments that estimate financial losses resulting from the disaster and estimated costs of reconstruction, including raised mitigation standards. The World Bank also could restructure the country's existing loan portfolio to allow for expanded recovery projects. In addition, World Bank projects that have not yet been approved but are in the application process can be redesigned to account for changes caused by the disaster.

Finally, an Emergency Recovery Loan (ERL) can be granted to specifically address recovery and reconstruction issues. ERLs restore affected economic and social institutions and reconstruct physical assets such as essential infrastructure. It is important to note that ERLs are not designed for relief activities. They are most appropriate for disasters that adversely impact an economy, are infrequent (recurrent disasters are accommodated by regular lending programs), and create urgent needs. ERLs are expected to eventually produce economic benefits to the borrowing government, and are usually implemented within 3 years and are flexible to accommodate the specific needs of each unique scenario. Construction performed with ERLs must use disaster-resistant standards and include appropriate mitigation measures, thus providing overall preparedness for the country affected. Once an ERL has been granted, the World Bank coordinates with the IMF, the UNDP, NGOs, and several other international and local agencies to create a strategy that best utilizes these funds within the overall reconstruction effort.

The World Bank has established a Hazards Risk Management Team (also called the Hazard Management Unit; HMU), to address disasters and risk management within the context of development lending. This unit was originally created in 1998 as the Disaster Management Facility. The HMU promotes effective consideration of hazard risk in project design and incorporation of mitigation measures into overall disaster management effort. The HMU also works to provide a more strategic and rapid World Bank response to disasters. The specific objectives of the HMU are to

- Improve the management of disaster risk in member countries and reduce vulnerability in the World Bank portfolio
- Promote sustainable projects and initiatives that incorporate effective prevention and mitigation measures
- Promote the inclusion of risk analysis in World Bank operations, analysis, and country assistance strategies
- Promote training in the areas of disaster prevention, mitigation, and response
- Identify policy, institutional, and physical interventions aimed at reducing catastrophic losses from natural disasters through structural and nonstructural measures, community involvement, and partnerships with the private sector

The World Bank works to increase resistance to repeat natural disasters through lending programs that include mitigation and preparedness. The nature of its mission—alleviating poverty—zis a mitigation measure. As part of its lending process, the World Bank conducts vulnerability and risk assessments, which necessitate the subsequent consideration of any findings in future World Bank loans. The World Bank is also a source of information on current hazard-resistant technology and provides the expertise for establishing and enforcing more effective building codes. As countries develop, they increase their capacity to prepare for and respond to disasters and establish the legal and political institutions that guide construction and settlement practices to ensure greater overall resilience. The World Bank is one of the most important players when it comes to ensuring that countries are able to do this.

The two lending arms of the World Bank are the International Bank for Reconstruction and Development and the International Development Association.

- *International Bank for Reconstruction and Development (IBRD).* Established in 1945, the IBRD reduces poverty in middle-income and creditworthy poorer countries. The IBRD attempts to promote sustainable development activities through its loans. It also provides guarantees and other analytical and advisory services. Following disasters, countries with strong enough credit can borrow or refinance their existing loans from the IBRD to pay the often staggering costs of reconstruction.
- *International Development Association (IDA).* The IDA lends to the world's poorest countries, classified as those with a 2010 income of less than $1135 per person. Sixty-four countries currently are eligible to borrow from the IDA. It provides interest-free loans and grants for programs aimed at boosting economic growth and improving living conditions. This need is almost always present in the aftermath of disasters, including those caused by violent conflict.

The International Monetary Fund

The IMF was established in 1946 to promote international monetary cooperation, exchange stability, and orderly exchange arrangements; to foster economic growth and high levels of employment; and to provide temporary financial assistance to countries to help ease balance of payments adjustment. It carries out these functions through loans, monitoring, and technical assistance.

Since 1962, the IMF has provided emergency assistance to its 184 member countries when they have been affected by natural disasters. IMF assistance is designed to meet immediate foreign-exchange financing needs that arise from shortfalls in export earnings and/or increased imports, among other things. Its assistance also helps the affected countries avoid a serious depletion of external reserves.

In 1995, the IMF began to provide this emergency assistance to postconflict situations to re-establish macroeconomic stability and the basis for long-term sustainable growth. This is particularly important when a country must cover costs associated with an "urgent balance of payments need, but is unable to develop and implement a comprehensive economic program because its capacity has been damaged by a conflict, but where sufficient capacity for planning and policy implementation neverthe-less exists" (IMF, 2005). IMF support must be part of a comprehensive international effort to address the aftermath of a conflict. Its emergency financing is provided to assist the affected country and to gather support from other sources.

In the event of an international disaster or CHE in a member country, the IMF utilizes its Emer-gency Assistance Specific Facility to provide rapid financial assistance. It is not uncommon for a coun-try to severely exhaust its monetary reserves in response to an emergency situation. In the event of a natural disaster, funding is directed toward local recovery efforts and any needed economic adjust-ments. The IMF will lend assistance only if a stable governing body is in place that has the capacity for planning and policy implementation and can ensure the safety of IMF resources. After stability has been sufficiently restored, increased financial assistance is offered, which will be used to develop the country in its postemergency status.

When a country requests emergency assistance, it must submit a detailed plan for economic reconstruction that will not create trade restrictions or "intensify exchange." If the country is already working under an IMF loan, assistance may be in the form of a reorganization of the existing arrange-ment. Separate emergency assistance loans are also available, and these do not involve the regular criteria under which the countries must normally operate. These loans are set at 25% of a country's preestablished lending quota, but have gone as high as 50% of the lending quota in extenuating cir-cumstances. This funding is provided only when the member country is "cooperating with the IMF to find a solution to its economic problems." Tables 10–2 and 10–3 list IMF emergency assistance from 1995–2010 for natural disasters and CHEs.

Emergency assistance loans are subject to regular IMF interest rates and must be repaid within 3 to 5 years. In certain cases, as decided by the IMF and according to specific criteria, recipients of emergency funding may benefit from the IMF Poverty Reduction and Growth Facility (PRGF). The PRGF is the IMF's low-interest lending facility for low-income countries. PRGF-supported programs are underpinned by comprehensive country-owned poverty reduction strategies. Under this program, the interest rate on loans is subsidized to 0.5% per year, with the interest subsidies financed by grant contributions from bilateral donors. This program has been available for postconflict emergencies since 2000, but in January 2005, following the South Asia tsunami events, the IMF Executive Board agreed to provide a similar subsidization of emergency assistance for natural disasters upon request.

Table 10–2   IMF Emergency Assistance Provided in Response to Natural Disasters, 1995–2009

Country	Year	Hazard	Amount ($mil)	% of Quota
Bangladesh	1998	Floods	138.2	25
Dominican Republic	1998	Hurricane	55.9	25
Haiti	1998	Hurricane	21.0	25
Honduras	1998	Hurricane	65.6	50
St. Kitts and Nevis	1998	Hurricane	2.3	25
Turkey	1999	Earthquake	501.0	37.5
Malawi	2002	Food shortage	23.0	25
Grenada	2003	Hurricane	4.0	25
Grenada	2004	Hurricane	4.4	25
Maldives	2005	Tsunami	6.3	50
Sri Lanka	2005	Tsunami	158.4	25
Bangladesh	2008	Floods	217.7	25
Dominica	2008	Hurricane	3.3	25
Belize	2009	Floods	6.9	25
St. Kitts and Nevis	2009	Hurricane	3.4	25

Source: Bretton Woods Project, 2005.

The government of a country devastated by disaster often requires technical assistance or policy advice because it has no experience or expertise in this situation. This is especially common in post-conflict situations, where a newly elected or appointed government has been established and officials are rebuilding from the ground up. The IMF offers technical assistance in these cases to aid these countries in building their capacity to implement macroeconomic policy. This can include tax and government expenditure capacity; the reorganization of fiscal, monetary, and exchange institutions; and guidance in the use of aid resources.

The Asian Development Bank

The Asian Development Bank (ADB) is a multilateral development financial institution whose primary mission is reducing poverty in Asia and the Pacific. ADB was established in 1966 by 31 countries from both within and outside the region, and has grown to include 67 members as of 2010. Forty-eight are from the region and 19 are from other regions. Its clients are the 67 member governments, who are also the ADB's shareholders.

The ADB provides emergency rehabilitation loans to its member countries following disasters. ADB determined that its assistance in this critical phase of recovery would allow an affected developing country to maintain its development momentum. Bank analysts found that, without such assistance, the affected country may reallocate its scarce budgetary resources away from development issues to cover disaster-related expenses, sidetracking development progress. Additionally, they found that the production of goods and services would quickly suffer or fail completely if the country could not perform adequate rehabilitation following a disaster.

Table 10–3   IMF Emergency Assistance Provided in Response to Complex Humanitarian Emergencies, 1995–2009

Country	Year	Amount ($mil)	% of Quota
Bosnia and Herzegovina	1995	45.0	25
Rwanda	1997	12.2	15
Albania	1997	12.0	25
Rwanda	1997	8.1	10
Tajikistan	1997	10.1	12.5
Tajikistan	1998	10.0	12.5
Republic of Congo	1998	9.6	12.5
Sierra Leone	1998	16.0	15
Guinea-Bissau	1999	2.9	15
Sierra Leone	1999	21.4	15
Guinea-Bissau	2000	1.9	10
Sierra Leone	2000	13.3	10
Republic of Congo	2000	13.6	12.5
FR of Yugoslavia	2000	151.0	25
Burundi	2002	12.7	12.5
Burundi	2003	13.4	12.5
Central African Republic	2004	8.2	10
Iraq	2004	435.1	25
Haiti	2005	15.5	12.5
Central African Republic	2006	10.2	12.5
Lebanon	2007	76.8	25.0
Côte d'Ivoire	2007	62.2	12.5
Côte d'Ivoire	2008	66.2	12.5
Guinea-Bissau	2008	5.7	25.0
Lebanon	2008	37.6	12.5
Comoros	2008	1.7	12.5
Guinea-Bissau	2009	2.7	12.5

Source: IMF Fact Sheet, 2010.

ADB assistance in emergencies began in 1987, but was initially extended only to smaller developing countries (e.g., the Maldives, Papua New Guinea, and the smaller Pacific island states). Loans were limited to $500,000 (increased to $2 million in 1997), with funded projects to be completed within 12 months of disbursement. The funding was designed to address only simple repair and rehabilitation activities as needed in the immediate aftermath of a disaster, with more comprehensive repair being covered by regular bank lending programs. Lending was designed to be provided within 6 weeks of being requested.

In 1989, emergency lending was extended to all developing member countries regardless of their size. This change included a fundamental shift in what the emergency loans would cover, from simple repairs to more comprehensive, informed rehabilitation activities. Most important, ADB wanted to ensure that projects funded by its loans reduced overall risk to the affected nation and its population. Other major changes in ADB emergency lending policy are included in the following list:

- Introducing a typology of the causes and effects of disasters
- More clearly defining the ADB's response during various phases of postdisaster situations
- Identifying the nature, focus, and coverage of rehabilitation projects
- Introducing detailed, yet simplified, guidelines for processing rehabilitation projects
- Targeting rehabilitation loans toward restoring infrastructure and production activities, including capacity building and modernization
- Mandating that risk analysis and disaster prevention measures be included in all ADB projects in disaster-prone developing member countries
- Closely coordinating disaster responses at all levels (local, national, and international) with those of other external funding agencies, NGOs, and community groups
- Specifying that disaster prevention and mitigation activities were to be promoted along with regional cooperation
- Including non-natural disasters, for example, wars, civil strife, and environmental degradation (ADB, 2005a)

Between 1987 and 2008, ADB provided $7 billion to disaster-affected countries in the form of 235 loans—a rate of approximately one loan per month. The vast majority of the ADB emergency loan services during this period were provided in response to natural disaster events, with the remaining dedicated to postconflict situations. These loans rarely averaged more than 6% of the total annual lending by ADB and were concentrated primarily in South Asia. (See Exhibit 10–14 for a discussion of the ADB's response to the 2008 Wenchuan earthquake.)

EXHIBIT 10–14: EMERGENCY LOAN REQUEST FROM CHINA FOLLOWING THE MAY 12, 2008, WENCHUAN EARTHQUAKE

Loan Sector: Transport, education

Project Description
The Project comprises two components: (i) reconstruction and upgrading of damaged roads and bridges in Sichuan and Shaanxi provinces, and (ii) reconstruction and improvements of damaged schools in Shaanxi Province. The project will rehabilitate and reconstruct 368 high-priority earthquake-damaged roads in the 19 worst affected counties of Sichuan Province and 10 subprojects in the four worst affected counties of Shaanxi Province. The project will rehabilitate and reconstruct 12 high-priority earthquake-damaged education facilities in the three worst affected counties in Shaanxi Province. These components are designed to be mutually supporting in achieving the overall objective of restoring the affected communities' access to infrastructure to pre-earthquake levels, and ensuring restored infrastructure is in strict compliance with the latest seismic code.

Rationale

Based on the government's damage and needs assessment and the request of the PRC Government, the project identifies specific sectors that require emergency assistance in two of the worst earthquake-affected provinces (i.e., Sichuan and Shaanxi). The project seeks to (i) build on the immediate relief provided by the Government in the earthquake-affected provinces; (ii) contribute to coordinated rehabilitation and reconstruction by different development partners and the government; and (iii) specifically address sustainable recovery priorities by providing indirect livelihood support through public infrastructure rehabilitation and reconstruction, which generates public employment and underpins the restoration of livelihood activities by rehabilitating roads, bridges, and schools. The project design draws on the ADB experience in delivering emergency assistance acquired in different developing member countries over the past two decades, and complements relief and other rehabilitation and reconstruction assistance provided by the government, United Nations agencies, NGOs, bilateral development partners, and the World Bank. By meeting the earthquake reconstruction needs of the next three years, the project is consistent with ADB's *Disaster and Emergency Assistance Policy* (2004). The Project supports the State Overall Plan for Post-Wenchuan Earthquake Restoration and Reconstruction approved by the Government on 19 September 2008.

Impact and Outcome

The impact of the project is accelerated restoration of education and transport infrastructure in earthquake-affected areas of Sichuan and Shaanxi provinces. The project will support the government's efforts to (i) restore the livelihoods and economic activities of the affected population; (ii) accelerate poverty alleviation in the earthquake-affected counties, many of which have a high incidence of poverty; and (iii) rehabilitate and reconstruct public and community-based infrastructure that is vulnerable to natural disasters. The outcome of the project is restoration of people's access to transport and education infrastructure to preearthquake levels in 19 counties of Sichuan and four counties of Shaanxi provinces.

Project Investment Plan

The total project cost is estimated at $441.6 million equivalent.

Financing Plan

A loan of $400 million from ADB's ordinary capital resources will be provided under ADB's London interbank offered rate (LIBOR)-based lending facility. The loan will have a grace period of 8 years with a maturity period of 32 years, an interest rate determined in accordance with ADB's LIBOR-based lending facility, a commitment charge of 0.15% per annum, and such other terms and conditions set forth in the draft loan and project agreements.

Period of Utilization

Until June 30, 2012

Estimated Project Completion Date

December 31, 2011

(Continued)

EXHIBIT 10–14: EMERGENCY LOAN REQUEST FROM CHINA FOLLOWING THE MAY 12, 2008, WENCHUAN EARTHQUAKE (CONTINUED)

Implementation Arrangements

As the project is for emergency assistance, implementation will start immediately after approval and be completed within 36 months.

Executing Agency

Sichuan Provincial Communications Department in Sichuan Province; and Hanzhong city government and Baoji city government in Shaanxi Province

Implementing Agencies

Sichuan Highway Administration Bureau in Sichuan Province; and county-level highway administration bureaus for roads and bridges, and county-level education bureaus for schools in Shaanxi Province.

Project Benefits and Beneficiaries

The project will bring benefits to the project area by (i) reconstructing and improving road conditions and accessibility in townships and in villages in the Sichuan and Shaanxi provinces, (ii) reconstructing and improving 12 schools in Shaanxi Province, and (iii) creating local employment opportunities from project construction and related activities. The project will provide equal benefits to females and males.

The economic benefits of the rural roads and bridges include (i) savings in vehicle operating costs as a result of improved traffic and road conditions, (ii) time-savings for rural road users, (iii) savings in road accident costs as a result of fewer accidents, and (iv) economic benefits from generated traffic. The reconstruction and upgrading of rural roads in Sichuan and Shaanxi provinces will benefit about 5.6 million people, three-quarters of whom are rural and one-third of whom are poor. As reliable transport to markets becomes more readily available, cash crop farming in remote or isolated areas will be stimulated and access to off-farm employment opportunities will be broadened.

The project will focus on reconstruction of and improvements to 12 model schools to appropriate design standards, including six junior secondary and six primary schools. This will bring immediate benefits to the schools' 16,600 students (including more than 8000 female students), and long-term benefits to future students drawn from the 460,000 residents of the areas serviced by the schools, about 40% of whom are from rural areas of remote counties. The project will contribute to the government's efforts to rebuild the economy, rehabilitate public infrastructure and utilities, reinstate seismic code compliance, and generate employment. The rehabilitation and reconstruction of damaged schools will enable education services to be restored and will offer long-term benefits for affected persons by supporting opportunities for employment and participation in economic activities.

Source: Asian Development Bank, 2009.

ADB also provides mitigation-related project loans and Regional Technical Assistance (RETA), aimed at reducing member countries' overall disaster vulnerability. Mitigation and preparedness projects are not considered "emergency" in nature, and are therefore funded through its regular lending activities. Because mitigation and preparedness activities are most often included as components within larger development projects, ADB does not maintain records of its total financial risk reduction-based lending. Projects may include resilience-increasing activities such as reforestation, watershed management, coastal protection, agricultural diversification, slope stabilization, and land-use planning, although the project's overall goal is more development oriented. RETA and single-country technical assistance activities have included hazard management and disaster preparedness software programs and infrastructure protection assistance. ADB has developed disaster management guidebooks and distributed them to members to help them apply the lessons to their development projects.

Finally, ADB assists countries in restarting rehabilitation and overall development in the aftermath of armed conflict. In the past, ADB postconflict intervention focused almost exclusively on infrastructure rehabilitation, an area in which the ADB has extensive experience. Its focus in this area began to shift in the 1990s to preventing conflicts and helping postconflict countries move along a solid path of economic and social development. ADB is now committed to assisting affected member countries develop mechanisms to effectively manage conflict, including addressing the problems of poor governance and corruption.

The Inter-American Development Bank

Established in December 1959, the Inter-American Development Bank (IADB) is the oldest and largest regional multilateral development institution. It was first created to help accelerate economic and social development in Latin America and the Caribbean. The IADB has been a pioneer in supporting social programs; developing economic, social, educational, and health institutions; promoting regional integration; and providing direct support to the private sector, including microenterprises.

The IADB addresses disaster and risk management through its Sustainable Development Department. Through the efforts and actions of this department and its Disaster Risk Management policy, the IADB addresses the root causes of the region's high vulnerability to disasters. Building on its mandate to promote sustainable development in Latin America and the Caribbean, the IADB works with countries to integrate risk reduction into their development practice, planning, and investment, and to increase their capacity to manage risk reduction. It also provides funding that directly or indirectly supports disaster mitigation and preparedness (including hazard risk management capacity development at the government level; see Exhibit 10–15). In their "Plan of Action: Facing the Challenge of Natural Disasters in Latin America and the Caribbean" (IADB, 2000), the IADB outlined their six strategic areas of assistance:

1. *National systems for disaster prevention and response.* Building national legal and regulatory frameworks and programs that bring together the planning agencies, local governments, and civil society organizations; developing national strategies for risk reduction; and assessing intersectoral priorities, backed by separate budgets
2. *Inserting prevention into the culture.* Developing and disseminating risk information, and empowering citizens and other stakeholders to take risk-reduction measures
3. *Reducing the vulnerability of the poor.* Supporting poor households and communities in reducing their vulnerability to natural hazards and recovering from disasters through reconstruction assistance

EXHIBIT 10–15: PRINCIPAL DISASTER-RELATED IADB LOANS, 2001–2005

Principal Loans Approved During 2001

- The bank approved a bi-national loan operation for a total of $21.8 million for Honduras and Guatemala to help the sustainable development of renewable resources and reduce the impact of natural disasters.
- A $32.7 million loan was approved for a socioenvironmental and forestry development program in Nicaragua, with an important disaster prevention and rehabilitation in rural areas component.
- The bank approved a $25 million loan, the first stage of a financing operation for a total of $69 million, to promote the sustainable development of the economically and environmentally vulnerable basins of Honduras.
- A $70 million loan to El Salvador was approved to help reconstruct the infrastructure harmed in low-resources communities affected in 2001 by two earthquakes.
- The bank approved an emergency loan to Peru for $20 million to temporarily recover and rehabilitate the communities affected by the earthquake that took place in Southern Peru.

Principal Loans Approved During 2002

- The bank approved a $40 million loan to handle natural resources in high basins in Guatemala through the conversion of production technologies for small farmer enterprises.
- In Guatemala, a $46.6 million loan for the reduction of urban poverty was approved. The loan includes a water-channeling component to prevent landslides in marginal and vulnerable areas.
- The bank approved a loan to Bolivia for $2.8 million to install warning systems and an emergency plan in case of natural disasters, and another one for $2.5 million to restore water production for the city of Tarija in the biological and land reserve harmed by a forestry fire.
- The bank approved a $20 million loan destined for the emergency situations caused by flooding in Jamaica and to restore basic services.

Principal Loans Approved or Under Review During 2005

- IADB approved a $16 million loan to Costa Rica for a sustainable development program in the Atlantic Region. The program will support economic and social projects, disaster risk mitigation, and local governance.
- In Ecuador, the bank has prepared a $5 million loan for disaster prevention and early warning at the Cotopaxi volcano.
- $5 million has been designed to improve early warning systems for flooding in Haiti.
- The bank is preparing a $17.7 million loan for the Bahamas to restore services after Hurricanes Frances and Isabel.

Source: IADB, 2005b.

4. *Involving the private sector.* Creating conditions for the development of insurance markets, encouraging the use of other risk-spreading financial instruments where appropriate, and designing economic and regulatory incentives for risk reduction behavior
5. *Risk information for decision making.* Evaluating existing risk assessment methodologies, developing indicators of vulnerability, and stimulating the production and wide dissemination of risk information
6. *Fostering leadership and cooperation in the region.* Stimulating coordinated actions and mobilizing regional resources for investments in risk mitigation

The IADB created two mechanisms to allow for rapid loan disbursement in times of disaster: the Disaster Prevention Sector Facility and the Facility for the Immediate Response to Natural and Unexpected Disasters (formerly the Immediate Response Facility).

In 2001 the IADB established the Natural Disaster Network, represented by each of its borrowing member countries. Network members meet annually to discuss topics related to disaster management, such as "National Systems for Risk Management" (2001) and "The Macroeconomic Financial Consequences of Natural Disasters" (2002). In 2003, they published the book *Disaster Risk Management* based on the 2002 and 2003 meetings. Other meetings, for which subsequent disaster management guides were created, include "Risk Management at the Local Level" (2003), "Environmental Management and the Use of Economic Instruments for the Reduction of Disaster Risk" (2004), "Cost-Benefit Analysis of Mitigation Investments" (2004), and "The Role of the Private Sector in Disaster Risk Management" (also in 2004).

The IADB revised its disaster risk management policy in 2008. The new policy is designed to improve the IADB's ability to assist member countries in reaching their development goals by supporting their disaster risk management efforts. (See Appendix 10–1 for the full text of the 2008 IADB Disaster Risk Management Policy Guidelines.)

The IFIs described above, while among the largest in existence, are but a sample of the IFIs and development banks that exist worldwide. For reference, other banks include:

- African Development Bank (AfDB)—www.afdb.org
- Bank for International Settlements (BIS)—www.bis.org
- Black Sea Trade and Development Bank (BSTDB)—www.bstdb.org
- Caribbean Development Bank (CDB)—www.caribank.org
- Council of Europe Development Bank (COEB)—www.coebank.org
- Development Bank of Southern Africa (DBSA)—www.dbsa.org
- European Bank for Reconstruction and Development (EBRD)—www.ebrd.com/
- Islamic Development Bank (IDB)—www.isdb.org
- North American Development Bank (NADB)—www.nadbank.org

Conclusion

Through their efforts to mitigate, prepare for, respond to, and recover from natural disasters, multilateral organizations have a major role in international disaster management. All nations are at risk from disasters and, likewise, all nations face the prospect of one day finding themselves requiring help from one or more of these organizations. Multilateral organizations direct the collective experience and tools of their Member States to benefit all nations in need of assistance—even the wealthiest ones. The progress witnessed by the international disaster management community in recent years can be directly traced to the work of these multilateral organizations, especially focused initiatives like the International Strategy for Disaster Reduction.

References

Asian Development Bank (ADB). (2009). *Proposed loan: Peoples Republic of China emergency assistance for Wenchuan earthquake reconstruction project.* http://www.adb.org/Documents/RRPs/PRC/42496-PRC-RRP.pdf.

Asian Development Bank (ADB). (2005a). *Review of Asian Development Bank policy and assistance.* www.adb.org/Documents/news/2005/nr2005162.asp.

Bretton Woods Project. (2005). *IMF and World Bank emergency response.* www.brettonwoodsproject.org/article.shtml?cmd%5B126%5D=x-126-108164.

Capacity for Disaster Reduction Initiative (CADRI). (2010). *Who we are.* http://www.unisdr.org/cadri/who-we-are.html.

Central Emergency Response Fund (CERF). (2010). *CERF annual report.* http://ochaonline.un.org/OchaLinkClick.aspx?link=ocha&docId=1165583.

Europa. (2006). *The Solidarity Fund.* Europa Web site. http://europa.eu.int/comm/environment/civil/prote/solidarity.htm.

Europa. n.d. *United in diversity.* Europa Web site. http://europa.eu.int/abc/panorama/index_en.htm.

European Union (EU). (2005). *Community cooperation in the field of civil protection* (July 12). http://europa.eu.int/comm/environment/civil/prote/cp01_en.htm.

Food and Agriculture Organization (FAO). (2006). *FAO's mandate.* www.fao.org/unfao/about/mandate_en/html.

Inter-American Development Bank (IADB). (2008). *Disaster risk management policy guidelines. March.* http://idbdocs.iadb.org/wsdocs/getdocument.aspx?docnum=360026.

Inter-American Development Bank (IADB). (2005b). *Advanced profile of the disaster risk management policy.* January. www.iadb.org/sds/doc/env-disasterpolicyadvancedprofile.pdf.

Inter-American Development Bank (IADB). (2000). *Facing the challenge of natural disasters in Latin America and the Caribbean.* www.iadb.org/sds/doc/env-disasteractionplan.pdf.

International Labour Organization (ILO). (2005). *Some 1.1 million jobs may have been lost in Pakistan due to quake* (October 17). ILO/05/41. www.ilo.org/public/english/bureau/inf/pr/2005/41.htm.

International Monetary Fund (IMF). (2005). *IMF emergency assistance: Supporting recovery from natural disasters and armed conflicts.* IMF Fact Sheet. www.IMF.org/external/np/exr/facts/conflict.htm.

NATO. (2010). *Pakistan earthquake relief operation.* NATO Website. www.nato.int/cps/en/natolive/topics_50070.htm?selectedLocale=en.

Office for the Coordination of Humanitarian Affairs (OCHA). (2010). *Annual report 2009.* Reliefweb.Int. www.reliefweb.int/rw/lib.nsf/db900sid/OCHA-85FM3C/$file/OCHA_AR2009_Hi%20Res.pdf?openelement.

Office for the Coordination of Humanitarian Affairs (OCHA). (2010). *CERF annual report 2009.* http://ochaonline.un.org/OchaLinkClick.aspx?link=ocha&docId=1165583.

Office for the Coordination of Humanitarian Affairs (OCHA). (2010a). *Organizational structure of OCHA. OCHA website.* http://ochaonline.un.org/OchaLinkClick.aspx?link=ocha&docid=1149592.

Office for the Coordination of Humanitarian Affairs (OCHA). (2006). *The Central Emergency Response Fund (CERF).* http://ochaonline.un.org/webpage.asp?page=2101.

Office for the Coordination of Humanitarian Affairs (OCHA). (2005). *OCHA organigramme.* http://ochaonline.un.org/webpage.asp?site=organigramme.

ReliefWeb. (2005). *UN presence in tsunami affected areas,* May 11. Map.

Skullard, R. (2005). *Japan diverts rice to tsunami survivors.* World Food Programme. www.wfp.org/english/?moduleid=139&key=1164&elemid=3.

UN Children's Fund (UNICEF). (2010). *Annual report 2009. UNICEF Website.* www.unicef.org/publications/files/UNICEF_Annual_Report_2009_EN_061510.pdf.

UN Children's Fund (UNICEF). (2005). *Indian Ocean earthquake and tsunami UNICEF response at six-month update.* UNICEF HQ04-0954.

UN News Centre. (2010). *Humanitarian action mid-year: Five billion dollars short.* UNOCHA. Reliefweb.Int, July 14. http://www.reliefweb.int/rw/rwb.nsf/db900sid/VVOS-87CQQW?OpenDocument.

UN News Centre. (2006). *UN launches landmark disaster relief fund to speed up emergency assistance.* (March 9). www.un.org/apps/news/story.asp?newsid=17748&cr=disaster&cr1=.

United Nations. (2010). *Humanitarian appeal 2010: Mid-year review.* http://ochaonline.un.org/humanitarianappeal/webpage.asp?Page=1868.

United Nations. (2010). *Organizational chart. UN Website.* www.un.org/aboutun/chart_en.pdf.

United Nations Department of Economic and Social Affairs (UNDESA). (2004). *Johannesburg plan of implementation.* www.un.org/esa/sustdev/documents/WSSD_poi_pd/English/Poitoc.htm.

United Nations Development Fund for Women (UNIFEM). (2005). *Asian tsunami: UNIFEM calls for greater role of women in recovery and reconstruction efforts.* Press Release. June 23.

United Nations Development Programme (UNDP). (2010). *2009 Annual report.* http://www.undp.org/cpr/AnnualReports/2009/annual_report_2009.pdf.

United Nations Development Programme (UNDP). (n.d. (a)). *Mission Statement.* www.undp.org/bdp/pm/docs/reference-center/chapter1/mission.html.

United Nations Development Programme (UNDP). (n.d. (b)). *Vulnerability reduction and sustainable development.* www.UNDP.org.in/dmweb/.

United Nations Educational, Scientific, and Cultural Organization (UNESCO). (2004). *UNESCO's mission.* www.unesco.org/science/earth/disaster/unesco_mission.shtml.

United Nations High Commissioner for Refugees (UNHCR). (2005). Pakistan earthquake: Airlift starts today. *UNHCR Briefing News,* October 14.

United Nations International Strategy for Disaster Reduction (UNISDR). (2001). *Framework for action for the implementation of the International Strategy for Disaster Reduction*. June. www.eird.org/eng/acerca-eird/marco-accion-eng/htm.

United Nations Joint Logistics Center (UNJLC). (2005). *About the UNJLC*. www.unjlc.org/9639/.

World Food Programme (WFP). (2005). *Fast food: WFP's emergency response*. www.wfp.org/aboutwfp/introduction/hunger_fight.asp.

APPENDIX 10–1

IADB Disaster Risk Management Policy Guidelines

March 2008

    http://idbdocs.iadb.org/wsdocs/getdocument.aspx?docnum=360026

I. Introduction

Purpose of the Guidelines

    1.1. The purpose of the present guidelines is to help Bank teams and borrowing member countries to implement Bank actions according to the principles of the Disaster Risk Management Policy (GN-2354-5) approved February 2007. The objectives of the Policy are (i) to provide effective and efficient support to borrowing members in reducing disaster risks and (ii) to facilitate rapid and appropriate assistance by the Bank to its borrowers after a disaster. The guidelines are part of the Bank's framework for the management of development risk at the country and project levels.

    1.1. There are four possible strategies to manage risks: (i) acceptance, when risks remain below levels deemed tolerable by the parties involved; (ii) prevention and mitigation; (iii) sharing, when risks can be effectively transferred to a third party, for example through insurance; and (iv) rejection ("avoidance"), when the level of risk exceeds the risk level deemed acceptable but cannot be lowered at a reasonable cost.

Directives of the Policy

    1.2. The Policy directives outline the actions that are to be used both by the IADB staff and by teams of the borrowers, who are responsible for

    (i) Country programming—Policy Directive A-1

    (ii) Preparation and execution of new projects—Directive A-2

    (iii) Loan reformulations for financing disaster response—Directive B-1

    (iv) Preparation and execution of reconstruction projects—Directive B-2

    1.3. The guidelines will contribute to the mainstreaming of disaster risk management (DRM) into the Bank's programming exercises with the borrowers, particularly in high-risk countries. To determine which of the IDB's borrowing member countries will require a country risk assessment, a provisional classification of all countries has been prepared.

    1.4. The guidelines will be used for the design and implementation of lending programs, technical cooperations, small projects, cofinancing, and preinvestment activities consistent with the identified risk level. They will address ways to manage risk in public and private sector projects, in order to improve project viability. Whenever significant risks due to natural hazards are identified in project preparation, appropriate measures will be taken to secure the viability of the project, including the protection of populations and investments affected by Bank-financed activities. The Bank has nonreimbursable resources that may be used to cover the transaction costs incurred with the implementation of these guidelines.

1.5. These guidelines will also recommend ways to evaluate the benefits and opportunity costs of loan reformulations and give guidance on how to ensure adequate transparency and effective monitoring, auditing, and reporting on the use of redirected funds. In addition, the guidelines describe precautions to be taken to avoid rebuilding or increasing vulnerability during rehabilitation and reconstruction.

1.6. The guidelines are designed to be flexible in their application to the various situations that borrowing member countries and the Bank may experience, in the face of natural hazards and disasters affecting their development prospects and performance.

Natural Hazards and Climate Change

1.7. The present guidelines apply to all natural hazards, including the hydrometeorological hazards—windstorms, floods, and droughts—that are associated with both the existing climate variability and the expected change in long-term climate conditions. Of note for risk assessments, climate change is expected to change some countries' disaster risk (their probable losses) by changing the characteristics of the hydrometeorological hazards.

1.8 Although uncertainty persists, recent advances in downsizing climate models are allowing disaster managers to better calibrate their risk assessments to understand potential impacts due to climate change at the subnational level. Tools for identifying such climate risk at the country and project levels, and measures for mitigating these increased risks to Bank investments (climate change adaptation) will be developed under Pillar 4 of the Bank's Sustainable Energy and Climate Change Initiative (SECCI) Action Plan.

II. Policy Directive A-1: Country Programming

Purpose and Scope

2.1. The purpose of this section is to provide guidance to Bank teams on the implementation of Directive A-1 of the Disaster Risk Management Policy, particularly for countries classified as having high disaster risk, as well as for those sectors that are associated with a high vulnerability to natural disasters and in which the Bank has identified opportunities for financing. In accordance with this Policy, the Bank will encourage countries to include proactive DRM in programming activities in those countries, as indicated in Directive A-1 of the Policy:

2.2. *A-1. Programming*

Dialog with borrowing member countries. The Bank will seek to include the discussion on proactive disaster risk management in the dialog agenda with borrowing member countries. The Bank will give due consideration to vulnerability associated with natural hazards and risk management in relation to the priority areas of intervention discussed and agreed with the borrowers for the development of country and regional strategies, and operational programs.

The Bank will identify countries according to their level of exposure to natural hazards based on existing indicators and Bank experience. For countries that are highly exposed to natural hazards, the Bank will identify their potential vulnerability as a major development challenge and propose a country level disaster risk assessment. When the assessments identify that potentially important disruptions in the country's social and economic development could be caused by disasters resulting from natural hazards, the Bank will encourage the inclusion of disaster risk management activities in the country strategy and operational program agreed with the borrower. These may include policy reforms, specific institutional strengthening and land-use planning activities, measures of financial protection such as through risk transfer, and investment projects conducive to reducing vulnerability at the national, regional, and municipal levels. Where the natural hazards may affect more than one country, the Bank will encourage a regional approach within the existing programming framework. The Bank will promote the use of the Disaster Prevention Sector Facility and the Disaster Prevention Fund, described in Section V of this policy, and other means it offers to finance the recommended actions resulting from the assessment process.

2.3. To meet the requirement of the DRM Policy to identify countries according to their level of risk exposure, a provisional country classification has been developed. The provisional classification will be subject to change, based on expert knowledge, and eventually on the complete data set of risk information derived from the implementation of the Bank's Indicators for Disaster Risk and Risk Management Program in its 26 borrowing member countries. The Indicators Program has been completed in 14 countries to date.

Programming Stages

1. Disaster Risk Information for Country Dialog and the Preparation of Country Strategies

2.4. **Country Disaster Risk Assessment:** As indicated in Directive A-1, countries that have been identified as being highly exposed to natural hazards will be encouraged by the Bank to include DRM as a priority area for Bank assistance. In those cases, the Bank will propose that a *country disaster risk assessment* be carried out. The assessment would give an overview of the risks facing a country; identify the sectors and geographical areas that should receive priority attention; and provide initial policy orientation, reviews of relevant institutional capacities, and assistance needs. These assessments may already exist, or may be put together from country and secondary sources.

2.5. The evaluation of the macroeconomic impacts as part of the country disaster risk assessment may allow for the identification of risk reduction needs and the quantification of possible resource gaps between available resources and funding needed for disaster response and recovery. Recommendations will be prepared concerning opportunities for the Bank to contribute to financial protection against disasters, as appropriate, such as direct funding for risk identification and support for risk transfer in financial markets in order to improve the effectiveness of the country's development efforts in the areas and sectors of Bank involvement.

2.6. **Identification of Opportunities for Bank Financing.** In line with the new country development risk framework, a more detailed disaster risk assessment will be recommended when disaster risks faced by certain areas/sectors of Bank involvement could significantly jeopardize the achievement of a country's development objectives. These sector-specific or area-specific assessments would analyze how these risks could affect specific areas/sectors and make recommendations on how best to address the risks identified. For this purpose, loans, technical cooperations, and nonfinancial Bank products for proactive DRM may be proposed within the country programming activities.

2. Implementation of the Country Strategy: Programming Dialogue and Portfolio Management

2.7. When deemed necessary by the Bank and if the borrower agrees, DRM activities will be included as in the implementation of the country strategy. The Bank will give due consideration to the following:

- In the programming and portfolio reviews, the Bank and the borrower may seek to implement risk reduction investments in the priority sectors and geographical areas through disaster prevention and mitigation measures. These investments may be financed with free-standing loans or as part of larger investment programs, Policy Based Loans (PBL), or private sector operations.

- Technical assistance may be considered for carrying out area- or sector-specific risk evaluations, strengthening risk management through policy reforms, organizational design, land-use planning activities, the preparation of new prevention loan programs, and supporting the implementation of financial protection schemes such as through insurance to cover disaster losses.

- Loan portfolio modifications will likely be necessary due to the occurrence of major disasters during the regular programming cycle. Borrowers may request new emergency or reconstruction financing and will have access to either new resources, for instance, through the Immediate Response Facility for Emergencies Caused by Disasters (GN-2038-12 and GN-2038-16), or "existing" resources, through loan reformulations (see Directive B-1).

2.8. The results of the DRM implementation in-country programming will be evaluated using the monitoring system defined in the Country Strategy document.

Regional Activities

2.9. The Bank may recommend activities of a regional nature whenever it is known that a particular disaster could affect several borrowing member countries simultaneously. Examples of this situation are the ENSO (*El Niño Southern Oscillation*) phenomenon, and the hurricanes and tropical storms in the Caribbean and Central America.

2.10. The regional activities that possibly involve Bank financing will be agreed beforehand with the affected borrowing member countries and may involve coordination with other international entities. The resulting operations to be included in the regional portfolio of the Regional Strategy document could be funded through Bank instruments, such as technical cooperation of the Regional Public Goods Program or Disaster Prevention Fund, or loans prepared in parallel, in close cooperation with the countries interested in a regional program.

III. Policy Directive A-2: Risk and Project Viability
Purpose and Scope

3.1. The purpose of this section is to provide guidance to project teams on the implementation of the Bank's Disaster Risk Management Policy Directive A-2: Risk and Project Viability. This Directive is designed to promote the incorporation of DRM in a systematic manner during project preparation and execution. The objective is to reduce risk to levels that are acceptable to the Bank and the borrower, as indicated in Directive A-2 of the Policy:

3.2. *Identification and reduction of project risk. Bank-financed public and private sector projects will include the necessary measures to reduce disaster risk to acceptable levels as determined by the Bank on the basis of generally accepted standards and practices. The Bank will not finance projects that, according to its analysis, would increase the threat of loss of human life, significant human injuries, severe economic disruption, or significant property damage related to natural hazards.*

During the project preparation process project teams will identify if the projects have high exposure to natural hazards or show high potential to exacerbate risk. The findings will be reported to the Bank through the social and environmental project screening and classification process. Project teams should consider the risk of exposure to natural hazards by taking into account the projected distribution in frequency, duration, and intensity of hazard events in the geographic area affecting the project. Project teams will carry out a natural hazard risk assessment for projects that are found to be highly exposed to natural hazards or to have a high potential to exacerbate risk. Special care should be taken to assess risk for projects that are located in areas that are highly prone to disasters as well as sectors such as housing, energy, water and sanitation, infrastructure, industrial and agricultural development, and critical health and education installations, as applicable. In the analysis of risk and project viability, consideration should be given to both structural and nonstructural mitigation measures. This includes specific attention to the capacity of the relevant national institutions to enforce proper design and construction standards and of the financial provisions for proper maintenance of physical assets commensurate with the foreseen risk. When significant risks due to natural hazard are identified at any time throughout the project preparation process, appropriate measures should be taken to establish the viability of the project, including the protection of populations and investments affected by Bank-financed activities. Alternative prevention and mitigation measures that decrease vulnerability must be analyzed and included in project design and implementation as applicable. These measures should include safety and contingency planning to protect human health and economic assets. Expert opinion and adherence to international standards should be sought, where reasonably necessary. In the case of physical assets, the Bank will require that, at the time of project preparation, the borrower establish protocols to carry out periodic safety evaluations (during construction as well as during the operating life of the project) and appropriate maintenance of the project equipment and works, in accordance with generally accepted industry norms under the circumstances. The Bank's social and environmental project screening and classification process will evaluate the steps taken by project teams to identify and reduce natural hazard risk.

3.3. Under the Bank's new risk management development effectiveness framework, a common approach to the management of project risks is proposed. Disaster risk is one of several project risks. These guidelines are an input to the Bank's approach on project risk management. They apply to Bank-financed investment loans and technical cooperation projects in the public and private sector as well as to operations supported by the Multilateral Investment Fund.

Disaster Risk Management Process

3.4. During the assessment, management, and monitoring of disaster risk at the project level, the disaster risk is reviewed at various stages of project preparation and implementation. On this basis, appropriate actions are taken to protect project benefits and outcomes.

3.5. Directive A-2 requires that the Bank's social and environmental project screening and classification process provide for project teams to identify and reduce disaster risk. The recommended DRM steps are as follows:

For All Projects:

- Project Screening and Classification

  Outcome: Identifies those projects where the DRM Policy is applicable and classifies as high, moderate or low risk.
  Document: Report of the Social and Environmental Safeguards Policy Filter (SPF) and Social and Environmental Safeguards Screening Form. Document: Disaster Risk Profile in the Environment and Social Strategy.

For High-Risk Projects:

- Disaster Risk Assessment (DRA), including disaster risk management plan

  Outcome: Provides a detailed evaluation of the impacts of the significant natural hazards identified during project classification on project components; and outlines appropriate risk management and mitigation measures.
  Document: DRA Report, prepared by the Borrower (this may be a stand-alone report or it may be incorporated into the environmental impact assessment report).

- Disaster Risk Management Summary

  Outcome: Provides information on the specific disaster risks associated with the project and the risk management measures proposed by the Borrower.
  Document: DRM Summary, for inclusion in the Environmental and Social Management Report (ESMR), prepared by Project Teams.

- Project Implementation, Monitoring and Evaluation

  Outcome: Identifies the approaches which the executing agency applies during project implementation; and which project teams apply during project monitoring and evaluation.

1. Project Screening and Classification

3.6. The Bank's social and environmental screening and classification system of projects will be used to filter and classify those projects for which disaster risk is likely to be an issue for project viability and effectiveness.

3.7. There are two possible types of disaster risk scenarios:

- Type 1: The project is likely to be exposed to natural hazards due to its geographic location.
- Type 2: The project itself has a potential to exacerbate hazard risk to human life, property, the environment or the project itself.

Disaster Risk Management Policy Filter (a component of the Safeguard Policy Filter)
   3.8. The purpose of this step is to establish, early in the project preparation process, whether natural hazards are likely to pose a threat to the project area during the execution (construction) period and/or the operational life of the project, due to Type 1 and Type 2 risk scenarios.

Project Classification
   3.9. *Type 1 Risk Scenario*: The level of disaster risk associated with a given project is dependent on the characteristics of the natural hazards as well as on the vulnerability of the sector and project area. The project is classified on the basis of an estimate of the impacts/losses due to the significant hazards associated with Type 1 risk scenario. Project teams classify their projects in terms of high, moderate, or low disaster risk on the basis of the (i) projected frequency of occurrence and magnitude or intensity of the hazard and (ii) estimated severity of the impacts associated with the hazard, i.e., the magnitude and extent of the likely social, economic, and environmental consequences of the hazard on the various project components and on the general zone of influence of the project. The classification process also provides project teams with a preliminary indication of the hazards likely to be of greatest significance, as well as their likely impacts on project components.
   3.10. This classification is included on the *Social and Environmental Safeguards Screening Form* and reported as part of the disaster risk profile presented in the *Environment and Social Strategy* document. The project team will report its findings to the Bank unit responsible for social and environmental screening and classification of projects, as part of the Bankwide safeguards and risk management procedure.

High-Risk Projects
   3.11. The project will typically be classified as high-risk if one or more of the significant natural hazards may occur several times during the execution (construction) period and/or the operational life of the project and/or the likely severity of social, economic, and/or environmental impacts in the short to medium term are major or extreme. These impacts are of sufficient magnitude to affect project viability and may affect an area broader than the project site. As such hazards may affect project viability, a more detailed investigation of disaster risk, in the form of a DRA, is required.

Moderate-Risk Projects
   3.12. The project will typically be classified as moderate risk if one or more of the prevalent natural hazards are likely to occur at least once during the execution (construction) period and/or the operational life of the project and/or the likely severity of impact in the short to medium term is average. These impacts are typically confined to the project site and can be mitigated at reasonable costs. Projects associated with a moderate disaster risk do not typically require a DRA. However, a more limited DRA may be required, depending on the complexity of the project and where the anticipated vulnerability of a specific project component may compromise the achievement of project outcomes.

Low-Risk Projects

3.13. The project will typically be classified as low risk if natural hazards are not likely to occur during construction and/or the operational life of the project and/or associated with a low severity of impact in the short to medium term. Those impacts that occur do not lead to a disruption in the normal functioning of the operation and can be corrected as part of project maintenance. The occurrence of the hazard event does not impact on the achievement of project outcomes. A DRA is not required.

3.14. *Type 2 Risk Scenario*: The impacts associated with Type 2 risk scenario are addressed under Directive B-3 of the Bank's Environment and Safeguards Compliance Policy (OP-703). Such impacts are thus considered and included in the categorization of environmental impacts.

3.15. The unit responsible for environmental and social risk mitigation reviews the classification of all operations and may recommend a new classification based on the review of the disaster risk profile presented in the *Environment and Social Strategy*. The unit and Line Divisions will need to agree on the final classification of the operations, the level of disaster risk assessment required, and a proposed strategy to address and manage the anticipated impacts.

2. Disaster Risk Assessment

3.16. For projects that are identified as high-risk, a DRA is required and is prepared by the Borrower. The objective of the assessment is to evaluate in greater detail the impacts of the significant natural hazards identified during project classification on project components. The results of the risk assessment will guide the selection of appropriate risk management and mitigation measures.

3.17. The *DRA Report*

- Evaluates the frequency, intensity, and severity of previous hazard events that have affected the project area, as well as those predicted to affect the site over the project's operational life.

- Identifies the vulnerability and probable losses of project components, i.e., the nature and magnitude of the probable social, economic, and environmental impacts due to each hazard; this includes both direct and indirect impacts.

- Provides a disaster risk management plan, including proposals for the design of disaster prevention and mitigation measures, including safety and contingency plans to protect human health and economic assets, and their estimated costs; an implementation plan; a monitoring program and indicators for progress; and an evaluation plan. The implementation plan includes protocols to undertake periodic safety evaluations from project implementation up to project completion and maintenance of project equipment and works.

3. Project Analysis

3.18. Project teams include a summary of the DRA Report in the Environmental and Social Management Report, which is reviewed by both the Bank unit responsible for environmental and social risk mitigation screening and the Sector Divisions Chiefs will sign off on the ESMR and safeguard compliance plan, including the DRM activities. The DRM Summary provides information on the specific disaster risks associated with the project and the risk management measures proposed by the Borrower.

3.19. The project's proposed management and mitigation measures should comply with international standards of good practice and relevant national laws and regulations, such as national planning policies, laws and regulations, as well as national building codes and standards.

3.20. Project teams will analyze the impact of the disaster risk prevention and mitigation elements in their assessment of project viability, verifying that identified hazard impacts on project components are reduced to acceptable levels.

4. Project Implementation, Monitoring and Evaluation

3.21. The Executing Agency is responsible for ensuring that all DRM activities (including prevention and mitigation measures) associated with the project are implemented in accordance with the provisions of the loan agreement. This includes periodic safety evaluations and appropriate maintenance during project implementation and through project completion. Project teams will monitor implementation to verify that the DRM actions in the project risk management plan are carried out effectively; they shall use standard monitoring (Project Performance Monitoring Report; PPMR) procedures.

IV. Policy Directive B-1: Loan Reformulation

Purpose and Scope

4.1. The loan reformulation addressed by these guidelines provides financing for postdisaster response to the impacts of natural hazard events and physical damage (such as structural collapse and explosions) caused by technological accidents or other types of disasters resulting from human activity. Loan reformulation includes the diversion of existing loan resources to specific activities within the same project or to another existing project, in order to finance unplanned disaster response. Reformulations may thus involve just a single loan or several operations.

4.2. Loan reformulation allows for the reallocation of resources from existing loans to other projects under certain circumstances, in the aftermath of disasters, as stipulated in Directive B-1 of the Policy:

4.3. *The Bank may approve the reformulation of existing loans in execution in response to disasters if: (i) a state of emergency or disaster has been officially declared by the government; (ii) the impact of the loan reformulation has been estimated taking into account the intended uses and project objectives of the loan or loans to be reformulated relative to the new proposed use of the funds, thereby creating the conditions for more informed decisions on the part of the approving authorities; (iii) adequate transparency and sufficient mechanisms for monitoring, auditing, and reporting the use of the redirected funds are in place, while taking into account the need of a timely response given the nature of the situation; and (iv) a significant share of the redirected funds will be earmarked to reduce the borrower's vulnerability to future disasters and improve the country's capacity for comprehensive disaster risk management.*

Reformulation Process

1. Declaration of State of Emergency, Originating Report and Loan Request

4.4. In order to be considered for loan reformulation funding in response to a disaster, the Government must have declared a state of emergency or its equivalent, for a region or the country as a whole, according to the laws and regulations of the country.

4.5. The Country Office should prepare an originating document after the formal declaration of state of emergency by the Government, recommending the decisions that should be taken in relation to the projects/programs potentially affected by the disaster.

4.6. The Bank may offer technical support to the government in preparing an official request for financing through loan reformulation, on the basis of the Originating Report.

4.7. Once a financing request is received, a project team is appointed, and the approval process of the reformulation operation(s) will follow the established Bank procedures on delegation of authority, according to regular Bank procedures.

2. Analysis of Projects for Reformulation

4.8. Once the Bank has received an official request from the borrowing country for financing disaster response, the possibility of using fresh IDB resources, such as through the Immediate Response Facility (GN-2038-12 and GN-2038-16), is analyzed. If their use is not considered feasible, the impact of the loan reformulation will be estimated by VPC, with support from VPS, taking into account the intended uses and project objectives of the loan(s) to be reformulated either: (i) as a provider of funding or (ii) as a recipient of resources.

4.9. The analysis for operations receiving funding in response to a natural hazard or physical damage from technological activities or other types of disasters resulting from human activity will reflect the nature of the projects, available information, and use of the reallocated resources for an emergency, rehabilitation, and reconstruction.

4.10. The revision of the portfolio in emergency situations should be done jointly with the Borrower. Those projects whose development objective is unlikely to be achieved should be considered first as candidates for reformulation. The team responsible for the portfolio analysis needs to determine performance indicators, based on the possible revisions and reformulations being considered.

Analysis of Loans Used as a Source of Funding

4.11. The impact of redirecting loan resources from existing loans will be estimated taking into account the intended uses and project objectives of the loan or loans to be used as a source relative to the new proposed use of the funds, thereby creating the conditions for more informed decisions. Resource transfers could be done between cost categories within a project (in which case more streamlined approval procedures will apply), or between separate loans as stipulated by Bank procedures.

4.12. For choosing existing projects as origin of resources, following factors (in order of priority) would be considered:

i. *Public sector projects*. Only public sector loans would be considered. Loans to the private sector should not be included in the package of loans for possible reformulation as a result of disasters.

ii. *Development impact in the reformulated operations*. The loans that are having a relatively low economic/financial impact in the country should be considered first as a source for redirecting resources from existing loans toward emergency funding. Redirecting resources that are within a loan generally have a smaller effect than those involving several operations. The original development objectives may not be achieved due to the new social or economic situation created by the disaster or it could be considered too expensive to reorient the resources within the old operation. Recommendations regarding the redirection of resources will be based on project performance indicators used by the Bank.

iii. *Level of execution*. Operations with a low level of physical execution or disbursements and commitments could be chosen for redirection, except for those loans with a very high development impact. The selection should not only be based on a low disbursement rate of the existing loans alone, but also on an analysis of the underlying causes of the poor performance and any remaining opportunities for attaining project goals.

iv. *Loans in affected sectors*. Resource transfers within an affected sector will be preferred due to the greater similarity of their respective objectives compared with those of loans in different sectors.

v. *Loans in affected region(s)*. In general, existing projects in the disaster area will not be used to provide resources to be transferred to other programs in the same area. However, when damage is so severe that the attainment of the original development objectives is in jeopardy, or the continuation of a certain component of the project as a whole is unjustifiable on account of excessive costs, parts or all of the undisbursed balances may be re-channeled toward emergency or rehabilitation and reconstruction projects in the same area.

Factors to Be Considered in Projects Receiving Funding

4.13. The following are the recommended actions to be considered by project teams, while preparing the funding analysis:

4.14 i. *Technical analysis*.

- For emergencies, the technical analysis will be aimed at re-establishing basic services and critical infrastructure in a time efficient manner.

- The attainment of fully functioning facilities and productive capacity through rehabilitation and reconstruction will be measured through a detailed technical analysis with the objective of reaching disaster resistance, and fulfilling technical standards across the board and performance criteria required by the Bank.

4.15 ii. *Socioeconomic analysis*.

- For emergency response, the socioeconomic analysis will be limited to the evaluation of the cost-effectiveness of restoring the basic services and critical infrastructure. If information is scarce, the analysis may be done based on comparable data from similar operations elsewhere. Any delays in the analysis and processing of the emergency financing may limit the Bank to have a meaningful contribution to resolve critical needs that are affecting the population, urgent re-establishment of basic services and critical activities.

- The analysis for rehabilitation and reconstruction investments will follow standard Bank practices. If future project benefits cannot be estimated, cost-effectiveness analysis will be carried out.

4.16 iii. *Evaluation of institutional capacity and coordination*. In order to gain sustainability, existing agencies are preferred to the establishment of new, ad hoc entities. A rapid analysis will be carried out of the institutional capacity, procurement management capability, and financial track record of the existing agencies. Based on its results, it will be determined if the resources will be disbursed on an ex post or on a concurrent basis.

The administrative and technical responsibilities of all the participating institutions in different sectors and means of coordination need to be clearly defined to facilitate successful execution in a limited time frame. Planned strategies and activities need to be coordinated with other international agencies participating in the postdisaster financing.

3. Transparency and Monitoring

4.17 i. *Procurement procedures.* The applicable Bank policy and rules will be followed for the procurement of goods and services. As an exception, for emergency situations, specific procurement procedures are available, in view of the special nature of these operations and the urgency involved.

4.18 ii. *Transparency in financing.* The financial management and evaluation of procurements, expenses, and the utilization of goods and services to be funded with Bank resources for emergency situations will be audited on a concurrent basis, following current Bank practices. For rehabilitation and reconstruction investments the review may be on a concurrent or ex post basis depending on risk of lack of transparency estimated by the project teams. Loan resources can be used to contract the services of independent public accountants to audit the operation's financial statements as required by the Bank.

4.19 iii. *Monitoring and evaluation.* Bank resources will be subject to review on a concurrent basis for emergency investments. For rehabilitation and reconstruction, an audit will be required on a concurrent or ex post basis, depending on the risk of lack of transparency as estimated by the project team. Data collection will be planned for monitoring and evaluation. Only direct project impacts will need to be evaluated.

4. Reducing Vulnerability to Future Disasters

4.20. Vulnerability should not be replicated when designing disaster response financing. In the preparation of reformulations for rehabilitation and reconstruction, a proportion of the resources of the operation should be allocated to prevention and mitigation activities. The percentage of the total cost that will be dedicated to prevention and mitigation should be defined and the viability of these investments assessed by the project team. The project team should also justify any potential deviations from international practices in these allocations for disaster prevention and mitigation.

V. Policy Directive B-2: Reconstruction
Purpose and Scope

5.1. The purpose of this section is to provide assistance to project teams on the implementation of Directive B-2: Reconstruction. Specifically guidance is provided on the precautions that country programming process and project teams should take to promote revitalization of development efforts in the aftermath of disasters, while ensuring that rehabilitation and reconstruction projects do not lead to a rebuilding of or an increase in vulnerability. As indicated in Directive B-2 of the Policy:

5.2. *Avoiding rebuilding vulnerability. Operations that finance rehabilitation and reconstruction after a disaster require special precautions to avoid rebuilding or increasing vulnerability.*

These include the precautions mentioned in A-2, as well as correcting deficiencies in risk management policies and institutional capacity as reflected in A-1. A significant share of the new investment will be earmarked to reduce vulnerability to future disasters and improve the country's capacity for comprehensive disaster risk management. Particular attention must be given to lessons learned from recent hazard events. The Bank will not assume that pre-disaster conditions persist in whole or in part in the affected area. Disaster risk assessment of the reconstruction project should be carried out taking into account the specifics of the area, the sector, and the infrastructure concerned, as well as the current environmental, social, and economic situation and any changes in the affected area as a result of the disaster.

5.3. Reconstruction may follow as a response to the impacts of natural hazard events, and physical damage (such as structural collapse and explosions) resulting from technological accidents or other types of disasters resulting from human activity.

Vulnerability Reduction Considerations

5.4. The guidelines for Directive A-2: Risk and Project Viability, as described in Section 4 of these guidelines, also apply to rehabilitation and reconstruction projects. For projects identified as high risk, the disaster risk assessment, and design and implementation of risk reduction measures, will incorporate the lessons learned from the disaster event, including the performance of the physical works, the relevant sectors, institutions, and other project components. Risk reduction measures will include enhancements in national, regional, and sectoral risk management policies and strengthening of institutional capacity.

5.5. In order to avoid the rebuilding of or an increase in vulnerability, a proportion of the resources of the operation will be allocated to prevention, mitigation, and risk transfer. The percentage of the total cost is at the discretion of the project team, but will be guided by international practices.

Source: IADB, 2008, http://idbdocs.iadb.org/wsdocs/getdocument.aspx?docnum=360026.

⋮⋮⋮ 11
Special Considerations

Introduction

International disaster management has become increasingly diverse, encompassing new areas of technical expertise not traditionally considered relevant to the profession. Specialists in many fields, including development, economics, public health, political science, communications, and engineering, just to name a few, are finding that their experience and knowledge are being called upon as nations continue to address the snowballing issues of global disaster risk.

Hazard vulnerability, disaster risk, and the management of humanitarian emergencies have risen to the top of the global policy agenda in recent years, and have remained there due to the persistence of catastrophic disasters. The disaster events of the twenty-first century have already shattered any assumptions that some nations have solved the disaster risk problem. Through their awesome and destructive fury, disaster events have proven that all nations, rich and poor, have much to learn about preparing and mitigating for, responding to, and recovering from the many forms of disasters that continue to plague us.

Chapter 1 described the increasing incidence of disasters throughout the world, and the growing hazard risk faced by the world's population. These trends continue despite considerable efforts to counter them and, without a more concerted effort to incorporate the global disaster risk reduction recommendations of the ISDR and other movements, nothing will change. During a recent 12-month period (from August 2009 to August 2010) the world community was confronted with yet another wave of deadly and destructive disaster events, indicative of what may be expected without greater disaster management efforts by governments around the world. Exhibit 11–1 lists a sample of these events.

As shown by the efforts of governments, nongovernmental organizations (NGOs), and multilateral organizations to find solutions to the skyrocketing financial and human losses of disasters, disaster management will remain a global topic of concern for many decades to come. Through the efforts of the International Decade for Natural Disaster Reduction (IDNDR) and the International Strategy for Disaster Reduction (ISDR), as well as by NATO, the EU, governments such as Canada, the United States, Australia, and New Zealand, and many others, NGOs including most notably the Red Cross/ Red Crescent Movement, more has been done in the past decade to reduce this threat than has occurred throughout history. And in response to the outpouring of concern by the world's population to the recent great loss of life and property resulting from the disasters listed in Exhibit 11–1, world leaders are beginning to take disaster threats even more seriously.

In coming years, as the international community seeks to control increasing global risk, and as the international disaster management community begins to assume a more central and organized stance, several key issues continue to be pose a challenge. While many of these problems have long

Exhibit 11–1: MAJOR FORMS OF DISASTERS EXPERIENCED BETWEEN AUGUST 2009 AND AUGUST 2010 AND THE COUNTRIES THAT EXPERIENCED THEM

- Avalanches (Canada, China, Scotland, Pakistan, United States, Afghanistan, Switzerland, Italy, Poland, Tajikistan, New Zealand, France)
- Commercial airplane accidents with 10 or more deaths (Pakistan, Russia, Lebanon, Libya, Afghanistan, Yemen, Cameroon, Romania, Papua New Guinea, Kazakhstan)
- Complex humanitarian emergencies (Pakistan, India, Sudan, Kyrgyzstan, Congo, Eritrea, Ethiopia, Kenya, Somalia, Uganda, West Africa, Zimbabwe, Central African Republic, Colombia, Balkans, Afghanistan, Iraq, North Korea, East Timor, Lebanon, Palestine, Sri Lanka, Yemen, Georgia, Indonesia)
- Epidemics and pandemics (United States, India, Brazil, Venezuela, Colombia, Dominican Republic, Mexico, Cuba, Worldwide—swine flu)
- Explosions (United States, China, India, Syria, Belgium, Canada, Pakistan, United Kingdom, Colombia, Russia, Australia)
- Extreme heat (United States, Australia, India, Brazil, Canada, China, Iraq, Saudi Arabia, Kuwait, Pakistan, Libya)
- Extreme meteorological storms (Philippines, Guatemala, Honduras, Mexico, Portugal, Canada, France, Spain, Belgium, United Kingdom, Bangladesh, India, China, Germany, United States, Pakistan, Vietnam, Japan)
- Famine exceeding 20% of the population (Ukraine, North Korea, Mongolia, Tajikistan, Pakistan, Cambodia, India, Bangladesh, Madagascar, Botswana, Mozambique, Zimbabwe, Zambia, Angola, Malawi, DR Congo, Republic of Congo, Rwanda, Burundi, Tanzania, Ethiopia, Central African Republic, Chad, Sudan, Niger, Yemen, Djibouti, Sri Lanka, Armenia, Bolivia, Dominican Republic, Haiti, Nicaragua)
- Flooding (Pakistan, United Kingdom, United States, China, India, Philippines, Australia, United Arab Emirates, Singapore, Poland, Niger, Turkey, Taiwan, Brazil, Saudi Arabia, Chile, Cambodia, Vietnam)
- Hurricanes (United States, Mexico, El Salvador, Canada, Nicaragua, Belize)
- Landslides/Mudslides (China, Uganda, India, Kenya, Mexico, Philippines, Yemen, Afghanistan, Peru, Turkey, Indonesia, Portugal, Canada, Italy, Taiwan, Spain, Bangladesh)
- Major bus accidents (United States, India, Pakistan, Turkey, Peru, China, South Africa, Australia, Afghanistan, United Kingdom, Switzerland, Samoa, Germany, Nepal)
- Maritime disasters (Indonesia, Philippines, Peru, Bangladesh, Turkey, India, Myanmar, Sierra Leone, Tonga, Yemen)
- Mass poisoning (Afghanistan, Nigeria, China)
- Mining accidents (China, United States, Turkey, Australia, Colombia, Poland, Slovakia, Russia)
- Rail accidents (India, Italy, Belgium, United States, Russia, Spain, Congo, Egypt, Pakistan, Australia)
- Severe drought (Australia, United States, India, China, Nepal, Thailand, Laos, Vietnam, Kenya, Somalia, Gambia, Nigeria, Ethiopia)
- Stampedes (India, Pakistan, China, Mexico, Mali, Morocco, Uganda, Kenya)

- Strong earthquakes 7.0 or greater (Haiti, Chile, Solomon Islands, Ryukyu Islands, Mexico, Indonesia, Sumatra, Vanuatu, India, Papua New Guinea, Philippines, New Zealand)
- Structural failures (Hong Kong, Belgium, Kenya, Bangladesh, Indonesia, India, Spain, Egypt, Turkey, Nigeria)
- Structure fires (United States, India, Bangladesh)
- Terrorist attacks (Iraq, Colombia, United States, Pakistan, Greece, Afghanistan, Russia, Thailand, India, China, Iran, Turkey, Israel, Sri Lanka, Somalia)
- Tornadoes (United States, Argentina, Brazil, Canada, Germany, China)
- Tsunamis (Samoa, Tonga, American Samoa, Chile)
- Typhoons (Philippines, Taiwan, Vietnam, Cambodia, Taiwan, China, Japan)
- Volcanoes (Iceland, Guatemala, Colombia, DR Congo)
- Widespread civil unrest (Thailand, Georgia, China, Lebanon, Mozambique, Uganda, Iraq, Suriname, Israel, Nigeria, Somalia, Pakistan, Egypt, Kenya, Afghanistan, Jamaica)
- Wildfires (United States, Australia, Greece)
- Windstorms (Nigeria, United States, Canada, South Africa, France, Germany, Spain)

existed without being adequately addressed, others are newly discovered and will require new solutions. In either case, these issues stand as challenges to the progress of international disaster management. This chapter presents several of these new and existing problems, which are certain to remain on the forefront of international disaster management for quite some time.

Coordination

Disaster response is becoming increasingly complex with each new event. Whereas dozens of agencies used to converge upon the scene of an earthquake or flood, there are now hundreds, and occasionally thousands. In response to the December 2004 tsunami events, for example, over 200 organizations addressed the single issue of water quality, while thousands more provided food aid, shelter, medical assistance, and many other victim and rehabilitation needs. Studies have found that despite coordination attempts, these responding agencies still tend to work independently and in an uncoordinated manner, resulting in unnecessary delays and inefficiencies in the distribution and provision of relief. Lags, gaps, and inaccuracies persist in the vital information upon which coordination depends. Even when the NGOs and local community organizations involved in response would like to work together, they are often left out of the coordination planning processes before and during disaster response.

Coordination in disaster response has always been difficult, especially in terms of civil–military cooperation. As the scope of disaster management grows, coordination will only grow in complexity until a suitable mechanism is agreed on by all actors. Previous shortfalls contributed to the creation of coordination mechanisms like the United Nations Office for the Coordination of Humanitarian Affairs (UNOCHA; see Chapter 10). UNOCHA has proven effective as a coordinator in several disaster responses because of its close relationship to the overall UN system, whose agencies maintain long-standing relationships with developing country governments, where the most catastrophic disasters are likely to occur. However, OCHA lacks the authority to ensure all participating response and recovery agencies operate "on the same page." While such authority is unlikely to be granted to any single national, international, or nongovernmental organization, greater trust in, understanding of, and positive experiences with organizations like OCHA may lead to increased participation in their coordination structures.

Increased coordination has been shown to reduce the period of time between when the disaster occurs and when relief is provided. It also helps to increase the area covered by assistance efforts, decreases costs associated with the provision of supplies and assistance, and standardizes the quality of relief, among many other positive results. Effective disaster response coordination is the foundation on which increased international disaster response capacity will be built.

The Media

It is well known that the news media capitalizes on the spectacular nature of crises and disasters, broadcasting vivid images, heartbreaking tragedies, harrowing tales of survival, and public accusations of blame. This kind of reporting attracts viewers or readers and increases ratings. For centuries, the news media has exploited death, destruction, and victimization—first in newspapers, and later on the radio and the television. Today, thanks to technological advances, the media has found access to once unimaginable places. Because of nonstop news coverage and the expansion of Internet- and wireless-based news services (such as cellular or handheld computer systems), the world today receives real-time disaster information, which only a decade ago would have been "old news" by the time it reached consumers.

Disaster management officials and the news media have traditionally enjoyed a love/hate relationship, with disaster management agencies viewing the media more as an adversary than an ally. The media, likewise, viewed responders as "standoffish," untrusting, and secretive. With the advent of effective media partnerships and increased disaster-specific education for members of the press, however, the news media is beginning to be recognized for the significant benefits it may offer disaster management. For instance:

- Through media partnership, more effective risk communication is possible. Chapter 5 described studies that identified the media as the primary source of risk reduction information for many significant hazards. The media is able to reach individuals and households in ways risk managers could never do on their own or through alternate sources.

- No system has proved more effective than the news media in alerting emergency management organizations and citizens alike about the onset of sudden disasters. Early warning messages broadcast by emergency managers via television, radio, and the Internet have proven highly effective. The news media has proven capable of transmitting messages about evacuation, medical assistance, and other emergency-related information. Additionally, emergency managers often learn of impending disasters by watching or listening to media outlets. The news media maintains some of the most effective methods for recognizing events in progress and transmitting that information rapidly. For instance, it was discovered in the after-action reporting on the response to the September 11, 2001, terrorist attacks in the United States that many, if not most, U.S. government officials first learned of the attacks from media giant CNN.

- The media is effective at alerting the world to slow-onset disasters that may otherwise go unnoticed until becoming a full-fledged catastrophe. Drought, famine, and many complex humanitarian emergencies (CHEs) develop over a long period of time, during which intervention is much more effective. Even where knowledge of certain slow-onset emergencies exists, the media provides images and stories that allow citizens to understand and prioritize the events in relation to other existing issues. The media thus can mobilize concerned citizens, who pressure governments and multilateral organizations to take proper action. This coverage is also effective in motivating the same concerned citizens to increase philanthropic giving, on which humanitarian organizations depend.

- The news media is effective at identifying corruption and mismanagement, helping to reduce both. In their investigative role, they help raise awareness about unethical and inappropriate forms of response and recovery that often stymie disaster management efforts. The information they gather proves valuable long beyond the disasters, as it is later used to guide the improvement and restructuring of future response and recovery efforts.

- The media is able to act as a member of the emergency management team if provided the tools to do so. The media relies on accurate data and informed officials to provide viewers with useable information. By providing the media with these resources, and helping them to understand the dynamics of disaster management, disaster managers can increase the likelihood that the public is well informed.

Of course, many of the grievances emergency managers have against the media are based in part on truth and experience—and many of these problems persist. For instance, the media is not consistently accurate in their emergency assessments, and has made some situations appear worse than they actually are. The media often select "experts" who are likely to provide alarmist viewpoints that reflect worst-case scenarios and extreme predictions. As a result, resources can be directed away from more important but less publicized issues.

The media can cause donor fatigue because of the excessive coverage of disaster after disaster. This blanket coverage can result in lower concern for the plight of disaster victims, which can negatively impact philanthropic giving. Donors may feel that the world's problems are so extreme that their individual efforts are meaningless, which leads them to decrease or even cease their giving.

Accuracy of information is also an issue of concern in relation to the media. Even when treated as a partner, the media may produce ill-informed messages that cause problems for both responders and citizens alike. Once a message has been broadcast, countering its negative consequences is very difficult.

And, finally, the media's tendency to inject immediacy and consequence into every story can incite the public into pressuring officials to make hasty decisions when proper (though time-consuming) assessment and consideration are required. This is most often the case in the disaster recovery period, when risk-reduction measures must be incorporated into reconstruction.

The news media is an important partner to the disaster management community and possesses many highly refined tools that emergency managers could better utilize. With technological advancements the news media have increased their ability to gather information and report it to ever-wider audiences in real time, enhancing their value as a partner. It is in the best interest of all emergency management organizations to work with the media, not against them, and to treat them as an effective component of the greater effort to tackle emergency management problems.

Institutional Capacity Development

In early 2010, two massive earthquakes struck just outside of major metropolitan cities in the Western Hemisphere within weeks of each other—the first outside of Port-au-Prince, Haiti (7.0 magnitude) and the second outside of Concepcion and Santiago, Chile (8.8 magnitude). The much larger event struck a country that had experienced many seismic events in the past (including the strongest quake ever recorded—the 9.5 magnitude Valdivia earthquake in Chile in 1960) and had likewise taken the necessary steps to reduce their hazard risk (e.g., seismic retrofits, building code enforcement, public preparedness, zoning, response capacity, etc.), and the death toll was limited to 521. However, in Haiti—where poverty and corruption were rampant, building codes were never applied or enforced, materials were of lackluster quality, and no culture of preparedness existed—the much smaller event left 230,000 killed and over 1 million homeless. The most logical explanation for such great variance between experiences is that these two countries significantly differ regarding their institutional disaster management capacity. At the time of the Haiti earthquake, the seismic potential was well known by government planners and academics alike, but the nation lacked any effective mitigation and preparedness programs that could have prevented many of the fatal structural failures. It also had not yet developed an effective response framework. The opposite could be said for Chile, which was a clear example of lives saved through effective disaster risk management (see Figure 11–1). Nations need comprehensive emergency management capacities to protect themselves from the consequences of disasters—not just one or two emergency management components.

The UN, through ISDR, has made institutional capacity building central to its risk-reduction efforts. While many nations have developed these necessary frameworks in recent years, as espoused by ISDR, they have done little to institutionalize emergency management at all government levels. Moreover, the mechanisms supported by those emergency management frameworks are rarely given

FIGURE 11–1 Chilean emergency responders manage the consequences of the 2010 earthquake. (Photo courtesy of Juan Edwardo Donoso, 2010)

adequate staff or funding to prove effective should a disaster actually occur. It is evident from the continued need for international intervention in disasters, despite these early improvements, that most nations have a long way to go.

Political Will

Disasters are political events; they can either glorify politicians or destroy them. Their spectacular nature demands the involvement of these chief executives and tests their leadership merit. How politicians manage these rare events can frame how their entire term in office is judged.

In the absence of disaster events, however, the field of emergency management falls low on many policy agendas. All governments operate on limited budgets, making it particularly difficult for poor nations' leaders to choose mitigation for disasters that may never occur during their tenure over projects that will generate instant gratification and recognition. A U.S. politician captured this sentiment when he said, "I won't lose my job for failing to mitigate, but I might lose my job if I botch a response" (Haddow, 2005).

The UN has identified increased political commitment to emergency management as one of the four principal objectives of the ISDR. Public officials must be convinced of the extensive benefits of comprehensive emergency management, including how much more cost-effective mitigation and preparation efforts are as compared to disaster recovery and response.

Compound Emergencies

Disasters do not occur in a vacuum in the real world. However, many disaster management–planning efforts approach each hazard as if it will occur in the absence of all other hazards. Unfortunately, it is common for two or more disasters to occur in succession or concurrently, resulting in what is called a "compound emergency." Mudslides in the midst of hurricanes, for example, are a compound emergency that has become commonplace in Central America during the past decade. The victims of the 2005 earthquake in South Asia experienced another form of compound emergency when they found themselves without adequate shelter or clothing in the midst of snowstorms and extreme cold following the destruction of their homes. The Indonesian victims of the 2004 tsunami events in Asia were still in the immediate aftermath of an earthquake as the waves of the tsunami crashed over them. And in Louisiana, New Orleans, residents had just endured a powerful hurricane when levees broke and a technologically induced flood inundated 80% of the city.

Compound emergencies stretch the emergency management capacities of even the most prepared nations. They are as much a real hazard as many other more common, individual hazards. By considering these multi-hazard disasters, both affected governments and responding international relief agencies can better address the consequences of each unique disaster that is guaranteed to occur, regardless of whether it is compound, complex, or simple.

Donor Fatigue

The engine that drives international emergency management is fueled by the philanthropic actions of nations, corporations, and individuals. Donors give generously each year in response to the collective catastrophic damage caused by disasters of all forms, in all parts of the world. The December 2004 tsunami alone generated over $7 billion in international donations from a full range of public and private sources. In August 2005, when Hurricane Katrina caused widespread destruction across the southeastern parts of the United States, international donors responded again, providing over $1 billion in financial and other assistance. But less than 2 months later, a 7.6 magnitude earthquake struck South Asia, leaving almost 80,000 people dead and over 3 million homeless. Donors did not respond with such generosity. In fact, 3 weeks later, the UN Flash Appeal of $312 million for Pakistan had received only $90 million (less than one-third) compared with over $800 million pledged within 1 week in response to the tsunami. (The overall UN Flash Appeal in response to the earthquake was $978 million, later revised to $1.293 billion.)

Related to donor fatigue is the finding of a study performed by acclaimed risk perception and disaster behavior scientist Paul Slovic that individuals experience what is called "psychic numbing" as the scale and scope of disaster events increase. This study found that, contrary to the belief that people are more philanthropic to large catastrophic events than small ones, people are actually less compelled to give as disaster statistics increase (based solely on the number of casualties). In other words, as the number of fatalities reported increases, the likelihood that individuals donate to that humanitarian effort decreases (Henderson, 2007).

In light of the growing number and size of disasters throughout the world, nations, corporations, and citizens are finding that they are running out of funds to dedicate to humanitarian assistance. With more disasters happening concurrently throughout the world, donors are having difficulty concentrating on more than one humanitarian effort at a time, with the more spectacular events receiving priority both in the press and from donors' pockets. Many humanitarian agencies and NGOs are finding that their response and recovery funding for certain disasters is not meeting needs, especially when multiple large-scale events are happening concurrently or in quick succession. The 2010 earthquake in Chile, for instance, suffered from the donor fatigue caused by the earthquake in Haiti just weeks prior. While donor giving spiked immediately after the Haiti earthquake was televised throughout the globe, there was no comparable spike in the immediate aftermath of the Chile quake, which occurred as daily footage from Haiti continued. Whether the disasters of 2004–2005 and 2010 are trend-setting or anomalous remains to be seen, but it would appear that the mere timing of an event in relation to other events can drastically affect the response and recovery assistance expected from the international community—most notably that of charitable giving.

Donors and recipient agencies must reassess how disaster funding is collected for and disbursed to emergency situations. The American Red Cross attempted to divert some of the billions of dollars it received in response to the September 11, 2001, terrorist attacks to allow the funding to address a much wider range of disaster-related needs, but public backlash for this led to a significant tarnishing of their reputation. In light of this experience, industry-wide consideration of how to fund multiple disasters has been necessary.

Corruption

Corruption exists to a varying degree in all countries' governments, businesses, and general population. Widespread corruption often leads to the types of vulnerabilities that cause humanitarian emergencies. A short list of examples of how corruption increases vulnerability includes:

- Building inspectors accepting payment to overlook violations
- Construction contractors substituting approved building materials for substandard materials that may result in structural weaknesses

- Government employees embezzling or sidetracking funding earmarked for disaster mitigation or preparedness
- Government executives misusing loans from the international community, resulting in underdevelopment coupled with high indebtedness
- Certain local leaders with political ties to the central government secure funding for emergency management activities, while those without political favor are unable to secure sufficient funding
- Transportation carriers failing to follow government safety regulations to cut operating costs: failing to properly train employees, neglecting maintenance, or failing to install proper safety equipment

Once a disaster occurs, existing corruption patterns do not vanish. Humanitarian emergencies are characterized by huge inflows of cash and supplies, both of which present new opportunities for corruption. Power has been abused in diverse ways in these situations, ranging from simple theft to systemic rape and murder. Disaster victims have been required to pay assessors to be included on relief and recovery registries; others have had to pay for or offer other favors to receive supplies and assistance that had been donated for uncommitted distribution. At times, relief supplies have simply disappeared, presumably into some official's personal possession. International NGOs and governmental agencies inadvertently contribute to this corruption by not fully understanding how such matters affect local politics and society. Ongoing discussions seek ways to reduce or prevent such actions in the future. Corruption not only undermines the work of response and recovery agencies but also causes additional suffering for victims.

State Sovereignty

International law states that nations retain their sovereignty even in the event of disasters or CHEs. Accordingly, affected governments must invite international response agencies to participate in response efforts before these organizations can provide humanitarian assistance. While most countries in need do not balk at requesting outside help, in some situations, much needed international assistance is not requested or is turned away at the border. The reasons why sovereignty may be invoked to prevent access by relief agencies are diverse. Aid refusal occurs in both rich and poor countries and for national, technological, and intentional disasters.

One of the most common reasons is that the affected country is concerned with "saving face," and believes that refusing assistance or failing to share information will help downplay the disaster and give the illusion of control. Because of this, China kept its disaster fatality information classified until September 2005—a practice that made the assessment of disaster magnitude almost impossible for outside response agencies. Another notorious example of face-saving occurred in Japan following the 1995 Kobe earthquake, when international search-and-rescue teams were denied entry for many days, closing the window of time when they could have been most effective.

Nations that are oppressive and maintain closed borders may also refuse assistance for fear of the outside influence rescuers may introduce. This is said to be the reason why Russia denied the entry of Japanese rescuers after the 1995 Sakhalin Island earthquake. (Russia was reputedly afraid that Japan would use its access to take control of the island.) It exhibited similar behavior in 2000, after the Kursk submarine disaster, when 118 sailors perished after Russia refused all international assistance. In one of the worst cases of an oppressive government hindering a much needed international humanitarian response, the government of Burma (Myanmar) blocked the entry of thousands of international responders amassed across the border in Thailand after Cyclone Nargis swamped the better half of the country's south on May 2, 2008 (see Figure 11–2). While accurate statistics may never be known, the UN estimated that 1.5 million people were affected in the event, and 135,000 people were killed or remain missing. Despite that the event was the most deadly worldwide in almost 40 years, the ruling junta waited a full week before allowing the inflow of supplies—only allowing aid workers to leave the delivered aid at the airport or other ports of entry to be managed without oversight by a military that had already illegally confiscated food aid from the World Food Programme (WFP) for personal use, or that claimed the donated goods were their own for propaganda purposes. On May 19, two and a half weeks after the disaster struck with millions facing starvation and exposure, a limited number of NGOs from within the region were allowed to begin providing humanitarian assistance, but it was too late for many. The junta has been accused of committing crimes against humanity and other international condemnation for their blocking of international relief, but this has done little to change the attitudes of the repressive regime and the same would likely be repeated in a future event.

Nations with a history of political rancor also have been known to refuse assistance from each other. Cuba and the United States regularly offer each other assistance in the aftermath of hurricanes, without any of this assistance ever having been accepted. A surprise reversal in behavior took place following the 2005 South Asian earthquake, when longtime rivals India and Pakistan allowed bi-national assistance in the disputed Kashmir region, despite decades of ongoing violence in the affected area.

FIGURE 11–2 Survivors of Cyclone Nargis seek refuge in Sanayaungchi Monastery, May 16, 2008. (Photo courtesy of UN/UNHCR, 2008)

Finally, governments of nations entrenched in violent conflict often refuse international assistance due to fears that responding governments or agencies will meddle in their political affairs in a way that is unfavorable to their position or hold on authority. Similarly, there may be no viable government to provide access or entry, as occurred in Somalia in 1993.

Equality in Humanitarian Assistance and Relief Distribution

Monetary value cannot be placed on human life. Equally, all people have the same unalienable rights regardless of their age, race, gender, religion, social class, or nationality. However, common inequalities and inconsistencies exist in the provision and distribution of humanitarian assistance by donors and relief and recovery personnel. These inequalities are persistent and follow many of the same patterns seen in development. As such, certain regions, nations, and populations receive less assistance than others in the aftermath of disasters.

At the victim level in the relief and recovery phases of disaster management, it is not uncommon for existing bigotries to influence the distribution of emergency assistance, and for certain groups in need of aid to be favored over others. In societies in which people are discriminated against or placed at a general disadvantage due to their race, gender, age, religion, social class, caste, physical ability, appearance, or other distinguishing characteristic, these already vulnerable populations become even more vulnerable.

One of the most typical forms of discrimination is gender bias, which is most common in societies in which gender roles are strictly defined and women are traditionally tasked with duties related to the home and children (duties that tend to increase in times of crisis). In these cultures, men are more likely to wait in relief lines for supplies, while women (as well as children and the elderly) become increasingly dependent on them for survival. This situation is exacerbated when a woman is a widow or single parent and is unable to compete for aid.

Another common form of discrimination is class bias. Although most obvious in social systems based on caste identity, underlying ethnic and racial divides often present similar problems. Avoiding these forms of bias can be difficult because the disaster management agencies involved in response must be aware of the discrimination to counteract its influence. For example, when host country nationals are hired by humanitarian agencies to assist in relief distribution, as is often the case, they can inadvertently inject existing ethnic or cultural biases into their efforts. Therefore, humanitarian agencies must be careful to balance the makeup of their employees in such situations.

Many NGO and governmental response agencies are continuously developing systems of relief and distribution that counteract the complex problems associated with discrimination. However, the difficult nature of this issue is highlighted by the fact that targeting specific groups, such as women or children, can lead to reverse discrimination. Any such bias can result in a decline in perceived legitimacy or impartiality of the assisting agency and/or exacerbation of the needs being addressed (Maynard, 1999).

Inequality in humanitarian assistance also occurs on a more global scale at the donor level. The reasons for this phenomenon, illustrated by the levels by which Flash Appeals are funded in comparison to each other, are less understood. Table 11–1 shows the highest and lowest levels of funding for CAP appeals from 2008–2010 (the five lowest and five highest of each year).

Through its Flash and Consolidated Appeals Processes (CAPs), the UN tasks the world community to assume the costs of response and recovery for the many international disasters that occur each year. Unfortunately, these appeals go largely unmet. Worse yet, there is significant irregularity in how these appeals are responded to, with some receiving significant donations and others receiving

Table 11–1   Levels of Funding for CAP Appeals, 2007–2009

2010		
Country	*Appeal*	*% Covered*
Top Five:		
Central African Republic	100,447,041	68
Occupied Palestinian Territory	804,522,005	70
Afghanistan	664,923,055	70
Madagascar	22,347,522	71
Pakistan	680,070,527	71
Bottom Five:		
Laos	10,153,872	42
Namibia	7,071,951	32
Burkina Faso	18,449,092	29
Philippines	18,449,092	22
El Salvador	18,449,092	0
2009		
Country	*Appeal*	*% Covered*
Top Five:		
Somalia	662,326,146	70
Bolivia	14,401,773	70
Zimbabwe	502,349,477	75
Chad	310,350,229	77
Central African Republic	117,755,845	91
Bottom Five:		
Haiti	17,086,986	33
Pakistan	55,102,503	30
Southern Africa	24,684,397	28
Honduras	17,086,986	10
Yemen	11,483,150	0
2008		
Country	*Appeal*	*% Covered*
Top Five:		
Swaziland	19,000,000	55
Lesotho	23,000,000	58
Mozambique	39,000,000	68
North Korea	15,000,000	83
Madagascar	19,000,000	89
Bottom Five:		
Nicaragua	42,000,000	27
Ghana	12,000,000	25
Dominican Republic	14,000,000	23
Zambia	9,000,000	7
Burkina Faso	6,000,000	2

Source: UNOCHA, 2010, 2009, 2008.

almost nothing. While 83% of the 2004 South Asian Tsunami Flash Appeal was met within weeks of the event, the South Asia Earthquake Flash Appeal (Pakistan) only raised 13% in the same time frame. Despite pleas by former UN Secretary General Kofi Annan and former Under Secretary General for Humanitarian Affairs Jan Egeland during the 2005 UN Donors Conference, donor nations only contributed an additional $15.9 million to the South Asia Flash Appeal, bringing the total amount of the appeal covered to 16%.

Part of the reason for this inequality is the inconsistent level of international attention to certain disasters, regardless of their severity. Some say that the 2004 tsunami events in Southeast Asia garnered so much international attention only because they struck tourist centers and therefore affected a more international range of victims. In stark contrast, the 2005 earthquake in South Asia fell off the international media agenda within days, while the emergency phase of the disaster was still ongoing. Presumably this was because the affected area was a war-torn region not very well known by the general global audience, and therefore unable to attract wide media attention (CNN, 2005b). Hurricane Katrina in the United States, on the other hand, which caused far fewer deaths (about 1000, as compared to over 70,000 in Pakistan and almost 300,000 in the tsunami events) received 24-hour news coverage for several weeks.

Climate Change and the Environmental Impact of Disasters

Statistical data give clear signs that the earth's climate is changing rapidly at a rate possibly exceeding 0.2 °C per decade. Whether these changes are part of a natural cycle or induced by human activities is still a major point of contention, but the fact that such change is occurring is undeniable. These climatic changes have been correlated with overall increases in sea and air temperatures, changes in the speed and direction of wind and sea currents, alterations to the polar ice caps and glacial ice, and variances in precipitation patterns, among other effects. One of the more troubling consequences of these changes has been a shift in the types and severity of hazards throughout the world.

The UN in particular, and the global community in general, have recognized that nations must adapt to these changes and prepare for a possible increase in catastrophic hazards. The risk, according to one humanitarian organization, is as many as one billion refugees worldwide by the year 2050, thanks in large part to forced migration caused by floods, drought, and famine (Eccleston, 2007). Several nations may already have had a hint of what may come. In 2005, for instance, the United States experienced a record year in terms of both the number of hurricanes that struck and the maximum recorded strength of a hurricane (Wilma), resulting in the costliest disaster season yet. Klaus Topfer, the executive director of the UN Environmental Program (UNEP), officially blamed climate change for the record flooding and fires in Europe during the summer of 2005. Since then, record temperatures and rainfall averages have continued to be broken year after year, raising the specter of a realization that the magnitude of climatological changes are not only irreversible in the short term, but that they are increasing in speed and intensity.

Climate change is an especially divisive topic because of its implications on global trade and the cost of business. Some nations have been reluctant to formally agree with observed climate change data or accept that human activities influence such change, because they would be pressured to drastically alter their industrial behavior. Their production costs presumably would increase, possibly causing them to lose a certain amount of business competitiveness.

As part of the January 2005 World Conference on Disaster Reduction, recognition that the world's nations must address climate change as part of a greater risk-reduction effort was reflected in the resulting Hyogo Framework for Action, which tasked signatories with

> Promot[ing] the integration of risk reduction associated with existing climate variability and future climate change into strategies for the reduction of disaster risk and adaptation to climate change, which would include the clear identification of climate related disaster risks, the design of specific risk reduction measures and an improved and routine use of climate risk information by planners, engineers and other decision-makers. (UNISDR, 2005)

However, because of the objections of several countries (including the United States) to prescriptive language in the document, as well as to the number of times the phrase "climate change" appeared in the framework, the only general, widely interpretive outcome likely to result is in terms of how nations actually prepare for the prospect of a future change in the world's climate. While some may see the devastating year endured by the United States following this conference as due justice, it remains to be seen whether any countries will have learned from the experience. In the meantime, however, many island states, most notably the Maldives, have already begun planning for inevitable rises in sea level that will threaten their very existence as a viable land mass. And in some cities, both Arctic (e.g., Shishmaref, Alaska) and tropical (Bangkok, Thailand), these effects have already resulted in the loss of habitable land.

A concept that is beginning to take hold in both the environmental and emergency management communities is that of "adaptation" (see Figure 11–3). Adaptation, which is similar to mitigation, describes changes that we make as a society to deal with the changing nature of our risk related to the changing nature of our climate. Cultures and nations are looking at different ways to live so that these inevitable changes impact our lives and livelihoods to a less dramatic degree. Adaptation will likely become central to the profession of emergency management as climate change–induced disasters become the norm.

Early Warning

Systems that allow for early warning are expensive, complex, and require active maintenance, traditionally making them a luxury for only the wealthiest nations. This disparity in early warning capacity became apparent in the minutes and hours before the December 2004 and September 2009 tsunamis struck, when the U.S. government and other industrialized nations' governments were fully aware of what was to come but were unable to turn that information into action due to a lack of early warning infrastructure in the affected nations.

Early warning, as described earlier in Chapter 4, requires much more than the equipment and expertise to recognize disasters before they happen. To be effective, an early warning mechanism must include public education, accurate risk perception, a communications system to relay the message, and an emergency management system to adequately coordinate the response. Even if the wealthy nations of the world offer to share their early warning technology, only one piece of the puzzle will have been put in place. Until at-risk nations can fill in the gaps, they will remain at risk from future

FIGURE 11–3 In Bangkok, Thailand, where the effects of global climate change and sea level rise are already being felt in the form of more prevalent floods, residents have begun to adapt to these conditions. Flooding that would cripple most other cities is now managed without much or any commitment by the emergency services, as people have taken measures to ensure the water does not affect their homes, businesses, transportation, or other facets of life.

preventable disasters. Early warning is one of the primary topics addressed by the Hyogo Framework for Action created at the 2005 World Conference on Disaster Reduction.

Linking Risk Reduction and Development

The practice of integrating disaster management and risk reduction into overall development activities was detailed in Chapter 1 and subsequently touched upon in other chapters. Only those countries that are able to reduce their disaster vulnerability will ever achieve sustainable development. Disasters reverse development progress by years or even decades and leave countries facing monumental debt for projects that were destroyed.

Development organizations are responsible for ensuring that the projects they fund or conduct reflect an effort to increase local resilience. The international donor community must not only continue to insist that development projects fully accommodate disaster risk reduction but also institute monitoring mechanisms to ensure that such standards are followed. Additionally, the international donor community must assess risk before disasters occur, so that risk-reduction measures may be adequately tied to development activities prior to devastating events.

These standards of development practice depend on the availability of accurate disaster-specific information, including hazard risk assessments, viable mitigation options, and the full range of alternate projects and project locations. Efforts to map the world's risk zones for this purpose have been made by many organizations, including the World Bank Group, the UN, the Pan American Health Organization (PAHO), and others, but all of these projects remain in their infancy.

Differentiating Between Recovery and Development

When any country is affected by a major disaster, there will be the repair and reconstruction of buildings, roads, bridges, factories, utilities, and other components of national wealth that allow the society to function. In many cases, it was the poor condition of some of these societal components that led to their vulnerability in the first place. Post-disaster recovery efforts seek to rebuild these structures and infrastructure, and allow the community to function. But organizations involved in recovery must face the quandary of deciding to what standards recovery will strive for.

Imagine, for example, a poor country and a rich country, both of which suffer devastating earthquakes that destroy every building. To rebuild both to their previous conditions would require much different financial investments given that the wealthy nation would require modern design, materials, and infrastructure, while the poor country may have seemed to be in a state of emergency before the event even occurred (as was the case in Haiti). However, it would not seem fair, or even wise, to try to return the residents of a disaster-affected city to a situation in which their development indicators are substandard (despite that this is what existed prior to the event). Recovery, then, can be considered a function of international development just as much as a function of emergency management. This requires that those tasked with disaster recovery from both the affected government and the donor nations and international organizations have a corresponding understanding of the longer term development goals when performing their recovery effort. The ongoing efforts in Haiti, following the 2010 events, are a prime example of the blurred lines between relief and development that require such an understanding among response and recovery planners.

Terrorism

As described in Chapter 2, terrorism is a hazard that has existed for centuries. Some nations, such as Israel, the United Kingdom, Turkey, Colombia, and Spain, have dealt with the scourge of terrorism for decades. Others, due to a real or perceived lack of risk, have done little or nothing to address this hazard. However, since the turn of this century, the desire to address the terrorism hazard has increased substantially in terms of national and international spending and cooperation. This new direction for emergency management may end up increasing vulnerability in other hazard areas that traditionally are more likely to occur.

Hazards are managed according to the two component factors of risk: the likelihood that the hazard will strike, and the expected consequences if it does. However, since the September 11, 2001, terrorist attacks in the United States: the March 11, 2004, terrorist attacks in Spain; and the July 7, 2005, terrorist attacks in London; a third element has been introduced into this equation: risk perception (specifically, the irrational fear associated with terrorist attacks). The result, it seems, is that disaster management resources are now not doled out according to proportional or measured risk, but rather concentrated on this newly recognized (but in reality, age-old) hazard. While the United States is most vehemently accused of taking such a direction, many other nations' government have followed suit.

In reality, the statistics related to terrorism risk do not support the disproportionate amount of funding and effort that recently has been dedicated to its treatment. Between 1998 and 2007, the number of people killed in terrorist incidents worldwide averaged about 3900 per year. But terrorists have done very little in comparison to nature's fury during this or any other period in recorded history.

Heat waves killed over 20,000 people in the past decade alone—15,000 in one year—while earthquakes have claimed tens of thousands of lives on multiple occasions. Annual hurricanes, floods, and earthquakes kill tens to hundreds of thousands and cause economic damages that overshadow those of 9/11. One of the natural events listed in Exhibit 11–1, the 2010 earthquake in Haiti, likely resulted in more deaths than all terrorist attacks recorded during the entire twentieth century. Add to these deaths the injuries, unemployment, and homelessness that accompany natural disasters, and the number of people affected rises to a staggering 170,000,000 each year.

The consequences of focusing too much on a single, low-likelihood threat like terrorism became apparent to the United States in August and September of 2005 when Hurricane Katrina struck. The U.S. disaster management agency, FEMA, had been retooled as a terrorism-response agency since 2001 and had lost the ability to adequately respond to a large-scale natural disaster like Katrina, which only years before it would have had no problem handling. Other nations should learn from the United States' mistake and ensure that their emergency management systems are based upon risk and not political pressures or misguided perceptions.

Global Disasters: SARS, Avian Influenza, Swine Flu, and Other Emerging Epidemics

Many of history's most devastating disasters, in terms of fatalities, have been pandemics. The twentieth century alone saw three major pandemic events (1918–1919, 1957, and 1968), the first of which resulted in as many as 50 million deaths before being brought under control. While public health facilities and capacities in many of the world's wealthier countries have come a long way since 1968, the ease and speed of modern global air travel and the interconnectedness of international commerce could lead to many more fatalities in an even shorter amount of time should an equivalent pandemic arise. The poor countries of the world still lack even the basic infrastructure to contain such a hazard on their own.

The global potential of a modern pandemic was first recognized in 2002 and 2003 when SARS suddenly emerged, quickly spreading to 8100 people in dozens of countries on six continents. Many countries acted individually in their approach to limiting the virus, and there were many inconsistencies in response actions. While some nations were able to fully limit the disease's fatality rate, others experienced fatality rates as high as 17%. (Several countries did experience even higher fatality rates but did not have enough cases to constitute an acceptable sample size.)

Following the narrowly averted SARS pandemic, world leaders called for greater international cooperation in tackling preparedness for and planned response to the next pandemic threat. Like many other disasters, however, once the SARS emergency was brought under control and no longer an emergency, it quickly fell off the media agenda. After the dust settled, little had been done to address the need for an international monitoring, detection, and management capacity for pandemics until swine flu emerged in 2009 and began moving between the human population at a rate that resulted in worldwide warnings and actual quarantines in several countries. Even though avian influenza further elevated the topic of pandemic potential, it was not until the high rates of transmission of swine flu occurred that many countries began to grapple with the difficulties associated with global disease management; namely, how they, as individual sovereign nations, could or would apply quarantines and other disease control mechanisms. Global public health departments and ministries have begun working together to ensure accurate and effective sharing of information and technologies (e.g., vaccines), which could presumably work to contain the disease as quickly as possible.

The need for an effective global disease containment system was first highlighted in November 2005, when the Asian Development Bank estimated that an avian influenza pandemic would cost the countries of Asia over $280 billion in losses (over 6% of GNP). The World Bank further added that these losses would come "not from death or sickness but from people and governments responding in an uncoordinated way" (CNN, 2005a).

The UN estimated that the avian influenza virus could kill as many as 150 million people worldwide if it mutated into a form easily transmissible between humans. The U.S. government was the first to formally begin developing a mitigation and preparedness program geared toward the pandemic hazard, with a $7.1 billion program that includes detection and containment systems, laboratory research into pathogens and the development of treatments and vaccines, and preparedness for government officials at all administrative levels. While this program includes approximately $250 million for a "global surveillance and preparedness network," which has helped the international community to more quickly recognize emerging epidemics in coordination efforts of the World Health Organization (WHO), it clearly focuses upon the needs of one nation. Each nation must develop a domestic capacity that allows it to effectively use the information from any detection system.

Conclusion

The future of international disaster management is bright. The twenty-first century has so far been marked by a succession of disaster events so devastating that the weaknesses they have exposed are impossible to ignore. These illuminating events have coincided with the culmination of the IDNDR and the commencement of the ISDR, and their timing has served to justify the need for both.

All evidence points to a worldwide recognition that more effort is required by all nations to reduce global vulnerability. The most notable of these forward steps is the Hyogo Framework for Action 2005–2015: Building the Resilience of Nations and Communities to Disasters. This framework, adopted by the Member States of the UN, outlines the disaster management priorities of the coming decade:

1. Ensuring that disaster risk reduction is a national and a local priority with a strong institutional basis for implementation
2. Identifying, assessing, and monitoring disaster risks and enhancing early warning
3. Using knowledge, innovation, and education to build a culture of safety and resilience at all levels
4. Reducing the underlying risk factors
5. Strengthening disaster preparedness for effective response at all levels

Although these priorities may appear elementary, they are the foundation of emergency management practice upon which every lesson included in this text is built. In January 2010, governments from around the world met in Hyogo, Japan, to discuss the progress that the signatory nations had made in the intervening 5 years (information on the Hyogo Mid-Term Review can be found at http://www.preventionweb.net/english/hyogo/hfa-mtr/?pid:73&pil:1). While there is still a long way to go for the global community, for many nations these small steps constitute a revolutionary change in a cultural and political mindset regarding responsible development practices, proactive hazard risk management reduction, and an appreciation of the value of the emergency management profession. While 5 more years is certain to be too short a time frame to solve our problems of hazard risk, the progress that will have been made toward these inspirational goals represents more advancement than has happened in previous 1000 years.

References

CNN. (2005a). *Bird flu could cost Asia $283bn* (November 3). http://edition.cnn.com/2005/BUSINESS/11/03/asia.birdflu.main.reut/index.html.

CNN. (2005b). *Pakistan: F-16 delay for quake aid* (November 4). http://edition.cnn.com/2005/WORLD/asiapcf/11/04/pakistan.quake.reut/index.html.

Eccleston, P. (2007). Climate change will make millions homeless. *The Daily Telegraph*, May 14.

Haddow, G. (2005). Personal Interview.

Henderson, M. (2007). We evolved to ignore mass misery. *Ottawa Citizen*, February 17.

Maynard, K. (1999). *Healing communities in conflict: International assistance in complex emergencies.* www.ciaonet.org/access/maynard/.

United Nations International Strategy for Disaster Reduction (UNISDR). (2005). *Hyogo Framework for Action 2005–2015.* www.unisor.org/wcdr/intergover/official/-doc/l.-docs/hyogo-framework-for-action-english.pdf.

United Nations Office for the Coordination of Humanitarian Affairs (UNOCHA). (2008). *Humanitarian appeal 2008.* http://ochaonline.un.org/humanitarianappeal/webpage.asp?Page=1637.

United Nations Office for the Coordination of Humanitarian Affairs (UNOCHA). (2009). *Humanitarian appeal 2010.* http://ochaonline.un.org/humanitarianappeal/webpage.asp?Page=1709.

United Nations Office for the Coordination of Humanitarian Affairs (UNOCHA). (2010). *Humanitarian appeal 2010.* http://ochaonline.un.org/humanitarianappeal/webpage.asp?Site=2010&Lang=en.

Index

Note: Page numbers followed by *b* indicate boxes, *f* indicate figures and *t* indicate tables.

A